WORD BIBLICAL COMMENTARY

WORD BIBLICAL COMMENTARY

VOLUME 9

Ruth, Esther

FREDERIC W. BUSH

WORD BOOKS, PUBLISHER • DALLAS, TEXAS

To My Wife, Bernice
Without whose support, tangible and intangible,
this work would never have seen the light of day

יודע כל־שער עמי כי אשת חיל את *(Ruth 3:11b)*

and to David Allan Hubbard
(who went to be with the Lord the very day this dedication was written)
For his constant encouragement, his insightful critique, and his warm friendship

בכל־עת אהב הרע *(Prov 17:17a)*

Word Biblical Commentary
RUTH, ESTHER

Library of Congress Cataloging-in-Publication Data
Main entry under title:

Word biblical commentary.

Includes bibliographies.
1. Bible—Commentaries—Collected works.
BS491.2W67 220.7'7 81-71768
ISBN 0-8499-0208-8 (v. 9) AACR2

Printed in the United States of America

Scripture quotations in the body of the text are the author's own. The author's own translation of the text appears under the heading *Translation.*

6789 QPF 987654321

Contents

ESTHER

Editorial Preface

The launching of the *Word Biblical Commentary* brings to fulfillment an enterprise of several years' planning. The publishers and the members of the editorial board met in 1977 to explore the possibility of a new commentary on the books of the Bible that would incorporate several distinctive features. Prospective readers of these volumes are entitled to know what such features were intended to be; whether the aims of the commentary have been fully achieved time alone will tell.

First, we have tried to cast a wide net to include as contributors a number of scholars from around the world who not only share our aims but are in the main engaged in the ministry of teaching in university, college, and seminary. They represent a rich diversity of denominational allegiance. The broad stance of our contributors can rightly be called evangelical, and this term is to be understood in its positive, historic sense of a commitment to Scripture as divine revelation, and to the truth and power of the Christian gospel.

Then, the commentaries in our series are all commissioned and written for the purpose of inclusion in the Word Biblical Commentary. Unlike several of our distinguished counterparts in the field of commentary writing, there are no translated works, originally written in a non-English language. Also, our commentators were asked to prepare their own rendering of the original biblical text and to use those languages as the basis of their own comments and exegesis. What may be claimed as distinctive with this series is that it is based on the biblical languages, yet it seeks to make the technical and scholarly approach to a theological understanding of Scripture understandable by—and useful to—the fledgling student, the working minister, and colleagues in the guild of professional scholars and teachers as well.

Finally, a word must be said about the format of the series. The layout, in clearly defined sections, has been consciously devised to assist readers at different levels. Those wishing to learn about the textual witnesses on which the translation is offered are invited to consult the section headed *Notes*. If the readers' concern is with the state of modern scholarship on any given portion of Scripture, they should turn to the sections of *Bibliography* and *Form/Structure/Setting*. For a clear exposition of the passage's meaning and its relevance to the ongoing biblical revelation, the *Comment* and concluding *Explanation* are designed expressly to meet that need. There is therefore something for everyone who may pick up and use these volumes.

If these aims come anywhere near realization, the intention of the editors will have been met, and the labor of our team of contributors rewarded.

General Editors: *David A. Hubbard* †
Glenn W. Barker †
Old Testament: *John D. W. Watts*
New Testament: *Ralph P. Martin*

Author's Preface

It is impossible to complete the writing of a commentary on a book of the Bible without, on the one hand, being immensely aware of how much one is indebted to the work of those who have gone before and without, on the other hand, feeling a deep sense of gratitude for the insight, understanding, and stimulation that their work has provided. In particular, most valuable has been the work on semantic structure by J. Beekman, J. Callow, and M. Kopesec; that on narrative interpretation by R. Alter, A. Berlin, and M. Sternberg; and above all, for the book of Ruth, the fine commentaries by E. F. Campbell, R. L. Hubbard, P. Joüon, W. Rudolph, and J. M. Sasson; and those of H. Bardtke, D. J. A. Clines, M. V. Fox, and C. A. Moore for Esther. My indebtedness to these and many other scholars in the difficult task of "commenting" on Ruth and Esther will be evident on almost every page.

In writing this commentary, particularly the *Comment* sections, I have always had (quite unconsciously at the beginning, I must confess) the needs and interests of the students who have sat for some thirty-one years now in courses on the grammar and exegesis of Hebrew and the other Semitic languages that it has been my privilege to teach at Fuller Theological Seminary. Hence, these sections are far more liberally sprinkled with grammatical explanations and with references to the standard grammatical and exegetical reference works than is normally the case in a work of this kind. I crave the general reader's indulgence in this regard, an aspect that otherwise would at times, I fear, seem unnecessary, and perhaps even pedantic.

As Rowley observed in 1946, the book of Ruth "abounds in problems for which no final solution can ever be found, since the materials for their solution have been denied us" (*The Servant of the Lord,* 171). Nevertheless, I have attempted explanations for several of these intractable problems. In attempting such, I do not presume for a moment to have found the final solutions of which Rowley speaks. I only hope to have thrown some further light on the issues and questions involved. Looking back, I have sometimes wished that I had followed Farrar's advice of a century ago in regard to the book of Daniel and obeyed "the wise exhortation of the Rabbis, 'Learn to say, "I do not know"'" (quoted by Goldingay in his author's preface to the Word Biblical Commentary on Daniel). The reader should also note that, since the writing of the commentary on the book of Ruth was completed in 1991, it has not been possible to include works that have appeared after that date.

I am indebted to John D. W. Watts, the Old Testament editor of the Word Biblical Commentary, first for the opportunity to contribute this volume to that series, and second for the remarkable forbearance he has shown in patiently awaiting its completion. Particular thanks are due to David A. Hubbard, my former colleague at Fuller Theological Seminary and the general editor of this series, for his continued encouragement and especially for his helpful criticism at each stage of the work. Finally, I am grateful to Fuller Theological Seminary for the sabbaticals that have provided most of the time to write, and in particular to the staff of the Word Processing Department of the School of Theology for their skill in turning my inimitable hieroglyphics into readable text.

FREDERIC WM. BUSH

Fuller Theological Seminary
June 7, 1996

Abbreviations

PERIODICALS, SERIALS, AND REFERENCE WORKS

AB	Anchor Bible
ABD	D. N. Freedman (ed.), *Anchor Bible Dictionary*
AfO	*Archiv für Orientforschung*
AJBI	*Annual of the Japanese Bible Institute*
AJSL	*American Journal of Semitic Languages and Literature*
ALUOS	Annual of Leeds University Oriental Society
ANET	J. B. Pritchard (ed.), *Ancient Near Eastern Texts*
AOAT	Alter Orient und Altes Testament
ArOr	*Archiv orientální*
ASTI	*Annual of the Swedish Theological Institute*
ATD	Das Alte Testament Deutsch
AUSS	*Andrews University Seminary Studies*
BA	*Biblical Archaeologist*
BASOR	*Bulletin of the American Schools of Oriental Research*
BAT	Die Botschaft des Alten Testaments
BDB	F. Brown, S. R. Driver, and C. A. Briggs, *Hebrew and English Lexicon of the Old Testament*
BHK	R. Kittel (ed.), *Biblia hebraica,* 3rd ed.
BHS	*Biblia hebraica stuttgartensia*
Bib	*Biblica*
BJRL	*Bulletin of the John Rylands University Library of Manchester*
BKAT	Biblischer Kommentar: Altes Testament
BL	H. Bauer and P. Leander, *Historische Grammatik der hebräische Sprache*
BibLeb	*Bibel und Leben*
BN	*Biblische Notizen*
BOr	*Bibliotheca Orientalis*
BR	*Biblical Research*
BS	*Biblische Studien*
BSac	*Bibliotheca Sacra*
BT	*The Bible Translator*
BZAW	Beihefte zur *ZAW*
Canaanite Myths	J. C. L. Gibson, *Canaanite Myths and Legends*
CB	The Century Bible
CBQ	*Catholic Biblical Quarterly*
CHALOT	W. L. Holladay, *A Concise Hebrew and Aramaic Lexicon of the Old Testament*
CTA	A. Herdner, *Corpus des tablettes en cunéiforms alphabétiques*

Dictionary	M. Jastrow, *Dictionary of Talmud Babli, Yerushalmi, Midrashic Literature and Targumim*
DISO	C.-F. Jean and J. Hoftijzer, *Dictionnaire semitiques de l'ouest*
EncJud	*Encyclopaedia Judaica* (1971)
EOL	*Ex Oriente Lux*
ExpTim	*Expository Times*
FOTL	The Forms of the Old Testament Literature
GBH	P. Joüon, *A Grammar of Biblical Hebrew,* tr. & rev. T. Muraoka
GCA	*Gratz College Annual of Jewish Studies*
Ges.-Buhl	*Gesenius' hebräisches und aramäisches Handwörterbuch über das Alte Testament,* rev. F. Buhl
GHB	P. Joüon, *Grammaire de l'hebreu biblique*
GKC	*Gesenius' Hebrew Grammar,* ed. E. Kautzsch, tr. A. E. Cowley
GMH	M. Segal, *A Grammar of Mishnaic Hebrew*
HALOT	*The Hebrew and Aramaic Lexicon of the Old Testament,* Eng. tr. of L. Koehler and W. Baumgartner, *Hebräisches und Aramäisches Lexikon zum Alten Testament*
HAR	*Hebrew Annual Review*
HAT	Handbuch zum Alten Testament
HDSS	E. Qimron, *The Hebrew of the Dead Sea Scrolls*
HebS	R. J. Williams, *Hebrew Syntax*
HS	*Hebrew Studies*
HSM	Harvard Semitic Monographs
HSS	Harvard Semitic Studies
HTR	*Harvard Theological Review*
HTS	Harvard Theological Studies
HUCA	*Hebrew Union College Annual*
IBH	T. O. Lambdin, *Introduction to Biblical Hebrew*
IBHS	B. K. Waltke and M. O'Connor, *An Introduction to Biblical Hebrew Syntax*
ICC	International Critical Commentary
IDB	G. A. Buttrick (ed.), *Interpreter's Dictionary of the Bible*
IDBSup	Supplementary volume to *IDB*
IEJ	*Israel Exploration Journal*
ILR	*Israeli Law Review*
ILOT	S. R. Driver, *Introduction to the Literature of the Old Testament*
Int	*Interpretation*
ITC	International Theological Commentary
JANESCU	*Journal of the Ancient Near Eastern Society of Columbia University*
JAOS	*Journal of the American Oriental Society*
JBL	*Journal of Biblical Literature*

JBLMS	*JBL* Monograph Series
JBR	*Journal of Bible and Religion*
JCS	*Journal of Cuneiform Studies*
JES	*Journal of Ecumenical Studies*
JETS	*Journal of the Evangelical Theological Society*
JJS	*Journal of Jewish Studies*
JNES	*Journal of Near Eastern Studies*
JNWSL	*Journal of North West Semitic Languages*
JQR	*Jewish Quarterly Review*
JR	*Journal of Religion*
JRAS	*Journal of the Royal Asiatic Society*
JSOT	*Journal for the Study of the Old Testament*
JSOTSup	Supplement to *JSOT*
JSS	*Journal of Semitic Studies*
JTS	*Journal of Theological Studies*
KAT	E. Sellin (ed.), Kommentar zum Alten Testament
KB^1	L. Koehler and W. Baumgartner, *Lexikon in Veteris Testamenti Libros*
KB^3	L. Koehler and W. Baumgartner, *Hebräisches und Aramäisches Lexikon zum Alten Testament*, 3rd ed.
KHAT	Kurzer Hand-Commentar zum Alten Testament
KTU	*Die Keilalphabetischen Texte aus Ugarit*, vol. 1, ed. M. Dietrich, O. Loretz, and J. Sammartin, AOAT 24 (1976)
Kutscher	E. Kutscher, *A History of the Hebrew Language*
Leš	*Lešonénu*
Mus	*Le Muséon*
NCBC	New Century Bible Commentary
NICOT	New International Commentary on the Old Testament
Or	*Orientalia* (Rome)
OTS	*Oudtestamentische Studiën*
RB	*Revue biblique*
RevELA	*Revue de l'organization internationale pour l'etude des langues anciennes par l'ordinateur*
RevQ	*Revue de Qumran*
RGG	*Religion in Geschichte und Gegenwart*
RHA	*Revue hittite et asianique*
RHPR	*Revue d'histoire et de philosophie religieuses*
RTP	*Revue de théologie et de philosophie*
SAT	Schriften des Alten Testaments
SBH	F. I. Andersen, *The Sentence in Biblical Hebrew*
SBLDS	SBL Dissertation Series
SBLSCS	SBL Septuagint and Cognate Studies

SBM	Stuttgarter biblische Monographien
SCM	Student Christian Movement
SEÅ	*Svensk exegetisk årsbok*
SGKAO	*Schriften zur Geschichte und Kultur des Alten Orients*
SJT	*Scottish Journal of Theology*
SSAW	*Sitzungsberichte der Sächsischen Akademie der Wissenschaften zu Leipzig, phil.-hist. Klasse*
Syntax	C. Brockelmann, *Hebräische Syntax*
TDOT	G. J. Botterweck, H. Ringgren, and H. J. Fabry (eds.), *Theological Dictionary of the Old Testament*
TGUOS	*Transactions of the Glasgow University Oriental Society*
THAT	E. Jenni and C. Westermann (eds.), *Theologisches Handwörterbuch zum Alten Testament*
TJ	*Trinity Journal*
TOTC	Tyndale Old Testament Commentaries
TPBT	*Technical Papers for the Bible Translator*
TSSI	J. C. L. Gibson, *Textbook of Syrian Semitic Inscriptions*
TynBul	*Tyndale Bulletin*
TZ	*Theologische Zeitschrift*
UF	*Ugarit-Forschungen*
USQR	*Union Seminary Quarterly Review*
UT	C. H. Gordon, *Ugaritic Textbook*
VT	*Vetus Testamentum*
WBC	Word Biblical Commentary
WMANT	Wissenschaftliche Monographien zum Alten und Neuen Testament
WO	*Die Welt des Orients*
WTJ	*Westminster Theological Journal*
WZKM	*Wiener Zeitschrift für die Kunde des Morgenlandes*
ZAW	*Zeitschrift für die alttestamentliche Wissenschaft*
ZBAT	Zürcher Bibelkommentare Alten Testament

MODERN TRANSLATIONS

JB	The Jerusalem Bible
JPS	Jewish Publication Society, *The Holy Scriptures*
KJV	King James Version (1611) = AV
Moffatt	J. Moffatt, *A New Translation of the Bible*
NAB	The New American Bible
NASV	New American Standard Version
NEB	The New English Bible
NIV	The New International Version (1978)
NJB	New Jerusalem Bible (1985)
NJPS	The New JPS

NRSV	New Revised Standard Version (1989)
REB	Revised English Bible
RSV	Revised Standard Version (NT 1946, OT 1952, Apoc. 1957)
TEV	Today's English Version

Texts, Versions, and Ancient Works

AT	The A-text of the book of Esther	*Meg.*	*Megilla*
Ant.	Josephus, *Antiquities*	*Midr. Esth. Rab.*	*Midraš Esther Rabbah*
b.	Babylonian Talmud	MT	Masoretic Text
B. Bat.	*Baba Batra*	OL	Old Latin
DSS	Dead Sea Scrolls	Sy	Syriac
L	Codex Leningradensis	Tg	Targum
LXX	Septuagint	Vg	Vulgate
m.	*Mishnah*	*y.*	Jerusalem Talmud

Biblical and Apocryphal Books

Gen	Genesis	Jer	Jeremiah
Exod	Exodus	Lam	Lamentations
Lev	Leviticus	Ezek	Ezekiel
Num	Numbers	Dan	Daniel
Deut	Deuteronomy	Hos	Hosea
Josh	Joshua	Joel	Joel
Judg	Judges	Amos	Amos
Ruth	Ruth	Obad	Obadiah
1–2 Sam	1–2 Samuel	Jonah	Jonah
1–2 Kgs	1–2 Kings	Mic	Micah
1–2 Chron	1–2 Chronicles	Nah	Nahum
Ezra	Ezra	Hab	Habakkuk
Neh	Nehemiah	Zeph	Zephaniah
Esth	Esther	Hag	Haggai
Job	Job	Zech	Zechariah
Ps(s)	Psalm(s)	Mal	Malachi
Prov	Proverbs	1–2 Esdr	1–2 Esdras
Eccl	Ecclesiastes	Jdt	Judith
Cant	Canticles, Song of Solomon	Tob	Tobit
Isa	Isaiah	Matt	Matthew

Hebrew Grammar

abs	absolute	c	common
acc	accusative	coh	cohortative
act	active	conj	conjunction
adj	adjective/adjectival	consec	consecutive
adv	adverb/adverbial	constr	construct
aor	aorist	dittogr	dittography
apoc	apocopated	fem, f	feminine

fut	future
gen	genitive
haplogr	haplography
hiph	hiphil
hithp	hithpael
hoph	hophal
impf	imperfect
impv	imperative
inf	infinitive
juss	jussive
masc, m	masculine
niph	niphal
obj	object
pass	passive
pf	perfect
pl	plural
poss	possessive
prep	preposition
pron	pronoun
pronom	pronomina
ptcp	participle
sg, s	singular
suff	suffix

MISCELLANEOUS

Akk.	Akkadian
Aram.	Aramaic
BH	Biblical Hebrew
ca.	circa
cf.	compare
chap(s).	chapter(s)
diss.	dissertation
E	Elohist
EBH	Early Biblical Hebrew
e.g.	for example
ed(s).	edition(s), editor(s), edited by
Eng.	English
EV	English versions
esp.	especially
et al.	and others
FS	Festschrift
hapax legomenon	sole occurrence
Heb.	Hebrew
id.	*idem,* the same
J	Yahwist
K	Kethib, the text as written
LBH	Late Biblical Hebrew
lit.	literally
MH	Mishnaic Hebrew
MS(S)	manuscript(s)
n(n).	note(s), footnote(s)
OT	Old Testament
pl.	plate
PN	personal name
Q	Qere, the text as read
repr.	reprint
rev.	revised by
SBH	Standard Biblical Hebrew
sc.	namely, that is to say
tr.	translated by
UP	University Press
v(v)	verse(s)
viz.	namely
vs.	versus
x	times (i.e., number of occurrences)
§	section/paragraph

Ruth

Main Bibliography

COMMENTARIES
(referred to in the text by authors' names only)

Bertholet, A. *Das Buch Ruth.* KHAT 17. Tübingen: Mohr, 1898. **Bettan, I.** *The Five Scrolls: A Commentary on the Song of Songs, Ruth, Lamentations, Ecclesiastes, Esther.* Cincinnati: Union of American Hebrew Congregations, 1940. **Campbell, E. F.** *Ruth.* AB 7. New York: Doubleday, 1975. **Gerleman, G.** *Ruth: Das Hohelied.* BKAT 18. Neukirchen: Neukirchener, 1965. **Goslinga, C. J.** *Joshua, Judges, Ruth.* Bible Student's Commentary. Tr. R. Togtman. Grand Rapids, MI: Zondervan, 1986. **Gray, J.** *Joshua, Judges, and Ruth.* CB. London: Nelson, 1967. **———.** *Joshua, Judges, Ruth.* NCBC. Grand Rapids, MI: Eerdmans, 1986. **Gressmann, H.** *Ruth.* SAT 1/2. 2nd ed. Göttingen: Vandenhoeck & Ruprecht, 1922. **Haller, M.** *Die Fünf Megilloth.* HAT 18. Tübingen: Mohr, 1940. **Hertzberg, H. W.** *Die Bucher Josua, Richter, Ruth.* ATD 9. 2nd ed. Göttingen: Vandenhoeck & Ruprecht, 1959. **Hubbard, R. L.** *The Book of Ruth.* NICOT. Grand Rapids, MI: Eerdmans, 1988. **Joüon, P.** *Ruth: Commentaire philologique et exégétique.* 1924. Repr. Rome: Pontifical Biblical Institute, 1953. **Keil, C. F.** *Joshua, Judges, Ruth: Biblical Commentary on the Old Testament.* Tr. J. Martin. Repr. Grand Rapids: Eerdmans, 1950. **Lattey, C.** *The Book of Ruth.* Westminster Version of the Sacred Scriptures. London: Longmans, Green, 1935. **Morris, L.** *Ruth.* In A. Cundall and L. Morris. *Judges, Ruth.* TOTC. Downers Grove, IL: InterVarsity, 1968. **Rudolph, W.** *Das Buch Ruth, Das Hohe Lied, Die Klagelieder.* KAT 17. Gütersloh: Mohn, 1962. **Sasson, J. M.** *Ruth: A New Translation with a Philological and a Formalist-Folklorist Interpretation.* 2nd ed. Sheffield: JSOT, 1989. **Slotki, J.** "Ruth." In *The Five Megilloth,* ed. A. Cohen. Soncino Bible. Hindhead and London: Soncino, 1967. **Trible, P.** "A Human Comedy." In *God and the Rhetoric of Sexuality.* Philadelphia: Fortress, 1978. **Waard, J. de,** and **Nida, E. A.** *A Translator's Handbook on the Book of Ruth.* Helps for Translators 15. London: United Bible Societies, 1973. **Witzenrath, H. H.** *Das Buch Rut: Eine literaturwissenschaftliche Untersuchung.* Munich: Kosel, 1975. **Würthwein, E.** *Die Fünf Megilloth.* HAT 18. 2nd ed. Tübingen: Mohr/Siebeck, 1969. **Zenger, E.** *Das Buch Ruth.* ZBAT 8. Zurich: Theologischer, 1986.

OTHER STUDIES

Anderson, A. A "The Marriage of Ruth." *JSS* 23 (1978) 171–83. **Ap-Thomas, D. R.** "The Book of Ruth." *ExpTim* 79 (1967–68) 369–73. **Baly, D.** *The Geography of the Bible.* Rev. ed. New York: Harper & Row, 1974. **Beattie, D. R. G.** "The Book of Ruth as Evidence for Israelite Legal Practice." *VT* 24 (1974) 251–67. **———.** "Kethib and Qere in Ruth IV 5." *VT* 21 (1971) 490–94. **———.** "A Midrashic Gloss in Ruth 2:7." *ZAW* 89 (1977) 122–24. **———.** "Redemption in Ruth and Related Matters: A Response to Jack M. Sasson." *JSOT* 5 (1978) 65–68. **———.** "Ruth III." *JSOT* 5 (1978) 39–48. **Berlin, A.** "Poetics in the Book of Ruth." In *Poetics and Interpretation of Biblical Narrative.* Sheffield: Almond, 1983. 83–110. **Bernstein, M. J.** "Two Multivalent Readings in the Ruth Narrative." *JSOT* 50 (1991) 15–26. **Bertman, S.** "Symmetrical Design in the Book of Ruth." *JBL* 84 (1965) 165–68. **Bewer, J.** "The Geʾullah in the Book of Ruth." *AJSL* 19 (1902–3) 143–48. **———.** "The Goël in Ruth 4:14,15." *AJSL* 20 (1903–4) 202–6. **Brenner, A.** "Naomi and Ruth." *VT* 23 (1983) 385–97. **Brockelmann, C.** *Hebräische Syntax.* Neukirchen: Moers, 1956. **Burrows, M.** "The Marriage of Boaz and Ruth." *JBL* 59 (1940) 445–54. **Bush, F. W.** "Ruth 4:17, A Semantic Wordplay." In *Go to the Land That I Will Show You.* FS D. W. Young, ed. J. Coleson and V. Matthews. Winona Lake, IN: Eisenbrauns, 1996. 3–14. **Campbell, E.** "The Hebrew Short Story: A Study of Ruth." In *A Light unto My Path.* FS J. M. Myers, ed. H. Bream, R. Heim, and C.

Moore. Philadelphia: Temple UP, 1974. 83–101. **Davies, E. W.** "Inheritance Rights and the Hebrew Levirate Marriage: Part 1." *VT* 31 (1981) 138–44. ———. "Inheritance Rights and the Hebrew Levirate Marriage: Part 2." *VT* 31 (1981) 257–68. ———. "Ruth IV 5 and the Duties of the Goʾel." *VT* 33 (1983) 231–34. **Dommershausen, W.** "Leitwortstil in der Ruthrolle." In *Theologie im Wandel: Festschrift zum 150 jährigen bestehen der Kathologisch-Theologischen Fakultät Tübingen 1817–1967.* Munich-Freiburg: Wewel, 1967. 394–407. **Ehrlich, A. B.** *Randglossen zur hebräischen Bibel: Textkritisches, Sprachliches und Sachliches.* VII. 1914. Repr. Hildesheim: Georg Olms, 1968. 19–29. **Eissfeldt, O.** "Sohnespflichten im Alten Orient." *Syria* 43 (1966) 39–47. **Fewell, D. N.,** and **Gunn, D. M.** "'A Son Is Born to Naomi!': Literary Allusions and Interpretation in the Book of Ruth." *JSOT* 40 (1989) 99–108. **Glanzmann, G.** "The Origin and Date of the Book of Ruth." *CBQ* 21 (1959) 201–7. **Gordis, R.** "Love, Marriage, and Business in the Book of Ruth: A Chapter in Hebrew Customary Law." In *A Light unto My Path.* FS J. M. Myers, ed. H. Bream, R. Heim, and C. Moore. Philadelphia: Temple UP, 1974. 241–64. **Gow, M.** "Literary Structure in Ruth." *BT* 35 (1980) 309–20. ———. "Ruth Quoque—A Coquette? (Ruth IV 5)." *BT* 41 (1990) 302–11. **Green, B.** "A Study of Field and Seed Symbolism in the Biblical Story of Ruth." Diss., Graduate Theological Union, 1980. **Gruber, M.** *Aspects of Nonverbal Communication in the Ancient Near East.* Rome: Biblical Institute, 1980. **Gunkel, H.** "Ruth." In *Reden und Aufsätze.* Göttingen: Vandenhoeck & Ruprecht, 1913. 69–92. **Hals, R.** *The Theology of the Book of Ruth.* Philadelphia: Fortress, 1969. **Hubbard, R. L.** "Ruth IV 17: A New Solution." *VT* 38 (1988) 293–301. **Humbert, P.** "Art et leçon de l'histoire de Ruth." In *Opuscules d'un Hebräisant.* Neuchâtel: Secrétariat de l'Université, 1968. 83–110 (= *RTP* 26 [1938] 257–86). **Hunter, A.** "How Many Gods Had Ruth?" *SJT* 34 (1981) 427–35. **Hurvitz, A.** "Ruth 2:7—'A Midrashic Gloss'?" *ZAW* 95 (1983) 121–23. **Hyman, R. T.** "Questions and Changing Identity in the Book of Ruth." *USQR* 39 (1984) 189–201. ———. "Questions and the Book of Ruth." *HS* 24 (1983) 17–25. **Jongeling, B.** "HZʾT NʿMY (Ruth 1:19)." *VT* 28 (1978) 474–77. **Köhler, L.** "Die Adoptionsform von Ruth 4:16." *ZAW* 29 (1909) 312–14. **Kutscher, E. Y.** *A History of the Hebrew Language.* Jerusalem: Magnes, 1982. **Labuschagne, C. J.** "The Crux in Ruth 4:11." *ZAW* 79 (1967) 364–67. **Lacocque, A.** "Date et milieu du livre de Ruth." *RHPR* 59 (1979) 583–93. **Lachemann, E. R.** "Note on Ruth 4:7–8." *JBL* 56 (1937) 53–56. **Leggett, D.** *The Levirate and Goel Institutions in the Old Testament.* Cherry Hill, NJ: Mack, 1974. **Levine, B.** "In Praise of the Israelite *Mišpāḥâ:* Legal Themes in the Book of Ruth." In *The Quest for the Kingdom of God.* FS G. E. Mendenhall, ed. H. B. Huffman, F. A. Spina, and A. R. W. Green. Winona Lake, IN: Eisenbrauns, 1983. 95–106. **Levine, E.** *The Aramaic Version of Ruth.* Rome: Pontifical Biblical Institute, 1973. **Lipiński, E.** "Le mariage de Ruth." *VT* 26 (1978) 124–27. **Loretz, O.** "The Theme of the Ruth Story." *CBQ* 22 (1960) 291–99. ———. "Das Verhältnis zwischen Rut-Story und David-Genealogie im Ruth-Buch." *ZAW* 89 (1977) 124–26. **May, H. G.** "Ruth's Visit to the High Place at Bethlehem." *JRAS* (1939) 75–78. **McKane, W.** "Ruth and Boaz." *TGUOS* 19 (1961) 29–40. **Meinhold, A.** "Theologische Schwerpunkte im Buch Ruth und ihr Gewicht für seine Datierung." *TZ* 32 (1976) 129–37. **Moor, J. de.** "Narrative Poetry in Canaan." *UF* 20 (1988) 149–71. ———. "The Poetry of the Book of Ruth (Part I)." *Or* 53 (1984) 262–83. ———. "The Poetry of the Book of Ruth (Part II)." *Or* 55 (1986) 16–46. **Mundhenk, N.,** and **Waard, J. de.** "Missing the Whole Point and What to Do about It—With Special Reference to the Book of Ruth." *BT* 26 (1975) 425–33. **Myers, J.** *The Linguistic and Literary Form of the Book of Ruth.* Leiden: Brill, 1955. **Nielsen, K.** "Le choix contre le droit dans le livre de Ruth: De l'aire de battage au tribunal." *VT* 35 (1985) 201–12. **Phillips, A.** "The Book of Ruth—Deception and Shame." *JJS* 37 (1986) 1–17. **Porten, B.** "The Scroll of Ruth: A Rhetorical Study." *GCA* 7 (1978) 23–49. **Prinsloo, W. S.** "The Theology of the Book of Ruth." *VT* 30 (1980) 330–41. **Rauber, D.** "Literary Values in the Bible: The Book of Ruth." *JBL* 89 (1970) 27–37. **Rebera, B.** "Yahweh or Boaz? Ruth 2:20 Reconsidered." *BT* 36 (1985) 317–27. **Richter, H.-F.** "Zum Levirat im Buch Ruth." *ZAW* 95 (1983) 123–26. **Robertson, E.** "The Plot of the Book of Ruth." *BJRL* 32 (1950) 207–28. **Rowley, H. H.** "The Marriage of Ruth." In *The Servant of the Lord.* Oxford: Blackwell, 1952.

169–94. **Sacon, K.** "The Book of Ruth: Its Literary Structure and Theme." *AJBI* 4 (1978) 3–22. **Sasson, J. M.** "The Issue of *Geʾullāh* in Ruth." *JSOT* 5 (1978) 52–64. **Schneider, T. R.** "Translating Ruth 4:1–10 among the Tsonga People." *BT* 33 (1982) 301–8. **Segert, S.** "Vorarbeiten zu hebraischen Metrik: III. Zum Problem der metrische Elements im Buche Ruth." *ArOr* 25 (1967) 190–200. **Staples, W.** "The Book of Ruth." *AJSL* 53 (1936–37) 145–47. ———. "Notes on Ruth 2:20 and 3:12." *AJSL* 54 (1938) 62–65. **Stinespring, W. F.** "Note on Ruth 2:19." *JNES* 3 (1944) 101. **Thompson, D.,** and **Thompson, T.** "Some Legal Problems in the Book of Ruth." *VT* 18 (1968) 79–99. **Vaux, R. de.** *Ancient Israel.* New York: McGraw-Hill, 1961. **Vellas, B.** "The Book of Ruth and Its Purpose." *Theologia* 25 (1954) 201–10. **Vesco, J.** "La date du livre de Ruth." *RB* 74 (1967) 235–47. **Vriezen, T. C.** "Two Old Cruces: a. Ruth iv 5." *OTS* 5 (1948) 80–88. **Wright, G.** "The Mother-Maid at Bethlehem." *ZAW* 98 (1986) 56–72.

Introduction

Canonical Status and Position

Bibliography

Beckwith, R. *The Old Testament Canon of the New Testament Church.* Grand Rapids, MI: Eerdmans, 1985. **Bentzen, A.** *Introduction to the Old Testament.* 3rd ed. Copenhagen: Gad, 1957. **Childs, B. S.** *Introduction to the Old Testament as Scripture.* Philadelphia: Fortress, 1979. **Eissfeldt, O.** *The Old Testament: An Introduction.* New York: Harper and Row, 1965. **Leiman, S.** *The Canonization of Hebrew Scripture: The Talmudic and Mishnaic Evidence.* Transactions of the Connecticut Academy of Arts and Sciences 47. Hamden, CT: Archon, 1976. **McDonald, L.** *The Formation of the Christian Biblical Canon.* Nashville: Abingdon, 1988. **Pfeiffer, R.** *Introduction to the Old Testament.* New York: Harper, 1948. **Soggin, J. A.** *Introduction to the Old Testament.* 3rd ed. Louisville, KY: Westminster/John Knox, 1989. **Sundberg, A. C.** *The Old Testament of the Early Church.* HTS 20. Cambridge: Harvard UP, 1964. **Wolfenson, L. B.** "Implications of the Place of the Book of Ruth in Editions, Manuscripts, and Canon of the Old Testament." *HUCA* 1 (1924) 151–78.

Apart from one late (ninth century A.D.) challenge by an obscure Nestorian Christian commentator (see Beckwith, *OT Canon,* 305), the testimony to the canonical status of Ruth in both Jewish and Christian sources is uniform and voluminous. Both the NT (Matt 1:5; Luke 3:32) and Josephus (*Ant.* 5.9.1–4) draw on its contents precisely as they do other OT books. The earliest lists of the books of the canon include it, both Jewish (*b. B. Bat.* 14b, quoting a rabbinic teaching dating to the first two centuries A.D.) and Christian (Melito, Bishop of Sardis in the second century A.D.). And almost every Jewish and Christian source thereafter does likewise, in particular Origen and Jerome, both of whom studied under Jewish scholars. Only one talmudic statement even implies that there might have been some question on the part of some authorities about its canonical status. Rabbi Simeon ben Yohai is quoted (*b. Meg.* 7a) as saying "Ecclesiastes is among the matters on which the school of Shammai was more lenient and the School of Hillel more stringent, but [all agreed that] Ruth, Song of Songs and Esther make the hands unclean" (i.e., are canonical; see Beckwith, *OT Canon,* 304–5). Since the rabbi felt the need to affirm the canonicity of Ruth, it is implied that there must have been some question raised (as there unquestionably was with Song of Songs and Esther). For suggestions about the grounds on which Ruth was questioned, see Leiman, *Canonization,* 190 n. 104.

Although the canonicity of Ruth has been virtually accepted without question (but for the instances mentioned above), its position in the canon has been variable and has occasioned considerable controversy. In KJV and all subsequent modern English translations that stem from Christian circles, the book is found between Judges and 1 Samuel. This is also its position in the German, French, Arabic, and Syriac Bibles and in the Vulgate, all of which, including KJV, follow the order of the Septuagint. However, in NJPS and the printed editions of the Hebrew Bible, Ruth is found in the third division of the Jewish canon, the

Kethubim or Writings. In the vast majority of Hebrew manuscripts and printed editions, Ruth is one of the five Festal Scrolls (Megilloth), which are grouped together because they are read at the five major festivals of the Jewish liturgical year.

Two different orders of the Festal Scrolls are found. The historically later order groups these scrolls according to the chronology of the liturgical year: Song of Songs at Passover (Nisan = March–April); Ruth at Shabuᶜoth (weeks or Pentecost, fifty days after Passover, hence May–June); Lamentations at Ninth of Ab (= August–September), the commemoration of the destruction of the temple; Ecclesiastes at Sukkoth or Booths (Tishri = September–October); and Esther at Purim (Adar = February–March). This order is that found in modern editions of the Hebrew Bible printed prior to 1937, based on the best medieval manuscripts then known. The earlier sequence is that found in the work of the Tiberian Masoretes (ninth–tenth centuries A.D.)—Ruth, Song of Songs, Ecclesiastes, Lamentations, Esther—the principle of which is generally considered to be the historical order of the era to which tradition assigned the books (Song of Songs being presumably the work of Solomon's youth, Ecclesiastes his old age). This is the order of *BHK* and *BHS,* based as they are on *Codex Leningradensis,* the earliest complete codex of the Hebrew Bible and generally considered to represent the work of the Ben Asher family of Masoretic scholars. (Those manuscripts and editions of the Hebrew Bible in which the five Festal Scrolls are placed after Deuteronomy do not reflect a Jewish tradition in which these books are considered to belong to the Prophets rather than the Writings. They are simply medieval arrangements made in order to place together conveniently those books that alone are read in their entirety in the course of the Jewish liturgical year [see Wolfenson, *HUCA* 1 (1924) 154–58].)

Although this is the position of Ruth in the vast majority of manuscripts and printed editions, it is relatively speaking a late one. It could not have arisen until after the period in which it became customary to read these five books at the major festivals of the Jewish year, which custom gradually arose during the sixth to the tenth centuries A.D. (see Wolfenson, *HUCA* 1 [1924] 163–67; Beckwith, *Canon,* 202–3). If one takes into account, however, earlier Jewish tradition, the position of Ruth within the Writings is a variable one and raises the question of which position is original, a question not without import for such issues as the dating of the book.

Prior to the period of the Masoretes, our evidence for the order and arrangement of the books of the OT canon (other than the five books of the Pentateuch) is limited and open to differences of interpretation. Other than the Dead Sea Scrolls, whose complete biblical manuscripts are few and constitute in each case a single book per manuscript, we possess no complete Hebrew manuscripts prior to the tenth century A.D. Our evidence consists, rather, of lists set forth in the extant literature, either from Jewish sources themselves or from Christian sources who cite the practice current among Jews of their day. Our only detailed evidence from Jewish sources (for the statement of Josephus, see below) is that of the Babylonian Talmud (*b. B. Bat.* 14b), which reports the order of the books of the Prophets and the Writings. Although the Babylonian Talmud dates to the late fifth–early sixth centuries A.D., the list itself is a *baraita,* i.e., a quote from the Tannaim, the rabbinic scholars who lived during the first two centuries A.D. (cf. Beckwith, *Canon,* 26–27). This passage places Ruth at the *beginning* of the Writings immediately prior to Psalms (see Beckwith, *Canon,* 122; the passage is quoted in full in Leiman, *Canonization,* 51–53; not surprisingly then, this order is followed in a number of medieval Hebrew manuscripts; see the table in Wolfenson, *HUCA* 1 [1924] 160–61). The rest of the five books that were later to become the Festal Scrolls are listed in the Writings as separate books but are not placed together as a group. Though not explicitly stated, the number of books thus listed is nineteen, eight in the prophetic division and eleven in the Writings, which, together with the five books of the Pentateuch, produces a canon comprising twenty-four books. This agrees with the number invariably given in numerous other passages of the Talmud (for a representative list, see Leiman, *Canonization,* 53–56), as well as that implied by 4 Ezra 14:44–48, dating to ca. A.D. 100 (cf. Beckwith, *Canon,* 240–41). To this evidence from Jewish sources must be added that of Jerome, writing toward the end of the fourth century A.D. In this connection it is significant that Jerome was a Hebrew scholar who studied under various rabbis (on the authenticity of his claim to be citing Jewish sources, sometimes disputed, see Beckwith, *Canon,* 119–22, 204–6). Jerome also knows of a Jewish view that essentially agrees with the Babylonian Talmud. In the *Prologus Galeatus* (his preface to the Vulgate translation of Samuel-Kings) he states, "some [i.e., Jews] set down . . . Ruth and Kinoth [Lamentations] among the Hagiographa, and think that these books ought to be counted [separately] in their computation, and that there are thus twenty-four books of the old Law" (bracketed comments added; for the passage see Beckwith, *Canon,* 120).

However, in the earlier part of this same discussion, in marked contrast to the above, he states that the Jews count the number of the books of the OT as twenty-two since they number twenty-two letters in their alphabet. He then lists the books in the order of the three divisions of the Jewish canon, and the count of twenty-two results from listing Ruth with Judges and Lamentations with Jeremiah. In regard to Ruth he states, "Then they add the Book of Judges; and in the same book they include Ruth, because the events narrated in it occurred in the days of the Judges" (see Beckwith, *Canon,* 120). Here Ruth is listed not among the Writings but in the prophetic corpus between Judges and Samuel, the same position it has in the Septuagint, the Vulgate, and the rest of the Christian tradition. The testimony of other Church Fathers that is often cited to the same or similar effect is problematic since it seems most probable that they are dependent on Christian views when it comes to the order and arrangement of the OT canon (see the remarks of Beckwith, *Canon,* 183–85 for Melito of Sardis, 185–87 for Origen). The earliest enumeration often cited is from the last decade of the first century A.D. by Josephus, who also gives the number of OT books as twenty-two but does not list them (*Against Apion* 1.7–8). To obtain this number, Josephus must have combined Lamentations with Jeremiah, and although it might mean that he reckoned Ruth with Psalms (as in the talmudic order), it is generally concluded that he must have combined Ruth with Judges (cf. Beckwith, *Canon,* 253).

This evidence from early Jewish sources for a position of Ruth in the corpus of the Prophets rather than the Writings has raised a considerable controversy over which position is chronologically prior. The question is of some moment, for the position of Ruth in the Writings is often taken to indicate that it must date to the post-exilic era (see the discussion in *Date* below). The vast majority of commentators have concluded that the tradition that places Ruth among the Writings rather than the Prophets must be original. This conclusion has most frequently been argued on the basis of the received and traditional view of the development of the Christian canon, often termed the Alexandrian Canon Hypothesis, which until recently has virtually held sway in scholarly circles since its proposal in the eighteenth century (cf. the earlier introductions of Pfeiffer [1941] and Bentzen [1948] and the third edition of Soggin [1987]). According to this view, the hellenized Jews of Alexandria (and the diaspora in general) arranged and ordered the books of the Jewish canon differently from their Palestinian brethren and also included therein the books known to Protestantism as the Apocrypha and in Roman Catholic tradition as deuterocanonical, as attested in the earliest comprehensive manuscripts of the Septuagint. This "Alexandrian" arrangement is secondary to and derived from the canon of the Jews of Palestine and was that adopted by the developing early Church (for a succinct statement of the hypothesis and its development, see Sundberg, *The OT of the Early Church,* 3–40). Given this view of two different Palestinian and Alexandrian canons, it has seemed clear to most commentators that the order and division of the canon that placed Ruth after Judges derives from this Alexandrian canon and not from the "Hebrew" canon of the Jews of Palestine; hence it is not original (see, e.g., Rudolph, 23–24).

Recent investigations and discoveries, however, have not only rendered the view of a wider Alexandrian canon untenable (see Sundberg, *OT Canon of the Early Church,* 51–74; Beckwith, *Canon,* 382–86) but have also made equally doubtful the concomitant and generally accepted view (cf., e.g., Eissfeldt, *Introduction,* 564–68) that the canon of the Hebrew Bible was completed in three stages: the Law by the end of the fifth century B.C., the Prophets by the end of the third century B.C., and the Writings by the end of the first century A.D., in connection with the illusory Council of Jamnia (see the succinct overview of Childs, *Introduction,* 53–54). Indeed, these investigations and discoveries have so demonstrated both the complexity of the process of canonization and the paucity of our information, despite the volume of new data from the discoveries in the vicinity of the Dead Sea, that no synthesis is currently possible (cf. the remarks of Childs, *Introduction,* 54–57, and note the radically different conclusions of Sundberg, *OT Canon of the Early Church;* Beckwith, *Canon;* McDonald, *Formation*). However, two of the developments that have destroyed the consensus are important for our considerations here. First, it has become clear that hellenistic Judaism was not largely independent of Palestinian Judaism; indeed, there was a close community of language and ideas between the two (see Beckwith, *Canon,* 30–31). Second, related to this state of affairs, the discovery of the Dead Sea Scrolls has confirmed that, as had been postulated earlier on literary grounds, the majority of the Apocrypha (including Tobit, Judith, Baruch, 1 Maccabees, and the Additions to Daniel) were originally written in Hebrew, probably by Palestinian Jewish authors.

The implications for our question are obvious. The testimony of the ancient authorities cited above demonstrates that both arrangements of the canon—that with Ruth among the Prophets after Judges and that with Ruth among the Writings immediately before Psalms—existed among the Jews of Palestine, dating at least earlier than the first two centuries A.D. (see Beckwith, *Canon,* 181–222). It is simply no longer possible to posit that Ruth was moved to the Prophets by hellenized Jews whose canon is reflected in the Septuagint. It can only be the case that these different arrangements of the Prophets and the Writings arose among different elements of the Jewish community and existed side by side at least until the time of Jerome, late fourth century A.D. How the one arrangement later became exclusive to the rabbinic tradition as reflected in the Talmud and the other to the stream of tradition ultimately reflected in the Septuagint is simply unknown. Nor do we have any information to decide which of the two may be earlier or original (contra Eissfeldt, *Introduction,* 569; Gerleman, 1; for the view that there was no "original" order, see Wolfenson, *HUCA* 1 [1924] 170–75). It can only be said that the more plausible view (see Beckwith, *Canon,* 256) is that the tradition that numbered the books as twenty-two, with Ruth after Judges, is a later development arising from the somewhat artificial assimilation of the number of the books to the number of the letters of the alphabet. There is no plausible reason for a supposed earlier arrangement of twenty-two to be expanded to twenty-four. If this is the case, then the position of Ruth in the Writings immediately before Psalms is earlier and in this sense original (cf. Beckwith, *Canon,* 158–59, 252–56; note also the remarks of Campbell, 34–36).

Text

Bibliography

Baillet, M., Milik, J. T., and **Vaux, R. de.** *Les 'Petites Grottes' de Qumrân.* Discoveries in the Judean Desert of Jordan 3. Oxford: Clarendon, 1962.

The text of Ruth upon which this translation and commentary are based is that of codex Leningrad B19[A], *Codex Leningradensis,* siglum L, as it appears in *BHS.* This codex is dated to A.D. 1008 or 1009 and, pending the eventual completion of the critical edition of the text of the Aleppo Codex by the Hebrew University Bible Project, is the only available exemplar of the vocalized text of the Ben Asher family of Tiberian Masoretes with a critical apparatus and is still "the oldest dated manuscript of the complete Hebrew Bible" (*BHS,* xi). On the basis of this text, Rudolph's judgment (25) that "the text of Ruth has been very well preserved" can hardly be gainsaid (cf. Gerleman, Hubbard, Sasson; contra Joüon). Only the last eight words of 2:7 present a textual conundrum incapable of solution, and this clause fortunately does not significantly affect a coherent understanding of that scene (see *Comment* thereto).

In regard to variant readings suggested by evidence in the versions, there are, in my opinion, only three passages where the text of the MT is inferior to such readings. In 1:13 הלהם is to be read for הלהן; in 4:4 תגאל for יגאל; and in 4:5 קָנִיתָה for קניתי. (See the discussion *in loco.*) Various commentators have suggested some two dozen or so further textual changes on the basis of readings in the LXX and Syr. (Rudolph, 25, for example lists seven further passages where he judges that the readings of the LXX merit priority.) Those that merit consideration will be discussed *in loco,* but none on close inspection presents a reading superior to the MT.

Further, a number of variants have been suggested on the basis of other Hebrew manuscripts and/or the Kethib/Qere readings of the MT (the apparatus of *BHS* records approximately eighteen such). Only five of these represent readings superior to the consonantal text of L. In 2:1 מודע is preferable to מידע; in 3:12 אם is to be deleted (Kethib *wĕlô* Qere following the *Masora*); in 3:14 מרגלתיו is to be read rather than מרגלתו and בטרם rather than בטרום; and in 4:4 ואדעה rather than ואדע (see the discussion *in loco*).

Finally, fragments of four manuscripts of Ruth have been unearthed in the discoveries at Qumran, two from cave 2, published in *Les 'Petites Grottes'* (71–75) and two from cave 4, as yet unpublished but studied by Campbell (40–41) from photographs. These texts are essentially Masoretic in type and evidence only one reading of consequence, namely, the variant מרגלתיו in 3:14 just noted.

Unity

Bibliography

Ap-Thomas, D. "Book of Ruth." *ET* 79 (1968) 369–73. **Berlin, A.** *The Dynamics of Biblical Parallelism.* Bloomington: Indiana UP, 1985. ———. *Poetics and Interpretation of Biblical Narrative.* Sheffield: Almond, 1983. **Brenner, A.** "Naomi and Ruth." *VT* 23 (1983) 385–97. **Bush, F.** "Ruth 4:17, A Semantic Wordplay." In *Go to the Land I Will Show You.* FS D. W. Young, ed. J. Coleson and V. Matthews. Winona Lake, IN: Eisenbrauns, 1996. 3–14. **Childs, B.** *Introduction to the Old Testament as Scripture.* Philadelphia: Fortress, 1979. **Eissfeldt, O.** *The Old Testament: An Introduction.* Tr. P. Ackroyd. New York: Harper and Row, 1965. **Fohrer, G.** *Introduction to the Old Testament.* Tr. D. Green. New York: Abingdon, 1968. **Glanzmann, G.** "The Origin and Date of the Book of Ruth." *CBQ* 21 (1959) 201–7. **Hoftijzer, J.** *The Function and Use of the Imperfect Forms with Nun Paragogicum in Classical Hebrew.* Assen: Van Gorcum, 1985. **Kirkpatrick, P. G.** *The Old Testament and Folklore Study.* JSOTSup 62. Sheffield: JSOT, 1988. **Kugel, J.** *The Idea of Biblical Poetry: Parallelism and Its History.* New Haven/London: Yale UP, 1981. **Loretz, O.** "Das Verhältnis zwischen Rut-Story und David-Genealogie im Rut-Buch." *ZAW* 89 (1977) 124–26. **May, H.** "Ruth's Visit to the High Place at Bethlehem." *JRAS* (1939) 75–78. **Moor, J. de.** "The Poetry of the Book of Ruth (Part I)." *Or* 53 (1984) 262–83. ———. "The Poetry of the Book of Ruth (Part II)." *Or* 55 (1986) 16–46. **Rowley, H.** "The Marriage of Ruth." In *The Servant of the Lord and Other Essays on the Old Testament.* 2nd ed. Oxford: Blackwell, 1965. 171–94. **Segert, S.** "Vorarbeiten zur hebräischen Metrik, III: Zum Problem der metrischen Elemente im Buche Ruth." *ArOr* 25 (1967) 190–200. **Shearman, S.,** and **Curtis, J.** "Divine-Human Conflicts in the Old Testament." *JNES* 28 (1969) 231–42. **Sheehan, J.** "The Word of God as Myth: The Book of Ruth." In *The Word in the World.* FS F. L. Moriarity, ed. R. Clifford and G. MacRae. Weston, MA: Weston College, 1973. 35–46. **Staples, W.** "The Book of Ruth." *AJSL* 53 (1937) 145–57. **Wilson, R.** *Genealogy and History in the Biblical World.* New Haven: Yale UP, 1977. ———. "The Old Testament Genealogies in Recent Research." *JBL* 94 (1975) 169–89. ———. *Sociological Approaches to the Old Testament.* Philadelphia: Fortress, 1984. **Wright, G.** "The Mother-Maid at Bethlehem." *ZAW* 98 (1986) 56–72. **Zevit, Z.** "Converging Lines of Evidence Bearing on the Date of P." *ZAW* 94 (1982) 481–511.

Almost all who have worked on the book of Ruth agree that it is a unity, with the possible exception of the genealogy in 4:22. There are, in my opinion, no unevennesses, incongruities, repetitions, changes in literary style and diction, or apparent seams as have led to theories of composite origin in other OT texts. Indeed, given the all-consuming interest in and predilection for genetic issues that until the last few decades have dominated biblical studies, it is probably significant testimony to the obvious unity of the book that the attempts to posit earlier sources for the narrative have been so few. Two theories, at least, have been advanced, based upon supposed sufficient unevennesses and difficulties in the narrative to warrant them and positing on these grounds earlier variant stories.

Glanzmann has proposed a three-stage development of the story based upon the view that several stages of composition must be postulated to explain certain linguistic features of the book (*CBQ* 21 [1959] 207). But the argument is simply non sequitur. Besides a nebulous "poetic character," which Glanzmann substantiates only by a passing reference to Myers' study (for which see below), his linguistic evidence for the first stage, taken to be an old poetic tale in oral form, is twofold. First, it is based simply on the book's onomasticon (all of which except Obed and Boaz occur nowhere else in the OT), which Glanzmann finds to be early and non-Israelite on the basis of comparisons with the Ugaritic onomasticon and which hence could not have been invented by a later author. However, apart from the general weakness of the "argument from silence" the view entails, later research has documented these names for the most part as general West Semitic and not limited to the second millennium B.C. (cf. the comments of Sasson, 17–21, 241; Hubbard, 88–90, 94–95). There is no evidence, then, that they are non-Israelite, nor need they be early. The second piece of evidence for this stage is the postulate that the imperfect forms with nun paragogicum, of which six are found in Ruth, are not characteristic of classical Hebrew prose but of "the oldest Hebrew poetry" (*CBQ* 21 [1959] 207). In fact, exactly the opposite is the case; cf. Hoftijzer's full study of these forms, which documents eighty-four uses in prose passages versus sixty-one in poetic texts, not all of which by any means are "old" (*Function and Use,* 5, 58). The evidence for the other two stages are the existence, on the one hand, of postulated "late" forms, taken to be evidence of "editorial work in the postexilic period" (*CBQ* 21 [1959] 204), and, on the other hand, the postulated classical, pre-exilic prose style of the rest of the narrative, interpreted as evidence of a pre-exilic "intermediate literary stage" (205). But if it were granted that the forms cited are late, the unexamined assumption that they are "editorial work" is based upon no evidence whatsoever and is most improbable. (For their interpretation as evidence of language change over time, based upon principles of historical linguistics, see the discussion in *Date* below.)

Recently, Brenner has suggested that "the book of Ruth is composed of two still distinct strands, a Naomi story and a Ruth story," each of which "originally belonged to a separate . . . folk-tale," and that "the seams which combine them are still discernible" (*VT* 23 [1983] 385). The "seams," however, never appear; the evidence for two "strands" is Brenner's opinion that there are "certain difficulties which cannot be easily dismissed" (385). Upon closer examination, however, these "difficulties" are such because Brenner chooses to make them so; i.e., a careful interpretation of the problem of the story, its plot, and the characterization of the chief protagonists reveals that these "difficulties" are an integral part of a smooth, well-told story. Thus, the problem of who is being redeemed in 4:13–17, Naomi, Ruth, or both (385–86), is one that Brenner seeks to establish by a passing reference in a footnote to Sasson's interpretation. In point of fact, Ruth is *not* described in 4:14–15 as the "agent of redemption" of Naomi (385–86). The "agent of redemption" of Naomi, rather, is clearly and unmistakably the child born to Ruth and Boaz. That Ruth is not thereafter mentioned is a coherent part of the resolution of the problem of the story set forth in 4:13–17 (see the *Explanation* thereto below), namely, the death and emptiness that have afflicted *Naomi's* life. Second, the "exchange of roles" and "dominant positions" of Naomi and Ruth in successive scenes (394, 386–87) pose also no real difficulty once the major problem is elucidated, to the resolution of which the plot of the story is devoted. Naomi is the major character in chap. 1 because that chapter is devoted to setting forth both the factual and the affective dimensions of the problem of the story, the death and emptiness that have afflicted her life (see the *Explanation* sections for 1:7–19a and 1:19b–22 below, and esp. Table 1 in *Genre* below). Similarly, there is nothing incongruous or "difficult" about Ruth's and Naomi's roles in chap. 2. Brenner badly understates Naomi's role and overstates Ruth's. Naomi's inactivity initially is consistent with her bitterness and despair so powerfully portrayed in chap. 1 and is not true of her through the whole chapter. On the contrary, in the third scene, vv 17b–23, she erupts into excited questions prompted by the large amount of grain Ruth has gleaned and the quantity of food left over from her noon meal. Moreover, upon hearing that Ruth's benefactor has been Boaz, she bursts into glad words of praise, calling on Yahweh to bless him. Naomi has come back to life again and so takes the initiative in the following scene. Nor does Ruth simply "act independently" and "dutifully share her plans with Naomi" (386). Rather, she seeks Naomi's permission for her gleaning (2:2; see *Comment* thereto), revealing Naomi's dominant role as mother-in-law throughout the story. In short, all of Brenner's supposed difficulties can be integrated into a coherent whole given a correct understanding of the problem of the story and its resolution as will be made clear in the following commentary.

Although not supposing separate stories later combined, Myers has argued for an earlier stage in which the story circulated orally in poetic form. Myers supports his theory in general by the rather subjective judgment that the scenes of the book are "fraught with poetic associations" (*Linguistic and Literary Form,* 34), and in particular by (1) finding that many specific words and phrases have parallels in OT poetry (34–36) and (2) attempting to scan a number of passages as poetic following the theories of meter and poetic parallelism then current (37–42). Even granting the validity of the theory of Hebrew poetry to which he subscribes, most scholars believe Myers has failed to establish his case. Segert (*ArOr* 25 [1967] 190–200), for example, notes that Myers often had to engage in emendation in order to get his poetic lines to scan metrically. More to the point, however, the easy differentiation between prose and poetry that characterized the older view has now been seriously challenged in favor of a far more complex taxonomy of "elevated style" in which the distinction between Hebrew prose and poetry is not sharp and clear cut and is sometimes difficult to make (see Kugel, *Idea,* 59–95, esp. 85; for a succint and helpful discussion, see Berlin, *Dynamics,* 1–7). Thus, de Moor has argued for a West-Semitic "narrative poetry" and rather successfully applied it to the book of Ruth (*Or* 53 [1984] 262–83; 55 [1986] 16–46). Whatever one concludes about the validity of such views, they demonstrate the fallacy of a theory of a "poetic original" for the book. And to give the coup de grâce to all such views, recent field research in folklore studies has demonstrated that to distinguish between oral and written texts on the basis of stylistic features is no longer tenable (see Kirkpatrick, *OT and Folklore,* 116–17, esp. 51–72).

There continue to be attempts, based upon a priori theories of the prevalence of myth and mythic ritual in Israelite religion, to argue that the story originated in and/or alludes to one or another of the fertility cult legends that are supposed to be endemic to the ancient world, Semitic or Greek (see Staples, *AJSL* 53 [1937] 145–47; May, *JRAS* [1939] 75–78; Shearman and Curtis, *JNES* 28 [1969] 231–42; Sheehan, "Word of God as Myth"; and recently Wright, *ZAW* 98 [1986] 56–72). The theories are based upon reading mythic associations into the personal and place names or into various parts of the plot. Thus, for example, Naomi's journey to Moab because of famine and her return when the earth again yields increase, a return that "culminates in a harvest festival marked by a 'union' which eventually results in a 'saviour'—a man born to be king" (Wright, *ZAW* 98 [1986] 59), is thought to reflect the "original legend," which "is the familiar one of the disappearing and returning vegetation deity of the Middle East" (59). Such views, deemed to be "manifest parallels" that are "self-evident" (59), are surely so only to those who come to the question already convinced. (For a cogent critique of the views of Staples and May, see Rowley, "Marriage of Ruth," 189 n. 2.)

It has most often been claimed that 4:18–22, the concluding genealogy, is not original to the story but is a secondary addition, and a number of scholars have included 4:17c, "he is the father of Jesse, the father of David," in that judgment as well. This latter view normally includes the concomitant conclusion that the story originally had nothing to do with David or his family line (e.g., Eissfeldt, *Introduction,* 479; Fohrer, *Introduction,* 250–51; Gray, *NCBC,* 372–74; Loretz, *ZAW* 89 [1977] 125–26; Würthwein, 1–3; yet note Childs, *Introduction,* 566, who claims that their secondary addition "says nothing about the historicity of the tradition which connects Ruth to David"). Most of those who have adopted this view have based it upon the argument of Eissfeldt (*Introduction,* 479) that 4:17a–b is a faulty name-giving and that thus the "splicing" of the later editor is here visible (e.g., Fohrer, Gray, Würthwein). However, if 4:17 is examined carefully in the whole context of the giving of names in the OT, it can be understood as a perfectly acceptable example of such whose specifics fit the context of this account of Naomi's restoration to life and fullness quite well (see Bush, "Ruth 4:17," 3–14, and the discussion in the *Comment* on 4:17). Further, recent scholarship has more generally concluded that any attempt to add to the story the false claim that David was descended from a Moabite great-grandmother would be utterly improbable (cf. Ap-Thomas, *ET* 79 [1968] 370; Gerleman, 7–8; Rudolph, 29). Especially would this be the case the later in Israel's history that the attempt is posited, for in the later period David had become the sacrosanct, holy king of Israel (Gerleman, 8–9) and the prototype of the Messiah (Rudolph, 29–30), while Moab is regarded ever more negatively (Deut 23:3–4).

A far larger consensus, however, has regarded the final genealogy itself (exclusive of 4:17c) as a later addition. This is based upon several arguments, none of which in my opinion is cogent. Thus, for those who date Ruth to the pre-exilic period, that the genealogy is later in date is clearly indicated by the formula of introduction וְאֵלֶּה תּוֹלְדוֹת, "these are the descendants of . . . ," and the verb form הוֹלִיד, "fathered." Since these are characteristic of the post-exilic Priestly document of the Pentateuch but not of the pre-exilic Jahwist or Elohist sources, the genealogy must date later and so be secondary (cf. Gerleman, 38). However, the post-exilic date of the Priestly document is increasingly coming under question, particularly through the application of principles of historical linguistics (cf. the bibliography in *Date* below, esp. the studies by Hurvitz), and several kinds of significant evidence now argue for a pre-exilic date (see, e.g., Zevit, *ZAW* 94 [1982]

481–511). In addition, if my argument from historical linguistics is cogent (see *Date* below), namely, that the language of Ruth dates at the earliest to the transitional period between Standard and Late Biblical Hebrew and if the Priestly source is pre-exilic (or even exilic), the fact that both P and Ruth draw upon the same stock of genealogical formulas is no grounds for postulating that 4:18–22 is a later addition.

It has also been argued on the one hand that the genealogy will not stand up to historical examination, since there must have been far more than ten generations in the time period from Perez to David (Rudolph, 72), and on the other that the genealogy is out of harmony with the rest of the story on the grounds that a skilled artist such as the author of Ruth would not complete his story by resorting to a genre so pedantic and aesthetically awkward or discordant (cf. Campbell, 15: "a distinct anticlimax to a story . . . complete without it"; Rudolph, 71: it "drastically detracts from the forceful, concise conclusion . . . in 4:17b"; similarly Joüon, 96; *ILOT*, 456). However, both of these evaluations of genealogy are seriously wanting. The first is a modern, Western estimate of the form and function of genealogies. Recent investigation and study of the nature of genealogies have greatly clarified their function and role in the kinship societies (similar in many respects to premonarchical Israel) that use them (see esp. Wilson, *Genealogy and History*). It was tacitly assumed in much of OT interpretation that genealogies were intended to be historical sources that preserved accurate data about kinship relationships between individuals and/or tribal and subtribal groups (see Wilson, *Genealogy and History,* 1–8; for a further critique, including extrabiblical genealogies, see Wilson, *JBL* 94 [1975] 169–78). In parallel genealogies the information is sometimes contradictory, and the genealogies most often are not long enough to account for the time that independent OT research indicates must have elapsed between early and late members of a given list without according an improbable, and often impossible, average number of years to each generation. Hence, the biblical genealogies were generally regarded as inaccurate and unreliable or else as late, artificial constructions that had only the literary function of linking sections of narrative (cf. Wilson, *JBL* 94 [1975] 169–78). Recent study, however, has radically changed this conception. It is now seen that, for the kinship societies that use them, genealogies are not intended to be historical sources. Rather, they are oral or written expressions or mnemonics of the kinship relationships that form the fundamental organizational principle upon which such societies are based.

In *function,* linear genealogies, such as Ruth 4:18–22 (as opposed to segmented genealogies, i.e., the "family tree" type; see Wilson, *Sociological Approaches*, 57–61), essentially are used to support a claim to a position, role, rights, or power in different social spheres, domestic, religious, political, or socio-juridical. In *form,* they exhibit two characteristics: depth (i.e., the number of names in the list) and fluidity. Normally, they are five to ten generations in depth, as most of the biblical genealogies are, e.g., besides Ruth, Gen 4:17–24; 5:1–32; 25:12–15; 1 Sam 9:1. Although they may exhibit fluidity for a number of reasons, the most common type results from the loss of names as new generations are added. The names at the end are the well-known recent generations, and the names at the beginning are the revered and honored founders whose prestige and power the genealogy is usually intended to invoke. Hence, loss of names, often termed "telescoping" (see Wilson, *Genealogy and History,* 33), usually occurs in the middle of the list. The genealogy in Ruth 4:18–22 can now be seen in a very different light against this background. Its depth, ten members, is not only paralleled by linear genealogies in the biblical record, e.g., Gen 5:3–32; 11:10–26, but it is also characteristic of the average maximum length both of written linear genealogies in the ancient Near East in general and of oral linear genealogies elsewhere (see Wilson, *Genealogy and History,* 133–34). It is thus plausible that this genealogy exhibits the "telescoping" characteristic of such genealogies. That this is the case may be supported by the following. The names of Perez and Hezron at the beginning of the list were apparently well fixed in the tradition as important ancestors of the tribe of Judah (see Gen 46:9; Num 26:21). At the end of the list appear the generations of Boaz, Obed, Jesse, and David, the recent generations; in addition, Boaz and Obed are pertinent to the story, and the sequence Jesse-David was well known elsewhere (e.g., 1 Sam 16:1–23; 17:12; 22:9; 25:10; 1 Kgs 12:16). It is also clear that the sequence Amminadab-Nahshon was well fixed in the tradition from the Mosaic period (see the references in *Comment* below). It is perhaps, then, significant that Ram and Salmon, which exhibit the widest variation in form and spelling in all the versional attestations (and for Salmon in the MT as well), are the two names that link, on the one hand, the patriarchal generations to those of the Mosaic era, i.e., Ram, and, on the other hand, the names of the Mosaic era to those of the recent generations, i.e., Salmon. And certainly since it does not intend to be a historical document, it does not have to "stand up to historical examination" (Rudolph, 72).

Since genealogies function to legitimate claims to position, role, rights, or power (see above), a persuasive case can be made that 4:18–22, rather than being an insipid anticlimax, brings closure to the whole by underlining the significance of the story's resolution, Naomi's return to life and fullness through the birth of Obed. That resolution led two generations later to David (see *Explanation* for 4:18–22; cf. also the comments of Hubbard, 19–22; Sasson, 181). Extremely pertinent here, and in my opinion quite persuasive, is Berlin's argument (*Poetics,* 109–10) for the poetic function of the genealogy as a *coda,* a story conclusion that completes the narrative discourse by relating the narrative to the reader's own time in a variety of ways (see Berlin, *Poetics,* 107–9). "The genealogy, then, is the narrator, as spokesman for the Israelite narrative tradition, viewing the story of Ruth and putting it in the proper context in that narrative tradition. It is a kind of prologue and epilogue rolled into one, providing material that surrounds the story. This does not mean that it is a late addition" (110).

It has been argued that the genealogy is in conflict with the narrative itself in that in the story Obed, as the offspring of a levirate marriage, must belong to the genealogical line of Elimelech-Mahlon, whereas the genealogy makes him the son of Boaz (e.g., Rudolph, 71). But again, the new evidence delineated above has documented that genealogies change in structure and content when their function changes. As Wilson has put it (*Sociological Approaches,* 59):

> The configuration of a given lineage may change depending on the social sphere in which it is functioning. Thus, for example, domestic relationships based on genuine kinship may not be the same as political or economic ties. As the lineage's structure changes, the genealogy that reflects that structure must also change in order to be an

> accurate representation of the lineage. This process may give rise to several apparently contradictory genealogies which are in fact accurate records of the lineage functioning in particular contexts.

Consequently, differing genealogies are in use at the same time in order to represent the differing functions that such genealogies express (cf. also Wilson, *Genealogy and History,* 46–47). The people who use them do not regard them as contradictory, for in each sphere in which they function, they are regarded as true. Hence, it is quite conceivable that, in the sphere of family inheritance, Obed would be regarded as belonging to the line of Elimelech-Mahlon in order to express his right to the usufruct of the land that once belonged to that line. However, in the political sphere, in order to express David's right to exercise royal leadership, descent would be expressed through Boaz (cf. the discussion of Hubbard, 19–20). Further, that there is a blatant contradiction between the genealogy and the narrative in this regard may well be based upon false premises. It assumes not only that the marriage of Boaz and Ruth is a levirate marriage but also that the son born of levirate marriage must necessarily be regarded as belonging exclusively to the genealogical line of the deceased brother. This is based upon a literal understanding of the language in Deut 25:6; Ruth 4:5, 10. That neither of these presumptions is correct is argued in the exposition of the story below (see for the first *Excursus: Levirate Marriage in the OT* following the *Comment* on 4:5 and for the second the *Comment* in 4:5 on the phrase "to raise up descendants [lit. 'name'] for the deceased on his inheritance").

In conclusion, the role of the genealogy as a fitting and appropriate capstone revealing the significance of the resolution of the story argues for its originality, as does its role in the overall structure of the book, wherein it functions chiastically as the structural counterpart of the prologue in 1:1–6 (see *Explanation* at 1:1–6; cf. the remarks of Hubbard, 17; see also the outline and Table 1. Discourse Structure below).

Authorship and Date

Bibliography

Andersen, F. I. *The Hebrew Verbless Clause in the Pentateuch.* New York: Abingdon, 1970. **Bergey, R.** "The Book of Esther—Its Place in the Linguistic Milieu of Post-Exilic Biblical Hebrew: A Study in Late Biblical Hebrew." Diss., Dropsie College, 1983. **Berlin, A.** *Poetics and Interpretation of Biblical Narrative.* Sheffield: Almond, 1983. **Bewer, J.** "The *Gᵉʾullah* in the Book of Ruth." *AJSL* 19 (1902–3) 143–48. ———. *The Literature of the Old Testament in Its Historical Development.* Rev. ed. New York: Columbia UP, 1933. 282–84. **Burrows, M.** "The Marriage of Boaz and Ruth." *JBL* 59 (1940) 445–54. **David, M.** "The Date of the Book of Ruth." *OTS* 1 (1942) 55–63. **Davies, E.** "Inheritance Rights and the Hebrew Levirate Marriage, Part II." *VT* 31 (1981) 257–68. **Freedman, D. N.** "The Spelling of the Name 'David' in the Hebrew Bible." *HAR* 7 (1983) 89–104 (repr. *Divine Commitment and Human Obligation: Selected Writings of D. N. Freedman. Vol. 2: Poetry and Orthography,* ed. J. R. Huddlestun. Grand Rapids, MI: Eerdmans, 1996. Chap. 11). **Gordis, R.** "Love, Marriage, and Business in the Book of Ruth: A Chapter in Hebrew Customary Law." In *A Light unto My Path.* FS J. M. Myers, ed. H. Bream, R. Heim, and C. Moore. Philadelphia: Temple UP, 1974. 241–64. **Guenther, A. R.** "A Diachronic Study of Biblical Hebrew Prose Syntax:

An Analysis of the Verbal Clause in Jeremiah 37–45 and Esther 1–10." Diss., University of Toronto, 1977. **Hallo, W.** "New Viewpoints on Cuneiform Literature." *IEJ* 12 (1962) 13–26. **Hurvitz, A.** "The Chronological Significance of 'Aramaisms' in Biblical Hebrew." *IEJ* 18 (1968) 234–40. ———. "Dating the Priestly Source in Light of the Historical Study of Biblical Hebrew a Century after Wellhausen." *ZAW* 100 (1988) 88–100. ———. "Linguistic Criteria for Dating Problematic Biblical Texts." *Hebrew Abstracts* 14 (1973) 74–79. ———. *A Linguistic Study of the Relationship between the Priestly Source and the Book of Ezekiel.* Paris: Gabalda, 1982. ———. "On 'Drawing off the Sandal' in the Book of Ruth." (Heb.) *Shnaton* 1 (1975) 45–59. **Kutscher, E. Y.** *A History of the Hebrew Language,* ed. R. Kutscher. Leiden: Brill, 1982. **Lacocque, A.** "Date et milieu du livre de Ruth." *RHPR* 59 (1975) 583–93. **Lambert, W.** "A Catalogue of Texts and Authors." *JCS* 16 (1962) 59–81. **Lamparter, H.** *Das Buch der Sehnsucht.* BAT 16. Stuttgart: Calwer, 1962. **Leggett, D.** *The Levirate and Goel Institutions in the Old Testament.* Cherry Hill, NJ: Mack, 1974. **Meinhold, A.** "Theologische Schwerpunkte im Buch Ruth und ihr Gewicht für seine Datierung." *TZ* 32 (1976) 129–37. **Mittelmann, J. M.** "Der altisraelitische Levirat." Diss., Leipzig, 1934. **Myers, J.** *The Linguistic and Literary Form of the Book of Ruth.* Leiden: Brill, 1955. **Niditch, S.** "Legends of Wise Heroes and Heroines: Ruth." In *The Hebrew Bible and Its Modern Interpreters,* ed. D. Knight and G. Tucker. Philadelphia: Fortress, 1985. 451–56. **Oesterley, W.,** and **Robinson, T.** *An Introduction to the Books of the Old Testament.* New York: Meridian, 1958. 83–84. **Pfeiffer, R.** *Introduction to the Old Testament.* New York: Harper, 1941. **Pirston, P.** "*Šalap̄*—An Unrecognized Aramaism." (Heb.) *Leš* 35 (1971) 318. **Polzin, R.** *Late Biblical Hebrew: Toward an Historical Typology of Biblical Hebrew Prose.* Missoula, MT: Scholars, 1976. **Qimron, E.** *The Hebrew of the Dead Sea Scrolls.* Atlanta: Scholars, 1986. **Rendsburg, G.** "Late Biblical Hebrew and the Date of 'P'." *JANES* 12 (1980) 65–80. **Richter, H.-F.** "Zum Levirat im Buch Ruth." *ZAW* 95 (1983) 123–26. **Rooker, M.** *Biblical Hebrew in Transition: The Language of the Book of Ezekiel.* JSOTSup 90. Sheffield: JSOT, 1990. **Segal, M.** *A Grammar of Mishnaic Hebrew.* Oxford: Clarendon, 1927. **Sternberg, M.** *The Poetics of Biblical Narrative.* Bloomington, IN: Univ. of Indiana Press, 1985. **Vesco, J.-L.** "La date du livre de Ruth." *RB* 74 (1967) 235–47. **Weinfeld, M.** "Ruth, Book of." *EncJud* 14:518–24. **Weiser, A.** *The Old Testament: Its Formation and Development.* New York: Association, 1961. 302–5. **Wolfenson, L. B.** "The Purpose of the Book of Ruth." *BSac* 69 (1912) 329–44.

AUTHORSHIP

Any attempt to discuss in any concrete manner the authorship of the book of Ruth is an exercise in futility for the simple fact that, like the rest of biblical narrative (except perhaps for the post-exilic "memoirs" of Ezra and Nehemiah), not only is the book anonymous but it gives not the slightest hint, directly or indirectly, of the identity of the writer as a historical person. Nor have any traditions regarding authorship been preserved in any of the literature of ancient Israel (excluding the very late rabbinic traditions). As far as anonymity goes, this practice follows that of the ancient world in general. When Hallo surveyed the many thousands of documents that have been recovered from the Assyro-Babylonian sphere in 1962 (*IEJ* 12 [1962] 14–15), he could state that ". . . there are only two Akkadian compositions (and at most one Sumerian one) which incorporate specific reference to authorship," and even in these cases the attribution is made in such exceptional circumstances that they "seem merely to prove the rule." Indeed, biblical narrative reveals such an utter lack of concern about the identity of its authors as to outdo that of the ancient world in general (see on this point Sternberg, *Poetics,* 65–66). For, however much the literature of Israel's neighbors was almost invariably anonymous, both the Egyptian and Mesopotamian spheres have left evidence that a concern about authorship was not at all unknown, at least in literate circles. Thus, in ancient Egypt one text names and sings the praises of her greatest authors (and so is dubbed by modern scholars the "Praise of Learned Scribes"; see *ANET,* 431–32). And in the Akkadian sphere fragments of a catalogue have been found among the remains of Ashurbanipal's library (mid seventh century B.C.) in which literary works are listed and ascribed to named scholars, a kind of bibliography (see Lambert, *JCS* 16 [1962] 59–77). Lambert interprets the catalogue as a "manifestation of critical scholarship" dealing with authorship (59; for similar evidence from Hittite and Ugaritic texts, see Sternberg, *Poetics,* 66). However, from this concern for authors and authorship, OT narrative diverges arrestingly. Rather, "Biblical narrative exhibits such a rage for impersonality as must lead to the conclusion that is writers actively sought the cover of anonymity. . . . Its culture's and its own remarkable powers of memory encompass everything but the names that produced it" (Lambert, *JCS* 16 [1962] 65–66). The book of Ruth partakes fully of this utter lack of indications of authorship. The writer never refers to himself (or herself?) in any way whatsoever, and there are no exact clues to the time and place of writing. Consequently, about the author as a historical person we can say nothing, apart (perhaps) from some general indication of the date of writing, to which we shall now turn.

DATE

Although the biblical author adopts such a posture as a storyteller as to leave his historical identity utterly shrouded in mystery, it may well be that he has left us sufficient clues in the handling of his tale that we can say something about the date at which the story was written. However, here, as much as in the matter of the author's historical identity, the investigation has been dependent upon criteria that are highly subjective (cf. the remarks of Würthwein, 6) and open to the most diverse interpretation and understanding, drawing upon such matters as (1) the ideology or theology supposedly extant in the narrative, (2) the nature of the socio-legal institutions presumably present in the text and their relationship to the nature of these institutions elsewhere in the OT, (3) the most probable setting in the OT period for the presumed purpose and intent of the story, (4) parallels between the events and characters of the narrative and those of other OT stories, or (5) the nature of the language of the text. Given such criteria, it is not surprising that the most diverse datings have been proposed, running from the Davidic era itself down to the latter part of the post-exilic period.

Indeed, revealing the subjective nature of such criteria, not infrequently much the same evidence has been used to argue for widely diverse datings. As regards the language of the story, it has very frequently been claimed that the large number of Aramaisms and late usages can only be explained if the book is post-exilic in date (so Gordis, "Love, Marriage, and Business," 244–46; Joüon, 11–13). For others, however, not only are the Aramaisms and late usages very few (Sasson, 244) and/or not demonstrably late (Campbell, 24–25; Hertzberg, 259; Hubbard, 26–27; Rudolph, 28), but the text contains demonstrably early linguistic features (Campbell, 25–26; Hubbard, 30–31; Myers, *Linguistic Form,* 8, 20, 32; Weinfeld, *EncJud* 14:521–22). Similarly, in the matter of the ideology of the story, it has been argued since the middle of the nineteenth century that the book advocates a spirit of universalism and tolerance of foreigners and mixed marriages, since Ruth is a Moabitess and is nonetheless accepted into Israelite society and marries Boaz, a righteous Israelite of substance and standing. Therefore, it is argued, the book is a product of the party favoring such a view and in opposition to the rigorist and exclusivist policies of Ezra and Nehemiah (Bewer, *Literature,* 282–84; Oesterley and Robinson, *Introduction,* 84; Weiser, *Old Testament,* 304; most recently, Lacocque, *RHPR* 59 [1975] 584, 87 and passim; for other bibliography, see Leggett, *The Levirate,* 147 n. 11). On the other hand, others have argued that the attitude in the book of Ruth of a willing and friendly incorporation of foreigners into Israel argues for a date in the pre-exilic period. In the post-exilic era such assimilation was a matter of religious commitment, not compassion or cultural assimilation as in Ruth (so Meinhold, *TZ* 32 [1976] 131–32; cf. also Hertzberg, 258–59; Lamparter, *Das Buch der Sehnsucht,* 16; Wolfenson, *BSac* 69 [1912] 337–39). Again, in contradistinction to such conclusions from the book's openness to Moab, Gordis argues that the book must be post-exilic since, in Ruth, Moab was no longer an actual enemy on Israel's borders as she was prior to the exile ("Love, Marriage, and Business," 245; cf. Gerleman, 7–8). One finds a similar situation when one turns to the matter of the socio-legal institutions presumed in the book. Thus, the vast majority of scholars have posited that the marriage between Boaz and Ruth is a levirate marriage. On the basis of this assumption, often tacit, some have argued that the way the levirate functions in Ruth is so different from that institution in Gen 38 and Deut 25 that in Ruth we must have a custom that either has long become outdated (so Lacocque, *RHPR* 59 [1975] 588–89) or has fallen into disuse (so David, *OTS* 1 [1942] 58–59; Vesco, *RB* 74 [1967] 242–43) or has become broadened or expanded in its application (so Davies, *VT* 31 [1981] 257–67). Hence, Ruth must be later than Genesis and Deuteronomy, and since these texts, it is assumed, date to the exile, Ruth must be post-exilic. Others, however, have argued on various grounds that the nature of the levirate in Ruth is such that it predates the legislation in Deuteronomy and so must be pre-exilic. Thus, Bewer (*AJSL* 19 [1902–3] 143–44) and Burrows (*JBL* 59 [1940] 450–54) propose that the levirate marriage of Boaz and Ruth is part of the clan responsibility devolving upon the *gôʾēl,* the "redeemer" (Hebrew גֹּאֵל, i.e., the relative with family obligations), and so represents an earlier stage than that of Deut 25, which is strictly limited to the immediate family (cf. also Hertzberg, 258–59; Richter, *ZAW* 95 [1983] 126). Exactly similar are those attempts to argue from the shoe custom in Ruth 4:7, often in comparison with that in Deut 25:9, that Ruth, on the one hand, must be later than the exile (Gray, *NCBC,* 367; Joüon, 13; Pfeiffer, *Introduction,* 718) or, on the other, earlier (Mittelmann, "Der altisraelitische Levirat," 23–24; Rudolph, 27–28; Weinfeld, *EncJud* 14:521).

Though other examples could be cited (cf. the summary of views in Meinhold, *TZ* 32 [1976] 129–30), these show how tenuous and tendentious are the arguments for the date of the book based upon criteria that are open to such diverse interpretations. Some of these arguments are based on presuppositions that upon closer examination are simply incorrect. This is particularly true of those many attempts to date the book on the presumption that the marriages referred to in 1:11–13 and in chaps. 3 and 4 are to be understood as levirate marriages, either identical, or closely related at least, to those in Gen 38 and Deut 25. For arguments that such is not the case, see *Excursus: Levirate Marriage in the OT* and the

Comment on 4:5. For a succinct survey documenting that results based upon such criteria are contradictory and inconclusive, see Niditch, "Ruth," 451–56, and for a more extensive treatment, see Hubbard, 24–46, or Sasson, 240–52.

Recently, however, developments in the understanding and critical evaluation of the dating of biblical Hebrew may give us more objective criteria for an approximate dating for the book of Ruth. These developments have come about through the application of the linguistic theory of diachrony, i.e., the nature and character of language change through time, to the study of the language of the OT. (For a succinct discussion of the linguistic theory involved, see Rooker, *Biblical Hebrew,* 1–21, or Bergey, "Book of Esther," 1–10.) Although, like all languages, the Hebrew of the OT period must have undergone a slow process of linguistic change, only relatively late in the elucidation of its grammar has it been discovered that its written remains give evidence of this fact (see Rooker, *Biblical Hebrew,* 23–33, for a short but helpful survey of the history of this discovery). Though other factors have been involved (notably theological views of the language as sacred and hence *sui generis*), this has undoubtedly resulted from the remarkable and surprising uniformity of the whole corpus of OT Hebrew, which is due to both the stabilizing force of the written religious medium that it constitutes (cf. the comments of Bergey, "Book of Esther," 10–12) and the homogeneity imposed upon it by the Masoretic traditionists who produced its present vocalized form. Nevertheless, despite this remarkable uniformity, the OT text does enshrine numerous significant traces of linguistic changes over time. The existence of such data was noted as early as the last century and by ca. 1900 it had in general become clear that at least two different phases of the language could be distinguished: one to be found in texts from the pre-exilic era and the other in those from the post-exilic period. Note especially the still important delineation of late features both in Driver's description of the linguistic characteristics of the post-exilic literature (*ILOT*, 473–75, 484–85, 504–8, 535–40, 553) and in BDB, passim. Based on work such as this, the existence of these two phases has been recognized in the standard grammatical treatises (see GKC § 2l, m, t–v; *GBH* § 3b; BL § 2q). Little was done, however, then or in the following decades, to delineate the specific features of these two phases of the language. But in the last few decades, the application of sound linguistic methodology and the availability of new comparative material, such as the Dead Sea Scrolls, have produced major progress in the elucidation of the historical phases of OT Hebrew (for a general discussion, see Kutscher, *History* §§ 17, 111–25). This is particularly true in regard to the determination of the linguistic character of the Hebrew of the literature of the post-exilic period, now generally called Late Biblical Hebrew (LBH), so much so that in 1988 Hurvitz could write: ". . . it is widely recognized in contemporary research that LBH constitutes a well-defined linguistic entity whose characteristics are manifested in every aspect of the language—orthography, grammar, vocabulary, and syntax" (*ZAW* 100 [1988] 90).

Indeed, several recent studies have attempted to delineate the features of a transitional stage between the language of the pre-exilic phase, now generally called Standard Biblical Hebrew (SBH), and the full-blown LBH of such texts as Ezra-Nehemiah, Chronicles, and Esther. In *Late Biblical Hebrew,* Polzin attempted to show that the language of those passages of the Pentateuch that are generally agreed by OT scholarship to belong to the Priestly source P is typologically later than the language of SBH as represented in three traditional corpora: (1) a sampling of the Pentateuchal source JE from Exodus and Numbers (for the delineation of which, see *Late Biblical Hebrew,* 117 n. 10), (2) the so-called Court History of 2 Samuel and 1 Kings (117 n. 11), and (3) a sampling of the language of the so-called Deuteronomic History (117 n. 12). Hence, Polzin argued, the language of P represented a transitional stage between SBH and LBH. Subsequent research has not substantiated this conclusion, however, but rather indicates that the language of P is substantially SBH (see Hurvitz, *Linguistic Study,* 163–71; Rendsburg, *JANES* 12 [1980] 65–80; Rooker, *Biblical Hebrew,* 35–53). Nevertheless, Polzin's pioneering work went a long way toward establishing the specific features of LBH, and a significant number of his criteria have been generally accepted. This further research has, however, rather clearly established that it is the language of the book of Ezekiel (most probably reflecting its exilic date and milieu) that best reflects a transitional stage between pre-exilic SBH and full-blown post-exilic LBH. This was argued first by Hurvitz in a number of works, notably *Linguistic Study,* based mainly upon lexicographical data, and then fully confirmed by Rooker in *Biblical Hebrew in Transition,* which took into account a much broader range of linguistic evidence, including orthography, morphology, and syntax, as well as lexicography.

Now the determination of the linguistic features of LBH has also of necessity resulted in the determination of a like number of the features of SBH, with which the LBH features contrast. Hence, with this wealth of data available for distinguishing whether a given corpus of OT Hebrew lies within the range of SBH, LBH, or the transitional stage between them, it is no longer possible, as has been the case in the ongoing dispute about the date of Ruth, simply to cite a few isolated linguistic features, often tacitly assumed to be "early" or "late," as an argument for the date of the book (see the examples given above, and cf., surprisingly, Rooker, *Biblical Hebrew,* 83). Rather, only a full examination of the linguistic features of the language of Ruth vis-à-vis those of SBH and LBH will suffice to determine, if possible, with which phase of OT Hebrew the book may belong.

Before turning to such an examination, however, a few brief comments on methodological considerations are necessary. First, it must be kept in mind that for a given linguistic feature to be regarded as LBH, as opposed to SBH, it must meet two linguistic criteria: the principle of linguistic contrast or substitution and the principle of linguistic distribution (see Hurvitz, *Hebrew Abstracts* 14 [1973] 75–76). The first establishes the differences between the two phases in the use of a particular grammatical or lexical feature in identical or similar contexts, thus establishing a possible diachronic development. Thus, for example, note the change from מַמְלֶכֶת, "kingdom," to מַלְכוּת, "kingdom," in identical context between 2 Sam 7:12 and 1 Chron 17:11 (see Rooker, *Biblical Hebrew,* 56–57). The second principle establishes that the change is widespread in the later language and not peculiar to one particular source. Thus, for example, מַלְכוּת, "kingdom," also occurs to the exclusion of מַמְלֶכֶת in Daniel and Esther, in the DSS, and is the only term employed in mishnaic Hebrew (see Rooker, *Biblical Hebrew,* 56–57). The first principle is necessary to obviate the possibility that a linguistic feature that is widespread in LBH but absent in SBH may be missing there simply because there was no occasion in SBH to use it (for examples, see Bergey, "Book of Esther," 187–88). The second principle is necessary to obviate the possibility that a linguistic feature that does contrast with SBH usage in only one LBH text may derive from the idiolect or genre and style of that one author.

Finally, the size of the book of Ruth must be taken into account. It is very small for statistical comparison, consisting of only 80 verses of narrative (excluding the genealogy in 4:18–22) with only 1,252 words. Given such a small corpus, a number of linguistic features occur only one, two, or three times. In each instance, the uncertainty of results based upon such a low frequency of occurrence must be taken into account. Particularly is this true in regard to those linguistic features that exhibit "variancy," i.e., alternative ways of expressing the same feature, which a speaker may freely choose at any given time, one usually more common, the other less so. The existence of such variants is common to all languages and is a significant factor (if not *the* significant factor) in language change (for a brief discussion, see Rooker, *Biblical Hebrew*, 17–21). One of the implications of this phenomenon is that the diachronic change in two stages of the language may consist not in the absolute displacement of one linguistic feature by an alternative one but rather by a change in the frequency of usage. A feature that was infrequent at one stage of the language becomes the dominant mode of expression at a later time. If this is the type of linguistic change involved in a given case, then a very small number of occurrences gives little indication of which stage of the language is represented.

In examining the linguistic nature of the book of Ruth, neither time nor space will permit here an independent examination of all or most of the linguistic features of Ruth followed by a comparison of these with the corresponding features of SBH and LBH (cf. the methodology of Guenther, "A Diachronic Study," 1–10, 189–90). Rather, we shall use those features that have been determined with reasonable certainty to be characteristic of LBH as opposed to SBH in the following recent works: Bergey, "Book of Esther" (hereafter *BE*); Guenther, "Diachronic Study" (hereafter *DS*); Hurvitz, *Linguistic Study* (hereafter *LS*); Polzin, *Late Biblical Hebrew* (hereafter *LBH*); and Rooker, *Biblical Hebrew in Transition* (hereafter *BHT*); together with one important study on a linguistic feature in Ruth, Hurvitz, *Shnaton* 1 (1975) 45–59. And we shall determine how many of these features in the book of Ruth exhibit the SBH form and how many the LBH form and so attempt to find where in the range SBH—transitional stage (Ezekiel)—LBH the book lies.

Standard Biblical Hebrew

In the following linguistic features, the form in Ruth aligns with SBH. They are not presented in any particular order.

(1) אנכי vs. אני. Although both forms of the first person singular independent pronoun occur throughout biblical Hebrew, the long form אנכי is much more frequent in SBH. In later texts the short form prevails more and more. Thus, Rooker (*BHT*, 72–73) notes that in the Pentateuchal corpus designated JE אנכי prevails over אני by a ratio of 81 to 48; in Jeremiah, however, אני prevails over אנכי by 54 to 37; and in the late books of Ezekiel, Haggai, Zech 1–8, Malachi, Ecclesiastes, Lamentations, Ezra-Nehemiah, Daniel, Chronicles, and Esther, one finds 265 uses of אני to only 5 of אנכי. In the DSS אני prevails almost exclusively (Qimron, *HDSS*, 57). Ruth patterns with SBH: אנכי is used seven times, אני twice.

(2) In LBH there is a marked decrease in the waw-consecutive tenses in general (see Guenther, *DS* § 9.2.4 and Table 9-4; Rooker, *BHT*, 100–102) and in the use of ויהי and והיה in particular (see Polzin, *LBH*, 56–58). In Ruth, however, the waw-consecutive tense is in full use throughout, there being only one use of the perfect tense plus waw-conjunctive in 4:7, for which see the discussion in LBH feature (6) below. In particular, the waw-consecutive plus perfect occurs some 15 times, evidencing a number of the uses characteristic of SBH: simple future (והיה, 4:15); introduction of temporal clause in the future (והיה, 3:13); to continue the jussive and imperative (ואכלת . . . וטבלת, 2:14; וידעת . . . ובאת . . . וגלית . . . ושכבתי, 3:4); subordinate clause of result (והיו, 1:11); the protasis of a condition (וצמת, 2:9); to form an imperative not dependent on a previous verb (והלכת . . . ושתית, 2:9; ורחצת . . . וסכת . . . וירדתי, 3:3; ופרשת, 3:9).

(3) The decrease in the waw-consecutive tenses occasioned a change in the form of the temporal clause consisting of a preposition, most frequently ב or כ, plus the infinitive or other substantive. In the SBH form of the idiom, the prepositional phrase is regularly preceded by ויהי/והיה; in LBH texts, ויהי/והיה is regularly lacking (see Bergey, *BE*, 52–55; Polzin, *LBH*, 56–67; Rooker, *BHT*, 103–5). The Ruth usage accords with SBH: 4 times the prepositional phrase occurs with ויהי/והיה (1:19; 3:4, 8, 13).

(4) In biblical Hebrew the conjunction אשׁר may be used to subordinate a substantival clause as the object of a verb, rather than the far more regular conjunction כי, "that." This usage is rare in SBH but occurs more frequently in LBH, until the use of כי died out completely in mishnaic Hebrew (MH), which used only the particle שֶׁ, the MH equivalent of אשׁר (see Bergey, *BE*, 61–64; Polzin, *LBH*, 128; Rooker, *BHT*, 111–12). Ruth patterns with SBH: אשׁר is not used, but כי occurs 6 times (1:6, 18; 2:22; 3:11, 14; 4:9).

(5) One type of the substantival clause introduced by כי or אשׁר that functions as the object of a verb, mentioned in (4) above, is of diachronic significance. This type of substantival clause consists of a personal pronoun subject plus nominal predicate. In the SBH pattern, the order of the clause is predicate-subject (for examples see Andersen, *Hebrew Verbless Clause* §§ 369, 372–74), whereas in LBH the order is subject-predicate (see Bergey, *BE*, 71–72). Two examples of this type of clause occur in Ruth with the order predicate-subject (1:18, 3:11), patterning with SBH.

(6) In SBH the use of ל to mark the direct object of a verb instead of the particle את does sporadically occur. In LBH, however, its use markedly increases (see Polzin, *LBH*, 64–66; Rooker, *BHT*, 97–99). The usage is completely lacking in Ruth, a phenomenon that accords with SBH, although the small size of the corpus of Ruth somewhat mitigates its weight.

(7) The plene spelling of the name David (i.e., with the addition of the vowel-letter yodh, דויד) rather than the defective writing (i.e., without the yodh, דוד), long recognized to be a late phenomenon, has recently been given a full treatment by Freedman (*HAR* 7 [1983] 89–104; cf. also Rooker, *BHT*, 68–71). The shift from the defective spelling in SBH to the plene in LBH is extremely consistent. Thus, in Samuel-Kings, Isaiah, Jeremiah, and Psalms, the plene form is found only 4 times and the defective 780. In the LBH books of Ezra-Nehemiah and Chronicles, the plene form is found 271 times, the defective 0. And Ezekiel seems to be transitional, with 1 plene spelling and 3 defective (see Rooker, *BHT*, 69;

Freedman, *HAR* 7 [1983] 95–96). Ruth patterns with SBH, with 2 occurrences of the defective spelling in 4:17, 22.

(8) With the alternative prepositional expressions . . . בין . . . ובין (lit. "between . . . and between . . .") and . . . בין . . . ל (lit. "between . . . to . . ."), the first is by far predominant in SBH; in LBH the second becomes more frequent than the first (see Rooker, *BHT*, 117–19). In 1:17 Ruth uses בין . . . ובין. Given the fact that both forms do occur in both SBH and LBH, a single occurrence of either form in the absence of other criteria is necessarily ambiguous. But given the significant number of criteria listed above that pattern with SBH, this usage may be said to exhibit a slight predilection in that direction.

(9) Occasionally the final nun of the preposition מן, "from," does not assimilate before a noun without an article. Although this occurs sporadically in SBH texts, it occurs with much greater frequency in the later texts and particularly the LBH texts of Nehemiah, Daniel, and Chronicles (see Polzin, *LBH*, 66; Rendsburg, *JANES* 12 [1980] 72). In Ruth the preposition מן occurs prefixed to 14 different substantives (without the article) a total of 21 times. Although both assimilated and unassimilated forms occur in both SBH and LBH texts, this number of different substantives and occurrences is much more probable in an SBH text than an LBH one.

(10) Finally, there is another linguistic feature that aligns Ruth with SBH. In the *Comments* on 1:8 and on 1:22, the occurrence of 7 examples of what appears to be the second or third person *masculine plural* pronoun suffix (5x), verbal suffix (1x), or independent pronoun (1x), all referring to two women, was noted, all of which are to be understood instead as examples of second or third person *dual* morphemes having common gender. Recently, Rendsburg has discussed the appearances of some 43 occurrences of dual pronoun suffixes in biblical Hebrew and has demonstrated their marked decrease in the later texts of the OT (*JANES* 12 [1980] 77). To Rendsburg's evidence must be added the 2 examples of the third person dual independent pronoun in Zech 5:10; Ruth 1:22. The evidence for the decrease in the use of the dual morpheme (a phenomenon in keeping with the disappearance of the dual in Egypto-Semitic in general, see Rendsburg, *JANES* 12 [1980] 77, esp. n. 55) is then as follows (excluding Ruth, where chronological orientation is at issue): in early works (P, JE, Judges, 1 Samuel), 24x; in exilic SBH works (Jeremiah, Ecclesiastes, Zechariah), 4x; in the transitional stage between SBH and LBH (Ezekiel), 4x; in works of uncertain date (Proverbs, Canticles), 6x; in unmistakably LBH works (Daniel, Ezra-Nehemiah, Chronicles, Esther), 0x. The lack of any appearances of the dual suffix in LBH must not be pressed, for it is likely that the opportunity for feminine duals, the only forms presenting evidence for the survival of the dual, simply does not occur. Nevertheless, the appearance of 7 forms of the dual in Ruth clearly shows that Ruth patterns with SBH in this linguistic feature.

These ten features clearly align Ruth with SBH. However, there are also a number of features that accord with LBH.

Late Biblical Hebrew

In the following linguistic features, the form in Ruth aligns with LBH. Again, the order in which they are presented is not pertinent to the discussion.

(1) In biblical Hebrew the pronominal object may be expressed in two different ways. It may be attached directly to the verb as a pronominal suffix, or it may be attached to the direct object marker אֶת־/אוֹת־ as a separate word. When in preverbal position for emphasis, the pronominal object must be attached to the object marker; hence no variation is possible. However, in post-verbal position, where the two different forms seem to be free variants, there is a marked difference in preference between SBH and LBH. Although SBH texts in general express the pronominal object more often with the suffix attached directly to the verb than attached to the object marker, in LBH texts the pronominal object is overwhelmingly attached directly to the verb (see Polzin, *LBH,* 28–31; Bergey, *BE,* 85–89; Guenther, *DS,* 89–92, 197–99). Thus, in the corpus of SBH texts surveyed by Polzin, the ratio is almost 2 to 1 in favor of the direct attachment of the suffix to the verb (see Polzin, *LBH,* 99–100). On the other hand, in Polzin's LBH sources, the direct attachment of the suffix to the verb prevails by a ratio of almost 17 to 1 (see Polzin, *LBH,* 28–31; the figures of Guenther, *DS,* 198, Table 9-5A, are very similar). The diachronic nature of the change is further confirmed by the fact that the pronominal object is attached directly to the verb in DSS Hebrew 250x as opposed to only 11x attached to the object marker when not required by syntax or morphology (see Qimron, *HDSS,* 75–76). The following example from a biblical quote in the DSS illustrates the diachronic nature of the phenomenon (see Qimron, *HDSS,* 76):

Num 30:6(ET 30:5): וְאִם־הֵנִיא אָבִיהָ אֹתָהּ, "if her father opposed her"
Temple Scroll 53:21: כי־הניאה, "because (her father) opposed her"

In this linguistic feature Ruth accords fully with the LBH pattern; there are 10 examples of the pronominal object attached directly to the verb (1:21; 2:4, 13, 15; 3:16, 13, 13; 4:15, 15, 16). There is not 1 example in which the pronominal object is attached to the object marker. The usage in Ruth here stands in sharp contrast not only to SBH but even to the exilic Jeremiah (combining the evidence from the prose sections sampled by Bergey [*BE,* 87] and Guenther [*DS,* Table 9-5], the ratio is 3 to 1 in favor of the verbal suffix [54 to 18]) and to Ezekiel (Bergey's sampling [*BE,* 87] gives 9 verbal suffix uses to 16 with the object marker).

(2) A second linguistic phenomenon in connection with the pronominal object also may exhibit a diachronically significant difference between SBH and LBH. In SBH, when the verb is a plural form ending in *-û,* written plene or defectively, and the pronominal object is either third person masculine or feminine singular, it is regularly attached to the object marker rather than directly to the verb, dramatically reversing the pattern noted in the first feature aligning Ruth with LBH. In LBH texts, however, these pronominal objects are almost invariably attached directly to the verb. (For the third masculine singular pronominal object in SBH and LBH, see Guenther, *DS,* 199–20, esp. Table 9-5C; Rooker, *BHT,* 86; and for the transitional phase represented by Ezekiel see Rooker, *BHT,* 87.) The third person feminine singular pronominal object occurs so infrequently in LBH as to preclude a definitive statement. Nevertheless, the following data agree with the pattern for the masculine suffix. In a sampling of early texts, the feminine suffix is attached to the object marker 7x (Gen 12:15, 15; 34:8, 21; Judg 15:6; 19:25; 1 Kgs 1:3) but to the verb 3x (Gen 34:10; 38:24; Judg 19:25). In late

texts Rooker notes one example in the transitional stage represented by Ezekiel (36:18, *BHT,* 87), and another example occurs in LBH in 1 Chron 11:14. Both are attached directly to the verb, in contrast to the pattern in the SBH texts noted above. The form תְּכְלִימוּהָ in Ruth 2:15 accords with the usage in Ezekiel and Chronicles, aligning Ruth with LBH.

(3) In his study of the use of the frequently synonymous prepositions ל and אל, Guenther found that in general the preposition used was verb specific (i.e., with few exceptions one or the other occurred with a given verb) and that with the verb אמר, "to say," the preposition most frequently used changed from אל in SBH texts to ל in LBH (*DS,* 96–99; 202–6, esp. Table 9-7; Guenther's evidence for verbs other than אמר is either too little to be significant or appears to be a phenomenon of the idiolect of the writer of Chronicles). Thus, in Guenther's evidence from the SBH corpus used by Polzin (see above), the verb אמר takes the preposition אל 162x to only 50x for ל, a ratio of 3.25 to 1 in favor of the former. However, in LBH texts the ratio is 18 uses of אל to 83 with ל, a ration of 4.5 to 1 in favor of the latter. This represents a fifteenfold change in the ratio from SBH to LBH. A similar phenomenon occurs with the use of the same prepositions with the substantive קרוב, "near, close." Whether used literally in a spatial sense or figuratively, often then referring to blood relationship, the substantive appears 16x in SBH texts with the preposition אל only (Gen 45:10; Exod 12:4; Lev 21:2, 3; 25:25; Num 27:11; Deut 4:7; 13:8; 21:3, 6; 22:2; 30:14; Josh 9:16; 2 Sam 19:43; 1 Kgs 8:46, 59). However, in later texts (apart from the chronologically uncertain Psalms, 34:19; 85:10, both of which use ל), *both* אל and ל occur. In the transitional stage represented by Ezekiel, one finds one example of אל (43:19) and one of ל (42:13) and in LBH one finds one example of אל (Esth 1:14) and one of ל (Neh 13:4). This diachronic change in the use of אל and ל is further substantiated by the fact that in MH אל is rare (Segal, *A Grammar of Mishnaic Hebrew [GMH],* 142). In the use of these prepositions with the verb אמר, "to say, speak," Ruth stands significantly closer to the LBH pattern with 8 examples with אל to 15 with ל, a ratio of 1.9 to 1 in favor of the latter. Also, the one use of קרוב ל- in Ruth (2:20) definitely patterns with the exilic to post-exilic usage.

(4) There are several lexical features in Ruth that definitely pattern with later rather than earlier usage. The first concerns the idiom for "to take a wife." In this idiom in biblical Hebrew, two synonyms for "to take" occur: לקח and נשׂא. In SBH the verb לקח is used to the virtual exclusion of נשׂא: לקח is used many dozens of times (e.g., 34x in Genesis alone), but נשׂא occurs only in Judg 21:23. In LBH texts, however, the two verbs are used with nearly equal frequency: לקח occurs in Ezra-Nehemiah 3x (Ezra 2:61 = Neh 7:63; Neh 6:18; 10:31) and in the sections of Chronicles not paralleled in Samuel-Kings 6x (1 Chron 2:19, 21; 4:18; 7:15; 2 Chron 11:18, 20); נשׂא occurs in Ezra-Nehemiah 4x (Ezra 9:2, 12; 10:44; Neh 13:25) and in the sections of Chronicles not paralleled in Samuel-Kings 4x (1 Chron 23:22; 2 Chron 11:21; 13:21; 24:3). Kutscher explains this change convincingly by noting that the verb לקח is used in biblical Hebrew mainly with the meaning "to take" but in MH mainly with the meaning "to buy" and that this change is already under way in LBH (see *History of the Hebrew Language* § 123, 82–83). This is unquestionable; besides Kutscher's example in the chronologically uncertain Prov 31:16, see Neh 5:2, 3; 10:32. Hence, to avoid misunderstanding, נשׂא began to be used for "to take a wife." In Ruth one finds one example of נשׂא (1:4) and one example of לקח (4:13), aligning Ruth with the late usage of LBH.

(5) לְקַיֵּם, 4:7. An accumulation of late features occurs in Ruth 4:7–8, two lexical and one syntactical. The form קִיֵּם, the piel stem of קוּם, with the meaning "to confirm, establish, effect" is unquestionably a late feature; for the evidence, see Hurvitz, *LS,* 32–35; cf. Rooker, *BHT,* 83–85; Bergey, *BE,* 40–42. The diachronic change meets the criterion of contrast in that the form of the verb with this meaning in SBH is exclusively the hiphil, הֵקִים. And the principle of distribution is met first by the fact that קִיֵּם occurs in biblical Hebrew only in LBH texts (Esther 7x, Ezekiel 1x, Ps 119 2x) and second by the fact that the root קוּם has virtually disappeared in MH except for the piel קִיֵּם, which is in widespread usage (see Segal, *GMH* §§ 109, 179–80; Hurvitz, *LS,* 34; and esp. Hurvitz, *Shnaton* 1 [1975] 48). LBH represents the transitional period of this linguistic change, for both forms appear therein (for הֵקִים, cf. Dan 9:12; Neh 5:13; 2 Chron 33:3). The usage in the book of Ruth fits this transitional stage, for the hiphil לְהָקִים occurs in 4:5, 10, whereas the piel appears in 4:7. The diachronic change of the latter in Ruth is nicely illustrated by the following parallel passages:

1 Kgs 2:4 לְמַעַן יָקִים יהוה אֶת־דְּבָרוֹ
"so that the LORD may effect his word . . ."

Ezek 13:6 וְיִחֲלוּ לְקַיֵּם דָּבָר
"and they hope to effect (their) word."

Ruth 4:7 וְזֹאת לְפָנִים . . . לְקַיֵּם כָּל־דָּבָר
"And this formerly was (the custom) . . . to effect any matter"

Though forms like this do occur rarely in biblical Hebrew and so are genuine variant Hebrew forms (see Segal, *GMH* § 180), it is highly probable that the *increase* in their usage in LBH and MH results from the influence of Aramaic, where they are very common. In this sense they are "Aramaisms" (see Hurvitz, *LS,* 34; Rooker, *BHT,* 85).

(6) וְנָתַן, 4:7. In the discussion of SBH linguistic feature (2) above, it was noted that one feature of LBH is a marked decrease in the waw-consecutive tenses in general (see bibliography there), in place of which one finds instead the simple tense with waw-conjunctive. Rooker (*BHT,* 101) notes the following example, where the writer of Chronicles uses the simple tense with waw-conjunctive in place of the waw-consecutive form in the parallel passage in Kings:

2 Kgs 23:6 וַיֹּצֵא אֶת־הָאֲשֵׁרָה . . . וַיִּשְׂרֹף אֹתָהּ . . . וַיָּדֶק
"And he brought out the Asherah . . . and burned it . . . and *ground it up*"

2 Chron 34:4 וְהָאֲשֵׁרִים . . . שִׁבַּר וְהֵדַק
"And the Asherim . . . he broke to pieces and *ground them up*"

This decrease in use in the consecutive tenses continued in the Hebrew of the DSS (Rooker, *BHT,* 101–2), and in MH they ceased to be used completely (Segal, *GMH* §§ 104, 308, 316). In the book of Ruth one finds in 4:7 the waw-conjunctive plus perfect form (וְנָתַן) to express temporal consecution in the past, instead of the waw-consecutive form (וַיִּתֵּן), which is the form used for this purpose throughout the rest of Ruth and almost invariably throughout SBH. It is highly probable that this syntactic change between SBH and LBH also results from the influence of Aramaic, which does not have the consecutive tenses (see the remarks of Rooker, *BHT,* 102).

(7) נעל + שׁלף, 4:7. The third feature of 4:7 that is very clearly late usage is the use of the verb שָׁלַף with נַעַל, "sandal(s)," to express the meaning "draw off." Joüon (11) identified the combination in 1924 as a "probable neologism," without providing evidence for his judgment. This evidence has now been convincingly supplied by Hurvitz (*Shnaton* 1 [1975] 45–59), who shows that the combination meets the criteria for linguistic change. First, it contrasts with SBH usage, in which the verb שׁלף occurs almost exclusively in the idiom חרב + שׁלף, "to draw the sword" (15x). It never occurs with נעל, "sandal." Rather, the verbs in this idiom are חלץ (Deut 25:9, 10; Isa 20:2) or נשׁל (Exod 3:5; Josh 5:15). Consequently, ". . . not by the lack of a suitable opportunity—nor by the lack of a fitting context—can one explain the absence of נעל + שׁלף from the early books of the Bible" (*Shnaton* 1 [1975] 46). Second, does it meet the criteria of linguistic distribution and concentration? Hurvitz argues that it does (46–49). First, he presents striking evidence that this linguistic change results from Aramaic influence. Thus, in the Palestinian Targumim (examples are given from Pseudo-Jonathan, Jonathan, Neofiti, and Shomroni, drawn from Pirston, *Leš* 35 [1971] 318) in Exod 3:5; Deut 25:9; Isa 20:2, the Aramaic verb שׁלף regularly translates both Hebrew חלץ and נשׁל. This strongly suggests that the late Hebrew expression נעל + שׁלף is a calque, i.e., a new expression created by the influence of an Aramaic background upon the speaker's Hebrew. There is, however, a complete lack of the idiom in the *Hebrew* literature of the Tannaitic age. In spite of this, Hurvitz argues that the conclusion is compelling on the grounds that this feature is not a single, exceptional, and isolated example in the text in which it occurs. There is, in point of fact, a singular concentration of such features in Ruth 4:7. Further, this verse is an insertion into the body of the narrative of chap. 4, either by the author or by a later hand. Therefore, it ". . . constitutes an independent 'unit' from a literary and linguistic examination" (*Shnaton* 1 [1975] 48). With this conclusion our own analysis of the structure of chap. 4 agrees completely (see my discussion in *Form/Structure/Setting* on 4:1–12, esp. the chart of the structure of vv 3–8). This digression, which anticipates the narrator's statement in v 8c, is inserted into the middle of the redeemer's response (vv 6–8) to Boaz's challenge in v 5. Because of its length, it causes the narrator to insert a second narrative introduction (v 8a) in order to clarify to his readers who is speaking to whom. Hence, it is legitimate to discuss this verse in isolation from the scroll of Ruth in general. And in this verse, Hurvitz notes (48), we have another undoubtedly late feature heavily influenced by Aramaic, לְקַיֵּם, see LBH feature (5) above. Hence, he concludes, we have such a concentration of late elements influenced by Aramaic as to tip the scales decisively in favor of the conclusion that the expression נעל + שׁלף is a late Aramaic calque. The evidence is even more compelling than this. To the late feature לְקַיֵּם we can now add the phenomenon of the waw-conjunction plus perfect form וְנָתַן, a late feature also resulting from Aramaic influence; see LBH feature (6) above. Hence, we have three late elements of Aramaic influence in this one verse. When one adds to the equation the further accumulation of late elements in the book of Ruth in general set forth in LBH items (1) through (4) above, the case seems conclusive indeed.

Whether this remarkable concentration of late elements influenced by Aramaic in Ruth 4:7 is evidence for the lateness of the book as a whole depends, of course, upon whether one considers the digression that 4:7 represents to have been added to the text by the author of the rest of the book or by a later hand. In agreement with the majority of modern commentators (see the comments of Berlin, *Poetics,* 99), in my opinion there is no unevenness or other incongruity of any kind in the structure of the text that precludes the conclusion that the digression is from the hand of the author of the rest of the narrative and not from a later hand. It can only be said that this very concentration of late elements of Aramaic influence constitutes an argument of some probability in favor of the possibility that 4:7 may be later than the rest of the book. If such could be shown, it still would not alter the evidence of נעל + שלף for the dating of Ruth, since that idiom also occurs in 4:8, the body of the narrative. Indeed, it is this appearance of the idiom that prompts the author to insert the digression of v 7 in order to explain it.

(8) שָׂבַר, 1:13. Given the clear evidence of late elements in the book of Ruth noted in LBH items (1) through (7) above, there is a much greater probability, drawing on the principle of concentration, that שָׂבַר, for which the evidence is not clear cut, is indeed another late feature that has entered the language under the influence of Aramaic. First, a possible case can be made for a contrast between classical and later literature as regards the semantic domain of "wait for, expect, hope." Thus, biblical Hebrew throughout knows the two close synonyms קִוָּה and יִחֵל (for their close synonymetry, cf. Mic 5:6; Isa 51:15; Job 30:2, where the two verbs appear in *parallelismus membrorum*). For their use in the classical period, note the following: קִוָּה, Gen 49:18; Hos 12:7; Mic 5:6; Isa 5:2, 4, 7; Jer 13:16; 14:22; יִחֵל, 1 Sam 13:8; Mic 5:6. For the late period, note the following: קִוָּה, Lam 2:16; Ps 119:95; יִחֵל, Ezek 13:6; Ps 119:43, 49, 74, 81, 114, 147. The verb שָׂבַר, however, outside of Ruth, does not appear at all in unmistakably early texts, but it does appear three times in clearly late texts (Pss 119:166; 145:15; Esth 9:1) and in two chronologically uncertain texts (Ps 104:27; Isa 38:18). In these passages it moves in the identical semantic range as the two earlier synonyms. Note the following contrast in early and late passages:

לישועתך קויתי יהוה	Gen 49:18
שברתי לישועתך יהוה	Ps 119:166

The appearance of the substantive שֵׂבֶר, "hope," in two late passages (Pss 119:116; 146:5) corroborates the late appearance of this root in biblical Hebrew. Second, a possible case can be made for the criterion of distribution. The root is very common in Aramaic texts with a meaning in the same semantic range, and, although seemingly much less common, it does occur likewise in MH (Jastrow, *Dictionary,* 951). The concentration of late elements in Ruth and particularly the concentration in 4:7–8 of three features resulting from Aramaic influence, support the notion that the use of שָׂבַר in 1:13 may be another late feature whose presence in the later literature results from Aramaic influence.

Two other vocables in Ruth have often been regarded in past discussions as "Aramaisms," the verb עגן and the vocable לָהֵן, both in 1:13. However, apart from the tenuous nature of the criteria used for identifying these words as "Aramaisms" (on the criteria for which see Hurvitz, *Hebrew Abstracts* 14 [1973] 74–79), the case for both is very weak on other grounds. For עגן, see the *Comment* on 1:13. The evidence for the Aramaic origin of לחן could hardly be more tenuous. It is based upon the supposed existence of a biblical Aramaic vocable לחן, "therefore," a meaning that occurs for this vocable almost solely in Dan 2:6, 9; 4:24. Although the context in those passages seems indeed to require some such sense, this hardly establishes such a separate Aramaic vocable, for the word לחן, on the contrary, is widespread in Aramaic in the sense "but, however." The tenuous nature of such a hypothesis is revealed by the fact that KB[2] (לָהֵן II, p.1090; cf. *CHALOT*, 410) treats the biblical Aramaic as a borrowing from Hebrew! Further, as Rudolph (40 n. 13a) notes, the translators of the LXX, Syr, and Tg, all of whom were familiar with Aramaic, did not recognize such a meaning for לחן in Ruth 1:13. And, of course, if our correction of the text here to לָהֵם (see *Comment*), following all the versions (see *Note* 1:13.a.), is correct, there is no such word to be identified as Aramaic.

The result of this comparison of the linguistic features of the book of Ruth with these LBH features and their SBH counterparts can be stated as follows. In general, ten features that align with SBH bear out the judgment of many scholars that the majority of the linguistic features of Ruth accord with those of SBH (cf. the oft-quoted judgment of Driver, *ILOT*, 454). However, there are also eight features that accord with LBH, the later phase of the language. Although three of these features, (2), (5), and (6), are found in the transitional phase represented by Ezekiel, both they and the other five features are much more representative of the post-exilic LBH phase of the language. This evidence suggests that the writer of the book of Ruth must have lived no earlier than the transitional period between the SBH and LBH phases of the language, i.e., the late pre-exilic to the beginning of the post-exilic era. He endeavored to write his narrative using the classical language of SBH, and he has been eminently successful both in grammar and vocabulary as is evidenced by the number of features that accord with SBH. But inevitably he could not avoid using several of the more subtle linguistic features of his own era. Any attempt to narrow the possible range within that transitional period can only be very tentative. However, the relatively small number of late linguistic features does suggest that Ruth is earlier than such exilic texts as Jeremiah, for which Bergey lists ten (*BE*, 176–77) and Rooker fifteen (*BHT*, 182–83), and Ezekiel, in which Rooker finds thirty-seven late features (*BHT*, 182–83). This would lead to a date in the late pre-exilic period. On the other hand, if the digression of 4:7 is from the author and not from a later hand, the fact that all three of the features therein result from the influence of Aramaic and that three of the other features, namely, LBH items (1), (3), and (4), clearly correlate with only LBH texts, would argue that the language of the author's era is later rather than earlier, leading to a date at the beginning of the post-exilic period. In my opinion, the latter seems more likely.

Genre

Bibliography

Alter, R. *The Art of Biblical Narrative.* New York: Basic Books, 1981. **Bar-Efrat, S.** *Narrative Art in the Bible.* Sheffield: Almond, 1989. **Beekman, J., Callow, J.,** and **Kopesec, M.** *The*

Semantic Structure of Written Communication. Dallas: Summer Institute of Linguistics, 1981. **Berlin, A.** *Poetics and Interpretation of Biblical Narrative.* Sheffield: Almond, 1983. **Campbell, E.** "The Hebrew Short Story: A Study of Ruth." In *A Light unto My Path.* FS J. M. Myers, ed. H. Bream, R. Heim, and C. Moore. Philadelphia: Temple UP, 1974. 83–101. **Coats, G.** "Balaam: Sinner or Saint." In *Saga, Legend, Tale, Novella, Fable: Narrative Forms in Old Testament Literature,* ed. G. Coats. JSOTSup 35. Sheffield: JSOT, 1985. 56–62. ———. *Genesis with an Introduction to Narrative Literature.* FOTL 1. Grand Rapids, MI: Eerdmans, 1983. ———. "Genres: Why Should They Be Important for Exegesis?" In *Saga, Legend, Tale, Novella, Fable: Narrative Forms in Old Testament Literature,* ed. G. Coats. JSOTSup 35. Sheffield: JSOT, 1985. 7–15. ———. "Tale." In *Saga, Legend, Tale, Novella, Fable: Narrative Forms in Old Testament Literature,* ed. G. Coats. JSOTSup 35. Sheffield: JSOT, 1985. 63–70. **Gottwald, N.** *The Hebrew Bible—A Socio-Literary Introduction.* Philadelphia: Fortress, 1985. **Gunkel, H.** "Ruth." In *Reden und Aufsätze.* Göttingen: Vandenhoek & Ruprecht, 1913. 65–92. ———. "Ruth." *RGG* (1930). 4:2180–82. **Hals, R.** "Legend." In *Saga, Legend, Tale, Novella, Fable: Narrative Forms in Old Testament Literature,* ed. G. Coats. JSOTSup 35. Sheffield: JSOT, 1985. 45–55. **Hirsch, E.** *Validity in Interpretation.* New Haven: Yale UP, 1967. **Humphreys, W.** "Novella." In *Saga, Legend, Tale, Novella, Fable: Narrative Forms in Old Testament Literature,* ed. G. Coats. JSOTSup 35. Sheffield: JSOT, 1985. 82–96. **Jolles, A.** *Einfache Formen.* Halle: Max Niemeyer, 1930. **Kirkpatrick, P.** *The Old Testament and Folklore Study.* JSOTSup 62. Sheffield: JSOT, 1988. **Knierim, R.** "Old Testament Form Criticism Reconsidered." *Int* 27 (1973) 435–68. **Long, B.** "Introduction to Historical Literature." In *1 Kings with an Introduction to Historical Literature.* FOTL 9. Grand Rapids, MI: Eerdmans, 1984. 1–8. **Longman, T.** "Form Criticism, Recent Developments in Genre Theory, and the Evangelical." *WTJ* 47 (1985) 46–67. ———. *Literary Approaches to Biblical Interpretation.* Grand Rapids, MI: Zondervan, 1987. **Lord, A.** *The Singer of Tales.* New York: Atheneum, 1965. **Milne, P.** "Folktales and Fairy Tales: An Evaluation of Two Proppian Analyses of Biblical Narratives." *JSOT* 34 (1986) 35–60. ———. *Vladimir Propp and the Study of Structure in Hebrew Biblical Narrative.* Sheffield: Almond, 1988. **Moor, J. de.** "Narrative Poetry in Canaan." *UF* 20 (1988) 149–71. ———. "The Poetry of the Book of Ruth (Part I)." *Or* 53 (1984) 262–83. **Niditch, S.** "Legends of Wise Heroes and Heroines: II. Ruth." In *The Hebrew Bible and Its Modern Interpreters,* ed. D. Knight and G. Tucker. Philadelphia: Fortress, 1985. 451–56. **Osborne, G.** "Genre Criticism-Sensus Literalis." *TJ* 4 (1983) 1–27. **Propp, V.** *The Morphology of the Folk Tale.* 2nd ed. rev. Tr. L. Wagner. Austin: Univ. of Texas Press, 1968. **Radday, Y.,** and **Pollatschek, M.** "Computerized Experiments with the Frequency Lists of the Five Scrolls." *RevELA* 2 (1978) 1–30. **Solomon, A.** "Fable." In *Saga, Legend, Tale, Novella, Fable: Narrative Forms in Old Testament Literature,* ed. G. Coats. JSOTSup 35. Sheffield: JSOT, 1985. 114–25. **Sternberg, M.** *The Poetics of Biblical Narrative.* Bloomington: Indiana UP, 1985. **Wellek, R.,** and **Warren, A.** *Theory of Literature.* 3rd ed. New York: Harcourt, Brace, Jovanovich, 1977.

A veritable ferment exists in modern literary criticism in regard to the underlying theory of the concept of genre, even to the point of so raising to autonomy the individuality of a literary work as to deny completely the validity of literary categories or types (cf. the remarks of Knierim, *Int* 27 [1973] 436–45; for a recent penetrating, though technical, overview of the modern debate and its significance for biblical study, see Osborne, *TJ* 4 [1983] 1–27). But, however difficult and elusive delineating an acceptable underlying theory may be, it is exceedingly hard to deny the existence of similarities between texts on many levels and to deny that the interrelationship between these similarities gives presumptive evidence of generic identity between them (for a helpful and nontechnical presentation of this view, see Longman, *Literary Approaches*). A working and helpful definition of genre from this point of view is that adopted by Osborne (*TJ* 4 [1983] 4–5) and Longman (*Literary Approaches,* 80–81) from the classical statement of Welleck and Warren

(*Theory of Literature*, 231–34), namely, that genre involves a grouping of literary works based on outer form, i.e., the structure of the text and the presence or lack of metrical rhythms of speech, and inner form, i.e., the nonformal aspects of the text (e.g., the mood, setting, function, narrative voice, and content).

Hirsch (*Validity*, 68–77) makes the exceedingly important point that the identification of genre will unquestionably impinge directly upon how a literary work is interpreted (cf. also Coats, "Genres," 7–11, and Longman, *WTJ* 47 [1985] 61–63). As Sasson (197) cogently observes, its identification, then, is not simply an exercise in classification. Having consciously or unconsciously made a determination of genre, the reader then has marked and definite expectations about both the nature and the meaning of the reality that is conveyed, as well as its affective dimension, how it will be heard. This can affect the interpretation of the meaning of both the whole work and individual elements within it. For the former, note Sternberg's example (*Poetics*, 30) of the transformation of Nathan's story of the Poor Man's Ewe-Lamb in 2 Sam 12 from "the history of an injustice to a fictional parable of injustice," without a single change in the story, simply by Nathan's enunciation of its purpose with the declaration "You are the man!" For an excellent example of the latter, note Sternberg, *Poetics*, 524 n. 3.

Further, the corollary necessarily follows that to make false assumptions about genre results in misunderstanding and misinterpretation (cf. Coats, "Genres," 10). Compare, for example, what radical differences exist between the meaning, nature, and purpose assigned to Ruth by Sasson and those assigned by Hubbard on the basis of genre identification. Sasson (197–221) classifies Ruth as a folktale (see below). Hence, he concludes that it is not "burdened . . . by a historical background" (216) and, on the same grounds (221), cites as "relevant" Gautier's judgment that "from the religious point of view, the import of the book is almost nil" (in Sasson, 249). By contrast, Hubbard (47–48) follows Campbell's postulate (4–10) that Ruth belongs to a group of OT "short stories" that includes Gen 24; 38, the Joseph cycle, and episodes from the Court History of David in 2 Sam 9–20 (Campbell, 5, 10). On this basis, he concludes that "the short story allows for the historical accuracy of the narrative" and hence that "the heart of the story is historical" (Hubbard, 48). Presumably on the same grounds, he can find significant theological meaning in it (66–74).

The determination of genre, then, is unmistakably of critical importance for the interpretation of the book of Ruth. But, the determination of the genres of OT narrative literature is a notoriously difficult task. True, ancient texts are unquestionably amenable to generic classification, perhaps even more so than modern literature. Since the structures of ancient life were far less individualistically ordered and conceived than in the modern West, literature conformed more significantly to typical forms and patterns than does literature in the modern world with its strong tendency toward the innovative and the iconoclastic (cf. the remarks of Longman, *WTJ* 47 [1985] 55–56; Knierim, *Int* 27 [1973] 435–36). However, the OT knows virtually nothing by way of generic classification of its literature, except for a very few terms for literary forms used in nontechnical and varied senses (e.g., משל *māšāl*, "proverb, parable"; for a similar lack in the Mesopotamian sphere, see Longman, *WTJ* 47 [1985] 55). It has not even preserved a vocable with the sense of "story, narrative." Hence, the practice has almost invariably been adopted of using genre designations for the OT drawn from fields of literature outside of and much later than the OT. Although in principle this is an acceptable practice (see the remarks of Longman, *WTJ* 47 [1985] 53–56), it has not always been carried out in a manner to preclude misunderstanding and misinterpretation. First, the terms that have been used have often lacked careful and precise definitions in their own field (note, for example, the comments of Kirkpatrick, *OT and Folklore,* 74–76, and Hals, "Legend," 45–50, on the variability in and difficulty of defining the meaning of the terms "saga" and "legend"). Hence, terms have not infrequently been used with significantly divergent meanings. Second, the terms used must have meanings appropriate to the nature of the OT texts and then be further refined by careful definition. Coats (*Genesis,* 4) has expressed it well:

> [I]f the technical vocabulary has currency relevant to the characteristics of the narrative genres identified from particular texts, not in abstraction from the texts, then it seems appropriate to define the vocabulary so that it can be used with precision and then to apply that vocabulary to the narrative units of the OT. The goal . . . is therefore to identify the major narrative genres, to suggest terminology for them, and then to provide sufficient definition to facilitate precision in their use. The goal does not call for a resolution of all the problems in the history of the terms. It calls only for identification of legitimate characteristics signaled by the terms so that the reader can know what they stand for. . . .

Past attempts to determine the genre of Ruth have been vitiated by methodological problems such as these. Discussions have most often taken as their point of departure the work of Gunkel ("Ruth" in *Reden und Aufsätze* [1913] and again in his article "Ruth" in *RGG* [1930]). Greatly influenced by the views of folk literature and oral tradition prevalent in his day (for which see the succinct study of Kirkpatrick, *OT and Folklore,* 23–34), Gunkel postulated that the content, the structure, and the poetic tone of a great deal of OT narrative, in particular the stories of Genesis, demonstrated that these narratives existed as oral folklore in poetic form before being committed to writing in their present prose form. Applying this to his study of Ruth, Gunkel described the book in general as "an artistic tale" ("Ruth" in *Reden,* 84), a "poetic popular saga" or an "idyllic" narrative ("Ruth" in *RGG* 4:2181). In particular, he observed that through the highly developed use of dialogue "a new genre emerges, which we can best term 'novella.' The Italian novellas of the Renaissance (the starting point of the modern novella) also arose out of the materials of folktales and saga, which came to be highly developed from an interest in the depiction of characters. One is therefore justified in speaking of a Ruth novella" ("Ruth" in *Reden,* 85). Here not only has a term been adopted from European literature, but a whole theory of literary development has been read back into the OT situation (for which see below). And in the discussion that has ensued, though Gunkel's term has frequently been used, it has not infrequently been given quite different, even contradictory, meanings. Thus, quite in contradistinction to Gunkel's understanding that the novella was interested in the depiction of characters through the highly developed use of dialogue, Gerleman (6) adopts the definition of Jolles (*Einfache Formen,* 192) that the novella "endeavors to relate an incident or occurrence of significant import in a way that gives to us the impression of a factual event, and indeed such that the event itself appears to us more important than the characters who experience it." It is mainly on this definition of the genre that Gerleman bases his view that "the real interest of the narrator" is "a particular event" and that "The specific event which is here related is the Judaizing of the Moabitess Ruth" (6–7). Würthwein (3–4), influenced by Goethe's definition of the novella, defines it, in a manner very similar to Gerleman, as concerned with "an 'unprecedented event' behind which the characters completely recede" (3), but then he concludes, contra Gerleman, that Ruth cannot possibly belong to this genre. To increase the confusion, Witzenrath (362–68) also adopts the term but defines it not on the basis of content but of form, which "comprises the structure or composition . . . , the management of plot and character in place and time and certain characteristics of style" (364).

The same difficulty attaches to Würthwein's discussion of genre (3–4). Having dismissed the term "novella" (see above), he documents at some length that the book is "interested in the characters and their behavior." This interest, he then argues, is to present these characters as exemplary models who are "simple people in a simple, rural milieu," with whom "everything goes its good, upright way." On these grounds, Würthwein deems Ruth a typical example of the "idyll," a term ultimately drawn from Greek literature, whose characteristic is "an orientation towards an ideal, innocent state, . . . as well as the appearance of few, mostly exemplary, simple characters" (4), to which "we may not pose . . . the question of historical reliability" (5). On the grounds of this identification of genre he deems that the purpose of the book is to give "an impressive artistic illustration" (6) of the Hebrew conception of חסד *ḥesed*, which he defines as "the duty of loyalty to family/community." But, although Würthwein's discussion of the exemplary nature of the characters is insightful, this alone does not establish that this is the main point and purpose of the story. One suspects that it is more the definition of the genre as "idyll" that determines this as its purpose than vice versa.

Another major difficulty connected with the determination of the genre of Ruth is that the number of examples of such narratives in the OT with which to compare it is so small. The determination of genre is a subtle affair, weighing the implications of such factors as style, form, content, and context. Hence, the larger the number of exemplars with which a work may be compared, the more likely is it that a sound determination of genre may be made. To solve this dilemma, Campbell (4–10, 18–23; cf. also id., "The Hebrew Short Story"), followed by Hubbard (47–48), attempts to set up a category of "Hebrew short story," which, he avers, "is a distinct and discrete form, with its own ground rules, its own purposes, its own range of content . . . , and its own style." This category includes "Genesis 24 and 38; the Joseph story; a number of the Judges narratives, including, for example, Judges 3:15–29 . . . and Judges 4; Ruth . . . ; and the Job prose story" ("The Hebrew Short Story," 90). In his commentary, he adds "several scenes in the Court History of David (2 Sam 9–20)" (5). However, both the criteria used to establish this category and the characteristics reputed to mark it are either far too general and imprecise or much too problematic to carry the case. Taking his point of departure from Myers' general observation of the similarity in language between Ruth and the JE narratives of the Pentateuch and the narrative portions of Joshua, Judges, Samuel, and Kings, Campbell simply then avows that this extends to literary structuring and theme as well. Nowhere is there even an attempt to demonstrate these general similarities, let alone the detailed comparative study necessary to establish that these texts are members of a single genre. One can only surmise that Campbell means to imply that his study of the "craft of the book of Ruth" ("Hebrew Short Story," 93–99) is to be understood as representative of the whole group. If we assume with Niditch ("Legends," 455) that this is the case, her criticism is cogent: "the literary traits shared by these works, such as vividness of color, the technique of repetition, and the use of foreshadowing" are "universal narrative techniques," rather than evidence for a distinctive genre of Hebrew short story. The same observation can in general be made about the other characteristics Campbell adduces for this category (5–6), particularly the use of "an artistic and elevated prose containing rhythmic elements that are poetic." This is characteristic not only of Hebrew narrative in general, as Campbell himself is aware ("this form . . . shares this special Hebraic prose, however, with other literary *Gattungen*" ["Hebrew Short Story," 99; cf. also "Narrative Poetry," passim]), but also of a very widespread category of Semitic narrative, a narrative style that de Moor terms "narrative poetry" (*Or* 53 [1984] 262–71). How, then, can it be a distinctive characteristic of a special category of "Hebrew short story"? In short, even if one overlooks the lack of any detailed study that establishes that these criteria are common to the reputed members of the category, they are far too broad to establish a distinctive genre of "Hebrew short story."

Equally troubling is the premise, common also to much of the discussion of other OT narratives ever since the work of Gunkel, that the form and style of these narratives demonstrates that the material circulated orally as folk literature, popular oral tradition, before being committed to writing. For instance, Campbell (18–23) argues that his postulated genre of "Hebrew short story" represents the final written form of stories that were originally composed and transmitted orally over generations by a guild of "Hebrew singers of tales." Campbell bases his argument on the field research of folklorists Parry and Lord on epic tales sung by balladists in the Balkans reported in Lord's *The Singer of Tales*. The primary evidence from the OT for such a postulate seems to be the literary style of "artistic and elevated prose containing rhythmic elements" (5) that were "probably at least partially mnemonic in purpose" ("Hebrew Short Story," 90). This hypothesis can no longer be seriously entertained. To begin with, the fact that this "poetic, rhythmic" style is characteristic of a very large range of narrative tradition from both the OT and other ancient Semitic literatures (see above) precludes it from being evidence for a specific guild of singers of a specific genre of "Hebrew short stories." Second, as Niditch observes ("Legends," 455), "Careful reading of Lord's work shows that Ruth has neither the usual percentage of formulaic language found in truly oral works (Lord: 47) nor the expected formalism of story pattern (Lord: 68–98)." Finally and conclusively, Kirkpatrick has recently explored the implications of contemporary folklore research for the widely prevalent theory of OT scholarship that behind much of the biblical material lies an oral literature. She presents substantive evidence that "distinguishing between oral and written texts on the basis of certain stylistic features is no longer tenable" and that indeed "even the presence of epithets or formulaic phrases in a written text is no sure touchstone of its orality" (*OT and Folklore*, 116–17; cf. esp. 51–65). Hence, it can no longer be concluded that the form of the text *necessarily* demonstrates that it once circulated in an oral form.

Likewise, similar strictures apply to the attempt of Sasson to determine the genre of Ruth (197–221, 225–40). Noting the utter lack of consensus about the question, Sasson moved in a new and creative direction. He adopted the structural analysis of fairy tales developed by the Russian folklorist V. Propp (*The Morphology of the Folktale;* cf. the detailed treatment by Milne, *Vladimir Propp,* 19–122, and the brief assessment by Kirpatrick, *OT and Folklore,* 79–81). Propp analyzed the plot development of a collection of some one hundred fairy tales, isolating some thirty-one different elements of plot, or "functions," that appeared in fixed sequence, determining the composition of each tale. Adopting Propp's analysis, Sasson attempted to show that the elements of the plot of Ruth correspond to Propp's functions and follow the same sequence. Unfortunately, his creative attempt must be judged as unsuccessful. First, the approach obviously required a subtle adaptation of Propp's model. Since Ruth clearly was not a fairy tale, Sasson accepted the view of some folklorists that Propp's "listings of functions and the types of character roles are equally applicable to folktales" in general (201). Nevertheless, directly repudiating the view of Campbell and others (see above) that "formulaicity, poetics" and "other modes of stock expressions" could establish that the present written text was preceded by an oral form of the story, he categorically states, ". . . it cannot be said that orally transmitted texts have been successfully identified within the OT" (214). Therefore, he is "careful to avoid calling *Ruth* a folktale." Rather, it has only "the form . . . of a folktale," and he advances the postulate: "Thus, it might well be that our *Ruth* was created *upon a folktale model* by scribally oriented intelligentsia" (Sasson, 214, italics in the original). (Unfortunately, Sasson's caution has not been emulated by Gottwald, who simply cites him to document his identification of Ruth as a "thoroughly credible folktale," *Hebrew Bible,* 554.) This interpretation, however, is most problematic. In regard to the view that Propp's work could be applied to folktales in general, Milne notes in her detailed review of Sasson's work (*Vladimir Propp,* 144–54) that Propp himself was quite explicit that the model he developed was valid only for the category of fairy tales that he studied, and she concludes, ". . . the notion that the model is as valid for all folktales as it is for heroic fairy tales is simply not correct" (*Vladimir Propp,* 146). In regard to the view that Ruth is not a folktale but only has the form of one, surely if Sasson's analysis is valid and Ruth's character roles and sequence of plot functions do indeed fit comfortably within Propp's model of the fairy tale/folktale, then the proper conclusion ought to be that this structural congruence demonstrates that here we do in fact have a folktale that has been reduced to writing.

However, even the validity of Sasson's analysis has been seriously called into question by Milne (*Vladimir Propp,* 148–53; cf. also Milne, *JSOT* 34 [1986] 43–45). She has rather convincingly shown that the manner in which Sasson interprets features of Ruth as examples of Proppian narrative functions is in many instances forced and improbable. "The text is made to fit the model, by reinterpretation where necessary, or the model is made to fit the text, often by a misunderstanding of what Propp had written about individual functions." Hence, she concludes, "Ruth does not fit the model comfortably at all" (*Vladimir Propp,* 172). There seems little doubt, then, that, whatever it may be, the genre of Ruth is not the folktale, nor is it modeled after one.

Though past attempts to delineate the genre of Ruth have been vitiated by methodological problems as the above considerations have shown, recent discussions present refinements that go a long way toward resolving these issues. Given the discussion of the general interpretation of narrative in Beekman, Callow, and Kopesec (*Semantic Structure*) and the discussion of some of the particular OT narrative genres pertinent to such a text as Ruth in Coats ("Tale"), Hals ("Legend"), Humphreys ("Novella"), and Long ("Introduction to Historical Literature"), it is possible to elucidate at least in general terms the genre of the book.

To begin with, it is very clear that Ruth does not belong to that category of OT narratives whose main purpose is to present in some detail a sequence of events in which the cause-effect relationship is dominant and whose intention is primarily to report events in their proper order (such as is described by Long, "Introduction"; cf. also the first group of OT narrative genres described by Coats, "Tale," 63). On the contrary, the narrative structure of Ruth is controlled by what Beekman, Callow, and Kopesec describe as a "problem-based plot" (*Semantic Structure* § 4.2.4). In such narratives, a problem or conflict of some kind gives rise to a series of actions and interactions that move toward a resolution, often including a heightening of tension or suspense that reaches a climax at or just before the resolution. The pattern of structural elements or discourse roles (see Beekman et al., *Semantic Structure* § 8.1) found in such a plot may be described as follows (see Beekman et al., *Semantic Structures* § 8.7.2; Coats, "Tale," 64–66; Longman, *Literary Approaches*, 93):

(a) *Setting.* Introduces the principal characters, along with whatever information about their circumstances and interrelationships necessary to enable the narrator to tell his story.

(b) *Problem.* A generic term: that lack, threat, loss, disaster, crisis, need, etc. that affects the principals so as to raise the need for resolution and increase tension for the readers.

(c) *Complication(s).* One or more events, relationships, circumstances, or sequences of the same that retard or move the problem away from resolution and increase tension and suspense.

(d) *Resolving Incident(s).* One or more events, relationships, circumstances, or sequences of the same that move the problem toward resolution but do not fully resolve it.

(e) *Resolution.* To the benefit or detriment of the characters involved, some kind of resolution of the problem that set the narrative in motion.

(f) *Dénouement.* The response to the Problem-Resolution pair. It reveals the consequences of the resolution—expressing what difference it makes for the principal character(s).

(g) *Conclusion/Coda.* That which completes the narrative discourse and brings the story to an end. It may include a "coda," i.e., material that completes the story by complementing the setting in that, as the setting "takes the audience back into the time of the story," the coda "takes the audience out of the time frame of the story and brings them back to real time" (Berlin, *Poetics*, 107).

As important to the analysis as the structural elements or discourse roles are the relations that link both the structural elements themselves and the individual parts that make up each element (Beekman et al., *Semantic Structure* § 8.1). In the chronologically sequential structural elements of narrative, two different relations exist. In the first instance, though there is a necessary chronological sequencing of events, the first event does not give rise to the second, i.e., is not its cause. Such a relation Beekman terms a progression. It is the last event of such a sequence that is prominent, so the members of the sequence are labeled *step*$_n$*-goal* (*Semantic Structure* § 8.6). In the second instance, the relation is that of cause-effect: the first event gives rise to the second. Here two distinctions are pertinent (*Semantic Structure* §§ 8.7, 8.7.1., 8.7.2). The relation may be such that the first event is the efficient cause of the second; it necessarily brings it about. Such a relation is deemed *stimulus-response.* In other cases, the first event is weaker than an efficient cause but does create the circumstances from which the following event or sequence of events flows. This relation is deemed *occasion-outcome.*

Using these structural roles and relations, the plot of the book of Ruth may be analyzed as in Table 1. Discourse Structure (for the structure and roles of the underlying scenes and episodes, see the *Form/Structure/Setting* sections in the following commentary).

For the purpose of brevity of description, the content summaries identifying the discourse roles in this chart are given as narration. This, however, almost completely obscures an important feature of the plot development of the book: namely, that the narrator primarily advances his plot line through *dialogue,* not through a detailed description of events. This is generally the case in OT narrative, so much so that Alter can affirm, "As a rule, when a narrative event in the Bible seems important, the writer will render it mainly through dialogue" (*Art,* 182; see esp. his insightful analysis of this trait, 63–87). This is supremely the case in Ruth. That this is so is signaled by so coarse a measure as word frequency, for though the normal expectation would be that grammar words, rather than content words, would there rank highest, the fact is that the word that occurs most frequently in the whole scroll is אמר, "to speak, to say" (see Radday and Pollatschek, *RevELA* 2 [1978] 4–5). Hence, it is not surprising that the narrated events are completely oriented to the needs of this "narration-through-dialogue" (Alter, *Art,* 69) rather than to a detailed narration of events that advances the plot of the story. Thus, in the plot structure above, the setting (1:1–2), the initial statement of the problem (1:3–5), the digression (2:1; cf. also 4:7), the first complication (2:23), and the conclusion/coda (4:17a–22) are succinct and spare narration. But, the two-step progression by which the problem is developed (1:7–19a; 1:19b–22), both long resolving incidents (2:1–22; 3:1–4:12), the resolution (4:13–17c), and the dénouement (4:17d) consist exclusively of dialogues. Several of these are long and complex (viz. 1:7–19a; 2:4–17a; 4:3–12), whereas their narrative elements are almost uniformly brief, even summary, introductions, transitions, and conclusions (see the particular *Form/Structure/Setting* sections below, esp. the diagrams for 1:7–19a; 1:19b–22; 2:4–17a; 2:19–22; 3:1–5; 3:6–15; 4:3–8). It is essentially through dialogue, then, that the plot is advanced.

Table 1. Discourse Structure of the Book of Ruth

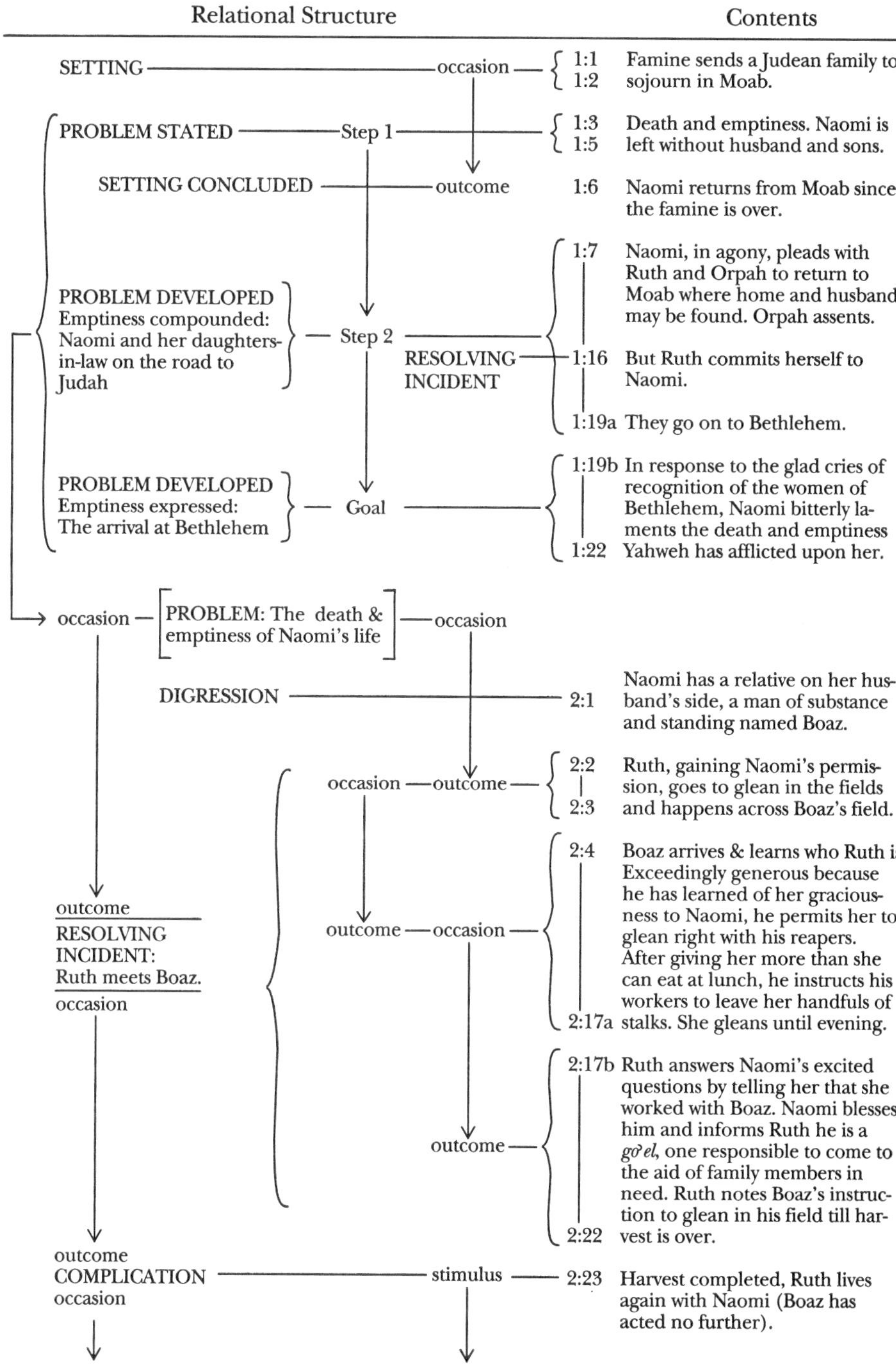

Relational Structure		Contents
SETTING — occasion	1:1–1:2	Famine sends a Judean family to sojourn in Moab.
PROBLEM STATED — Step 1	1:3–1:5	Death and emptiness. Naomi is left without husband and sons.
SETTING CONCLUDED — outcome	1:6	Naomi returns from Moab since the famine is over.
PROBLEM DEVELOPED Emptiness compounded: Naomi and her daughters-in-law on the road to Judah — Step 2	1:7	Naomi, in agony, pleads with Ruth and Orpah to return to Moab where home and husband may be found. Orpah assents.
RESOLVING INCIDENT	1:16	But Ruth commits herself to Naomi.
	1:19a	They go on to Bethlehem.
PROBLEM DEVELOPED Emptiness expressed: The arrival at Bethlehem — Goal	1:19b–1:22	In response to the glad cries of recognition of the women of Bethlehem, Naomi bitterly laments the death and emptiness Yahweh has afflicted upon her.
occasion — PROBLEM: The death & emptiness of Naomi's life — occasion		
DIGRESSION	2:1	Naomi has a relative on her husband's side, a man of substance and standing named Boaz.
occasion — outcome	2:2–2:3	Ruth, gaining Naomi's permission, goes to glean in the fields and happens across Boaz's field.
outcome RESOLVING INCIDENT: Ruth meets Boaz. occasion; outcome — occasion	2:4–2:17a	Boaz arrives & learns who Ruth is. Exceedingly generous because he has learned of her graciousness to Naomi, he permits her to glean right with his reapers. After giving her more than she can eat at lunch, he instructs his workers to leave her handfuls of stalks. She gleans until evening.
outcome	2:17b–2:22	Ruth answers Naomi's excited questions by telling her that she worked with Boaz. Naomi blesses him and informs Ruth he is a *gō'ēl*, one responsible to come to the aid of family members in need. Ruth notes Boaz's instruction to glean in his field till harvest is over.
outcome COMPLICATION occasion — stimulus	2:23	Harvest completed, Ruth lives again with Naomi (Boaz has acted no further).

Table 1—*Continued*

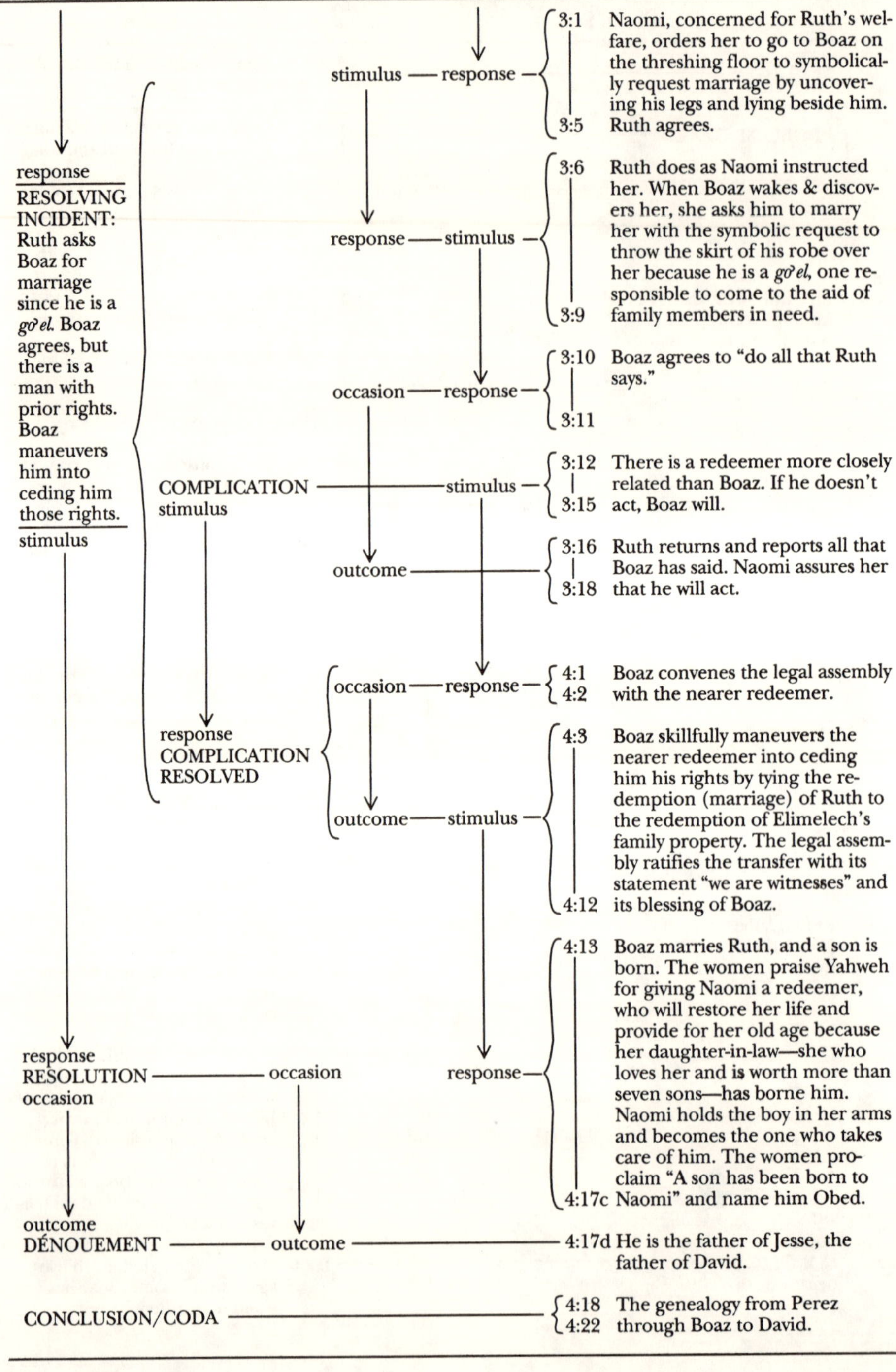

stimulus — response
3:1–3:5 Naomi, concerned for Ruth's welfare, orders her to go to Boaz on the threshing floor to symbolically request marriage by uncovering his legs and lying beside him. Ruth agrees.
response
RESOLVING INCIDENT: Ruth asks Boaz for marriage since he is a *gō᾿el*. Boaz agrees, but there is a man with prior rights. Boaz maneuvers him into ceding him those rights.
stimulus
response — stimulus
3:6–3:9 Ruth does as Naomi instructed her. When Boaz wakes & discovers her, she asks him to marry her with the symbolic request to throw the skirt of his robe over her because he is a *gō᾿el*, one responsible to come to the aid of family members in need.
occasion — response
3:10–3:11 Boaz agrees to "do all that Ruth says."
COMPLICATION stimulus — stimulus
3:12–3:15 There is a redeemer more closely related than Boaz. If he doesn't act, Boaz will.
outcome
3:16–3:18 Ruth returns and reports all that Boaz has said. Naomi assures her that he will act.
occasion — response
4:1–4:2 Boaz convenes the legal assembly with the nearer redeemer.
response COMPLICATION RESOLVED
outcome — stimulus
4:3–4:12 Boaz skillfully maneuvers the nearer redeemer into ceding him his rights by tying the redemption (marriage) of Ruth to the redemption of Elimelech's family property. The legal assembly ratifies the transfer with its statement "we are witnesses" and its blessing of Boaz.
response RESOLUTION occasion — occasion — response
4:13–4:17c Boaz marries Ruth, and a son is born. The women praise Yahweh for giving Naomi a redeemer, who will restore her life and provide for her old age because her daughter-in-law—she who loves her and is worth more than seven sons—has borne him. Naomi holds the boy in her arms and becomes the one who takes care of him. The women proclaim "A son has been born to Naomi" and name him Obed.
outcome DÉNOUEMENT — outcome — 4:17d He is the father of Jesse, the father of David.
CONCLUSION/CODA — 4:18–4:22 The genealogy from Perez through Boaz to David.

Given this analysis of the structure of Ruth, it is clear that its genre is to be distinguished from the "tale" as defined by Coats (see "Tale"). The tale is short, moving briskly from problem to resolution, and simple both in the interrelationship of structural elements (i.e., no complications or subplots) and in the depiction of characters. Further, the tale is primarily interested in an *event* and its implications, not in the characterization of the principal character. As we shall see below, the situation is otherwise with Ruth.

Particularly helpful for the elucidation of the genre of Ruth is Humphreys' attempt to define "novella" in the OT (see "Novella"). Humphreys begins with a brief description of the designations "short story," "novella," and "novel" in modern Western literary criticism ("Novella," 82–85). He then seeks to apply these modern definitions of genre to OT narrative, answering the question of their suitability in the positive, since "the essential issue is . . . the presence . . . of material that essentially fits the descriptive criteria that define a specific genre designation" ("Novella," 85; cf. the discussion above). Humphreys finds that, though there are no novels in the OT, there are short stories and ". . . a limited range of novellas and novella-like material" ("Novella," 85). As examples of the former, he cites Gen 24 and Ruth (and perhaps the stories of Dan 1–6 and Jonah, though these exhibit elements characteristic of fables), and for the latter the story of Samson (Judg 13–16), the story of Joseph and His Brothers (Gen 37–50), and the story of Esther and Mordecai in the book of Esther.

The most obvious differences between the short story and the novella as they are defined by Humphreys are the features of length and complexity. In general, the short story will be briefer than the novella and will have fewer characters, a less complex plot structure, and a more limited time frame ("Novella," 84).

But most important and most insightful is Humphreys' observation that the most essential distinction between the short story and the novella in the OT is the same as that between the modern genres of short story and novella/novel, namely,

> . . . the short story *reveals* the nature of a character or situation while a novel *develops* characters or situations. James Joyce speaks of the "epiphany quality" of the short story, its quality of revelation. Through a compact series of events or stress situations a character is made clear and distinct to the reader or a situation's true quality is revealed. By contrast, over a much wider range of events and situations the characters of a novel grow and/or deteriorate; they are seen to evolve as they shape and are shaped by events and situations. ("Novella," 84)

So, likewise, it is the development of—and not simply the revelation of—characters and/or situations that essentially sets the OT novella apart from the short story ("Novella," 84, 92–93). On the other hand, the short story

> . . . reveals the quality of a situation and/or character. Jonah, Ruth, and even Daniel and his companions are essentially the same at the end of each story as at the outset; they do not grow or develop before us. We just recognize with greater clarity the character of each as the story progresses. They share in the "epiphany quality" of which Joyce spoke. ("Novella," 85)

Clearly, in terms of length and complexity of plot, the book of Ruth stands between the tale as defined by Coats and the novella as defined by Humphreys.

And clearly it partakes of the "epiphany quality" of which Humphreys speaks. It intends to reveal its characters, not develop them.

And against this background a further refinement of the genre of the book also can be made clear. Though the "epiphany quality" of a short story may in general intend to reveal the quality of situations or characters, it is unmistakable that the book of Ruth primarily does the latter. Its all-encompassing intent is to depict the quality of its characters, not that of a situation or a sequence of events (in contrast to the situation in Esther; see the *Genre* section in *Introduction* to Esther).

This can be demonstrated by an examination of the narrator's characterization of his three major characters, Naomi, Ruth, and Boaz (on these as the three full-fledged or "round" characters of the narrative, see Berlin, *Poetics,* 83–86). This he accomplishes primarily in two ways. First, he portrays character indirectly through the speech and actions of his protagonists, the most common method of OT characterization (cf. Bar-Efrat, *Narrative Art,* 64–92; Berlin, *Poetics,* 33–42; and esp. Alter, *Art,* 114–30). Indeed, he devotes not a single statement to the direct description of character through either the report of outward appearances or the report of motives and inner life. Nor, apart from the important digression in 2:1 with which he introduces Boaz to us, do we hear a single word of direct evaluation (both of which are on occasion used elsewhere in the OT; cf. Bar-Efrat, *Narrative Art,* 48–64; and esp. Alter, *Art,* 114–19). Rather, as Berlin puts it (*Poetics,* 105), he "prefers the more sophisticated technique of embedded evaluation . . . accomplished by having the characters register the evaluation, either by their words or actions." And in Ruth, in keeping with the central role of dialogue in the plot development of the book (see above), direct speech, either by a character himself or herself or by others about him or her, is the primary means by which character is revealed, with actions playing an underlining and corroborating role. Second, the narrator of Ruth very effectively employs contrast between the principal protagonists and certain minor characters whom Berlin helpfully designates "agents," since they either play a role in plot development and/or function as aids in characterization of the principals (see *Poetics,* 23–24, 85–86). In Ruth the agents are Orpah in contrast to Ruth, the "nearer redeemer" (i.e., the relative with family obligations) in contrast to Boaz, and the women of Bethlehem in relation to Naomi. These devices of characterization are used by the narrator to portray Ruth and Boaz especially, but also Naomi, as the virtual enfleshment of *ḥesed,* that quality of kindness, graciousness, and loyalty that goes beyond the call of duty.

Since the first words that a character utters constitute "an important moment in the exposition of character" (Alter, *Art,* 74), it is not surprising that the first words that Ruth individually speaks in the story in 1:16–17 set forth the fullest expression in the whole narrative of the love and loyalty that will uniformly mark her character throughout, emphasized by the rich and expressive parallelism of Hebrew poetry (see the analysis of Ruth's speech in 1:16b–17e in *Form/Structure/Setting* for 1:7–19a; on the significance of this commitment, see the *Explanation* for 1:7–19a and the *Theology* section below). As is the pattern throughout, such words of love and loyalty had proleptically been symbolically expressed by the action that preceded them, as she physically clung to her mother-in-law (v 14c). All her words and actions that follow merely corroborate this loving commitment and loyalty: in the initiative that she takes to provide the wherewithal to sustain their lives by offering to glean in the fields, properly first seeking Naomi's permission (2:2); in the deference and respect she shows toward Boaz in response to his unexpected magnanimity, proper to her position as a stranger and a foreigner, expressed in both words (2:13) and actions (2:10, cf. *Explanation* for 2:4–17a); and in her obedient response in both word (3:5) and deed (3:6–7) to Naomi's risky scheme for her on the threshing floor, a course of action that entailed the greatest risk to both her reputation and her person (cf. *Explanation* for 3:1–5). This character of loving devotion and loyalty is expressed not only by Ruth's own words and actions but also by the repeated evaluation of other characters. In 2:11 in brief compass and in language redolent with praise and admiration Boaz affirms as accomplished fact what Ruth had promised to Naomi: "... you have left your father and your mother and the land of your birth and have come to a people you did not previously know," on the basis of which he implores Yahweh to grant her full reward (2:12). And in 3:10, in response to her request for marriage, he dubs this same promise and its fulfillment an act of *ḥesed.* In giving assent to her request, he appropriately sums up her character with the affirmation that "everyone in town knows that you are a woman of worth [אשת חיל]" (3:11), an evaluation from the lips of Boaz that reflects the narrator's own evaluation of him as איש גבור חיל, "a man of substance and standing" (2:1). In 4:15 the narrator places in the mouths of the women of Bethlehem his final evaluation of Ruth as they assure Naomi that the child of Ruth and Boaz will restore her life and provide for her old age because "... your daughter-in-law who loves you has given him birth—she who is more to you than seven sons" (cf. Würthwein, 4). In a culture that places such value upon the acquiring of a male descendant and in a context in which the acquisition of but one son is seen to mean so much (4:17b), the assurance that Ruth is more to Naomi than seven sons—the ideal number in the estimation of Israel—amounts to an encomium.

In like manner the character of Boaz is set forth. The first assessment of him is given not in his own words, as with Ruth, but with the omniscient narrator's own evaluation as he introduces us to him in 2:1 in a digression laden with possibilities. Here he identifies him as איש גבור חיל, "a man of substance and standing." Though this identification places most of its stress upon his ability and resources (see *Comment* thereto), i.e., his "substance," it also implies reputation and honor, i.e., his "standing." If this assessment places most of its emphasis upon the means and influence he possesses to improve the lot of the two widows, leaving somewhat in question whether he has the will, his intent is immediately and resoundingly revealed in his speech and actions in the scene on the harvest field that ensues. Here his magnanimity and generosity far exceed anything that law and custom require, so much so that Ruth, on the one hand, cannot comprehend the grounds for his action (2:10, 13) and Naomi, on the other, when she hears about it, blesses Yahweh for Boaz's *ḥesed* to the living and the dead (2:19–20; for the details of Boaz's beneficence see *Explanation* for 2:4–17a and the *Theology* section below). And even though his actions on his own initiative go no further than this remarkable beneficence (2:23, see Table 1 above), he responds in the affirmative to Ruth's request for marriage without a moment's hesitation (3:9–10), signaling his full and ready willingness to take on the responsibilities inherent in his role as "redeemer," one responsible to come to the aid of family members in need (see *Comment* on 2:20). Not only in regard to the two women does Boaz exercise the responsibility that devolves upon him. There is a "nearer redeemer," i.e., one more closely related and hence with prior rights (3:12), and so propriety dictates that he should have the opportunity to act first (3:13). Once again ". . . Boaz is given his opportunity to show his worthiness; for it is one feature of Boaz's valor that he will not even usurp another man's right to act responsibly" (Campbell, 137).

The narrator reveals Boaz's character of loving devotion through his own words and actions and also by the statements of others, as he has done with Naomi. When Naomi learns that Ruth's exceedingly gracious benefactor has been Boaz (3:17–19), she designates his actions as *ḥesed* (3:20; for this interpretation, see *Comment* thereto), revealing that she recognizes in him not just one who is a "redeemer" but one who has signaled that he will meet such responsibilities to the full. Her assessment of his probity and rectitude is fully confirmed when she sends Ruth to him on the threshing floor, symbolically to request marriage by uncovering his legs and lying beside him, with only the affirmation that "he will tell you what do" (3:4). The same confidence in his character is expressed by her assurance to Ruth, after hearing "all that the man had done for her" (3:16c), that he ". . . will not rest this day unless he has settled the matter" (3:18).

Not only are Ruth and Boaz presented to us as exemplary persons through their own words and deeds and the evaluation of others, but the story also provides each of them with contrasting characters, "against whose 'normal' conduct theirs stands out in relief all the more luminously" (Würthwein, 4; on contrast in characterization, see Berlin, *Poetics,* 40–41, 85–86; Alter, *Art,* 71–74). The contrast is effected by both actions and words. Thus, Ruth's actions contrast sharply with those of Orpah: Ruth "clung" to Naomi while Orpah "kissed her mother-in-law farewell," the contrast effected by content as well as by syntax (1:14; see *Form/Structure/Setting* for 1:7–19a). Even more striking is the contrast in speech, presenting a stark example of what Alter calls "contrastive dialogue" (*Art,* 72–74), for the narrator allows us not a single word from Orpah's lips (she *must* have said something!) in contrast to Ruth's moving and passionate speech (1:16–17). And so does the nearer redeemer function for Boaz. Faced with the advantageous responsibility of redeeming the land of Elimelech, he responds with alacrity with a two-worded assent: אנכי אגאל, "I'll redeem!" (4:4). But, faced with the dual responsibility of marrying the nubile widow Ruth and raising an heir to the land (4:5), he declines with a lame excuse that reveals concern for his own patrimony and interests but none for Ruth and the line of Elimelech (4:6; for this interpretation, see *Comment* on 4:6c and *Explanation* for 4:1–12). These brief, self-serving utterances contrast sharply with the demand of the faithful Boaz that the legal assembly exercise its notarial function and certify his acceptance of both obligations (4:9–10; see *Explanation* for 4:1–12). Equally striking is the contrast in action. The nearer redeemer seals his refusal by symbolically removing his sandals (4:7–8), an action that, though doubtless literally different in meaning (see *Comment* on 4:7), could hardly fail in the circumstances to bring to the minds of the readers the shameful חליצה ritual of levirate marriage in which the widow removed the sandals of her brother-in-law who likewise refused to do his duty (Deut 25:9–10). And Boaz? The narrator sets his seal to Boaz's fulfillment of his obligations by relating the most important of them, his marriage to Ruth, in five short clauses, the longest of which in Hebrew comprises but four words: "So Boaz took Ruth, and she became his wife. And when they came together, Yahweh caused her to conceive, and she gave birth to a son" (4:13). And well does the narrator confirm the contrast, by refusing to name the closer relative, designating him pejoratively "Mr. So-and-So" (אלמני פלני, 4:1d; cf. *Comment* on 4:1 and *Explanation* for 4:1–12).

Though the characterization of Naomi may appear at first glance to be rather more ambiguous than that of Ruth and Boaz, a careful reading will show that such is not really the case. True, she plunges to the depths of dark despair in both her response to the initial refusal of her daughters-in-law to return to Moab—in which in her anguish she posits absurdities and impossibilities (see *Explanation* for 1:7–19a)—and in her response to the glad cry of recognition of the women of Bethlehem, "Is this really Naomi?" in which she denies the meaning of her name "Pleasant" by renaming herself "Bitter" (see *Explanation* for 1:19b–22). Admittedly, in both responses she openly voices her complaint in blunt and bitter terms that it is Yahweh himself who is the cause of the death and emptiness that have afflicted her life (1:13, 20–21). But, our narrator uses Naomi's honest and forthright lament and complaint not to portray her character in negative hues but rather to depict the affective dimensions of the desolation and emptiness of a woman "left alone without her two boys and without her husband" (1:5) in a world where life depends upon men (see *Explanation* for 1:19b–22).

Moreover, since a character's opening words are important for the exposition of character (Alter, *Art,* 74), that the narrator's characterization of Naomi is positive is first of all to be seen in her opening words in the story in 1:8–9, which exhibit only care and concern for her daughters-in-law and none for her own situation. This same concern she expresses throughout (cf. 2:22), especially in 3:1–2. Here the hiatus in the plot development, occasioned by Boaz's failure to act beyond his beneficence on the harvest field (2:23; see the discourse structure outlined in Table 1 above), is moved forward specifically and solely by Naomi's concern for Ruth's welfare: "Must I not seek for you home and husband, *so that all will go well for you?*" (see *Comment* on 3:1 and *Explanation* for 3:1–5).

Second, such a positive characterization is reflected in the way in which the reversal of her despair and emptiness is portrayed in the resolving incident in 2:2–22 and in the resolution and dénouement in 4:13–17c (see Table 1 above). In the first, her response to Ruth's return from gleaning in the fields (2:17–22) is a surprising reversal indeed. For prior to this response, apart from the laconic, almost lethargic, two words (in Hebrew) with which she gave Ruth permission to glean (2:2), the last word we heard from Naomi was the fourfold flood of bitter complaint against Yahweh himself (1:20–21). But now, seeing only the abundant grain Ruth has gleaned and the leftovers from her noon meal (2:18), she expresses surprise and excitement with prolix speech consisting of redundant and repetitive questions (2:19a–c; see *Comment* on 2:19). Then she follows that, almost inexplicably, with words of blessing addressed to Yahweh (but without using his name!). And when Ruth responds with the information that the name of the man with whom she worked was Boaz, Naomi suddenly takes the name of Yahweh on her lips (2:20), only not now in blunt and bitter complaint but in words of praise and blessing, triggered by the possibilities latent in Boaz's identity as a "redeemer." Truly, ". . . with the advent of this understanding comes an upward surge of her spirit, a lifting from the depths. . . . and we know that Naomi, who was herself among the dead, lives again" (Rauber, *JBL* 89 [1970] 32–33). In the dénouement in 4:16–17c this "lifting from the depths" finds its full expression when the emptiness expressed by Naomi's bitter words, "Full was I when I went away; / But empty has Yahweh brought me back" (1:21), is balanced by her tender and touching action, "Naomi took the boy and held him to her breast and became the one who took care of him" (4:16).

Clearly, then, through his varied and unremittingly positive characterization of Ruth, Boaz, and Naomi, the narrator presents them as exemplary characters, quite in contrast to the vast bulk of the rest of OT narrative, which dramatically depicts the moral ambiguity and even downright contradiction that mark the character of the human agents through whom God works. That is, the narrator presents the major characters of his story as models for his readers to emulate. Hence, at a very significant level, the book of Ruth intends to function in the manner that Hals suggests for the genre that he labels "legend," i.e., to "portray the virtue of fidelity" and so to "focus on the element of the *imitabile*" or "go thou and do likewise" ("Legend," 51–52; cf. also Coats' third category of OT narrative genres, "Tale," 63–64). That is, it intends to edify as much as to inform and entertain. The genre of Ruth, then, can be defined as "an edifying short story."

Finally, although God is not one of the characters of the narrative and it is not possible to speak in any way of a "characterization" of him (on the characterization of God in OT narrative, see the perceptive remarks of Sternberg, *Poetics*, 322–25), he is nonetheless present in the story, as in all OT narrative. However, the Ruth narrator's portrayal of God and his action places the book far to one side of the OT artistic perspective, for God's role in the story and his control of events are very much behind the scenes and in the shadows. He is not one of the dramatis personae of the narrative, as he is, for example, in a number of the Abrahamic narratives (Gen 12–22). There are no miracles, nor are there any acts of sacrifice or other cultic activity. No prophetic or charismatic figure appears at all. The protagonists never refer to God's past guidance of the events of the story or its outcome (as, e.g., Joesph does in Gen 45:5–7; 50:19–20), nor do they call upon God specifically to direct the events of the narrative (as, e.g., the servant does in the story of the wooing of Rebekah, Gen 24:12–14). And yet, for all its reticence, the story subtly evidences the same view of reality as does the rest of OT narrative, namely, that God exercises absolute sway over the affairs and actions of his world, human and otherwise. This is evidenced first of all by the way in which, in keeping with the rest of the OT, the name of Yahweh so frequently rushes to the lips of the main characters in words of praise and invocation whenever the context calls for the expression of thanksgiving, or blessing or resolve (see Hals, *Theology*, 3–19). Thus does Naomi bless her daughters-in-law (1:8–9) and Boaz (2:20); twice does Boaz so bless Ruth (2:12; 3:10); thus do the assembled elders and people bless Boaz (4:11–12); and in the dénouement so do the women of the town bless Naomi (4:14). This extends from everyday greetings as Boaz meets his workers on the harvest field (2:4) to the oath with which Ruth affirms the constancy of her commitment to Naomi (1:17). Apart from general words of blessing, we also find expressed the conviction that it is Yahweh who provides widows a new home and husband (1:8–9); it is he who repays good deeds with a full reward (2:12); it is he who provides abundant descendants and offspring (4:11–12); and it is Yahweh who has redeemed Naomi's life through the birth of the child to Ruth and Boaz (4:14). Second, though the narrator laconically reports the death and deprivation that have afflicted the life of Naomi in terms that utterly avoid any implication of divine causation (1:3–5), Naomi unflinchingly and unrelentingly attributes these events to the direct action of God: ". . . bitter indeed has the Almighty made my life! . . . empty has Yahweh brought me back. . . . Yahweh has spoken against me, and the Almighty has pronounced disaster upon me" (1:20–21). Finally, that the narrator himself fully shares the views of his protagonists is unmistakable given that two of his narrative statements express the divine sovereignty over both nature and the events of the story. In 1:6 he asserts that Naomi heard in Moab ". . . that Yahweh had seen to the needs of his people by giving them food," and in the dénouement of the story he affirms that, when Boaz and Ruth came together in marriage, ". . . Yahweh caused her to conceive, and she gave birth to a son" (4:13).

Clearly, at every level of the story the author affirms the uniform OT conviction that the world is fully and uniformly under the control of an all-powerful and all-knowing God. However, though all OT narratives mix the overt and implicit guidance of God over the affairs of his world, in the book of Ruth the stress is overwhelmingly on the implicit nature of God's all-causality. The resolution of the death and deprivation that have afflicted the life of Naomi is effected by God almost completely through the ordinary hopes, intentions, and purposes of the human protagonists of the story. This is stressed by the fact that at one point he overtly includes even the "accidental" events of the lives of his characters (Hals, *Theology*, 14–15). First he proleptically introduces Boaz to us in a digression as a relative of Naomi's on her husband's side and a man of substance and standing, thus subtly suggesting some role for him in the resolution of the death and deprivation that have afflicted the lives of the two widows (2:1). Then he tells us that, when Ruth went to the fields to glean, "she happened to come upon the field of Boaz" (2:3). Not only Boaz's faithfulness and Naomi's risky plan (chap. 3) but also Ruth's accidental steps are part of the control God effects over his world behind the scenes and in the shadows.

Theme, Purpose, and Theology

Bibliography

Beekman, J., Callow, J., and **Kopesec, M.** *The Semantic Structure of Written Communication.* Dallas: Summer Institute of Linguistics, 1981. **Berlin, A.** *Poetics and Interpretation of Biblical Narrative.* Sheffield: Almond, 1983. **Clines, D.** *The Esther Scroll: The Story of the Story.* JSOTSup 30. Sheffield: JSOT, 1984. ———. "Story and Poem: The Old Testament as Literature and as Scripture." *Int* 34 (1980) 115–27. ———. *The Theme of the Pentateuch.* JSOTSup 10. Sheffield: JSOT, 1978. **Dommershausen, W.** "Leitwortstil in der Ruthrolle." In *Theologie im Wandel.* Munich-Freiberg: Wewel, 1967. 394–407. **Hals, R.** "Ruth." *IDBSup* 758–59. ———. *The Theology of the Book of Ruth.* Philadelphia: Fortress, 1969. **Murphy, R.** *Wisdom Literature: Job, Proverbs, Ruth, Canticles, Ecclesiastes, Esther.* FOTL 13. Grand Rapids, MI: Eerdmans, 1981. **Rauber, D.** "Literary Values in the Bible: The Book of Ruth." *JBL* 89 (1970) 27–37.

Sakenfeld, K. *Faithfulness in Action.* Philadelphia: Fortress, 1985. ———. *The Meaning of Hesed in the Hebrew Bible: A New Inquiry.* Missoula: Scholars, 1978. **Sternberg, M.** *The Poetics of Biblical Narrative.* Bloomington: Indiana UP, 1985.

THEME AND PURPOSE

Opinions about the purpose of Ruth are as diverse and contradictory as those about its date (for which see *Date* above). For a survey of older views, see Dommershausen, "Leitwortstil," 394–95; and for more recent opinions, see Hubbard, 35–39; Murphy, *Wisdom Literature,* 86–87. Such diversity naturally results from such a subtle and complex literary creation as the book of Ruth, which has many possible levels of meaning (see in this regard the insightful comments of Rauber, *JBL* 89 [1970] 35–36; Clines, *Int* 34 [1980] 118–23). Yet there has been a strong tendency in discussions of the meaning of Ruth to raise to autonomy as *the* one meaning of the text one of the concerns that the book is alleged to address, with greater or lesser validity as the case may be.

However, even though the subtlety of the narrative genre means that its meanings are multivalent, it is not only possible to determine from the discourse structure, contents, and mood of the text what those meanings may be, but it is also possible to determine from the *prominence* given to these features of the text which of these possible meanings are primary and which are secondary. Most helpful in this regard is the discussion of prominence in narrative discourse by Beekman, Callow, and Kopesec. Prominence, which consists simply of making one or more parts of a discourse unit more important than other parts (*Semantic Structure* § 2.3.1.c), is a meaning feature of every semantic unit in all genres. Beekman begins by distinguishing between the *theme* of a narrative and a *précis* or brief statement of the narrative events in chronological sequence. The theme involves "the central ideas and theses at various hierarchical levels in the composition" expressing "the logical relationship of the units, not just their chronological sequence" (*Semantic Structure* § 10.3.1). In this regard Clines' discussion of the theme of a narrative work provides further relevant and insightful definition (*Theme,* 17–18). Clines observes that the theme of a narrative is not a statement that is merely a compressed narrative but rather a statement of "plot with an emphasis on conceptualized meaning," which focuses the significance of the plot and states its implications. Alternatively, he adopts the definition of Thrall and Hibbard that the theme "is the central and dominating idea . . . the abstract concept which is made concrete through its representation in person, action, and image in the work." Or again, it is a rationale of the content, structure, and development of the work, i.e., "an account of why the material is there, and of why it is presented in the order and shape in which it is" (*Theme,* 18). Clearly, then, it is the prominence of the structural elements that constitute the plot that will be the significant feature in giving an account of why these structural elements are there, i.e., in determining the theme. In narrative discourse, the structural elements—or discourse roles—primarily consist of a chain of elements dominated by the relationship of cause-effect (see the discussion of the roles of stimulus-response or occasion-outcome under *Genre* above), and in such a relationship effects are naturally more prominent than causes (*Semantic Structure* § 10.3.1). Therefore, in the words of Beekman, Callow, and Kopesec (*Semantic Structure* § 10.3.1):

> Since the final response in a chain usually represents the Resolution or Outcome to the story, there is a movement from the information with lesser prominence to that with more prominence or significance, from the standpoint of the author's purpose. The statement of the theme for such units would come from the Resolution or Outcome, together with whatever information from the Problem or Occasion that needs to be stated in order that the statement of the Resolution or Outcome makes sense. The final response(s) of an episode are thus the most prominent units within the episode.

Further, in the more complex discourse structure, which has both a resolution and a dénouement (or outcome), both the resolution and the dénouement should be regarded as prominent and included in the statement of the theme (*Semantic Structure* § 10.3.1). Finally, Beekman observes that in narrative discourse *participants* function like *topics* in hortatory and expository discourse in that they are given prominence either naturally or through some special marking device. Hence, in stating the theme one must determine the status of each of the participants since each one's prominence will determine what role that one will play in the theme statement (*Semantic Structure* § 10.3.2).

Let us, then, apply this understanding of the prominence of participants and discourse elements to determine the theme of Ruth, beginning with the participants. Unquestionably the most important character in the book is Naomi. This can be established at every level of the story. It is she alone about whom the problem of the narrative is posited (1:3–5), and there her centrality is given marked prominence in two ways. First, that Naomi is the principal character is effected by the subtle reversal of patriarchal identities: "Naomi, wife of Elimelech" (lit. "his") in v 2 becomes "Elimelech, husband of Naomi" in v 3 (see *Explanation* for 1:1–6). Second, that it is *her* loss and emptiness that are the problem of the narrative is stressed when the narrator leaves the particularity and individuality of his narrative in v 5 and makes a general statement for his readers to ponder, "the *woman* was left alone without her two boys and without her husband." Likewise, she alone is the subject of the resolution and dénouement (4:13–17c). It is for giving *Naomi* a redeemer who will restore *her* life and provide for *her* old age that the women praise Yahweh (4:14–15). And the child's significance is revealed by the women's proclamation, "A son has been born to *Naomi!*" (v 4:17c; see *Explanation* for 4:13–17). This is further corroborated by the fact that every other character stands in relation to her (see Berlin, *Poetics,* 83–84). The important relationship of Ruth and Orpah is to Naomi as "daughters-in-law," not to their husbands (we do not even know to which of Naomi's sons they are married until the scene with the legal assembly in 4:1–12 requires a full legal identity for Ruth, v 10). The same is true for Boaz. When the narrator first introduces him to us in an important digression, it is as a relative of Naomi's, albeit by marriage: "Now Naomi had a relative on her husband's side, . . ." (2:1). And when Naomi reveals to Ruth who he is, his identity is "*our* relative, . . . one of *our* redeemers" (2:20). Finally, this is confirmed by the way she is named. Throughout, when not viewed through the eyes of Orpah or Ruth as "mother-in-law," she "stands independently, known only by her proper name" (Berlin, *Poetics,* 87).

Ruth and Boaz are also full-fledged characters and important to the plot as the means by which the problem in the story is resolved. Supremely is this the case with Ruth, so much so that she is the focus of the interest point of view in the story (see Berlin, *Poetics,* 84). Thus, she plays the major role in every resolving incident in the narrative: 1:16–17; 2:2–22; 3:1–4:12. Indeed, she is absent only in 4:1–12, the unit in which Boaz negotiates with the nearer redeemer. But this unit is of secondary importance in the plot development, for it functions there only as the resolution of the complication introduced by the existence of this man. And Boaz is important to the plot structure not only as the means, with Ruth, for the resolution of the problem but also as the source and instigation of the two complicating incidents, namely, his failure to act beyond his beneficence on the harvest field (2:23) and his insistence on respecting the rights of the closer relative (3:12–15; 4:1–12). Finally, both the importance of Naomi and Ruth to the plot and the sophistication of the author's narrative technique are signaled by the fact that each plays in a subordinate way the role of the other. Thus, by the very commitment and loyalty to Naomi that constitutes the first incident that moves the bitter emptiness of Naomi's life toward resolution (1:16–17), Ruth also involves herself in that very lack. And though obviously her decision and request to glean in the fields would have had as its object the relief of her own hunger as well as Naomi's, the narrator first brings Ruth's lack explicitly to expression by Naomi's enunciation of her responsibility to seek for her home and husband so that all would be well for her (3:1). And though Ruth's lack of home, husband, and the wherewithal to sustain life is described in the succinct and staccato statements of 4:13, the minor role that Ruth's lack plays in the plot is signaled by the fact that this summary does not function primarily to express such a fulfillment but to be a narrative introduction to the resolution of Naomi's emptiness (4:13–15; see *Form/Structure/Setting* for 4:13–17 and *Explanation* for 4:13–17). Likewise with Naomi does the author exhibit the subtlety and sophistication of his narrative technique. For, in her dramatic new initiative in 3:1–4, which sprang exclusively from her loving concern about Ruth and had as its limited objective the end of the destitution and reproach of Ruth's widowhood (3:1; see above), Naomi also unwittingly played a role in the resolution of her own loss and emptiness. When Ruth grounded her request for marriage in Boaz's responsibility as a גאל *gôʾel,* a "redeemer" (3:9), she opened to Boaz the possibility of both redeeming the field of Elimelech and marrying Ruth, the wife of the deceased Mahlon, for the purpose of raising an heir to continue the line of Elimelech and to inherit the field he has redeemed (4:9–10)—a course of action that would resolve Ruth's widowhood and end the loss and emptiness of Naomi's life as well (see *Explanation* for 4:1–12). The most important character, then, in the problem, resolution, and outcome is Naomi, though Ruth plays a secondary role therein. All three play roles in the resolving incidents, though Ruth and Boaz are the most important. Boaz is also important as the source of the complications in the plot.

In the light of the assumption of the vast majority of the interpreters of the book that the problem of the story is the provision of an heir to the family line of Elimelech, let us note the almost inconsequential role played in the story by Elimelech and his sons Mahlon and Chilion. The only role they play is in the setting—they are part of the information about the circumstances and relationships of the principal character, Naomi, that is necessary for the narrator to be able to tell his story. Though they appear again later in the story, their role there is the same, "bits of information" (Berlin, *Poetics,* 86) about the circumstances (4:3, 9, 10) and/or relationships (2:1) of the principals necessary to the plot. They play no role whatsoever in any of the structural elements of the plot; they are indeed "proper names without characters attached to them" (Berlin, *Poetics,* 86).

With this understanding of the status of the participants and the prominence of the structural elements of resolution and dénouement, the theme of the book of Ruth can be determined from Table 1 (see in *Genre* above). First of all, it is supremely important to note that the discourse structure unmistakably and emphatically makes clear that the problem of the story is the death and emptiness that have afflicted the life of Naomi. This is expressed by the way the narrator identifies her in 1:3–5 and names her throughout (see above) and by the fact that, after the setting (1:1–2, 6) and the statement of the problem (1:3–5), he devotes the next two scenes primarily to depicting the affective dimensions of this problem—the bitterness, anger, and despair that Naomi feels (see *Explanations* for 1:7–19a and 1:19b–22). Nothing is said here, or alluded to in any way, about the problem of providing a male heir for the line of Elimelech (see *Explanation* for 1:19b–22). A glance at the resolution and dénouement of the story confirms this understanding of the problem of the story. Though a son born to Ruth and Boaz is mentioned (4:13), his significance relates entirely to Naomi. Yahweh is not celebrated by the female chorus because he has not left the line of Elimelech without an heir but because he has not left Naomi without a "redeemer" to restore her to life and provide for her old age (4:14–15). Nor do they celebrate his identity by the cry "A son has been born to Elimelech" but rather by "A son has been born to Naomi" (4:17). (For arguments that, when Naomi refers to Boaz as a *gôʾēl* in 2:20 and when Ruth does also in 3:9, neither of them implies a responsibility to perform a levirate marriage or redeem the land of Elimelech, see *Comment* on 2:20 and *Excursus: The Relationship between Ruth's Request and the Question of Levirate Marriage.*) Finally, the discourse structure further conclusively demonstrates that the question of an heir for the line of Elimelech is but a secondary concern to the story, given that it surfaces only in 4:5–6 as part of Boaz's scheme to induce the closer relative to cede to him his prior right to redeem the field of Elimelech and marry Ruth (see the *Comment* on the clause "to raise up the name of the deceased on his inherited property," 4:5d, esp. *Excursus: Levirate Marriage in the Old Testament* and the *Comment* on 2:6). That is, its only role in the story is as part of the resolution of a subordinate plot development, namely, the existence of the closer relative, who has prior rights in family matters, a complication that must be resolved before the resolving incident of Boaz's assent to do all that Ruth has requested may go forward (see Table 1 in *Genre*). Unquestionably, the problem of the story is the death and emptiness that have afflicted the life of Naomi.

Second, it is also important to note that the story has both a resolution and a dénouement (and accompanying conclusion/coda) and that both of these are prominent and essential for the theme. The resolution, as we have noted, devoted itself exclusively to depicting the total reversal of the death and emptiness that afflicted the life of the woman who "was left alone without her two boys and without her husband" (1:5; see above). But the dénouement, 4:17d, expressing the consequences of the resolution, what difference it makes for the principals (see the definitions of the discourse roles under *Genre* above), is a delightful, though not unanticipated (see the *Explanation* for 1:1–6), surprise. The birth of Obed not only restored Naomi to life and fullness but led two generations later to David. This outcome expresses the significance of the story, for the resolution has meaning by virtue of all that the son of Ruth and Boaz meant for Naomi (and Ruth) and also by virtue of the fact that it provided an integral link in the family line that led to David. As Berlin has perceptively observed, by providing the story with this coda, which serves to situate its characters among the body of known personalities in the main narrative tradition from Genesis to Kings, the narrator brings closure to his story by stating its relevance. "The connection with David tends to elevate the status of the story as much as the story tends to elevate David" (*Poetics,* 110).

In enunciating the theme, it is important to take into account that the narrator primarily advances his plot through dialogue and that through this dialogue he reveals the quality of the characters of his story (see the discussion of *Genre* above), presenting them as the virtual enfleshment of *ḥesed,* that quality of kindness, graciousness, and loyalty that goes beyond the call of duty. It is as much, if not more, the quality of their character that moves the story forward as the actions they perform. That is, the theme must take into account the genre of the book as an *edifying* short story that places significant stress on the *imitabile,* "go thou and do likewise."

The theme of the book of Ruth, then, can be stated in full as follows: (1) the loving loyalty, faithfulness, and obedience of Ruth the Moabitess, expressed in her commitment to her mother-in-law, Naomi, which transcended the claims of religion and national origin; (2) the kindness, graciousness, and sagacity of Boaz, expressed in his benevolence and his faithfulness to family responsibilities, in regard both to marrying Ruth the Moabitess and to redeeming the field of Elimelech on behalf of Naomi, all of which transcended the claims of self-interest; (3) the loving concern of Naomi for the welfare of her daughter-in-law, expressed in her risky scheme to induce Boaz to marry Ruth; and (4) Yahweh's gracious provision of fruitfulness for field and womb; all have provided a son to restore Naomi's life and provide for her old age, reversing the death and emptiness that had afflicted her. This story of *ḥesed* was of utmost significance, for its outcome, its dénouement, was the preservation of the family line that led from Perez through Boaz and Obed to David.

Having determined that the genre of the narrative is the edifying short story and having elucidated the specific theme that engenders its plot, it is now possible to ascertain which are primary among the many levels of meaning that come to expression in such a subtle and complex literary creation. First, as both the discussion of the theme of the book and its genre, particularly its characterization through dialogue (see *Genre* above) have revealed, the primary intention of the author is to present Ruth, Boaz, and Naomi as models for his readers to emulate. They portray in dramatic and concrete form what *ḥesed* looks like in the sphere of interpersonal and family obligations and responsibilities. By his portrayal of the significance of this enfleshment of *ḥesed,* namely, that it provided an integral link in the family line that led to David, he focuses sharply on the element of the *imitabile.*

Second, though it is certainly incorrect to say that God is the primary actor (so Campbell, 29) or the major character (so Rudolph, 33), for his role is effected in a subtle and indirect manner, the story affirms, fully in keeping with the rest of OT narrative, the absolute sway that God exercises over the affairs and actions of his world, human and otherwise. This extends from the expressions of thanks or resolve of the protagonists, to their assessment of the source of good or evil in the world, to the narrator's own explicit statements reflecting Yahweh's sovereignty over both nature and the events of the story (1:6; 4:13; see the role of God in the story described in *Genre* above). However much God's all-causality is implicit, acting through the ordinary hopes, intentions, and purposes of the human protagonists, this is a story of the divine providential guidance in the lives and fortunes of this one family.

Third, the prominence of the story's discourse roles of dénouement and conclusion/coda provides significance for the story, but it also focuses attention beyond the story. Not only does the connection with David elevate the story, but the character of the story elevates David (Berlin, *Poetics,* 110). This is primarily effected by the characterization of its principal protagonists, reflecting David's worth through the quality of life of his forebears. It is also effected by the story's stress on the guidance of God in the life of this family (see above), presenting "the providential care that was working behind the choice of David" (Murphy, *Wisdom Literature,* 87).

THEOLOGY

From this analysis of the genre, theme, and purpose of the book, the major theological emphases flow, however subtly they are expressed in such a literary vehicle. The story portrays in the dramatic and concrete form of the words and deeds of its protagonists what in the sphere of interpersonal and family obligations constitutes *ḥesed* while focusing sharply on the element of the *imitabile,* "go thou and do likewise." Hence, one of its major theological emphases is that the reader should emulate such a style of life. What such a lifestyle involves becomes clear from Sakenfeld's examination of this concept when used between human beings in both the secular and religious spheres of life (see *The Meaning of Hesed,* 233–34; *Faithfulness in Action,* 39–42). Two aspects of an act of *ḥesed* are of particular importance. First, there is the emphasis that such an act is, as Sakenfeld terms it, a "free act"; i.e., the one performing the act may have a privately or publicly recognized responsibility in the matter because of the relationship in which he or she stands to the one in need, but there is no binding legal obligation; he or she is free not to act without incurring serious repercussions. That is, to put it positively, the act is one of gracious and loving kindness. Second, equally important is the fact that such an act involves an extraordinary element of mercy or generosity, a "going beyond the call of duty." This is especially to be seen in the lifestyle modeled for us by both Ruth and Boaz in those actions that the narrator specifically designates *ḥesed* through the embedded evaluation of his characters, namely, Ruth's commitment to Naomi in chap. 1 (see 3:9) and Boaz's generosity to Ruth in chap. 2 (see 2:20). Thus, Ruth's devotion to Naomi in 1:16–17, expressed in the moving parallelism of Hebrew poetry (see *Form/Structure/Setting* for 1:17–19a), encompasses all of the activities of life, expressed by the merism "to travel" and "to lodge, spend the night," and extends to the end of life itself: even in the place of burial will they be united. It transcends the bonds of community and religion: Naomi's people and Naomi's God will henceforth be hers. And, giving the ring of truth to her words, she takes the name of Yahweh on her lips in a solemn oath that only death will finally separate her and Naomi. Ruth's action as *ḥesed* can hardly be more eloquently expressed than in the words of Trible (173):

> Ruth stands alone; she possesses nothing. No God has called her; no deity has promised her blessing; no human being has come to her aid. She lives and chooses without a support group and she knows that the fruit of her decision may well be the emptiness of rejection, indeed of death. Consequently, not even Abraham's leap of faith surpasses this decision of Ruth's. And there is more. Not only has Ruth broken with family, country and faith, but she has also reversed sexual allegiance. A young woman has committed herself to the life of an old woman rather than to the search for a husband. . . . One female has chosen another female in a world where life depends upon men. There is no more radical decision in all the memories of Israel.

Boaz's actions in chap. 2 also meet the same criteria. His magnanimity knows no bounds. The instant his overseer informs him of Ruth's identity (2:6), he accords her exceptional privileges. Not only may she glean in his field (2:8 b–c), but she is to glean beside the women harvesters who are binding the cut grain into bundles and sheaves (2:8d–9b), a region normally off-limits to gleaners (see *Comments* on 2:8 and 2:9 for this interpretation), ordering his men not to interfere with her (2:9c). He then grants her access to their water supply (2:9d). In the second episode of the scene (2:14–16; see *Form/Structure/Setting* on 2:4–17a), he welcomes her to the intimate circle of their noon meal, giving her so much food she cannot eat it all (2:14). When she resumes gleaning, he orders his workers not only to permit her to glean between the sheaves themselves but also to pull out stalks of grain from the handfuls they have cut and leave them for her—an unheard-of favor! And when in the third scene Naomi reveals to Ruth who Boaz is (2:20), Ruth remembers, in sudden comprehension, that he granted her these same privileges until the whole harvest was completed (2:21).

The author emphasizes that this conduct of Ruth and Boaz is marked by an element of freedom from legal responsibility, of gracious and loving kindness that goes beyond the call of duty, by providing for each of them a contrasting character who models the choice not to act: Orpah in contrast to Ruth and the nearer redeemer, Mr. So-and-So, in contrast to Boaz (Campbell, 29–30). Indeed, Orpah's previous course of action in relation to her dead husband and her mother-in-law are designated by Naomi as *ḥesed* (1:8). The narrator implies no judgment whatsoever upon her decision to accede to Naomi's importuning and return home. Her decision is the sound and reasonable one: she opts for the possibility of home and husband (1:9a) and for her own community and faith (1:15). But her decision to accede to the dictates of community and custom merely demonstrates that Ruth's remarkable action is indeed one of gracious and loving kindness that goes beyond the call of duty. In like manner does the nearer redeemer function in respect to Boaz's further demonstration of *ḥesed*—his actions of redeeming the field of Elimelech and marrying Ruth. These are shown to meet the demands of *ḥesed* by the actions of Mr. So-and-So. First, his acts are "free": not only may he freely assent (4:4), but he may also freely decline (4:6a). Second, that the combination of the two is an exceedingly generous and gracious action is revealed by the reason he gives for his refusal: he could perform both only at the risk of bringing ruin upon his own estate (4:6b). Boaz, however, accepts the rights proffered to him both by the symbolic rite of the transfer of sandals (4:7–8; see

Comment) and by his public announcement that formally executes the transfer (4:9–10, a "performative" utterance, "I hereby acquire . . ."; see *Comment*), calling on the legal assembly to notarize the transaction. That actions immediately followed his words is a foregone conclusion, confirmed by the narrator's succinct summary introducing the next scene (4:13). In contrast to Mr. So-and-So's refusal to act beyond the demands of proper self-interest, the selfless generosity of Boaz expressed in the fullness and detail of his formal public announcement before the legal assembly stands out in bold relief.

Finally, these foils for Ruth and Boaz, whose actions, though legal and correct, do not constitute *ḥesed* indicate that, as Campbell (29) insightfully observes, "The Ruth story does not represent the style of life which exercises caring responsibility as a foregone conclusion for God's people. It is portrayed as attainable but elusive." This points up all the more sharply the manner in which the story holds up before us the quality of life of Ruth, Boaz, and Naomi as exemplary, worthy of imitation.

Another important theological emphasis of the book stems from the manner in which the divine role in the story is portrayed. As was noted above in the discussion of *Genre,* the narrator's portrayal of God and his action places the book far to one side of the OT artistic perspective. Though the story affirms that God exercises absolute sway over the affairs and actions of his world, human and otherwise, the stress is overwhelmingly on the implicitness of his providence. God's providence is not really "hidden" in the book of Ruth (as Hal puts it, *Theology,* 15–19). Rather, Clines' observation about its expression in the book of Esther is equally valid for Ruth: ". . . there is nothing *hidden* or *veiled* about the causality of the events . . . : it is indeed *unexpressed* but it is unmistakable, given the context within which the story is set" (*Esther Scroll,* 156). As in the book of Esther, so in Ruth, it takes divine and human causality to transform Naomi's life from death and emptiness to life and fullness. This coincidence of divine and human action is subtly and powerfully expressed in one wordplay, which produces a "moment of imaginative splendor and depth" (Rauber, *JBL* 89 [1970] 33). In explaining to Ruth that the reason for his generosity is his knowledge of all that she has done for Naomi (2:11), Boaz prays that her reward might be full from Yahweh, under whose "wings" (Hebrew כנף in the dual) she has come to take refuge (2:12). Then, Ruth voices her request for marriage on the threshing floor symbolically, requesting Boaz to throw his "wing" (כנף, referring here to the skirt of his robe) over her. She who came to find shelter under Yahweh's "wing" will find her full reward from Yahweh when the man who voiced such a petition spreads his "wing" over her in marriage. Not only does God act in the acts of *ḥesed* done by human characters (Hubbard, 71), but the reversal of the death and deprivation that have afflicted Naomi's life is effected by him through their ordinary hopes, intentions, and actions, including a "young girl's accidental steps and an old woman's risky plan" (Hals, *IDBSup,* 759). This is very different from the stress in much of the rest of OT literature on the overt, and at times supernatural, nature of divine guidance. Thus, the book of Ruth affirms that God often effects his purposes in the world through the ordinary motivations and events of his people—ordinary people like Ruth and Boaz, or like you and me, the ripple of whose lives stirs little beyond the pool of their own community—and in particular through their acts of gracious and loving kindness that go beyond the call of duty.

Outline

Act 1. Prologue and Problem: Death and Emptiness (1:1–22)

Scene 1. Setting and Problem. A Judean family dies in Moab: Naomi is left without husbands and sons (1:1–6)

Scene 2. Emptiness Compounded: Naomi and her daughters-in-law on the road to Judah (1:7–19a)

Scene 3. Emptiness Expressed: Naomi arrives at Bethlehem with Ruth (1:19b–22)

Act 2. Ruth Meets Boaz, Naomi's Relative, on the Harvest Field (2:1–23)

Scene 1. Ruth goes to glean—and happens upon the field of Boaz, Naomi's relative (2:1–3)

Scene 2. Ruth and Boaz meet on the harvest field: Boaz is exceedingly generous (2:4–17a)

Scene 3. Naomi evaluates the meeting: Boaz is one of their redeemers (2:17b–23)

Act 3. Naomi Sends Ruth to Boaz on the Threshing Floor (3:1–18)

Scene 1. Naomi reveals her plan for a home and husband for Ruth (3:1–5)

Scene 2. Ruth carries out Naomi's plan, and Boaz offers to be the redeemer (3:6–15)

Scene 3. Naomi evaluates the encounter: Boaz will act (3:16–18)

Act 4. Resolution and Epilogue: Life and Fullness (4:1–22)

Scene 1. Boaz acquires the right to redeem Naomi and Ruth (4:1–12)

Scene 2. A son is born to Ruth and Boaz: Naomi is restored to life and fullness (4:13–17)

Scene 3. Epilogue. A Judean family restored: The line of David (4:18–22)

Act 1
Prologue and Problem: Death and Emptiness (1:1–22)

Scene 1
Setting and Problem. A Judean Family Dies in Moab: Naomi Is Left without Husband and Sons (1:1–6)

Bibliography

Baly, D. *The Geography of the Bible.* Rev. ed. New York: Harper and Row, 1974. **Berlin, A.** *Poetics and Interpretation of Biblical Narrative.* Sheffield: Almond, 1983. **Cohen, S.** "Ephrathah." *IDB* 2:122. **Dommershausen, W.** "Leitwortstil in der Ruthrolle." In *Theologie im Wandel.* Munich-Freiberg: Wewel, 1967. 394–407. **Fawcett, S.** "Rachel's Tomb." *IDB* 4:5. **Gottwald, N.** *The Tribes of Israel.* Maryknoll, NY: Orbis, 1979. **Harvey, D.** "Ruth, Book of." *IDB* 4:131–34. **McDonald, J.** "The Status and Role of the Naʿar in Israelite Society." *JNES* 35 (1976) 147–70. **Moor, J. de.** "The Poetry of the Book of Ruth (Part I)." *Or* 53 (1984) 262–83. **Myers, J.** *The Linguistic and Literary Form of the Book of Ruth.* Leiden: Brill, 1955. **Porten, B.** "The Scroll of Ruth: A Rhetorical Study." *GCA* 7 (1978) 23–49. **Rauber, D.** "Literary Values in the Bible: The Book of Ruth." *JBL* 89 (1970) 27–37. **Sacon, K.** "The Book of Ruth—Its Literary Structure and Theme." *AJBI* 4 (1978) 3–22. **Smith, G.** *The Historical Geography of the Holy Land.* 1894. Repr. London: Collins, 1973. **Stager, L.** "The Archeology of the Family in Ancient Israel." *BASOR* 260 (1985) 1–35. **Staples, W.** "The Book of Ruth." *AJSL* 53 (1936–37) 145–47.

Translation

1 *During the time when the Judges ruled,*[a] *there was a famine in the land, and so a certain man*[b] *went from Bethlehem in Judah*[c] *to live in the territory*[d] *of Moab together with*[e] *his wife and his two*[f] *sons.* 2 *The man's name was Elimelech, the name of his wife Naomi, and the names of his two sons Mahlon and Chilion—Ephrathites from Bethlehem in Judah.*[a] *They came to the territory of Moab, and there they stayed.*

3 *Then Elimelech, Naomi's husband, died, and she was left alone with her two sons.*[a] 4 *They took Moabite wives, the name of one being Orpah and the other Ruth, and they lived there about ten years.* 5 *Then both Mahlon and Chilion also died, and the woman was left alone without her two boys and without her husband.*

6 *Then she set out with her daughters-in-law*[a] *and returned from the territory of Moab, for she heard there*[b] *that Yahweh had seen to the needs of his people by giving them food.*

Notes

1.a. Lit. "and it was in the days of the judging of the Judges." Some MSS of the LXX omit "the days of," and Syr omits the inf שׁפט. These readings probably represent the translators' attempt to render the Heb. of the MT rather than evidence for a different Heb. text.

1.b. Lit. "a man."

1.c. Or perhaps "Bethlehem of Judah"; see *Comment.*

1.d. Whether the spelling here (שְׂדֵי) should be understood as a rare form of the masc sg constr (so, e.g., Campbell, 50; Myers, *Literary Form,* 9; Rudolph, 37) or as masc pl constr (so Hubbard, 86, n. 15; Joüon, 32; cf. GKC § 93ll; the pl constr elsewhere is fem, שְׂדוֹת) is difficult to decide and immaterial as far as meaning is concerned (see *Form/Structure/Setting*).

1.e. Lit. "he and . . ."

1.f. Some LXX MSS and Syr omit the word "two."

2.a. See *Note* 1.c.

3.a. The Heb. would be more correctly translated "she and her two sons were left alone," but this then creates a problem in Eng. with the unspecified "they" as the subject of the next verb. This is not a problem in Heb. since the Heb. verb distinguishes masc and fem gender in its morphology.

6.a. Lit. "she and her daughters-in-law"; see *Comment.*

6.b. Lit. "in the territory of Moab." That the narrator would have used שְׂדֵי מוֹאָב in 6a as masc pl constr to mean "fields of Moab" but שְׂדֵה מוֹאָב here to mean "country of Moab" (Hubbard, 97 n. 3) is most improbable. See *Comment* on v 1.

Form/Structure/Setting

The first act of the book of Ruth consists of 1:1–22. In it our author gives us the initial setting and circumstances of his story: he tells us that famine has sent an Ephrathite family from Bethlehem to sojourn in Moab, where all its male members die; he introduces us to all but one of the principal characters of the tale, leaving only Boaz for the next scene; and he sets forth the major problem of the book: What will happen to a woman in a patriarchal society when all the men of the family have died? All these data are presented in succinct form in this the opening episode, vv 1–6 (see below). Hence, the question needs to be raised, should not these opening verses be given independent status as the statement of the problem, for which all that happens subsequently is the resolution, so that the rest of chap. 1, vv 7–22, constitutes an independent scene recounting the first step in that resolution? Indeed, some of the data of the first chapter seem to corroborate such a division. Thus, the return to Judah (v 7) could be understood as the first step in Naomi's transformation from death and emptiness to life and fullness. And surely vv 7–22 tell us how it was that Ruth the Moabitess "returned" to Judah—she whose faithfulness and loyalty will constitute the major means by which Naomi's transformation will be effected. However, the unity of 1:1–6 with the following two sections, 7–19a and 19b–22, can be seen at all levels of analysis. First, the conditions that distinguish the boundaries of the unit, creating the major break in the discourse, clearly occur at 1:22 and 2:1 (see the discussion there), not at 1:6 and 1:7. In fact, the transition from the opening section to the following is so gradual that there is real ambiguity in determining clearly whether the first unit closes with v 5, 6, or 7 (see the discussion below). Second, the unity of 1:1–22 is demonstrated by the commonness of its content. The theme of this opening act is sounded incessantly by the frequency of occurrence of the verbs הלך, "to travel, go, walk," and שׁוב, "to return." הלך is used 1x in the opening scene, 8x in the second, and 1x in the third, while שׁוב, the verb that above all sets the theme of this section (cf. Dommershausen, "Leitwortstil in der Ruthrolle," 396–

98), occurs 12x. It refers 6x to a return to Moab, all in the second scene, and 6x to a return to Judah, spread through all three scenes: 1x in the first (v 6), 2x in the second (vv 7, 10), and 3x in the third (vv 21, 22, 22). Further, the coherence of the content of the whole section is further effected by the use of other verbs from this same semantic domain: בוא, "to come, enter," 4x; יצא, "to set forth," 1x; גור, "to sojourn," 1x; ישב, "to dwell, remain," 1x; and לין, "to stay, spend the night," 2x.

Finally and conclusively, although the developments in the events noted above, namely, Naomi's return to Judah and Ruth's insistence on coming with her, could be considered logical steps toward the resolution of the story, it is very clear that, as steps in the plot, our narrator uses these developments far more to set forth the problem of his story—to depict the desolation, despair, and emptiness of Naomi's life—than as steps in the resolution of her plight. This can be seen most clearly in the content of these scenes, particularly in his characterization of Naomi. Although the primary statement of the problem the story will address is related in vv 3–5 of the opening section (see *Explanation* below), the pain and poignancy of that problem, its affective dimensions, are revealed in his depiction of Naomi in the two following scenes. (1) In the second scene, this is depicted in his characterization of Naomi's pain and anguish as she faces in dialogue with the two young women the bitter choice of sending them back to Moab (where they have some hope of life again)—and returning home utterly alone—or dragging them with her into the hopelessness of her widowed and lonely state in a foreign land (for details see *Explanation* for the following scene, vv 7–19a). (2) It is above all depicted in the way in which our narrator devotes the whole content of the arrival scene, vv 19b–22, exclusively to describing Naomi's bitter despair in her anguished response to the delighted cry of recognition with which the women of Bethlehem greet her (vv 20–21). Furthermore, Ruth's presence with Naomi is presented in this last scene not as a step toward the resolution of Naomi's state but as a poignant commentary on the depths of her despair, for her bitter cry that Yahweh has brought her back empty is belied by Ruth's presence with her, a presence that, though ignored by Naomi, is stressed by the narrator in the last verse of the scene (see *Comment* and *Explanation* for 1:22). In addition, this unity is strongly corroborated by the parallelism of the structure of this opening scene with that of the last; see *Form/Structure/Setting* on 4:1–12 below.

On these grounds, we contend that the opening act comprises 1:1–22, consisting of three scenes, vv 1–6, 7–19a, and 19b–22, and that the major purpose of this act is to set forth the problem of the death and emptiness of the life of Naomi, to the resolution of which the rest of the story will be devoted. In this connection, cf. the insightful analysis and comments of Rauber, *JBL* 89 (1970) 29–30.

The first scene of this opening act, then, consists of vv 1–6, and the major structural problem in connection with it is its ending. Some commentators end the pericope with v 5 (Campbell, Gerleman, Gray, Hubbard, Joüon, Morris, de Waard-Nida); some with v 6 (Hertzberg, Sasson); and others with v 7a (i.e., after ושתי כלתיה עמה, "her two daughters-in-law with her," Bertholet, Gressmann, Haller, Rudolph, Trible). On the grounds of rhetorical and structural considerations, Porten (*GCA* 7 [1978] 23–24) ends the pericope with v 6, and, on the same grounds, Sacon (*AJBI* 4 [1978] 4–5) with v 7b. On the basis of his analysis of the book of Ruth as narrative poetry, de Moor concludes the unit with v 5 (*Or* 53 [1984] 274, 280).

In my opinion, the critical question is whether v 6 belongs with what has preceded or with the section to follow. Since it is a transitional passage, good arguments can be found for placing it with either one. I have chosen to see it as the concluding statement of the opening pericope for the following reasons. Even though vv 3–5 form a subunit tightly bound together by the close parallelism of vv 3 and 5 (which form a striking inclusio, see below), thus leaving v 6 as a separate entity, v 6 is antithetically parallel to v 1, providing a chiastic contrast in content: there was a famine / went to Moab (v 1); returned from Moab / Yahweh . . . (gave) food (v 6) (see Porten, *GCA* 7 [1978] 24). Note how v 6 looks backward with its "return . . . from the territory of Moab" while v 7 looks forward with its "return to the land of Judah." Second, v 6 provides the conclusion to the initial circumstances and setting, namely, the journey to Moab because of famine (v 1) and the return from Moab because the famine is over. It also forms, however, a preview and content summary of all that will be revealed in more detail in the following two scenes and as such provides the transition to the story of the return told in those scenes, in which our narrator will set forth the affective dimensions of the problem he here simply states.

This opening pericope clearly divides into three sections. Vv 1–2 describe the setting, the characters, and the initial circumstances of the book. They are framed as a unit by the contrast between "went from Bethlehem in Judah" in v 1 and the summary statement at the end of v 2: "they came to the territory of Moab and there they stayed." Vv 3–5 form a tightly constructed chiasm framed by an identically parallel inclusio:

A **Then died Elimelech, the husband of Naomi, and she was left alone** with her two sons. v 3
B *They took* Moabite wives, the name of one Orpah and the other Ruth, v 4a
B′ *And they lived* there about ten years. v 4b
A′ **Then died also both Mahlon and Chilion, and the woman was left alone** without her two boys and without her husband. v 5

V 6, as noted above, rounds off and brings to a conclusion the initial circumstances of vv 1–2: "went to Moab" is balanced by "returned from Moab," while "famine" is balanced by "food." The verse concludes with a lovely alliteration לָתֵת לָהֶם לָחֶם *lātet lāhem lāḥem,* "by giving them food," which rings with associations in sound and meaning with the family's place of origin בית לחם, "Bethlehem."

In regard to time, our narrator dates his story only in the most general terms: lit. "in the days of the judging of the Judges," v 1. To attempt to date the story more precisely, then, such as suggesting that it implies the period between the Judges Ehud and Jephthah (Sasson, 15; cf. Hubbard, 84), is to go beyond the intent of the author. He clearly intends to tell us simply that his story took place in the period after the settlement of the land but before the monarchy existed in Israel. It does not seem at all likely that there is some stress on either the Judges or "judging" (contra Campbell, 57). Neither does this expression ring with connotations similar to English "once upon a time." By referring to a definable time period in the history of his people, he implies that the events he is about to relate do belong to his people's past (see also Sasson, 14). It is quite incorrect to call this expression a "characteristic folk-tale description of a time long past" (Harvey, *IDB* 4:131–34). It does not clearly give any indications as to how far in the past this period is. Once Israel's whole socio-juridical system changed with the establishment of the monarchy, this would be the natural way to refer to the previous period.

In regard to place, our story involves a family from Bethlehem in Judah, and the resolution of the problem here related will be worked out exclusively within the confines of that village scene. (On the physical nature and environs of the Israelite village in the Judean and Samarian hill country, see Stager, *BASOR* 260 [1985] 1–35.) Bethlehem is situated approximately five miles southwest of Jerusalem. It figures in some of the earliest stories of the period after the settlement of the land by Israel. The Levite who became the priest of Micah in Ephraim and who later migrated north with the Danites came originally from Bethlehem (Judg 17–18). It was also the home of the concubine whose brutal death in Gibeah of Benjamin was the cause célèbre that brought on the Benjaminite war (Judg 19). By far its most famous claim to fame, however, is its identification as the birthplace of David (1 Sam 16:1–13). As such, it is also expected to be the home of the coming Messianic king (Mic 5:2[Eng. 5:1]). Whether it is attested in the Amarna texts from the fourteenth century B.C. is disputed (see Campbell, 54).

Bethlehem lies on a pronounced ridge some 2400 feet above sea level. To the east and at a lower elevation lie broad fertile fields producing the characteristic crops of the region, grain, olives, and grapes. To the west, however, lies the prominent height of Har Gillo, cutting the town off from the western slopes of the central mountain ridge. This means that Bethlehem lies slightly in the rain shadow, for the eastern slopes receive far less rain than those west of the water parting, desert conditions prevailing very quickly to the east of the high point of the central mountain ridge (see Baly, *Geography*, 183, and esp. Smith, *Historical Geography of the Holy Land*, 211–12). When the rains failed, the desert conditions of the Wilderness of Judea quickly invaded the towns that lay along its western edge, such as Bethlehem.

Because of the famine, Elimelech and his family remove to שׂדי מואב, which we have translated "the territory of Moab." The word שׂדה can mean (1) "open country, open field (as opposed to villages or cities)" and (2) "plot of (arable) land, field (of an individual)." On this basis one might conclude that שׂדי מואב referred to some particular portion of the land of Moab. However, whenever שׂדה occurs in construct with a geographical name it means (3) "region, territory, domain." Thus, for example, שׂדה אדום, "domain of Edom," occurs in apposition to ארץ שׂעיר, "land of Seir," in Gen 32:4 (cf. also Judg 5:4), both referring to the country of Edom. Hence, our narrator informs us only that they went to live in the "territory" or "region" of Moab.

The country of Moab lay almost directly east of Judah on the other side of the deep depression of the Jordan Rift Valley, which is filled with that body of water known as the Dead Sea. It comprised three regions: (1) the "plains of Moab" (Num 22:1), a region on the east side of the Jordan rift valley just north of the Dead Sea where the valley floor reaches back into the eastern scarp of the Transjordanian plateau in a great "bay"; (2) the מישׁר (Deut 3:10), a level tableland east of the Dead Sea, 2000–2400 feet high, stretching from the northern end of the Dead Sea to the Arnon River, which flows into the sea about halfway down its length; and (3) the heartland of Moab, the higher tableland reaching heights above 4000 feet, stretching from the Arnon to the Zered, which empties into the southern end of the Dead Sea (see Baly, *Geography*, 202, 229–33). Since our narrator is totally silent about where in Moab the family of Elimelech took up residence, speculation will add nothing to his story. One can only note that the probabilities considerably favor the northern tableland over the more remote southern region.

Comment

1 וַיְהִי בִּימֵי שְׁפֹט הַשֹּׁפְטִים, "During the time when the Judges ruled." The book opens with a characteristic Hebrew temporal clause introduced by the waw-consecutive form of the verb היה, "to be," followed by the temporal expression (GKC § 111g), in this case consisting of the preposition בימי, "during the time that" (lit. "in the days of"), followed by the infinitive construct שפט plus its cognate subject שפטים, "Judges." Although this exact construction is unknown elsewhere in the OT (Campbell notes only Gen 36:31 as a close parallel), its meaning is quite clear. The word יום, "day," is the usual term for expressing time in a durative sense (Joüon, 31; cf. esp. 1 Sam 22:4; 2 Chron 26:5). Some have alleged that the fact that Ruth begins with the waw-consecutive form of the verb היה implies that it was, or was thought to be, the continuation of another text (cf. GKC § 49b n. 1; Joüon, 31). However, a number of books of the OT begin with a waw-consecutive form of the verb (Leviticus, Numbers, Joshua, Judges, 1 Samuel, 2 Kings, Ezekiel, Esther, Nehemiah, and 2 Chronicles) and, although some of these doubtless were originally parts of a larger whole (notably Leviticus, Numbers, 2 Kings, 2 Chronicles), it is not possible that they all were (certainly not Ezekiel and Esther). There can be no doubt that Ruth always formed a separate literary entity and was never part of a larger work (so also Gerleman, Hubbard, Rudolph; see the excellent discussion of Morris, 245 n. 1).

וַיְהִי רָעָב בָּאָרֶץ, "there was a famine in the land." Since this "certain man" and his family went to Moab to escape the famine, it is clear that our author uses אֶרֶץ, "land," here in its traditional sense of the land of Israel proper, i.e., Cisjordan, as often in the OT (cf., e.g., Judg 18:2; 1 Sam 14:29). To charge, as Gerleman (14) does, that a migration from Judah to Moab is hardly conceivable, since Moab lies climatically in the same region as Judah and has the same rainfall, not only makes nonsense of the story but is not borne out by the facts. The amount of rainfall in Palestine in a given year in modern times has varied widely from region to region—and even village to village (see Baly, *Geography*, 69–76)—and Amos 4:7–8 rather clearly suggests that the same conditions existed in the OT period. The sharp scarp of the Transjordanian plateau, which in places is higher than Cisjordan, causes considerable rain to fall on its western margin as the winds, sucked down by the Jordan rift valley, rise again to surmount it. Scott notes (*IDB* 3:622) that in the dry year of 1931–32 more rain fell in southern Moab than at Bethlehem, illustrating the feasibility of the situation described in our story. A famine in Judah could well have left parts of Moab sufficiently unaffected to provide a haven (cf. Hubbard, 87 nn. 19, 22).

וַיֵּלֶךְ אִישׁ מִבֵּית לֶחֶם יְהוּדָה, "and so a certain man went from Bethlehem in Judah." It is syntactically impossible to tell whether "from Bethlehem in Judah" modifies the verb "went" (i.e., "went from Bethlehem in Judah") or the noun "man" (i.e., "a man from Bethlehem in Judah"). On the grounds that, in introducing a new character, it is common to supply his address as well as his name, Andersen takes it with the noun "man" (*SBH,* 90; cf. Hubbard, 83 n. 2). The translation chosen here is based on rhetorical considerations, namely, that "went from Bethlehem in Judah" and "came to the territory of Moab" form an inclusio, framing vv 1–2 as a subunit (see *Form/Structure/Setting* above; cf. Joüon, 31; Campbell, 50). The expression בית לחם יהודה is either a compound name, "Bethlehem-Judah," or a construct expression, "Bethlehem of Judah." The specification "of Judah" is necessary in order to be exact since בית לחם, literally "place of food/bread," means something like "granary" (Morris, 248) or "storehouse," and hence there was another city with the same name in Zebulun (Josh 19:15).

לָגוּר בִּשְׂדֵי מוֹאָב, "to live in the territory of Moab." גור is a technical term expressing the position in society occupied by a גר, often translated "resident alien," a position intermediate between a native and a foreigner. The גר, since he lived among people to whom he had no blood relationship or tribal affiliation, had only the rights and status that the hospitality of the native population accorded him. (For a description of these rights in Israel, see *TDOT* 2:443–48; de Vaux, *Ancient Israel,* 74–76.) It is a reasonable assumption that some similar status would also have existed in Moabite society. That such was the case would be virtually certain if the restoration of the term גר as a social category of persons in line 16 of the stela of Mesha, king of Moab, is correct (see Gibson, *TSSI* 1:75, 80–81). One could translate the verb לָגוּר, as "to live as a resident alien" but, besides being cumbersome, that implies a modern legal status no doubt markedly different from that of ancient Palestine. The verb in and of itself does not necessarily connote a temporary stay (contra Morris, 247), for many "resident aliens" lived in a community more or less permanently. A move because of famine, however, would normally suggest that it was not intended to be permanent.

שְׂדֵי מואב, "territory of Moab," is spelled this way four times in Ruth (1:1, 2, 6, 22) and three times as the normal singular construct form שְׂדֵה (1:6; 2:6; 4:3; see Myers, *Linguistic and Literary Form,* 9). Although it is possible that שְׂדֵי is the plural construct form, that form elsewhere is שְׂדוֹת. Since a singular absolute form שָׂדַי occurs elsewhere (predominantly in poetry), it is probable that שְׂדֵי is singular, not plural, and is an older orthographic variant for שְׂדֵה (see GKC § 93ll; for a contrary opinion, see Hubbard, 86 n. 15).

הוּא וְאִשְׁתּוֹ וּשְׁנֵי בָנָיו, lit. "he and his wife and his two sons." The independent pronoun הוא, "he," is not emphatic here. When one adds a second subject (here "his wife and his two sons") to a nominal subject (here איש, "man") after a separating word or phrase, a resumptive pronoun is necessary (see *GBH* § 146.c.2; *IBHS* § 16.3.2.c).

2 אֱלִימֶלֶךְ . . . נָעֳמִי . . . מַחְלוֹן וְכִלְיוֹן, "Elimelech . . . Naomi . . . Mahlon and Chilion." The names of the family members need not detain us long, for our author makes no play on their meaning, with the exception of Naomi. His example, unfortunately, has not been followed by some modern discussions, one of which has sought in the names symbolic meanings connected with fertility cult myths (see Staples, *AJSL* 53 [1936–37] 145–57). It is important, however, to observe that, although all four occur only here in the OT, three of them are well attested in extrabiblical literature of the Late Bronze Age (ca. 1400 B.C.) and the fourth is of a similar pattern. Elimelech occurs both in the Amarna texts and at Ugarit, while Chilion is found in both syllabic and alphabetic texts from Ugarit.

Although Mahlon is not attested, it is built on identically the same pattern as Chilion. The name נעמי *Noʿŏmî* means "good, pleasant, lovely," an etymology that will be used by our narrator in v 22. The name occurs at Ugarit, and the form, ending in *-î,* possibly originally *-iya* or *-aya,* is widely attested in female names from Ugarit and among the female Amorite names from Mari. (For documentation, see esp. Hubbard, 88–90.) Since our author makes no wordplay upon them (apart from Naomi), the etymologies of these names, although frequently discussed by commentators, are of no relevance for the meaning of our story. Hence, they will not be discussed here (for detailed treatment, see Hubbard, Campbell, or Sasson). It should be noted, however, that supposed etymologies for Chilion and Mahlon, yielding the meanings "extermination" and "sickness," respectively, have often been used to posit that they are fictitious names invented to fit their role in the story.

אֶפְרָתִים מִבֵּית לֶחֶם יְהוּדָה, "Ephrathites from Bethlehem in Judah." Of more importance to the story than the etymologies of the names (see *Explanation*) is the identification of this family as "Ephrathites" from Bethlehem. In Judg 12:15; 1 Sam 1:1; 1 Kgs 11:26, the gentilic אפרתי refers to people from Ephraim and indeed in these passages clearly is the gentilic form of the tribal and geographic name אפרים, "Ephraim." On the other hand, 1 Sam 17:12, as well as our passage, knows of the Ephrathites as a portion (probably a "clan," see below) of the population of Bethlehem. Further, the geographic term אפרתה/אפרת is unmistakably an alternate name for Bethlehem in 4:11, and the compound name "Bethlehem-Ephrathah" in Mic 5:1 (Eng. 2) is deemed "little to be among the clans [אלפי] of Judah." In addition, the author of Chronicles knows אפרתה/אפרת as the wife of Caleb who bore to him Hur, the "father of Bethlehem" (1 Chron 4:4; but cf. 1 Chron 2:50–51). Finally, Gen 35:16–19; 48:7 narrates that Rachel died in childbirth "while there was still a distance of ground to come to Ephrathah" (35:16; 48:7) and was buried "on the road to Ephrathah, that is, Bethlehem" (36:19; 48:7). There is nothing that compels one to locate this Ephrathah in Benjamin (contra Fawcett, *IDB* 4:5; Stager, *BASOR* 260 [1985] 23), even though the OT also knows a tradition that locates Rachel's tomb in the territory of Benjamin (1 Sam 10:2), presumably near Ramah (Jer 31:15), and even though the identification of Ephrathah with Bethlehem in Gen 36:19; 48:7 is very likely a later addition to the text (see also the remarks of Gottwald, *Tribes of Israel,* 268–69). Further (contra Cohen, *IDB* 2:122), the juxtaposition of Ephrathah with "the fields of Jaar" (שדי יער) as parallel pairs in the poetry of Ps 132:6 in no way demands that Ephrathah is a northern region on the basis that שדי יער is a variant form of Kiriath-Jearim (קרית יערים) and that the parallelism with Ephrathah is synonymous. It surely is not out of place in a psalm that extols David for bringing the ark to Jerusalem (vv 1–5, 8) to mention both the place of David's origins, Ephrathah, and שדי יער (i.e., Kiriath-Jearim), the site from which he brought the ark to Jerusalem after its twenty-year sojourn there (1 Sam 7:1–2). As a geographical entity, Ephrathah was probably at one time not an alternate name for Bethlehem but a site nearby, one of the tributary villages (Hebrew בנות, lit. "daughters") within the territory of Bethlehem. Gottwald (*Tribes of Israel,* 269) may well be correct in suggesting that it lay in the direction of Tekoa to the southeast on the grounds of its connections with Caleb (1 Chron 2:19, 24, 50–51; 4:4). In the sense in which it is used here, however, it figures not as a village but as the name of one of the משפחות, the "clans," that formed the population of Bethlehem (cf. Hubbard, 91). As Gottwald (*Tribes of Israel,* 269) observes:

> . . . it seems a reasonable assumption that the region known as Ephrathah was inhabited by a single *mishpāḥāh* and that when Elimelech's family members are called "Ephrathites" it means more than that they lived in Ephrathah; it means that they were of the protective association of families known as *mishpaḥath* Ephrati (compared to Saul's *mishpaḥath* Matri, or possibly *mishpaḥath* Bichri). Micah still remembers that Ephrathah was counted "among the *ʾalphē* Judah" (*ʾeleph* here replacing the more common *mishpaḥath*), a memory probably kept alive by the prominence of the *ʾeleph* of David. The proposal that the *mishpaḥath* Ephrati of Elimelech and Boaz inhabited a sub-section of larger Bethlehem fits well with the general conception of the story. If the entirety of Bethlehem was one *mishpāḥāh* or only a part of a still more widely dispersed *mishpāḥāh* (as would appear to be the case if we follow Numbers 26:19–22 in believing that there were only five *mishpāḥōth* in all Judah), then the singling out of Boaz as "known kinsman" of *mishpaḥath* Elimelech is foolish. If all Bethlehemites were from the same *mishpāḥāh* as Elimelech, then all Bethlehemites would have been "known kinsmen" of Elimelech. The excitement and suspense of the story depends upon the fact that only some Bethlehemites are of Elimelech's *mishpāḥāh.*

All of this would serve, of course, to give added point to the identification of Elimelech's family as "Ephrathites." The language here is strikingly reminiscent of the identification of David in 1 Sam 17:12: "David was the son of an Ephrathite from Bethlehem in Judah . . ." (see *Explanation*).

וַיִּהְיוּ שָׁם, "and there they stayed." The verb הָיָה, "to be," is used here in the sense of "to remain, stay." This meaning is not infrequent or unusual (contra Campbell; cf. Exod 34:28, Judg 17:12; BDB, III.2, p. 226; *HALOT,* 3.b, p. 244). Hubbard (91) may well be right in observing that the omission of a time reference, which often accompanies the idiom, may suggest that the sojourn in Moab would be of indefinite duration.

4 וַיִּשְׂאוּ לָהֶם נָשִׁים מֹאֲבִיּוֹת, "They took Moabite wives." The idiom נָשָׂא אִשָּׁה, "to take a wife," occurs elsewhere only in Chronicles, Ezra, and Nehemiah, i.e., in post-exilic texts. The earlier idiom is לקח אשה. This has often been used as one piece of evidence for a post-exilic date for the book (see *Introduction*).

עָרְפָּה . . . רוּת, "Orpah . . . Ruth." As with the names of the characters given in v 2 above, our author makes no play on the meanings of the names Ruth or Orpah; hence, the involved discussion of their possible etymologies brings no enlightenment to our story (see again for details Hubbard, Campbell, or Sasson). It should be noted, however, that a supposed etymology for Orpah, yielding the meaning "she who turned her back," has often been used as evidence that this name is also fictitious, invented to fit her role in the story.

וַיֵּשְׁבוּ שָׁם כְּעֶשֶׂר שָׁנִים, "and they lived there about ten years." The context in general, and in particular the masculine plural form of the verb following upon the change to masculine plural in the verb of the previous clause (for which see *Note* 3.a.), is very strongly in favor of the meaning that it is the two sons (and Naomi) who lived there about ten years (so Joüon, 34), rather than that the two sons were married for ten years (contra Hubbard, 91 n. 2; Campbell, 58; cf. Sasson, 21). This and the appended approximative כ, "about," makes it unlikely that there is any conscious echo here of Gen 16:3 (contra Sasson, Hubbard). Even less likely is it that "the passage of ten years makes the audience anticipate . . . the birth of children" and hence that the text "quietly introduces one of the book's dominant themes, the problem of heirs" (Hubbard, 95).

5 וַתִּשָּׁאֵר הָאִשָּׁה מִשְּׁנֵי יְלָדֶיהָ וּמֵאִישָׁהּ, "and the woman was left alone without her two boys and without her husband." The idiom השאר מן, lit. "to be left from," is used here in a unique sense. Elsewhere in this idiom the preposition מן, "from," has its partitive force (e.g., Deut 3:11, "Only Og King of Bashan *was left from* the survivors of the Rephaites"; cf. Exod 10:5; Josh 13:12). The force of מן, here, however, is "without," a meaning not listed by BDB or Ges.-Buhl (Joüon, 35), but see GKC § 119w and *HebS* § 321. As Joüon (35) notes, the use of ילד, "boy, youth," to refer to a married man occurs only here. The choice likely results from two factors: (1) it forms an inclusio with 4:16 where Naomi cradles a new ילד in her arms (Campbell, 56), and (2) it expresses the poignancy of the mother's loss more than would the prosaic בן, "son." On its use in comparison to synonyms, see McDonald, *JNES* 35 (1976) 150.

6 וַתָּקָם הִיא וְכַלֹּתֶיהָ וַתָּשָׁב מִשְּׂדֵי מוֹאָב, "Then she set out with her daughters-in-law and returned from the territory of Moab." The syntax here is striking. Although the singular form of the Hebrew verb ותקם, "then she set out," which stands prior to its compound subject, is quite regular (cf. GKC §§ 146f, g), it is at variance with normal Hebrew syntax for the succeeding predicate ותשב, "and returned," whose subject must be the preceding compound, "she and her daughters-in-law," to be singular rather than plural (cf. GKC §§ 145s, u). Further, even more striking is the continuation of this feminine singular construction in both the following subordinate clause of reason, כי שמעה, "for she heard," and the succeeding sequential main clause ותצא, "so she set forth," v 7. The net effect of this is that the true subject of all these clauses is simply "she," i.e., Naomi alone, and not "Naomi and her daughters-in-law," which compound phrase is the literal subject of the first clause. To reflect this, one must not render the first clause with a compound subject, "she and her daughters-in-law set out," but rather with "she set out with her daughters-in-law." For the significance of this, see the *Comment* on v 7 and the *Explanation.*

לָתֵת לָהֶם לָחֶם, "by giving them food." This use of the infinitive construct of נתן, "to give," plus the preposition ל is the equivalent of the English gerund with the preposition "by," expressing means, i.e., "by . . . -ing" (see *HebS* § 195; *IBHS* § 36.2.3.e).

Explanation

As the section on *Form/Structure/Setting* has revealed, our author describes in the opening section, vv 1–2, the initial setting and circumstances of his story: famine sends a family from Bethlehem to sojourn in Moab. Since these facts are incidental to the major problem of the story, giving only the background and setting, they are stated in only the broadest of terms. We do not know the cause, severity, or extent of the famine, and it is dated only "during the time when the Judges ruled." Nor are we given the slightest information as to the destination of this family; they simply went to reside "in the territory of Moab." And although he gives us the names of the members of this family—a man Elimelech, his wife Naomi, and two sons Mahlon and Chilion—our narrator, in the main, has touched the canvas of his story with broad brush strokes only, unrelieved by detail. Yet in one place at least he has flecked that canvas not only with detail but with repetition, which, hence, is highlighted, so it behooves us to note this with care. Although he tells us nothing more than that a famine occurred to occasion a family's migration to a foreign land, and although he gives us not one word as to their actual destination in the whole country of Moab, he twice tells us the origin of this family born to trouble. They are not just from Judah but from Bethlehem in Judah (vv 1 and 2); they are not just Bethlehemites but very specifically "Ephrathites from Bethlehem in Judah" (v 2). In the period in which the story was told, this foregrounding of origin in such repeated detail could hardly fail to raise in the minds of its hearers connections with the most famous Ephrathite from Bethlehem in Judah—David son of Jesse. Note the language of 1 Sam 17:12, "Now David was *the son of an Ephrathite from Bethlehem in Judah* whose name was Jesse . . . ," and see *Comment* on v 2. Hence, suggestions about the end of the story in 4:17, and the appended genealogy, were already woven subtly into the tapestry of its opening verses. So, though that ending doubtless still came as a delightful surprise, it was nonetheless an expected and anticipated one.

While noting the implications of this highlighted detail, it is also important to stress the *lack* of implications in the broad general statements with which our author sketches in the rest. There is not the faintest suggestion, for example, that there is any opprobrium to be attached to the move to Moab or that the famine is Israel's punishment for her sin. Especially there is not the slightest hint that the tragic deaths of Elimelech and his sons in any way resulted from their having forsaken their people in a time of trouble or their having moved to Moab where the sons married Moabite women. Later rabbinic exegesis used such themes of retribution and punishment to the full (for details, see Campbell), but they are read into the story, not out of it. In point of fact, a plausible case can be made for the existence, at times, of reasonably friendly relations between Judah and Moab in the period prior to the Israelite monarchy (note Deut 2:8–9, 28–29 and especially 1 Sam 22:3–5, which tells of David taking his parents to the king of Moab at Mizpah of Moab when he became a fugitive from Saul; see Campbell and note the comments in *IDB* 3:414–15). The attitude expressed in Deut 23:3–6 is that of a much later period. Hence, as Campbell notes, the events recorded are certainly plausible. However, apart from the issue of the plausibility of the story, none of this is relevant to its meaning simply because the author leaves all such questions totally in the background—by design, in my opinion. To raise such questions, indeed to give any more details, would have been a distraction, for the complete journey to and from Moab and its cause are but the background and setting for the main problem the story addresses, which is depicted in the second section, vv 3–5.

Famine has driven a family to Moab, yes, but that event is not the stuff that makes a good story—at least not this good story. The stuff of this story is the death and deprivation succinctly but powerfully portrayed in the short section, vv 3–5, so strikingly bracketed by the journey to Moab because of famine (vv 1–2) and the notice of the return from Moab because Yahweh has provided food (v 6). Here form and content unite to highlight the theme of death and deprivation: v 5 is chiastically parallel to v 3, identical in structure and closely related in content (see *Form/Structure/Setting*). The tragic picture of the widow left alone with two sons, so succinctly recounted in v 3, is given momentary respite through the marriage of the two sons to Moabite wives (v 4a). But the possibility of the continuation of the family, first postponed by ten years without progeny (v 4b), is then dramatically ended (cf. Trible, 167): both Mahlon and Chilion also died, "and the woman," the narrator tells us, "was left alone without her two boys and without her husband."

Here our narrator sets forth unmistakably for us the major character and the major problem of his story. He achieves this by the subtle way that Naomi's identity shifts within the pericope through the way he *names* her (on the general subject of naming in narrative poetics, see A. Berlin, *Poetics,* 59–61). In vv 1–2 he calls her "his [i.e., Elimelech's] wife." Yet never again throughout the rest of the story is she ever identified as "Naomi wife of Elimelech." She is simply "Naomi" or, from the point of view of Ruth or Orpah, "mother-in-law." Not even in the legal negotiation between Boaz and the nearer redeemer at the city gate in chap. 4 (so Berlin, *Poetics,* 87), where a legally exact definition would seem most appropriate (note Ruth's identity; see below), does Boaz call her "wife of Elimelech" but only "Naomi, who returned from the territory of Moab" (4:3), or simply "Naomi" (4:9; strikingly in contrast with "Ruth the Moabitess, wife of Mahlon," 4:10). That Naomi is the principal character is subtly effected here in v 3 at the beginning of the story by the way the narrator identifies Elimelech: "Then died Elimelech *the husband of Naomi.*" Here normal patriarchal identities are reversed: instead of "Naomi wife of Elimelech" we have "Elimelech husband of Naomi." By this reversal, Naomi is given center stage; the tale to come is her story. Throughout, when not viewed through the eyes of Orpah or Ruth as "mother-in-law," she "stands independently, known only by her proper name" (Berlin, *Poetics,* 87). Indeed, "a man's world is to tell a woman's story" (Trible, 166).

Further, through the way our narrator refers to Naomi in this pericope, he also delineates clearly the major problem of his story. In its chiastic parallelism, v 5 is closely related in content to v 3, but it is also strikingly different. In his choice of one word in the final clause, the narrator suddenly leaves the particularity and individuality of his story and makes a general statement for his audience to ponder: "The *woman,*" he says, "was left alone without her two boys and without her husband." He does so "for the emotional effect of the phrase—a woman stands alone" (Berlin, *Poetics,* 87). In this way he sets forth powerfully and poignantly the major problem the story will address and resolve: What will happen to a woman in Israel's patriarchal world, in which, as all his hearers knew so well, all power and privilege were vested in the male members of the family, when suddenly all of them are gone?

> From wife to widow, from mother to no-mother, this female is stripped of all identity. The security of husband and children, which a male-dominated culture affords its women, is hers no longer. The definition of worth, by which it values the female, applies to her no more. The blessings of old age, which it gives through progeny, are there no longer. Stranger in a foreign land, this woman is a victim of death—and of life. (Trible, 167–68)

In v 6, the author brings full circle the opening and incidental circumstances: Naomi (and her daughters-in-law) returned from Moab. The verb "return" (שׁוּב),

new to this section, both completes the introduction and looks ahead to the next scene, a scene dominated by the theme of "returning." Thus far, outside of the tantalizingly veiled allusions contained in the identity of this family as "Ephrathites from Bethlehem in Judah," the introductory scene has not given the slightest hint as to how this desperate state of affairs will be resolved. Is there hope for Naomi (and her two daughters-in-law)? As the next scene will reveal, Naomi bitterly does not think so. However, in the way the narrator states the reason for her return in the final clause of v 6, he raises *our* hopes and expectations, for he interprets the physical facts in the light of his covenant faith: "she heard," he tells us, "that Yahweh had seen to the needs of his people by giving them food." Those who hear the story and share such a theology can only wait to see how and in what way Yahweh will likewise remember Naomi. Does he perhaps even mean that this is the form in which Naomi heard or interpreted the facts? We cannot be sure, but, if so, it will not be until much later that Naomi can see beyond the circle of bitterness and despair that now surrounds her (see 2:20). For the nonce, she has been, like Job, "rendered bereft of those things which provide her security and she cannot comprehend why (see 1:20–21)" (Campbell). But that is to anticipate our author's story.

Scene 2
Emptiness Compounded: Naomi and Her Daughters-in-law on the Road to Judah (1:7–19a)

Bibliography

Aejmelaeus, A. "Function and Interpretation of כי in Biblical Hebrew." *JBL* 105 (1986) 193–209. **Barr, J.** "Why? in Biblical Hebrew." *JTS* 36 (1985) 1–33. **Brichto, H.** "Kin, Cult, Land, and Afterlife—A Biblical Complex." *HUCA* 44 (1973) 9–24. **Dillard, R.** *2 Chronicles.* WBC 15. Waco, TX: Word, 1987. **Dommershausen, W.** "Leitwortstil in der Ruthrolle." In *Theologie im Wandel.* Munich-Freiburg: Wewel, 1967. 394–407. **Fewell, D.,** and **Gunn, D.** "'A Son Is Born to Naomi!': Literary Allusions and Interpretation in the Book of Ruth." *JSOT* 40 (1988) 99–108. **Gruber, M.** *Aspects of Nonverbal Communication in the Ancient Near East.* Rome: Biblical Institute, 1980. **Hunter, A.** "How Many Gods Had Ruth?" *SJT* 34 (1981) 427–35. **Hyman, R. T.** "Questions and the Book of Ruth." *HS* 24 (1983) 17–25. ———. "Questions and Changing Identity in the Book of Ruth." *USQR* 39 (1984) 189–201. **Moor, J. de.** "The Poetry of the Book of Ruth (Part I)." *Or* 53 (1984) 262–83. **Porten, B.** "The Scroll of Ruth: A Rhetorical Study." *GCA* 7 (1978) 23–49. **Rauber, D.** "Literary Values in the Bible: The Book of Ruth." *JBL* 89 (1970) 27–37. **Rendsburg, G.** "Late Biblical Hebrew and the Date of 'P.'" *JANES* 12 (1980) 65–80. **Schoors, A.** "The Particle כי." *OTS* 21 (1981) 240–76. **Thompson, D., and Thompson, T.** "Some Legal Problems in the Book of Ruth." *VT* 18 (1968) 79–99. **Vesco, J.** "La date du livre de Ruth." *RB* 74 (1967) 235–47. **Vriezen, T.** "Einige Notizen zur Übersetzung des Bindeswort *kî*." In *Von Ugarit nach Qumran,* ed. J. Hempel and L. Rost. BZAW 77. Berlin: de Gruyter, 1958. 266–73.

Translation

[7]*So she set forth from the place where she had been staying,*[a] *together with her two*
daughters-in-law, and they took[b] *the road to return to the land of Judah.* [8]*Naomi said to*
her two daughters-in-law, "Come, return each of you to her mother's[a] *house! May Yahweh*
deal[b] *kindly and faithfully with you as you have done with the dead and with me.* [9]*May*
Yahweh grant that each of you may find repose in the house of a husband."

And she kissed them good-bye, and they all wept and sobbed loudly.[a]

[10]*But they said to her, "No, we want to*[a] *go with you back to your people!"*

[11]*Then Naomi replied, "Go back, my daughters! Why do you want to come with me?*
Do I yet have sons within me[a] *to become*[b] *husbands for you?* [12]*Go back, my daughters!*
Go! For I am too old to have a husband. Even if I said that there was hope for me—
indeed, if I had a husband this night[a] *and actually bore sons—*[13]*would you wait for*
them[a] *until they grew up? Would you go without a husband for them?*[a] *No, my daugh-*
ters! For my life is much too bitter for you[b] *to share, for Yahweh has stretched out his*
hand[c] *against me."*

[14]*They continued to weep loudly.*[a] *Then Orpah kissed her mother-in-law farewell,*[b] *but*
Ruth clung to her.

[15]*"Look," said Naomi,*[a] *"your sister-in-law has gone back to her people and to her god.*
Go back[b] *after your sister-in-law!"*

[16]*And Ruth said,*

"Do not press me to leave you,
To turn back from following you.[a]
For wherever you travel, I will travel;
And wherever you stay, I will stay.
Your people will be my people,
And your God, my God.
[17]*Where you die, I will die;*
And there shall I be buried.
Thus may Yahweh do to me and more also[a]*—*
Nothing but death will separate me from you!"

[18]*When Naomi*[a] *saw that she was determined to go with her, she said no more.*[b] [19a]*Then*
the two of them went on until they arrived at Bethlehem.

Notes

7.a. On this meaning of היה, see *Comment* on v 2 above.

7.b. Lit. "And they went on." See *Comment.*

8.a. LXX[B] reads the same as MT; LXX[A] (and some other LXX MSS) reads some form of "father," while Syr expands: "your country and the house of your parents." These variants reveal translators wrestling with a difficult text and demonstrate that the MT reading is original.

8.b. K (יעשה) shows the full form of the impf rather than the shortened form of the juss (יעש), which the vowel pointing of Q supplies. The juss sense is required, but either form is correct, since the full form of the impf of verbs ל״ה is frequently used with the sense of the juss. See GKC § 109a n. 2.

9.a. Lit. "they lifted their voices and wept." See *Comment.*

10.a. Heb. נשוב. For the use of the simple impf to express the nuance "want to," cf. GKC § 107n; *GBH* § 113n.

11.a. Lit. "in my insides, abdomen."

11.b. In a rather rare use (cf. *GBH* § 119 n. 2), the pf with waw consec (והיו) after a nominal clause expresses result here. See *IBHS* § 32.2.4.a.

12.a. Several MSS of the LXX and Syr omit הלילה, "tonight" (considering it indecent?—so Campbell, Rudolph, Gerleman). Other LXX MSS misread it as חלילה, "profaned." The MT is unquestionably the original text.

13.a. The LXX, Syr, Tg, OL, and Vg all read "for them," with the pronoun "them" clearly referring to the sons that Naomi mentions in the protasis in v 12; hence, they read the suffix as 3rd masc pl. This would require הלהם rather than MT's הלהן. See *Comment.*

13.b. Heb. מכם. For the interpretation of the masc pl here as originally a dual ending, see *Comment* on עמכם in v 8.

13.c. Lit. "the hand of Yahweh has come forth against me." See *Comment.*

14.a. Lit. "They lifted up their voice and wept still more." See *Comment.* The form וַתִּשֶּׂנָה, from נשׂא, lacks the quiescent aleph; the full form occurs in v 9 (see GKC §§ 74k, 76b).

14.b. Since נשׁק here has the force "to kiss farewell" (see *Comment* on v 9), the added phrases of Syr, "she turned and went," and the LXX, "she returned to her people," are clearly not original, despite de Moor's arguments on poetic grounds (*Or* 53 [1984] 281).

15.a. Lit. "she said." In Heb. style, the change in subj does not need to be specifically stated. Eng. style, however, requires identifying the speaker.

15.b. The LXX (throughout) and Syr have "an attractive addition here" (Campbell, 73). After the verb, they read the equivalent of גם את, "you too" (Joüon, Campbell). As Campbell notes (73), this might represent an independent text tradition, lost in the forerunners of the MT.

16.a. Heb. לשוב מאחריך, lit. "to turn back *from after* you." In such idioms, מאחרי has the meaning "from following" (see BDB, 4.a[*a*], p. 30, and compare 1 Sam 24:2; with עלה, cf. 1 Sam 14:46).

17.a. Lit. "and thus may he add."

18.a. Lit. "when she . . ." Again Heb. style does not express the change in subj. In contrast, some LXX MSS and Syr add "Naomi." Eng. style also needs the subj made explicit. On the expression of the temporal clause by simple juxtaposition, see *HebS* § 496; GKC §§ 111d, 164b.

18.b. Lit. "She ceased to speak to her."

Form/Structure/Setting

The form of this whole scene differs from that of the introductory pericope in two striking and important ways. First, our narrator does not, except at one point (v 19a), move events forward in great leaps by using broad, general statements as he did in the first section. Instead, he now relates certain incidents in considerable detail; indeed, in this scene he brings the action to a full halt partway on the journey home and relates to us an extended conversation between Naomi and the two young women. Second, he does not primarily relate to us what the protagonists of his story are thinking or feeling or what their intentions were by making narrative statements about them. Rather, he communicates this information by letting us hear them speak; i.e., his favorite literary device here, as well as in the rest of the book, is *dialogue.* As Joüon (12 n. 1) puts it, "The story could have been told in a few verses. But, what produces in part the charm of the narrative is that the author, instead of telling us who his characters are and what they do, has them speak. More than half the book is in dialogue (exactly 55 verses out of 85)." The task of the interpreter is thereby made more difficult, for the feelings, intentions, and actions of the characters of the story are portrayed indirectly and subtly. Yet by this method of portrayal, the individuals of the story emerge as persons with life and flesh and feelings in a way that simple narrative statements about them could hardly portray.

On the basis of both form and content, this scene divides unmistakably into three dialogues, each separated by narrative transitions and the whole enclosed by a narrative introduction and conclusion, as follows:

A	Narrative Introduction	v 7	Naomi and her daughters-in-law set forth to return to the land of Judah.
B	Dialogue 1	vv 8–9a	Naomi urges the young women to return home and blesses them.
C	Narrative Transition	v 9b	She kisses them farewell, and they all weep.
D	Dialogue 2	vv 10–13	The young women refuse, insisting that they will go with her, and Naomi replies, urging them to return home with an impassioned plea.
C´	Narrative Transition	v 14	They all continue to weep while Orpah kisses Naomi farewell, but Ruth clings to her.
B´	Dialogue 3	vv 15–18	Naomi urges Ruth to follow Orpah's example and return home. Ruth refuses in a dramatic and moving speech of commitment to Naomi. Seeing Ruth's determination, Naomi ceases urging her to leave.
A´	Narrative Conclusion	v 19a	The two of them proceed until they come to Bethlehem.

This carefully constructed scene is a chiasm, formed around the second dialogue (vv 10–13), which is the high point of Naomi's attempt to persuade her daughters-in-law not to return with her to Judah. The narrative introduction (A) and conclusion (A´) both correspond and contrast in content and form. In A, the three women *set forth* (תצא) on the journey and *go* (תלכנה) on their way; in A´, Naomi and Ruth *go on* (תלכנה) until they *arrive at* (באנה) Bethlehem. The repetition of ותלכנה, "they went (on)," and the appropriate chiastic contrast of יצא, "to set forth," and בוא, "to arrive," form an inclusio clearly marking the beginning and end of the passage.

Dialogues 1 (B) and 3 (B´) correspond in that in B Naomi opens the dialogue by urging the young women to return home and then invokes the name of Yahweh to bless them, whereas in B´ Ruth brings the dialogue to a close by reducing Naomi to silence through her moving speech of commitment, at the end of which she invokes the name of Yahweh in an oath. The narrative transitions C and C´ form a dramatic inclusio that ties the whole passage together, for they contain the same actions of kissing good-bye and weeping loudly. These two actions are, however, arranged chiastically and combined with one dramatic contrast in content:

X	9c	She kissed them good-bye,
Y	9d	and they all wept and sobbed loudly.
Y´	14a	They continued to weep loudly.
X´	14b–c	Then Orpah kissed her mother-in-law good-bye, but Ruth clung to her.

The contrast in meaning comes with the reversal of subjects and objects in X and X´ (see Trible, 171). Orpah's kiss of farewell signals her decision to leave as Naomi wishes. Ruth's action is equally expressive, but it signals her refusal to accept leaving. In the Hebrew, her action is strongly contrasted with that of Orpah's by the inversion of subject and object:

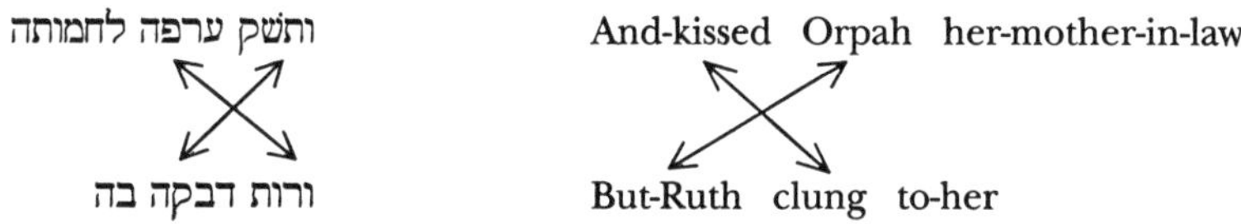

ותשק ערפה לחמותה
ורות דבקה בה
And-kissed Orpah her-mother-in-law
But-Ruth clung to-her

The hinge of the chiasm is vv 10–13, comprising the young women's initial refusal and Naomi's reply. In it she addresses them three times, each time as "my daughters" (11b, 12a, 13c). Her impassioned plea builds up through each of the three units, which consist of carefully balanced couplets (see also Porten, *GCA* 7 [1978] 27–28). The first unit consists of a pair of rhetorical questions:

11b "Go back, my daughters!
11c Why will you come with me?
11d Do I yet have sons within me . . . ?"

The second unit first answers these rhetorical questions and then continues with a balanced conditional sentence that concludes with another pair of rhetorical questions, each pair introduced by the same Hebrew particle:

12a "Go back, my daughters! Go!
(כי) 12b For I am too old to have a husband!
(כי) 12c Even if I said that there was hope for me—
(גם) 12d indeed if I had a husband this night
(וגם) 12e and actually bore sons—
(הלהן) 13a Would you wait for them until they grew up?
(הלהן) 13b Would you go without a husband for them?"

The third unit consists of a couplet that reaches an irrefutable conclusion by moving from the absurdity of the previous rhetorical questions to the statement of Yahweh's past action (Porten, *GCA* 7 [1978] 27–28):

13c "No, my daughters!"
(כי) 13d For my life is much too bitter for you to share,
(כי) 13e for Yahweh has stretched out his hand against me."

Note how each of the last four sets of couplets begins with the same Hebrew word and how the final couplet is emphasized by the poignant alliteration of mem and yodh: כי־מר־לי מאד מכם כי־יצאה בי יד־יהוה *kî mar lî meʾōd mikkem kî yāṣĕʾāh bî yad Yhwh.*

Finally, Ruth's moving speech of commitment to Naomi in vv 16–17 consists of a series of five pairs of clauses that compose another chiasm:

A	Do not press me to leave you, To turn back from following you.	16b	Introductory imperative
B	For wherever you travel, I will travel; And wherever you stay, I will stay.	16c 16d	Verbal sentence pair
C	Your people will be my people, And your God, my God.	16e 16f	Nominal sentence pair
B´	Where you die, I will die; And there shall I be buried.	17a 17b	Verbal sentence pair
A´	Thus may Yahweh do to me and more also— Nothing but death will separate me from you!	17c–d 17e	Concluding oath

The introductory imperative, A, and concluding oath, A´, enclose three pairs of parallel clauses, B, C, and B´.

The outer pair B and B´ correspond in form and content. In form they are verbal sentences, contrasting with the nominal construction of C. In content they encompass all of life. The first pair of clauses, B, set forth opposite activities, "travel" (הלך) and "stay" (לין), a literary device (merism), which is equivalent to saying "everywhere": whatever activity in life Naomi engages in, so also will Ruth. The third pair of clauses, B´, takes Ruth's commitment to the end of life itself: not even the place of burial will separate her from Naomi. In the short, staccato pair of nominal clauses, C, enclosed by B and B´, Ruth picks up the language used by Naomi in v 15, when she urged Ruth to follow Orpah's example and return to "her people and her god," and rejects her argument by the affirmation "Your people will be my people, and your God, my God."

Finally, this clear structure and balance strongly suggest that de Moor erred in his decision *not* to combine vv 6–14 (his "Canto B") and vv 15–22 (his "Canto C") into one larger unit (*Or* 53 [1984] 283).

Comment

7 וּשְׁתֵּי כַלֹּתֶיהָ עִמָּהּ, "together with her two daughters-in-law." This clause is markedly circumstantial (see *HebS* § 494), thus enabling the author to make Naomi alone the subject of the verb in the main clause. Contrast the compound subject of the first verb of v 6. On the reason for this construction, see *Explanation.*

וַתֵּלַכְנָה בַדֶּרֶךְ לָשׁוּב אֶל־אֶרֶץ יְהוּדָה, lit. "and they went on the road to return to the land of Judah." With the verb ותלכנה, our author finally adopts the plural form of the verb that the implied subject (Naomi and the two young women) leads one to expect (see *Explanation*). For a smooth English translation, we have rendered "they went on the road" by "they took the road." The clause beginning לשוב, "to return," can only be an adverbial clause of purpose modifying the verb ותלכנה, "they traveled." The infinitive לשוב cannot be understood as a gerund modifying "road," i.e., "road leading back" (contra Campbell, 64).

8 לֵכְנָה שֹּׁבְנָה אִשָּׁה לְבֵית אִמָּהּ, "Come, return each of you to her mother's house." The feminine plural imperative לֵכְנָה, lit. "go," must be understood as the "expletive" use, i.e., an introductory word used to gain attention, much as English "come, come on" (see BDB 5.f[2], p. 234; *HALOT,* 2, p. 246; cf. 1 Sam 9:9). A more colloquial rendering might be "Well!" or "Well now!" (cf. Rudolph, "Wohlan"). The usage in v 12 is quite different (contra Campbell).

That Naomi urges the young women to return "each to her *mother's* house" seems most unusual, for elsewhere in the OT a widow returns to her father's house (e.g., Gen 38:11; Lev 22:13; cf. Num 30:17; Deut 22:21; Judg 19:2, 3). The commentaries engage in a number of rationalizing explanations: e.g., the fathers are already dead; mothers are named since they know best how to console; the reference suggests the existence of a matriarchal society (cf. Rudolph, Campbell). All of these are either strained or improbable or both. Dommershausen's explanation ("Leitwortstil in der Ruthrolle," 397) that the words were chosen to achieve parallelism and alliteration between the expressions אשה לבית אמה in v 8 and אתך נשוב לעמך in v 10 is very forced, while the suggestion of Campbell (64) and Hubbard (102–3), based on references to the "mother's house" in Gen 24:28; Cant 3:4; 8:2, that the phrase is used here because the mother's house was customarily the locus for discussion and planning for marriage is predicated on the slimmest of evidence. The best we can do is observe that the OT does refer to the mother's house in Gen 24:28 (which passage also refers to the father's house in v 23; as Campbell notes) and Cant 3:4; 8:2, which could mean either that wives could have separate areas of residence in the polygamous patriarchal family or that the family residence could be referred to as the "mother's house" under appropriate circumstances. However that may be, granted the availability of this way of speaking, it can be argued that it is singularly appropriate here: it emphasizes the contrast Naomi wishes to make—a widow should return to her mother and not stay with her mother-in-law (Porten, *GCA* 7 [1978] 26; cf. Trible, 169).

יַעַשׂה יְהוָה עִמָּכֶם חֶסֶד כַּאֲשֶׁר עֲשִׂיתֶם . . ., "May Yahweh deal kindly and faithfully with you as you have done . . ." In the forms עמכם, "with you," and עשיתם, "you have done," in v 8, we have masculine plural forms instead of the expected feminine plural forms. This occurs in five other places in Ruth: לכם, "to you," 1:9, 11; מכם, "more than you," 1:13; and שתיהם, "the two of them," 1:19, 4:11. This phenomenon, which occurs more frequently in the later books (*GBH* § 149b), has been regarded as a result of the influence of the colloquial language on the literary idiom (GKC § 135o). Campbell (65), however, has given a full presentation of the explanation of F. I. Andersen that these forms in Ruth are the remains of an early Hebrew dual suffix that ended in *-m* just as the masculine plural suffix did, but with a different vocalization (cf. also Rendsburg, *JANES* 12 [1980] 77). In support of the thesis, it is worth noting that those Semitic languages that do have a dual, such as Arabic and Ugaritic, do indeed build those forms that do not distinguish gender by a vocalic modification of the *masculine* form. In the course of the development of the language, the dual ceased to be used, so these forms in the text of the OT were replaced by the standard masculine and feminine plural forms. All seven such "confusions" in Ruth are indeed cases in which the suffix refers to two women. The hypothesis is most attractive. It must be noted, however, that there are four occurrences of suffixes referring to two women that are *feminine* plural—להן, "(she kissed) them," 1:9b; באנה, "their coming," 1:19 (2x); and עליהן, "over them," 1:19—and so could not be originally duals later repointed. But once the dual was lost in the spoken language, such (largely unconscious?)

corrections to conform to current usage would inevitably have taken place. (On the form המה in v 22, see the *Comment* there.)

כַּאֲשֶׁר עֲשִׂיתֶם עִם־הַמֵּתִים וְעִמָּדִי, "as you have done with the dead and with me." "The dead" here is simply Naomi's way of referring in general to her two sons, now deceased, formerly the husbands of the two young women. She obviously refers to the faithfulness of Ruth and Orpah both to her and to these dear departed during the ten years (v 4) of their married life together. There is no need to force the significance of "the dead" and conclude with Hubbard (104) that "their kindness to her in some unspecified way benefited the dead, that is, that loyalty to her was loyalty to the dead and vice versa. The words may have assumed a belief that the dead experienced in the afterlife the fortunes of their living relatives, . . ."

9 יִתֵּן יְהוָה לָכֶם וּמְצֶאןָ, "May Yahweh grant that each of you may find." The syntax here is difficult. It consists of a jussive verb יתן, "may (Yahweh) grant," followed by a clause consisting of the connective ו, "and," joined to an imperative מצאן, "find." Many commentators (e.g., Gerleman, Rudolph, Sasson) follow Joüon (*GBH* § 177h) in seeing the second clause as the object of the first verb, "grant." Campbell (66) objects to this on the basis that in none of the other examples of the phenomenon is the second verb an imperative. He proposes adopting the analysis of GKC § 110i, which cites a number of passages where a jussive form is resumed with an imperative plus "and" and expresses an intended consequence (e.g., Gen 20:7), i.e., "may Yahweh grant to you so that you may find." The difficulty with this solution is that we are then left with no object for the verb "grant" in the first clause. The various objects supplied by the versions really only show that they too were wrestling with unusual syntax (so also de Waard-Nida). Since it seems quite unlikely that the object of the verb "grant" would have disappeared from the whole Hebrew textual tradition, we have adopted Joüon's solution, in spite of the lack of a close parallel to the case here (cf. Hubbard, 98 n. 11).

מְנוּחָה אִשָּׁה בֵּית אִישָׁהּ, lit. "repose each in the house of her husband." It is syntactically most improbable, if not impossible, to understand אשה בית אישה as in apposition to מנוחה with Witzenrath (18, 99; followed by Hubbard, 98 n. 13: "a place of settled security, namely a home with her husband"). To begin with, אשה is patently not in apposition with מנוחה but forms the subject of the verb as the distributive "each," which regularly construes with the plural verb (cf. GKC § 139b n. 1). Second, the appositive regularly follows the head noun immediately, without any intervening vocable. Third, it is most improbable for the appositive to be definite, "the house of her husband," and the head noun indefinite, simply מנוחה, "repose, place of rest." Hence, בית אישה must be adverbial, as it has generally been taken by commentators (cf. Gerleman, 17; Joüon, 37, Rudolph, 40; Sasson, 24; and others). In such locative adverbial expressions using בית, "house of," one may have either בית alone, with the locative sense implied, or specifically בבית, "in the house of" (e.g., cf. in very similar context Num 30:4 vs. 30:11; 2 Kgs 11:4b vs. 4d; cf. *GBH* § 133c; Brockelmann, *Syntax* § 81a).

וַתִּשַּׁק לָהֶן וַתִּשֶּׂאנָה קוֹלָן וַתִּבְכֶּינָה, "She kissed them good-bye, and they all wept and sobbed loudly." נשק can mean simply "to kiss," but it is used here and elsewhere (cf. Gen 31:28; 1 Kgs 19:20) as a gesture of farewell (cf. Hubbard, 98 n. 14). On this gesture, cf. Gruber, *Aspects of Nonverbal Communication*, 330–34. The idiom

ותשאנה קולן ותבכינה, "they lifted up their voices and wept," is an example of hendiadys. The one meaning conveyed by the two coordinated expressions is "to weep with loud cries and sobs" (see de Waard-Nida, 13; for the force of the idiom "to raise the voice," cf. Isa 52:8). The force of this idiom would not be conveyed by a literal translation, for English idiom is different. The "all" is necessary; without it the translation would most likely be taken to mean that only the two girls wept. However, the feminine plural suffix on קולן, "their voices," shows that all three did so (contra de Waard-Nida, 13; cf. Campbell, 66).

10 כִּי־אִתָּךְ נָשׁוּב לְעַמֵּךְ, "No, we will go with you back to your people!" (For the nuance "want to" for the imperfect tense, see *GBH* § 113n.) The force of כי here is problematic. It could simply be understood as an example of the so-called recitative use introducing direct discourse (cf. *HebS* § 452; GKC § 157b). But the context rather clearly implies an adversative sense. כי, however, regularly has an adversative force only after a preceding negative clause (*HebS* §§ 447, 555; GKC § 163a). Without a preceding negative, the idiom is regularly לא כי (e.g., Gen 18:15; 19:2; for a full list, see Joüon, 38). Consequently, Joüon (38; followed by Rudolph, 40) feels it necessary to read לא either instead of or after the לה immediately preceding כי־אתך. However, כי alone can express adversative/negative if a preceding negation is implied (cf. KB[3] 3.c.; Brockelmann, *Syntax* § 134a; e.g., Gen 31:16; cf. Campbell, 66, and note esp. Schoors, *OTS* 21 [1981] 253). Rudolph appeals to the negative adverbs used here by LXX, OL, and Syr. But this in no way necessarily implies a different Hebrew text. These versions either understood כי itself as an adversative (as just noted) or else translated according to sense. By placing אתך, "with you," before the verb, emphasis is placed upon it. We have attempted to express this by the order "to go with you back . . ." instead of "to go back with you . . ."

11 לָמָּה תֵלַכְנָה עִמִּי, "Why will you come with me?" It is important to recognize that this question is not eliciting facts or seeking an explanation. It is an example of the use of questions in what Hyman calls "the critical/corrective sense" (see *HS* 24 [1983] 17–24) and what BDB ([a], p. 554) calls "in expostulation." Hyman explains in *USQR* 39 (1984) 190:

> The context of chapter 1:8–14 and the accompanying imperatives which she uses indicate that, on the contrary, Naomi is critical of Orpah and Ruth and seeks to correct their behavior. A triple transformation—which is necessary when a question functions in a critical/corrective manner—shows the real meaning of Naomi's question. (The triple transformation, which an addressee performs automatically and instantly, consists of switching the valence of the question from positive to negative or vice versa: changing the grammatical form from interrogative to declarative and/or imperative; and modifying the words themselves in order to arrive at the question's emotional meaning.) Transformed, the question reads, "You are wrong to go with me; you should not go; there is no point to it."

Naomi is not seeking information, nor is she expressing "joyful acknowledgement tinged with a slight reproach at the excessive kindness or consideration of another" (Barr, *JTS* 36 [1985] 33). She is expostulating. Her following utterances corroborate this, both in their form as rhetorical questions and in their content (see *Explanation*). That such expostulation is implied by the use of למה instead of

מדוע (Hyman, *HS* 24 [1983] 19–20) cannot be substantiated, however; see Barr, *JTS* 36 (1985) 1–33.

הַעוֹד־לִי בָנִים בְּמֵעַי, "Do I yet have sons within me . . . ?" Naomi does not use one of the ordinary words for "womb" here (e.g., רחם or בטן) but a more general term, מעים, used of men or women, that means "insides, intestines, abdomen, inner parts." When used of a woman outside of the Ruth passage, it occurs only in poetic parallelism with the more specific term בטן, "womb, belly" (Gen 25:23; Isa 49:1; Ps 71:6). Used by itself, then, it has a more general force than "womb."

12 כִּי זָקַנְתִּי מִהְיוֹת לְאִישׁ, "For I am too old to have a husband." The force of מן in מהיות is not strictly comparative. If so, Naomi would be saying "I am older *than* . . ." Rather, this is the use described in GKC § 133c, called by others "the absolute comparative (or elative)" (*HebS* § 318) or "the comparative of compatibility" (*IBHS* § 14.4f), expressing the idea that the quality involved is "too great/small, much/little for" (cf. Exod 18:18). This use, quite clear here, will be important for the exegesis of v 13. The idiom היה לאיש, "to belong to a man (as wife)," using the idiom for "to have," היה ל׳, "to be to," is the regular idiom for "to have a husband" (cf. KB^3 7.b.; e.g., Jer 3:1). Naomi, of course, does not mean in this context that she is too old to marry, regardless of how Israelite society resolved the status of an older widow without sons. She means she is too old to have sexual relations that would result in pregnancy (cf. Sasson).

כִּי אָמַרְתִּי יֶשׁ־לִי תִקְוָה גַּם הָיִיתִי הַלַּיְלָה לְאִישׁ וְגַם יָלַדְתִּי בָנִים, "Even if I said that there was hope for me—indeed if I had a husband this night and actually bore sons." In agreement with most commentators, it is best to take the last three clauses of v 12, beginning with כי, and the first two clauses of v 13, each of which commences with הלהן, as a complex conditional sentence, in spite of the difficulties. That the apodosis begins at the start of v 13 is certain, however one construes the problematic הלהן, but the construction of the protasis is less clear. The uncertainty is occasioned by (1) the fact that כי rarely introduces a contrary-to-fact condition; (2) the lack of any waw connective between the first two clauses (the second clause beginning with גם, not וגם); (3) the difficulty of interpreting the force of the . . . גם וגם, which introduces the last two clauses; and (4) a certain semantic inappropriateness between the first clause, which speaks only of having hope, and the second two, which speak specifically of having a husband that night and bearing sons. Let us deal with these problems in the order mentioned: (1) The use of כי to introduce a contary-to-fact condition is rare but not unexampled: e.g., Jer 51:53; cf. *HebS* § 517; *GBH* § 167i. The perfect tense of the following verb is normal for such a condition (*HebS* § 516; GKC § 159l). It is the perfect tense of the verb in this clause that makes it impossible to understand it as a result clause attached to the preceding sentence: "I am too old to have a husband *that* I might say: 'I have hope!' . . . ," so that the next sentence begins with the following clause introduced by גם (contra Campbell, 68). However, rather than the conditional sense per se, it makes better sense in the context to understand the כי here as a concessive, "even if, although," as noted by Vriezen ("Einige Notizen zur . . . *kî*," 268–69; cf. *HebS* § 448), although the difference in meaning between the conditional and concessive conceptions is slight indeed, particularly here (cf. the remarks of Schoors, *OTS* 21 [1981] 271). (2) and (3) The two clauses introduced by גם could then be understood as further concessive clauses (cf. *HebS* § 382; Hubbard, 107

n. 7). However, the lack of waw connective on the first גם makes this problematical. In this light the two clauses are best understood as further conditional/concessive clauses with the conditional/concessive particle understood from the first clause (cf. the similar phenomenon with אם in Esth 8:5). The גם in each clause has then intensive force (*HebS* § 379; GKC § 153; so also Rudolph), and there is no connective ו, "and," between these two clauses and the first because they are parenthetical—Naomi specifies in detail what she means by having hope: "Even if I said that there was hope for me—indeed had a husband this night and bore sons." This relieves the semantic inappropriateness between the clauses, mentioned above, which arises if they are understood as coordinate: "Even if I said there was hope for me and even if I had a husband this night and bore sons." Hubbard's view (107 n. 8) that the second גם has "additive" force, "and also," is most improbable in the context. Campbell (67) attempts to handle the גם . . . וגם by finding in Ps 119:23 another example of גם introducing the protasis of a conditional sentence that contains a perfect verb. This passage is far better understood, however, as a further example of the concessive clause noted above (cf. also Ps 95:9; Neh 6:1, among others).

13 הֲלָהֵן תְּשַׂבֵּרְנָה עַד אֲשֶׁר יִגְדָּלוּ, "would you wait for them until they grew up?" The form הֲלָהֵן has been much discussed. As pointed, it can be the interrogative particle הֲ plus the preposition לְ, "to, for," plus the third person feminine plural pronominal suffix הֵן, "them." The feminine plural suffix makes most difficult sense in the context. Gerleman's view (17) that the feminine plural here has a neuter sense and refers to the condition Naomi has just mentioned in the protasis is most unlikely (Rudolph, 40). Holladay accepts this etymology but assumes the derived sense of "therefore," borrowed by biblical Aramaic (*CHALOT*, הֵן II, p. 82; לָהֵן, p. 173; לָהֵן I, p. 410). Others suggest that it is a borrowing of the identical Aramaic particle appearing in Dan 2:6, 9; 4:21, meaning "therefore" (see *Introduction*). But, whatever its origin, the emphatic repetition of a particle with such a meaning here and in the next clause seems most improbable (Joüon, 39–40). Therefore, since all the versions (see *Note* 13.a.) read "for them," obviously referring to Naomi's postulated sons mentioned at the end of v 12, and since such an adverbial phrase repeated in emphatic position at the head of this clause and the next makes perfect sense in the context, we have followed most commentators and have accepted the emendation of the MT to הלהם (e.g., Campbell, Joüon, Morris, Rudolph; cf. Hubbard).

The verb שׂבר in the piel stem means "to hope, expect, wait for." Outside of the Ruth passage, it is used only in Pss 45:15; 104:27; 119:166; Isa 38:18; Esth 9:1, while the noun form שֵׂבֶר, "hope," appears in Pss 119:116; 146:5. Although rarely used, its meaning is clear. (On its possible Aramaic origin, see *Introduction.*)

הֲלָהֵן תֵּעָגֵנָה לְבִלְתִּי הֱיוֹת לְאִישׁ, "Would you go without a husband for them?" The MT verb תֵּעָגֵנָה is anomalous and probably incorrect. Not even its root is clear. If it is from עגה (עגי), it should be pointed תֵּעָגֶינָה; if from עגן, it should be תֵּעָגַנָּה (GKC § 51m; BL § 49v, p. 352). The root עגי does not exist in either Hebrew or any cognate language with a suitable range of meaning. (The meaning of the Ugaritic form *ʿgw* cited by Campbell is utterly unknown, even its Semitic origin being uncertain; cf. Sasson, 25.) עגן occurs, however, in the Aramaic and Hebrew of the Mishnah, where, in technical legal contexts, it refers to the status of married women when the whereabouts and continued existence of the husband is unknown. It is posited that in this context the verb means "to prevent a woman from contracting a new marriage" (see KB^3, III, p. 742; Gerleman, 19). On this basis, translations such as "to shut oneself up" (Gerleman, Rudolph), or "withhold oneself from (someone)" (Rudolph), or "keep oneself continent" (Joüon) have been adopted. However, in the present state of our knowledge, one ought to avoid adopting too technical and precise a meaning for the Ruth passage on the basis of this usage (Campbell, Sasson). As Campbell notes, the technical legal background and meaning of the terms in the Mishnah are obscure and may well derive from rabbinic exegesis of this very passage. The LXX (*κατέχω*) and the OL (*detineo*) used verbs with the meaning "hold back, refrain." Since some such meaning fits the context, this seems the most prudent course at the present time (cf. Hubbard, 112).

Sasson's view (22, 25–26) that the idiom היות לאיש, "to have a husband," refers here, as in v 12, to marital intercourse, "the pleasure of marital embraces," overinterprets the phrase, especially in the light of the uncertainty of the meaning of the verb תעגנה. There is nothing in Naomi's words in this context to suggest that she is using the phrase in this sense.

אַל בְּנֹתַי כִּי־מַר־לִי מְאֹד מִכֶּם, "No, my daughters! For my life is much too bitter for you to share." The adverb אל, which normally negates the jussive, is used here as an emphatic negative (*HALOT,* 1.a, p. 48), with ellipsis of the verb (*HebS* § 403). It is normally thus used to reject a demand (Brockelmann, *Syntax* § 56a; *GBH* § 160j; cf. Gen 19:18; Judg 19:23). The grounds for the rejection are introduced by כי as is also often the case with לא (BDB, 1.a[d], p. 519). This reveals the force with which Naomi viewed Ruth's and Orpah's determination to go with her (v 10).

The meaning of the clause כי־מר־לי מאד מכם is far from clear. In context the meaning accorded the phrase must meet two criteria. First, if the introductory כי is understood in its causal sense, the meaning of the clause must provide grounds for Naomi's emphatic rejection of the young women's refusal to separate themselves from her (see above; so also Rudolph, Gerleman). Second, it must fit with the following sentence, also introduced by כי, "for, because." At least the following four translations are grammatically possible: (1) "For things are very bitter for me because of you" (so RSV, JB, GNB); (2) "For things are far more bitter for me than for you" (so NJPS, NASV, NEB, NIV, Campbell, Hubbard, Sasson); (3) "For things are too bitter for me for you (to share)" (so NAB; Brichto, *HUCA* 44 [1973] 12–13; Joüon; cf. also *GBH* § 141i; Rudolph); (4) The first כי could bear the concessive sense "although" (Vriezen, "Einige Notizen zur . . . *kî,*" 268–69). In the first interpretation, the מן of מכם is interpreted in its causal sense (see BDB, 2.f; *HebS* §§ 319, 535). Campbell (70–71) objects to this translation on the grounds that the specific and unexpressed cause must be something that the two young women have done and they have done nothing to cause Naomi's bitterness. But the cause itself is unspecified and left to the context, and the context clearly implies that the cause is the situation the young women find themselves in, i.e., without husbands or prospects. Campbell considers this possibility but objects that this interpretation of "because of you" gives a nuance to מן for which there is no biblical parallel. This scarcely follows; the nuance of meaning given to מן here is simply causal. Surely the situation in which the young women find themselves is just as much a possible cause of Naomi's bitter state as something they might have done! However, as Gerleman observes (19), this translation does not fit the following sentence at all well. If Naomi is very bitter on account of the two young women, one would surely expect that the reason given would relate to them, e.g., "since you have no husbands" or the like. Nor does it provide very convincing grounds for her continued attempt to persuade them to return home (Rudolph, 41). The second translation is quite possible. It takes the מן of מכם in its simple comparative sense (*HebS* § 317), and, contrary to the first, it fits with the context preceding it and following it reasonably well. The third translation understands the מן of מכם in a different sense (though a valid one, contra Campbell, 71; Sasson, 27), i.e., that described in v 12, the absolute or "elative" use, in which the idea is expressed that the quality involved is "too much/little for" (so Joüon, Rudolph; cf. *IBHS* § 14.4f). This translation is preferable, for it fits the following clause better than the previous translation and provides better grounds for Naomi's rejection of the young women's refusal to leave her. Vriezen's proposal that the first כי is concessive, "although," simply does not make sense in the context (cf. the remarks of Schoors, *OTS* 21 [1981] 272).

On Campbell's highly adventuresome speculation that מאד here might once have been an epithet for God, see the remarks of Sasson (27).

כִּי־יָצְאָה בִי יַד־יְהוָה, "for Yahweh has stretched forth his hand against me." Hubbard (107 n. 13) follows Campbell (61; cf. Sasson, 22) in taking the כי as asseverative, "indeed." However, this sentence, because of the semantic content of the two sentences, must inevitably be construed as giving the grounds or reason for the statement in the preceding sentence. Hence the כי, whose meaning is regularly causal, can only be so understood here, particularly in light of the serious doubt cast upon the emphatic interpretation of the particle by the study of Aejmelaeus (*JBL* 105 [1986] 193–209).

Although the idiom יד־יהוה יצאה ב׳, "the hand of Yahweh has come forth against . . . ," occurs only here, its meaning is abundantly clear (contra Sasson), since idioms such as היתה יד יהוה ב׳, "the hand of Yahweh was against . . ." and שלח יד ב׳, "to send a hand against," with both God and man as subject, are very frequent (cf. Hubbard, 113).

14 וַתִּבְכֶּינָה עוֹד, lit. "and wept still more." On the meaning of the idiom "lift up the voice and weep," see *Comment* on v 9. עוד here does not mean "again"; it stresses the idea of continuance (see BDB, 1.a[b]; note the comments of de Waard-Nida, 16; cf. Gen 46:29).

וְרוּת דָּבְקָה בָּהּ, "but Ruth clung to her." The order of the clause here, ו + subject + verb, expresses the simultaneity of Ruth's and Orpah's actions (*HebS* § 573[5]; *GBH* § 118f) as well as contrasting them.

15 הִנֵּה שָׁבָה יְבִמְתֵּךְ אֶל־עַמָּהּ וְאֶל־אֱלֹהֶיהָ, "Look, your sister-in-law has gone back to her people and to her god." The exact force of יבמתך, translated here "your sister-in-law," is not easy to elucidate. Other than this verse, it occurs only in Deut 25:7, 9 in the passage on the levirate law. On the grounds of the Deuteronomy passage, it is possible to understand the meaning of the word as a technical term specifically restricted to the designation of the wife of the deceased in a levirate marriage (so Campbell, 72–73; cf. also Thompson, *VT* 18 [1968] 84–85; Vesco, *RB* 74 [1967] 243). It is to be observed, however, that this term is not used in Gen 38:8, 9 in the story of Judah and Tamar, where precisely this technical force is appropriate. There the narrator uses אשת אח, "brother's wife," instead. Although by no means conclusive, this data seems to indicate that the terms יבמת and אשת אח are simply synonymous, meaning "sister-in-law," especially when the evidence of the passage here is taken into account, where יבמת means "wife of the husband's brother." This usage is directly paralleled by the synonymous אחות אב, "father's sister," and דודה, "aunt," in Lev 18:12, 14 (Leggett, *The Levirate,* 43 n. 33). Further evidence in this direction is the appearance of *yabamum* in an Old Babylonian text from West Semitic circles found at Tell al-Rimah where the meaning "brother-in-law" nicely fits the context (for text and discussion, see Sasson, 29). Although far from conclusive (the word thus far appears in no other texts, and its meaning is based on the hypothesis that the Hebrew term is cognate, as Sasson notes), this argues in favor of the more general sense. (For possible but very problematic connections with the term *ybmt lʾimm* at Ugarit, an epithet of the goddess Anat, see Campbell, 73, and Thompson, *VT* 18 [1968] 84.)

Since the religion of Moab presumably was polytheistic, as was that of all of Israel's neighbors, it is possible that the plural אֱלֹהֶיהָ should be understood literally, "her gods," with LXX, Vg, RSV, NRSV, NJPS. But the word אלהים is regularly plural (a plural of majesty) when referring to the God of Israel. Hence, since Chemosh was the national god of Moab (1 Kgs 11:33), the singular seems preferable, with most modern translations (cf. Hunter, *SJT* 34 [1981] 427–35). Hunter attempts, however, to read out of the story implications that suggest that Naomi and Ruth both regarded Ruth's god and Naomi's god as equally real—hence אלהים should be rendered "god," with lower case "g" in both this verse and v 16, where Ruth makes her declaration that Naomi's אלהים will be her אלהים. But this is to make the narrative and the narrator speak to concerns that are simply not addressed. It further ignores the fact that this is a story told by Israelites to Israelites. That Naomi's words assume the reality of the worship of Chemosh, the god of Moab, in Moab, admits of no doubt. Beyond that, the story does not commit itself (cf. Hubbard, 116; Morris, 260).

16 אֶל־אֲשֶׁר תֵּלְכִי אֵלֵךְ וּבַאֲשֶׁר תָּלִינִי אָלִין, "wherever you travel, I will travel, and wherever you stay, I will stay." Whether the verb לין has its common meaning here of "spend the night" (cf. 3:13) or a more general sense of "dwell, stay" (e.g., Josh 3:1; so Hubbard, 117) is hard to determine and of little moment, for the significance of the choice of words here is that הלך, "go, travel," and לין, "spend the night, stay," are opposites, creating a merism, equivalent to saying "all of life" (see *Explanation*). In this light, Campbell's restriction (73–74) of the sense to the current journey home to Bethlehem quite misses the point.

17 כֹּה יַעֲשֶׂה יְהוָה לִי וְכֹה יֹסִיף כִּי הַמָּוֶת יַפְרִיד בֵּינִי וּבֵינֵךְ, "Thus may Yahweh do to me and more also—Nothing but death will separate me from you!" Ruth uses here the formula of imprecatory oath (GKC § 149d; *GBH* § 165a). In all the twelve uses of this formula, the calamity that the speaker invokes is never named, since OT culture (in keeping with the rest of the ancient Near East) accorded such power to the spoken word. It may well be that the imprecation was accompanied by some symbolic gesture (Campbell, 74), but we have no evidence of the existence of such, let alone its nature. In one form of the oath (used five times in Samuel-Kings), the content of the oath itself is expressed as a conditional clause, using on the one hand אם, "if," to express what the speaker swears will *not* happen (1 Sam 3:17; 25:22;

1 Kgs 20:10; 2 Kgs 6:31) and on the other hand אם לא, "if not," to express what he swears *will* happen (2 Sam 19:14). In six of the other seven occurrences (1 Sam 14:44; 20:13; 2 Sam 3:9; 1 Kgs 2:23; 19:2; Ruth 1:17), the content of the oath is not expressed as a conditional clause but is a positive statement introduced by the asseverative use of the particle כי, "truly, indeed" (see *HebS* § 449; BDB, 1.c, p. 472). Joüon is undoubtedly correct in observing that this use of כי in imprecatory oaths comes from its occurrence in oaths that use the formula נשבע כי (see *GBH* §§ 165a, b). In each of the five occurrences in Samuel-Kings, the oath introduced by כי expresses what the speaker was determined *will* happen (contra Campbell, 74; Hubbard, 119 n. 33, who maintain that 1 Sam 14:44; 2 Sam 3:9; 1 Kgs 2:23; 19:2 are ambiguous in meaning). The syntax, then, is unambiguous: Ruth is swearing that death alone will separate her from Naomi. To render ". . . if even death separates me from you," as some translations and commentators do (e.g., RSV, JB, Campbell, Hubbard), would require, according to the above analysis, either that the oath clause be negated (המות לא יפריד) or that it be introduced by אם, not כי. There is no conflict with the statement "Where you die, I will die; And there shall I be buried" in the first half of the verse (contra Hubbard, 119–20), for that expression deals specifically with the place of burial and so relates, as the previous expressions have done, to Ruth's commitment of all of her life to Naomi, even including the place of burial. The nuance "nothing but" must be gained from the context, as sometimes occurs in Hebrew (Joüon, 42; cf. Gen 32:11; 2 Kgs 13:19), in this case signaled by the emphatic position of the subject המות before the verb יפריד (Gerleman, Joüon, Rudolph).

18 וַתֵּרֶא כִּי־מִתְאַמֶּצֶת הִיא, "When she [Naomi] saw that she was determined." The force of the hithpael of אמץ here is difficult to assess. It is used in only two other contexts in the OT—1 Kgs 12:18 = 2 Chron 10:18; 2 Chron 13:7—each of which requires meanings significantly different from one another and from the meaning required by the context here in Ruth. To trace an etymology on the basis of the semantic range "to be strong" reflected in the meanings of the root in other stems (e.g., Schreiner, *TDOT* 1:324; followed by Hubbard, 121) is invalid semantically. Hence, we have only the context to guide us (note the remarks of Dillard on the meaning of 2 Chron 13:7: *2 Chronicles,* 107–8). This requires some such meaning as "to be firmly resolved, be determined." The participle expresses durative action in past time (*HebS* § 213), stressing the continuous nature of Ruth's resolve, a nuance difficult to bring out in translation.

וַתֶּחְדַּל לְדַבֵּר אֵלֶיהָ, "She said no more (to her)." Trible (172–73), in her rhetorical study of Ruth, speaks of Ruth's "separation" from her mother-in-law and of Naomi's "withdrawal" from Ruth, based on Naomi's silence here and on the fact that she does not speak again to Ruth in this scene. This analysis is followed up by Fewell and Gunn in their "reading" of Naomi's character, *JSOT* 40 (1988) 99–108. Based on Naomi's "silence" and on a supposed literary allusion in Ruth 1 to the Judah-Tamar episode of Gen 38, Fewell and Gunn argue not simply for a Naomi who has withdrawn from Ruth but for a Naomi whose silence "emerges as resentment, irritation, frustration, unease. Ruth the Maobite is to her an inconvenience, a menace even" (104). But this reads far more into the story than it can bear. Naomi's silence here receives no stress whatsoever. The sentence simply means that she ceased any longer to importune Ruth to return to Moab. The text does not say "she spoke to her no longer." The verb used is חדל, which used intransitively means "to stop, cease," e.g., Exod 9:29; but with the infinitive as direct object or with the infinitive plus ל, it means "to stop, cease to do something," e.g., Gen 11:9. The text clearly means, then, "She ceased to speak to her (*about going home*)." Further, our narrator tells us nothing about what happened on the journey; he gives us only the most concise summary statement: "the two of them went on until they arrived at Bethlehem" (v 19a). Our narrator has used the scene exclusively to report this series of dialogues between Naomi and her daughters-in-law (see *Form/Structure/Setting* and esp. *Explanation*). About all else he leaves us totally uninformed.

Further, Fewell and Gunn's attempt to use literary allusion to Gen 38 is forced and illusory. Judah's journey to the Adullamite, during which his two sons and his spouse die, functions so differently in Gen 38 as to make any "structural reminiscence" forced indeed. And the allusion to Judah's words to Tamar "to return to her father's house," supposedly provided by Naomi's words to Ruth and Orpah "to return to your mother's house," is surely belied by (1) the narrator's choice in the Ruth story of the unusual "mother's house" and (2) the fact that Judah said "return (or remain?) *as a widow* to your father's house," while Naomi's urging is specifically so that Yahweh may grant that "each of you may find repose in the house of a husband," i.e., *cease to be widows!* How can such tenuous literary allusion suggest that Naomi views Ruth with the same suspicion as Judah did Tamar, i.e., "considering her to be the cause of the trouble (namely, the deaths of his two sons)" so that "Ruth, then, would be to Naomi as Tamar is to Judah, an albatross around her neck" (*JSOT* 40 [1988] 103)?

Fewell and Gunn do read Naomi's words correctly in one respect: ". . . at the heart of all her utterance in this chapter (as can be shown by a close rhetorical analysis of the passage) is Naomi's bitter sense of deprivation" (*JSOT* 40 [1988] 101), for our narrator clearly uses both the dialogue here and that between Naomi and the women of Bethlehem in the next scene to fill in the affective dimensions of the problem of the death and emptiness afflicting Naomi's life that he so briefly sketched in vv 1–5 (see *Explanation*).

19a וַתֵּלַכְנָה שְׁתֵּיהֶם עַד־בֹּאָנָה בֵּית לָחֶם, "Then the two of them went on until they arrived at Bethlehem." For the view that the suffix ־הם on שתיהם is the vestigial remains of a dual, rather than masculine plural, see *Comment* on v 8 above. The third person feminine plural suffix ־אנה, instead of the more common ־אן (see GKC § 91f) might have been used to provide alliteration with ותלכנה (Joüon, Sasson).

Explanation

As was noted in the discussion of the unity of 1:1–22 in the *Form/Structure/Setting* section of the opening scene, this scene sets forth an important development in the event line of the story, the return to Judah. Vocabulary alone reflects this fact, for the verbs הלך, "go, travel," and שׁוב, "return, go back," dominate the language, each occurring eight times in the passage. The scene is not, however, a narrative of events that could be entitled "How Naomi and Ruth returned to Judah." Form and content both make this clear. In form it is not a narrative of events at all. Apart from a brief narrative introduction (v 7) and the briefest of narrative conclusions (v 19a), it is devoted exclusively (see *Form/Structure/Setting*) to the dialogue that took place between the three women somewhere on the road that led to Judah—a painful dialogue about who is returning where. Are the two young women going with Naomi or returning to Moab? It is reflected in content in the very way our author uses the verb שׁוב, "return": only twice does it refer to a return to Judah, once in the narrative introduction in v 7 and once in the affirmation of the two young women in v 10 that they intend to return with Naomi. The other six occurrences refer to a return to Moab, four of them being commands from Naomi in her impassioned appeals to the two young women to go back to Moab. Hence, at this level of the story—the event line—the scene does not really relate how it was that Naomi and Ruth returned from Moab but rather how the summary statement in preview in v 6, "She [Naomi] returned from the territory of Moab," could have become the summary statement in retrospect in v 22: "So Naomi returned, and Ruth the Moabitess, her daughter-in-law, was with her—she who *returned* from the territory of Moab."

This suffices for the surface level of the story—the sequence of events. At the level of the plot line, it is clear that our author uses these developments far more to continue to set forth the problem that he has so far only briefly described—the loss and emptiness afflicting Naomi. This can be seen in the content of the dialogue (specifically his characterization of Naomi); in the undertone of complaint with which she commands the two young women to return to Moab in vv 8–9; in her anguished, almost angry, appeal to them to go home in vv 11–13, buttressed with absurdities and climaxed with a bitter charge against Yahweh himself; and in the silence with which she greets Ruth's passionate vow of love and commitment in vv 16–18 (see details below).

The conflict over the women's destination is subtly introduced in the very language of vv 6–7, the narrative transition that closes the first scene and opens this one, setting the stage for the dialogue. The syntax of these verses is unusual and striking. In v 6 the narrator fails to shift to the plural with the verb ותשׁב, "and she returned," in spite of the plural subject preceding (see *Comment* thereto), thereby making "Naomi" alone the subject of the closely joined verbs. This is reinforced by "Naomi" standing alone as the subject of the verb "heard" in the following subordinate clause. V 7 is even more striking. Even though he has already introduced the subject "she [Naomi] and her two daughters-in-law" at the beginning of v 6, he does not simply say "So they-went-forth [ותצאנה] from the place where they-were-staying [היו]." Instead both verbs are singular, the subject being "Naomi" alone, and the two young women are included only in the appended circumstantial clause, "her two daughters-in-law with her" (see *Comment* on v 7). They are not said to "return" or "hear" or "set out"; they are only "with their mother-in-law." The plural is finally adopted only in the last clause, "and they took the road to return . . ." Hence, only Naomi is "returning to Judah," even though from the outset she is accompanied by her daughters-in-law. Our author thus skillfully suggests in the minds of his hearers the ambiguity and uncertainty of the position and intentions of the two young women. What are they doing by accompanying Naomi? In this way we are quite prepared for the dialogues that follow in vv 8–17 as the three women wrestle painfully with this very question.

Naomi opens the dialogue in v 8 by frontally attacking the problem: she commands each of them to go back to Moab and buttresses this dismissal by imploring

Yahweh to bless their return by granting them each another home. The ambiguity of the situation of the three of them skillfully expressed in the narrative introduction, coupled with this specific demand, reveals the mixed feelings and difficulty of Naomi's position. To have Orpah and Ruth return to Moab means that she must journey home utterly alone and desolate, having lost all. But to have them return to Judah with her means asking them to renounce all hope of the life she now implores Yahweh to give them. Faced with this dilemma, she has no real choice. To the calamity of losing home, husband, and sons, she must now add another, inflicted this time by herself (Campbell, 82). She must return home alone. Her first words of dismissal indeed carry an undertone of complaint (Campbell, 82). They are also said with feeling and with pain, for they all immediately break into loud sobs and tears (v 9c).

The parting, however, is not to be so easy. Neither of the young women can simply acquiesce in such a solution (v 10): "No," they cry, "*with you* will we return . . ." (see *Comment*).

Naomi responds to this refusal with three separate speeches (vv 11–13; see *Form/Structure/Setting*) in each of which she now addresses them poignantly as "my daughters." In the first (v 11) she buttresses her demand that they return home with a blunt rhetorical question, positing an impossibility, the sharp tone of which is set by her choice of the term "insides" instead of "womb": "Do I yet have sons in my insides to become husbands for you?" In the second (vv 12–13b) she answers this question with a statement of fact, "I am too old to have a husband," and then continues with an unlikely (or contrary-to-fact) condition whose protasis considers the possibility of the very fact she has just denied: "Even if I said there was hope for me—indeed if I had a husband this night and bore sons . . ." She answers this impossible condition with two rhetorical questions that border on the absurd, "Would you wait for them until they grew up? Would you go without a husband for them?" In the third address (13c–d), she concludes with an emphatic "no" and gives as the reason that her lot in life is far too bitter for them to share. She then sets the seal on her insistence with the bitter complaint that the cause of her calamity is none other than Yahweh himself, who has stretched out his hand against her. The form and tone of this series of rhetorical questions and conditions, all of them impossibilities, show that Naomi is not engaging in logical argument. She is not really giving reasons at all. Rather, this is the anguished, almost angry, cry of a woman overwhelmed by the bitter knowledge that she must return home alone and cannot drag two young women into the hopelessness of her widowed and lonely state, although they seem set on accompanying her.

Her anguished appeal is met with two opposite responses. Orpah assents to Naomi's urging and kisses her mother-in-law farewell. Her decision is the sound and reasonable one; she opts for her community and her faith: she "returned to her people and her god" (v 15a). As Campbell (82) and Trible (172) stress, the story implies no negative judgment on Orpah's action. She has obeyed Naomi, thereby reducing her pain, and she acts as the demands of community and custom dictate. But though her course of action may be right and reasonable, it means she can play no further role in Naomi's world, and she passes from the story. Our author affords us not even a single glimpse of her lonely journey home.

Ruth's response is as expressive as Orpah's farewell kiss: she now physically clings to her mother-in-law. Having succeeded with Orpah, Naomi responds to Ruth's action by urging her to follow her sister-in-law's example (v 15).

To this last demand from Naomi, Ruth responds with an eloquent and moving declaration (vv 16–17), which expresses such radical commitment to her mother-in-law that it encompasses not only every living action but extends to the end of life itself—even in the place where they are buried will they be united (see *Form/Structure/Setting*). Her commitment to Naomi transcends even the bonds of racial origin and national religion: Naomi's people and Naomi's God will henceforth be hers. And, giving the ring of truth to her words, she then immediately takes the name of Yahweh on her lips in a solemn oath that only death itself will finally separate them. Such radical commitment relieves Naomi from feeling responsible for the unknown fate that will follow upon Ruth's going with her, so she does not again enjoin her to go back. Instead, seeing Ruth's determination, she importunes her no longer (v 18). Our narrator describes no warm embrace, no loving words of gratitude for such commitment. Surely such a lack of reaction to Ruth's warm and impassioned devotion speaks volumes about the bitterness that consumes Naomi in her return. She cannot refuse a commitment that brooks no refusal, but she cannot offer more than silent acquiescence. Immediately our author then concludes the episode, "Then the two of them went on until they came to Bethlehem" (v 19a). The journey is left untold but for this briefest of summaries. With such scenes our author has well begun to fill in the affective dimensions of the death and emptiness he so sketchily outlined by his statement "the woman was left alone without her two boys and without her husband" (v 5).

And what of Ruth? Her very presence with Naomi and above all the ringing words with which she expresses this commitment constitute a countermovement to Naomi's emptiness and loss, presaging life and fullness. But these words and actions also constitute one of the most striking examples in all of OT literature of that loving and sacrificial loyalty that the Hebrew language designated *ḥesed* (cf. 1:8; 3:10), for Ruth's devotion to Naomi caused her to cast aside all concern for her future and security and to break the bonds even of community and religion. Phyllis Trible observes (173) that in the entire epic of Israel only Abraham himself matched such radical commitment, but he had a call from God and was a man in a man's world with a wife and family for support. On the other hand,

> Ruth stands alone; she possesses nothing. No God has called her; no deity has promised her blessing; no human being has come to her aid. She lives and chooses without a support group and she knows that the fruit of her decision may well be the emptiness of rejection, indeed of death. Consequently, not even Abraham's leap of faith surpasses this decision of Ruth's. And there is more. Not only has Ruth broken with family, country and faith, but she has also reversed sexual allegiance. A young woman has committed herself to the life of an old woman rather than the search for a husband . . . . One female has chosen another female in a world where life depends upon men. There is no more radical decision in all the memories of Israel.

A young woman has committed herself to the life of an old woman, yes. But Naomi cannot yet appreciate the significance of this commitment—as her reaction to their arrival in Bethlehem in the next scene will reveal.

Scene 3
Emptiness Expressed: Naomi Arrives at Bethlehem with Ruth (1:19b–22)

Bibliography

Berlin, A. *Poetics and Interpretation of Biblical Narrative.* Sheffield: Almond, 1983. **Dommershausen, W.** "Leitwortstil in der Ruthrolle." In *Theologie im Wandel.* Munich-Freiberg: Wewel, 1967. 394–407 **Hyman, R. T.** "Questions and Changing Identity in the Book of Ruth." *USQR* 39 (1984) 189–201. ———. "Questions and the Book of Ruth." *HS* 24 (1983) 17–25. **Jongeling, B.** "HZ'T NᶜMY (Ruth 1:19)." *VT* 28 (1978) 474–77. **McDonald, J.** "Some Distinctive Characteristics of Israelite Spoken Hebrew." *BO* 32 (1975) 162–75. **Myers, J.** *The Linguistic and Literary Form of the Book of Ruth.* Leiden: Brill, 1965. **Pedersen, J.** *Israel, Its Life and Culture I–II.* London: Oxford, 1926. **Rauber, D.** "Literary Values in the Bible: The Book of Ruth." *JBL* 89 (1970) 27–37. **Rebera, B.** "Identifying Participants in Old Testament Dialogue." *BT* 33 (1982) 201–7. **Vaux, R. de.** *The Early History of Israel.* Philadelphia: Westminster, 1978.

Translation

19b *When they entered*[a] *Bethlehem, all the women of the town buzzed with excitement because of them, saying,*[b] *"Is this really Naomi?"*[c] 20 *She replied to them,*

"Don't call me, 'Pleasant';[a] *call me 'Bitter'!*[a]
For bitter indeed has the Almighty made my life!
21 *Full was I when I went away;*[a]
But empty has Yahweh brought me back.
Why do you call me 'Pleasant'?
When Yahweh has spoken[b] *against me,*
And the Almighty has brought disaster upon me!"

22 *So thus Naomi returned, along with Ruth the Moabitess, her daughter-in-law—she who returned from the territory of Moab. And they arrived in Bethlehem at the beginning of the barley harvest.*

Notes

19b.a. On the form of the suffix here, see *Comment* on v 19a.

19b.b. Lit. "the whole town was abuzz because of them, and they [fem pl] said, . . ." See *Comment.*

19b.c. Lit. "Is this Naomi!"—an exclamation not a question; see *Comment.*

20.a. "Naomi" means "pleasant, lovely"; "Mara," "bitter," a play on words. See *Comment.*

21.a. Lit. "I full went away." See *Comment.*

21.b. Lit. "testified." The versions (LXX, Vg, Syr, and OL) all read the verb here as עִנָּה, a piel stem of the root ענה, and so render "to afflict, cast down" and the like (so RSV). But, since this verb nowhere else takes ב with its object (Joüon; Myers, *Linguistic and Literary Form,* 22) and the MT form עָנָה ב, "to testify against," makes good sense in the context, the MT is doubtless to be preferred. See *Comment.*

Form/Structure/Setting

This scene describes the arrival of Naomi and Ruth in Bethlehem and characterizes Naomi's arrival home by setting forth a dialogue between her and the women of the town. It begins with a temporal clause introduced by ויהי, a construction regularly used to open a new section of narrative (GKC §§ 111f, g), and this temporal clause repeats the information of v 19a, עד־בואנה בית לחם, "until they entered Bethlehem." This in turn forms an inclusio with the closing summation of v 22c, והמה באו בית לחם, "They arrived in Bethlehem . . ."

The final verse of the scene, v 22, provides closure for the whole act. The opening word of the first sentence of v 22, ותשׁב, "and she returned," reiterates the theme word of the whole passage, שׁוב, and forms an inclusio with the identical summary statement of v 6, the sentence that brought the first scene to a close and formed a transition to the next. An even more dramatic inclusio is formed by the relative clause by which Ruth is identified in v 22b, "she who returned from the territory of Moab." Here both the verb שׁוב, "to return," and the expression שׂדי מואב, "the territory of Moab," take us back to the opening pericope, vv 1–6. Further, the temporal clause at the end of v 22, stating when they arrived at Bethlehem, that is, "at the beginning of the barley harvest," substantiates the statement in v 6 that Yahweh had provided food for his people, and both these references bring resolution to the famine of the opening sentence. The skill of our narrator is obvious in the use of the phrase "the barley harvest" for the dual purpose of providing closure for this scene and linking with the next scene in which Ruth gleans in the fields of this same harvest. Finally, this closure is also signally effected by the syntax of the final clause. By beginning with the independent pronoun "they," placed before the perfect verb "arrived in," our author breaks the chain of chronological succession achieved by the previous sequence of waw-consecutive verb forms. On the use of such "circumstantial" clauses to mark the beginning and end of an episode, see *SBH,* 78, 80–82.

Here also, as in the previous scene, our narrator uses dialogue rather than narrative to communicate. The whole passage consists simply of the dialogue between Naomi and the women, vv 19d–21, sandwiched between one narrative statement, vv 19b–c, which introduces the scene, and a second narrative statement, v 22, which concludes it (see the diagram). The dialogue is triggered by the women's glad cry of recognition, v 19d. Naomi's response, vv 20–21, divides into two sections, closely united in form and content. Each section begins with a wordplay on the meaning of her name, which has just echoed so happily on the lips of the women of the town, each wordplay intending to deny that she is what the meaning of her name implies, "pleasant, lovely" (see *Comment*). In the first wordplay, W (v 20b), she denies the meaning of her name by demanding that she be called Mara, "Bitter," the antonym of "Naomi" (see *Comment*). In the second wordplay, W´ (v 21c), she uses a rhetorical "why" question that is intended to reject the identity implied (see *Comment*). Each wordplay is followed by the grounds for the denial. These two statements are couplets, A–B and B´–A´, that relate to each other chiastically: A and A´ use "Shaddai" and are parallel in structure and content, while B and B´, though quite different in structure and content, are parallel in their use of "Yahweh." B in turn consists of two clauses that are chiastic, both in content: "I" vs. "Yahweh," "full" vs. "empty," and "went-away" vs. "brought-me-back"; and in sentence order: S–Adv–V vs. Adv′– V′–S′. This throws the subject of each sentence into bold relief, sharply contrasting Naomi's initial state with what Yahweh has subsequently done to her. The narrative conclusion, v 22, brings closure to this scene as well as to the whole act (see diagram of the structure of 19–22).

The Structure of vv 19b–22

N Intro. When they entered Bethlehem, the whole town hummed with excitement at them. 19b–c

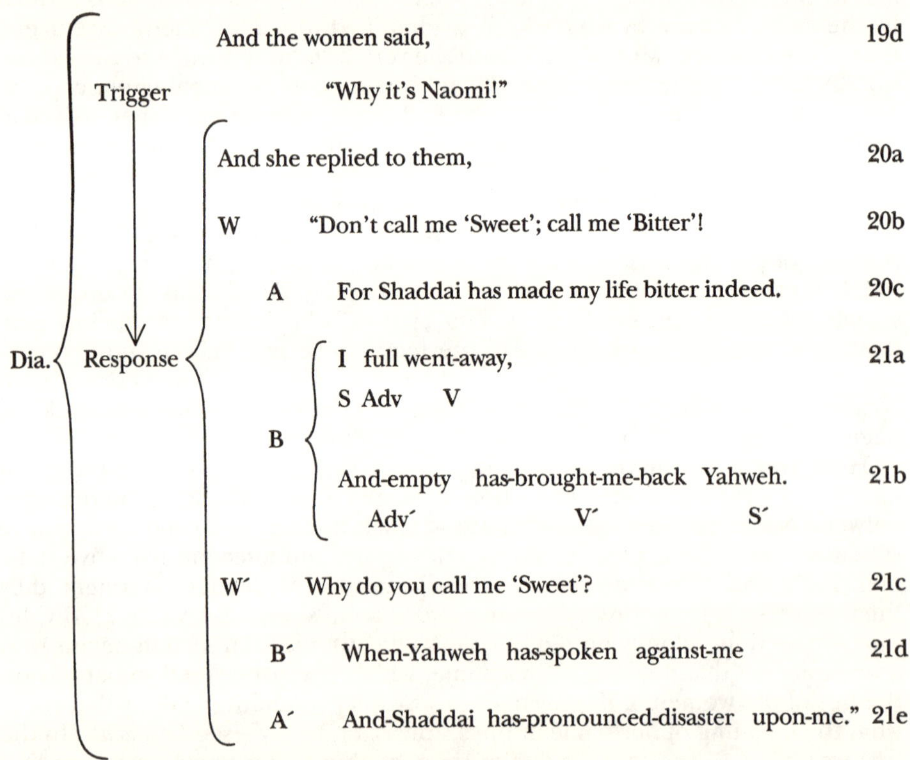

And the women said, 19d
Trigger
"Why it's Naomi!"
And she replied to them, 20a
W "Don't call me 'Sweet'; call me 'Bitter'! 20b
A For Shaddai has made my life bitter indeed. 20c
Dia.
Response
I full went-away, 21a
S Adv V
B
And-empty has-brought-me-back Yahweh. 21b
Adv′ V′ S′
W′ Why do you call me 'Sweet'? 21c
B′ When-Yahweh has-spoken against-me 21d
A′ And-Shaddai has-pronounced-disaster upon-me." 21e

N Concl. So Naomi returned, and Ruth the Moabitess, her daughter-in-law, was with her—she who returned from . . . Moab. And they arrived in Bethlehem at the beginning of barley harvest. 22

Comment

19b וַתֵּהֹם כָּל־הָעִיר עֲלֵיהֶן, lit. "The whole town was abuzz because of them." Both the root and the meaning of the verb וַתֵּהֹם are uncertain. First, the roots נהם, המם הום/הים, המה all exist with a meaning in the range of "hum, buzz, growl, roar" (doubtless all expansions of an original onomatopoetic root הם *hm*; cf. *TDOT* 3:419), from which have come the figurative senses "to resound with excitement, be in an uproar, be restless, turbulent, bring into confusion." Second, the form itself, as pointed, could be either a qal stem of הום (see GKC § 72h) or a niphal of המם (for similar forms, see GKC § 67t) or הום (for similar forms, see GKC § 72v). Given the variety of forms that occur from these roots, it is non sequitur to posit that the LXX *ἤχησεν*, "resounded," reflects the reading ותהם from המה (Joüon, Rudolph; cf. the remarks of Gerleman, 17). In fact, the same form וַתֵּהֹם also occurs in 1 Sam 4:5, referring to the glad sound of the Israelite camp when the ark of the covenant arrived, and in 1 Kgs 1:45, referring to the excited acclamation that greeted Solomon's anointing. However, related forms from these same roots can refer to the uproar and tumult of city streets (Isa 22:2; Prov 1:21) or the roar of the surf (Isa 17:12; Jer 6:23). Hence, however MT's וַתֵּהֹם is parsed, it could have here either of two senses. On the one hand, it could be taken to express agitation and consternation or, on the other, delighted excitement. Which nuance is to be understood depends upon the meaning accorded to the following question, "Is this Naomi?" for which see below.

The phrase "the whole town" is an example of synecdoche, a figure of speech in which the whole stands for a part (or vice versa); i.e., "one speaks of 'the whole town' when in reality one means only a large part of the inhabitants of the town" (de Waard-Nida, 20). As the feminine plural form of the next verb reveals, "the whole town" in this case means the women of Bethlehem (see below).

וַתֹּאמַרְנָה הֲזֹאת נָעֳמִי, lit. "and they [fem] said, 'Is this Naomi'?" If the subject of the first clause of v 19b is translated literally, "And the whole town . . . ," then this clause cannot simply be rendered "and they said . . ." (so LXX, KJV) since "they" would then naturally be taken to refer to this subject, namely, "the whole town," whereas the feminine plural form of ותאמרנה makes it clear that the women of the town are meant (cf. the discussion in Rebera, *BT* 33 [1982] 203). In point of fact, however, the first clause should not be translated literally. Joüon (43) and de Waard-Nida (20) are quite correct in noting that this feminine plural would imply to the native speaker that the specific meaning of the vague figure of speech "the whole town" (see above) is the women of Bethlehem (cf. also Trible, 174). This is made virtually certain by the pointed omission here of a specific subject for the verb ותאמרנה, "and they said," such as הנשים, "the women." Some such rendering of the two clauses as we have given is necessary to communicate the subtle effect of the Hebrew idiom.

The question "Is this Naomi?" effected by the interrogative particle הֲ is not addressed by the women to Naomi but rather to one another, creating the excited commotion expressed by ותהם. It is not a real question, expecting a "yes/no" answer (contra Hyman, *HS* 24 [1983] 17), but a rhetorical question having the force of an exclamation (cf. *GBH* § 161b, and the discussion of the question in v 11 above). Such an expression can convey a variety of emotions, running from surprise and joy through doubt and uncertainty to consternation and concern (cf. Hyman, *USQR* 39 [1984] 192). Jongeling (*VT* 28 [1978] 474–77) compares such passages as 1 Kgs 18:17, where Ahab expresses his astonishment at seeing Elijah with the question "Is that you, you disturber of Israel?" which means "So there you are, you disturber of Israel!" (cf. also 1 Kgs 18:7). When these possibilities are combined with the ambiguity of meaning expressed by the verb ותהם (see above), the scene can be understood in two quite different ways. On the one hand, the "noisy hum" with which the city resounds (expressed by the verb ותהם) and the question "Is this Naomi?" would both convey consternation and concern, perhaps because of Naomi's aged and careworn condition (Rudolph, 44). On the other hand, the "noisy hum" could express delighted excitement and the rhetorical question astonished and joyful recognition. The meaning intended would have been clearly conveyed by the tone with which the narrator voiced the question. The evidence is very strongly in favor of the latter alternative, a point of view that has been persuasively argued by Jongeling (*VT* 28 [1978] 474–77). In the first place, the verb expresses joyous elation in two other similar contexts (see above). But, above all, Naomi's response, in which she immediately challenges the tone of their exclamation by demanding that they change her name from Naomi, "Pleasant," to Mara, "Bitter," makes much better sense if she is reacting to glad and joyous recognition rather than shocked and amazed consternation and concern. The question, then, expresses surprised and delighted recognition: "Can this really be Naomi?" (Hubbard, 123), or even "Why, it's Naomi!"

20 אַל־תִּקְרֶאנָה לִי נָעֳמִי קְרֶאןָ לִי מָרָא, "Don't call me 'Pleasant'; call me 'Bitter'!" Naomi engages in a play on words, which our translation attempts to capture. "Naomi" means "pleasant, lovely," while מרא comes from the root מרר, "to be bitter." The word מרא exhibits the unusual feminine singular absolute ending א־, instead of the normal ה־ (see GKC § 80h). This occurs sporadically in the Hebrew portions of the OT and can be explained by the hypothesis that, during the transmission of the text, scribes accustomed to writing the Aramaic ending א־, occasionally substituted it for the Hebrew one. The change to מרי, "my bitter one" (Joüon, 44; JB/NJB footnote), has no grounds whatever, especially since it is most unlikely that the ending *-î* on "Naomi" has anything to do with the first person singular pronominal suffix "my." See *Comment* on v 2. Likewise, Sasson's attempts (32–34) to find an etymology for מרא and so interpret it as a true proper name is quite beside the point, for the play on words clearly understands the word to be connected with מרר, "bitter."

הֵמַר שַׁדַּי לִי מְאֹד, "for bitter indeed has the Almighty made my life." The order places marked emphasis on the verb המר, for in spoken Hebrew the subject normally precedes the verb. On this point, see McDonald's study of direct speech in OT Hebrew, *BO* 32 (1975) 163–66, and compare the order in the last two clauses of v 21, ויהוה ענה בי ושדי הרע לי.

As a synonym for Yahweh, Naomi uses the divine name שדי *Shaddai.* The translation of this name is highly problematical since both its meaning and its etymology remain obscure (see de Vaux, *The Early History of Israel,* 276–78). Following the tradition of the LXX's *παντοκράτωρ* and the Vulgate's *omnipotens,* English translations have almost universally translated it "the Almighty." The name appears most often in the earlier literature in passages involving blessing and cursing (cf., e.g., Gen 17:1; 28:3; 35:11; Num 24:4, 16; see Joüon, 44), frequently in contexts expressing judgment (e.g., Isa 13:6; Joel 1:15; Job 5:17) and power (e.g., Ezek 1:24;

10:5; Pss 68:15; 91:1). Hence, it is used most appropriately in the context of Naomi's bitter complaint in Ruth. (As a result, also, the traditional translation "the Almighty" captures this connotation very well—certainly better than the transliteration *Šaddai* would do.) Also pertinent for the Ruth story is the distribution of the name in the OT. As Campbell documents (76–77), the name was in full use in the period prior to the monarchy, after which it largely fell out of use until appearing again as an archaism in Job and in a few late prophetic passages. Hence, as far as its period of use is concerned, it is also quite appropriate on the lips of Naomi.

The reason Naomi gives for calling herself מרא, "Bitter" instead of נעמי, "Pleasant," כי־הֵמַר שדי לי מאד, "for bitter indeed has the Almighty made my life," is strikingly parallel to the reason she gave in v 13 for refusing Ruth and Orpah's announced intention to accompany her to Judah, כי־מר־לי מאד מכם, "my life is much too bitter for you." The difference relates to the distinct development in her complaint. In v 13 she attributes the cause of her complaint to God somewhat obliquely: "My life is much too bitter for you to share," she says, "for Yahweh has stretched out his hand against me." Here the verb "to be bitter" is in the causative stem with "the Almighty" as subject, directly charging God with her unhappy lot: "For bitter indeed has the Almighty made my life!"

21 אֲנִי מְלֵאָה הָלַכְתִּי וְרֵיקָם הֱשִׁיבַנִי יְהוָה, "Full was I when I went away; / But empty has Yahweh brought me back." The order of the first two clauses of this verse is not normal for the purposes of emphasis. In the first place, the two adverbs מלאה, "full," and ריקם, "empty," stand before the verb, instead of after, and so are stressed. I have attempted to capture this in translation by radically altering the syntax of the first clause: "Full was I when I went away." Second, the subject of the second clause יהוה, "Yahweh," is reserved to the end, producing chiasm (see *Form/Structure/Setting*) and providing marked contrast between Naomi's circumstances and Yahweh's action. The use of the independent pronoun אני, "I," in conjunction with the fully inflected verb form הלכתי, "I went away," is not emphatic, however. This is a standard feature of spoken Israelite Hebrew (see McDonald, *BO* 32 [1975] 166–67).

וַיהוָה עָנָה בִי וְשַׁדַּי הֵרַע לִי, "When Yahweh has spoken against me, / And the Almighty has brought disaster upon me!" The expression ענה ב means "to respond/speak against" (BDB, 3.a, p. 773), usually used in a juridical context where it has the technical force "to testify against" (Exod 20:16; Num 35:30). Even though, as Myers observes (*Linguistic and Literary Form*, 22), in none of the other uses in the OT is Yahweh regarded as testifying against someone, there is nothing inherently implausible in such a statement. Naomi adopts juridical language and conceives of Yahweh as having given testimony against her—from such a source, irrefutable!

Campbell (77) is correct in contending that the juridical force of the first verb will carry over to the second in the synonymous parallelism of this poetic couplet, so that in this context the verb הרע ב״ does not so much refer to the infliction of calamity as to the pronouncing of the sentence of the same.

22 וַתָּשָׁב נָעֳמִי וְרוּת הַמּוֹאֲבִיָּה כַלָּתָהּ עִמָּהּ הַשָּׁבָה מִשְּׂדֵי מוֹאָב, "So thus Naomi returned, along with Ruth the Moabitess, her daughter-in-law—she who returned from the territory of Moab." The waw-consecutive form ותשב here does not express chronological sequence, which is its regular use in a narrative in past time. Rather, its relationship is logical not chronological; it introduces a recapitulation (see GKC § 111k; *GBH* § 118i; cf. Hubbard, 128 n. 1).

In the final clause, the verb form הַשָּׁבָה is accented by the Masoretes on the penult, thus making it the perfect tense, not the participle (cf. the remarks of *IBHS* § 19.7c, d). The article then has a relative force, "who, the one who" (GKC §§ 138i, k). There seems merit in Joüon's suggestion (45), followed by Campbell (78), that the choice of the perfect instead of the participle (which would also be perfectly correct grammatically and would make little difference in meaning) resulted from the Masoretes' desire to express more precisely the past time of the action.

The structure of this recapitulation is striking. At the conclusion of the previous scene in v 19a, our narrator again used the plural verb ותלכנה, "they went on," which he had finally adopted in his narrative introduction to that scene in v 7 (see *Comment* and *Explanation* thereto). Here, however, he makes Naomi alone the subject of the verb "returned" and includes Ruth in an appended circumstantial clause. By so doing he provides at one level a more obvious inclusion with the same verb form in v 6 (see *Form/Structure/Setting*). But his structure actually stresses Ruth's "return" rather than that of Naomi, for by including Ruth in an appended circumstantial clause, he is able to add to her name the relative clause השבה משדי מאב, "she who returned from the territory of Moab." By this structure alone, he gives Ruth's "return" prominence. The significance of this structure is missed and misunderstood by those who judge the clause to be a duplication in content after ותשב (Witzenrath, 14) and stylistically awkward and clumsy (Rudolph, 44; Witzenrath) and so wish to delete it as a superfluous addition brought in from 2:6c. However, it is precisely this unusual structure and syntax (but hardly awkward or clumsy) that the narrator uses to give to Ruth's "return" remarkable prominence. This is further heightened by the identification he gives her, using her full name "Ruth the Moabitess," hence underlining her foreign origin (on this as her full name, see *Comment* on 2:21). This is most appropriate here: the narrator stresses the astonishing "return" of a foreign woman. On the significance of this, see *Explanation.*

וְהֵמָּה בָּאוּ . . ., "and they arrived . . ." The use of the third person *masculine* independent pronoun to refer to the two women instead of the feminine הנה is troubling. The use of the pronoun itself, placed before the verb, occasions no difficulty (contra Campbell, 78); in this way our author avoids the use of the waw-consecutive form, which would imply sequence (Joüon; see *Form/Structure/Setting*). But, as Campbell notes, if the hypothesis of a dual suffix adopted in the *Comment* on v 8 is valid, then it cannot be said that the text of Ruth exhibits confusion in the grammatical distinction of gender. Further, the use of masculine for feminine forms of the independent pronoun is very rare in the OT (*GBH* § 149c). For these reasons Campbell adopts Freedman's suggestion (derived from Dahood's commentary on Psalms) that המה is not the pronoun but an emphasizing particle *hm(t)* found in Ugaritic, and so he translates "Now as it happened . . ." But this particle is problematic in Ugaritic itself, and the independent pronoun seems required by the syntax (see above). It seems far more likely that we have here an original third person *dual* independent pronoun, built on the form of the third person masculine plural (as in Ugaritic and Arabic, where the form is *humâ,* by coincidence very similar to the form we have in our text). If this hypothesis is granted, then we do not have a single example of confusion in grammatical gender in either suffixed or independent pronouns in Ruth.

Explanation

As our examination of the structure of this scene has revealed (see as well the structure of the whole chapter discussed in the opening scene), its whole purpose is to present to us Naomi's response to the cry of recognition, "Is this Naomi?" with which the women of the town greeted her. The tone of this query signaled that it was not really a question at all but an exclamation of astonished and joyful recognition: "Can this really be Naomi!?" (see *Comment* on v 19b). In Naomi's response, our author brings to full measure the affective dimensions of the loss and emptiness of her life, whose bare outlines he began to fill in through the painful dialogue of the last scene. If there an undertone of complaint accompanied her words of dismissal to her two daughters-in-law (vv 8–9) and if that undertone became a major motif in her pain-filled cry urging their return home (vv 11–13), in this scene it bursts forth as the sole and all-absorbing theme. To do this our author throws Naomi's feelings into bold relief by contrasting them with the joyful exclamations with which the city rang. Sunk in the depths of her bitter affliction, Naomi cannot bear to hear her name resounding in happy surprise on the lips of the ladies of Bethlehem. For in Hebrew thought, one's name can be expressive of one's character, being, and personality (see *IDB* 3:501). So Naomi challenges the tone and content of their glad and delighted cries by twice denying the meaning of her name. First with a command and then with a question, she affirms that she who was once named "Pleasant" can now only be called "Bitter," for "bitter indeed has the Almighty made my life!" Full she went away, but empty has God brought her back. How can they call her "Pleasant" when the Almighty has pronounced disaster upon her?

It is important to note that Naomi's world view does not permit her to rail at fate or chance or circumstances. Rather, she lays responsibility for her empty life directly at the feet of God: "Empty has *Yahweh* brought me back. . . . *Yahweh* has spoken against me!" What are we to think of such open complaint against God? Does the story intend, as Rudolph (33) alleges, that we should learn from Naomi how Yahweh shames those of little faith? Perhaps so, but can such a view square with what one might call the OT's "theology of complaint"? As Campbell observes (83), in the OT,

> not only is complaint tolerated by God, but it can even be the *proper* stance of a person who takes God seriously! Anyone who ascribes full sovereignty to a just and merciful God may expect to encounter the problem of theodicy, and to wrestle with that problem is no sin even when it leads to an attempt to put God on trial.

Naomi here does not evidence little faith; rather, with the freedom of a faith that ascribes full sovereignty to God, she takes God so seriously that, with Job and Jeremiah (and even Abraham, Gen 15:2), she resolutely and openly voices her complaint. With this robust example of the honesty and forthrightness of the OT's "theology of complaint," our author depicts in somber and expressive hues the desolation, despair, and emptiness of the life of a woman "left alone without her two boys and without her husband" (v 5) in a world where life depends upon men.

And so the curtain comes down on the first act: Naomi has returned home, empty, unfulfilled, and bitter. Though this is the main point of the scene, two other observations cry out to be made. First, not only has Naomi returned home; so has Ruth. This our author makes clear in his closing summation. In the structure of this sentence, he gives all the prominence to Ruth (see *Comment* on v 22): "So thus Naomi returned, along with Ruth the Moabitess, her daughter-in-law—she who *returned* from the territory of Moab." Here our author has come full circle. In vv 6–7 only Naomi was said to "return to Judah"; the two young women were only "with" their mother-in-law. The only thing predicated of all three was "they took the road to return . . ." (see *Comment* on v 7). Even here in the first clause of v 22, his statement is "So thus Naomi returned . . ." In a real sense only Naomi and Orpah have returned home, but here our narrator consciously and deliberately refers to Ruth in the same manner. Having never been in Judah, she nonetheless has "returned." Thus he indicates that this is a real return for Ruth. Indeed, if her arrival at Bethlehem is to be such, she must find adoption by the people and God of Israel (cf. Dommershausen, "Leitwortstil in der Ruthrolle, " 398). This she intends: "Your people will be my people and your God my God" (v 16). Our storyteller affirms that the people of Israel will complete the process—how yet remains to be told.

Second, Naomi has returned home empty, unfulfilled, and bitter, yes. Her journey has been a journey into the depths, and she can see nothing else, true. But there is more. In Naomi's anguished response to the delighted cries of the women of Bethlehem—all absorbed in her own world of pain and bitter affliction—she fails even to acknowledge Ruth's presence with her, a presence whose accomplishment transcended the call of faith and home and hope! Her whole complaint is voiced in the singular: ". . . bitter indeed has the Almighty made *my* life . . . empty has Yahweh brought *me* back . . . the Almighty has pronounced disaster upon *me!*" It is indeed, as Rudolph (44) avers, a subtle touch of the narrator that has Naomi utter her complaint as though Ruth, whose words of loving commitment still ring in our ears, were not there at all! By so telling the story, our author subtly presages hope. Yahweh has indeed *not* brought Naomi back empty, and the final word to this effect lies with the narrator when, in his closing summation, he gives all the prominence to describing Ruth's arrival as a *return* (see above and the *Comment* on v 22). Indeed, the countermovement to death and emptiness was already sounded in the previous scene in Ruth's affirmation, "wherever you go, I will go; and wherever you stay, I will stay" (v 16). So "we know that Naomi is not alone and will not be" (Rauber, *JBL* 89 [1970] 30). This commitment of a young woman to the life of an old woman in the darkest hours that women in a man's world can face is already a signal step toward a dawn for Naomi's dark night of despair. In the life of Israel, God has given his people food (v 6b) so that famine (v 1) has given way to barley harvest (v 22c). As for the famine in the life of Naomi, "So Naomi returned, *along with Ruth the Moabitess, her daughter-in-law—she who returned from the territory of Moab.*"

Finally, in the light of concerns and emphases that will surface more clearly later in the story, it is important to emphasize that the problem that forms the core of our story, to describe the pain and desolation of which our author has devoted this first act, is the death and emptiness that have afflicted the life of this woman Naomi in the loss of the only identity for a woman to which her patriarchal world gave value, that of wife and mother.

> The security of husband and children, which a male-dominated culture affords its women, is hers no longer. The definition of worth, by which it values the female, applies to her no more. The blessings of old age, which it gives through progeny, are there no longer. (Trible, 167–68)

It must be stressed that in this whole act in which the problem of the story is set forth and its affective dimensions so poignantly portrayed, nothing is said whatever about the male concern of providing an heir for the family line of Elimelech and Mahlon (contra Hubbard, 39, 131), a concern that will arise later in the story. Indeed, instead of raising this concern, Naomi commands Orpah and Ruth to return to their mother's house in Moab and beseeches Yahweh that there they might find home and husband (vv 8–9). Her speculation about a future husband and sons for herself (vv 12–13) arises out of concern to provide security for her daughters-in-law and not to continue the male line of her deceased husband and sons (Trible, 192; cf. also the remarks of Berlin, *Poetics,* 105–6). This same concern for the security of home and husband—the only vocation their patriarchal world afforded them—will be the primary agenda that motivates the plans and actions of these women throughout the story. This must be stressed, for many commentators have done violence to the narrative by reading it so exclusively through the lenses of its patriarchal world as to read such male issues as levirate marriage and its purpose into scenes and conversations where such do not exist at all. Pedersen can even carry this practice to the extreme of reading such an agenda into this first act (*Israel,* 80):

> It is not the individual affection of Ruth for Noami which the narrator wants to praise in her. This feeling exists and is beautifully expressed, but the feeling of Ruth is of a much deeper and more far-reaching kind; she acts in loyalty towards her husband and his family . . . . Naomi . . . calls herself "the bitter" (1, 20). That which lies behind Naomi's feelings is that the house of her husband is blotted out by the death of her childless sons. Her soul is bound up with the house of her husband . . . . Ruth . . . might have taken the advice of Naomi and . . . her desire for children might then have been amply fulfilled. But for Ruth it was not enough to get children; she wanted to fulfill her obligation of honour towards her deceased husband . . . .

Surely such a misreading of both the intentions of the narrator and the feelings of the protagonists, in which the expressed affection of one woman for another cannot be taken at face value and, further, cannot compare to the totally unexpressed loyalty a woman has to her husband, which is "of a much deeper and more far-reaching kind"—surely such a misreading springs from the chauvinism of the interpreter and not from the story itself! It is a mistake to make the purpose of raising an heir to the deceased head of the family the exclusive purpose of each of the protagonists at every point and so dismiss the equally valid and legitimate concern of these women to find for themselves the security of home and husband—the only identity their patriarchal world afforded them.

Act 2
Ruth Meets Boaz, Naomi's Relative, on the Harvest Field (2:1–23)

Scene 1
Ruth Goes to Glean—and Happens upon the Field of Boaz, Naomi's Relative (2:1–3)

Bibliography

Andersen, F. I. "Israelite Kinship Terminology and Social Structure." *BT* 20 (1969) 29–39. **Borowski, O.** *Agriculture in Iron Age Israel.* Winona Lake, IN: Eisenbrauns, 1987. **Geus, C. H. J. de.** *The Tribes of Israel.* Amsterdam: Van Gorcum, 1976. **Gottwald, N.** *The Tribes of Israel.* Maryknoll, NY: Orbis, 1979. **Hals, R.** *The Theology of the Book of Ruth.* Philadelphia: Fortress, 1969. **Thompson, D.,** and **Thompson, T.** "Some Legal Problems in the Book of Ruth." *VT* 18 (1968) 79–99.

Translation

[1]*Now Naomi had a relative*[a] *on her husband's side,*[b] *a man of substance and standing*[c] *from the clan of Elimelech, whose name was Boaz.*

[2]*And Ruth the Moabitess said to Naomi, "I would like to go to the fields*[a] *to glean behind someone in whose eyes I might find favor." And Naomi said*[b] *to her, "Go ahead,*[c] *my daughter."*

[3]*So she went on her way and gleaned*[a] *in the fields behind the reapers, and as it happened she came upon*[b] *the field of Boaz,*[c] *who was from the clan of Elimelech.*

Notes

1.a. On the K vs. Q problem here, see *Comment.*

1.b. Lit. "To Naomi was a relative of her husband."

1.c. Lit. "mighty in wealth/ability/power." See *Comment.*

2.a. Lit. "field." See *Comment.*

2.b. Lit. "she said."

2.c. לכי is the imperative of permission, not of command; see GKC § 110b; *GBH* § 114n; cf. 2 Sam 18:23.

3.a. The Heb. lit. reads, "And she went and came and gleaned." A literal rendering in Eng. is far too overloaded. A few LXX MSS, Syr, and Vg also omit the second verb, doubtless for the same reason. It is very unlikely that this evidence implies different Heb. recensions, here conflated (so Campbell, 42); see *Comment.*

3.b. Lit. "her chance chanced upon . . ." On the translation, see *Comment.*

3.c. Lit. "the portion of the field [a collective; see *Comment* on v 2] belonging to Boaz." See *Comment.*

Form/Structure/Setting

The second act of the book of Ruth consists of the whole of chap. 2. Between two short scenes involving Ruth and Naomi, one introductory (vv 1–3), the other an epilogue (vv 18–23), is sandwiched the principal scene (vv 4–17). This scene features the meeting between Ruth and Boaz as she gleans in his field. The unity of the section is signaled by its formal characteristics (see below) and by the cohesion of its chronology and the coherence of its content. Ruth's activities continue from her journey to the fields after securing Naomi's permission (vv 2–3), through the overseer's timing of her activities with "from the morning until now" (v 7), through Boaz's kind invitation at the noon meal (v 14), to her gleaning in the field until evening (v 17), and end with her return to the city and her report to Naomi on the day's events (vv 18–22). The concluding comment reports that she continued gleaning until the end of the harvest period (v 23). The coherence of its content is effected by repeated reference throughout to the same semantic domain, i.e., the activities and persons involved in the harvesting of grain: (1) the place: "field" (שׂדה), 7x; (2) the personnel: "reapers" (קצרים), 6x; "men and women workers" (נערים, נערות), 7x; "overseer" (נער נצב על), 2x; (3) the activities: "to harvest" (קצר), 1x; "to gather" (אסף), 1x; "to glean" (לקט), 12x; "to thresh" (חבט), 1x; (4) the product: "harvest" (קציר), 3x; "stalks" (שׁבלים), 1x; "bundles" (צבתים), 1x; "sheaves" (עמרים), 2x; "barley" (שׂערים), 2x; "wheat" (חטים), 1x.

The beginning boundary of the introductory scene, and indeed of the whole act, is signaled by a digression (v 1), addressed by the narrator to his readers, which breaks off the story line to introduce to us proleptically the major new character in the ensuing scene. Its form is a nominal clause with the order predicate-subject, breaking the chronological sequence of waw-consecutive verbal forms. The closing boundary is marked by a brief report of what Ruth proceeded to do (v 3a), thus concluding the introduction and forming a transition to the next scene by providing a succinct summary of its content. The section is marked by chiasm:

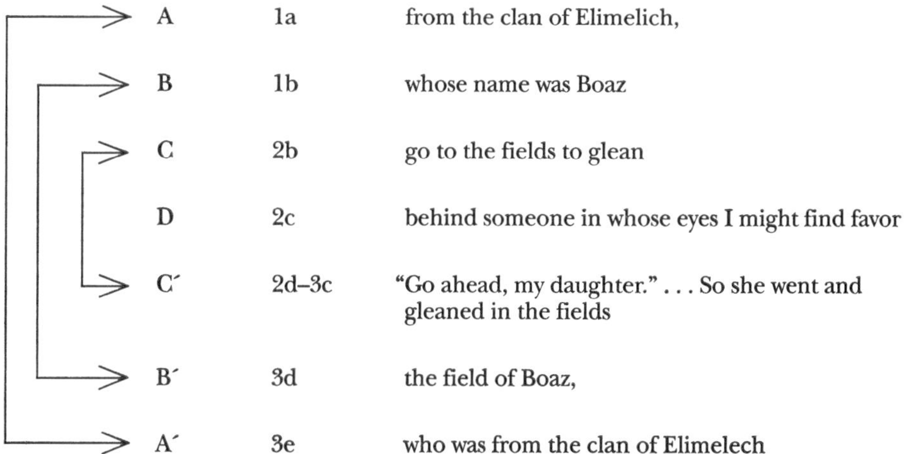

A 1a from the clan of Elimelich,
B 1b whose name was Boaz
C 2b go to the fields to glean
D 2c behind someone in whose eyes I might find favor
C′ 2d–3c "Go ahead, my daughter." . . . So she went and gleaned in the fields
B′ 3d the field of Boaz,
A′ 3e who was from the clan of Elimelech

Comment

1 וּלְנָעֳמִי מֹידַע לְאִישָׁהּ, lit. "to Naomi was a relative of her husband." The K, to be read מְיֻדָּע, occurs six times elsewhere (2 Kgs 10:11; Pss 31:12; 55:14; 88:9, 19; Job 19:14) meaning "close associate, intimate friend." The Q (which is also the reading of a large number of Hebrew MSS) reads מוֹדַע, a word of uncertain meaning that occurs elsewhere only in Prov 7:4. Although either meaning fits the general context in Prov 7:4, the term אחות, "sister," which occupies the corresponding place in the parallel clause is distinctly in favor of "relative." The term מודעת, the feminine form of מודע, occurs in 3:2, but the context there makes the meaning no clearer than here. In 2:20 Naomi says that Boaz is קרוב לנו, "a relative of ours." Further, in 2:20; 3:9, 12, and elsewhere, he is called a גאל *gôʾēl* to Naomi and Ruth, a term meaning a *relative* who is obligated to come to the aid of family members in need (see the discussion in the *Comment* on 2:20). Therefore, since Boaz is being introduced to us proleptically in a digression calculated to raise our interest and pique our curiosity, it seems far preferable with the vast majority of commentators to read the Q and understand the general meaning to be "relative" (contra Sasson, 39). Further, to state that Naomi had a "relative of her husband" is necessary in order to make clear that the blood relationship was with her husband and not with her (since Israelite marriage was endogamous). It is most important to the development of the story to know that Boaz is a blood relative of Elimelech since only upon such relatives fell the social responsibilities of the גאל, "the redeemer," a concept that surfaces in chaps. 3 and 4. Campbell (89–90) develops an elaborate hypothesis in which he renders מידע as "covenant-brother" and defines it as "an archaic term belonging to a societal structure that reaches beyond blood ties," which "adds the dimension of covenant responsibility to that of family responsibility." It connotes "responsibility inherent in covenant ties, relationships entered into voluntarily rather than through the accident of blood connection" (109). This hypothesis is based upon a tenuous reconstruction of 2 Kgs 10:11 (following the LXX) and upon an equally tenuous parallel with the use of the verb ידע in treaty/covenant terminology. The story, as we have noted above, makes clear that the responsibilities for the two women incumbent upon Boaz result from his blood relationship with Elimelech. It seems even less probable that the storyteller would introduce him here by a term that refers to voluntary relationships than that he would identify him by the term "friend." Finally, Joüon's suggestion (46) that the term מידע bears the technical force "relative by marriage" (*adfinis* rather than *cognatus*) is excluded because this would render the following phrase, "of her husband," completely redundant.

אִישׁ גִּבּוֹר חַיִל מִמִּשְׁפַּחַת אֱלִימֶלֶךְ, "a man of substance and standing from the clan of Elimelech." איש גביר חיל means literally "a man mighty in חיל." Since חיל can bear several meanings—"strength, power, ability, wealth"—the exact meaning of גביר חיל depends upon the context in which it is used. In a military setting it refers to a warrior, particularly one who has distinguished himself in armed combat. In other contexts it can refer to wealth (2 Kgs 15:20) or ability (1 Kgs 11:28), and it always designates one who possessed social standing and a good reputation. In this context it connotes not only wealth but also ability and honor (cf. *TDOT* 2:374; Campbell, 90).

Boaz is identified as belonging to the same משפחה, "clan," as Elimelech. This further identification of Boaz is not so repetitious after מידע, "relative," as to require that it has been secondarily introduced here from 2:3d (contra Witzenrath, 15). Nor is it so redundant a statement as to require that מודע means "friend" (contra Hubbard, 132–33). Though obvious after the previous statement that Boaz is Naomi's relative on her husband's side, it is used for emphasis and literarily to provide an inclusio with v 3 (see *Form/Structure/Setting*). The משפחה was a social unit that stood between the tribe (שבט or מטה) and the extended family (בית אב). All those who belonged to the same משפחה claimed descent from a common ancestor, usually one of the grandsons of Jacob/Israel, who was considered the progenitor of the משפחה, the "subtribe," or "phratry," to use Andersen's term (*BT* 20 [1969] 34–38). The משפחה was possibly the most important single group in the social structure of ancient Israel (cf. Andersen, *BT* 20 [1969] 34–38; de Geus, *Tribes of Israel,* 136–39). It set the bounds of recognized kinship and formed the basic endogamic unit of society. Hence, there can be little doubt that Boaz and Elimelech were kinsmen, although the relationship was doubtless relatively distant, since it was the בית־אב, the extended family (lit. "father's house"), that contained the more closely related kin group, such as uncles, aunts, and cousins of the nuclear family head. (See the discussion of Gottwald, *Tribes of Israel,* 261–70.)

וּשְׁמוֹ בֹּעַז, "whose name was Boaz." Boaz occurs as a personal name only in Ruth. Its etymology is obscure and much debated, particularly since it occurs also as the name of one of the pillars stationed before the entrance of the temple of Solomon (1 Kgs 7:21). Since our author makes no play on the meaning of Boaz's name, a discussion of its origin will add nothing to the understanding of the story. For possible etymologies, see the discussions of Campbell and Sasson.

The introduction of a new character into the narrative by a circumstantial nominal clause of the type [X] ושמו/ושמה, "whose [lit. 'and his/her'] name was [X]," is fairly common (ca. 30x) in the OT. Sasson (42–43), however, alleges that in about two dozen of these instances the narrator consistently introduces material of major import to the narrative immediately after such an introduction, whereas in only three passages is a new character so introduced without immediately proceeding to recount his activities. He thus implies that the pattern of the majority of the occurrences should also be the case here in Ruth and that this then is a further argument for his theory that vv 2–3 assert that Ruth deliberately set out to find Boaz's field. But the evidence can just as plausibly be argued to prove the opposite. In 1 Sam 21:8 Doeg the Edomite and in 2 Sam 4:4 Mephibosheth are both introduced proleptically into the respective narratives in order to account for their roles in events subsequent to the immediate scene, Doeg in 1 Sam 22:9–10 and Mephibosheth in 2 Sam 9:1–8. Such proleptic introductions occur also with other characters in OT narrative who are not introduced by the naming formula in question. Thus Amasa is introduced proleptically in 2 Sam 17:25, preparatory to the role he plays in the events reported in 2 Sam 19:11–14; 20:4–13. Consequently, Gerleman (25) is correct in noting that it is quite in keeping with Hebrew narrative style, and quite in order, that the story should introduce Boaz in 2:1 to return to him only later in the narrative. Sasson has missed the narrator's skill as a storyteller: by introducing Boaz prematurely, and withholding his name until the end of the introduction, he has aroused interest, created suspense, and suggested importance (Trible, 175).

2 אֵלְכָה־נָּא הַשָּׂדֶה, "I would like to go to the fields." The form אלכה־נא, the first person cohortative plus the particle נא, is a frequent idiom in polite requests. Campbell (91) argues for a nuance of firm determination on Ruth's part: "I am going out . . . ," basing his view on Lambdin's discussion of the meaning of the particle *-nā* (*IBH,* 170–71). Lambdin's discussion, however, deals primarily with the use of the particle with imperatives when the speaker regards his command as consequent upon his former statement or upon the general situation in which it is uttered. Neither seems at all pertinent here. There is no preceding statement, nor does anything in the context suggest that this is a declaration of firm determination after Ruth has sized up her situation (contra Campbell, Hubbard). Rather the idiom is used with *the cohortative form of the first person,* which regularly functions as a polite request, frequently addressed to someone in a position of authority or respect (e.g., Exod 4:18; 2 Sam 15:7; esp. Deut 3:25; see *GBH* § 114d; GKC § 108c). The expression can have the force suggested by Campbell when it is a resolution addressed to the self (e.g., Exod 3:3; Isa 5:1; cf. GKC § 108b), but here Ruth addresses her mother-in-law, under whose authority she clearly regards herself to be (see Thompson, *VT* 18 [1968] 96) since Naomi's status and age accord her Ruth's respect and obedience (contra Campbell, 111). Hence, the context demands a polite request, not a blunt announcement of what she intends to do. Finally, that this is demanded by the context is made clear by Naomi's response, "Go ahead, my daughter," an imperative of permission (see *Note* 2.c.), which is "a response to a petition in cohortative form" (Hubbard, 136 n. 4). The context is very similar to that of v 7, where exactly the same form, the first person cohortative with *-nā,* also appears (cf. the remarks of Campbell, 94).

השדה is singular here, but it is used collectively to refer to the arable land of the town whose individual fields are owned by the male heads of the families of Bethlehem (cf. *Comment* on v 3 below). In the context, the plural makes better sense in English.

וַאֲלַקֳטָה בַשִּׁבֳּלִים, "to glean stalks of grain." The speaker avoids the perfect with waw consecutive, וְלִקַּטְתִּי, which would express sequence—"I would like to go . . . and then glean . . ."—as in 2:7. The use of a cohortative joined with simple waw to another cohortative (or jussive or imperative) implies subordination, expressing purpose or result (see *IBH,* 118–19; *HebS* §§ 187, 518). The piel stem of the verb לקט is used elsewhere in the OT seven times to mean "gather, pick up (materials, e.g., arrows, wood)," always with the object expressed. It is used in a more technical sense to mean "glean (ears of grain)," with the object expressed, three times outside the book of Ruth: Lev 19:9; 23:22; Isa 17:5. In Isa 17:5 the object is שבלים, "ears of grain," as in Ruth 2:2. In all of these occurrences, the verb governs its object directly; only here does it do so with the preposition ב. The force of this, consequently, is difficult to assess. It is very difficult to take it as locative, "in, among," or partitive, "some" (so BDB, 3, p. 544, followed by Morris, 269 n. 1; cf. Hubbard, 136 n. 3). Since one gleans ears, not "among ears," the first is obvious and the meaning "some" would be expressed by מן (Joüon, 47)—no such meaning is attested for ב. Joüon, followed by Gerleman and Rudolph, posits a ב*-participative,* "to glean *at* the ears of grain," i.e., "to work at gleaning, to participate in the gleaning," (cf. Ges.-Buhl, B.1.b, p. 80; BDB, I.2.b, p. 88). However, it seems more likely that this is an example of the use of the preposition ב with various classes of verbs, for which no simple explanation in terms of the common meanings of ב may be found (cf. BDB, II.3, p. 89; IV, p. 90). The context shows that the idiom, however it is construed, simply means "I would like to glean ears of grain." Since it seems more natural in English, we have not expressed the object of the verbal phrase, שִׁבֳּלִים, "stalks of grain," in the translation. The term refers to the cut ear of grain with the stalk attached (cf. Borowski, *Agriculture,* 57–58, 61).

אַחַר אֲשֶׁר אֶמְצָא־חֵן בְּעֵינָיו, "after someone in whose eyes I might find favor." It is grammatically possible to understand the idiom אחר אשר in two quite different ways. On the one hand, the preposition אחר, "after, behind," governs the noun clause אשר אמצא־חן בעיניו. In this noun clause, the verbal phrase אמצא־חן בעיניו, "I might find favor in his eyes," is nominalized by the relative particle אשר, which has here an unexpressed antecedent, "(one) who," to which unexpressed antecedent the pronoun "his" refers, i.e., "behind (one) who I might find favor in his eyes" = "behind one in whose eyes I might find favor." (For such a usage, see GKC §§ 138e, f; *HALOT,* אשר A.8, p. 98.) On the other hand, the combination אחר אשר can belong to that type of construction in which the relative particle אשר is appended to a preposition and forms a *conjunction* that governs verbal clauses, e.g., כאשר, "as, when"; על אשר, "because" (cf. GKC §104b). It occurs in this usage elsewhere only in Ezek 40:1, where it is clearly temporal, "after." However, the synonym אחרי occurs five times in the compound אחרי אשר with a causal force, "since, seeing that." Almost all commentators and translators have understood אחר אשר in the Ruth passage to belong to the first category of uses of the compound. However, Sasson (42–43) has argued for the second interpretation, rendering the clause literally "since I shall find favor in his eyes." The pronoun "his" then can only refer to Boaz, who has been mentioned in the preceding verse. Sasson uses this interpretation as the first link in the chain of his argument that Ruth deliberately set out from the start, with Naomi's acquiescence (v 2c), to meet Boaz specifically and gain his attention and favor. Although such a translation is grammatically possible, the context utterly precludes it, since in the context the suffix "his" on "his eyes" cannot refer to Boaz. Boaz thus far has been mentioned in the story only in v 1, which is an aside from the narrator to his readers. There is no indication that Naomi and Ruth have mentioned him or thought of him as a possible answer to their problems. Sasson (43) seeks to obviate this difficulty simply by stating that the change from indirect discourse in 2:1 to direct discourse in 2:2 should not refute his thesis. But this is a misunderstanding of the nature of v 1, which makes a statement *about* Naomi. It does not make a statement *about her knowledge* at that moment, as Sasson's translation implies: "Now Naomi knew of an acquaintance of her husband . . ." (38; but cf. his literal translation, 39). As a statement about Naomi, it is a digression, an aside, which communicates information from the narrator to his hearers but does not imply in the least that this is knowledge that Naomi and Ruth share. Finally, Sasson's view that Naomi and Ruth both concurred in Ruth's plan to meet Boaz and gain his favor cannot possibly square with vv 19–20, for it is clear that here the name of Boaz comes as a surprise to Naomi and that here she informs Ruth who he is for the first time. Hence, the only plausible translation of the clause in the context is ". . . to glean behind someone in whose eyes I might find favor." (See also the remarks of Hubbard, 138–39 n. 13.)

Finally, we have to ask what Ruth means by the expression "someone in whose eyes I might find favor." As commentators have observed (e.g., Campbell, Keil, Rudolph), the legal statements in Lev 19:9–10; 23:22; Deut 24:19–21 expressly grant to the poor, the resident alien, the widow, and the orphan the legal right to glean in the harvest fields. However, the large number of passages in the law that accord special privileges to the widow (e.g., Exod 22:22–24; Deut 10:18; 14:29; 16:11; 24:17) and those in the prophets and elsewhere that charge Israel with their oppression (e.g., Isa 1:23; 10:2; Jer 7:6; Job 24:3, 21; Ps 94:6) clearly attest that the refusal of this right must have been common. Therefore, the simplest understanding of Ruth's words is that she "wants to glean behind someone who would benevolently allow it" (Keil, followed by Rudolph). However, a number of commentators (e.g., Campbell, Gerleman, Hubbard, Joüon; cf. NEB) understand the phrase to mean that Ruth will or must (so Gerleman, who then concludes that the author of Ruth did not know the laws of Leviticus and Deuteronomy!) seek permission from the harvesters or the owner of the field before gleaning. However, the laws granting the right to glean do not require that the gleaner request permission; indeed, they imply just the opposite. Consequently, since Ruth's words about "someone who will look on me with favor" fit the context of the frequent denial of the right to glean, they do not imply that she needs to or will seek permission.

3 וַתֵּלֶךְ וַתָּבוֹא וַתְּלַקֵּט בַּשָּׂדֶה, lit. "and she went and came and gleaned in the fields." These three tightly sequential verbs constitute a summary statement of what the ensuing scene describes in detail. The combination of הלך, "to go, move, walk," and בוא, "to come, come in," in summary statements, though overloaded if literally translated (see *Notes*), is a frequent idiom in OT narrative style (cf. Judg 19:10; 1 Sam 22:5; 1 Kgs 14:17; 2 Kgs 4:25; cf. Hubbard, 140 n. 4). We have attempted to render the force of the combination with "she went on her way." This does not imply that all three actions took place before the statement that follows, "and as it happened she came upon . . . ," for that clause is not sequential in time with these clauses (see Campbell, 92, and the following *Comment*).

וַיִּקֶר מִקְרֶהָ, lit. "and her chance met/came across." The waw-consecutive form here does not express temporal sequence as it usually does in past narrative (GKC § 111a). Here it expresses concomitant circumstance (cf. Joüon, 48; *GBH* § 118k; *IBHS* § 33.2.2). Here our narrator begins to set forth the details of the summary statement just made. Although the noun מקרה occurs in 1 Sam 6:9; 20:26 with the meaning "accident, chance," the idiom קרה מקרה occurs elsewhere only in Eccl 2:14, 15, where it is usually translated "fate befalls, overtakes." In our context the idiom does not express the modern idea of "chance" or "luck," for that is foreign to OT thought (see *Explanation*). Rather, it signifies that Ruth, *without any intention to do so,* ended up gleaning in the field that belonged to Boaz. The translation "as it happened she came upon" expresses nicely the absence of volition on Ruth's part. The meaning of the expression presents the gravest of difficulties for Sasson's view, discussed above, that Ruth set out to glean with the express intention of meeting (and pleasing) Boaz, for it can hardly be construed "to emphasize Ruth's good fortune, not so much that Boaz turned out to be the owner of the field which she happened to reach, but that she located Boaz's plot *without wasting precious time searching for it*" (Sasson, 45—italics in the original).

On the contrary, the clause shows clearly that Ruth set out to glean with no intention at all of finding Boaz's field.

חֶלְקַת הַשָּׂדֶה לְבֹעַז, lit. "the portion of the fields belonging to Boaz." According to GKC § 129d, the genitive "of Boaz" is expressed here by the preposition ל, "to," because the construct phrase חלקת השדה is a compound representing one united idea, "the individual field" (lit. "the portion of the fields"), contra *IBHS* § 9.7b. This can clearly be seen in 2 Kgs 9:25–26, where the expression חלקת השדה in v 25 is referred to by חלקת alone in v 26. Hence, the expression unambiguously means "the field of Boaz," whereas חלקת שדה בעז *could* be understood to mean "the portion of Boaz's field." See the similar expression in 4:3; cf. Gen 33:19; Josh 24:32.

Explanation

The second act of the book, 2:1–23, reveals the first concrete step toward the resolution of Naomi's lonely and bitter state, namely, the meeting between Ruth and Boaz. Our narrator begins this act in the drama with a scene, short and introductory, that explains how this meeting came about. It is well calculated to raise intriguing questions and possibilities and so to arouse and hold our interest. It commences not with an advance in the story line but with a digression in which the narrator addresses us, his readers, and introduces us to Boaz. Boaz, he informs us, is a man of substance and standing in the community from the same "clan" as Elimelech, and he stresses Boaz's kinship with Naomi through her husband. By so doing, and above all by introducing him proleptically to us in a digression, our narrator skillfully arouses our interest and creates suspense (cf. Trible, 175). This interest is heightened in v 2 with Ruth's words about gleaning behind someone in whose eyes she might find favor. After our introduction to Boaz, such language almost teasingly suggests that this will be he. Suggestion soon gives way to expectation at the end of the scene when we learn that Ruth, totally unaware of his existence, happens upon his field. This expectation will be fulfilled, of course, when Boaz immediately puts in his appearance at the beginning of the next scene. Obviously this man will play a role in the story, but what?

After the digression of v 1, the story resumes, not with Naomi but with Ruth the Moabitess. Still absorbed with the bitter affliction and emptiness of her life, Naomi remains inactive and but for two words keeps her silence. It is Ruth who takes the initiative to provide the wherewithal to sustain their life by offering to glean in the fields. True to her character, in deference to her mother-in-law she politely requests her acquiescence. Naomi responds with nothing more than two words of assent: "You-may-go, my-daughter." Is it advanced age that keeps her from gleaning with Ruth in the fields, or has she pursued her suffering into the withdrawal of despair? Our storyteller gives us no hint. Or does he? In fact, the only words he grants to Naomi between her bitter complaint to the women of Bethlehem and her suddenly interested questions when she sees the quantity of grain Ruth has gleaned (v 19) are these two words of dismissal to Ruth to glean alone in the fields wherever haply she might.

The narrator concludes this brief scene with a summary statement (v 3) in the form of a preview whose details will be supplied in the following scene. This preview is stated so that he can tell us that Ruth, when she went out to glean, "happened to come across" Boaz's field. One must be careful not to read modern secular conceptions of "fate" or "luck" or "chance" into this language. In the OT view God directly controlled all that happened (cf., e.g., Amos 3:6b; Lam 3:37–38; Isa 45:1–8). That this is the view of our author is abundantly clear from the way he attributes both the end of the famine in 1:6 and Ruth's conception in 4:13 directly to the divine causality. Hence, "chance" means here, as also in Ecclesiastes, "that which happens without the intention or assistance of those involved and thereby expresses the conviction of the narrator that men cannot determine the course of events" (Gerleman, 25). This sentence indeed "smacks of hyperbole—striking understatement intended to create the exact opposite impression" (Hubbard, 141). As Hals (*The Theology of the Book of Ruth,* 12) has put it,

> . . . the author's real meaning in 2:3b is actually the opposite of what he says. The labelling of Ruth's meeting with Boaz as "chance" is nothing more than the author's way of saying that no human intent was involved. For Ruth and Boaz it was an accident, but not for God. The tenor of the whole story makes it clear that the narrator sees God's hand throughout. In fact the very secularism of his expression here is his way of stressing that conviction. It is a kind of underplaying for effect. By calling this meeting an accident, the writer enables himself subtly to point out that even the "accidental" is directed by God.

After the narrator identifies the owner of the field in which Ruth gleaned, he piques our interest by reminding us of Boaz's relationship to Naomi. Boaz, a man of substance and standing, is related to Naomi through her husband, and Ruth, looking to glean behind someone in whose eyes she might find favor, has come by "chance" to glean in his field. What this portends our narrator now proceeds to tell.

Scene 2
Ruth and Boaz Meet on the Harvest Field: Boaz Is Exceedingly Generous (2:4–17a)

Bibliography

Alter, R. *The Art of Biblical Narrative.* New York: Basic, 1981. **Barthélemy, B.,** et al. *Preliminary and Interim Report on the Hebrew Old Testament Text Project.* Vol. 2. New York: United Bible Societies, 1979. **Beattie, D. R. G.** "A Midrashic Gloss in Ruth 2:7." *ZAW* 89 (1977) 122–24. **Berlin, A.** *Poetics and Interpretation of Biblical Narrative.* Sheffield: Almond, 1983. **Borowski, O.** *Agriculture in Iron Age Israel.* Winona Lake, IN: Eisenbrauns, 1987. **Dalman, G.** *Arbeit und Sitte in Palästina.* Vol. 3. 1933. Repr. Hildesheim: Georg Olms, 1964. **Daube, D.** *Studies in Biblical Law.* London: Cambridge UP, 1947. **Driver, G. R.** "Affirmation by Exclamatory Negation." *JANES* 5 (1973) 107–14. **Ehrlich, A. B.** *Randglossen zur hebräischen*

Bibel: Textkritisches, sprachliche und sachliches. Vol. 7. 1914. Repr. Hildesheim: Georg Olms, 1968. 19–29. **Hubbard, R.** "The Events of Ruth 2:1–16: A Proposal." Paper read at the SBL Annual Meeting, 1985 (kindly supplied by the author). **Humbert, P.** "Art et leçon de l'histoire de Ruth." In *Opuscules d'un Hébraïsant.* Memoires de l'Université de Neuchâtel 26. Neuchâtel: Secrétariat de l'Université, 1958. 83–110. ———. "En marge du dictionnaire hébraique." *ZAW* 62 (1949–50) 199–207. **Hurvitz, A.** "Ruth 2:7—'A Midrashic Gloss'?" *ZAW* 95 (1983) 121–23. **Kennedy, A.** "The Root GʿR in the Light of Semantic Analysis." *JBL* 106 (1987) 47–64. **Levine, E.** *The Aramaic Version of Ruth.* Rome: Biblical Institute, 1973. **Lys, D.** "Résidence ou repos? Notule sur Ruth ii 7." *VT* 21 (1971) 497–501. **MacIntosh, A.** "A Consideration of Hebrew נער." *VT* 19 (1969) 471–79. **Myers, J. M.** *The Linguistic and Literary Form of the Book of Ruth,* Leiden: Brill, 1955. **Nötscher, F.** "Zum emphatischem Lamed." *VT* 4 (1954) 372–80. **Porten, B.** "The Scroll of Ruth: A Rhetorical Study." *GCA* 7 (1978) 23–49. **Stager, L.** "The Archeology of the Family in Ancient Israel." *BASOR* 260 (1985) 1–35. **Trible, P.** "Woman in the OT." *IDBSup,* 963–66.

Translation

4 *And wouldn't you know it,*[a] *Boaz came from Bethlehem! He said to the reapers, "The LORD*[b] *be with you!" and they replied to him, "The LORD bless you!"*

5 *Then Boaz said to his servant in charge of*[a] *the reapers, "To whom does this young woman*[b] *belong?"*
6 *And the servant in charge of the reapers replied, "She is a*[a] *Moabite young woman who came back with Naomi from the territory of Moab.*
7 *She asked, 'May I glean stalks of grain and gather them in bundles*[a] *behind the reapers?' So she came and has remained here. From morning until just now*[b] *she has stopped*[c] *only a moment."*

8 *Then Boaz said to Ruth, "Listen carefully,*[a] *my daughter! Don't go to glean*[b] *in any other field; indeed, do not go beyond*[c] *the boundaries of this one. But right here you are to stick close to my young women.*
9 *Watch closely*[a] *where the workers are harvesting*[b] *and follow*[c] *behind the women.*[d] *I am herewith ordering*[e] *the young men not to interfere with*[f] *you. If you are thirsty,*[g] *then go and get a drink from the jars that the young men have filled."*[h]

10 *She bowed down, touching her forehead to the ground,*[a] *and said to him, "How have I earned your favor*[b] *so that you pay such attention to me, though I am a foreigner?"*

11 *And Boaz replied,*[a] *"I have been fully informed of all that you have done for*[b] *your mother-in-law since your husband's death—how you have left your father and mother and the land of your birth and have come to a people you did not previously know.*
12 *May Yahweh repay your good deed, and may your reward be full from Yahweh, the God of Israel, under whose wings you have come to find shelter!"*

13 *And she said, "You are most gracious,*[a] *sir,*[b] *for you have eased my mind and given encouragement*[c] *to your maidservant, though I myself will never be the equivalent of one of your maidservants."*[d]

14 *At mealtime Boaz said to her,*[a] *"Come over*[b] *here. Have*[c] *some food,*[d] *and dip your bread*[e] *in the wine vinegar." So she sat down beside the reapers. He handed her some roasted grain, and she ate all she wanted,*[f] *and then she still had some left over.*[g]
15 *Then she rose to glean, and Boaz commanded his workers,*[a] *"Even between the sheaves themselves let her glean, and do not scold her.*
16 *In fact, be sure to pull out some stalks from the handfuls for her and leave them behind for her to glean, without rebuking her!"*

17[a] *So she gleaned in the field until evening.*

Notes

4.a. Lit. "And behold!" See *Comment.*

4.b. Although we have elsewhere translated יהוה, the personal name of God, as "Yahweh," the traditional rendering "LORD" sounds more natural in Eng. in conventional greetings such as these.

5.a. Lit. "the one who was stationed over . . ."

5.b. הנערה. Since Ruth has been married for some time, possibly as much as ten years (see *Comment* on 1:4b), the translation "young woman" seems more appropriate than "girl."

6.a. Rudolph's view (46) that the definite article is to be placed on נערה מואביה (with the LXX) on the grounds that the overseer supposed that Boaz had already heard about Ruth's return is to be rejected. It is just as plausible to assume that the overseer is not sure that Boaz knows about the situation. At least this is what the MT reading presumes (on the indefinite nature of the following השבה, see *Comment*).

7.a. The phrase ואספתי בעמרים, "and gather them in bundles," is omitted by Syr and Vg. On the principle of the more difficult reading, the MT is much to be preferred (contra TEV, de Waard-Nida, Gerleman). See the *Comment.*

7.b. The LXX reads ἑσπέρας, "evening" (Heb. ערב), for עתה, "now." MT is to be preferred; see *Comment.*

7.c. This translation reads שָׁבְתָה, "she has stopped," instead of MT's שִׁבְתָּהּ, "her sitting," and omits the following word, הבית, "the house." See *Comment.*

8.a. Lit. "Have you not heard?" See *Comment.*

8.b. לִלְקֹט, inf constr of לקט, is used in the qal with the technical sense "to glean" only here.

8.c. תַּעֲבוּרִי. The long *û* in the penultimate syllable is highly unusual, particularly when there should be no vowel in the syllable at all: the expected form is תַּעַבְרִי. If not a mistake, this may be evidence for a penultimate accent (perhaps in the colloquial dialect?). Cf. GKC § 47g.

9.a. Lit. "Let your eyes be on the field."

9.b. Lit. "they[masc pl]-are-harvesting," i.e., the masc pl referring to a mixed group of male and female servants. See *Comment.*

9.c. Lit. "go."

9.d. Lit. "them [fem pl]." See *Comment.*

9.e. Lit. "Have I not ordered?" See *Comment.*

9.f. לבלתי נגעך. Ordinarily נגע, "touch (to do harm)," does not govern its obj directly, as here, but takes a prep, usually ב. Joüon quite persuasively argues that the use of the direct obj here is conditioned by the fact that the obj is a pronom suff (see *GBH* § 125b).

9.g. וצמת < צמא, "to be thirsty." Since the aleph was lost in pronunciation (quiesced), it has been lost in the orthography as well; cf. ותשׂנה < נשׂא in 1:14 above. The form is usually considered to have been treated as if it were a ל״ה verb (GKC § 75qq; *GBH* § 78g).

9.h. Lit. "go to the (water-)jars and drink from what the young men have drawn." The reordered sentence is much more natural in Eng.

10.a. Lit. "she fell on her face and did obeisance to the ground." With de Waard-Nida (32), I choose to avoid the lit. translation "she fell on her face," since in Eng. this usually connotes an accidental rather than an intentional act. For the nature of the gesture, see *Comment.*

10.b. Lit. "Why have I found favor in your eyes . . . ?" On the expression, see the *Comment* on v 2.

11.a. Lit. "answered and said to her."

11.b. את expresses advantage here; see *HebS* § 341.

13.a. Lit. "I am finding" or "May I find favor in your eyes," an expression of thanks. See *Comment.*

13.b. Lit. "my lord."

13.c. Lit. "spoken to the heart of." See *Comment.*

13.d. Lit. "I myself am not as/like one of your maidservants." See *Comment.* In the context, the Heb. text is much to be preferred to the LXX, OL, and Syr, which omit the negative, producing some such meaning as "and I am indeed only one of your maidservants." See *Comment.*

14.a. לָה. For some reason, the Masoretes did not indicate with mappiq the consonantal nature of the ה here as the 3 fem sg pronom suff, i.e., לָהּ; see GKC § 103g.

14.b. גֹּשִׁי. This form is quite anomalous. One expects גְּשִׁי. Since the impf and the masc sg impv have an *a*, the *ō* is also unusual. Four such forms of the impv occur, however, so the anomaly is well attested; see GKC § 66c.

14.c. Lit. "eat."

14.d. לחם means not only "bread" but "food" in general; cf. 1 Sam 14:24–30. The more general sense fits this context better than "bread."

14.e. פתך, lit. "your morsel, piece (of bread)." The phrase is often explicit: פת־לחם, "morsel of bread" (e.g., Gen 18:5).

14.f. Lit. "she ate, and she was satisfied."

14.g. וַתֹּתַר. The hiphil impf consec form here has pataḥ in the final syllable, whereas one expects ṣērē; cf. וַיּוֹתֵר, 2 Sam 8:4. It is usually explained as an indication of pause; see GKC § 53n (but cf. § 69v!).

15.a. Lit. את־נעריו, "his young men," or better "his young people" (Campbell) since it seems probable that the masc pl is used in passages such as this to refer to workers of both sexes; see the *Comments* on vv 8 and 9.

Form/Structure/Setting

This, the second and principal scene, constitutes the bulk of the chapter, stretching from v 4 to v 17a. The opening boundary is clearly marked, both by its form and its content. In form it departs from the waw-consecutive verbs used in the closing summary statement that precedes it, consisting rather of the והנה + subject + verb construction, thus avoiding any expression of chronological sequence and making the narrative graphic and vivid (see *Comment*). As for content, it takes us back to and resumes the digression introduced in v 1, for it depicts the arrival of Boaz, the new character in the scene, whose proleptic introduction in v 1 has foreshadowed with distinct anticipation just such a development as is now described.

The end of the scene is equally clear, for the narrative summary in v 17a, "So she gleaned in the field until evening," takes us back to the closing summary statement of v 3, "So she went and came and gleaned in the field," showing that the preview there has now been told in full. It is tempting to end the scene with v 18a, "And she lifted (it) and came to the city" (cf. B. Porten, *GCA* 7 [1978] 33), for this would complete the journey begun by Ruth in the opening section. But in my opinion, the last half of v 17, which describes what an exceedingly large amount of grain Ruth had gleaned, properly belongs with the next scene, for it sets the stage for Naomi's wide-eyed and glad surprise at Ruth's success (v 19). Further, since the *beginning* of Ruth's journey is related in the *concluding* statement of the *opening* scene, the pronounced symmetry of the chapter speaks strongly in favor of the view that the *conclusion* of that journey is related in the *opening* statement of the *concluding* scene. Here Ruth's activities indeed come full circle as she and Naomi evaluate what has transpired.

The unity of this section is strongly marked by the cohesion of its chronology and the coherence of its content, for which see the remarks on the form and structure of the whole chapter in *Form/Structure/Setting* for 2:1–3.

As far as structure is concerned, the scene breaks into two episodes framed by a brief narrative introduction, v 4a, and conclusion, v 17a (see the diagram): In the first episode, vv 4b–13, the narrative statements are only the barest necessary to provide coherent introduction to the conversations involved. The episode consists almost exclusively, then, of dialogue, one between Boaz and his workers (A), the other between Boaz and Ruth (B), each of which centers its attention on Ruth and Boaz to the exclusion of all else. Even the opening dialogue of A, vv 4b–e, in which Boaz and his workers exchange greetings, has only a functional value related to the main purpose. It delays the action and increases the suspense of the reader who already knows Boaz's identity (v 1) and knows that he must play some unknown role in the resolution of the problem of the book. The same purpose explains the seemingly overloaded repetition of the identity of the "overseer" as "the servant who is in charge of the reapers" in vv 5, 6. Failure to recognize

The Structure of Ruth 2:4–17a

Episode			Verses	Content	Function	
		Narrative Introduction	4a	Boaz arrives.	opens the scene	
Episode 1: vv 4–13	A	Conversation between Boaz and his workers about Ruth and her gleaning	4b–e	Boaz greets his workers.	delays action and creates suspense	
			5	Boaz asks his overseer about Ruth.	Question: ↓	Trigger ↓ Response
			6–7	The overseer responds.	Answer:	Trigger ↓ Response
	B	Conversation between Boaz and Ruth: He grants her exceptional rights and explains why	8–9	Boaz commands Ruth to glean right behind his workers.	Command: ↓	Trigger ↓ Response
			10	Ruth asks why she is thus favored.	Question: ↓	Trigger ↓ Response
			11–12	Boaz tells Ruth he knows of her faithfulness and blesses her.	Answer: ↓	Trigger ↓
			13	Ruth expresses gratitude and thanks.	Evaluation:	Response
Episode 2: vv 14–16	B´	Actions involving Boaz and Ruth: He grants her exceptional privileges at the noon meal	14a, b	Boaz invites Ruth to sit and eat with his workers.	Command: ↓	Trigger ↓
			14c	Ruth complies.	Execution:	Response
			14d	Boaz gives her an excess of food.	Narrative Statement	
	A´	Conversation between Boaz and his workers about Ruth and her gleaning	15a	Ruth goes to glean.	Narrative Statement:	Trigger ↓
			15b–16	Boaz commands his workers to give her extraordinary privileges.	Command:	Response
		Narrative Conclusion	17a	Ruth gleans until evening.	Concludes the scene	

this function prompts Witzenrath (15) to delete the second occurrence as dittography. In the concluding dialogue of A, vv 5–7, Boaz asks his overseer for the origin of the unknown young woman gleaning in his field, and the overseer responds, both identifying Ruth and informing him of her request to glean and probably (the latter half of v 7 is most obscure; see *Comment*) of her early morning activity. This response sets in motion the dialogue between Boaz and Ruth, B, which forms the high point of the scene. In this four-part conversation, each speech is both a response to the stimulus of the previous one and a trigger that provides the stimulus for the following reply. Thus, the overseer's response identifying Ruth (vv 6–7) prompts Boaz's *commands* to Ruth that she should stick close to his workers with access to their water supply (vv 8–9), leading Ruth to *question* why she, a foreigner, should be so favored (v 10). This triggers Boaz's *answer* praising her faithfulness to Naomi and invoking therefore Yahweh's blessing upon her (vv 11–12), which in turn prompts Ruth's closing *evaluation* of Boaz's kindness and favor through her reply of gratitude and thanks (v 13).

The second episode, vv 14–16, consists more of narrative, less of dialogue, delineating Boaz's further action on Ruth's behalf. In the first, B´, he invites Ruth to join his workers at the noon meal and provides her such an abundance of food that she has an excess left over (v 14). In the second, A´, he gives his workers commands that carry his largesse far beyond the gracious allowances he granted her previously in vv 8–9.

These two episodes are chiastically balanced: A and A´ consist of conversations between Boaz and his workers about Ruth and her gleaning, while B and B´ constitute conversations between Boaz and Ruth in which he accords her extraordinary privileges beyond anything that custom dictated for the destitute who gleaned in Israel's fields.

Comment

4 וְהִנֵּה־בֹעַז בָּא, "And wouldn't you know it, Boaz came." This construction, והנה + subject + verb, does not express chronological sequence with the preceding string of waw-consecutive verbs that form the summary statement closing the previous scene. Further, the form בא can be either the participle or the perfect tense. Campbell argues for the participle, citing a subgroup of והנה clauses "employing the participle only, used when a scene has been set and then just the right thing happens, with little or no lapse of time, and with a distinct hint of wonder at the cause" (93). However, the examples Campbell cites differ from the Ruth passage at one crucial point. In these examples, the והנה clause is preceded either by a series of discrete temporally sequential events that have already been concluded prior to the action reported by the והנה clause (2 Sam 16:1; 18:31; Ruth 4:1), or the narrator explicitly expresses the simultaneity of the events by some such phrase as "was still speaking" or "had not finished speaking" (Gen 24:15; 1 Kgs 1:22, 42). Our passage, however, is preceded by a narrative statement (v 3) that presents a succinct summary and preview of the whole scene. Hence, the action it describes has clearly not been completed when the event introduced by והנה takes place.Thus, it is preferable, in my opinion, to understand the verb בא as a perfect tense. The construction simply leaves unexpressed how long a time elapsed between Ruth's arrival at the field and that of Boaz (contra Sasson, 46, who posits that the phrase means that Ruth and Boaz arrived "within seconds of each other," and de Waard-Nida, 27, who conclude that the perfect tense form of בא suggests that Boaz arrived several hours later).

Campbell is quite right, though, when he observes that the use of והנה imparts "a distinct hint of wonder." The construction is "very freq. in historical style, . . . making the narrative graphic and vivid, and enabling the reader to enter into the surprise or satisfaction of the speaker or actor concerned" (BDB, 244; on such "surprise" clauses, see *SBH,* 94–95). However, the surprise or unexpected element that הנה introduces functions on a number of different levels. Recently Berlin (*Poetics,* 91–95) has provided a very helpful study of these different uses. She distinguishes three such uses in Ruth: (1) in direct discourse as an emphatic, registering attention or surprise, as in 1:15 above; (2) in narration as an indicator of "point of view," i.e., the perspective from which an event or character is viewed, for "a character is not perceived by the reader directly, but rather mediated or filtered through the telling of the (implied) author, the narrator, or another character" (43), e.g., as in 3:8 below; (3) the usage in the verse under consideration. Berlin clearly shows that the use here does not have a chronological function, as most commentators have understood (e.g., NIV "Just then"; TEV "Some time later"; cf. the comments noted above), for the suddenness that it expresses in the presentation of information to the reader (or to a character) "has nothing to do with the time lapse between events; it has to do with the abrupt or unexpected way in which the new fact is introduced in the narrative" (*Poetics,* 93). That is, it again expresses point of view. However, the point of view expressed here is not that of one of the characters of the narrative—certainly not Ruth, for she does not know who Boaz is or that he was coming from Bethlehem (Berlin, *Poetics,* 93–94). Rather, the point of view is that of *the narrator to his reader.* As we noted above in the *Explanation* to the previous scene, the narrator has already piqued our interest by proleptically introducing Boaz to us in a digression (v 1), subtly made us wonder about his connection with the "someone in whose eyes I might find favor" of whom Ruth speaks in v 2, and then heightened our expectation with the information in v 3 that she "happened to come upon" his field. And so now he confirms what we suspected all along with the "surprise" phrase והנה, "And look!" The difficulty is to capture this in translation. Berlin's "At that point" or "Just then" (*Poetics,* 94) does not do well here, for each almost inevitably connotes a temporal sense. To capture the sense of "surprised" (and delighted!) confirmation that our narrator shares with this readers, we suggest "Wouldn't you know it!" or "Of course!"

יְהוָה עִמָּכֶם . . . יְבָרֶכְךָ יְהוָה, "The LORD be with you! . . . The LORD bless you!" When a nominal clause is used to express a wish (*HebS* § 551) and the predicate is a prepositional phrase, the normal order is subject-predicate (*HebS* § 580); hence, there is no emphasis on יהוה in the first clause. Such conventional greetings are still in use in Arabic, e.g., *ʾAllâh maʿak,* "God be with you!" In verbal clauses expressing a wish, the verb is jussive, and the normal order is predicate-subject (*HebS* § 546), as in the second clause.

5 לְמִי הַנַּעֲרָה הַזֹּאת. Boaz's question is not "*Who* is this young woman?" but "*To whom* . . . ?" As Myers observes (*Linguistic and Literary Form,* 23), the construction למי with a personal subject occurs elsewhere only in Gen 32:18; 1 Sam 30:13. On the basis of these passages, Campbell (93–94) argues that the question is more general than simply one of identification and paraphrases it "Where does this young woman fit in?" But Campbell's analysis presents no concrete evidence that the expression means anything more than its literal meaning expresses, "To whom does this young woman belong?" In ancient Israelite society in general, the community to which one belonged—at all levels, family, clan, tribe, nation, village—was central to one's identity and status. To be resident outside that community was to be a גר *gēr,* "resident alien" (see *Comment* on 1:1), without rights and status. In particular, a woman had no independent status and identity in Israel's patriarchal world. She belonged to and lived under the authority of her father when unmarried and her husband when married (cf. Trible, *IDBSup,* 964). Given such an understanding of identity, the question "To whom do you belong?" is quite natural (cf. Gen 32:18; 1 Sam 30:13). Particularly instructive is Saul's question to Abner regarding David: בן־מי־זה הנער, "Whose son is this young man?" (1 Sam 17:55; note 17:56, 58), as well as the question of Abraham's servant to Rebekah: בת־מי את, "Whose daughter are you?" (Gen 24:23). In the case of Ruth, however, Boaz does not know whether to ask "whose daughter" or "whose wife" she is, since she is a stranger. So he must naturally ask the general question. In the light of these considerations, it is most improbable that the question implies that Boaz wished to betray no unseemly curiosity about Ruth's person (Rudolph, 46), since she is a female (Gray, *NCBC,* 391). Finally, that the choice of the term נערה, "young woman," is used designedly by the narrator in order to raise questions in our minds occasioned by the other possible meanings of the word, namely, "(female) servant" or "marriageable young woman" (so Hubbard, 146–47), is most unlikely. It is simply the natural term to use for an unknown young woman (cf. the use of the masculine equivalent for David in 1 Sam 17:55–58). The most that can be said is that it implies Ruth's youth vis-à-vis Boaz.

6 נַעֲרָה מוֹאֲבִיָּה הִיא הַשָּׁבָה . . ., "She is a Moabite young woman—the one who came back . . ." Classifying clauses (*HebS* § 577, distinguished from those that *identify* the subject) normally have an indefinite predicate and the order predicate + subject (*HebS* § 579), as here (cf. 1 Sam 15:29). The form הַשָּׁבָה is again pointed as a perfect (see the *Comment* on 1:22). It seems likely in cases like these that the article loses its determination in a relative force. To translate the phrase as definite ("She is the Moabite young woman who . . . ," so Sasson, 38) is to understand the predicate as an identifying, rather than classifying, clause, which requires not only a definite rather than indefinite predicate but also the order subject + predicate (*HebS* § 578; see also *Note* 6.b.).

7 אֲלַקֳטָה־נָּא וְאָסַפְתִּי בָעֳמָרִים אַחֲרֵי הַקּוֹצְרִים, "May I glean stalks of grain and gather them in bundles behind the reapers?" The Hebrew of v 7 is fraught with problems. It is extremely difficult to make the apparent meaning of this clause fit coherently with the rest of the chapter, and it is very difficult to make sense at all of the rest of the verse as it stands. The meaning and relationship of the first two words is reasonably clear. The cohortative אלקטה־נא is continued by a perfect with waw consecutive, ואספתי, expressing sequence: "I would like to glean and (then) gather." Contrast this with the use in v 2 of a second cohortative (ואלקטה) to continue a previous cohortative (אלכה־נא), a construction that expresses purpose: "I would like to go . . . to glean." The second sequential verb, "and gather," refers to the fact that the work of gleaning involved picking up individual stalks of grain and gathering them into bundles. In this context (see below), it seems far less likely that the sequence is logically consequent, "Let me glean and (so) gather," contra *IBHS* § 32.2.2b.

The force of the phrase ואספתי בעמרים, "and gather them in bundles," however, is unclear in the context and much disputed. It is often rendered "and gather among the sheaves" (NASV; NEB; NIV; RSV; cf. Campbell, 94; Rudolph, 46 n. b; Sasson, 38, 48). The preposition ב can bear the meaning "among" (cf. BDB, 2, p. 88; note esp. 2 Sam 15:31). However, major problems are raised by such a translation. First, it stretches credulity to the breaking point to believe that Ruth would make a request so contrary to customary practice. In OT times, grain was reaped as follows (see Boroswki, *Agriculture,* 57–61; Dalman, *Arbeit und Sitte* 3:41–44, 46–50): The reaper (קצר) grasped a handful of standing grain (קמה) with one hand (Ps 129:7a) and cut it with a sickle (Jer 50:16) held in the other (Isa 17:5; see the illustration in Borowski, *Agriculture,* 59). This handful of cut grain (שבלים—the ears with attached stubs of stalk) was laid on the ground behind him. These "handfuls" were in turn gathered into "bundles" (עמרים; cf. KB[3], 804) by the "bundler [מעמר] who fills his arms" (Ps 129:7b; see esp. plate 5 in Dalman, *Arbeit und Sitte,* vol. 3). These "bundles" were probably then bound into sheaves (אלמים or אלמות, Gen 37:7; Ps 126:6; cf. Borowski, *Agriculture,* 60–61), although it is also possible that עמרים, "bundles," and אלמים, "sheaves," are synonymous. The ordinary privilege of gleaning required that the gleaners work only in that part of the field in which the work of harvesting described above had been completed and the sheaves removed to the threshing floor (see Dalman, *Arbeit und Sitte* 3:46–47, 62; and esp. Deut 24:19; cf. deWaard-Nida, 30; Hubbard, 148, 176; and esp. Joüon, 50). Most probably, this is what is implied by the expression "to glean *behind* (someone)," used by Ruth in v 2 and by the narrator in the summary statement of v 3, and by the expression "follow *behind* the women workers," used by Boaz in his instructions to Ruth in v 9. Ruth was a stranger and a foreigner. It would be almost unthinkable for her to have requested the right to glean "among the sheaves," a right of gleanage that far exceeded anything accorded by custom to native Bethlehemites. It could have caused her only the ill will and enmity of all the other women whom circumstances (cf. Deut 24:19) had also driven to the exigencies of the poverty stricken. Indeed, if the above interpretation is correct, then the rendering of v 7 by "may I glean and gather *among* the sheaves *behind* the reapers" is simply a contradiction in terms. In this light, it is not insignificant to note that the expression "behind the reapers" or its equivalent is missing in v 15, where Boaz does command his workers to let Ruth "glean between the sheaves." And finally, it is incongruous for Ruth to request this privilege here in v 7 and for Boaz not to grant it until v 15 after the break for the noon meal (v 14). Consequently, most commentators have sought a meaning for the expression other than "glean *among* the sheaves."

However, two recent commentators, Sasson and Hubbard, have attempted with considerable insight and ingenuity to make this translation fit with a coherent interpretation of the chapter. Both have followed the lead of Campbell, who wonders whether we should not understand the verse to mean that Ruth asked for permission to glean among the sheaves but had received no answer from the overseer, "because the owner of the crop had not yet arrived, and in the overseer's view the owner alone was the one to grant it" (Campbell, 96). In favor of this view, Campbell argues, is the possibility that the following phrase, ותבוא ותעמוד,

can then be taken "in its literal and regular sense: 'she arrived and has stood waiting for permission before she begins . . .'" (96; see the discussion below). Although suggesting that Boaz gave his permission in the sequel, Campbell does not offer a complete interpretation of the scene. He only notes that the proposal requires understanding v 3a to be a summary of the action that the whole episode spells out. In particular, he does not discuss the phrase ואספתי בעמרים in connection with the hypothesis and, indeed, seems to imply that Ruth requested only the ordinary rights of gleanage.

Sasson (44–48), however, takes the proposal that one step further. He understands ואספתי בעמרים to mean "and gather among the sheaves," and with Campbell he takes ותעמוד to mean "she stood waiting," to which clause he joins the following temporal phrases, yielding the translation "She requested permission to glean, and to gather grain among the sheaves behind the reapers. She arrived and has been waiting from daybreak until now" (38). On the basis of this interpretation, Sasson (47) posits that Ruth "was deliberately presenting the overseer with a request he was not in a position to grant," to glean among the sheaves themselves, rather than in that part of the field where the harvesting had been completed and the sheaves removed to the threshing floor. He uses this understanding to buttress his view, discussed above, that Ruth with Naomi's collusion deliberately set out to meet Boaz and gain his favor. For, by making a request that could not be fulfilled by a mere overseer, she "was assured of meeting Boaz, since the latter could hardly fail to notice her as she stood by" (48). In Sasson's view of the continuation of the scene (48–57), Boaz does not immediately respond to Ruth's request. In the dialogue that follows (vv 8–13), he grants her only the ordinary rights of gleanage (49–50), which Ruth then set about doing at the conclusion of her conversation with him recorded in vv 8–13 (44, 49). It is only after pondering her request during the rest of the morning and during the break for the noon meal (54–55) that in v 15, after the meal, Boaz finally grants her request (56).

But this interpretation fails to give a coherent understanding of the scene at very significant points. First, it must be said that, although v 3a is a summary statement for which this whole scene spells out the details (see *Comment* above), its most natural implication is that the gleaning of which the narrator there speaks is in process as he tells us of Boaz's arrival in v 4. Sasson himself feels the force of this, commenting about v 3: "Ruth arrives at the fields and begins gleaning." Since, however, this does not fit with his view that "Ruth did not begin gleaning until after her interview with Boaz," he suggests that it may be best to translate the verse "She proceeded to begin gleaning in the field behind the reapers" (44). It is hard indeed to see how this either fits the Hebrew or implies that Ruth did not begin gleaning until much later. Second, if Boaz accorded Ruth only the ordinary rights of gleanage in his response in vv 8–9 instead of the special request to glean between the sheaves, it is very hard to understand her dramatic and astonished response to him in v 10, in which she prostrates herself on the ground and asks, incredulously, "How have I earned your favor so that you pay such attention to me. . . ?" (see the discussion below). This is hardly what one would expect if her request had not at all been met, and Sasson recognizes the incongruity, for he observes, rather understatedly, that her action "is somewhat an exaggerated display of gratitude for the limited amount of privilege which Boaz granted Ruth" (51). Third, if Ruth began gleaning according to the normal pattern after her conversation with Boaz in vv 8–13, it is surprising that the narrator says nothing whatsoever about it. Indeed, the abrupt transition from the morning's conversation in vv 8–13 and Boaz's words to her at the break for the noon meal in v 14 rather clearly imply no change in her activities in the meantime.

Finally, two factors speak conclusively against Sasson's interpretation. First, as Hubbard notes ("The Events of Ruth 2:1–16," 5), Boaz's words of permission in v 15 are directed to his workers, not to Ruth, and only after Ruth got up to resume gleaning. In this view then, Ruth received the answer to her major request indirectly, by overhearing a command directed to others. As Hubbard observes, given the story's pattern of face-to-face dialogues, should we not expect Boaz to answer her directly? Second and most important, as we noted in the *Comment* on vv 1–2 above, Sasson's view that Ruth set out from the beginning deliberately to meet Boaz and gain his favor cannot be sustained. Hence, Ruth cannot have adopted this course in order to meet Boaz, and consequently, we are left without a reason for Ruth to make such a request—a request that, as we noted above, so far exceeded what custom accorded native poor people that it would have been unthinkable for a stranger and a foreigner.

Hubbard (149 n. 41), on the other hand, follows Sasson in understanding Ruth to be requesting in v 7a that she might "glean and gather among the sheaves" and in understanding v 7b to mean that she "stood waiting" for the owner of the field to respond to her request (149, 152). But he departs from Sasson in stating that Boaz grants her request in his first words to her in vv 8–9a (154; also "The Events of Ruth 2:1–16," 8) rather than in v 15b. What, then, of Boaz's command in v 15b, "Let her glean between the sheaves," addressed to his workers after the noon meal reported in v 14? In Hubbard's view (176) this is Boaz's instruction to his workers implementing the permission granted Ruth in vv 8–9a before the meal. And the statement immediately preceding, "She rose to glean" (v 15a), records the *beginning*, finally, of Ruth's gleaning (175, 178). In this view, then, vv 7–16 compose one long, continuous sequence of events in which Ruth's request is reported (v 7), Boaz grants it (vv 8–9), and the conversation occasioned by her surprise at his action ensues (vv 10–13), followed by the report of the noon meal (v 14), the onset of Ruth's gleaning (v 15a), Boaz's instructions to his workers implementing his permission (v 15b), and his further magnanimity toward her (v 16).

But this interpretation, ingenious though it be, likewise seems problematic on several counts. First of all, it is difficult to view vv 7–16 as one long continuous sequence, for the most natural interpretation of the language of v 14, "Then Boaz said to her *at the mealtime*" (see below), implies a break of some length between the previous conversation and that about to ensue. Hubbard himself suggests that they "probably met sometime in mid-morning and shared the meal about midday" (171 n. 2) and speaks of "a pregnant, pause of unknown duration . . . between vv 13 and 14" that "introduced a new short scene" (172). Why, then, did Ruth not set about gleaning in the interim? Indeed, does not Boaz's initial summons, "Come over here and eat," imply that she is then some distance away? Second, Boaz's language in vv 8–9a can only with great difficulty be understood as a response to a request to "glean among the sheaves." It rather comprises instructions that she should limit her gleaning to his field alone. In Hubbard's own words (154), "He formally authorized Ruth to remain in his field." Third, Ruth's dramatic reaction to Boaz's words, in which she is "surprised" and "astonished" (Hubbard, 161) is hard to understand if he has done nothing more than grant her request. It can hardly be explained by his granting her access to his workers' water supply (v 9d). Finally, and most conclusive, since Hubbard (138–39; esp. n. 13) rejects Sasson's view that Ruth deliberately set out to meet Boaz and win his favor, she cannot then have adopted this course in order to meet him. Hence, his view likewise gives no reason that can explain the impropriety of such an action on her part (see the discussion above).

Consequently, it seems most unlikely that a coherent interpretation of the scene can be given if the translation "glean among the sheaves" is adopted, so the phrase must have some other meaning. To begin with, it is not possible to take עמרם, "bundles," as the object of אסף, "to gather," governed by the preposition ב (contra Barthélemy et al., *Preliminary and Interim Report* 2:138), for the verb אסף occurs some eighty times meaning "gather, collect" and never elsewhere governs its object with a preposition. Hence, citing Syr and Vg (see *Note* 7.b.), some have simply omitted the phrase (e.g., JB; TEV; Gerleman; Witzenrath; Dalman, *Arbeit und Sitte* 3:47). Others emend עֳמָרִים to read עֲמִרִים, understood to be a defectively written plural of עָמִיר, "cut grain," meaning "stalks of grain" (Joüon, Rudolph, Haller). Besides the fact that this is purely hypothetical, it also leaves the problem of the anomalous preposition ב unexplained. To take this as another example of the problematic ב participative as in v 2 above (Zenger, 55) does not in the least commend itself. Equally unlikely is the view of those who emend וְאָסַפְתִּי to the feminine plural participle, אֹסְפוֹת, yielding the translation "the women gathering the sheaves," which is then transposed after "behind the reapers" (Hertzberg, Würthwein) or deleted as a gloss (Gray, *CB*). A solution, however, is suggested by the manner in which the verb לקט is used in Ruth. Elsewhere this verb is used ten times, and the object of the gathering or gleaning is always explicitly stated (see, e.g., Lev 19:9, 10; 23:22; Isa 17:5). However, here in Ruth 2, the verb occurs twelve times, and the object "ears of grain" is only once explicitly stated, where (v 2) it is problematically related to the verb by the preposition ב (see *Comment* above). In every other occurrence (vv 3, 7, 8, 15[2x], 16, 17[2x], 18, 19, 23) the object is not stated. In these passages, then, the verb לקט means "to glean ears of grain"; i.e., its object is implied in its specialized sense in this context (which is the case even if בעמרים is taken to mean "among the sheaves"). This being the case, it seems plausible to understand this implied object of the verb אלקטה־נא, "May I glean (ears of grain)," as the understood object of ואספתי, "and gather," and to take the phrase בעמרים as an adverbial expression of manner, "in bundles" (cf. NAB; Barthélemy et al., *Preliminary and Interim Report* 2:138). It is not uncommon for the object to be implied in such a manner as this when the context makes it clear what is meant; cf. the following passage from the Yavneh-Yam inscription (*TSSI* 1:48): ויקצר עבדך ויכל ואסם כימם, "And your servant reaped and measured and stored (grain) for the (agreed) days" (lines 4–5). Further, such a usage fits well within the range of meanings of the preposition ב that *HebS* § 252 terms that of "norm, expressing a state or condition" (contra deWaard-Nida, 88 n. 17; cf. also BDB, I.6, p. 88). Such an understanding provides a reason for the addition of "and gather" to "may I glean," for otherwise the two verbs move in the same semantic field. This, as we shall show below, yields a coherent interpretation of the events of the scene.

וַתָּבוֹא וַתַּעֲמוֹד, "So she came and has remained here." The exact meaning of the remainder of the verse is highly problematic. For a summary of some nineteen different renderings up to 1971, see Lys, *VT* 21 (1971) 497–99. If the conclusions we have come to above are cogent, ותעמוד cannot mean "she has stood waiting" (contra Campbell, Hubbard, Sasson). As these scholars note, Rudolph's rendering, "she has been on her feet" (so NEB), i.e., "working continuously," goes well beyond the attested usage of the verb עמד. However, עמד can bear the meaning "remain, stay" (cf. BDB, 3.b, p. 764; *HALOT* 3.c, p. 841; note Rudolph's literal translation, 46 n. c). In Deut 5:31; 2 Kgs 15:20 it is the antonym of שׁוב, "return," and in Exod 9:28 of שׁלח, "send away." This meaning makes good sense in the context. (Indeed, Rudolph's translation, 47 n. c, is but a contextual rendering of this more literal sense.) In this light, the emendation to the otherwise unattested ותעמור, "she gleaned stalks" (Rudolph, 46), is unnecessary. The statement "And she came and has remained here" is the overseer's way of indicating that Ruth acted upon the implied permission that he gave.

מֵאָז הַבֹּקֶר וְעַד־עַתָּה זֶה שִׁבְתָּה [הבית] מְעָט, "From morning until just now she has stopped only a moment." Since מאז can govern an infinitive (a *verbal* noun: Exod 4:10; Lachish Letters 3:7 [see *TSSI*]), as numerous prepositions do, with the meaning "since, from the time of," there is nothing syntactically problematic (contra Campbell, 95) in finding it governing a *noun* in the same sense (so Rudolph, 46; cf. BDB, 23; *HALOT* אז 4.b, p. 26; as Brockelmann, *Syntax*, § 111e, indicates, מן alone can be used in just the same sense: Gen 46:34; cf. also Joüon, 50). This makes unnecessary the suggested emendation to מאר, "from the light (of)" (Rudolph, 46).

Contrary to the MT pointing, which joins זה to the following words, the words עתה זה probably belong together as an idiom meaning "now, just now" (cf. BDB, 4.h, p. 261; GKC § 136d), rather than understanding זה itself as an adverb of time (joined with the following words, BDB, 4.i, p. 261; so Sasson, 48). The LXX reads *ἑσπέρας*, "evening" (Heb. ערב), for עתה, "now," an impossibility, since ahead lies the noon meal and an afternoon of work (cf. v 17).

It is quite unclear, despite the MT accent on וַתַּעֲמוֹד, which indicates a major break, whether the phrase "from the morning until now" goes with the preceding or following clause, especially since the latter is virtually unintelligible. If our conjecture regarding the meaning of the following clause is anywhere near correct, the phrase is best taken with it, on the grounds that "the emphasis . . . is not upon 'remaining,' but upon the fact that Ruth continued working and thus did not rest from daylight until the time of this conversation between Boaz and the servant" (de Waard-Nida, 30; cf. Gerleman, 23).

The last four words according to the MT accentuation, זה שִׁבְתָּהּ הַבַּיִת מעט, can hardly be original, for "this (or "here" or "now") her sitting the house little" does not make sense. The translation "her sitting (i.e., resting) in the house <has only been> for a moment" (Barthélemy et al., *Preliminary and Interim Report* 2:139) reads much into the Hebrew and cannot fit the context. The problem with the text must have originated prior to the LXX, for the readings of all the ancient versions vary so widely that it is obvious that they represent attempts to deal with a difficult text. None are acceptable alternatives to the MT. For a brief but cogent discussion of the value of these readings, see Beattie's discussion (*ZAW* 89 [1977] 122). Beattie's ingenious solution, in which he interprets the phrase as a pre-

LXX midrashic gloss on ועד עתה, is unconvincing; Hurvitz (*ZAW* 95 [1983] 121–22) shows that Beattie's interpretation of the clause as rabbinic Hebrew is not syntactically acceptable. In addition, one might add that the reason given for providing a gloss on "until now" is implausible; there is no evidence whatever in the rather voluminous midrashic literature for a Hebrew equivalent of the Aramaic verb בות, "to spend the night." Hurvitz (*ZAW* 95 [1983] 122–23) suggests accepting the phrase זֶה שִׁבְתָּהּ הַבַּיִת מְעָט as it stands to mean "Ruth's stay in 'the house' was very brief" (123). He understands its jumbled syntax to be an artistic device of the narrator intended to convey the sense that the overseer "speaks in an apologetic and confused manner because he is not sure whether the 'boss' will approve of the fact that the overseer has given Ruth his permission to stay . . . *inside* the house reserved specifically for Boaz's workers" (122). Apart from the fact that this understanding of the words is overly subtle and requires reading into the scene a scenario for which no other hint exists except the confused phrase itself, it posits the existence of a "house" in the midst of the fields (for criticism of which, see below). Finally, Lys (*VT* 21 [1971] 497–501), followed by Hubbard (150–52), divides the last four words into two separate statements, yielding, "this (field) is ['has been'—Hubbard] her residence; the house little." Besides the difficulty of understanding what a house is doing out in the fields (Hubbard's postulate, 151, that it refers to the house in town where Ruth otherwise stayed is most improbable), and being as cryptic and elliptical as to be virtually unintelligible, such an interpretation, which presumes that Ruth has been standing there waiting all morning, seems precluded by the discussion above.

A tolerable sense may be achieved with little emendation by reading שבתה as שָׁבְתָה, "she stopped/rested." One could then understand הבית as adverbial, "in the house," except that the sense obtained is impossible. First, the normal sense of בית, "house," is excluded, for there could hardly have been a permanent dwelling out in the fields, and, second, there is no precedent anywhere in the OT for translating בית as "hut, shelter" as is often done (cf. in this regard, *TDOT* 2:111–15). As Rudolph notes, even the existence of a hut or shelter seems difficult given its lack of mention in v 14. For this reason, we have followed the large number of translators and commentators who have dropped הבית from the text (e.g., Gerleman, Hertzberg, Joüon, Rudolph, Würthwein, de Waard-Nida, JB, NAB, NEB, RSV, TEV), even though the reason usually given (dittography, since it shares two consonants with שבתה) is forced and improbable. Although rare, the use of מעט in a temporal sense, "a little while," does occur; cf. Job 24:24.

8 הֲלוֹא שָׁמַעַתְּ בִּתִּי, lit. "Have you not heard, my daughter?" Hebrew often uses the negative question in such a way as to be emphatically affirmative. Although it can hardly be said that the interrogative particle itself functions as an interjection (so Zenger, 55), the whole construction certainly has an exclamatory effect: "Listen carefully, my daughter!" The same idiom occurs in v 9 and in 3:1, 2. See GKC § 150e and especially Driver, *JANES* 5 (1973) 107–14.

אַל־תֵּלְכִי לִלְקֹט בְּשָׂדֶה אַחֵר וְגַם לֹא תַעֲבוּרִי מִזֶּה, "Don't go to glean in any other field; indeed, do not go beyond the boundaries of this one." The second clause, וגם לא תעבורי מזה, is usually translated "Do not leave this one," or "Do not go away from here," or the like. When this is done, the sense seems redundant and the order of the two clauses rather incongruous and unnatural, since the first clause says essentially the same thing. One would normally expect the more general request to be stated first: “Don’t leave this field, and don’t go to glean in another” (cf. the comments of de Waard-Nida, 31). The גם, “also,” in the second clause then seems quite superfluous (Campbell) as well. It is simply omitted in almost all the modern translations (e.g., JB, NAB, NEB, NIV, RSV). However, the problems of redundancy and unnatural order do not arise if one understands עבר מן to mean “to go beyond (the limits of).” Thus, note 2 Sam 15:32 , דוד בא עד הראש, “David went as far as the summit,” followed by 16:1, ודוד עבר מעט מהראש, “And David went a little beyond the summit” (cf. Hubbard, 155; and note also 2 Sam 15:24; Cant 3:4). Further, וגם then makes excellent sense in its frequently attested emphatic or intensifying sense “even, just, indeed,” rather than that of addition (cf. *HebS* § 379; and esp. Hubbard, 152 n. 3; note also v 16 below). Boaz’s admonition is necessary since fields in the ancient Near East were separated by no clearly visible boundaries (see the discussion and the examples of Sasson, 45). Hence, Ruth must be careful not to go beyond the boundaries of Boaz’s field and glean unintentionally on an adjoining plot. Such a meaning is corroborated by the fact that Boaz uses the prohibitive form לא plus the imperfect, a more emphatic negative than אל plus the jussive used in the first clause (GKC § 107o; *HebS* § 173). Since Boaz is granting her more than the ordinary rights of gleanage (see below), she must not inadvertently glean in some other field. Further, when this meaning is recognized, כה, “right here,” in the next clause makes perfect sense (contra Joüon, 52; cf. Campbell, 97; Rudolph, 47).

Sasson attempts to understand the verb here in its figurative sense of “transgress, go beyond the limits of (a command or legal precept).” However, besides fitting this context rather poorly, when used in this sense, the verb always governs its object directly, without the preposition מן.

וְכֹה תִדְבָּקִין עִם־נַעֲרֹתָי, “But right here you are to stick close to my young women.” תדבקין represents the use of the imperfect indicative to express a command (*HebS* § 173). It has a stronger force than the imperative, continuing the emphatic command of the previous clause; hence, we have rendered it “You are to . . .” The form תדבקין exhibits the morphology of the second person feminine singular imperfect with the so-called paragogic nun (cf. GKC § 47o; probably, with Myers, *Linguistic and Literary Form,* 17, an archaism). Strikingly, such forms occur in three other places in Ruth, one of which is Ruth’s quote of Boaz’s words (2:21) and two of which are in Naomi’s speech (3:4, 18; cf. Campbell, 97). One can add to this that Boaz also uses two third person masculine singular forms with the same morphology in the very next verse (v 9). Quite remarkably, the idiom here and in 2:21 (where Ruth quotes Boaz) is unusual in another respect: only here does the verb דבק take the preposition עם; elsewhere in the OT it normally takes ב, including two occurrences in Ruth in the author’s narrative framework (1:14; 2:23). The author employs unusual syntax and archaic morphology (as also with Naomi). We shall note similar phenomena in Boaz’s speech below. עם can mean “beside”; see *HebS* § 329; BDB 2, p. 768.

Joüon (52) is puzzled over the feminine plural form נערתי, “my young women.” He notes that the masculine plural form occurs in v 9 and that Ruth uses the masculine plural in v 21, where she quotes to Naomi similar words of Boaz. It is his opinion that if there were both men and women working at the harvesting, Boaz would have told Ruth to go and drink with the women rather than the men (v 9) and that she would have sat down beside the women and not the men (v

14). He thus corrects the text to read the masculine form throughout. Campbell (97), however, is quite correct in observing that the masculine plural forms refer not only to males alone but also to groups composed of both sexes, the context making clear which is meant (cf. also the remarks of Zenger, 53).

Joüon's emendation is not only unnecessary but actually would eliminate the critical and important part of Boaz's instructions. In a discussion of harvesting personnel, G. Dalman (*Arbeit und Sitte* 3:17; cf. also Borowski, *Agriculture,* 59) has observed that the נערות, "women workers," mentioned here would have walked behind the reapers as מעמרות, "bundlers" (Ps 129:7), binding the handfuls of cut grain into sheaves (see the description of harvesting in the *Comment* on v 7 above). Most commentators agree (e.g., Campbell, 98; Gerleman, 23; Gray, 391; Rudolph, 49). Furthermore, the verb he uses is significant. דבק is always used in idioms referring to extremely close physical proximity. In poetic imagery it refers to the clinging of skin to bone (Job 19:20) or stain to the hand (31:7). In 2 Sam 23:10 it refers to a warrior's hand cleaving to the sword from constant use, and it was used above in 1:14 to describe Ruth's clinging to Naomi. Since the semantic range of the word overlaps with that of such English words as "cling, cleave, stick to, hold onto," we have chosen the translation "stick close to" as a suitable and expressive contextual rendering. If this understanding is correct, Boaz is urging Ruth to "stick close to" the women workers who are gathering up the cut grain and binding them into sheaves; i.e., she is to glean in that portion of the field normally off limits to gleaners (cf. also Dalman, *Arbeit und Sitte* 3:62).

9 עֵינַיִךְ בַּשָּׂדֶה אֲשֶׁר־יִקְצֹרוּן וְהָלַכְתְּ אַחֲרֵיהֶן, lit. "Let your eyes be on the field where they [masc pl] are harvesting and go behind them [fem pl]." The first clause cannot be taken as a subordinate circumstantial clause, "keeping your eyes on the field" (contra Campbell, 98; Rudolph, 47; cf. Gerleman, 23). Such circumstantial clauses regularly follow the clauses they modify and are joined to them with the connective וְ (cf. *HebS* § 582). The order here, subject + predicate, is the order expected with desiderative clauses (*HebS* § 551) when the predicate is a prepositional phrase (*HebS* § 580; cf. יהוה עמכם above, v 4).

Although the masculine plural verb form here may be an example of the Hebrew tendency to use the third person masculine plural of the verb in place of the feminine plural (GKC § 145u; *GBH* § 150c), such a tendency seems to be markedly absent in the book of Ruth (see the *Comment* on vv 8; 1:22b). Further, the verb קצר probably refers to the whole process of harvesting performed by both the men and the women. Hence, the subject of the masculine plural verb is doubtless the harvesters en masse. Ruth, then, is to watch closely where "they," i.e., the harvesters, are working but "go behind them [fem pl]," i.e., the young women referred to above. This confirms completely the interpretation offered above that Ruth is being given special privileges. It simply is not possible that the feminine plural here refers to the gleaners (so de Waard-Nida, 31; NEB), for in what sense could they be said to belong to Boaz ("*my* young women," v 8)?

הֲלוֹא צִוִּיתִי אֶת־הַנְּעָרִים לְבִלְתִּי נָגְעֵךְ, lit. "Have I not ordered the young men not to bother you?"—another example of the use of "affirmation by exclamatory negation" (see *Comment* on v 8). The perfect tense of צויתי cannot refer to actions Boaz has previously taken (contra Sasson, 49), for he did not know of Ruth's presence prior to his arrival and, after greeting the harvesters, he has spoken only to his overseer and now to her. Nor can the expression possibly be taken to refer to Boaz's command in v 15, ולא תכלימוה, "and do not rebuke her" (contra Hubbard, 158). Apart from the fact that the verb here, נגע, is different from the one used there, the time gap of some length that is clearly implied between vv 13 and 14 (see above) together with the whole noon meal (v 14) precludes such a reference, for the idiom relates to the present. It is an example of the use of the perfect to express the coincidence of the assertion itself and the accomplishment of the action it expresses (see GKC § 106i; *GBH* §112g; *HebS* § 164). As de Waard-Nida note (89 n. 25), only a few commentators have correctly rendered the present tense of the expression.

נגע means literally "to touch"; see, e.g., Gen 3:3. It can mean "to strike violently, injure" (e.g., Gen 32:26) but also "to trouble, molest, interfere with" (2 Sam 4:10; Jer 12:14). This is the sense it has here. Since Boaz has accorded her the right to "stay close beside" (דבק, v 8) his women workers and so to glean in a portion of the field normally off limits to gleaners, he instructs his workers not to interfere with her. Recognizing this removes the incongruity that troubles Sasson (50), i.e., that of harvesters molesting gleaners exercising their customary rights, and there is no need then to posit with Sasson that the command relates to the permission granted Ruth in the next clause to drink from the harvesters' water supply. The MT accentuation correctly connects the command with the preceding clauses. This recognition also reveals how mistaken is Stager's use of the passage as an illustration of his judgment that "'youths' were often a lecherous lot" (*BASOR* 260 [1985] 26; cf. also *HALOT,* 1.b, p. 668).

וְצָמִת וְהָלַכְתְּ, "If you are thirsty, then go." The conditional relationship is frequently expressed by simple juxtaposition of clauses (*HebS* § 512) and frequently employs the perfect with waw consecutive (GKC § 164b[4]).

וְשָׁתִית מֵאֲשֶׁר יִשְׁאֲבוּן הַנְּעָרִים, lit. "and drink from what the young men have drawn." Noting that nothing in the text indicates water, Joüon (54) suggests that the jars contained wine. Not only is this most improbable, but, as Campbell (98) notes, the verb שׁאב refers exclusively to the drawing of water. On the practice of keeping water in jars on the harvest field because of the heat in Palestine at the time of harvest, see Borowski, *Agriculture,* 61.

10 וַתִּפֹּל עַל־פָּנֶיהָ וַתִּשְׁתַּחוּ אָרְצָה, lit. "She fell on her face and did obeisance to the ground." This action is a gesture that consisted of dropping to the knees and touching the forehead to the ground; see the description and references in *TDOT* 4:250. Although it is usually reserved for deity and royalty, it also is used with lesser personages as a gesture of greeting or paying homage (e.g., Gen 23:7; 33:3; 2 Kgs 2:15; see Gruber, *Aspects of Nonverbal Communication,* 187–99, 303–10). As Gruber shows (98–100), the gesture occurs in Gen 48:12; 2 Kgs 4:37, as well as here, as a posture expressing gratitude.

Both Ruth's action and her accompanying words show that she is exceedingly surprised at—indeed can hardly believe—what Boaz has said to her, showing that he must have granted her far more than she had requested. Sasson, however, interprets Boaz's words in the preceding vv 8–9 to mean that he "is permitting little more than the customs of gleaning required of him" and that his speech "shows him exceeding the 'correct' behavior of a *gibbôr ḥayil* by very little indeed" (49). Consequently, Sasson is struck by the incongruity of Ruth's reaction in v 10, deeming it "somewhat an exaggerated display of gratitude" (51). To make sense of such an exaggerated display, he interprets Ruth's words and actions as attempts to "elicit further statements from Boaz" (51), understanding that she is engaged in "overtures" (52) and "in eliciting acts of kindness" from him (53). However, not only are such interpretations far too subtle for statements and actions that are anything but self-serving overtures and are clearly motivated by puzzled gratitude, but all such understandings become utterly unnecessary as soon as it is seen that Boaz has granted privileges that go beyond the normal rights of gleanage (see above). Further, given Sasson's interpretation, Boaz's words in v 11, which Sasson deems "a generous accolade to Ruth's deeds" (52), hardly fit as an answer to her puzzled query if he has not granted her request—and indeed has done nothing more than custom demands.

לְהַכִּירֵנִי וְאָנֹכִי נָכְרִיָּה, "so that you pay such attention to me, though I am a foreigner." The infinitive with ל can express result or consequence (*HebS* § 198). On the meaning, see BDB, 1, p. 648. Given the use of the verb elsewhere (esp. in Ps 142:4), the word is not "bent semantically" (Campbell, 98) to achieve the wordplay.

Many have noted the delightful play on words here—one metaphoric, playing on the two opposing meanings of the root נכר in להכיר, "to recognize, pay attention to," and נכריה, "foreign woman," and the other parasonantic, playing on the recurring consonants *n* and *k* in the three words (see particularly Sasson, Campbell). Daube's suggestion (*Studies in Biblical Law,* 7) that the term is here colored by legal usage, so that it means something like "to acknowledge as . . . גר, as a person to be protected," does not at all fit the context.

The circumstantial clause ואנכי נכריה (*HebS* § 494) is clearly concessive in force, "though I am a foreigner," as such clauses often are (cf. GKC § 141e; *HebS* § 528).

In the light of the identity that will be accorded Ruth by Boaz in chap. 4, it is important to note in passing that there is no indication in this passage that she has the status of "wife of Mahlon."

11 הֻגֵּד הֻגַּד לִי, "I have been fully informed." The force of this common Hebrew emphatic construction depends both on the semantic content of the verb involved and on the context. The same idiom in Josh 9:24 seems to lay stress on the certainty of the fact. Here the stress seems to be much more on the extent of the information Boaz has received (cf. Hubbard, 153 n. 6).

וַתַּעַזְבִי . . ., "how you have left . . ." The waw-consecutive verb here is epexegetical (giving further information); see *GBH* § 118j, where Joüon cites the similar syntax of 1 Kgs 18:13. The LXX uses πῶς, "how." To place an "and" between the two sentences (Campbell, 86, 99) is to obscure the relationship totally.

12 יְשַׁלֵּם יְהוָה פָּעֳלֵךְ, "May Yahweh repay your good deed." The syntax here is not so unique as Campbell (99) alleges. Most often the person repaid, if stated, is expressed by the preposition ל, "to," while the deed or action or situation for which recompense is made is expressed as the direct object of the verb (e.g., Job 34:11; Jer 51:34). The use of the preposition כ, "according to," to introduce the action for which the recompense is to be made is in reality a different, though related, form. Campbell's suggestion (99–100) that the noun פֹּעַל is an archaic word that has a renaissance in the exilic period has much merit.

13 אֶמְצָא־חֵן בְּעֵינֶיךָ אֲדֹנִי, "You are most gracious, sir." The exact force of these words is much disputed. Since the verb is in the imperfect, the expression does not refer to what has already transpired between Boaz and Ruth, for that would use the perfect, and, besides, this has already been expressed by Ruth in v 10. The form grammatically could simply be making a declarative statement about the present,

"I am finding favor in your eyes" (so Moffatt). But this seems excluded by v 10, in which Ruth states that she has already earned Boaz's favor. The form could be taken as a cohortative since ל״א verbs such as מצא rarely add the cohortative ה when used with the cohortative force (see *GBH* § 114b n. 1). In this sense, it would express a wish for the present or future, "May I find favor in your eyes" (cf. Hubbard, 153 n. 9). But again, such a wish seems out of place given Ruth's statement in v 10. Further, all such senses fit poorly with the causal clauses that follow. By far the best interpretation is that of A. Ehrlich, who understands the phrase as an expression of thanks (*Randglossen zur hebräischen Bibel,* 7:24; see *HALOT,* 2, p. 332; cf. also Gerleman, Rudolph, de Waard-Nida), in much the same way that English "You are most gracious, sir!" expresses thanks. That the phrase is used in this sense seems most clear from such contexts as Gen 47:25; 1 Sam 1:18 (cf. the remarks of Alter, *Art,* 85); 2 Sam 16:4. Not only is an expression of thanks most natural and fitting now that Ruth knows the reason for Boaz's remarkable beneficence, but it also accords well with the causal clauses introduced by כי, "because, for," that follow. Sasson's translation, "I must have pleased you," receives no corroboration from his grammatical discussion (53) and seems dictated by the needs of his theory that Ruth is "eliciting acts of kindness from Boaz."

כִּי נִחַמְתָּנִי וְכִי דִבַּרְתָּ עַל־לֵב שִׁפְחָתֶךָ, "for you have eased my mind and given encouragement to your maidservant." The piel of נחם most often refers to the comforting or consoling of the bereaved (Gen 37:35), but the verb can have the more general sense of "reassure, relieve the mind"; cf. Gen 50:21, where Joseph reassures his brothers regarding his intentions toward them after the death of their father. This is a most helpful context for our Ruth passage, for the parallel expression there is likewise דבר על לב, literally "speak to the heart (of)." As Campbell notes, this idiom has a wide range of meanings: (1) "to speak tenderly" to a woman (to win her affection and consent, Gen 34:3; Judg 19:3; Hos 2:16); (2) "to speak compassionately" to someone in deep affliction and distress (Isa 40:2, where it also parallels the piel of נחם, "to console"); or (3) "to speak reassuringly or encouragingly" to those who for various reasons need such (Gen 50:21; 2 Sam 19:8; 2 Chron 32:6), which clearly is the meaning conveyed in our context. Boaz has certainly relieved Ruth's mind and encouraged her, for she is a destitute foreigner who has gone out to glean, ignorant of what she will meet, and Boaz's kindness has just assured the success of her mission.

Ruth here refers to herself as a שפחה, "maidservant," while in 3:9 she uses the closely related term אמה. Although שפחה and אמה are frequently synonymous, there does seem good evidence that שפחה, when used distinctively, is the more deferential term since it refers to women who belong to the lowest rung of the social ladder (cf. 1 Sam 26:41, and see the helpful comments of Sasson, 53–54). Although the choice of terms here does permit the play on words with משפחה, "clan, subtribe," in 2:1, 3 (so Campbell, 101), it seems more likely that it indicates Ruth's humility: "the designation שפחה, as low as it is, is yet too elevated for her" (Joüon, 57).

וְאָנֹכִי לֹא אֶהְיֶה כְּאַחַת שִׁפְחֹתֶיךָ, "though I myself will never be the equivalent of one of your maidservants." This is another concessive circumstantial clause; see the *Comment* on v 10c above. The tense of the expression לא אהיה is almost invariably taken as present (e.g., Campbell, Gerleman, Rudolph, Sasson). However, Joüon is quite correct when he observes that the normal expression for "I am not" is either אינני or, more emphatically, לא הייתי, using the perfect of a stative verb for a present condition (see *HebS* § 161; GKC § 106g), e.g., Gen 42:31. Joüon thus avoids the present indicative "I am not" in favor of the nuance "I do not claim to be." However, in spite of his appeal to Isa 3:7, such a nuance for the imperfect cannot be established. Apart from some unusual passages in Job, where it is used in contexts that are clearly past tense, the verb form אהיה or its negative לא אהיה is elsewhere (some thirty-seven times) invariably future. In my opinion, that makes it very difficult to take it in any other sense here, a sense that quite fits the context. The force of the expression "though I myself will never *be like* one of your servants" seems best expressed in English by some such translation as "be the equivalent of" or "have the same standing as" (cf. de Waard-Nida). This seems preferable to such a translation as Campbell's: "I am not even (as worthy) as one of your maidservants!"

As Rudolph (47) observes, the phrase is an expression of humility, which is lost by interpreting the לא as some form of emphasizing particle meaning "surely, only" (F. Nötscher, *VT* 4 [1954] 375) or by understanding the passage as the use of the negative to express a strongly affirmative sense ("Shall I indeed not be!" Driver, *JANES* 5 [1973] 108).

14 לְעֵת הָאֹכֶל, "at mealtime." The MT accentuation joins this temporal phrase with the preceding words of the narrator and not with Boaz's words that follow. The OL and the LXX do the opposite. The MT division is followed by all modern translations and commentators. The point is of some importance both for the narrative flow of the text and for its division into episodes. If the temporal phrase is part of Boaz's words, then his instructions to Ruth continue unbroken through the first half of v 14. The resumption of the narrative that occurs with "So she sat down . . ." would then create a clumsy break in the flow of the action from v 4, and the narrative would lose all coherence. Our narrator is far too skillful an artist for such an incongruity! On the contrary, we must understand an unknown interval (Joüon, 57, regards it as "rather considerable") comprising the rest of the morning's work, between the close of the dialogue in v 13 and Boaz's words to Ruth at the noon meal in v 14.

וְטָבַלְתְּ פִּתֵּךְ בַּחֹמֶץ, "and dip your (piece of) bread in the wine vinegar." The exact nature of חמץ, here translated "wine vinegar," is uncertain. From Num 6:3 it is evident that it is a drink that can be made from either wine or שכר, another alcoholic drink; Prov 10:22 indicates that it could set the teeth on edge, while Ps 69:22 suggests it was not a beverage for slaking the thirst (cf. Hubbard, 173). The best we can conclude is that it was a refreshing sour condiment. It is usually translated "vinegar" (cf. Borowski, *Agriculture,* 113). Rudolph (49) notes that the Babylonian Talmud (*b. Šabb.* 113b) states that חמץ is good for countering the heat (cf. Dalman, *Arbeit und Sitte* 3:18).

וַיִּצְבָּט־לָהּ קָלִי, "He handed her some roasted grain." The verb צבט occurs only here in the OT, and its meaning is quite uncertain. It occurs in mishnaic Hebrew with the meaning "seize, grasp," but only in contexts describing that part of a vessel or jar by which it is handled (see Jastrow, *Dictionary* 2:1258). The same basic meaning is suggested by the Ugaritic term *mṣbṭm* (*UT* 19.2139), which occurs in contexts suggesting some such sense as "tongs, handles" (Sasson, 55). The Arabic *ḍbṭ*, "to hold fast," provides evidence in the same direction. But such a meaning does not fit this context at all. One can only surmise that the meaning developed from "hold, handle" to "hand (over), pass," which may well be correct, although we have no evidence at the present time. The same can be said for Gerleman's suggestion (27) that the word has a very specialized meaning connected with the preparation of roasted grain. The LXX and Vg use words with the general meaning of "to heap up," which causes one to suspect that they read the verb as צבר (BDB, 840). A number of translations and commentaries adopt this rendering (e.g., Campbell, Joüon, Rudolph; cf. the discussion of Hubbard, 174). Campbell (103) supports it by observing that it accords with the end of the verse, where Ruth, having eaten her fill, has a surplus. However, the translation "to hand (over)" is not less fitting for this reason, for one only needs to understand that he gave her more than she could eat.

קָלִי, "roasted grain" (on the meaning, see Lev 2:14), has been a very common food in the Near East. Passages such as 1 Sam 17:17; 25:18 demonstrate that it was a staple food for many elements of OT society. Compare also the observation from the nineteenth-century explorer and archeologist Edward Robinson (cited by Joüon, 59–60), who notes that in 1838 in Palestine its use was so ordinary among the laboring classes that it was sold in the marketplace.

וַתֹּאכַל וַתִּשְׂבַּע וַתֹּתַר, lit. "she ate and was satisfied and had some left over." As Sasson notes (56), this sequence of three waw-consecutive verbs, with their terse staccato form, is intended to indicate how generous was the quantity of roasted grain that Boaz gave to Ruth. We have attempted to express this by translating the last verb "and then she still had some left over."

15 גַּם בֵּין הָעֳמָרִים תְּלַקֵּט וְלֹא תַכְלִימוּהָ, "Even between the sheaves themselves, let her glean, and do not scold her." Emphasis is placed upon "even between the sheaves" by placing it first in the clause. The hiphil of כלם can mean "to put to shame, disgrace" (Prov 25:8; 28:7) and "harm, injure" (1 Sam 25:7), but twice in Job, in contexts clearly referring to speech, it means "abuse, reproach, revoke" (Job 11:3; 19:3). Clearly it must have a meaning close to this here. Boaz is not concerned about improper advances from the men (Campbell, 103) or that they will "harm" her (Gerleman, 22; "molest," NJB), or "abuse, revile" her (Rudolph, 46; "insult," NASV), but that they might "scold" or "reproach" her (so RSV, NAB, NEB; cf. Hubbard, 177) for gleaning in a location normally prohibited.

16 וְגַם שֹׁל־תָּשֹׁלּוּ לָהּ מִן־הַצְּבָתִים, "In fact, be sure to pull out some stalks from the handfuls for her." The sense of וגם here is not addition but emphasis (*HebS* § 379), "indeed, in fact," as in v 8 above. Boaz restates exactly what he means by "let her glean between the sheaves." שֹׁל־תָּשֹׁלּוּ can only be the emphatic use of the infinitive absolute with the finite verb. We have rendered its force by the expression "be sure to." The form שֹׁל is normally the form of the infinitive construct of ע״ע verbs, but occasionally it is used for the infinitive absolute (cf. GKC § 113x; BL § 36j´). For the command force of the imperfect indicative, see *HebS* § 173. This is stronger than the imperative; cf. v 8 above.

The precise meaning of this clause is difficult because שלל is used here in a sense it bears nowhere else in the OT, while צבתים occurs only here. שלל occurs only with meanings in the range of "to plunder, despoil." However, Arabic knows a cognate word *sll* with the meaning "draw out (a sword)," and some such meaning seems to fit the context here (contra Joüon, 61). Concerning צבתים, most recent commentators have followed Dalman (*Arbeit und Sitte* 3:42; cf. P. Humbert, *ZAW* 62 [1949–50] 206–7) in understanding, by analogy to Arabic practices, that the word refers to the handfuls of grain held in one hand by the reaper (while he wielded the sickle with the other). This would yield the translation "Pull out (some ears of grain) from the handfuls" (e.g., Campbell, Gerleman, Rudolph, Sasson). This requires that the object of the verb "pull out," translated "some" or "some stalks," be understood from the context. Joüon notes (61) that, in the absence of any other object for the verb, מן־הצבתים would ordinarily be understood to mean "some handfuls" rather than "from the handfuls." However, that Boaz would have instructed them to pull out handfuls from the gathered bundles (עמרים, see above, v 7) surely stretches kindness to the point of incredibility. To have them deliberately leave stalks of grain for her was doubtless itself unprecedented largesse (cf. Rudolph, 50).

וַעֲזַבְתֶּם וְלִקְּטָה. The perfect with waw-consecutive ולקטה here expresses result (cf. *HebS* § 525; *GBH* § 119e). עזב here is not "leave undisturbed, let alone" (BDB, 1.f, p. 737) but "leave behind, abandon" (Joüon, 61–62).

וְלֹא תִגְעֲרוּ־בָהּ, lit. "and do not rebuke her." The verb גער here and in Gen 37:10; Jer 29:27 is usually translated "rebuke, reprimand." MacIntosh (*VT* 19 [1969] 473–74) argues, on the basis of usage elsewhere, that the verb here refers to "angry protest rather than rebuke in a moral, judgmental sense." Since the context shows that Boaz wanted his workers not to reprimand her (because she was gleaning in an otherwise illicit area), the distinction means little. In a more recent study, Kennedy (*JBL* 106 [1987] 60–64) comes to the conclusion on the basis of structural semantics that, in contexts with Yahweh as subject, גער refers to "an explosive blast" of Yahweh's breath that "brings about the total capitulation . . . of the forces of chaos or the human enemy in such a way as to end once and for all the threat posed thereby" (58–59). In applying this to Ruth 2:16, he concludes that in such a context the clause would mean "don't hoot at her or treat her in such a way as to send her away frightened and helpless," i.e., don't rebuke her with loud, angry expostulations.

Explanation

In 2:1–3, the short scene introductory to this act, the narrator skillfully aroused our interest and created suspense by introducing Boaz, a man of standing in the community who is related to Naomi's husband, Elimelech. Interest and suspense are further heightened at the conclusion of the scene when Ruth, having gone out to glean, stumbles unaware upon his field. Having piqued our interest, our narrator does not long leave us hanging; Boaz immediately appears on the scene in v 4, and the possible significance of what is about to transpire is signaled by the "wouldn't you know it!" with which his arrival is introduced. Having put in his appearance, Boaz's first words are an exchange of greetings with his workers (v 4b–c). We must not be misled by this into thinking that our narrator's purpose is to convey to us a chronicle of the events of the day. He intends no such thing: in fact, the specific information given to us about what happened is so minimal as to make a coherent account of these events most difficult indeed. Rather, the whole narrative narrowly and exclusively centers its attention upon the conversation and the relationship between Boaz and Ruth, to the exclusion of all else. Nothing extraneous to this central purpose is included. The greetings of v 4 only build up the suspense already begun (see *Form/Structure/Setting*). But not for long. Boaz immediately queries his overseer about the identity of the unknown young woman he finds gleaning in his field by asking about her origins (v 5). There then follows the tight series of stimulus-response–related dialogues that constitute the rest of the first episode of this scene (vv 5–13; see *Form/Structure/Setting*).

In the first dialogue, the overseer identifies Ruth by national origin, "a Moabite young woman," and by the family to which she, by choice, now belongs, "who returned with Naomi." This was all that he was asked. The rest of his answer, given voluntarily, relates that she asked permission to glean behind the reapers (v 7—on the difficult phrase here, see *Comment*) and goes on to stress at least the length of time she has been there, and probably also (the verse is most unclear, see *Comment*) her diligence in working all morning with hardly a pause.

Boaz then addresses Ruth twice, and she answers twice. His first words to her are not only kindly but generous beyond anything she could have expected from a landowner unknown to her. Not only is she to glean in his field and to be careful not to go beyond its bounds (v 8b–c), but she is to "stick close to" his "women workers" and "follow behind them" (vv 8d–9b); i.e., he grants her the right to glean right beside the women who are binding the cut grain into bundles and sheaves, a region of the field normally off limits to gleaners (see *Comment*). He then orders his men not to interfere with her and gives her access to their water supply (v 9c–d). Ruth can hardly believe her ears. So stunned and puzzled by such unexpected generosity is she that she falls to the ground in gratitude in the oriental posture of obeisance (see *Comment*) and asks how it is that she a foreigner should be so favored (v 10). Boaz's reply constitutes the high point of the scene (vv 11–12). Briefly and in language redolent with praise and admiration, he now affirms as accomplished fact what Ruth in 1:16–17 had solemnly vowed to Naomi in her stirring words of commitment in Moab: "you have left your father and mother and the land of your birth and have come to a people you did not previously know" (v 11). As Trible (177) observes, this description of her actions validates the analogy between Ruth and Abraham that her previous words to Naomi implied. Boaz then beseeches Yahweh to repay her good deed and prays that her reward might "be full from Yahweh, the God of Israel, under whose wings you have come to find shelter" (v 12). Realizing now the basis on which this unknown landowner has been so inexplicably kind and generous, Ruth expresses her thanks and relief (v 13).

It is obvious that Boaz's solicitous attention and kindness to Ruth directly result from his desire to repay her faithfulness and commitment to Naomi. Hence, his own actions already constitute a significant although small step in fulfilling the blessing he is uttering. We the audience suspect that he is to have a much larger role in bringing that blessing into reality! A young woman did indeed commit herself to the life of an old woman rather than to the search for a husband (see *Explanation* to 1:7–19a), but that commitment has now brought the generous and solicitous attention of a "man of substance and standing." Does it presage more? Boaz's blessing hints tantalizingly that it does.

In the second episode (vv 14–17a), Boaz's magnanimity is significantly extended and expanded, almost as if to give concrete reality to the blessings he has just voiced. He welcomes her to the intimate circle of their noon meal, invites her to partake, and bestows so much roasted grain upon her that she eats all she wants and has some left over. Then, when she resumes gleaning, he orders his workers to let her glean between the sheaves themselves without trouble and even commands them without fail to pull out stalks of grain from the handfuls the men cut (see *Comment*) and leave them behind for her—an unheard-of favor! He concludes by charging them once again not to drive her away.

Ruth's reaction to all of this is exemplary: she shows the deference and respect proper to her circumstances as a stranger and a foreigner. Though gleaning was a right accorded the poor by custom (Lev 19:9–10; 23:22; Deut 24:19), she seeks the permission of the overseer before commencing (v 7). In response to Boaz's inexplicable generosity, she expresses commendable and respectable gratitude (v 10), and in response to his words of praise and his blessing, she utters appropriate words of thanks, grounding them in the reassurance and encouragement he has given her, yet conceding that she "will never be the equivalent" even of one of his menial servants. In her first response Ruth makes mention of her status: "though I am a foreigner" (v 10). This concessive clause reveals that, given this status, Ruth finds Boaz's generosity and kindness hard to comprehend, even though it is based on what she has done for her mother-in-law. Sasson (51) is quite right in noting the significance of Humbert's comments ("Art et leçon," 92–93) at this point:

> "the foreigner (*nŏkrî*) is one to whom, etymologically, one pays no attention, that one does not recognize as belonging to him, and here Boaz has clearly paid attention to her, for he has recognized that she belongs to him (*hikkîr*). This statement (v 10) assumes its full import only if Ruth reckons as properly "familial" the reception she has received from Boaz, a reception which astonishes her and for which she asks the reason, since she is still at this moment ignorant of her kinship with this man.

However, Ruth is not, in a calculating manner, "broadly hinting acceptance into Boaz's clan" (Sasson, 51); rather, Ruth recognizes that Boaz is treating her as if she were a "member of the clan" and is utterly nonplussed that he does so. Boaz clearly implies more than Ruth can understand to be possible! And her puzzlement at her familial reception is intended by our author to be a delight to us the audience, for we know full well who Boaz is—our author suggestively introduced him to us at the very beginning of the act. He also intends to hold us in suspense, for surely Ruth must soon learn somehow who this man is, and surely this relationship will result in something more than extraordinary rights of gleanage.

The scene ends with a narrative conclusion that summarizes the rest of the day and brings us to the evening and the end of Ruth's gleaning. With the expectations created by the irony of Ruth's situation—this man treats her like a member of the family, but she has no idea who he is—we anticipate her return to Naomi, who surely will know who Boaz is!

Scene 3
Naomi Evaluates the Meeting: Boaz Is One of Their Redeemers (2:17b–23)

Bibliography

Aejmelaeus, A. "Function and Interpretation of כי in Biblical Hebrew." *JBL* 105 (1986) 193–209. **Albrektson, B.** "The Swedish Old Testament Translation Project: Principles and

Problems." *TPBT* 29 (1978) 101–13. **Barthélemy, B.** et al. *Preliminary and Interim Report on the Hebrew Old Testament Text Project.* Vol. 2. New York: United Bible Societies, 1979. **Beattie, D.** "Redemption in Ruth and Related Matters: A Response to Jack M. Sasson." *JSOT* 5 (1978) 65–68. ———. "Ruth III." *JSOT* 5 (1978) 39–48. **Dalman, G.** *Arbeit und Sitte in Palästina.* Vol. 3. 1933. Repr. Hildesheim: Georg Olms, 1964. **Daube, D.** *Studies in Biblical Law.* London: Cambridge UP, 1947. **Glueck, N.** Ḥesed *in the Bible.* Cincinnati: Hebrew Union College, 1967. **Gunkel, H.** "Ruth." In *Reden und Aufsätze.* Göttingen: Vandenhoeck & Ruprecht, 1913. 69–92. **Mitchell, W. M.** *The Meaning of BRK "To Bless" in the Old Testament.* Atlanta: Scholars, 1987. **Pardee, D. G.** "The Preposition in Ugaritic." *UF* 8 [1976] 221–23. **Rauber, D.** "Literary Values in the Bible: The Book of Ruth." *JBL* 89 (1970) 27–37. **Rebera, B.** "Yahweh or Boaz? Ruth 2:20 Reconsidered." *BT* 36 (1985) 317–27. **Sakenfeld, K.** *The Meaning of Hesed in the Hebrew Bible: A New Inquiry.* Missoula, MT: Scholars, 1978. **Schoors, A.** "The Particle כִּי." *OTS* 21 (1981) 240–76. **Stinespring, W. F.** "Note on Ruth 2:19." *JNES* 3 (1944) 101. **Talmon, S.** "The New Hebrew Letter from the Seventh Century B.C. in Historical Perspective." *BASOR* 176 (1964) 29–38.

Translation

[17b]*And when she threshed the barley she had gleaned,*[a] *it came to a full ephah,*[b] *and*
[18]*she carried it*[a] *into the town. Her mother-in-law saw what she had gleaned, and she brought out and gave to her the food she had left over from her noon meal.*[b]

[19]*So her mother-in-law said to her, "Where did you glean today, and where*[a] *did you work? May he who paid you such attention be blessed!" Then she told her mother-in-law with whom*[b] *she had worked and said, "The name of the man with whom I worked today is Boaz."*

[20]*Naomi said to her daughter-in-law, "May the* LORD *bless him,*[a] *for he has not neglected to show kindness to the living and the dead!"*[b] *Then she*[c] *said to her, "The man is a relative of ours; he is one of those responsible for us."*[d]

[21]*Then Ruth the Moabitess*[a] *said, "Why, he even said to me, 'Stick close to my workers*[b]
until they have completed all my harvest.'" [22]*Then Naomi said to Ruth her daughter-in-law, "Yes, my daughter, the best thing for you is to go out*[a] *with his women workers;*[b] *then no one will harm you in some other field."*

[23]*So she gleaned close beside Boaz's young women*[a] *until the barley and wheat harvests were finished. Then she lived*[b] *at home with her mother-in-law.*

Notes

17b.a. Lit. "what she had gleaned."

17b.b. Lit. "ephah of barley."

18.a. Lit. "She carried it and went."

18.b. Lit. "what she had left over from her being satisfied" (if from the qal inf constr) or "her satiety, abundance" (if from the noun שֹׂבַע). Whichever form one chooses, the reference is to the food she had left over from her noon meal (v 14).

19.a. אָנָה normally means "whither, to where?" (BDB, [a], p. 33). However, in the same way that שָׁמָּה, "thither, to that place," can mean simply "there, in that place" (cf. 1:7), אָנָה here must mean simply "where" (see BDB, [b], p. 33).

19.b. The LXX reads "where she had worked," clearly an accommodation to the form of Naomi's question (Gerleman, Rudolph).

20.a. Lit. "Blessed be he by Yahweh." Again, in a conventional saying like this, "LORD" sounds more natural in translation than Yahweh (see *Note* 2:4.b.).

20.b. Lit. "since he has not forsaken his *ḥesed* with the living and with the dead"; see *Comment.*

20.c. Lit. "Naomi."

20.d. Lit. "he is among our redeemers"; see *Comment.* מִגֹּאֲלֵנוּ must be understood as defective writing for מִגֹּאֲלֵינוּ; i.e., the pl noun plus 1 c pl suff. Such defectively written forms do occur; see GKC § 91k.

21.a. The LXX, Syr, OL, and Vg omit "the Moabitess," and the first three add לחמותה, "to her mother-in-law." MT is to be retained, contra Rudolph, Joüon.

21.b. Lit. "young men/male servants," but it seems very likely that the masc pl is used here to refer to the whole body of reapers, male and female. See *Comment* on v 9.

22.a. Lit. "Best it is, my daughter, that you go out . . ." See *Comment.*

22.b. Lit. "young woman/female servants."

23.a. Lit. "She kept close to Boaz's young women to glean."

23.b. Heb. וַתֵּשֶׁב את־חמותה. A few Heb. MSS read וַתָּשָׁב אל חמותה, "she *returned* to her mother-in-law," a reading that is followed by Vg. As Rudolph observes, such a reading implies that she came home to Naomi each evening, which is self-evident, and so the MT is to be retained.

Form/Structure/Setting

Scene 3, vv 17b–23, forms the epilogue of the second act. The beginning boundary admits to some doubt, since v 17 is transitional in nature. We have chosen to begin the scene with v 17b since v 17a rather clearly forms a closing summary to the main scene describing Ruth's gleaning in the field. V 17b, stressing as it does the large quantity of grain that Ruth threshed from her gleanings, clearly leads into Naomi's surprised reaction and excited questions in v 19. The end of the scene is unmistakable, for it consists of a narrative summary that rounds out the whole act, both by repetition of the old information that Ruth did indeed stay close to Boaz's young women to glean and by introduction of the new information that she did so until the end of the whole spring harvest season and then stayed home with her mother-in-law. The phrase "until the end of the barley harvest" also carries us back to the end of scene 2, when Naomi and Ruth arrived at Bethlehem "at the beginning of the barley harvest" and signals to us that we have in some sense come full circle.

The unity of the section both internally and as part of the whole act comprising chap. 2 is effected by its chronological cohesion with the larger pericope and by the repetition of key terms from the semantic domain of the harvesting and gleaning of grain, both of which are discussed in detail in the introductory scene above. In addition, the section repeats references to the food Ruth had "left over from her noon meal" (v 18; cf. v 14); Naomi echoes her daughter-in-law's words (v 10) in blessing the one who "gave her such attention" (v 19), and twice the passage speaks of "sticking close to" Boaz's workers (vv 21, 23), repeating Boaz's earlier admonition (v 8).

The narrative introduction (vv 17b–18) and the narrative summary (v 23) enclose a dialogue between Ruth and Naomi that exhibits a chiastic structure with the high point at the center being Naomi's revelation to Ruth of Boaz's family and social relationship to them (see the table). In dialogue A–B Naomi begins with excited questions prompted by the large quantity of grain and the left-over food Ruth brought home, and Ruth responds by identifying the man with whom she worked. This response is carefully calculated to increase our suspense and interest. The author first makes a narrative statement, "She told her mother-in-law with whom she worked," and then repeats the content by quoting Ruth's exact words, in which she leaves the climactic name of Boaz to the very end! At the center of the chiasm, C, Naomi's reply follows a similar pattern (see also Trible,

179), first blessing Boaz before stating the crucial information that he is a relative and a redeemer. The narrator even separates the blessing of Boaz and his identity into two separate statements, further highlighting who he is. Dialogue B´–A´ creates the chiastic structure that gives prominence to C since this time Ruth begins the exchange by responding almost wonderingly to Naomi's revelation with the statement about Boaz's invitation to glean with his workers until the end of harvest, to which Naomi responds with a positive evaluation.

The Structure of vv 19–22

		Verses	Content	Function	
Dialogue:	A	19a–b	Naomi asks where Ruth worked and blesses the one who paid her attention.	Question: ↓	Trigger ↓
	B	19c–d	Ruth responds that she worked with a man named Boaz.	Answer	Response / Trigger ↓
	C	20a–b	Naomi blesses Boaz and informs Ruth he is a relative and redeemer.	Statement:	Response / Trigger ↓
Dialogue:	B´	21	Ruth responds that Boaz told her to stay with his workers until the end of the harvest.	Statement: ↓	Response / Trigger ↓
	A´	22	Naomi agrees that Ruth should stay with Boaz's young women.	Evaluation	Response

Comment

17b וַתַּחְבֹּט אֵת אֲשֶׁר־לִקֵּטָה, lit. "she beat out what she had gleaned." The verb חבט means literally "to beat" and refers to the practice of threshing small quantities of grain by beating the stalks and ears with a stick (cf. Judg 6:11; for the use of a stick, cf. the "beating out" of seeds of certain spices in Isa 28:27). On the practice in antiquity, see Borowski, *Agriculture,* 63; Dalman, *Arbeit und Sitte* 3:61, 92, especially plate 25.

וַיְהִי כְּאֵיפָה שְׂעֹרִים, "and it came to a full ephah (of barley)." Although the preposition כ here is almost invariably taken in its fairly common sense of "about, approximately" (cf. *HebS* § 257), Campbell notes with approval the suggestion of Talmon on the basis of a usage in the Yavneh-Yam inscription (*BASOR* 176 [1964] 33) that the preposition כ here should carry the meaning "exactly" (the so-called *kaph veritatis*). Since the point in this passage is to stress the extremely large amount of grain that Ruth threshed from her gleanings, this is just the meaning the context requires.

An ephah was a dry measure equivalent to one tenth of a homer, the homer (חֹמֶר *ḥōmer*) being the amount that one donkey (חֲמוֹר *ḥămôr*) could carry. Obviously it was a substantial amount for one woman to glean in one day, but determining the size of the ephah in modern equivalents has not yet been possible with certainty, particularly since the size may have varied throughout the long course of OT history (note esp. the well-taken caveat of de Vaux, *Ancient Israel,* 201–2). Two different estimates are currently in vogue (see *IDB* 4:834; Campbell, 104, gives a full discussion), on the basis of which an ephah would be equivalent to either 22 or 36.4 liters respectively (approximately 5.8 or 9.6 U.S. gallons). On the basis of United States government standards, these quantities of barley would weigh slightly less than thirty or fifty pounds! Whatever may be the accuracy of these estimates, the amount is clearly intended to be extremely large for one day's gleaning, particularly given the estimate cited by Sasson (57) that the ration of grain per day for a male worker at Mari in the Old Babylonian period rarely exceeded one to two pounds. (Cf. also the remarks of Hubbard, 179.)

18 וַתֵּרֶא חֲמוֹתָהּ, "Her mother-in-law saw." Syr and Vg do not read the qal וַתֵּרֶא, "(her mother-in-law) saw," of the MT but the hiphil וַתַּרְא, "she showed (her mother-in-law)," as do a very few Hebrew MSS (see Campbell). Many modern commentaries and translations adopt the change (e.g., Gerleman, Rudolph, de Waard-Nida, JB, NAB, RSV, TEV), on the grounds that the same subject throughout the verse creates a smoother text (e.g., Rudolph, de Waard-Nida, Zenger). However, the lack of את, the sign of the definite direct object, before חמותה, "her mother-in-law," and the criterion that the more difficult reading is to be preferred strongly favors the MT pointing (so also Campbell, Joüon, Sasson; Barthélemy et al., *Preliminary and Interim Report* 2:140; cf. NRSV).

19 אֵיפֹה לִקַּטְתְּ הַיּוֹם וְאָנָה עָשִׂית, "Where did you glean today, and where did you work?" The apparent redundancy of the two questions has occasioned problems for translators. Joüon, for example, emends the second to read ואת־מי, "with whom," instead of "where." The two questions seem to our manner of thinking to be in the wrong order, since the more general question should come first (de Waard-Nida). Gerleman, therefore, understands אנה in its more usual sense of "whither" (see *Note* 2:19.a.) and treats the sentence as a condensed way of speaking: "whither (did you go and) did you work?" (accepted by de Waard-Nida; cf. NAB). However, the redundancy can be understood perfectly well in context as a prolix way of speaking (Rudolph) occasioned by Naomi's amazement at the quantity of grain and food that she has just seen (v 18). That the two questions do not inquire after a geographical location, but about the owner of the field, is made clear by the blessing that follows (cf. Zenger, 60). Stinespring's proposal to render אנה with "to what purpose" (*JNES* 3 [1944] 101) makes no sense in the context.

יְהִי מַכִּירֵךְ בָּרוּךְ, lit. "Let-be he-who-noticed-you blessed." As Campbell notes, this form of the blessing formula, using the jussive of the verb "to be," יהי, occurs outside this passage only in 1 Kgs 10:9 (= 2 Chron 9:8) and Prov 5:18. The first passage blesses Yahweh himself and the second "your fountain," a metaphor for a man's wife. It cannot really be said that this is an unusual blessing form except perhaps statistically. It is simply a variant form in which the jussive force is expressed by the verb יהי, "let be," whereas the more common form expresses the wish with a nonverbal clause (ליהוה) X ברוך. "May X be blessed (by Yahweh)" (see *HebS* § 551). The word order here is not unusual (contra Campbell, 105); it is the normal and expected word order in a verbal clause: i.e., verb-subject-predicate/object (cf. יקם יהוה את־דברו, "May Yahweh confirm his word!" 1 Sam 1:23; see *HebS* §§ 184, 546). Thus, there is no emphasis on מכירך, "he who noticed you" (contra Campbell).

וַתַּגֵּד לַחֲמוֹתָהּ אֵת אֲשֶׁר־עָשְׂתָה עִמּוֹ וַתֹּאמֶר שֵׁם הָאִישׁ אֲשֶׁר עָשִׂיתִי עִמּוֹ הַיּוֹם בֹּעַז, "Then she told her mother-in-law with whom she had worked and said, 'The name of the man with whom I worked today is Boaz.'" Both Campbell and Sasson note the redundant nature of the language in these two sentences. To obviate this redundancy, which he believes "may not be legitimate," Sasson (59) seeks to understand the two clauses, אשר עשתה עמו and אשר עשיתי עמו, as identical but for the person of the verb, in two quite different ways, basing his interpretation on the nuance of the meaning of the two verbs הגיד and אמר, which introduce the two clauses. On the basis that הגיד "presumes that an elaborate retelling of events was presented by Ruth upon her return home," he translates the first clause "that which she accomplished with him," and sees it as "but a phrase used to avoid repeating details of Ruth's interview with Boaz" (59). On the basis, however, that the verb אמר is "much more precise, often times demanding that a definite statement follow," he renders the identical clause in the second sentence "with whom I dealt" (57). But the two verbs in and of themselves simply do not bear such narrow and specific meanings. The hiphil verb הגיד in a context such as this simply means "to tell, inform"; in itself it implies nothing whatever about the nature of that which is to be told. In context, this can be a single fact (e.g., Gen 24:23) or an account (e.g., Gen 24:28). Hence, the clause must be translated the same way in both parts of the sentence. Indeed, this seems virtually demanded by the context, for Naomi's question "Where did you work?" is far more plausibly answered by Ruth telling her with whom she worked than by an account of what she accomplished with the man. As Hubbard (184) puts it, "Syntactically, the direct address specified the content of the indirect address (i.e., 'to be specific, she said . . .')." Campbell's assessment of the redundancy (106) is the correct one: our narrator slows his pace once more to gain effect. By repeating the clause "(the man) with whom she worked," a clause replete with the alliterative repetition of shin and ayin (see Porten, *GCA* 7 [1978] 36; Hubbard, 185), he postpones Ruth's revelation of the name to the very end and so creates suspense. Further, by greatly expanding the subject of Ruth's nonverbal identifying sentence (*HebS* § 578) by such repetition, he places great emphasis on the name "Boaz"—an emphasis awaited by us the readers with delighted and expectant anticipation, for we know that Naomi will know who this man is (see *Explanation*)!

20 בָּרוּךְ הוּא לַיהוָה אֲשֶׁר לֹא־עָזַב חַסְדּוֹ אֶת־הַחַיִּים וְאֶת־הַמֵּתִים, "May the LORD bless him, for he has not neglected to show kindness to the living and the dead!" The translation of this sentence depends upon the decision one makes in regard to two grammatical ambiguities. First, it is not clear whether חסדו, "his *ḥesed*," is the subject or object of the verb עזב, "forsake, withhold," and, second, it seems uncertain whether the antecedent of אשר, "who," is "Yahweh" or "he" (i.e., Boaz). In regard to the first, there is no substantive difference in meaning whichever way one construes the clause. However, it is far more likely in a context such as this that the verb עזב, "abandon, forsake," would have a personal subject (either Yahweh or Boaz) than an impersonal one (חסד) (cf. the remarks of Hubbard, 185–86).

The second ambiguity, whether the antecedent of אשר is Yahweh or Boaz, has been much debated. In his study of חסד, Glueck argued that Boaz is the antecedent (*Ḥesed in the Bible,* 41–42), his most cogent arguments being the parallelism in content with 1:8 and the parallelism in form with 2 Sam 2:5. In 1:8, the doing of חסד with the living and the dead is predicated of humans, and in 2 Sam 2:5 the antecedent of the אשר clause cannot be Yahweh but only the human subject involved. Most recent commentators have disagreed with Glueck and, with little comment or discussion, have stated that the antecedent must be Yahweh (e.g., Gray, *NCBC,* 393; Hertzberg, 270; Morris, 280; Rudolph, 50; de Waard-Nida, 42). Campbell (106) and Sakenfeld (*The Meaning of Hesed,* 104–7) both argue that Yahweh is the antecedent on the grounds of a comparison with the similar construction in Gen 24:27 (cf. also Gerleman, 28; Zenger, 61), where the antecedent of the relative clause is unmistakably Yahweh. Campbell adds the further grounds that Naomi's blessing is general, not specific, since she speaks of doing *ḥesed* to החים, "the living [masc pl], " a quite general expression, whereas a specific reference to the two women would be feminine plural. In answer to this, however, Rebera (*BT* 36 [1985] 320) correctly observes that the masculine plural החים, "the living," is the only such form available in OT Hebrew to refer to persons, male or female, since the feminine noun (חיה, pl חיות) refers exclusively to animals. In favor of Yahweh as the antecedent, Sakenfeld (106) adds the further grounds that Boaz's action of allowing Ruth to glean a few stalks of grain can hardly be regarded as *ḥesed* to the dead husbands or to Ruth herself. However, this rather badly misjudges the significance of Boaz's actions. In the light of the understanding of the scene worked out above, Naomi can indeed construe Boaz's actions as an act of *ḥesed* (as such an act has been elucidated by Sakenfeld herself, 233–34): (1) Naomi knows they spring from an existing relationship: Boaz is a relative (2:20; cf. Rebera, *BT* 36 [1985] 323–24); (2) it involves an urgent need on the part of the recipient: the two women are destitute and without means; (3) it is a free act on Boaz's part: he has responsibility as a relative, but no legal obligation; and (4) it involves "going beyond the call of duty": from the moment he knew who Ruth was, he treated her in an extraordinarily generous manner (see the last scene). It is not only the large amount of grain that Ruth has gleaned that prompts Naomi's outburst of blessing but also the food Ruth brought home from her noon meal.

Although in v 19 Naomi immediately blesses this unknown person, she cannot yet deem the action *ḥesed.* As soon as she knows it is Boaz, however, a second invocation is called for, blessing him for *ḥesed* because she recognizes that his actions spring from his relationship to both women through his kinship with Elimelech (Rebera, *BT* 36 [1985] 324). Hence, her blessing is followed by her explanation to Ruth that "the man is a relative of ours; he is among those who have the responsibility of redeeming us" (v 20d–e). Boaz's actions then, are very properly deemed *ḥesed* by Naomi.

Regarding the comparison with Gen 24:27, the definitive treatment of Rebera (*BT* 36 [1985] 317–27) has demonstrated that it is erroneous, for Gen 24:27 differs from Ruth 2:20 in both form and function. It is an *ascription of praise to Yahweh,* of the form . . . ברוך יהוה אשר, "blessed be Yahweh who . . . ," in which the אשר

clause states the grounds on which Yahweh is praised (cf. the exactly parallel clause in Ruth 4:14). On the other hand, Ruth 2:20, exactly parallel to 2 Sam 2:5 (contra Zenger, 61), is an *invocation of Yahweh* to bless someone, of the form [N] ברוך . . . ליהוה אשר, "blessed by Yahweh be [N] who . . . ," in which the אשר clause states the grounds on which the invocation of Yahweh for blessing is made (see *TDOT* 2:284). Compare 3:10, where the grounds for the blessing are stated in a separate sentence, but the causal connection is obvious, and 1 Sam 23:21, where the grounds are introduced by כי, "because," rather than אשר. Indeed, as Rebera (*BT* 36 [1985] 323) points out, אשר in Ruth 2:20 could well be taken as a causal connective, "since . . . ," making the grounds explicit, as many translations do in 2 Sam 2:5. Further, the idiom עזב מעם in Gen 24:27 is *not* a synonym of עזב את in Ruth 2:20 (contra Campbell, 106). The preposition מעם invariably means "from," involving a sense of motion, action, direction, or source (see *HALOT,* עִם 4, p. 840). Hence, the idiom עזב מעם can only mean something like "withhold from" (= "refuse, deny," *HALOT,* עזב 4, p. 807), as the very similar idioms כרת חסד מעם/הסיר, "remove/cut off *ḥesed* from" (1 Sam 20:15; 2 Sam 7:15), show.

Finally, in *IBHS* § 11.2.10.d, p. 207, the phrase is translated, "May he be pronounced blessed *to* Yahweh" and not "*by* Yahweh." This is based upon the view of D. G. Pardee (*UF* 8 [1976] 221–23) that the construction is the passivization of the active construction "I bless him to Yahweh," i.e., "I commend him for blessing to Yahweh," and not of "May Yahweh bless him," because of the appearance of this active construction, i.e., ברוך + personal name + [ל + divine name], in Ugaritic, Phoenician, Aramaic, and the Hebrew of the Arad letters (cf. Scharbert, *TDOT* II.1.i, 2:287). If such an analysis is correct, it makes virtually certain that the following אשר clause gives the grounds for which the person is commended to Yahweh for blessing rather than being a relative clause modifying Yahweh. However, given the frequency and variety of blessing formulas in the Hebrew of the OT, the complete lack of this active construction therein raises serious questions about the validity of the analysis for OT Hebrew (cf. the remarks of Mitchell, *The Meaning of BRK,* 111–12; Scharbert, *TDOT* 2:287).

In light of the above, it seems unquestionable that Boaz is the antecedent of the relative clause. Of all the modern renditions, only NIV has correctly so translated. The clause [N] עזב חסדו את, lit. "he forsook his *ḥesed* with (someone)," is an antonym of [N] עשׂה חסד את, "to do *ḥesed* with (someone)." We have therefore rendered it "he has not neglected to show kindness."

קָרוֹב לָנוּ הָאִישׁ מִגֹּאֲלֵנוּ הוּא, lit. "The man is a relative of ours; he is among our redeemers." Naomi explains her blessing of Boaz by observing not only that he is a relative (see 3:1 and *Comment* thereto) but also that he is among their "redeemers" (on the plural form, see *Note* 2:20.d.). The context here makes it clear that Naomi is not using גאל *gôʾēl,* "redeemer," in any of its technical legal senses. When used in this legal sense, it refers to that family member upon whom was incumbent the following: (1) the responsibility to receive the payment of restitution that accompanies a guilt-offering (אשׁם *ʾāšām;* cf. Lev 5:20–26[Eng. 6:1–7]) in the event of the death of the relative to whom this restitution was due (Num 5:5–8); (2) the "redemption of blood," i.e., blood vengeance (Num 35:9–28; Deut 19:6–13); (3) the "redemption of persons," i.e., the responsibility to purchase the manumission of a relative who has been forced by poverty to enter into slavery to a non-Israelite (Lev 25:47–55); (4) "the redemption of land," i.e., the responsibility to purchase family property that, because of poverty, must be or has been sold outside the family (Lev 25:24–25; see the detailed discussion in the *Comment* on 4:4 below). The first three legal obligations of the גאל have no bearing on the events and social situations of the book of Ruth at all. And, although the fourth, the redemption of land, does figure importantly in the legal scene at the gate in chap. 4, that Naomi at this point in time had as a viable option the legal right to the redemption of land to which she then would have rights as the widow of the deceased owner, or in any other capacity, makes nonsense of the story. For if she had such rights, it is incredible that neither she nor Boaz has made any move in the matter, and instead Ruth has been forced to glean in the fields, the vocation of the destitute. No, Naomi is using גאל in a more general sense, that sense with which it is frequently used in reference to God's actions on behalf of his people. In this nontechnical sense, the idea of payment, prominent in the legal meaning, is not involved. David Daube (*Studies in Biblical Law,* 40) has put it well:

> "To buy back" is not a perfectly accurate translation of גאל. It would be safer to translate "to take back," seeing that the word is as often as not employed where he who recovers makes no payment. The word simply denotes the rightful getting back of a person or object that had once belonged to one but had been lost.

In such usage it means "to deliver a member of one's kinship group (family, clan, tribe, or people) from evil of any kind." The evil involved may be general (e.g., all harm, Gen 48:16; distress of various kinds, Ps 107:2; even death and Sheol, Lam 3:53–58; see *TDOT* גאל III.1, 2, 2:352–53), or it may be specific. Several such passages are pertinent to the usage in Ruth. In Ps 72:14 the king is said to redeem the poor and needy from oppression and violence, and in Isa 54:4–8 Yahweh is the גאל who removes the reproach of widowhood from Israel and becomes her husband (cf. Prov 23:11). As Beattie cogently observes (in connection with Ruth's use of גאל in 3:9, *JSOT* 5 [1978] 44):

> Ruth used the word as descriptive of Boaz in the part he has already played in the story. In welcoming Ruth to his fields, feeding her at meal-times and making sure that she gleaned ample grain to sustain herself and her mother-in-law, Boaz could be said to have redeemed Ruth and Naomi from their destitution.

In my opinion, this is just the sense that Naomi uses here in 2:20. It is also in this sense that we must understand the use of גאל in 4:14 to refer to the child born to Ruth and Boaz: he will restore Naomi to life and sustain her old age (v 15a; see *Comment* there; cf. Beattie, *JSOT* 5 [1978] 66). Since there is no similar institution in modern Western society, there is no word in English remotely equivalent. We have chosen to render the plural term here "those responsible for us." In later passages where this translation does not fit well, I use the term "redeemer." On the question of translation, see the helpful remarks of Albrektson, *TPBT* 29 (1978) 106–7.

21 וַתֹּאמֶר רוּת הַמּוֹאֲבִיָּה, "Then Ruth the Moabitess said." It has seemed incongruous to some, apparently including some of the ancient translators (see *Note* 2:21.a.), that Ruth's origin should be mentioned again here (e.g., Rudolph, 51).

Consequently, some modern translators adopt the reading "to her mother-in-law," which replaces "the Moabitess" in the LXX, Syr, and OL (Joüon, Rudolph, JB; NJB includes both!). However, given the account of Ruth's origin in chap. 1, the words of the overseer to Boaz identifying her as "a Moabite young woman who came back with Naomi" (2:6), and Ruth's own stress on her foreignness in her response to Boaz's kindness (2:10), her foreign origin was not only well known to the inhabitants of Bethlehem but would have been clear to the readers of the story as well, whether the author occasionally added the gentilic term or not. Rather, the occasional use of "Ruth the Moabitess" instead of "Ruth" occurs because this is simply her full name. In the Israelite setting where she was a גרה, a "resident alien," the patronymic, the addition of which normally formed the full name with native Israelites, was replaced by the gentilic, in just the same way that most other foreigners who were permanently domiciled in Israel were regularly identified by their country or region of origin. Thus, note "Uriah the Hittite" (2 Sam 11) vis-à-vis "Uriah Son of Shemaiah from Kiriath-jearim" (Jer 26:20–23), or the Philistine "Ittai the Gittite" (2 Sam 15:19–22; 18:2–12) vis-à-vis "Ittai Son of Ribai from Gibeah of Benjamin" (2 Sam 23:29). The family or clan of origin of such foreigners would have had no standing and little meaning in the Israelite setting, so the gentilic replaces the patronymic. In 2 Sam 11 "Uriah the Hittite" is used where the full name is appropriate (vv 3, 6, 21, 24; cf. 2 Sam 12:10); elsewhere either form may be used, but the form without the gentilic is more common, as in Ruth. Thus, Ruth's full name was "Ruth the Moabitess" (exactly as Uriah's was "Uriah the Hittite"), and her full name is used in the narrative where appropriate, as in 1:22 (see *Comment* there) and especially in 4:5, 10, where Boaz identifies her in the formal public setting of the legal assembly. Elsewhere the narrator may use either form of her name. Although it is certainly possible that the choice of the full name over the short form could be used in order to place emphasis upon foreign origin, there is certainly nothing in this context (or in that of v 2 above) that makes such stress the least bit appropriate (contra Hubbard, 190).

גַּם־כִּי אָמַר אֵלַי, "Why, he even said to me." The meaning of the idiom גם כי in this syntactic setting must be determined from context. In its six other occurrences, it functions as a subordinating conjunction introducing concessive clauses (*HebS* § 530), which cannot be the case here. BDB (כִּי 1.d, p. 472) helpfully takes it to be an example of idioms in which כי is added to adverbs or interjections "to add force or distinctness to the affirmation which follows." In this light, it can be taken to be a more emphatic form (since כי is added) of the intensifying use of גם (BDB, 2, p. 169; KB[3], 5, p. 188). It is a synonym, then, of אף כי, which can be used in exactly the same way (e.g., Ezek 23:40; cf. *IBHS* § 39.3.4.d). This sense eminently fits the context: having learned who Boaz is, Ruth is struck by his willingness to grant her the privilege of gleaning right beside his reapers until the harvest is over. This makes much better sense than to use an etymology that gives the phrase the meaning "also (it is) that," i.e., "besides, in addition, moreover" (so BDB, גַּם 6, p. 169; cf. *GBH* § 157a n. 2; Schoors, *OTS* 21 [1981] 261; yet see n. 119), adopted by Gerleman, Joüon, Rudolph, JB, NJB, NASV, RSV. Ruth is not so much adding a new piece of information to her report to Naomi as she is expressing understanding of Boaz's actions, now that she knows of his relationship to them, including the fact that he has accorded her the same extraordinary gleaning rights (דבק עם; see *Comment* on v 8d) throughout the rest of the harvest. Consequently, we have rendered the phrase, "Why, he even said to me." NEB catches the force well (contra de Waard-Nida, 93 n. 78) with "And what is more . . ."; cf. NAB, NIV.

עַד אִם־כִּלּוּ אֵת כָּל־הַקָּצִיר אֲשֶׁר־לִי, "until they have completed all my harvest." עד אם is a rare form of the conjunction עד, "until," governing a verb, which usually has the form עד אשר (BDB, II Conj. 1.a, b, pp. 724–25). Normally our author uses עד אשר (1:13; 3:18) or עד plus the infinitive (1:19; 2:23; 3:3) to express this same sense (Joüon, 65). Given the expression עד־כלות, "until (they) finished," in the author's narrative summary in v 23, it is hard to avoid the conclusion that this is another example of unusual speech on the part of Boaz (here quoted by Ruth), as Campbell (107) notes. Williams (*HebS* § 457) understands the particle אם to introduce an element of doubt, citing this passage, but there is surely none such in this context (or in Gen 24:19, 33; Isa 30:17?).

Twice in these last two clauses, in words of Boaz quoted by Ruth, Boaz avoids the simple pronominal suffix in favor of the expanded form אשר־לי, "which is mine." This is considered to be emphatic by Rudolph (51; cf. Hubbard, 190 n. 44), but he must then delete the second occurrence since there is patently no need for emphasis on the pronoun in "my harvest" (cf. also, Witzenrath, 15). GKC (§ 135m n. 3) simply lists the form as a free variant of the simple preposition; i.e., it is purely a matter of style. We agree with Campbell that it is chosen by our author to give Boaz's speech a stilted, formal style.

22 טוֹב בִּתִּי כִּי תֵצְאִי עִם־נַעֲרוֹתָיו, lit. "Best is it, my daughter, that you go out with his young women." טוב must be understood as the comparative/superlative use of the adjective (see *GBH* § 141g). As Joüon points out, when the comparison has a single member (i.e., when that to which the comparison is made is omitted), the simple adjectival form must suffice; cf. 2 Sam 18:3 (Joüon, Rudolph). This is a far preferable understanding of the construction than to consider טוב as an expletive "good!" followed by the emphatic כי, "indeed" (given as alternative renderings by Campbell, 107; Sasson, 62), especially given the questions raised about the emphatic use of כי by Aejmelaeus (*JBL* 105 [1986] 204–5). Finally, since there is no appreciable difference morphologically between the comparative and the superlative in Hebrew, this is best taken as a superlative (so NEB).

Although Boaz's words in v 21, quoted by Ruth, speak of נערים, which we have interpreted to refer to the whole group of harvesters, men and women, Naomi in her response speaks specifically of the נערות, the "young women." As Campbell (107) notes, her counsel here is very similar to that of Boaz in v 8. Naomi's use of the term does not mean that she opposes Boaz's women workers to his male workers (contra Hubbard, Rudolph); i.e., "It is better that you go out with his women (rather than his men)." Most likely the reference means nothing more than the fact that Naomi assumes that Ruth's closest and most natural associations would be with the young women who gather the cut grain into bundles and sheaves (see *Comment* above). Indeed, since she uses the verb יצא, "to go out, go forth," she may mean "go forth (to the fields)" with these women.

וְלֹא יִפְגְּעוּ־בָךְ בְּשָׂדֶה אַחֵר, "then no one will harm you in some other field." The verb פגע means "to meet, encounter." When the encounter is with hostile intentions, it can mean "to fall upon, attack." Usually the context makes clear that the intent of the attack is to kill (cf. Judg 15:12 vis-à-vis v 13), but without such implications from context, some phrase must be added to show that death was the result (cf. 1 Kgs 2:25, 46). The verb, then, means "to attack physically with the intent to do harm" (cf. REB). Naomi, consequently, uses a much stronger word than Boaz did in either v 9 or v 15, and it seems unmistakable that she is concerned for Ruth's safety (contra Sasson, 62). Doubtless it was possible that she could be driven off by overzealous harvest hands or other gleaners greedy for the scanty leavings of the reapers. Sasson's attempt (62) to understand the verb to mean "entreat, urge, press," yielding the translation "and not be pressed into another field," is unconvincing, even if פגע could be taken to mean "coerce, compel" rather than "beseech, implore" (cf. 1:16). The meaning "offend, insult" (Rudolph, NAB) is unwarranted. NEB's rendering "let no one catch you" (taking the verb to mean "to meet"?) is most difficult in the context. Does it imply that she should not be apprehended in some other field (that is, by Boaz; so Morris, 281–82)?

23 עַד־כְּלוֹת קְצִיר־הַשְּׂעֹרִים וּקְצִיר הַחִטִּים, "until the barley and wheat harvests were finished." Campbell (108) shows from Deut 16:9–12 and from the Gezer Calendar that the time period from the beginning of barley harvest to the end of the wheat harvest was normally seven weeks, concluding at Pentecost, and that the period of the year was approximately from late April to the beginning of June. For ancient readers of the story, who well knew the length of time involved in these activities of the agricultural year, the point is well made: Ruth has gleaned for a very considerable period—the whole harvest of both crops—but nothing further has developed between her and Boaz. A development that appeared to hold the promise of a solution to their widowed and helpless state seems to have resulted in nothing more than the provision of food for a season.

There is a problem raised, however, by the statement that Ruth gleaned until the end of the wheat harvest, for the next scene takes place on the threshing floor during the threshing of *barley* (3:2). On these grounds, Gunkel ("Ruth," 75) and Bertholet (410) delete "and the wheat harvest" as a gloss. But there is not a shred of textual evidence to support such surgery. It is entirely possible that the *threshing* of barley continued past the end of the *harvesting* of wheat.

וַתֵּשֶׁב אֶת־חֲמוֹתָהּ. There are two possible ways of understanding this phrase: (1) "And she lived with her mother-in-law" (i.e., while she was gleaning) or (2) "Then she stayed (at home) with her mother-in-law" (i.e., after she finished gleaning). Sasson opts for the first, translating "Meanwhile she lived with her mother-in-law" and arguing that the storyteller is "emphasizing . . . that . . . Ruth was not so completely taken into Boaz's *familia* that she no longer dwelled with Naomi" (62). This interpretation is based on his contention (Sasson, 42–61) that Ruth has cleverly prevailed upon Boaz to accord her status as a member of his family. But, as we have already shown above, this is a misunderstanding of the meaning of Ruth's actions and words. Rather (see *Explanation* to the last scene), Boaz has treated her as a member of his family because of her relationship and commitment to Naomi from the moment that he learned who she was. The most natural understanding of the waw-consecutive form ותשב is to take it in its regular sense of temporal (or logical) sequence, "Then she stayed at home." This sentence in the concluding summary thus makes the same point as the reference to the length of time Ruth gleaned (see above and note the remarks of Hubbard, 193). Although Boaz's relationship to the two widows and his extraordinary kindness to Ruth have hinted strongly that he will play a major role in the solution to their problems, that expectation seems to have died aborning: Ruth and Naomi live together in much the same status as when the chapter opened.

Explanation

In this the concluding scene Ruth and Naomi evaluate the events of the day. Ruth's contribution throughout has been consistent with her character. Her actions have sprung from her loyalty and commitment to Naomi. She went to glean in the field to provide food for the two of them, and, as Trible (180) observes, her response to Naomi's explanation of Boaz's identity bears out her commitment. Hearing that Boaz has the responsibilities of a relative and redeemer, understanding dawns upon her, and suddenly his inexplicable benevolence is comprehensible. Almost wonderingly, she remembers his further words and assures her mother-in-law that their source of sustenance and support will continue throughout the harvest season (v 21). It is very clear, in the light of developments to come, that she does not think of Boaz as a prospective husband for herself or as the means to provide a male heir for the line of her deceased husband. As her first act upon returning home was to give Naomi food (v 18), so now her last words in the scene affirm the continuance of this provision (Trible, 180). This activity she faithfully pursues until the end of both barley and wheat harvests, and then she continues to live with her mother-in-law (v 23).

For Naomi, however, the scene means nothing less than a return to life. She had begun her journey home from Moab with the painful dialogue with Ruth and Orpah that ended with her silent acceptance of Ruth's resolve to return with her (1:8–18), and she had concluded that journey at Bethlehem in the black despair and emptiness that climaxed in open and bitter complaint against Yahweh himself (1:20–21). Even at the beginning of the day, still absorbed in her affliction and emptiness, she had responded to Ruth's proposal to glean in the fields with naught but two brief words of assent (2:2). But now, startled by the large amount of grain Ruth has produced and the quantity of food left over from her meal, Naomi asks excited questions about where Ruth has worked and blesses proleptically whoever it was that paid her such attention. The whole exchange is fraught with delightful irony, for we, the hearers, realize that each of the women knows more than the other: Ruth knows that she worked with Boaz but does not know who Boaz is, while Naomi has no idea that Ruth has worked all day with Boaz, but knows very well who he is! Ruth replies to Naomi's questions unaware of the significance of what has happened and in "enormous and touching innocence" (Rauber, *JBL* 89 [1970] 32) leaves out the name of the man who has been so inexplicably attentive and generous until the very end of her response: "The name of the man with whom I worked today is Boaz!" As soon as Naomi hears that it is Boaz who has showered such kindness and attention upon Ruth, she sees and understands full well the possibilities latent in that reality and so breaks forth into glad words of praise and blessing for him. One cannot but affirm with Rauber (*JBL* 89 [1970] 32) that "with the advent of this understanding comes an upward surge of her spirit, a lifting from the depths . . . and we know that Naomi, who was herself among the dead, lives again." The reason for Naomi's glad cry of blessing she leaves to the end: "The man is a relative of ours; he is among our redeemers." The "redeemer" in Naomi's usage here refers to that family member who has a moral responsibility to come to the aid of family members in need (see *Comment*). As Naomi's glad cry invoking Yahweh to bless Boaz who "has not neglected to show kindness to the living and the dead" has revealed, she recognizes in him not just one who has this responsibility but also one who has clearly signaled that he is willing to meet that responsibility to the full.

Now, as Rebera insightfully observes (*BT* 36 [1985] 324), it is most important for the development of the story to recognize that Naomi blesses *Boaz,* not *Yahweh,* for his *ḥesed* (see *Comment* on v 20). On the one hand, this signal indication of Boaz's willingness to "do *ḥesed,*" i.e., to act sacrificially in a manner faithful to the obligations of his kinship, forms "the logical base upon which the entire strategy, with which the third act begins, depends for its success" (*BT* 36 [1985] 324). On the other hand, this recognition is also important for the correct assessment of the stages in the story's resolution of the death and emptiness that have afflicted Naomi.

> For Naomi, who at 1.20–21 delivers a scathing indictment of Yahweh as her oppressor, to declare the munificence of his *ḥesed* conduct at 2.20 without any redress is to scuttle the plot and reduce everything that follows to a disappointing anticlimax. The vindication of Yahweh is not to be found in the utterances of Naomi but in the utterances of the women in 4.14 to whom Naomi addressed her indictment in 1.20–21. (Rebera, *BT* 36 [1985] 324)

Naomi has indeed come back to life—as her glad cry of blessing for Boaz reveals—but at this stage of the story it is a rebirth of hope. "Yahweh had seen to the needs of his people by giving them food" (1:6c), and now Boaz's *ḥesed* has given them a share in that provision. Naomi's new life springs from the hope that these actions may presage further acts of *ḥesed.* Does she perhaps hope that they might even go so far as to relieve the death and emptiness that childlessness and widowhood represented for these women who live in a man's world? That she identifies him as "one of our redeemers" perhaps hints that she does.

The conclusion of this scene, however, presents to us suddenly a most puzzling impression of Boaz. Our narrator very carefully and deliberately drew our attention to him at the very beginning of the act. He introduced him to us in a digression that was well calculated to raise intriguing possibilities and so to incite our interest: Boaz is a man of substance and standing in the community from the same "clan" as Elimelech and so related to Naomi (v 1). Our interest was further heightened when Ruth, going out to glean unaware, happened "by chance" across his field. Boaz then immediately put in his appearance, and his almost excessive kindness and benevolence to Ruth have further sustained our interest and curiosity. And now Naomi's sudden return to life and hope at the mention of his name and her revelation that he is one of a group of relatives with socially imposed responsibilities for her and Ruth have virtually confirmed our impression that in this man will lie the solution to their problems. Yet, with the concluding verse of this scene, our narrator brings the whole forward thrust of the narrative suddenly and completely to a halt. "So she gleaned close to Boaz's young women," he tells us, "until the barley and wheat harvests were finished"—a period of some seven weeks!—"and then she lived at home with her mother-in-law"! Once again they exist in much the same state as when they first returned home from Moab, for the end of the harvest season must ultimately mean for them the return of famine and emptiness. At the end of chap. 1 the narrator presaged hope (1:22c), while Naomi languished in bitter despair (1:20–21); here at the end of chap. 2 Naomi lives again (2:20), but our narrator has returned us full circle to the clouded and uncertain state that existed before Ruth set out to glean (Trible, 181). He drops not a single hint as to how the story will move forward. Further progress toward resolution waits in suspense for an impetus from some quarter, as do we, the hearers. At the beginning of the act, initiative for progress in the story had devolved upon Ruth since Naomi was wrapped up in the silence of her bitter despair. In the next act, however, it will be Naomi, brought to life again by the possibilities latent in Boaz's willingness to "show kindness to the living and the dead," who will provide a new and startling impetus.

Act 3
Naomi Sends Ruth to Boaz on the Threshing Floor (3:1–18)

Scene 1
Naomi Reveals Her Plan for a Home and Husband for Ruth (3:1–5)

Bibliography

Anderson, A. A. "The Marriage of Ruth." *JSS* 23 (1978) 171–83. **Bernstein, M. J.** "Two Multivalent Readings in the Ruth Narrative." *JSOT* 50 (1991) 15–26. **Bewer, J. A.** "The Goēl in Ruth 4:14, 15." *AJSL* 20 (1903–4) 202–6. **Borowski, O.** *Agriculture in Iron Age Israel.* Winona Lake, IN: Eisenbrauns, 1987. **Brongers, H. A.** "Bermerkungen zum Gebrauch des Adverbialen *wᵉʿattāh* im Alten Testament." *VT* 15 (1965) 290–99. **Brown, M. L.** "'Is it not?' or 'Indeed!': *HLʾ* in Northwest Semitic." *Maarav* 4 (1987) 201–19. **Dalman, G.** *Arbeit und Sitte im Palästina.* Vol. 3. 1933. Repr. Hildesheim: Georg Olms, 1964. **Dommershausen, W.** "Leitworstil in der Ruthrolle." In *Theologie im Wandel.* Munich-Freiberg: Wewel, 1967. 394–407. **Fewell, D. N.,** and **Gunn, D. M.** "'A Son Is Born to Naomi!': Literary Allusions and Interpretation in the Book of Ruth." *JSOT* 40 (1989) 99–108. **Gow, M.** "Literary Structure in Ruth." *BT* 35 (1980) 309–20. **Green, B.** "The Plot of the Biblical Story of Ruth." *JSOT* 23 (1982) 55–68. **Humbert, P.** "Art et leçon de l'histoire de Ruth." In *Opuscules d'un Hébräisant.* Memoires de l'Université de Neuchâtel 26. Secrétariat de l'Université: Neuchâtel, 1968. 83–110. **Kruger, P. A.** "The Hem of the Garment in Marriage: The Meaning of the Symbolic Gesture in Ruth 3:9 and Ezek. 16:8." *JNWSL* 12 (1984) 79–86. **McDonald, J.** "Some Distinctive Characteristics of Israelite Spoken Hebrew." *BO* 32 (1975) 162–75. **Nielsen, K.** "Le choix contre le droit dans le livre de Ruth." *VT* 35 (1985) 201–12. **Sacon, K.** "The Book of Ruth—Its Literary Structure and Theme." *AJBI* 4 (1978) 3–22.

Translation

1 *Then Naomi, her mother-in-law, said to her, "My daughter, must I not seek* [a] *for you home and husband* [b] *so that all will be well for you?*[c] 2 *So then, is not Boaz, whose young women you have been with, a relative* [a] *of ours?*[b] *And look, tonight he is winnowing barley at the threshing floor.*[c]

3 *"So, wash yourself, put on perfumed oil, put on your dress,*[a] *and go down*[b] *to the threshing floor; but do not make your presence* [c] *known to the man until he has finished eating and drinking.* 4 *Then, when he lies down, note the place where he is lying, and go, uncover his legs and lie down.*[a] *Then he will tell you what to do."*

5 *And Ruth said to her, "All that you say,*[a] *I will do."*

Notes

1.a. Here in vv 1 and 2 we have the Heb. use of the negative question to express a strongly affirmative sense; see *Note* 2:8.a. Whether or not הלא in v 2 is actually a hitherto unrecognized emphatic interjection הלוא, "indeed," and not the interrogative particle ה + the neg. לא, as is argued by Brown (*Maarav* 4 [1978] 218), is immaterial, for the meaning is the same, an emphatic affirmation. The impf (אבקש) in an independent clause in v 1 may express a variety of nuances; here the injunctive force of "must" seems most appropriate (for which see *HebS* § 173; esp. *GBH* § 113m).

1.b. Lit. "a place of rest"; see *Comment.*

1.c. אשר ייטב־לך. Grammatically this relative clause could either be attributive, modifying מנוח, i.e., "a place of rest which will be good for you" (cf. NAB), or adverbial, modifying אבקש and expressing its intended result, i.e., "Must I not seek . . . so that it will go well for you." For the latter, see *HebS* §§ 465, 527. In the context the meaning intended is rather clearly adverbial, particularly since the idiom is almost invariably impersonal (Rudolph, Campbell; contra Zenger, 65).

2.a. מֹדַעְתָּנוּ. The form of the suffix ־ָנוּ instead of ־ֵנוּ occurs only here (except for a doubtful form in Job 22:20); cf. GKC § 91f.

2.b. See *Note* 1.a.

2.c. Lit. "he is winnowing the threshing floor of barley." See *Comment.*

3.a. The K reads the sg, שִׂמְלָתֵךְ, but the Q the pl, שִׂמְלֹתַיִךְ. In the context here, the pl would connote the same sense as Eng. "clothes," which does not fit the context well at all. The same K-Q readings are found in 2 Sam 12:20, where again the K is preferable. See the *Comment.*

3.b. The form of the verb here, וירדתי, preserves the yodh of the original form of the 2nd fem sg ending of the pf tense, i.e., *-tîy*, a form that is also preserved whenever a suffix is added (see GKC § 44h).

3.c. Lit. "do not make yourself known."

4.a. On the yodh attached to the 2nd fem sg suff here, see the remarks in *Note* 3:3.b.

5.a. Q adds the vowels for אֵלַי, "to me," after the verb תאמרי, "you say"; some Heb. MSS have the Q reading, and LXX MSS, OL, and Syr add these words in translation. The K is to be preferred, since the addition of the word is more likely than its omission.

Form/Structure/Setting

The third act consists of 3:1–18. Its structure is completely parallel to the previous act, for it too comprises two shorter scenes, one introductory and the other an epilogue, and a much longer central scene between Ruth and Boaz. In my opinion the material divides most naturally as follows: scene 1, vv 1–5; scene 2, vv 6–15; scene 3, vv 16–18. This division is based on locale and content: scene 1 takes place at Naomi's home and comprises Naomi's advice and instructions to Ruth plus Ruth's statement of compliance; scene 2 takes place on the threshing floor, describing how Ruth carried out Naomi's instructions and how Boaz responded; and scene 3 takes place at Naomi's home once more and comprises Ruth's report of the encounter and Naomi's evaluation. Further, certain formal and structural characteristics corroborate such a division. The first scene is clearly enclosed by the statements "Then Naomi . . . said to her" (v 1) and "Ruth said to her" (v 5). V 6 forms both a transition between the first two scenes and a content summary that, by previewing the events about to transpire, marks the beginning of a new episode. The second scene is enclosed by the statements "So she went down to the threshing floor" (v 6) and "then he went to the city" (v 15) and is marked by its chiastically structured account of Ruth's and Boaz's words and deeds (see *Form/Structure/Setting* thereto). The beginning of the third scene is marked by the statement "She came to her mother-in-law" (v 16). Recently, however, Gow (*BT* 35 [1980] 309–20) and Sacon (*ABJI* 4 [1978] 3–22) have argued for a division based on the temporal sequence, producing the sections (1) at evening, vv 1–7; (2) at midnight, vv 8–14a; and (3) at dawn, vv 14b–18. This, however, accords with neither the content division nor the formal characteristics outlined above.

The Structure of Naomi's Proposal, vv 1a–5

	Form	Verses	Content	Function	
	Narrative	1a	"Naomi . . . said to her"	Introduction	
Naomi's Assertions	Naomi states the problem	1b	בתי הלא אבקש, "My daughter, must I not seek . . ."	A Problem	Trigger
	and posits Boaz as solution	2a	ועתה הלא בעז, "So then, is not Boaz . . ."	B Solution	
Naomi's Instruction	Statement: where Boaz will be	2b	הנה הוא זרה, "Look, he's winnowing . . ."	X	Response
	4 imperatives (waw + perfect)	3a–d	ורחצת וסכת ושמת . . . וירדתי, "Wash, anoint, put on . . . , go down . . ."	Y	
	negative imperative	3e	אל־תודעי, "Do not make yourself known . . ."	Z	
	positive imperative	4b	וידעת, "Then note . . ."	Z´	
	3 imperatives (waw + perfect)	4c–e	ובאת וגלית . . . ושכבתי, "Go, uncover . . . and lie down . . ."	Y´	
	Statement: what Boaz will do	4f	והוא יגיד לך, "And he will tell you . . ."	X´	
	Narrative	5	"Ruth said to her . . . "	Conclusion	

As with the previous act, there is a marked unity to this section, created by the closeness of its chronology and the coherence of its content. The dialogue between Naomi and Ruth in scene 1 takes place during the day. Scene 2 occurs during the ensuing evening, midnight, and dawn, whereas scene 3 transpires at dawn with a reference to an expected dénouement the following day (v 18). As Dommershausen has noted ("Leitwortstil," 402–5), the key terms binding this unit together by their repetition and interrelationship are the following: גרן, "threshing floor" (vv 2, 3, 6, 14), which defines the locale of the action; שכב, "to lie down" (vv 4[3x], 7[2x], 8, 13, 14), and גאל, "to redeem" (9, 12[2x], 13[4x]). שכב and גאל express the principal concepts of the scene that advance the story's plot. שכב, "to lie down," is used not only in its literal meaning "to lie down (to sleep)" but also as an action through which Ruth expresses symbolically her request for marriage to Boaz. In this sense it relates to and moves in the same semantic field as גאל, "to redeem," that of family social responsibilities (see *Comment* and *Explanation*).

The carefully balanced structure of the opening scene comprises Naomi's proposal, vv 1a–4d, and Ruth's acquiescence, v 5. The narrative introductions, "Naomi said to her," v 1a, and "Ruth said to her," v 5a, form an inclusio, framing the scene. In between, Naomi's assertions and instructions form a carefully balanced whole, marked by chiasm (see the table, The Structure of Naomi's Proposal, vv 1a–5). The opening words of her proposal, vv 1b–2a, form a couplet A–B, consisting of a pair of negative questions that actually constitute strong affirmations (see *Note* 1.a.). They relate to one another as problem-solution. These in turn trigger the following set of six clauses, arranged in a closely balanced chiasm effected by both vocabulary and sentence type (cf. the remarks of Zenger, 65).

Comment

1 מָנוֹחַ, "a home and a husband." Here the word מנוח, "place of tranquility and repose," refers to the condition of security and rest afforded a woman in Israelite society by marriage; cf. 1:9. It seems preferable in translation to make the basis of this security explicit since the literal meaning in English, "place of rest," would not be taken to refer to marriage. In the light of what will ensue, let us note here that Naomi's whole concern is her responsibility to see that the destitute state and reproach that widowhood represented in Israelite society is resolved for Ruth. There is absolutely no indication that her real concern—or even a secondary concern—is to provide an heir for the family line of Elimelech.

This must be stressed for it has most often been posited that Naomi's concern here, and indeed her primary concern throughout (see the quote from Pedersen in the *Explanation* to 1:19b–22), was to carry out the levirate obligation and provide a son to carry on the line of Elimelech. Thus, for example, Leggett (*The Levirate*, 189) rightly observes, "the events in chapter three point overwhelmingly to Naomi contemplating the possibility of a marriage between Boaz and Ruth." From this he immediately assumes, without further consideration or discussion of Naomi's purpose in this marriage, that what she is proposing is a *levirate marriage:* "It remains to be seen whether Naomi considers Boaz *bound* to perform the levirate duty or whether one considers it to be his *duty* as goel." (Compare also the remarks of Rudolph, 53–54, Goslinga, 535, Würthwein, 17; cf. Hubbard, 205.)

However, that such motives were primary in the mind of Naomi at this point in the story does not spring from a careful exegesis of the passage but from the a priori view that the marriage of Boaz and Ruth was a levirate marriage. But the text does not suggest in any way that Naomi is concerned here about an heir for the line of Elimelech. Indeed, she gives as the intended result of her seeking a home and husband for Ruth "so that all may be well for you," v 1. If she had in mind an heir for Elimelech, rather than providing for Ruth, surely she would have expressed herself differently, perhaps using language similar to that used by Boaz in 4:5 when he wishes to espouse that very purpose: "so that you may raise up the name of the deceased on his inheritance," or the like. On the contrary, Naomi is narrowly and specifically concerned for the welfare of Ruth. This was realized long ago by Bewer: "the whole story bears witness that Naomi had not been planning how to raise seed for her son Mahlon, but how to secure Ruth's fortune" (*AJSL* 20 [1903–4] 203; cf. also the remarks of Humbert, "Art et leçon," 98). On this score, Trible (192–93) notes that when women speak of marriage, not only here but throughout the book, they do not voice a concern about restoring the name of the dead. Thus, Naomi dismisses her daughters-in-law in chap. 1 with the command that they return home to Moab and beseeches Yahweh to grant each of them security in the house of a husband (1:8–9; cf. the remarks of Anderson, *JSS* 23 [1978] 178). "Even her speculation about a future husband and sons for herself bespeaks concern for her daughters-in-law rather than for the name of her dead husband and sons" (Trible, 192–93). Cf. also our discussion of the meaning of Ruth's request in 3:9.

2 וְעַתָּה הֲלֹא בֹעַז מֹדַעְתָּנוּ, "So then, is not Boaz a relative of ours?" The introductory word ועתה regularly introduces a logical step in an argument, often a consequence or a conclusion; see BDB, 2.a, p. 774. As Brongers (*VT* 15 [1965] 293–94) puts it, the particle "falls back on the past and, making deductions from that, seeks to draw the consequences for the situation in the present or the future." Hence, Naomi is proposing Boaz as the answer to her problem of security and home for Ruth based on the fact that he is a family member, a מודעת. In connection with the view espoused in the comment on v 1 above that Naomi is concerned specifically with a home and husband for Ruth (and not to provide an heir for the family line of Elimelech), it is worth noting here that Naomi does not ground her presentation of Boaz as the answer to her problem of security for Ruth on the fact that he is a גאל *gô᾽ēl*, "redeemer," but only on his position as a מודעת, "relative." Actually, given the understanding of the meaning of Naomi's use of גאל, which we have espoused in 2:20 (and will espouse in 3:9), it would have been quite fitting if she had done so. However, the lack of use of the term here at least prevents those who would say that the duties and obligations of the גאל also included the levirate obligation from claiming that this is a concern of Naomi's here.

מֹדַעְתָּנוּ, "relative of ours." מודעת is the feminine form of מודע, the Q reading that was adopted in 2:1; see *Comment* there. A very few terms that refer to masculine persons can take a feminine ending in Hebrew: e.g., קהלת, "speaker (in the assembly)"; cf. GKC §§ 122p, r, s. The word here seems to be simply a synonym of מודע. Joüon's suggestion (66; cf. *GBH* § 89b), followed by Hubbard (199), that the feminine form here has an intensive force, "near-relative," drawing on Arabic usage, does not commend itself. Campbell's need to emend the text by adding the preposition מן, "from," to the front of the word is based upon his understanding that the feminine term is a collective, naming the larger entity of which מודע, "covenant-brother" (see *Comment* in 2:1), designates a single member. Although the feminine singular substantive (particularly participles) can function as a collective (cf. GKC § 122s), both Campbell's need to emend the text and the tenuous nature of his hypothesis that the meaning of מודע is "covenant-brother" (see *Comment* on 2:1) make this suggestion most unlikely. From context and its clear relation to מודע in 2:1 (see *Comment* there), the word must bear the meaning "relative, kinsman." The word is given considerable stress by a reversal of normal sentence order. It is placed immediately after the subject, ahead of the relative clause "whose young women you have been with," which should normally immediately follow the noun it modifies (cf. Ruth 2:19g; cf. Hubbard, 199 n. 16).

הוּא זֹרֶה אֶת־גֹּרֶן הַשְּׂעֹרִים, "He is winnowing barley at the threshing floor." The literal Hebrew, "He is winnowing the threshing floor of barley," is problematic. If the text is correct, then we must understand גרן, "threshing floor," to stand by metonymy for "the product of the threshing floor," i.e., the threshed grain, consisting of a mixture of straw, chaff, and the kernels of grain that must be separated. Campbell's objection (117), followed by Hubbard (200 n. 18), that there would then be syntactic difficulty with the resulting construct chain is hard to follow, for the addition of "barley" simply specifies which crop (barley or wheat) was being winnowed. It is certainly true, however, that the mention of winnowing barley here seems to create a problem with 2:23, where it was stated that Ruth "gleaned until the barley and wheat harvests were finished." The winnowing of barley must have continued past the end of the harvesting of wheat (cf. the remarks of Zenger, 66). Sasson (130–31) speculates that the mention of barley alone here was intended to signal to the audience the cleverness of Boaz in not waiting until the end of the wheat harvest (some two to four weeks later) to summon the legal assembly and present his case (4:1–12). But, apart from the difficulties with this view raised by Hubbard (200 n. 19), two further considerations make it most improbable. First, it is Naomi who determines the timing of these events, and, as we noted above, her sole concern is the possibility of a marriage for Ruth. Second, the narrator has already informed us that Ruth gleaned in Boaz's field until the end of both barley and wheat harvests and then continued to live at home with her mother-in-law (2:23). Apart from implying that the events here recorded occur after that time, it hardly seems likely that Boaz would have permitted Ruth to continue to glean in the fields like a pauper for several more weeks once he had announced to the legal assembly his commitment to marry her (4:10). To obviate the difficulty, Campbell proposes to read the consonants שערים not as שְׂעֹרִים, "barley," but as שְׁעָרִים, "gates," understanding it to be an adverb designating the locale of the threshing floor. The reading is certainly possible (in unpointed Hebrew texts, sin and shin were undifferentiated), and it is true that in the OT (1 Kgs 22:10) and at Ugarit mention is made of a threshing floor clearly adjacent to a city gate. Nonetheless, Campbell's proposal is not convincing. First, the references to "going down" from the city to the threshing floor in 3:3, 6 show (cf. Sasson, 64; Zenger, 66) that the threshing floor must have been some distance from the city. Second, the use of the plural to refer to a single gate of a city is quite unexampled, both in Ruth (4:1, 10, 11) and in the rest of the OT. Campbell's use of 2 Sam 18:24 to suggest that such is possible is quite irrelevant, for the form there is clearly dual, referring to the recesses of a double- or triple-entry gate (as Campbell himself shows). Third (as Zenger, 66, notes), the text in v 17 would also have to be emended to support Campbell's theory, for it is specifically barley that Boaz gives to Ruth to take with her. The biggest problem with the proposal, however, is that it seems totally superfluous and unnecessary for Naomi to state that the threshing floor was near the city gate, since every resident of Bethlehem would have known full well where it was located.

הַלָּיְלָה, "tonight." As Joüon notes, "tonight" is used here in the sense of "this evening" as also in Josh 2:2. Winnowing in Palestine consisted of throwing the mixture of straw, chaff, and grain up into the wind by means of a fork with large teeth. The chaff was blown away farthest from the winnower, the straw less far, while the heavier kernels of grain fell back onto the threshing floor (cf. Borowski, *Agriculture,* 65–66). The wind necessary for this operation was normally the regular onshore breeze that springs up from the Mediterranean daily about two o'clock in the afternoon and continues through the evening hours until sunset (see Baly, *The Geography of the Bible,* 46). Dalman (*Arbeit und Sitte* 3:127–29) notes that the wind must not be too strong, since then the heavy material is blown away with the light. He notes that in summer the west wind blows very strongly in the afternoon but drops off in the evening, so that the evening hours provide the most desirable wind conditions. If these conditions pertained in the OT period, as seems most probable, then the text is quite accurate in speaking of Boaz winnowing in the evening (contra Campbell). Rudolph notes in this regard the rendering of the Targum, "in the night wind until morning," and Gen 3:8a. Campbell (119) and Hubbard (201 n. 16) may well be right in suggesting that the choice of הלילה, "tonight," rather than הערב, "this evening," may have been dictated by thematic considerations, i.e., to orient the audience to the timing of the scene about to unfold in the dark of the night.

3 וְרָחַצְתְּ, "So, wash yourself." The syntax here is quite unusual in that it begins with a perfect verb form with waw consecutive. As Campbell notes, it is common to have the perfect with waw consecutive *continue* a series begun with imperatives, but it is rare for a series of commands to begin with such a form. Joüon understands the form as a future of command, "you will wash." The usage is usually explained as an independent use of the perfect with the waw consecutive to express a command, developed because it so frequently was used in Hebrew style to continue a series of imperatives (see GKC § 112x, aa).

וָסַכְתְּ, "put on perfumed oil." "Anoint" is not a good translation here because the English word "to anoint" has come to have primarily a technical, religious or ritualistic sense. The verb סוך, however, is used to refer to the application of oil to the body in the regular toilette, and it frequently takes as direct object שמן, "(olive)oil." There can be little doubt that the oil was perfumed (see *IDB* 3:593–95, 732), but it must be stressed in this connection that this was part of the normal toilette for both men and women (cf. Deut 28:40; Mic 6:15; 2 Sam 12:20; 2 Chron 28:15). In a hot climate and in a culture where bathing was only an occasional luxury since water was scarce and personal hygiene was at most in a primitive stage of development, perfumed oil was used as a cosmetic to counteract body odors.

וְשַׂמְתְּ שִׂמְלֹתֵךְ עָלַיִךְ, "put on your dress." The type of garment represented by the word שמלה *śimlāh,* here translated "dress," can be determined with reasonable certainty from its usage in the OT. It was a large, outer (cf. Isa 9:5) garment, doubtless covering the entire body and extending well down on the legs. The size is revealed in Exod 22:25–26, where the word is used to describe the garment of the poor man taken as security for a loan, which must be returned to him before sunset since it is his only covering while sleeping. In v 26 it is specifically called "his שׂמלה for his body" (compare also Gen 9:23). It is also clear that it was a garment that was worn by both men and women, although there apparently were differences between the two (Deut 22:5). In most uses in the OT the word has a generic meaning best translated by English "clothing" (e.g., Gen 35:2; Deut 8:4; 10:18; 22:3; Josh 7:6; Isa 4:1). It is very clear that it does not in *any* context mean "dressy clothes" or "best clothes."

What is Naomi's purpose in instructing Ruth to bathe, put on perfumed oil, and don her שׂמלה? To answer this, commentators have referred to several passages where a similar sequence of actions occurs. The passage most frequently invoked has been Ezek 16:8–12, a passage in which the relationship between Yahweh and Jerusalem is depicted using the metaphor of the espousal of a bride and groom in language that is sexually quite explicit. Since numerous elements of this passage have parallels with this and succeeding verses in Ruth, it is worth quoting the passage in full:

> [8]Then I passed by you and looked, and lo! you were at the age for love. So I spread the skirt of my robe over you and covered your nakedness. I gave you my oath and entered into covenant with you, says the Lord Yahweh, and you became mine. [9]Then I bathed you with water, washed the blood from you, and put perfumed oil upon you. [10]I clothed you with an embroidered dress and fine leather sandals; I dressed you in fine linen and covered you in sumptuous attire. [11]I decked you out in jewelry: I put bracelets on your arms, a chain around your neck, [12]a ring on your nose, earrings in your ears, and a lovely crown upon your head.

Since in vv 9–10 the same three actions of bathing, anointing with oil, and being clothed occur in the same order as in the Ruth passage, a number of scholars have understood Naomi's instructions to be the bride's preparations for marriage, so that Ruth comes to Boaz "so to speak as a bride" (Hertzberg, 274; cf. also, e.g., Humbert, "Art et leçon," 98–99; Sasson, 66–68; Würthwein, 17; Zenger, 66–67). But the two passages differ significantly and critically in the type of clothing named. The bridal preparations involved the wearing of "an embroidered dress, . . . leather sandals, . . . fine linen, and . . . sumptuous attire," together with jewelry of various kinds (Ezek 16:10–12). Naomi, however, simply instructs Ruth to put on the prosaic שׂמלה. And surely for Ruth to appear before Boaz on the threshing floor in her "bridal gown" (so to speak) would have been an action so brazen and malapropos as to produce the opposite effect that Naomi intends! On the other hand, a number of scholars have understood the actions involved to be those a woman engaged in when she was "dressing up" in order to attract a man (Gerleman, 31; Hubbard, 201; Rudolph, 54). In all probability this interpretation also lies behind the translation of שׂמלה, as "best clothes" (NAB, NASV, NIV, RSV, TEV). But again, a woman's preparations and attire when she was seeking to be attractive to men involved much more than simply bathing, putting on perfumed oil, and wearing a שׂמלה. In Jdt 10, Judith prepares herself to "captivate the eyes" (Jdt 10:4) of

Holophernes. Removing the garments of her widowhood, she not only bathed and perfumed herself but also put on "festive attire" (not a שמלה) and "sandals . . . , anklets, bracelets, rings, earrings, and all her other jewelry" (v 4).

There is one passage, however, that is almost directly parallel to Ruth 3:3. In 2 Sam 12:20, when David learned of the death of his child born to Bathsheba, "he washed himself and put on perfumed oil and changed his שמלה." It is also clear from other passages that mourning practices involved refraining from washing oneself or anointing oneself with oil (2 Sam 14:2), together with the wearing of "garments of widowhood" (Gen 38:14, 19) or else the usual garment unwashed for the period of the mourning. Hence, the most likely explanation of Naomi's instructions to Ruth is that they mean that she should end her period of mourning (cf. Green, *JSOT* 23 [1982] 61) and so signal her return to the normal activities and desires of life, which, of course, would include marriage. This change in her appearance, with its symbolic meaning, would indicate to Boaz both her availability and the seriousness of her intentions.

אַל־תִּוָּדְעִי לָאִישׁ עַד כַּלֹּתוֹ לֶאֱכֹל וְלִשְׁתּוֹת, "do not make your presence known to the man until he has finished eating and drinking." As many have noted, the statement "he felt at peace with the world" (lit. "his heart was good") in v 7 shows rather clearly the reason for this advice: Naomi desired Boaz to be in as receptive a mood as possible, a "mellower-than-usual condition" (Campbell, 122).

4 וִיהִי בְשָׁכְבוֹ, lit. "and let it be when he lies down." The form ויהי, waw connective + the qal jussive third person masculine singular from היה, is unusual. The more usual form in such a context would be the waw consecutive + qal perfect (cf. v 13). Thus Joüon (69; cf. *GBH* § 119z) deems it incorrect. But Rudolph's response (52) is certainly apropos: here it is a matter of a command, hence the jussive (cf. also GKC § 112z). Hubbard's suggestion (202), based on the three other occurrences of the form in 1 Sam 10:5; 2 Sam 5:24; 1 Kgs 14:5, that the form is a rhetorical device of spoken Hebrew meaning "Now this is crucial," seems most improbable, particularly in 1 Sam 10:5; 1 Kgs 14:5, where a jussive is quite inappropriate.

וְגִלִּית מַרְגְּלֹתָיו, "uncover his legs." The noun מרגלות is related to the noun רגל, "foot, leg." It is used in three other places in this chapter (vv 7, 8, 14), and elsewhere only in Dan 10:6. In Dan 10:6 it is coordinate with זרעות, "arms," in the description of a man, so that there it clearly means "legs." The *–ôt* ending is a special use of the feminine plural morpheme to designate a plural quality that is not a countable multiplicity but involves some sense on the part of the speaker that the referent is composite (as, e.g., the plural morpheme in such English words as "scissors," "trousers," etc. does), e.g. פנים, "face," מים, "water" (see esp. *IBHS* §§ 7.1d and 7.4.1c; GKC § 124a, b; *HebS* § 11). Similar to מרגלות is the word מראשות, "the region of one's head" (Gen 28:11, 18). Hence מרגלות means "legs, the region of the legs" (cf. Campbell, 121; contra Hubbard, 121 n. 30). As Dan 10:6 shows, it refers to a larger region of the body than the feet, in the same way that רגל can mean "leg, lower leg," as well as "foot" (cf. 1 Sam 17:6; Deut 28:57). Consequently, Naomi most probably means that Ruth should uncover the lower half of Boaz's body and lie down there close beside him, not simply "at his feet" as is often understood (e.g., Morris, 286; Hubbard, 121), so that "both lie beside one another as husband and wife" (Zenger, 67).

Since רגל, "foot, leg," can be used as a euphemism for the sexual organs, male or female (cf. BDB, 1.f, p. 920), some have suggested that מרגלות functions in that same way here (Trible, 198 n. 23). However, there is nothing in the context to suggest such a sense (cf. Sasson, 70), and the clear way in which our author seeks to be provocative by being ambiguous (cf. the remarks of Campbell, 121, 131–32) is strongly against such a view. In fact, one could plausibly argue that our author chose this (rare?) word deliberately in order to avoid the possibility of such an implication, which would clearly have been there if he had used the word רגל, "foot." That sexual overtones are present in the action of a woman uncovering a man's legs in the dark of the night and lying down, there can be no doubt. But, that our author intended the explicitly sexual sense "uncover his genitals and lie down" is in my opinion utterly improbable (see *Explanation*). Equally improbable is the view of Nielsen, *VT* 35 (1985) 204–7. Arguing on the grounds that Ruth's action of uncovering the lower body of a man is the only place in the OT where a woman "uncovers" a man and that such an action is incredible (given the case of the "lady wrestler" in Deut 25:11–12, who is punished by having her hand cut off for seizing the genitals of a man who is fighting with her husband), Nielsen (206) argues that גלה (piel) is to be translated "undress" and that מרגלות is to be taken as adverbial, "at his feet." Since the שׂמלה that Naomi commands Ruth to put on is "the only covering of the poor" (which Nielsen, 205 n. 6, takes literally, citing Exod 22:26; but surely the man who gave up his outer garment as a pledge did not then go about nude?), Ruth then lay down nude at the foot of Boaz's bed, an act that Nielsen adjudges to be "an appropriate manner of indicating her availability"! However, such an interpretation can meet neither the demands of language nor the content of the story. The piel stem of גלה in such a passage as Ruth 3:4, 7 cannot bear the meaning "to undress oneself." The passages cited by Nielsen to establish this meaning use either the hithpael (Gen 9:21) or the niphal stem (Exod 20:26; 2 Sam 6:20). The piel stem of גלה, however, is invariably transitive and hence requires an object to complete its meaning. In the one passage cited by Nielsen in which it does not have an object, Isa 57:8, the context makes it very clear that an object is to be understood, as Nielsen (206) notes. Further, it is quite impossible to understand the syntax of מרגלתיו, "his legs," in any other way than as the direct object of the verb. Nielsen appeals to vv 8, 14 as examples of the use of מרגלתיו as an adverb of place, "where," but the verb in vv 8 and 14 is the intransitive verb שׁכב, "to lie down," a construction that requires that the word be understood adverbially. This construction is in no sense comparable to the transitive construction with גלה in vv 4 and 7. Second, the content of the story precludes such a reading. Boaz does not awake and discover the female form at his legs until "in the middle of the night" (or perhaps "at midnight"?). Are we to presume that Ruth lay naked by his legs throughout the intervening period of, presumably, several hours? Finally, one can only comment that such an action is so inconsistent with the character of Ruth as portrayed in the story as to be utterly implausible. After such an action, one wonders how Boaz could possibly have grounded his assent to her request in the fact that "everyone in town knows that you are a worthy woman" (v 11). Surely such an action would be so much more "unimaginable that the narrator could hardly have made his readers accept it" (Nielsen, 206) than the action of uncovering his legs.

5 כֹּל אֲשֶׁר־תֹּאמְרִי אֶעֱשֶׂה, "All that you say, I will do." Joüon (70) finds this to be a deferential expression specifically relating to the future, since "all that you have just said" would require the perfect. However, the imperfect is used in a similar expression in 2 Sam 9:11 to refer very clearly to the instructions just given by David (cf. Rudolph, 53). Furthermore, Boaz uses the same expression in responding in v 11 to Ruth's request, and it cannot be understood as a "deferential expression specifically relating to the future" on the lips of Boaz. Finally, GKC § 170h lists examples where both perfect and imperfect are used to refer to actions that have just occurred. The sentence order here, object-verb, does not necessarily place emphasis on the object, for such inverted order seems to be the norm in spoken Hebrew (see McDonald, *BO* 32 [1975] 164–65).

Explanation

As we noted in the *Explanation* to the previous scene, the whole forward thrust of the narrative came to a halt with the concluding verse of that scene, and progress toward resolution waited there in suspense, as did the hearers, for an impetus from some quarter. The wait is short-lived indeed. Naomi, having come back to life, now takes charge, as Ruth did at the beginning of the previous act (2:2). This first scene begins with neither a digression (cf. 2:1) nor further narrative statement but rather with surprising words from Naomi—words that constitute a signal indication that Ruth's loving commitment to Naomi (1:16–17) is matched by Naomi's equal concern for Ruth. Ruth had reversed sexual allegiance and committed herself to her mother-in-law rather than returning home to Moab where she had the hope of finding a husband. So Naomi recognizes her responsibility to do all she can to find for Ruth the security—the home and husband—she has given up, so that "all may be well for her" (v 1). It is important to note this, for most commentators have understood that Naomi's primary purpose here was to provide an heir for the family line of Elimelech by engineering a levirate marriage for Ruth, but there is nothing in this text to indicate this (see *Comment* on v 1). On the contrary, Naomi is narrowly and specifically concerned for the welfare of Ruth. It is wrong to read the text as if these women could not and did not pursue their own purposes and seek to find as full an answer for their own needs as their culture permitted them, independently of the agendas and roles imposed upon them by the patriarchal world that was theirs. That Naomi recognizes that other agendas exist—and perhaps even that there is a hierarchy of rights in the matter that must be addressed—is strongly suggested by the fact that she gives Ruth no instructions on what to do beyond the symbolic request for marriage and informs her that Boaz will tell her what to do (v 4). Note, however, that Naomi's motivation for suggesting this appeal springs specifically out of her concern for a secure future (מנוח, v 1) for Ruth, not out of a desire to fulfill an obligation of levirate marriage and provide an heir to the line of Elimelech. That concern will be raised by Boaz in the next chapter.

Naomi then proposes (v 2; note the "So then," and see *Comment*) that Boaz is the answer to the problem of home and husband for Ruth based upon the fact that he is a relative. As is clear from her oblique reference to the previous relationship between Ruth and Boaz contained in the clause "whose young women you have been with" (v 2), Naomi hopes that Boaz's past kindness and generosity mean that he can be prompted to act upon whatever family responsibilities this relationship entails. But Boaz, though he has been magnanimous almost to an extreme in providing them sustenance during the harvest season, has thus far not acted any further upon whatever obligations these may be. So Naomi concocts a dangerous and delicate scheme. She instructs Ruth to bathe, to put on perfumed oil, and to put on her "dress," i.e., to remove the symbols and the garments of her widowhood (for this interpretation of v 3 see *Comment*), thus indicating her intention of engaging once again in the normal activities and relationships of life. She is thus available for the marriage that Naomi seeks for her. Naomi then instructs Ruth to engage in a series of actions whose exact intent and purpose are not obvious at all, though clearly they must relate somehow to the attainment of Naomi's goal, a home and husband for Ruth. Ruth is to go down to the threshing floor, where Boaz is winnowing barley, but she is not to let him know she is there until he has finished eating and drinking. Then, when he has lain down for sleep, she is to "uncover his legs" and lie down. Since Ruth is first to "note where he is lying" (v 4), it seems clear that Naomi intends her to lie down by his legs after he has gone to sleep (which she does, vv 7–8). Thus she gives Ruth no instructions whatever about communicating verbally with Boaz. Naomi's instructions clearly imply that Boaz will understand the meaning of Ruth's actions, i.e., of her uncovering his legs and lying down there. As we have noted, v 1 clearly shows that Naomi understands that her instructions to Ruth constitute a course of action designed to acquire for Ruth a home and a husband. In the ensuing scene, when Ruth carries out Naomi's instructions, she does not leave it to her actions alone to convey to Boaz her intentions but voices her request (v 9; see *Comment* thereto), and Boaz clearly understands both actions and request to be a request for marriage (v 10).

It is also important, however, to note that the actions themselves and the vocabulary involved throughout this scene and the next are laden with sexual overtones. Even though it is scarcely probable that the word מרגלתיו, "his legs," is functioning here as a euphemism for the sexual organs (see *Comment*), it is nonetheless clear that the word is intentionally ambiguous, leaving it quite uncertain how much of the lower half of Boaz's body is uncovered. Second, the use of the verb גלה, "uncover," governing a noun for "the region of the legs," could hardly fail to bring to mind at least two idioms: (1) the use of the expression "to uncover [גלה] the skirt [כנף; cf. Ruth 3:9] of the father's robe" (e.g., Deut 23:1; 27:20); and (2) the similar expression "to uncover the nakedness" (e.g., Lev 18:6–19; Ezek 22:10), both of which are euphemisms for sexual intercourse. Similarly, though the verb שׁכב, "to lie down," is used in our passage in the sense "to lie down to sleep" in v 4, it also occurs frequently in the idiom "to lie down with a woman." In this light, Campbell (131) is indeed correct when he observes that it is quite incomprehensible that a Hebrew storyteller could use such terms all in the same context and not suggest to his audience that a sexually provocative set of circumstances confronts them. Further, he is also correct, and this needs to be stressed, when he affirms that our narrator is not simply interested in titillating his audience, nor are his literary allusions intended to imply that the purpose of Naomi's plan was the sexual entrapment of Boaz (contra Fewell and Gunn, *JSOT* 40 [1989] 106). True, he has used language capable of double entendre, and he leaves unstated and hence shrouded in ambiguity exactly what transpired between this man and this woman on the threshing floor in the dark of the night. However, he has depicted both of them throughout his narrative as people of unmatched integrity (cf. 2:1; 3:11) whose lives exhibit that faithful loyalty to relationships described by the Hebrew word חסד *ḥesed* (see 1:8; 2:20; 3:10), and so it is clear that his silence means to imply that they met this moment of choice with that same integrity. As Campbell (132) has so insightfully put it:

> What now happens at the threshing floor is as essential to the story-teller's purpose as what happened on the Moabite highway between Ruth and Naomi, or what happened in the harvest scene when Boaz praised an impoverished widow who was gleaning, or what will happen in the solemn civil hearing at the city gate. At each of these points in the story, a moment of choice is presented to both actors and audience, and at each of these points the choice is made in favor of what righteous living calls for.

What then is the role of such sexually provocative language within this chapter? Why does the author choose words that carry overtones contradictory to the simple sense of the narrative? Bernstein's interpretation (*JSOT* 50 [1991] 16–20) is most attractive and illustrates once again our narrator's skill: it is a conscious literary device. The episode on the threshing floor, in keeping with biblical narrative in general, does not describe or express anything of the emotions of the characters toward each other. Hence,

> the artistic function of the conflicting connotations of words versus sentences must be to furnish, on a level beyond the literal, the sense of the sexual and emotional tension felt by the characters in the vignette. The narrative tells us straightforwardly that no sexual intercourse has taken place on the threshing floor, that final resolutions await the scene at the city gate. All the while, however, the vocabulary of the scene indicates that it might have, that the atmosphere was sexually charged. Thus the ambivalence. The words point, beneath the surface, to the might-have-been which the characters felt might be, while the combinations of the words emphasize the opposing reality. The author of Ruth is relying upon ambiguity of language to depict the tension of emotion, enabling him to convey the atmospherics of the scene without digressing from his narrative to describe them. (Bernstein, *JSOT* 50 [1991] 19–20)

Finally, in terms of the story line itself, we might ask why Naomi devises such a means of proposing marriage between Boaz and Ruth. We can only surmise, but the surmise seems highly probable. In the more general circumstances of the case, Boaz is clearly much older than Ruth, possibly of Naomi's own generation (see *Comment* on 2:1) and so has little reason to expect that such a marriage would be acceptable to Ruth, as his own words in 3:10 make clear (see *Comment* thereto). More to the point, the need for Naomi's scheme only makes sense if Boaz's family relationship to Naomi and Ruth is sufficiently distant that it would not naturally occur to him to act and that no social opprobrium would attach to his failure to do so (see *Comment* on 2:20). Naomi clearly hopes that the prospect of marriage to the young and obviously attractive Ruth will provide the motivation needed to prompt Boaz to act. And clearly the motivating element in the method she has chosen for the proposal requires no further comment.

And what of Ruth? The course of action outlined by Naomi entails the greatest risk to both her reputation (cf. v 14) and her person. True, both in his characterization of Boaz when he introduced him to us in 2:1 and in recording Boaz's actions and words throughout chap. 2, the narrator has signaled to us that Boaz is a generous and kind man of integrity who is faithful to his responsibilities. Nevertheless, the course of action outlined by Naomi could result, as far as Ruth could know, in several eventualities vastly different from the home and husband intended. At least the following seem possible (cf. Zenger, 67). (1) Since Ruth has not contracted a new marriage, she is still the wife of Mahlon (cf. 4:5, 10), so Boaz could charge her with failing in her family responsibilities and possibly even brand her an adulteress. (2) He could use the night's opportunity for his sexual pleasure and then with male bravado malign her character and perhaps even charge her with prostitution. (3) He could deride her request for marriage to him, the wealthy and powerful landowner, as delusions of grandeur. Yet, Ruth raises neither question nor objection but simply responds, "All that you say I will do," demonstrating once again the radical extent of her commitment to and trust in Naomi. In the scene that follows she immediately puts actions to her words, although, as we shall see, not with a blind obedience that enslaves her to every detail. That Naomi (and the narrator?) envisage no such eventualities as those suggested above is unmistakably indicated by the fact that she concludes her instructions with the open-ended declaration, "He will tell you what to do." Naomi seems certain of Boaz indeed, and we the audience have every warrant from his actions in the previous scene to concur in her trust. Nonetheless, we wait in suspense. Will it all turn out as Naomi has planned? What indeed does she suppose that Boaz will tell Ruth to do?

Scene 2
Ruth Carries out Naomi's Plan, and Boaz Offers to Be the Redeemer (3:6–15)

Bibliography

Aejmelaeus, A. "Function and Interpretation of כי in Biblical Hebrew." *JBL* 105 (1986) 193–209. **Beattie, D.** "Kethibh and Qere in Ruth IV 5." *VT* 21 (1971) 490–94. ———. "Redemption in Ruth, and Related Matters: A Response to Jack M. Sasson." *JSOT* 5 (1978) 65–68. ———. "Ruth III." *JSOT* 5 (1978) 39–48. **Berlin, A.** *Poetics and Interpretation of Biblical Narrative.* Sheffield: Almond, 1983. **Bernstein, M. J.** "Two Multivalent Readings in the Ruth Narrative." *JSOT* 50 (1991) 15–26. **Blau, J.** *An Adverbial Construction in Hebrew and Arabic: Sentence Adverbials in Frontal Position Separated from the Rest of the Sentence.* Proceedings of the Israel Academy of Sciences and Humanities 6/1. Jerusalem: Israel Academy of Sciences and Humanities, 1977. **Burrows, M.** "The Marriage of Boaz and Ruth." *JBL* 59 (1940) 445–54. **Daube, D.** *Studies in Biblical Law.* Cambridge: Cambridge UP, 1947. **Gordis, R.** "Love, Marriage, and Business in the Book of Ruth: A Chapter in Hebrew Customary Law." In *A Light unto My Path.* FS J. M. Myers, ed. by H. Bream, R. Heim, and C. Moore. Philadelphia: Temple UP, 1974. 241–64. **Green, B.** "The Plot of the Biblical Story of Ruth." *JSOT* 23 (1982) 55–68. ———. "A Study of Field and Seed Symbolism in the Biblical Story of Ruth." Diss., Graduate Theological Union, Berkeley,

1980. **Leggett, D.** *The Levirate and Goel Institutions in the Old Testament.* Cherry Hill, NJ: Mack, 1974. **Levine, E.** *The Aramaic Version of Ruth.* Rome: Biblical Institute Press, 1973. **Loretz, O.** "Das hebräische Verbum *LPT.*" In *Studies Presented to A. Leo Oppenheim.* Chicago: University of Chicago Press, 1964. 155–58. **McDonald, J.** "Some Distinctive Characteristics of Israelite Spoken Hebrew." *BO* 32 (1975) 162–75. ———. "The Status and Role of the Naʿar in Israelite Society." *JNES* 35 (1976) 147–70. **McKane, W.** "Ruth and Boaz." *TGUOS* 19 (1961–62) 29–40. **Meek, T.** "Translating the Hebrew Bible." *JBL* 79 (1960) 328–35. **Muilenberg, J.** "The Linguistic and Rhetorical Usages of the Particle כי in the Old Testament." *HUCA* 32 (1961) 135–60. **Mundhenk, N.,** and **de Waard, J.** "Missing the Whole Point and What to Do about It—With Special Reference to the Book of Ruth." *BT* 26 (1975) 425–33. **Rauber, D.** "Literary Values in the Bible: The Book of Ruth." *JBL* 89 (1970) 27–37. **Robertson, E.** "The Plot of the Book of Ruth." *BJRL* 32 (1950) 207–28. **Rowley, H.** "The Marriage of Ruth." In *The Servant of the Lord.* Oxford: Blackwell, 1952. 169–94. **Sakenfeld, K. D.** *Faithfulness in Action: Loyalty in Biblical Perspective.* Philadelphia: Fortress, 1985. ———. *The Meaning of Hesed in the Hebrew Bible: A New Inquiry.* Missoula, MT: Scholars, 1978. **Sasson, J.** "The Issue of *Geʾullāh* in Ruth." *JSOT* 5 (1978) 52–64. **Speiser, E.** "'Coming' and 'Going' at the City Gate." In *Oriental and Biblical Studies.* Philadelphia: University of Pennsylvania Press, 1967. 83–88. **Staples, W.** "Notes on Ruth 2:20 and 3:12." *AJSL* 54 (1938) 62–65. **Sternberg, M.** *The Poetics of Biblical Narrative.* Bloomington: Indiana UP, 1985. **Thompson, D.,** and **Thompson, T.** "Some Legal Problems in the Book of Ruth." *VT* 18 (1968) 79–99. **Weismann, Z.** "The Nature and Background of *bāḥūr* in the Old Testament." *VT* 31 (1981) 441–50.

Translation

6*So she went down to the threshing floor and did just as*[a] *her mother-in-law had instructed her.*[b] 7*When Boaz had eaten and drunk,*[a] *he felt at peace with the world,*[b] *and he went and lay down to sleep*[c] *at the end of the heap of grain,*[d] *and she came quietly, uncovered his legs,*[e] *and lay down.*

8*In the middle of the night,*[a] *the man awoke with a shudder,*[b] *turned over,*[c] *and here someone*[d] *was lying beside him!*[e] 9*He said, "Who are you?" and she replied, "I am Ruth, your handmaid; spread the skirt of your robe*[a] *over your handmaid, for you are a redeemer."*

10*"May you be blessed by the LORD, my daughter!" he said.*[a] *"This last act of yours is more loyal and gracious than the first,*[b] *in that you haven't gone after the young men, whether rich or poor.*[c] 11*So now, be assured,*[a] *my daughter, all that you say*[b] *I will do for you, for everyone in town*[c] *knows that you are a woman of worth.* 12*Now,*[a] *truly I am a redeemer, but there is a redeemer more closely related than I.* 13*Stay here tonight and in the morning, if he will redeem you, good, let him redeem you; but, if he is not willing to do so,*[a] *then, as the LORD lives, I will redeem you myself. Lie down until morning."*

14*So she lay there beside him*[a] *until morning. Then she arose before*[b] *one person could recognize another,*[c] *and Boaz thought,*[d] *"It must not be known that the woman came to the threshing floor."* 15*"Hold out*[a] *the shawl you are wearing,"*[b] *he said, "grasp it tightly."*[c] *She held it tightly, and he put*[d] *six measures of barley into it and lifted it*[e] *upon her. Then he*[f] *went to the city.*

Notes

6.a. כְּכֹל. With almost all recent commentators, the כְּ here is to be understood as the so-called *kaph veritatis,* expressing the nuance "exactly as, entirely as." See *HebS* § 257. See also *Note* 2:17b.b. A few Heb. MSS, Syr, and Vg omit כְּ, making the clause the direct obj of the verb "did." Since this would normally require אֶת־כָּל, the reading doubtless arose through haplogr.

6.b. צותה. This form is the pf 3rd fem sg of the verb צוה, "to command, instruct," plus the 3rd fem sg pronom suff. It is explained by positing that the ה of the 3rd fem sg suff *-hā* has assimilated regressively to the ת of the suffixal form of the pf 3rd fem sg verb, i.e., **ṣiwwat-hā* > *ṣiwwattāh;* see GKC § 59g.

7.a. The Heb. is lit. "And Boaz ate and drank and his heart was good." It is better in Eng. to bring out the implied causal relationship between Boaz's eating and drinking and his subsequent pleasant mood by the use of the subordinate clause.

7.b. Lit. "his heart was pleasant/good." See *Comment.*

7.c. This is the clear implication of the Heb. לִשְׁכַּב, in this context.

7.d. Although ערמה can simply mean "heap," contents unspecified, in such a context as this it clearly means the heap of threshed grain; cf. also Neh 13:15.

7.e. On this translation, see *Comment* on 3:4.

8.a. The phrase is not as precise as Eng. "at midnight" (RSV).

8.b. The verb elsewhere means "tremble"; see *Comment.*

8.c. Or "groped about." See *Comment.*

8.d. Lit. "And behold a woman was lying." The lit. Heb. "woman" is here equivalent to the Eng. indefinite pronoun "someone"; see *Comment.*

8.e. Lit. "at his legs." On this translation, see *Comment* on 3:4.

9.a. Lit. "your skirt." see *Comment.*

10.a. LXX and Syr supply the subordinate conj "for, because" here, expressing explicitly the logical connection of the two clauses. This is doubtless an interpretive addition of the translator, not evidence for such a particle originally present in the Heb.

10.b. Lit. "you have made your latter חסד better than the first."

10.c. Lit. "whether poor or rich." In Eng. the reverse order seems far more natural (de Waard-Nida, 55).

11.a. Lit. "have no fear."

11.b. A few Heb. MSS and almost all the versions add אלי, "to me," doubtless an interpretive addition; see *Note* 5.a. above.

11.c. Lit. "all the gate of my people."

12.a. Omitted in LXX, doubtless because of the difficult and overloaded syntax of the first five words; see *Comment.*

13.a. Lit. "to redeem you."

14.a. Lit. "at his legs"; see *Comments* on vv 4, 8. The word מרגלתו lacks the expected yodh between the taw and the waw, i.e., תיו־, manifestly simply a copyist's error.

14.b. The K form בטרום, instead of the usual and frequent (some 53x) Q בְּטֶרֶם, is inexplicable and doubtless erroneous.

14.c. Lit. "before a man could recognize his fellow."

14.d. Lit. "and he said." See *Comment.*

15.a. הָבִי, lit. "give, make available"; see *Comment.* The form here is unusual. One expects הֲבִי; see GKC § 69a.

15.b. Lit. "which is upon you."

15.c. MT וְאֶחֱזִי. For the unusual vocalization of this verb, see GKC § 64c. Here אחז is treated as a strong verb with a *u-theme vowel, contrary to the usual pattern (for which see GKC § 68b). Some MSS have the weak verb vocalization וֶאֱחֱזִי (Rudolph, 56).

15.d. Lit. "measured."

15.e. Lit. "placed it."

15.f. A number of Heb. MSS, Syr, and Vg read "she went."

Form/Structure/Setting

This, the second and central scene of act 3, depicts in deeds and words the response of Ruth and Boaz to Naomi's daring plan revealed in the first scene. For the characteristics of form and content that determine this division into scenes, see the discussion of the form and structure of the whole chapter given above for the introductory scene. The opening of this scene is signaled by the summary statement, "So she went down to the threshing floor and did just as her mother-in-law had instructed her," for which summary the following verses fill in both the details and the dénouement. The scene is framed by the striking contrastive opening and closing two-word clauses, ותרד הגרן, "she went down to the threshing floor," and ויבא העיר, "he went to the city," signaling that the initiative for progress in the story has passed from Ruth and Naomi to Boaz.

This scene divides into two episodes, each with two subsections chiastically arranged, as follows:

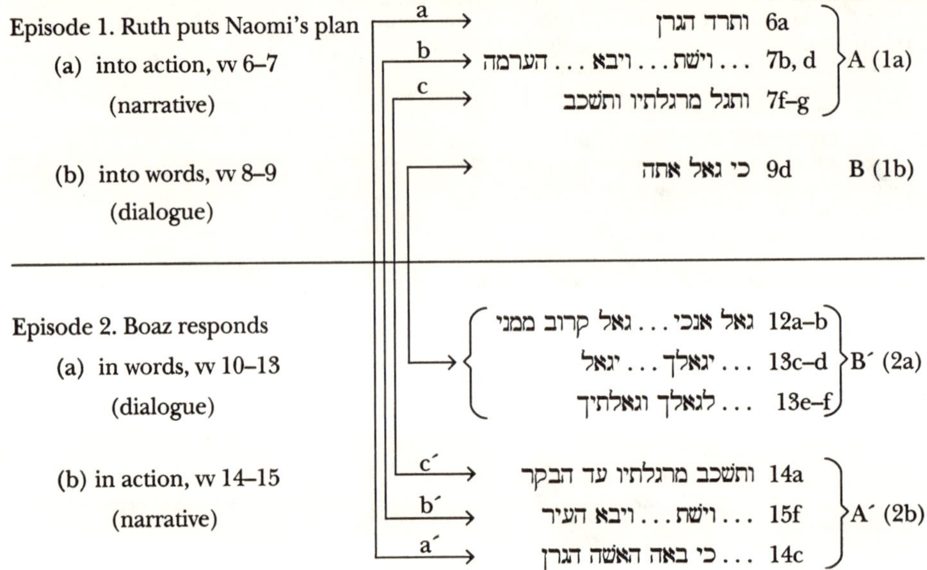

Episode 1(a) formally corresponds with 2(b) in that both are narrative, while episode 1(b) formally corresponds with 2(a) in that both are dialogue. The chiastic arrangement includes content, for symbolic actions of petition and promise (A and A´) encircle words of request and assent (B and B´). In addition, parallel and repeated phrases unite and reinforce the chiasm. In A and A´, these form inclusios for the scene as a whole. Thus, "she went down to the threshing floor" in Aa is paralleled by "the woman came to the threshing floor in A´a´; "she uncovered his legs and lay down" in Ac parallels "she lay by his legs until morning" in A´c´. Porten (*GCA* 7 [1978] 39) has noted "the surprising mixture of identical words, related expressions and similar sounds" in Ab and A´b´:

Ab "he ate, drank (וישת) . . . *came to* . . . the pile (הערמה)
A´b´ "he measured six (measures of) barley, put (וישת), . . . *came to* . . . the city (העיר)

Likewise, the use of גֹּאֵל, "redeemer," in B (v 9) is paralleled by the sixfold use of גאל in B´, twice in the identical form גֹּאֵל in v 12, and four times in forms of the verb גָּאַל in v 13.

Finally, Boaz's response to Ruth's request in episode 2 is stressed by its expanded length and careful construction. It is divided into four parts. Part 1 consists of words of praise for Ruth's choice of Boaz rather than the young men of the town (v 10). This is followed by two consequences (vv 11 and 12), each introduced by ועתה, "so now." Part 2, the first consequence, consists of Boaz's basic and general assent, grounded in the fact that everyone in town knows Ruth's worth (v 11). The second consequence, however, introduces a major complication in strictly parallel clauses (v 12):

12a אנכי	כי אמנם כי אם גאל	"Truly a *gô'ēl* (am) *I*"
12b קרוב ממני	וגם יש גאל	"There is a *gô'ēl* nearer than *I*"

The last part (v 13) gives Boaz's instructions for the resolution of this surprising development, consisting of four clauses chiastically arranged:

X 13a *Stay here tonight* and *in the morning,*

Y 13b if *he will redeem you,*
13c good, *let him redeem you;*

Y′ 13d but, if he is not willing *to redeem you*
13e then, as the LORD lives, *I will redeem you*

X′ 13f *Lie down until morning*

Here "night surrounds morning; the immediate situation encircles the coming resolution; instruction encompasses condition and promise" (Trible, 185).

Comment

7 וַיִּיטַב לִבּוֹ, lit. "his heart was good." This idiom expresses a feeling of euphoria and well-being resulting from a wide variety of causes (cf. 1 Kgs 8:66; Judg 18:20). It is often a synonym of שׂמח, "to be glad/happy" (e.g., 1 Kgs 8:66; Eccl 11:9), whereas its antonyms are עני, "oppressed, depressed" (Prov 15:15), כעשׂ, "grief" (Eccl 7:3), and כאב לב, "anguish of heart" (Isa 65:14). In several contexts, as here, the state of well-being is brought on by eating and drinking (Judg 19:6, 22; 1 Kgs 24:7). However, the statement leaves quite ambiguous whether wine was included (cf. the remarks of Zenger, 69–70; contra Joüon, 70). Note that this narrative statement makes explicit the effect desired by Naomi when she instructed Ruth not to make herself known to Boaz until he had finished eating and drinking (v 3). We have chosen to translate the Hebrew idiom by the English "to be at peace with the world" since this expression seems to leave the question of the extent that Boaz was under the influence of wine as ambiguous as does the Hebrew.

וַתָּבֹא בַלָּט, "and she came quietly." Whether בלט means "quietly" or "secretly" (a case can be made for either meaning; cf. the remarks of Hubbard, 209 n. 23; Joüon, 71) is of little moment for the meaning of our passage, for in either case it signals that Ruth came in a manner intended not to disturb the sleeping man. Berlin (*Poetics,* 90–91) seeks to see a contradiction between Ruth's performance here and Naomi's previous instructions, asserting that Naomi intended Ruth to approach Boaz before he fell asleep. She attributes this to Ruth's misapprehension of Naomi's ultimate intentions: "She did not realize that her mission was a romantic one, thinking rather that she was there on secret legal business" (91). Apart from the fact that the text gives not the slightest hint that Ruth understood her task and purpose any differently from Naomi's intent, Naomi's instructions to "note the place where he is lying" clearly imply that she is to wait until he has fallen asleep before approaching, uncovering his legs, and lying down. Berlin avoids the implication of this sequence by making this phrase an aside: "And when he is lying down—and you will know where he is lying—you will come and . . ." (90). But the verb וידעת is perfect with waw consecutive following a jussive and can only be understood as imperatival in force and hence sequential (the following verb is another perfect with waw consecutive).

8 וַיֶּחֱרַד הָאִישׁ וַיִּלָּפֵת. The exact meaning of these two clauses is uncertain. First, חרד in the qal stem means "to tremble." Although most frequently used in contexts where the trembling results from fear or deadly peril (e.g., 1 Sam 14:15; Isa 4:5, 19:16; Ezek 32:10), it can refer to trembling or shuddering resulting from other causes (cf. Gen 27:33; Exod 19:18; Ezek 26:16). In one context, it can mean "trouble oneself anxiously for" (2 Kgs 4:13). Whether fear is the cause of the trembling is determined then by the context (contra Sasson, 74). Consequently, a number of scholars (e.g., Campbell, Hubbard, Joüon, Trible), finding nothing in the context to occasion fear on Boaz's part, assume that the trembling results from the cold occasioned by the uncovering of his feet or legs. But there is nothing in the text or context to suggest that Boaz trembles from the cold. Most probably the verb in a context such as this means "to wake with a shudder or start" (so Gerleman, Hertzberg, Rudolph, Würthwein). There is, however, an element in the context that suggests that this experience would have been full of fear and apprehension, viz. "in the middle of the night," for the middle of the night is in the OT frequently a time of deadly peril. It was in the middle of the night that Yahweh in the form of the "destroyer" (Exod 12:23) passed through Egypt to kill all the first born (Exod 11:4; 12:29). In the middle of the night, Jacob wrestled with the "man" at the ford of the Jabbok (Gen 32:23–32); Job 34:20 knows of sudden death in the middle of the night; and Ps 91:4–5 speaks of finding shelter with Yahweh so "you will not be afraid of the terror by night" (cf. Zenger, 70). To this OT evidence Sasson (74–78), followed by Zenger (70–71), adds the general fear in the ancient Near East of female night-demons (some called *Lilū/Lilīt;* cf. Isa 34:14) who attack sleeping men (occasionally sexually). Altogether, given this background, it does indeed seem highly plausible that OT people would interpret someone's starting from sleep in the middle of the night to be an exceptionally fearful and dreaded experience. However, Sasson (78) specifically connects the trembling in fear with Boaz's discovery of a female form next to him: "upon awakening, Boaz discerns the figure of a woman. Fearing that it might be that of a Lilith, he shudders in fear." But such a specific connection is syntactically most improbable. To support his interpretation, Sasson must give the following clause a causal sense, positing that "the use of a participial form in connection with the demonstrative particle *hinnēh* . . . gives 'there was a woman lying close to him' an explicative purpose"; i.e., "it provides the audience with an explanation that accounts for Boaz's violent behavior" (80). However, such an understanding of the construction cannot be substantiated, in particular not by the passages Sasson gives for support.

The idiom ו + הנה + participle almost invariably sets forth an action that is temporally or logically subsequent to the clause(s) preceding (e.g., Gen 24:30; Judg 11:34; cf. esp. *SBH,* 94–96, and the discussion below). Such is the case here. As a result of the two actions ויחרד האיש וילפת, whatever their precise meaning, Boaz became aware of the presence of someone beside him. Nevertheless, even though such a specific connection is not expressed, it is clear that the background Sasson elucidates would mean that the Israelite reader would hear and perceive Boaz's experience as a very frightening and threatening one.

Second, the meaning of the niphal stem of לפת in this context is quite obscure. The root occurs in the OT only twice outside our passage: in the qal stem in Judg 16:29 and in the niphal again in Job 6:18. Only in the qal stem in the Judges passage is the meaning clear: "to take hold of, to grasp." This is also the meaning of the root in Akkadian. Given this range of meanings, Loretz ("Das hebräische Verbum *LPT,*" 155–58) has argued for a meaning "to touch, to grasp" in all three OT passages. In the Ruth passage, Loretz argues for a meaning "to grope" (see also KB^3, 507). In his interpretation (followed by Campbell), Boaz awoke trembling from the cold, felt around with his hand in order to cover himself again, and unintentionally struck against Ruth lying beside him. However, since there is nothing in the context that remotely suggests that Boaz's shuddering results from the cold, one is at a loss to understand for what reason Boaz "groped about." Such an interpretation leaves too much to the imagination of the reader to be intelligible.

Other commentators refer to the Arabic cognate *lafata,* which means "to turn, twist, bend" (Gerleman, Joüon, Rudolph), leading to the rendering adopted by most modern English translations, "he turned (over)" (RSV, NAB, NEB, NIV). If, as we have contended, Ruth is lying beside Boaz, or at least beside his legs, rather than strictly "at his feet," then such a meaning renders the whole sequence of events comprehensible: Boaz awoke with a start or shudder (cause unknown), rolled over, and became aware that someone lay beside him. In our present state of knowledge, this seems the most plausible interpretation.

וְהִנֵּה אִשָּׁה שֹׁכֶבֶת מַרְגְּלֹתָיו, lit. "and here a woman was lying beside him." The introductory particle והנה, lit. "and behold," introduces a "surprise clause" (*SBH,* 94; cf. *Comment* on 2:4), which not only makes the scene lively and vivid but also presents it to us very graphically from Boaz's own point of view (cf. Berlin, *Poetics,* 91–92). We have attempted to convey both the surprise and the perspective by the rendering "and here someone was," recognizing that Hebrew morphology requires the noun to be more gender specific than does a language such as English. Berlin (*Poetics,* 152 n. 6) is doubtless correct in observing:

> But the usage of "woman" can be explained by the necessity of Hebrew grammar, which must choose between איש ("man") and אשה ("woman") in order to say "someone." My feeling is that the sense of the verse is "*hinneh,* someone was lying at his feet," but since the reader knows that it is Ruth, it would be too incongruous to use the masculine for the impersonal.

Consequently we have chosen the impersonal "someone" rather than "woman."

9 אֲמָתֶךָ, "your handmaid." In 2:13 Ruth had designated herself, deferentially, as a שפחה, "a maidservant" (see *Comment* there). The choice of the socially higher term here is doubtless dictated by the fact that Ruth is about to suggest marriage to Boaz (see below). Hence she designates herself as a אמה, that class of females who "might be taken by a freeman either as a concubine or as a wife" (Sasson, 81). It is of considerable significance here that Ruth does not assume, or accord herself, the identity of "wife of Mahlon" (or "wife of the deceased"), the identity Boaz will give her in 4:5, 10; see *Explanation.*

וּפָרַשְׂתָּ כְנָפֶךָ עַל־אֲמָתְךָ, "spread your *kānāp̄* over your handmaid." The interpretation of this and the following clause is crucial for understanding what now transpires between Ruth and Boaz. Unfortunately, their precise significance is ambiguous, and diverse interpretations have consequently been placed upon them. To begin with, very few commentators, in wrestling with the meaning of this verse, have taken into account the implications of the content and purpose of Naomi's instructions to Ruth in vv 1–4 above. There (see *Explanation* thereto) Naomi affirmed her responsibility to find a home and husband for Ruth (v 1) *and* also affirmed that Boaz, being a relative, could be the answer to that need. Further, Naomi obviously expects that Boaz will understand the meaning of the action of uncovering his legs and lying down there (v 4), for she does not tell Ruth to say anything to Boaz but asserts that Boaz himself will tell Ruth what to do. Ruth agreed to do all that Naomi had said (v 5) and, as the text has affirmed (v 6), has indeed thus far done exactly that (v 7). Therefore, *unless the import of her words clearly indicates otherwise,* we have every reason to expect that here, when she departs from Naomi's instructions and makes her desires known verbally, she will still be pursuing the same ends and purposes (i.e., a home and a husband, v 1) that Naomi originally voiced.

In this context, then, what is the meaning of Ruth's request, "Spread your *kānāp̄* [כנף] over your handmaid"? The word כנף bears two meanings pertinent to its usage in Ruth: "wing," as in 2:12, and "skirt (of a garment)" (cf. Hag 2:12). Identifying the meaning intended here is further complicated by whether the word כנף is singular or dual/plural. The MT vocalization understands the text as the defectively written dual/plural כְּנָפֶךָ (for כְּנָפֶיךָ, a reading found in some Heb. MSS), but the consonantal text, LXX, and Syr read the singular כְּנָפְךָ. In Deut 23:1; 27:20; Ezek 16:8, the removal or the spreading of the "skirt" of a man's robe over a woman is used as a euphemism for the consummation of marriage, and in these passages כנף is unmistakably singular. Since v 10 demonstrates that Boaz understood Ruth's words as a symbolic request for marriage, there seems little doubt, with most commentators (see the list in Leggett, *The Levirate,* 197 n. 53), that the singular is the correct reading. Further, significant evidence for this understanding is to be found in the considerable evidence in the ancient Near East in general for the use of the hem of the man's garment in symbolic acts expressing the dissolution of the marriage bond (see P. A. Kruger, "The Hem of the Garment in Marriage," *JNWSL* 12 [1984] 79–83). The same action of covering the woman with the robe symbolic of marriage also occurs in the later customs of the Arabic world (see Gerleman, 32; Leggett, *The Levirate,* 197 n. 53).

The meaning of this figurative expression is made particularly clear in Ezek 16:7–8. In that passage, the relationship between Yahweh and Israel is depicted as that of the bridegroom and the bride, using language that is sexually explicit:

> 7. . . So you grew up, became tall, and attained womanhood; your breasts were formed and your hair had grown, but you were naked and bare. 8Then I passed by you and

looked, and lo! you were at the age for love. So I spread the skirt of my robe over you and covered your nakedness. I gave you my oath and entered into covenant with you, says the Lord Yahweh, and you became mine.

In discussing the interpretation of the phrase, Beattie has argued that "such a close physical proximity is indicated that the expression readily connotes an invitation to sexual relations, just as would an invitation, in English, to go to bed, but I cannot see how the idea of marriage may be found in it" (*JSOT* 5 [1978] 43). However, Naomi has marriage in mind for Ruth in the beginning of the chapter, and Boaz immediately thinks of marriage upon hearing Ruth's words; hence marriage must be implied in some way. Therefore, Beattie argues that Ruth offers herself to Boaz and simultaneously asks for his protection by cleverly choosing the word כנף, which he has previously used with this meaning (2:12), and in this idea of protection "there should probably be found a gentle hint at marriage." Beattie concludes with the observation that "The situation, however, is not that Ruth demanded or even explicitly requested marriage, but rather that Naomi conceived the plan of putting the idea into Boaz's head by putting Ruth into his bed" (43). But surely a view that Naomi and Ruth concocted a plan to induce Boaz to marry Ruth by having her seduce him on the threshing floor in the middle of the night is totally incompatible with the general character of both women. Green has put it well: "we can assume on the basis of the rest of the story that the actions of the characters are not only not contrary to the law but that their actions are virtuous beyond the demands of the law" ("Field and Seed Symbolism," 84 n. 4; cf. the remarks of Bernstein, *JSOT* 50 [1991] 16–17). However that may be, Beattie's view is totally incompatible with Boaz's response to her request in the ensuing verses. There he designates her proposal a better act of gracious loyalty (חסד; see *Comment* below) than she performed previously in her devotion to Naomi, and he grounds his acquiescence to her request in the fact that she is a אשת חיל, "worthy woman" (v 11). Clearly Boaz heard her words to mean something other than simply "Sleep with me"!

It is equally difficult to sustain such a meaning for the phrase in Ezek 16:8, quoted above. Although the phrase there may bear only the literal sense "I covered you with my robe" (so Beattie, *JSOT* 5 [1978] 47 n. 9), in the light of the following phrases, "I gave you my oath and entered into covenant with you," it more likely is meant figuratively, i.e., "I married you." Since the speaker is Yahweh, it can hardly mean "to have sexual relations."

The plural reading of the Q, doubtless to be translated "Spread your wings over your maidservant," is probably to be understood as a request for protection (cf. Rudolph, 55; Leggett, *The Levirate,* 193). However, as Beattie notes (*JSOT* 5 [1978] 42), a request for protection from a woman to a man in such a context as this would be understood as a request for marriage. Indeed, the MT pointing may well be occasioned by the desire to avoid the overt sexual implications of the singular, while obtaining essentially the same meaning.

כִּי גֹאֵל אָתָּה, "for you are a redeemer." The most natural and obvious translation of the particle כי here is the causal sense, "for, because," and virtually all commentators and translations have so understood it. Recently, however, in the interests of sustaining his view that the marriage of Ruth to Boaz is not a levirate marriage, Sasson (81–82; cf. id., "The Issue of *Geʾullāh,*" 53) has sought to make the last two clauses coordinate and independent. He says, "In that fateful night, Ruth sought two things. She asked Boaz to marry her . . . and asked him to become her mother-in-law's redeemer" ("The Issue of *Geʾullāh,*" 62–63, 68 n. 18). In order to establish this interpretation, Sasson seeks to understand the כי here not as the causal conjunction "for, because" but as the corroborative or emphatic adverb "indeed." His primary evidence for this interpretation is his view that Boaz responds in vv 11–13 to two issues: in v 11 he agrees to her proposal of marriage, and in vv 12–13 he deals with the issue of redemption (see *Ruth,* 81; id., "The Issue of *Geʾullāh,*" 54–58; cf. also Green, *JSOT* 23 [1982] 63). This argument is non sequitur. The fact that Boaz dealt with these two issues, Ruth's request for marriage and his position as גאל, "redeemer," in no way requires that Ruth made two separate requests. But Sasson's argument here is really beside the point, for the particle כי in this context can only be understood in its causal sense. All the examples of an emphatic force for כי in GKC §§ 148d, 159ee, to which Sasson refers, are either exclamations or conditional clauses (for other examples, see *HebS* § 449), hence radically different in syntax from the clauses here. Further, in those examples where interpreters have argued for an emphatic meaning for כי (cf. Meek, *JBL* 79 [1960] 45–54; Muilenberg, *HUCA* 32 [1961] 135–60), the causal connection between the two clauses has become so loose and indirect that translations into other languages using conjunctions expressing cause, reason, motivation, or explanation seem patently jarring or questionable (see the discussion by Aejmelaeus, *JBL* 105 [1986] 204–5, who questions the emphatic interpretation even in these cases). Such is clearly not the case here. Indeed, as Beattie notes (*JSOT* 5 [1978] 65), even if one were to grant Sasson's contention and give כי a corroborative force here, the second clause must, because of the semantic content of the two clauses, still inevitably be construed as giving the grounds for the request made in the first clause.

Excursus: The Relationship between Ruth's Request and the Question of Levirate Marriage

Some of the most difficult problems of interpretation of the book of Ruth relate to understanding the role of the גאל *gôʾēl,* "redeemer," in Hebrew society. Ruth bases her request for marriage on Boaz's position as a גאל, and chap. 4 introduces the responsibility of the גאל to recover or retain family property, together with the apparent implication that these two duties are somehow related. This raises the question of how the marriage of Ruth and Boaz is related to the so-called levirate marriage prescribed in Deut 25:5–10 (which also forms the major problem in the story of Judah and Tamar in Gen 38) and whether and how this social institution is related to the responsibilities of the גאל, and in particular to the land-redemption rights and duties of the גאל that surface in chap. 4.

Although variations in detail are endless, in general almost all commentators have argued as follows: (1) Ruth 4:5, 10 show that Boaz's marriage to Ruth was a levirate type of marriage, similar at least to that prescribed in Deut 25:5–10. Even though Boaz was not a *levir* (Heb. יבם), a "brother-in-law," this was a levirate marriage because 4:5, 10 specify that the purpose of the marriage to Ruth was "to raise up the name of the deceased on his inheritance so that the name of the deceased shall not be cut off from his brethren" (4:10), which is similar to the purpose given for levirate marriage (cf. Deut 25:6). (2) In 3:9 Ruth bases her request that Boaz accept the levirate marriage responsibility on the fact that he is a גאל, "redeemer." Therefore, one of the legal responsibilities of the "redeemer" was to perform the levirate marriage, even though the passages in the OT legal corpora dealing with redemption never touch upon the levirate obligation; nor do the passages dealing with the levirate ever call the one responsible for this obligation a "redeemer." (3) In chap. 4 land that belonged to Elimelech suddenly surfaces in the story, and Boaz calls upon the redeemer more closely related than he to act upon his rights and duties as redeemer and buy back (or preempt the sale of) this land. Further, the standard interpretation argues, Boaz uses the implications of the redeemer's double responsibilities of "levirate" marriage to Ruth and of redemption of the land of Elimelech to induce the unnamed גאל, who has prior rites, to cede those rights and responsibilities to him. Boaz then redeems the land and marries Ruth. For representative treatments, see the discussion of Campbell, 132–37; Thompson and Thompson, *VT* 18 (1968) 79–99, and for a full treatment, see Leggett, *The Levirate*.

Recently a number of studies have sought to solve the many difficulties that arise in applying the postulates outlined above to the exegesis and interpretation of chaps. 3 and 4 of Ruth by denying that the marriage between Ruth and Boaz is connected in any way with levirate marriage. See in particular Beattie, *VT* 21 (1971) 490–94; *VT* 24 (1974) 251–67; *JSOT* 5 (1978) 39–48; *JSOT* 5 (1978) 65–68; Gordis, "Love, Marriage, and Business," 241–64; Sasson, *JSOT* 5 (1978) 49–64; *Ruth*, 125–29, 143–46.

It is not pertinent to our purposes here to present a full discussion of what can be ascertained from the biblical texts about the nature and history of the social institutions of the levirate and redemption in ancient Israel, but it will be necessary when we come to the passages that raise those issues to touch upon those institutions in a manner sufficient, if possible, to elucidate the social and legal background that will clarify what is happening between the characters in our story. To do this, it will be extremely helpful to set forth certain principles inherent in such a task and dictated in large part by the nature of the material at our disposal. To begin with, I concur with Beattie (*JSOT* 5 [1978] 39–40) in the principles of storytelling that must be followed by a narrator if a narrative such as Ruth is to function effectively as a story. Beattie outlines three such principles. *First,* the narrative must be coherent and intelligible. The reader must be able to follow what is happening and how any given incident relates to what precedes and follows it; i.e., there must be no discontinuities that render the story unintelligible. *Second,* closely related to the above, the narrator must supply sufficient information so that his readers may understand what happens and why. Information decisive for understanding the story will not have been omitted, such that one cannot explain developments or fill in gaps. (I am not referring here to the way in which a narrator deliberately leaves "gaps" that create ambiguities in the story line or plot development, so that the reader must entertain various options to fill them. For the interpretation of such in the story of David and Bathsheba, see Sternberg, *Poetics,* 186–299.) For example (as Green, "Field and Seed Symbolism," 73, notes), if it had been necessary to presume a meeting between Boaz and Naomi between the events of chaps. 3 and 4 in order to understand the developments of chap. 4 (so Robertson, *BJRL* 32 [1950] 220), the narrator would have so stated. *Third,* the story must be credible; i.e., the narrator cannot create situations that his readers know to be legally, or otherwise, impossible (e.g., if widows could not legally inherit or own land, then the narrator cannot depict a widow doing so). This principle assumes, of course, that both the narrator and his readers know the legal and social mores and obligations that pertained in the period in which the story is set. As Beattie notes (*VT* 24 [1971] 253), it is rather clearly indicated that the author of Ruth so assumed since he was concerned enough that social customs be clear to his readers to explain the obsolete legal custom of the shoe transfer in 4:7. A further difficulty that greatly complicates the matter for us, however, is the distance in time, and hence in culture and social institutions, that now separate us from the original narrator. Since our knowledge of the nature and history of ancient Israel's legal and social institutions is incomplete, it is highly probable, if not virtually certain, that there are understandings shared by the ancient narrator and his readers that partially or totally escape us. It is antecedently possible then, perhaps likely, that situations and developments will occur in the story for which we simply do not have an adequate explanation and understanding. Every attempt will have to be made to provide such, but it is highly unlikely that certainty will ever be attained. As Rowley put it, the book of Ruth "abounds in problems for which no final solution can ever be found, since the materials for their solutions are denied us" ("The Marriage of Ruth," 171).

In the second place, it is important to recognize the implications of the nature of Israelite (and ancient Near Eastern) casuistic law noted by Campbell (133–35; cf. also the comments of Gordis, "Love, Marriage, and Business," 256–58, and Thompson and Thompson, *VT* 18 [1968] 83–84). Campbell observes that we must not be misled by such terms as "law-code" and "legislation" into thinking that collections of ancient case law functioned as codes of law do in modern Western countries. We must not regard the OT codes of law as comprehensive and all inclusive, intended to regulate the legal needs of life by a system of courts, lawyers, judges, and police. On the contrary, legal decisions were made by the town elders on the basis of local legal precedents, preserved primarily orally. These differed from those of other communities, even though communication between communities on legal matters doubtless created a certain degree of uniformity, particularly between towns in the same geographical area. Codes of law, such as Hammurabi's Code or those of Exodus or Deuteronomy, resulted from political attempts to normalize practice and functioned as legal precedents intended to serve as references for settling cases, particularly difficult ones. Their purpose was illustrative and didactic; consequently, they are anything but complete and comprehensive. As a further result, the customs and legal practices followed in the *narratives* in the Bible often do not agree with the legal formulations in the *codes*. In this light, it is quite incorrect to conclude that Boaz's marriage to Ruth can have nothing to do with levirate marriage as prescribed in Deut 25:5–10, simply because the Deuteronomy passage specifies that the obligation rests upon "brothers dwelling together" (25:5), while Boaz is a more distant relative (so Gordis, "Love, Marriage, and Business," 246). It is further to be noted in this regard that we cannot expect terms used by ordinary people in narratives to be employed with the kind of legal precision that would be found in a law code. As Beattie succinctly puts it (*VT* 24 [1974] 252), "what the law-code calls 'larceny' the storyteller may be excused for calling 'theft.'"

With these principles in mind, let us return to the question of the implications of the fact that Ruth bases her request that Boaz marry her on his role as a גאל. The situation presumed in the text is as follows. Naomi's instructions to Ruth in vv 1–4 above have as their sole expressed purpose the provision of "home and husband" for Ruth in order to remove the destitute state and reproach of her widowhood. In particular, there is not one word in her intentions and instructions that suggests that she really has in mind the providing of an heir for Elimelech and Mahlon, or even that she has this end in view in addition to providing for Ruth. On this point, see the discussion in *Comment* on 3:1. Further, Naomi logically concludes in v 2 (see the remarks on ועתה in *Comment*) that Boaz may be the means to procure home and husband on the basis that he is a relative, the very same expectation that she voiced when she first heard his name from Ruth after her first day's gleaning in 2:20: "The man is a relative of ours; he is one of our redeemers." There we argued that Naomi used גאל in its general nonlegal sense of "one who, by virtue of kinship ties, is responsible to deliver one from evil (e.g., poverty, injustice, oppression, slavery)"; see *Comment* on 2:20 and *Comment* on 3:2. From that point to this in the story, nothing has changed in the relationship between Boaz and the two widows Naomi and Ruth, related to him by marriage. Hence neither Naomi *nor Ruth* could possibly have in mind, in this context any more than previously, an obligation on Boaz's part to redeem land sold by Elimelech to which they would have some right as widows of the deceased members of that family line; i.e., they could not be using גאל in its technical legal sense. Apart from the fact that this would render Naomi's and Ruth's previous actions incredible and unintelligible, Ruth is using Boaz's role as a גאל, "redeemer," as a grounds for her request that he marry her. It is also not possible that Ruth is here using the term גאל in a technical sense referring to a legal responsibility of the גאל to perform the duty of levirate marriage. Apart from the difficult question of whether the legal responsibility of גאלה, "redemption," included the duty of levirate marriage, assuming such a legal responsibility on Boaz's part, to which Ruth now refers, again renders the story incredible and unintelligible. If such a responsibility existed, why would Naomi (who certainly would have been more cognizant of it than Ruth the Moabitess) have sent Ruth on her risky and provocative excursion to the threshing floor? It seems even less likely that Ruth, independently and without Naomi's knowledge, raises a legal responsibility that Naomi never thought of (contra Sasson, 83). If Ruth is using גאל in the same sense as Naomi has used it (2:20), then it is simply not possible that Ruth "did not realize that her mission was a romantic one, thinking rather that she was there on secret legal business" (Berlin, *Poetics,* 91). No, the only interpretation that renders the story coherent, credible, and intelligible is that Ruth is using גאל in its general sense as defined above—i.e., she says, ". . . spread the skirt of your robe over your handmaid [= marry me], for you are a גאל [= you are one who has responsibility to care for family members in need]."

Nor does it seem likely, as Hubbard (213) proposes, that Ruth intended her words to go beyond Naomi's intentions:

> . . . Ruth's statement implied—the first hint of the subject—that the proposed marriage aimed to benefit Naomi, probably by providing her with the very heir heretofore tragically absent from the story. . . . Naomi's instructions intended simply to obtain a husband for Ruth. . . . By invoking the *gôʾēl* custom on her own initiative, however, Ruth subordinated her own happiness to the family duty of providing Naomi an heir.

Hubbard (51–52; cf. also 187) has already persuasively argued that Ruth is using the term גאל here in 3:9 in the same sense as Naomi used it in 2:20, namely, to refer to the responsibility of the גאל to marry the widow of a deceased relative. Hence, since the symbolic act Ruth speaks of in her request ("spread the skirt of your robe over me," 3:9a) relates specifically and narrowly to marriage (so Hubbard, 212), how could she in the grounds for her request ("for you are a *gôʾēl*") suddenly be using the term to imply a responsibility to benefit *Naomi* by providing her with an heir? Note that she has not identified herself to Boaz immediately prior by saying "I am Ruth, wife of the deceased" (or "wife of Mahlon"; cf. her identity in 4:5, 10). Rather, she has called herself simply "Ruth, your handmaid," an identity that stressed her status as one eligible for marriage to a man of Boaz's position (as Hubbard notes, 211), not as the widow who must raise an heir to her husband's estate. In this light, it is difficult to see how Ruth could be using גאל in any different sense than Naomi did in 2:20 or than is implied in her reference to Boaz as a relative in 3:1–2. It does seem very likely that Boaz, in his response to her request in 3:12–13, speaks almost enigmatically in such a way that *he* seems to have more in mind that simply marriage (as we shall argue below), but Ruth in 3:9 surely does not. (On this understanding of Ruth's words, see also the remarks of Daube, *Studies in Biblical Law,* 40, 44–45; Gordis, "Love, Marriage, and Business," 253; and esp. Beattie, *JSOT* 5 [1978] 44–45.) When Ruth does more than mutely obey the instructions Naomi gave her that she should lie down at Boaz's legs and that he would tell her what to do, she is neither changing those instructions nor violating them but simply putting in words what Naomi voiced in her opening statement in vv 1–2: "Must I not seek for you home and husband . . . ? So then, is not Boaz . . . a relative of ours?"

10 בְּרוּכָה אַתְּ לַיהוָה, "May you be blessed by Yahweh." On the form of this blessing, see the remarks on יְהִי מַכִּירֵךְ בָּרוּךְ in 2:19.

הֵיטַבְתְּ חַסְדֵּךְ הָאַחֲרוֹן מִן־הָרִאשׁוֹן, "This last act of yours is more loyal and gracious than the first." The literal Hebrew reads "you have made your last חסד [*ḥesed*] better than the first." What Boaz means by Ruth's "last חסד" is made explicitly clear by the following clause, "in that you have not gone after the young men, whether rich or poor" (on the syntax of this clause, see below). Clearly, the "last חסד" Boaz refers to is in some sense Ruth's proposal of marriage. However, what Boaz means by Ruth's first act of חסד is left totally to the implications of the context. What it is, nonetheless, seems clear enough: it can surely be nothing but Ruth's gracious commitment to Naomi, knowledge of which Boaz has already voiced (2:11), an interpretation that has been espoused by nearly all commentators. Recently, however, Sasson (84) has attempted to understand Boaz's words in a radically different manner. According to him, "rather than evoking events which transpired months in the past, Boaz was responding to Ruth's immediate statement of v 9. In praising the 'last (deed),' Boaz singles out her unselfish attempt at finding a *gôʾēl* to resolve her mother-in-law's difficulty as worthier than her self-serving hope to acquire a husband" (cf. *JSOT* 5 [1978] 55). This is based, as Sasson specifically states, on his view of v 9 as two separate requests that Ruth makes of Boaz. Since, as we have argued above, that interpretation of v 9 is both syntactically and semantically impossible, so also is this understanding of v 10. Further, to sustain this view, Sasson must ignore the clear syntactic connection between the clause "you have made your last *ḥesed* better than the first" and the immediately following clause, "not going after the young men whether poor or rich." He treats them as independent sentences: "You have acted in a worthier fashion in the last instance than in the first. There will henceforth be no need to seek men whether poor or rich" (72). This understanding of the syntax of the sentence is quite unsupported by the Hebrew (see *Comment* below).

Clearly, then, Ruth's first act of חסד is her radical loyalty and commitment to Naomi, and her last act of חסד is her proposal of marriage to Boaz. But surely it seems somewhat incongruous that Boaz designates Ruth's request for marriage to him, rather than to a younger man, as a "better act of חסד" than her radical loyalty to Naomi! Especially does this seem to be the case given the meaning of חסד when used between human beings deduced by Sakenfeld (*The Meaning of Hesed,* 24, 233–34; cf. id., *Faithfulness in Action,* 13, 39–42). In her careful examination of the term, Sakenfeld finds that it denotes a loyal and gracious act that (1) springs from an existing relationship; (2) involves an urgent need on the part of the recipient; (3) is a free act of the one performing it, i.e., an act of moral not legal responsibility; and (4) involves an extraordinary element of mercy or generosity, a "going beyond the call of duty." Given this understanding of the meaning of חסד, Boaz's comparison does indeed seem incongruous, and there certainly seems merit in Sasson's criticism of this view (*JSOT* 5 [1978] 55): "how could one not find fault with a man who chooses to value a marriage proposal over an act of mercy?" Either Boaz speaks hyperbolically, or the narrator intends him to use very puzzling language (see below).

No such problem of incongruity between the nature of Ruth's request and Boaz's designation of it as an act of חסד is perceived in the standard view of the book. In that view, Ruth's reference to Boaz as a גאל is understood to mean that she is requesting him to fulfill the duty of levirate marriage in order to raise an heir for the line of Elimelech and Mahlon. Therefore, the "last חסד" of Ruth is to be understood as Ruth's faithfulness to her dead husband in the continuance of his name and family, rather than pursuing her own desires and fortunes in a marriage to a younger man (e.g., Gerleman, 32; Hubbard, 213–14; Joüon, 74; Morris, 290; Rudolph, 56). It is just this line of interpretation that Sakenfeld uses in including this passage in those pericopes that she investigates in order to establish the meaning of חסד (*The Meaning of Hesed*, 42–43). In actuality, however, it is difficult to make this view of Ruth's request fit the definition of חסד as determined by Sakenfeld. According to her study, חסד involves an act that is a free act, i.e., one of moral but not legal responsibility, and it involves an element of "going beyond the call of duty." In the standard view of the book, however, the levirate obligation is as legally binding on the widow as on the deceased's brother, and it functions not just as a means to provide an heir for the deceased but also to provide for the security and protection of the widow (see *Excursus: Levirate Marriage in the OT* following *Comment* on 4:5d below). In this case, Ruth is simply carrying out what law, custom, and her own interests demand. How is this an example of חסד? However inaccurate the interpretation may be, it is doubtless Boaz's designation of Ruth's marriage request as an "act of חסד" that has formed one of the strongest, and apparently clearest, reasons for the view that this request is really a request for Boaz to fulfill the legal duty of levirate marriage (see, e.g., the comments of Burrows, *JBL* 59 [1940] 450; Mundhenk and de Waard, *BT* 26 [1975] 431; or McKane, *TGUOS* 19 [1961–62] 31).

As attractive as this view seems at first glance, it is not possible, as we have argued above, that Ruth is using גאל in this technical, legal sense (apart from the question of whether the one performing the levirate could be referred to as a גאל, "redeemer"). Further, as Gordis cogently argues ("Love, Marriage, and Business," 248), followed by Sasson (127; cf. id., *JSOT* 5 [1978] 56) and also Beattie (*JSOT* 5 [1978] 68), the clause "in that you have not gone after the young men whether rich or poor" makes it clear that Ruth was, as Sasson puts it, "a free agent when it came to remarriage." This observation is not only correct but well taken. That Ruth could have sought marriage with any of the men of the town means that she was under no legal obligation to become the wife of Mahlon's closest relative in order to raise up an heir for her dead husband, i.e., to carry out an obligation as legally requisite as that of the levirate prescribed in Deut 25:5–10. Nor, as we have argued above, is there the slightest hint in any of the conversations between Naomi and Ruth, or between Ruth and Boaz, that either of the women is acting upon any responsibility to do so, whether under legal or moral suasion.

However, this discussion is of value in noting the significance of Ruth's grounding her request on Boaz's status as a גאל, "redeemer." Does Boaz's "puzzling language," his designation of her "last חסד," her proposal of marriage, as better than her first, suggest that, because of her reference to "redemption," he understands her to be asking for more than marriage? In other words, even though Ruth *meant* no more than a request for marriage, does Boaz *hear* more than that? The language he will use in what follows (vv 11–13) will even more strongly suggest that he does. But, in what other way than in a marriage for Ruth do Ruth and Naomi stand in need of "redemption"? The story thus far has given us no sure clue.

לְבִלְתִּי־לֶכֶת אַחֲרֵי הַבַּחוּרִים, "in that you haven't gone after the young men." This use of the infinitive (negated by לבלתי, as regularly; cf. *GBH* § 124e) is explanatory or epexegetical. It "makes precise or explicates the preceding" (*GBH* § 124o), like the English gerundive expression "in doing something" (cf. *HebS* § 195; *IBHS* § 36.2.3e).

As a number of commentators have noted (e.g., Campbell, 124; Sasson, 85), the expression הלך אחרי (lit. "to go, walk after") often bears the pejorative sense "to whore after" (as the Targum to Ruth so rendered it [see Levine, *Aramaic Version,* 90]), but such a rendering, however common elsewhere, is totally out of place here. Campbell cites passages such as Gen 24:5, 8, 39; 1 Sam 25:42 in which a woman follows after messengers after a marriage proposal has been made and accepted. He therefore concludes that Ruth had received marriage proposals, probably from the youths who harvested Boaz's crop. There is not the slightest hint in the context, however, that the phrase is being used in such a specific, almost technical, sense. Nor does Prov 7:22 seem at all pertinent (contra de Waard-Nida, 55), for the meaning there is the literal one, "to walk after" (cf. vv 6–10, 13). The expression is used in a wide variety of derived and figurative senses, springing from the literal meaning of "walk behind, after; follow after" (Gen 32:20). One of the most frequent meanings is "to adhere to, become a partisan of," used religiously, either of Yahweh (Deut 13:5) or of foreign gods (Judg 2:12). In a related sense, it is used of the unfaithful wife "pursuing, adhering to" her lovers (Hos 2:7; note the parallel used of רדף, "pursue," in v 9). Such a specific sense is not at all pertinent, of course, in the context of Ruth 3:10. But, the two contexts are close enough to make it highly plausible that here it means "to pursue (for the purpose of marriage)" (cf. Hubbard, 214). One must recognize, however, that such a meaning implies a far more subtle and subdued range of activities than the freedom to act that modern Western society gives a woman in such matters. TEV captures it nicely with "you might have gone looking for."

בַּחוּרִים, "the young men." The word בחור means "young man," i.e., one "fully grown, vigorous, unmarried" (*HALOT,* 1, p. 114). This is made clear by the number of passages where it parallels בתולה, "young (unmarried) woman" (Isa 23:4; 62:5), and contrasts with זקן, "old man" (Jer 31:13; Prov 20:29). On this usage, and on the distinction in meaning and usage between בחור and נער, see McDonald, *BO* 32 (1975) 166–68. That it refers to men who, although fully grown, are young is convincingly shown in such a passage as Eccl 11:9, where the בחור is admonished to rejoice in his ילדות, "youth." Boaz chooses the term here, then, to refer to that group of men the majority of whom are unmarried by reason of age. These are the men most available to a widow in a polygamous society, since economics prescribed that few men could take more than one wife. The article, then, is most likely used in its generic sense, i.e., indicating a class of individuals (cf. *HebS* § 92; GKC § 126m), in all probability those of the village of Bethlehem (Morris, 209). These considerations, especially the study of McDonald cited above, speak strongly against Sasson's view (85) that בחור means men in the prime of their lives, neither נערים, "adolescents, youths," nor זקנים, "old men," but men with sufficient means either to marry Ruth or fulfill the requirement of redemption (cf. also Weismann, *VT* 31 [1981] 441–50).

11 וְעַתָּה, "So now." The use of this particle indicates that Boaz is now drawing the logical consequence of what he has just said. See *Comment* on 3:2. Inasmuch as Ruth has demonstrated anew her extraordinary loyalty (חסד), Boaz states the consequence: he will do all that she has asked.

בִּתִּי אַל־תִּירְאִי, "be assured, my daughter," lit. "my daughter, do not fear." Joüon (74) says that these words, "after the words that Boaz has just addressed to Ruth, have a completely attenuated sense and give the impression of a conventional phrase." They have the sense, then, of "be assured" or "set your mind at rest" (NEB), intended to alleviate any concern Ruth might have that Boaz might refuse her request. De Waard-Nida (55), following Gerleman (32), contend that the object of Ruth's fear is not that Boaz will refuse to help her but "the possibility that the people of the town will oppose her because she is of Moabite origin." On this basis, de Waard-Nida defend TEV's restructuring of the sentence, in which the order of the next two clauses is reversed, so that the clause "for all my fellow-citizens know that you are a woman of worth" directly follows the clause "have no fear." But, it is exactly the order of the Hebrew sentence (and hence the need to restructure to make the sense clear in English) that precludes such an understanding! Rather, as Rudolph (56) has it, Boaz "gives her the testimonial that she enjoys the best reputation in 'the gate of his people' . . . , and he promises, therefore, to comply with her request." Therefore, this phrase, lit. "have no fear," does not constitute the main clause, the consequence introduced by ועתה, "so now," as Sasson (86) concludes. Hence Sasson's observations regarding the force of ועתה when followed by the imperative are not relevant to the interpretation of the passage.

כֹּל אֲשֶׁר־תֹּאמְרִי אֶעֱשֶׂה־לָּךְ, "all that you say I will do for you." On this expression, see *Comment* on 3:5. Such an all-inclusive response seems a little out of place. She has, after all, requested only that he marry her. Or is such language simply formulaic? Such a response is surely a further hint that Boaz has heard her request to involve more than just marriage, or is it?

כָּל־שַׁעַר עַמִּי, "everyone in town," lit. "all the gate of my people." This is an unusual expression, which, strangely enough, occurs in a literal sense in two poetic passages, Mic 1:9 and Obad 13 (cf. v 11), referring to Jerusalem. It seems clear that the word "gate" is used here metaphorically, although some have taken it in the literal sense, rendering something like "all the people of the gate" (e.g., Gerleman, Wurthwein, NASV). Since such a metaphorical use occurs only here, the exact sense is unclear. Rudolph (55) understands the phrase to mean "the public opinion of Bethlehem," while Gray (*NCBC*, 395) understands "gate" to be used for "city" by synecdoche, "here with particular reference to the gate . . . as the place of business and gossip." Since the gate is the place where legal and business transactions were carried on (cf. chap. 4), Campbell (124) argues that the phrase carries the connotation of "the legally responsible body of the town." In a similar vein, Speiser ("Coming and Going at the City Gate," 85) appeals to similar meanings for the Akkadian *bābtu*, "gate," and translates "gate" here as "assembly, community." Some such translation seems close to the meaning here, and so we have rendered "all the assembly [lit. 'gate'] of my people" as "everyone in town." Whatever the exact nuance of the expression, the sense is clear: it was a matter of common knowledge.

אֵשֶׁת חַיִל, "a woman of worth." The phrase here rather clearly stresses "the quality of Ruth's person" (Campbell, 125; contra Sasson, 87–88). The virtues of the אשת

חיל extolled in Prov 31:10–31 are her faithfulness to her social, religious, and family responsibilities. Just such responsibilities Ruth has carried out relative to Naomi. As most commentators have noted, Boaz's description of Ruth here matches precisely the narrator's identification of Boaz in 2:1.

12 וְעַתָּה כִּי, "Now." In v 11 Boaz has given a positive response to Ruth's request for marriage. But she has grounded that request on Boaz's position as a גֹּאֵל, "redeemer," and that fact has further consequences that neither Naomi nor Ruth envisaged. To these consequences, Boaz turns with words that can only leave his readers mystified regarding the full implications of their meaning and that hence increase the suspense and anticipation of events to come. We have opted to interpret the first כי of the sentence as an example of the use of כי to separate the sentence-adverbial from the rest of the sentence (with Blau, *Adverbial Construction,* § 2:1:4, p. 27; cf. esp. p. 26 n. 15), the function originating in the adverbial as a logical predicate (see Blau, *Adverbial Construction* § 1:7). This seems preferable to other options. The regular causal force, "since, because," adopted by Sasson (89) is rendered most improbable by the context. The clause it here introduces, "truly I am a redeemer, but there is a redeemer more closely related than I," is semantically most inappropriate as a cause or reason for the following injunction, "Stay here tonight" (v 13a; contra Sasson, 89; see also below). Almost as attractive in context as the view adopted above is the concessive force, "although, even if" (with almost all modern English translations; cf. Hubbard, 217, but can his translation, 208, "since" be so understood?). However, given the remarks of Aejmelaeus (*JBL* 105 [1986] 198–99) on the uncertainty of כי introducing real concessions, the concessive force is less likely here.

אָמְנָם כִּי אם גֹּאֵל אָנֹכִי, "truly I am a redeemer." The syntax of this clause is complicated by an apparent excess of asseverative and emphatic expressions. Elsewhere in the OT not only does the particle אָמְנָם (variant form אֻמְנָם) function as the asseverative, "truly, verily" (on which see *IBHS* § 39.3.4b), but so does the synonymous compound אמנם כי (Job 12:2), and perhaps also כי אמנם (Job 36:4, but כי here may well have a causal sense; cf. the remarks of Blau, *Adverbial Construction,* 26 n. 15). Moreover, כי־אם can function as an emphasizing expression (e.g., 1 Sam 21:6), quite frequent in oaths (cf. *HALOT,* B.1.b, p. 471). Given the uncertainty that כי אמנם does function as an asseverative in Job 36:4 (see above), the first כי in the sentence is best taken with ועתה; see the previous entry. Whether one then accepts K אמנם, "truly," + כי־אם, "indeed," or Q אמנם כי, "truly" (the following אם not being read), makes little difference to the sense (see the remarks of Blau, *Adverbial Construction,* 26 n. 15), though the former seems somewhat overloaded. In support of Q, it can plausibly be argued that the mistaken אם arose by dittography from the preceding כי אמנם (so, e.g., Gerleman, Gray, Rudolph).

Finally, two understandings of the passage depart rather radically from those commonly adopted. First, Sasson (88–99; followed by Hubbard, 208 n. 12) avers that both of the clauses of v 12, between ועתה, "now," and ליני, "spend the night" (the first word of v 13), are "parenthetical asides, spoken by Boaz in order to clarify his orders of verse 13." Sasson adopts this understanding in order to have two parallel uses of ועתה plus the imperative in vv 11 and 12–13 to function as two responses parallel to the two requests that he contends Ruth has made in v 9. But v 9 cannot be understood as comprising two requests (see *Comment* there), nor can v 11 be understood as ועתה plus the imperative (see *Comment* there). Likewise, in the context here, the logical consequence anticipated by the particle ועתה can hardly be the imperative, לִינִי, "spend the night," but surely must consist of the surprising complication of the existence of another redeemer nearer in kin than Boaz, which Boaz reveals in this verse.

Second, Staples (*AJSL* 54 [1938] 62–65) must understand v 12 in some other sense than the customary translation in order to support his argument that only one person at any one time could be designated "redeemer." To do so, he argues as follows: (1) the first כי belongs with אמנם to form an asseverative expression; (2) the second כי is an emphatic, as in oaths; and (3) the אם is an example of a rare negative particle. On these grounds Staples translates the sentence, "But now, as a matter of fact, I am really not [your] gô[>]ēl, but you do have a gôēl, one who is more closely related [to you] than I." However, the hypothesis that requires such a rendering is not acceptable, and the sense so obtained does not fit the context. As Rudolph (55) notes, the logic that concludes that only one person could be designated a "redeemer" is convoluted; the potential redeemer could just as well be called a redeemer as the actual one (cf. 4:4, 6). The interpretation that אם is here a negative, although grammatically possible (see GKC § 149e), makes most difficult sense in this context, for the second clause "but there is a גאל more closely related than I" clearly implies that Boaz also belongs to this category of people.

וְגַם יֵשׁ גֹּאֵל קָרוֹב מִמֶּנִּי, "but there is a redeemer more closely related than I." Given that the adversative sense sometimes assumed for גם (cf. BDB, גם 5; Joüon, 75) is problematical, it is best to take the compound וגם in its emphasizing force (cf. *CHALOT,* גם 11b), with the adversative sense signaled by the semantic contrast of the two clauses. This clause reveals that there was a hierarchy of responsibility and privilege among those subject to the obligation of caring for family members in need. Naomi and Ruth have requested Boaz to marry Ruth on the basis that he is subject to such moral obligations, and Boaz has agreed, vv 9–11. But there is another relative whose family relationship accords him prior rights and responsibilities. These Boaz will respect.

13 לִינִי הַלַּיְלָה, "Stay here tonight." As Sasson (90) observes, the verb לון denotes the passage of time rather than expressing the manner in which that time is spent, such as שׁכב, "lie down." As such, it avoids the possible sexual connotations of the latter, signaling that they met the temptation of such a setting with the same integrity that characterized their conduct throughout (cf. Hubbard, 218). As Boaz's next words will disclose, whether Ruth will marry Boaz or the just-revealed "nearer redeemer" will wait for the morning to decide. In the meantime, no taint of scandal will further complicate the matter. Many commentators speculate on the reason for Boaz's injunction, most expressing the danger inherent in a woman journeying home alone at night (cf. Cant 5:7). Our narrator, however, leaves the reason totally to his reader's imagination, another of the ways that he leaves his narrative ambiguous and hence somewhat provocative.

אִם יִגְאָלֵךְ, "if he will redeem you." Three times in this verse Ruth is explicitly the object of the verb גאל in the form of the second person feminine singular pronominal suffix, as here, and once implicitly, the object being understood. In my opinion, it is clear that Boaz must be using גאל, "to redeem," here to mean "to act as a *gô[>]ēl* by marrying the widow of a deceased relative," the same sense in which Ruth used the term גאל in 3:9 and the only sense in which the term has been used thus far in the context. Daube is quite correct (*Studies in Biblical Law,*

45) when he gives as one of the occasions on which perforce one had to rely on one's relatives, *qua* redeemers, "when a man died leaving a wife with no children, his nearest relative had to 'take back' [i.e., 'redeem'] the widow—who otherwise would be lost to the family and, mostly, destitute herself—by marrying her" (bracketed comment mine), citing Ruth 3:13. It is important to note that the purpose of this marriage is the protection and support of the widow, not the provision of an heir for the deceased; i.e., the verb גאל, "redeem," here is no more being used to refer to a legal obligation incumbent on a near relative to contract a levirate marriage than the noun גאל, "redeemer," was in 3:9 (see *Comment* there), contra the vast majority of commentators (e.g., Campbell, 132; Gray, *NCBC*, 395; Morris, 292–93; Rudolph, 56; de Waard-Nida, 53, 57 n. 20). As we have argued, the levirate obligation of marrying the widow of a deceased brother to raise up a descendant for the deceased has not surfaced thus far in the story at any point. Naomi's instruction to Ruth in 3:1–4 and Ruth's words to Boaz in 3:9 have had as their object not a levirate marriage but solely the removal of the destitution and disgrace of Ruth's widowhood. Furthermore, as the *Comment* on 4:5 will show, the marriage spoken of in that verse and in 4:10 is an example not of the legally required obligation of levirate marriage per se, incumbent upon the brothers of the deceased, but of a voluntary, moral obligation, which, for want of a better term, we shall designate a "levirate-type responsibility" (see the discussion there), which Boaz raises there for the first time.

Beattie (*JSOT* 5 [1978] 44–46) has proposed that גאל, "redeem," in 3:13 bears a very different sense from that which it carries in 3:9. Although Beattie avers that Ruth uses גאל in 3:9 in the general sense of "the part he has already played in the story" (44), i.e., as the one responsible to come to the aid of family members in need (see *Comment* on 2:20), he argues that "something new is introduced" in vv 12–13 and that "there is a certain degree of mystery" about Boaz's words therein (45). The identity of that "something new," according to Beattie, is not made clear until chap. 4, where Boaz is "acting as a *gôʾēl* in a technical sense and buying from them the property which had been left to them by Elimelech and Mahlon." Hence, "the meaning of Boaz's statement in iii 13 is simply that this anonymous redeemer would be offered the option of redeeming the land" (46). Beattie, then, contends that Boaz uses גאל, "redeem," in v 13 in the technical sense of the obligation of the גאל, "redeemer," to redeem land. But there is nothing whatsoever in the context to indicate that Boaz is using גאל here with any different meaning than Ruth has given it in 3:9. To support his argument, Beattie argues that in v 13 Boaz "must be referring to something other than what Ruth had asked for. It is nonsense, otherwise, for Boaz to say in v. 11, 'I will do all you say'" (*JSOT* 5 [1978] 46). This is simply non sequitur. In v 9 Ruth has said, in essence, "Give me the protection of marriage, for you are a *gôʾēl.*" In praising her in v 10, Boaz has clearly shown that he understands her to be asking for marriage. In v 11 he says, "I will do for you all that you say." He does not say specifically "I will marry you." When, then, in v 12 he introduces as a further consequence of her request that there is another גאל more closely related than he (i.e., with prior rights) and then speaks of the possibility of this man "redeeming" Ruth, in what other way we can possibly understand his words than to mean marriage? When Beattie notes "Nothing is said about the sphere of activity in which this other *gôʾēl* may choose whether or not to act" (*JSOT* 5 [1978] 46), he is totally ignoring the fact that the context has made it quite clear in what sense he is to act. Therefore, vv 12–13 indicate that there was an order of precedence according to which one relative would act as גאל rather than another in the matter of the moral obligation, the family responsibility, to marry the widow of a relative, just as there was an order of preference in the matter of the legal obligation to redeem land.

We do agree with Beattie, however, when he observes that the use of the verb גאל here is "deliberately equivocal language . . . . Boaz does *not* say, 'If he will not marry you, I will marry you myself'" (*JSOT* 5 [1978] 45). Once again by his choice of language our narrator strongly hints that Boaz has heard Ruth's proposal as more than a request for marriage. He uses the verb גאל, "redeem," with a double entendre, and there is an element of mystery involved (as Beattie alleges), for nothing in the story has suggested thus far in what other sense Ruth and Naomi may be in need of "redemption."

That v 13 speaks four times of either the nearer redeemer or Boaz "redeeming" Ruth is the final telling piece of evidence that Sasson's proposal that Ruth in 3:9 made two separate requests (see *Comment* thereto), one for marriage for herself and the other for redemption for Naomi, is an untenable hypothesis. Not only does Sasson (90) note the serious problems these data present, finally concluding (91–92) that "perhaps the best approach is to admit many difficulties in incorporating these data in the scheme of our tale," but also he translates the verb גאל with the attached direct object suffix "to redeem *for* you" (72; cf. also 90), a use of the objective pronominal suffix unparalleled elsewhere to my knowledge.

Hence, it is prima-facie evident that Boaz means by the verb "redeem" here at least what Ruth meant in 3:9, "to act as the *gô'ēl* by marrying the widow of a deceased relative." He may be using it with a double entendre—in which case the narrator both increases our suspense and piques our curiosity and interest by speaking somewhat mysteriously, for no other need for redemption for Ruth and Naomi has heretofore surfaced in the story. In my opinion this is exactly what he is doing. But he is not using "redeem" in a totally different sense from Ruth's use in 3:9.

14 The sequence of the last two clauses here is difficult. While the Hebrew states that it was Ruth who arose before one person could recognize another (ותקם, "she arose"), it is Boaz's words in the clause that follows (ויאמר, "and he said"), not spoken to Ruth (as האשה, "the woman," makes clear), that seem to give the grounds for such an action. Commentators adopt a number of stratagems to resolve the difficulty. Joüon (77) proposes to read ויקם, "he arose." But there is no textual warrant for such a change, for all the versions read the feminine form of the verb. Rudolph (55–56), rejecting Joüon's emendation, proposes to add בדברו, "at his bidding," after ותקם, "she arose," but, again, not a single Hebrew MS or ancient version gives any evidence of such a reading. Syr resolved the difficulty by making Ruth the subject of the last clause, rendering, "she said to him, 'No one should know that I came to you at the threshing floor,'" while Vg did so by making Boaz's words a warning spoken directly to Ruth. The difficulty is best resolved by observing that, even though the Hebrew MS idiom "to say to oneself, to think" is most often expressed by the phrase "to say in the heart," the verb "to say" alone, without the addition of the adverbial phrase "in the heart," can be used in this sense (e.g., Gen 20:11; see BDB, 2, p. 56; cf. the *Comment* on this use in 4:4 below). Further, our storyteller first describes what Ruth did and then what Boaz thought, for the waw consecutive with which the second clause begins, ויאמר, "and he said," precludes understanding Boaz's words as antecedent to Ruth's action.

15 הָבִי הַמִּטְפַּחַת, "Hold out the shawl." The imperative הָבִי is unusual in several respects. It occurs only in speech in the OT. The root is generally taken to be יהב, on the basis of the occurrence of this root in Aramaic/Syriac, Arabic, and Ethiopic with a meaning in the general semantic range of "to give." Except when it is used as an exhortatory interjection (meaning "come, come now!" e.g., Gen 11:3, 4, 7), it is a colloquialism used in contexts similar to the Ruth passage to express what one wishes to have provided or made available (cf. Gen 29:21; 30:1). In our passage, it means something like "hold out, make available."

הַמִּטְפַּחַת, "the shawl." The word מטפחת occurs elsewhere only in Isa 3:22 in a long list of women's jewelry and attire, in which the meanings of most items are as obscure and uncertain as מטפחת. Since, however, the items mentioned include none of the terms for ordinary garments or clothing in general (e.g., בגד, שׂמלה, or כתנת), it seems most unlikely that מטפחת is a synonym of שׂמלה and simply refers to the same garment mentioned in 3:3 (contra Campbell, 120; Joüon, 78). Further, it is also unlikely that Ruth could have used the only outer garment she was wearing to carry the very large portion of grain that Boaz is about to give her. Hence, some such rendering as "shawl" seems to meet the criteria demanded: it was a piece of outer clothing, yet large enough and strong enough to hold a considerable amount.

וַיָּמָד שֵׁשׁ־שְׂעֹרִים, lit. "and he measured six (measures) of barley." The omission of the measure involved in stating quantities of weight and volume is common enough in the OT when the context would have made the measure obvious (cf. Brockelmann, *Syntax* § 85e; *GBH* § 142n). Unfortunately, our knowledge of the normative term expected in speaking of the measurement of particular commodities is so limited that the particular volume measure here implied, which must have been clear to the original hearers of the story, is quite unknown to us. In addition, our knowledge of the precise modern equivalents of the volume and weight measures in use in the OT is also uncertain, so there is considerable uncertainty as to what quantity of barley Ruth shouldered and carried home. The measures of dry volume that produce weights of grain that are within reason for a healthy young peasant woman to carry (in some sort of garment, it is important to note) are three, the ephah (איפה), the seah (סאה), and the omer (עמר). According to the information presented in the *Comment* on 2:17, an ephah of barley would weigh a little less than 30 or 50 pounds, so six such measures would weigh something under 180 or 300 pounds, depending upon which modern equivalent is adopted (see the discussion in Campbell, 104), a weight that surely seems prohibitive for a woman to carry by any means, let alone in some sort of garment! Since the omer is one tenth of an ephah, the weight of grain involved would be about 18 or 30 pounds. This is considerably less than Ruth was able to glean in a day (cf. 2:17), probably too small an amount. The seah was about one third of an ephah (its exact relationship to the ephah is uncertain; see *IDB* 4:834–35), making the weight involved about 60 or 100 pounds, an amount that would certainly be possible for a strong young peasant woman, accustomed to such burdens, to carry. That such an amount could have been carried in some type of garment seems quite problematical, however. See the comments of Sasson, 96.

וַיָּבֹא הָעִיר, "Then he went up to the city." The majority of modern translations (e.g., JB, NASV, NEB, NJPS, RSV, TEV) and many recent commentators adopt the reading "*she* went up" here, a reading attested by a considerable number of Hebrew MSS, Syr, and Vg. But the MT reading of the masculine, referring to Boaz, is clearly to be preferred (cf. NRSV). In the second place, as Rudolph (56) and Sasson (98) have observed, such an emendation means that a very short clause beginning ותבוא would both close v 15 and open v 16, an inelegant redundancy hardly to be expected from a writer whose mastery of style has been evident throughout. Second, the main actor in the preceding sequence of clauses has been Boaz, so it is entirely expected that our narrator will finish describing what Boaz did before turning to tell of Ruth's actions. Indeed, without this clause, we would hear nothing about any further actions of Boaz until the opening clause of the next act in 4:1.

Explanation

As was noted in the section on *Form/Structure/Setting,* this scene depicts in both deeds and words the response, first of Ruth and then of Boaz, to Naomi's daring and shocking plan proposed in the previous scene. The first section (vv 6–7) and the last (vv 14–15) consist of narrative: in the first, Ruth puts Naomi's plan into action, and in the second, Boaz responds to Ruth with deeds. These narrative sections form the frame for the central sections of dialogue.

The first part of the narrative frame, vv 6–7, consists of a summary statement (v 6), for which the following verse fills in the details. In doing so, it repeats both the content and order of Naomi's instructions given in vv 3–4, and it adds three elements not mentioned by Naomi that seem not insignificant. (1) "When Boaz had eaten and drunk," we are told, "he felt at peace with the world." This surely hints that he will be receptive to the request that Ruth's actions will symbolize. (2) "Then," we are told, "he went and lay down to sleep at the end of the heap of grain." In the words of Trible (183),

> "At the end of the heap of grain": a minor detail yet important for the execution of the plan. The phrase suggests an area separate from the other sleepers and accessible to the waiting woman. Is this detail another hint of that blessed chance which aids these women in their struggles for life? Earlier Ruth happened to come to the field of Boaz (2:3). Does Boaz happen now to lie at the corner of the threshing floor? We cannot be sure.

But such a suggestive touch is fully in keeping with the subtle and expressive style of our narrator! (3) He then adds that Ruth came *quietly,* uncovered his legs, and lay down. By this addition—she did so in such a manner as not to disturb the sleeping man (see *Comment*)—our narrator wished to stress that Ruth carried out Naomi's instructions to the letter. Such repetition slows the pace of the account and heightens our suspense. Ruth has placed herself in a most delicate and risky situation—asleep with Boaz on an isolated corner of the threshing floor! What will be the outcome of such a provocatively sensual action?

Having set the scene with this narrative summary, our narrator then devotes minimal time, space, and words to the events that transpired. He introduces the dialogue between Boaz and Ruth with a staccato series of three sequential clauses (literally translated), "And it was in the middle of the night and the man shuddered awake and turned over," followed by the nonsequential, vivid, and graphic clause (capturing the scene from Boaz's point of view) "and here someone was lying beside him" (see *Comment*). Clearly, the center of his interest is the words that pass between Ruth and Boaz in the darkness of the threshing floor in the middle of the night; i.e., once again he moves his story forward principally through dialogue. The first words (v 9a) are those of Boaz as, startled, he seeks the identity of the unknown person lying beside him. Ruth's first words (v 9b) simply respond to this inquiry by giving her name and identifying herself as a "handmaid," a term that, though deferential, accords her a status compatible with the position her actions symbolically seek (see *Comment*). It is also important to note that she does not identify herself to Boaz as "wife of Mahlon" (or "wife of the deceased"), the identity Boaz gives her in 4:5, 10, as might be expected if she was indeed calling upon Boaz to take on the responsibility of levirate marriage for the purpose of raising an heir to the line of Elimelech, as is most often assumed (see esp. the discussion of the nature of the "levirate-type" marriage responsibility of the fourth chapter of Ruth following the *Comment* on 4:5d below and the *Explanation* thereto). Like Naomi when she concocted this bold stratagem (see above), Ruth is not here concerned to continue a male line. Rather, her goal is a woman's goal, namely, to be married, the only honorable security afforded a woman in her patriarchal world. The depth of her concern to achieve it is reflected in the risky scheme she so readily pursues.

With the words that follow, however, Ruth seems to modify the script of Naomi's instructions—somewhat surprisingly, given that our narrator has already told us, both in Ruth's own words (v 5) and in his own words (v 6), that she did exactly as Naomi had instructed. Naomi's instructions clearly stated that at this point Boaz would take over: "Then he himself will tell you what to do" (v 4d). Ruth, however, does not wait for a response from Boaz. She puts Naomi's plan into words, and in so doing tells Boaz what to do, "Spread the skirt of your robe [Heb. 'your *kānāp̄*'] over your handmaid, for you are a redeemer." Yet in so doing she does *not* rewrite the script that Naomi had written for her. On the contrary, Ruth uses an idiom that expresses in language the same meaning as the symbolic action that Naomi had instructed her to perform. Naomi had said, "uncover his legs and lie down" (v 4), and Ruth performed exactly this symbolic action (v 7). Now she uses the spoken idiom that both constitutes the natural and necessary complement to that action, "Spread the skirt of your robe [Heb. *kānāp̄*] over your handmaid," and bears the same meaning, i.e., "marry me" (see *Comment*). Both action and idiom lack nothing in clarity, and Boaz instantly comprehends, as v 10 makes clear. In addition, by putting such words in the mouth of Ruth, our narrator skillfully creates a wordplay with the expression Boaz used to bless her on the occasion of their first meeting on the harvest field in 2:12. Rauber (*JBL* 89 [1970] 33) has well caught the significance of this:

> In Boaz's mind this triggers a memory, recalls to him his previous words, "And a full reward be given thee of the Lord GOD of Israel, *under whose wings thou art come to trust.*" Once this correspondence has been made, the full meaning and implications of his

> previous words flood in upon him. . . . In a moment the process of understanding is completed. Everything culminates and merges in this image of ingathering: the wings of the LORD sweeping in to himself the people, the arms of Boaz gathering in to himself the maiden Ruth, the arms of the young men drawing into the barns the grain. It is a moment of imaginative splendor and depth.

She who came to find shelter under Yahweh's "wing" will find her full reward from Yahweh when the man who himself voiced such a blessing spreads his "wing" over her in marriage!

Ruth's words to Boaz, however, do not stop with this polite but firm request. She continues by grounding her request in the fact that Boaz is a גאל, "redeemer," i.e., that he is one who is called on to deliver a family member from evil and trouble, particularly poverty, oppression, or injustice (see *Comment* on 2:20). This fact makes it incontrovertible that, however much the time, place, and circumstances of her symbolic action ("she uncovered his legs and lay down") and the words with which she interprets it ("spread the skirt of your robe over me") are replete with sexual imagery and implications, her words do not simply invite Boaz to the pleasures of sexual embrace. Indeed, on the contrary, she, a foreign woman, calls an Israelite man to responsibility (Trible, 184). That Boaz would act in a responsible and caring way must surely have been what Naomi had in mind when she concluded her description of the symbolic action of uncovering Boaz's legs and lying down with the statement that "he will tell you what to do." However, under the exigencies of this moment, lying there beside Boaz on the threshing floor in the middle of the night, Ruth very understandably did *not* leave the meaning of that moment to Boaz's interpretation of mute metaphors and the inarticulate implications of symbolic action! Rather, she put the meaning of the moment into words and told Boaz what to do. Then, doubtless again under the exigencies of her situation, she grounded her request in Boaz's position as a גאל, a "redeemer." In so doing, as the story will quickly make clear, she opened to Boaz the possibility of a resolution of their plight that neither she nor Naomi envisaged for a moment!

The suspense created by Naomi's audacious plan, heightened in the opening episode by the detailed account of how Ruth carried it out, now subsides as Boaz gives his assent in vv 10–11. Characteristically, his opening words are words of blessing for Ruth. The reason for that blessing suggests, at first glance, that Boaz perceives the meaning of that moment from the perspective of his own limited world as fully as Ruth did from hers, for his first reaction seems to spring not from any sensitivity to the boldness of Naomi's plan or the precariousness and ambiguity of Ruth's situation but from a deep feeling of gratitude to Ruth that she has sought him out for marriage rather than seeking the young men of the town (v 10c). It would seem that he is so caught up in his own world of pleasure in her choice that he not only dubs it a kind and gracious act (חסד) but hyperbolically deems it more kind and gracious than her previous commitment to Naomi (v 10b)! And yet, is he only speaking hyperbolically? The extravagant language he uses to respond to a request for marriage, however gratifying, causes us to wonder. Has he perhaps understood her request to encompass more than simply marriage? If so, in what other way could he have understood her words? The story thus far has given us no sure clue. There is only a sense that Boaz's response somehow seems not to fit. Or does it?

The logical consequence (note the introductory "So now") of such a kind and gracious act almost necessarily follows: "be assured, my daughter, all that you say I will do for you, for everyone in town knows that you are a woman of worth" (v 11). Suspense seems to have fully given way to assurance, and the dénouement that will turn plight to plenty seems surely but a short step away—especially since Boaz's words of praise, calling her a "woman of worth" (אשת חיל), bring immediately to mind the narrator's description of Boaz in 2:1 as a "man of substance and standing" (איש גבור חיל). "Female and male; foreigner and native; youth and age; poor and wealthy—all these opposites are mediated by human worth" (Trible, 184). Such appropriateness of character in two such different people seems indeed to assure us that the requested marriage is a foregone conclusion. It is another measure of the skill of our storyteller that such a subtle assurance should be expressed immediately prior to the complication that seems to throw it all in doubt! Yet again, does he refer only to marriage when he says to her, "*All* that you say I will do"? Surely he simply means marriage. Or does he?

Boaz's words of response do not end, however, with this unqualified statement of assurance. The first logical consequence is balanced by a second (v 12a; see *Form/Structure/Setting*), this time attendant upon the fact that Ruth has grounded her request in Boaz's position as a גאל, "redeemer." Though Boaz is certainly a redeemer, there is a redeemer more closely related than he (v 12), and propriety dictates that he should have the opportunity to act first (v 13). "From a storytelling point of view, this has the marvelous effect of creating one more suspenseful moment, in which Boaz is given his opportunity to show his worthiness; for it is one feature of Boaz's valor that he will not even usurp another man's right to act responsibly!" (Campbell, 137). Suspense had subsided in the face of Boaz's unqualified assurance; in the face of his probity suspense returns full force.

Along with suspense, however, there is also mystery, for once again Boaz's language makes one wonder if he refers to more than she is asking. Four times in v 13, twice of the nearer relative and twice of himself, he speaks of "redeeming" Ruth. Naomi and Ruth have requested of Boaz only marriage to Ruth, and the word גאל, "redeemer," has been used thus far in the story only in the general sense of the moral obligation of a man to come to the aid and succor of family members in need. Surely, then, Boaz must be using the verb גאל, "to redeem," here in the same general sense. But, as Beattie observes (*JSOT* 5 [1978] 45), he could have said, "If he will not marry you, I will do so." Since he speaks of "redeeming" Ruth and this verb can bear at least three specific technical senses (see *Comment* on 2:20), does he mean something other than or more than marriage? If so, to what could he refer? In what other way does Ruth stand in need of "redemption" than the removal of the destitution and opprobrium of widowhood? The story so far has not given us the slightest clue. So Boaz must mean simply marriage. Or does he mean more than that?

The concluding frame for this remarkable dialogue constitutes the fourth episode, vv 14–15, again narrative. Here the next morning Boaz engages in symbolic actions that signify promise, corresponding to Ruth's symbolic action of petition the previous evening. Our narrator presents Ruth's actions and Boaz's thoughts as sequentially distinct events: "So she lay there beside him until morning. Then she arose before one person could recognize another, and Boaz thought 'It must not be known that the woman came to the threshing floor.'" Campbell (126) has doubtless caught the significance of this sequence: "The storyteller is getting across the idea that both Boaz and Ruth take the initiative in the progress toward resolution of what has now become their common cause." Boaz's symbolic action of promise then immediately follows: he filled her shawl full with an extremely generous gift of grain (see *Comment*), v 15, parallel to his generous provision of grain for Ruth to glean upon the occasion of their first meeting (2:14–17). Besides providing Ruth with a "cover" for her return home from the threshing floor, his gift is an earnest of his actions to come—actions that will permanently put an end to their plight.

The passage concludes with the almost laconic two-word statement, "Then-he-went to-the-city." This statement contrasts strikingly with the two-word clause that opened the scene, "Then-she-went-down to-the-threshing-floor" (v 6a). At the beginning of chap. 2, the initiative for progress in the story had devolved upon Ruth, since Naomi was wrapped up in the silence of her bitter despair. At the beginning of this chapter, the initiative had passed to Naomi, who had come to life again upon learning that Ruth's benefactor was Boaz. The contrast here of these opening and closing statements signals that the initiative for progress in the story has now passed from Ruth and Naomi to Boaz. As Naomi will realize when she receives the gift (v 18), we shall not have long to wait for Boaz to act to bring the whole problem to resolution.

Scene 3
Naomi Evaluates the Encounter: Boaz Will Act (3:16–18)

Bibliography

McDonald, J. "Some Distinctive Characteristics of Israelite Spoken Hebrew." *BO* 32 (1975) 162–75.

Translation

[16]*She came to her mother-in-law, who said,*[a] *"How do things stand with you,*[b] *my daughter?" So Ruth*[c] *told her all that the man had done for her.* [17]*"And," she said, "he gave me these six measures of barley,*[a] *'because,' he said,*[b] *'you must not go back empty-handed*[c] *to your mother-in-law!'"* [18]*Then Naomi said, "Now you must wait,*[a] *my daughter, until you learn how the matter*[b] *will turn out, for the man will not rest this day unless he has settled it."*[c]

Notes

16.a. Lit. "and she said."
16.b. Lit. "who [i.e., 'in what condition'; see *Comment*] are you, . . . ?"
16.c. Lit. "she."

17.a. Lit. "these six measures of barley he gave me." See *Comment.*

17.b. Q adds the vowels for אֵלַי, "to me," after the verb "he said," a reading attested by several of the versions. Though it is possible that the word was omitted by haplogr before אל (Gerleman, 30; Hubbard, 223; Joüon, 79), it is not necessary (Rudolph, 52). The shorter text is more likely original, as in vv 5 and 11.

17.c. Lit. "empty."

18.a. Lit. "sit down."

18.b. The word דבר, "matter," here inexplicably does not have the definite article, although it does later in the sentence.

18.c. Lit. "the matter."

Form/Structure/Setting

This, the concluding scene, consists of a brief dialogue in which Ruth reports to Naomi the results of the night's encounter. For the criteria of form and content that determine this division into scenes, see the discussion of the form and structure of the whole act given for the introductory scene. The scene opens with the narrative statement "she came to her mother-in-law," which contrasts sharply with the concluding statement of the previous scene, "He went to the city," marking the boundary of the pericope. The content of the scene consists of a short tripartite dialogue structured as follows:

Verse	Form	Content	Function
16b	direct quote	Naomi's question	trigger ↓
16c	narrative statement	Ruth's reply	response
17	direct quote		trigger ↓
18	direct quote	Naomi's conclusion	conclusion

It begins with Naomi's initial question asking Ruth how things stand with her, v 16b. This is followed by the report of Ruth's response, vv 16c–17, which then triggers Naomi's conclusion, v 18. The way the narrator reports Ruth's response, vv 16c–17, centers attention on only one of all the things that Boaz said and did, for the whole course of the night's events is set forth in the brief narrative statement "So Ruth told her all that the man had done for her." But the account of Boaz's magnanimous gift of grain is given in a direct quote of Ruth's words, within which is included a direct quote of Boaz's reason for the gift, thus focusing all our attention on this symbolic act and its meaning. Contrary to the preceding two acts, there is no concluding narrative statement.

Comment

16 מִי אַתְּ בִּתִּי, lit., "who are you, my daughter?" This literal meaning is difficult to understand in the context. It is impossible to understand this as Naomi's response to Ruth's knocking on the door, for the response to such a stimulus would more naturally be "who is there?" or "Is that you, Ruth?" and some further response from Ruth would be necessary, certainly different from that narrated in the clause following (v 16c; Rudolph, 57). Syr apparently took the text in just this literal sense and so was impelled to insert "She said to her, 'I am Ruth.'" LXX[B] handled the difficulty by simply not translating the two words מי את. As Campbell (129) notes, these attempts to handle this difficulty demonstrate the correctness of the text. Campbell very perceptively also notes that the vocative "my daughter," the term of address to Ruth regularly used by Naomi and Boaz (cf., e.g., 2:2, 8, 22; 3:1), clearly indicates that the question is not asking for identification; contrast the identical words in 3:9, where Boaz does not add "my daughter" and very specifically seeks identification (so also Sasson, 100). Most commentators (e.g., Campbell, Joüon, Rudolph) interpret מי here as an "accusative of condition" = "as who?" i.e., "in what condition or capacity?" (cf. BDB, 566; and esp. *IBHS* § 18.2d), citing as parallel its usage in Amos 7:2, 5: מִי יָקוּם יַעֲקֹב, "In what way/how can Jacob exist?" (cf. Isa 51:19). That מִי functions here as an "accusative" in a nominal sentence creates no grammatical difficulty (contra Hubbard, 224 n. 5), for designating the usage as an "accusative" is purely a matter of nomenclature. It could just as well be designated an adverbial usage (cf. *HebS* § 123). The impersonal pronoun מָה, "what," is used in a very similar way in Judg 18:8 (Goslinga, 541). Since Ruth's response is to tell Naomi all that Boaz had done for her (v 16c), some such sense is required by the context. Gerleman's attempt (33) to interpret the particle מִי here as purely an interrogative particle, yielding the question "Is it you, Ruth?" also does not commend itself since it too requires some other response from Ruth than an account of the night's activities.

17 שֵׁשׁ־הַשְּׂעֹרִים הָאֵלֶּה נָתַן לִי, "He gave me these six measures of barley." Although the inverted word order—object-verb—in which there is no emphasis implied, seems standard for spoken Hebrew (see McDonald, *BO* 32 [1975] 164–65), this would seem to be the exception, for the context, particularly the demonstrative pronoun האלה, "these" (behind which one can almost see Ruth pointing emphatically with her finger; so Hubbard, 225), rather clearly implies emphasis.

אַל־תָּבוֹאִי רֵיקָם, "You must not go back empty-handed." Interestingly, these words of Boaz, which Ruth quotes, were not recorded when the scene was related in v 15. From this fact, Sasson (151) sees merit in the suggestion that Ruth made up the statement in order to promote Boaz as a benefactor of Naomi so as to ease her anxiety over risking the loss of her daughter-in-law. In his view, it would be much more subtle and sensitive on the part of the narrator to assign the pregnant use of ריקם, "empty," here, employed to reflect the reversal of Naomi's "emptiness" expressed in 1:21, to Ruth who heard the first use of the word from the depths of Naomi's despair, rather than to the wealthy Boaz who could have used it only accidentally. In a more subtle analysis, Berlin suggests (*Poetics,* 97–98) that the narrator may have had Ruth use direct speech here in order to represent thought or interior monologue. She observes,

> If . . . we regard direct speech as stylistically preferable but semantically equivalent to indirect speech . . . , we can then transform the quoted direct speech into indirect discourse. We would then render Ruth's speech as "He gave me these six measures of barley because he thought that I should not come empty handed to my mother-in-law." This is Ruth's perception, psychologically and ideologically, of Boaz's action . . . . We don't know why Boaz gave Ruth the barley; we know only why Ruth thought Boaz gave it to her.

In my opinion, however, the narrator rather clearly implies that these are Boaz's own words. To begin with, he first relates Ruth's response to Naomi's inquiry *with indirect speech,* using a most *general narrative summary,* "So Ruth told her all that the man had done for her." Then, however, he has Ruth relate *with direct speech one detail* of all that happened, namely, the gift of the six measures of barley, within which she cites *a direct speech of Boaz* giving the reason for the gift. By means of this structuring of Ruth's response (see *Form/Structure/Setting*), the narrator throws all the stress on the gift and, in particular, on the reason for it. Further, this stress is intended to communicate to us (and to Naomi!) the seriousness of Boaz's intentions (see *Explanation*). Surely, then, he intends to imply that this really is Boaz's purpose in giving the gift of grain and not just Ruth's impression of the same.

18 שְׁבִי, "Now you must wait" (lit. "stay!"). The verb ישב can be used in the sense "remain, stay; remain at home" (BDB, 2.a, p. 442; *HALOT,* 4, p. 444). Here it is used in the sense of "sitting still," the emphasis being "not so much upon the location as upon the attitude which Naomi thinks Ruth is justified in having" (de Waard-Nida, 61).

אֵיךְ יִפֹּל דָּבָר, "how it will turn out." The use of נפל, "to fall," to mean "to result, turn out" occurs only here.

כִּי־אִם, "unless," introduces exceptive clauses (*HebS* § 556; GKC § 163c); i.e., it introduces a condition that must be fulfilled before the preceding statement can take effect.

Explanation

The closing scene reports the dialogue between Ruth and Naomi that ensues upon Ruth's return home. The tension with which Naomi must have awaited Ruth's return from carrying out her daring and risky play is reflected in the words with which she greets her. These words were not spoken with equanimity. Almost breathlessly Naomi asks Ruth how she is as a result of the night's events. Significantly, our narrator does not quote Ruth's words in answer to this eager question but states her reply only in a narrative summary, "So Ruth told her all that the man had done for her" (v 16c). Further, Ruth's words did not stop with the answer to Naomi's question. She continued on, and, as the section on *Form/Structure/Setting* has indicated, her further response centers all our attention on Boaz's magnanimous gift of grain by relating this event alone in a direct quote of Ruth's words. In addition, our narrator chooses to give the reason for Boaz's gift here, rather than in the scene itself (3:15), by having Ruth quote his very words: "because you must not go back empty to your mother-in-law." The reason for this stress is not hard to find and is important. Naomi's plan, introduced at the beginning of the previous scene, concerned only a resolution of the destitution and disgrace of Ruth's widowhood through marriage (3:1), as did Ruth's request and Boaz's response on the threshing floor (3:9–11). Further, Boaz's promise that either he or the nearer redeemer would act in the morning related specifically only to "redeeming" Ruth (3:13). But what of Naomi? How will the death and emptiness she has experienced, the major problem posed in chap. 1, be transformed into life and fullness? Surely, the way in which our narrator has Ruth quote Boaz's very words, in which he insists that she not return "empty" (ריקם) to her mother-in-law, signals that the munificent gift of grain Boaz sends to Naomi is a portent that the resolution he has promised will also encompass her return to life and fullness, for this is the same word Naomi used in her bitter complaint in 1:21: "Full was I when I went away, but *empty* [ריקם] has Yahweh brought me back." "With a single word the resolution of one part of Naomi's plight is accomplished" (Campbell, 129). Further, as Sasson (102) insightfully notes, it is a subtle and sensitive touch of our narrator that these words of Boaz, explaining the gift, which is his pledge that Naomi's emptiness is over, are placed in the mouth of Ruth, who not only "heard it from the depths of Naomi's despair," but whose very presence there with Naomi, ignored and unacknowledged in the blindness of her bitterness, was clear evidence that her emptiness even then was to some extent illusory and most certainly temporary.

Naomi's response to Ruth reveals that she grasps full well the meaning of Boaz's symbolic gift. She counsels Ruth to sit tight, "until you learn how the matter will turn out, for the man will not rest this day unless he has settled it" (v 18). Her confidence in Boaz's integrity is undiminished; it remains as complete as when she sent Ruth on her symbolic journey to the threshing floor with only the instructions "he will tell you what to do" (3:5). However, even though she has no doubt that Boaz will act, and act with integrity, what he will do she describes only with the vague expression "how the matter will turn out." Ruth reported "all that the man had done for her" (v 16b), apparently reporting explicitly Boaz's words and actions. Does Naomi envisage that Boaz will do more than marry Ruth, prompted by his promise that either he or the nearer redeemer will "redeem" her (3:13)? The story has thus far not given us the slightest clue what Naomi could possibly conclude that Boaz means when he speaks of "redeeming" Ruth other than marrying her. The way in which our narrator has reported the munificent gift of grain, coupled with the slightly incongruous way in which Boaz has responded to Ruth's request (see *Explanation* to previous scene), subtly suggests that the dénouement Naomi so confidently expects will resolve much more than just marriage for Ruth. Skillfully and tantalizingly, our narrator has given us not a single clue how and in what way this dénouement will come.

This exchange between Ruth and Naomi comprises the last words that either of them will utter in the entire story. Poised on the threshold of fulfillment, they both step aside. "The drama ceases to be their story and becomes the story about them" (Trible, 187). Boaz clearly now takes center stage and the imminence of his action is indicated both by Naomi's assertion and by the fact that this act ends differently from the two preceding ones. Our narrator concluded the first act with a pointed allusion to the barley harvest (1:22b), subtly suggesting the end of famine and emptiness. At the end of the second act, he brought all progress in the story to a halt by noting that, when the harvest was over, Ruth still lived with her mother-in-law (2:23b), signaling the return of famine and emptiness. But this act concludes with no such narrative statement (Trible, 187). Our narrator leaves ringing in our ears only Naomi's supremely confident words that Boaz will not rest this day unless the matter is settled. Boaz's symbolic gift of grain indicated to Naomi that he would act and, by centering all attention on this gift and the reason for it in Ruth's report of the night's events, the narrator signals to us that his story now rushes irrevocably toward resolution.

Act 4
Resolution and Epilogue: Life and Fullness (4:1–22)

Scene 1
Boaz Acquires the Right to Redeem Naomi and Ruth (4:1–12)

Bibliography

Andersen, F. I. *The Hebrew Verbless Clause in the Pentateuch.* JBLMS 14. Nashville: Abingdon, 1970. ——— and **Freedman, D. N.** *Hosea: A New Translation with Introduction and Commentary.* AB 24. Garden City, NY: Doubleday, 1980. **Anderson, A. A.** "The Marriage of Ruth." *JSS* 23 (1978) 171–83. **Ap-Thomas, D. R.** "The Book of Ruth." *ExpTim* 79 (1967–68) 369–73. **Baker, D. W.** "Further Examples of the *WAW EXPLICATIVUM.*" *VT* 30 (1980) 129–36. **Barthélemy, D.,** et al. *Preliminary and Interim Report on the Hebrew Old Testament Text Project.* New York: United Bible Societies, 1979. **Beattie, D. R. G.** "The Book of Ruth as Evidence for Israelite Legal Practice." *VT* 24 (1974) 251–67. ———. "Kethibh and Qere in Ruth IV 5." *VT* 21 (1971) 490–94. ———. "Ruth III." *JSOT* 5 (1978) 39–48. **Berlin, A.** *Poetics and Interpretation of Biblical Narrative.* Sheffield: Almond, 1983. **Bernstein, M. J.** "Two Multivalent Readings in the Ruth Narrative." *JSOT* 50 (1991) 15–26. **Bewer, J.** "The Geʾullah in the Book of Ruth." *AJSL* 19 (1902–3) 143–48. **Boecker, H. J.** *Law and Administration of Justice in the Old Testament and the Ancient Near East.* Tr. J. Moiser. Minneapolis: Augsburg, 1980. ———. *Redeformen des Rechtslebens im Alten Testament.* WMANT 14. Neukirchen: Neukirchener, 1964. **Brichto, H. C.** "Kin, Cult, Land, and Afterlife—A Biblical Complex." *HUCA* 44 (1973) 9–24. ———. *The Problem of Curse in the Hebrew Bible.* JBLMS 13. Philadelphia: Scholars, 1963. **Burrows, M.** "Levirate Marriage in Israel." *JBL* 59 (1940) 23–33. ———. "The Marriage of Boaz and Ruth." *JBL* 59 (1940) 445–54. **Coats, G. W.** "Widow's Rights: A Crux in the Structure of Genesis 38." *CBQ* 34 (1972) 460–66. **Daube, D.** *Studies in Biblical Law.* London: Cambridge UP, 1947. **Davies, E. W.** "Inheritance Rights and the Hebrew Levirate Marriage: Part 1." *VT* 31 (1981) 138–44. ———. "Inheritance Rights and Hebrew Levirate Marriage: Part 2." *VT* 31 (1981) 257–68. ———. "Ruth IV 5 and the Duties of the Gōʾēl." *VT* 33 (1983) 231–34. **Dearman, J. A.** *Property Rights in the Eighth Century Prophets.* Atlanta: Scholars, 1988. **Dombrowski, B. W.** "The Meaning of the Qumran Terms 'TʿWDH' and 'MDH.'" *RevQ* 7 (1969–71) 567–74. **Driver, S. R.** *A Treatise on the Use of the Tenses in Hebrew.* 3rd ed. Oxford: University of Oxford Press, 1892. **Epstein, L. M.** *Jewish Marriage Contract: A Study in the Status of Women in Jewish Life.* New York: Jewish Theological Seminary, 1927. ———. *Marriage Laws in the Bible and in the Talmud.* HSS 12. Cambridge, MA: Harvard UP, 1942. **Geus, C. H. J. de.** *The Tribes of Israel.* Amsterdam: Van Gorcum, 1976. **Gibson, J. C. L.** *Canaanite Myths and Epics.* Edinburgh: Clark, 1977. **Gordis, R.** "Love, Marriage, and Business in the Book of Ruth: A Chapter in Hebrew Customary Law." In *A Light unto My Path.* FS J. M. Myers, ed. H. Bream, R. Heim, and C. Moore. Philadelphia: Temple UP, 1974. 241–64. ———. "On Methodology in Biblical Exegesis." *JQR* 61 (1970) 93–118. **Gordon, C. H.** *Forgotten Scripts: Their Ongoing Discovery and Decipher-*

ment. New York: Basic, 1982. ———. "*WM-* 'and' in Eblaite and Hebrew." In *Eblaitica: Essays on the Ebla Archives and Eblaite Language.* Vol. 1, ed. C. H. Gordon, G. Rendsburg, and N. Winter. Winona Lake, IN: Eisenbrauns, 1987. 29–41. **Gottwald, N.** *The Tribes of Israel.* Maryknoll, NY: Orbis, 1979. **Gow, M.** "*Ruth Quoque*—A Coquette? (Ruth IV 5)." *TynBul* 41 (1990) 302–11. ———. "The Significance of Literary Structure for the Translation of the Book of Ruth." *BT* 35 (1984) 309–20. **Houston, W. J.** Review of *Ruth,* by J. Sasson. *JSOT* 16 (1980) 69–71. **Köhler, L.** "Justice in the Gate." In *Hebrew Man.* London: SCM, 1956. 149–75. **Labuschagne, C. J.** "The Crux in Ruth 4:11." *ZAW* 79 (1967) 364–67. **Lachemann, E. R.** "Note on Ruth 4,7–8." *JBL* 56 (1937) 53–56. **Leggett, D.** *The Levirate and Goel Institutions in the Old Testament.* Cherry Hill, NJ: Mack, 1974. **Levine, B.** "In Praise of the Israelite *Mišpāḥâ:* Legal Themes in the Book of Ruth." In *The Quest for the Kingdom of God.* FS G. E. Mendenhall, ed. H. B. Huffmon, F. A. Spina, and A. R. W. Green. Winona Lake, IN: Eisenbrauns, 1983. **Levine, E.** *The Aramaic Version of Ruth.* Rome: Pontifical Biblical Institute, 1973. **Lipiński, E.** "Le Mariage de Ruth." *VT* 26 (1978) 124–27. ———. "Sale, Transfer, and Delivery in Ancient Semitic Terminology." *SGKAO* 15 (1982) 173–85. **Mace, D.** *Hebrew Marriage: A Sociological Study.* London: Epworth, 1953. **Malamat, A.** "Mari and the Bible: Some Patterns of Tribal Organization and Institutions." *JAOS* 82 (1962) 143–50. ———. "Organs of Statecraft in the Israelite Monarchy." In *The Biblical Archeologist Reader 3,* ed. E. F. Campbell and D. N. Freedman. Garden City, NY: Doubleday, 1970. 163–98. **McDonald, J.** "Some Distinctive Characteristics of Israelite Spoken Hebrew." *BO* 32 (1975) 162–75. **McKane, W.** "Ruth and Boaz." *TGUOS* 19 (1961–62) 29–40. **McKenzie, J. L.** "The Elders in the Old Testament." *Bib* 40 (1959) 522–40. **Morgenstern, J.** "The Book of the Covenant, Part II." *HUCA* 7 (1930) 159–85. **Neufeld, E.** *Ancient Hebrew Marriage Laws.* London/New York: Longmans, Green, 1944. **Niditch, S.** "The Wronged Woman Righted: An Analysis of Genesis 38." *HTR* 72 (1979) 143–49. **Parker, S.** "The Marriage Blessing in Israelite and Ugaritic Literature." *JBL* 95 (1976) 23–30. **Pedersen, J.** *Israel, Its Life and Culture I–II.* London: Oxford, 1926. **Porten, B.** "The Scroll of Ruth: A Rhetorical Study." *GCA* 7 (1978) 23–49. **Rendsburg, G.** "Eblaite *Ù-MA* and Hebrew *WM-.*" In *Eblaitica: Essays on the Ebla Archives and Eblaite Languages.* Vol. 1, ed. C. H. Gordon, G. Rendsburg, and N. Winter. Winona Lake, IN: Eisenbrauns, 1987. 33–41. **Richter, H.-F.** "Zum Levirat im Buch Ruth." *ZAW* 95 (1983) 123–26. **Rowley, H. H.** "The Marriage of Ruth." In *The Servant of the Lord.* Oxford: Blackwell, 1952. 169–94. **Sacon, K.** "The Book of Ruth: Its Literary Structure and Theme." *AJBI* 4 (1978) 3–22. **Sasson, J. M.** "The Issue of GEʾULLAH in RUTH." *JSOT* 5 (1978) 52–64. **Schneider, T. R.** "Translating Ruth 4:1–10 among the Tsonga People." *BT* 33 (1982) 301–8. **Speiser, E. A.** "Of Shoes and Shekels." *BASOR* 77 (1940) 15–20. **Thompson, D.,** and **Thompson, T.** "Some Legal Problems in the Book of Ruth." *VT* 18 (1968) 79–99. **Tucker, G. M.** "Witnesses and 'Dates' in Israelite Contracts." *CBQ* 28 (1966) 42–45. **Vriezen, T. C.** "Two Old Cruces: a. Ruth iv 5." *OTS* 5 (1948) 80–88. **Weiss, D. H.** "The Use of קנה in Connection with Marriage." *HTR* 57 (1964) 243–48. **Westbrook, R.** *Old Babylonian Marriage Laws.* Horn, Austria: Berger, 1988. ———. "Redemption of Land." *ILR* 6 (1971) 367–75. **Wolff, H. W.** *Hosea: A Commentary of the Book of the Prophet Hosea.* Tr. G. Stansell. Philadelphia: Fortress, 1974.

Translation

[1]Now Boaz went up to the city gate[a] and sat down there, and just then the redeemer about whom[b] Boaz had spoken came passing by. Boaz[c] said, "Come over here and sit down,[d] So-and-So," and he came over[e] and sat down. [2]He [Boaz] then procured ten[a] of the elders of the city and said, "Sit down here," and they sat down.

[3]Then he said to the redeemer, "Naomi, who has returned[a] from the territory of Moab, is hereby surrendering her right[b] to the field[c] of our brother Elimelech. [4]And I thought I should inform you of it and say,[a] 'Acquire it in the presence of those sitting here and in

the presence of the elders of my people. If you want to exercise your right of redemption, do so.[b] *But if you do not,*[c] *tell me, so that I may know;*[d] *for no one but you has the right to do so and I after you."*[e] *The redeemer replied,*[f] *"I am willing to redeem it."*

5 *Then Boaz said, "On the day you acquire the field from Naomi, you acquire*[a] *Ruth the Moabitess, the wife of the deceased, in order to raise up descendants*[b] *for the deceased on his inheritance."* 6 *Thereupon the redeemer replied,*[a] *"Then I for my part cannot redeem it*[b] *lest I bring ruin upon my own estate.*[c] *You then take on my redemption responsibility,*[d] *for I cannot do so."*[e] 7 *Now this was the custom in former times in Israel in regard to the transfer of the right of redemption*[a] *in order to effectuate any such transaction: a man took off his sandals*[b] *and gave them to the other party.*[c] *This was the form of ratification in Israel.* 8 *Then the redeemer said to Boaz, "You acquire the right,"*[a] *and he took off his sandals.*[b]

9 *Then Boaz said to the elders and to*[a] *all the people, "You are witnesses this day that I am hereby acquiring from Naomi the right to all that belongs to Elimelech and all that belongs to Chilion and Mahlon.* 10 *And I am also hereby acquiring the right to take Ruth the Moabitess, the wife of Mahlon, as my wife in order to raise up descendants for the deceased on his inheritance so that the memory*[a] *of the deceased may not perish from among his brothers and from the gate of his town*[b]*—you are witnesses this day!"* 11 *And all the people who were in the gate and the elders said,*[a] *"We are witnesses! May Yahweh make the woman who is entering your house like Rachel and Leah who together built up the house of Israel, so that you may flourish in Ephrathah and gain renown*[b] *in Bethlehem,* 12 *and may your family line*[a] *be like that*[b] *of Perez whom Tamar bore to Judah through the offspring*[c] *that Yahweh will give you by this young woman!"*

Notes

1.a. The Syro-hexapla adds "(of) the city" after שׁער, "gate." On the rendering "city gate," see *Comment.*

1.b. With words of saying or speaking, when that which is spoken about is a relative clause beginning with אשׁר, the preposition expressing "about, concerning" (על, ב, ל) is regularly omitted; see Joüon, 80; *GBH* § 158i.

1.c. Lit. "he."

1.d. Lit. "Turn aside and sit down here."

1.e. Lit. "turned aside."

2.a. Lit. "ten men."

3.a. הַשָּׁבָה. For the use of the pf tense with the definite article, see the remarks on the identical form in *Note* 1:22.b.

3.b. For this rendering of מכרה, see *Comment.* Some MSS of the LXX read here *ἥ δέδοται Νωεμειν*, "which was given to Naomi." Such a reading is impossible, for it leaves the sentence without a main clause. Other LXX MSS read *ἀποδίδοται* or *ἀπέδοτο*, all of which show that the Heb. form was understood to be the pf, not the ptcp (see *Comment*).

3.c. Lit. "portion of field." On the expression, see *Note* 2:3.d.

4.a. Lit. "saying."

4.b. Lit. "exercise your right of redemption."

4.c. Lit. "if you will not exercise your right of redemption." The Heb. text actually reads יגאל, 3rd masc sg, rather than the expected תגאל, 2nd masc sg. See *Comment.*

4.d. K is the impf ואדע, Q the coh ואדעה. Since the previous impv, הגידה, "tell me," carries the coh suff, Q seems the preferable reading.

4.e. Lit. "there is no one except you to redeem and I after you."

4.f. Lit. "he said."

5.a. Reading Q קניתה rather than K קניתי (cf. *BHS,* n. b). See *Comment.*

5.b. Lit. "name."

6.a. Lit. "Then the redeemer said."

6.b. Lit. "I cannot redeem for myself."
6.c. Lit. "inheritance."
6.d. Lit. "redeem for yourself, you, my redemption."
6.e. Lit. "redeem."
7.a. Lit. "in regard to the redemption-right and the transfer," a hendiadys; see *Comment.*
7.b. Lit. "sandal," a collective; see *Comment.*
7.c. Lit. "his fellow, neighbor."
8.a. LXX adds the obj *τὴν ἀγχιστεῖαν μου*, "my kinship-rights," doubtless an explanatory addition.
8.b. Lit. "sandal"; see *Note* 7.b. The LXX and OL add here "and gave them to him," suggesting the addition of ויתן לו (cf. v 7b). Contra Joüon, 88; Rudolph, 60 (who explains the elision on the grounds of homoioteleuton, the scribe's eye passing from the first לו to the second), the MT is to be retained. It is far more likely that the words are an addition than that they were original and later omitted.
9.a. Contra Joüon (88), there is no need to read ולכל; the repetition of the prep is not required in Heb. See *Comment* on נגד in v 4.
10.a. Lit. "name." See *Comment* on the same expression in v 5.
10.b. Lit. "place, locality." *BHS* misreads the implications of the LXX tradition when it bases upon it the reading מעמו, "from his people," for virtually the whole LXX tradition contains expressions involving *φυλή*, "clan, tribe, assembly," a translation that reflects the derived sense of שער, i.e., "legal assembly," with "excellent insight" (Campbell, 124 [on 3:11]).
11.a. On the variant LXX reading, see *Comment.*
11.b. Lit. "name."
12.a. Lit. "house."
12.b. Lit. "the house of."
12.c. Lit. "seed."

Form/Structure/Setting

The fourth act comprises 4:1–22. It divides on the basis of form and content into three sections, consisting of two scenes, 4:1–12 and 4:13–17, and an epilogue consisting of the genealogy of David, 4:18–22. This structure departs radically from the A/short—B/long—A/short pattern of the two previous chapters. Instead, the structure parallels that of the first chapter, providing balance and closure for the book as a whole in a full resolution of Naomi's problem, which was so poignantly portrayed in chap. 1. Death and emptiness are transformed into life and fullness.

In the opening scene, 4:1–12, Boaz acquires the right to redeem the field of Elimelech and to marry Ruth, thus providing an heir to inherit the field and care for Naomi. This scene is parallel to 1:7–19a in that it consists of a dialogue between Boaz, the nearer redeemer, and the legal assembly, in the course of which the redeemer withdraws, just as 1:7–19a consists of a dialogue between Naomi, Ruth, and Orpah, in the course of which Orpah departs. When Boaz acquires the right to marry Ruth in 4:1–12, this resolves the question of a home and husband for her, the very point at issue between Naomi and the two young women in 1:7–19a and that which Ruth appeared to forfeit when she committed her life to Naomi. The second scene in chap. 4, vv 13–17, is strikingly parallel to 1:19b–22. Here the women of the town joyously celebrate the son born to Ruth and Boaz as the one who restores life and fullness to Naomi, just as in 1:19b–22 it was the women of the town to whom Naomi poured out her bitter tale of bereavement and loss. Finally, in chiastic order, the epilogue, vv 18–22, recounting the family line of David, is parallel to 1:1–6, for it documents ten generations of birth in Israel, parallel to the account of ten years of death in Moab (cf. Porten, *GCA* 7 [1978] 23, 48).

The beginning boundary of the first scene, vv 1–12, is clearly marked by the change from the sequential waw-consecutive verb form, which always stands first in its clause, to the nonsequential waw + subject + perfect construction, ובעז עלה, "And Boaz went up." The unit is delineated by the inclusio formed by השער, "the gate," and אנשים מזקני העיר, "men from the elders of the city," vv 1–2, repeated in כל־העם אשר־בשער והזקנים, "all the people in the gate and the elders," v 11. This division is corroborated by an analysis of the content, for vv 1–2 constitute the convening of the legal assembly, while v 11a–b recounts the carrying out of the function for which it was convened, the notarizing of the transfer of rights effected by the negotiations narrated in vv 3–10. The only question that remains is whether the blessing of the elders and the people in the gate, vv 11c–12, belongs with this pericope or begins the next. Sacon (*AJBI* 4 [1978] 15–17) and Gow (*BT* 35 [1984] 316–18) have argued the latter point of view. Sacon bases his division, on the one hand, on the close and careful structure of vv 5–10. But a careful analysis of the structure does not corroborate such a division; see below. On the other hand, he argues that 11c–12, the blessing of the elders and the people, forms a necessary part of the next scene, which thus forms "two parallel sets of blessings and their results." This, however, misunderstands the form and structure of that pericope; see the discussion there. Gow grounds his conclusion on a revision of the text based on the LXX form of v 11a (see *Comment*), arguing that the LXX presumes a subject + perfect construction, והזקנים אמרו, thus indicating a new section. But it is not at all certain that the Greek order here reflects such a Hebrew construction. It may render the waw consecutive imperfect (see *BHS* n. a-a). However that may be, we are called upon to exegete the text as we have it, not as we wish it to be, and Gow himself observes (*BT* 35 [1984] 316) that the MT implies a division after v 12. Further, Gow's emendation destroys the chiastic parallelism of the pair of narrative introductions to the second dialogue of this opening scene (see below) and removes one half of the inclusio that helps produce closure (see above). In my opinion, the blessing is a fitting conclusion to the function of the legal assembly, for it devotes its attention narrowly and exclusively to the size, prosperity, and fame of the family line of Boaz, a subject that dovetails nicely with the exclusively patriarchal concerns of the legal assembly and the negotiations it ratifies, whereas in the following scene, through the blessing enunciated by the women of the town, all attention is centered upon restoration of life, fullness, and felicity for Naomi through the child born to her by Ruth, who "loves her" and is "more to her than seven sons" (v 15; see *Explanation*).

This scene, 4:1–12, divides logically and structurally into three episodes, as follows:

Episode 1	vv 1–2	Boaz convenes the legal assembly
Episode 2	vv 3–8	Boaz negotiates with the nearer redeemer
Episode 3	vv 9–12	The legal assembly ratifies the agreement and blesses Boaz

Structurally, episode 1 consists of an account of the assembling of the three parties necessary for the negotiation and its ratification: Boaz, the nearer redeemer, and the legal assembly. The presence of each necessary party is signaled by the conclusion "he/they sat down":

The Structure of vv 1–2

1. Boaz	ובעז עלה השׁער Boaz went up to the gate	1a	A	Statement
	וישׁב שׁם and sat down there	1b	C	Statement
2. The *Gô*ʾ*ēl*	והנה הגאל עבר Just then the *gô*ʾ*ēl* came along	1c	A´	Statement
	ויאמר סורה שׁבה־פה He said, "Come over here and sit down"	1d	B	Summons
	ויסר וישׁב He came over and sat down	1e	C´	Compliance
3. The Legal Assembly	ויקח עשׂרה אנשׁים מזקני העיר He procured ten of the elders of the city	2a	A´´	Statement
	ויאמר שׁבו־פה He said, "Sit down here"	2b	B´	Summons
	וישׁבו And they sat down	2c	C´´	Compliance

Episode 2, the negotiation, divides structurally into two sections, (a) vv 3–4 and (b) vv 5–8, each of which is a three-part dialogue in which Boaz addresses the nearer redeemer and he responds (see the table The Structure of vv 3–8). Each section begins with a statement by Boaz. In the first section, Boaz's statement (S) is followed by a demand by Boaz ($D_{B\rightarrow G}$) and concludes with a declaration of assent on the part of the nearer redeemer (A_G). In the second, Boaz's statement (S´) is followed by a demand by the nearer redeemer ($D'_{G\rightarrow B}$) and concludes with a symbolic action of renunciation on the part of the nearer redeemer (R_G). This structure exhibits straight parallelism overall. S is parallel to S´ in that both involve information about the field, in S to the effect that Naomi is surrendering her rights to it, in S´ to the effect that when the redeemer acquires those rights, he also acquires Ruth in order to produce descendants for the deceased. D´ is antithetic to D and is chiastic in content. It is antithetic in that the direction of the demand is from Boaz to the redeemer in (a), $D_{B\rightarrow G}$, but from the redeemer to Boaz in (b), $D_{G\rightarrow B}$. It is chiastic in that the order of Boaz's demand is קנה, "acquire," followed by גאל, "redeem," whereas that of the redeemer is גאל, "redeem," followed by קנה, "acquire." The third element is antithetically parallel: an assent, A_G, by the redeemer in (a), a symbolic act of renunciation, R_G, in (b). This three-part structure is obscured by the digression of v 7–8a (cf. Berlin, *Poetics,* 99), which not only greatly enlarges the section giving the redeemer's demand upon Boaz but, because it is inserted in the middle of the redeemer's response, causes the narrator for the sake of clarity to insert a second narrative introduction informing his readers again who is speaking to whom (v 8a).

Episode 3 consists of a dialogue between Boaz and the legal assembly in which Boaz calls upon the assembly to give legal standing to the negotiations just concluded by publicly ratifying their result. Boaz's address to the assembly is enclosed by an identical inclusio consisting of the summons to witness, between which is his formal affirmation of his acquisition of the rights to the property and the woman, chiastically structured (see the table The Structure of vv 9a–11b). The scene as a whole is tied together and given unity because Boaz's affirmation, labeled a–b–c in the table, resumes the content of S and S´, the two statements of the previous episode, all three elements resumed from S´ and the first from S.

The Structure of vv 3–8

(a) vv 3–4				
	3a	ויאמר לגאל B →G		Narrative introduction
S	3b	a חלקת השדה אשר . . . לאלימלך [מכרה] נעמי	S	Statement by Boaz
$D_{B \to G}$	4c	. . . [קנה]	קנה	
	4de	אם־תגאל גאל	$D_{G \to B}$	Demand by Boaz
	4fgg	ואם־לא תגאול. . .	גאל	
	4ij	כי אין זולתך לגאול		
	4k	ויאמר G →B		Narrative introduction
A_G	4l	אנכי אגאל	A_G	Assent by redeemer
(b) vv 5–8				
	5a	ויאמר בעז B →G		Narrative introduction
S´	5b	a . . . [קנותך] השדה מיד נעמי b ומאת רות . . . אשת־המת [קניתי] c להקים שם־המת על־נחלתו	S´	Proposal by Boaz
	6a	ויאמר הגאל G → B		Narrative introduction
$D´_{G \to B}$	6b	לא אוכל לגאול־לי		
	6c	פן־אשחית את־נחלתי	גאל	
	6d	גאל־לך אתה את־גאלתי		
	6e	כי לא־אוכל לגאל		
	7a	וזאת. . . (Digression)	$D´_{G \to B}$	Counter-proposal by redeemer
	7b	שלף איש נעלו (Digression) וזאת. . .		
	8a	ויאמר הגאל לבעז G →B (Digression)		
	8b	[קנה] לך	קנה	
R_G	8c	וישלף נעלו	R_G	Symbolic act of renunciation by redeemer

The Structure of vv 9a–11b

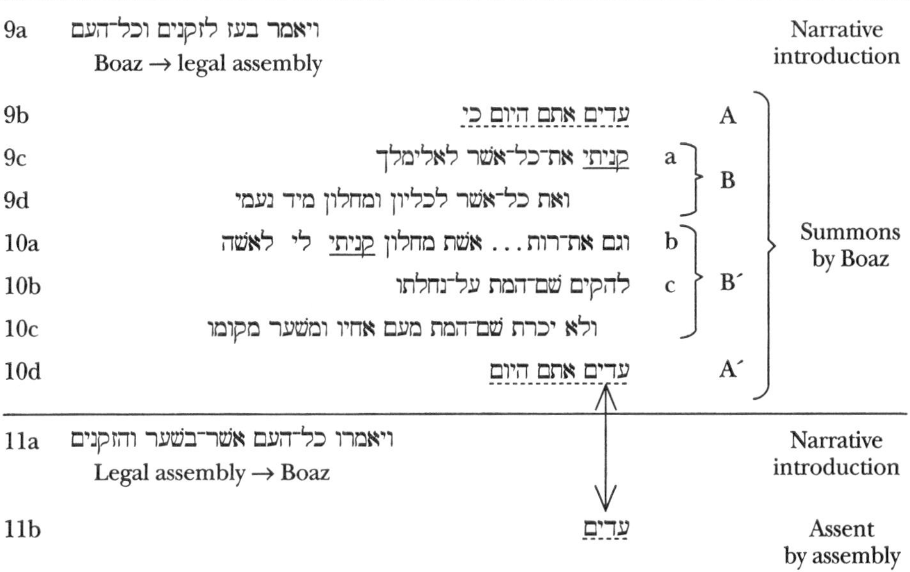

Finally, the scene concludes in vv 11c–12 with the blessing of the legal assembly. This blessing is structured chiastically, both in syntax, the outside members (AB–B´A´) using the jussive mood, the center (C) using the imperative, and in content (see the table The Structure of vv 11c–12).

The Structure of vv 11c–12

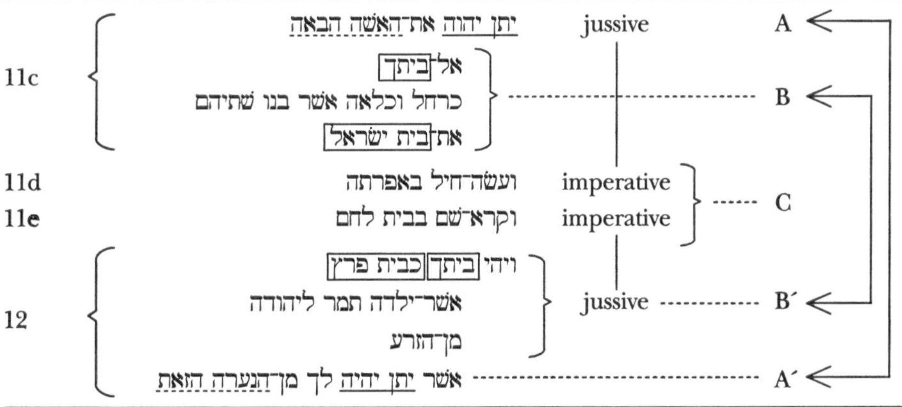

Such a structure places emphasis on the central element (C), the blessing of Boaz himself. Though it begins and ends with the bride-to-be, she is not named and is mentioned in both frames solely as the means through which the family line may be produced, in much the same way that her identity is "wife of the deceased" in the negotiation (v 5b) and "wife of Mahlon" in the ratification (v 10a); see *Explanation.*

Comment

1 וּבֹעַז עָלָה, "Now Boaz went." This construction, with the subject preceding the perfect verb, avoids expressing any temporal sequence with the preceding events and breaks the succession of waw-consecutive constructions employed to relate sequentially the events of the previous scene, signaling the beginning of a new scene (see *Form/Structure/Setting*). Since no sequence is implied, the time relationship expressed by this construction is ambiguous; it may be earlier, simultaneous with, or later than the preceding, and examples of all three such relationships occur in OT Hebrew (see *GBH* §§ 118 d–f). The order, with the subject preceding the verb, places no emphasis upon the subject, i.e., "Boaz"; this is the normal order when the perfect is used to avoid the imperfect with waw consecutive (see *GBH* § 166a; *HebS* § 573[4]). For this reason, Campbell's translation (140), "As for Boaz, he had gone up," should be avoided. Since the time sequence implied by the construction is ambiguous and there is nothing in the immediate context that suggests the specific time relationship between Boaz's ascent to the city gate and Ruth's conversation with Naomi just related, it seems preferable to leave the translation equally ambiguous. Thus we have avoided both "In the meantime Boaz went up" and "Boaz had gone up." Although our narrator expresses no precise chronological relation to the preceding, he clearly implies that Boaz proceeded without delay to fulfill his promise to Ruth in 3:13 that he would take care of the matter "in the morning."

הַשַּׁעַר, "the city gate." Since שׁער regularly refers to the gate of a city or town (and only rarely the gate of a fortress, palace, or temple), while the English word "gate" has a much broader meaning and usage, it is necessary to make clear that the gate of the city is meant (cf. deWaard-Nida, 63).

וְהִנֵּה, "and just then," renders the force of the construction ו + הנה + verb (on which see the remarks on the same construction in *Comment* on 2:4). The participle here expresses the durative nature of the action.

פְּלֹנִי אַלְמֹנִי, "So-and-So." This expression is an example of a wordplay termed "farrago" (see Sasson, *IDBSup*, 969). In such an expression, the elements involved often rhyme, and not infrequently one or more of them are without meaning outside of the given expression (e.g., English "hodge-podge"). The idiom occurs in two other contexts in the OT in the phrase אל מקום פלני אלמני (1 Sam 21:3; 2 Kgs 6:8), where it is clear that the narrator does not wish to give the name of the place meant; i.e., this phrase means something like English "such and such a place." Further, the phrase is rendered by some LXX MSS as ὁ δεῖνα, "such a one" (cf. Matt 26:18), and by the supplementing hand of the OL as *quicumque es*, "whoever you are." Finally, given that words cognate to the first element, פלני, occur in Jewish Aramaic, Syriac, Arabic, and a modern dialect of Ethiopic with the meaning "someone, a certain one," it seems reasonably clear that the expression means something like English "so and so," an expression used when the speaker cannot recall or does not want to use the name.

Given these rather clear facts, and given the fact that this type of wordplay idiom gains meaning almost exclusively from the context in which it is used (even more so than word meanings in general), it seems of little value to present here the quite hypothetical etymologies that have been suggested for each of the two words. (For those interested, the extended coverage given in Campbell, 142, or

Rudolph, 59, may be consulted.) In like manner, Campbell's highly speculative attempt (42) to use renderings in various versions whose meanings lie in the range of "secret, hidden" to suggest that some "connotation of secrecy was bound up" with the meaning of the phrase is most unlikely. It is far more likely that such renderings in the versions are attempts to translate an unknown and difficult phrase on the basis of the etymologies of the words involved than that they reflect the actual meaning of the phrase.

Although the meaning of the phrase seems relatively clear, the reason for its use is less so. To begin with, we must understand that the phrase originates with the narrator, not with Boaz (cf. the remarks of Berlin, *Poetics,* 99–101). It is manifestly most improbable that Boaz would not know the name of a fellow citizen in a small town like Bethlehem, let alone that of the relative who possesses the family rights as redeemer that stand immediately prior to his own (3:12). This makes the view of McDonald (*BO* 32 [1975] 173) that the expression "seems to suggest something akin to a homely American addressing a stranger as 'Mac'" most improbable. Further, it is crucial in understanding our author's intent and purpose in using such a wordplay to recognize that he could very easily have had Boaz address the nearer redeemer without using either his name or the expression פלני אלמני at all. As Campbell (141) notes, the sentence structure of v 1 does not require using a name. Thus the narrator could simply have had Boaz use no vocative word of address at all in speaking to the nearer redeemer, just as he did in giving Boaz's words to the elders in v 3. Or he could have had Boaz use the common vocative of polite address אדני, "sir," instead of פלני אלמני (cf. the very similar words of Jael to Sisera in Judg 4:18). So the question is not the one asked by Campbell, "why the anonymity?" for which he can find no adequate answer, but rather why the narrator chooses to emphasize that he does not name the nearer redeemer by having Boaz address him with this characteristic wordplay customarily employed when a name is unknown or avoided. Surely such a pointed way of underscoring the namelessness of this man in a narrative that so carefully names the other protagonists (cf. 1:2, 4; 2:1) subtly creates a less than favorable impression of him and prompts us to suspect a pejorative purpose in the choice of the expression (cf. the comments of Zenger, 81, and *Explanation*).

If this understanding of the significance of the phrase is correct, then to translate it with some such rendering as "friend/my friend" (NASV, NIV, RSV, TEV) or to indicate that Boaz actually used the man's name by paraphrasing with the Vg, "calling him by name" (NAB, NEB, Rudolph), is to miss completely the meaning of the narrator's pointed omission. To catch his nuance, we have followed those who render the expression "So and So" (NJPS, Gerleman, Hertzberg, Joüon, Sasson, Würthwein).

2 וַיִּקַּח עֲשָׂרָה אֲנָשִׁים מִזִּקְנֵי הָעִיר, "And he procured ten of the elders of the city." This contrasts markedly with the way that Boaz summoned the nearer relative. Since this man came passing by as Boaz took his seat in the city gate (see *Comment* on "just then" in v 1), he simply called him to come over (סורה) and sit down. But לקח means not only "to take" but also "to get, procure; fetch, bring" (cf. Gen 27:13; see BDB, 4.b, 6, p. 543). It can also mean "to have (someone) brought" (cf. 1 Sam 17:31; Jer 37:17; see *HALOT,* 5, p. 534). This strongly suggests the possibility that Boaz did not simply wait in the gate with the other redeemer until ten of the town's elders chanced to pass through on their way to the fields, but he summoned them, particularly since in v 2b he simply says to them, "sit down here," rather than "turn aside [סורו] and sit down." On the other hand, to have chosen ten men as they passed through the gate would undoubtedly not have taken an inordinate amount of time, since the great majority of the men of the town, including many of its leading citizens who would have formed the cadre of "elders" (see the next *Comment*), would have had to pass through the gate in the early morning on their way out to work the fields. However, the choice of verb here strongly suggests that the meaning "he had (them) brought" is the more probable sense, especially since the legal forum was not constituted of elders alone (see the following).

In ancient Israel, legal authority was invested in the "legal assembly." It is generally held that membership in this body extended to all the male citizens of the town. Numerous passages in the OT demonstrate that the legal forum comprised not just the elders or the officials (שׂרים) but also the rest of the eligible male citizens who assembled on such an occasion (cf., e.g., Gen 23:10, 18; 34:24; 1 Kgs 21:13; Jer 26:11, 12, 16; 32:12; see Köhler, "Justice in the Gate," 151–53; Boecker, *Law and the Administration of Justice in the OT,* 32–33). These men were those who, in the words of Köhler ("Justice in the Gate," 153), "occupy their own property, who do not stand under any kind of tutelage, and can claim the four great rights—marriage, cult, war, and the administration of law." Köhler continues (153):

> The supreme right, in which is experienced the pride and worth of a healthy man, who is of age, has his own property and is recognized by his fellows, is the right to take part and to speak in the legal assembly. It is the meeting place of those who really matter.

Within the membership of this assembly, there existed also a group or collegiate body known in the OT as the זקנים, "elders." Particularly when qualified by an appended genitive, such as "city," "land," or "people," as here, the term "elder" designated the holder of an office rather than a member of a particular age group. In the general governance of the cities and tribal territories of ancient Israel, the elders appear as the governing body (both independently and in conjunction with the leader of the community) and as a part of the legal assembly (see McKenzie, *Bib* 40 [1959] 523–27; *TDOT* 4:126–28). Who the elders were, how they were chosen, and what their specific responsibilities and privileges were vis-à-vis the assembly at large are matters of considerable uncertainty and debate (cf. McKenzie, *Bib* 40 [1959] 532–40; de Geus, *The Tribes of Israel,* 139–41; on the role of the body of elders under the monarchy, see Malamat, "Organs of Statecraft," 167–75). Both of these elements, i.e., the eligible male citizens of the town and the elders, were present in the body to which Boaz presented his civil action. This is confirmed by the statement in the opening part of the civil procedure that the option of redeeming the field is presented to the nearer redeemer "in the presence of הישׁבים [lit. 'those sitting (here)'; see below] and the elders of my people," v 4. Likewise, when Boaz calls upon the legal assembly to notarize the proceeding, he summons "the elders and all the people," v 9, and it is "all the people who were in the gate and the elders," v 11, who respond. The legal assembly met at no set times, nor was there a building set apart for the purpose of conducting legal proceedings. The assembly was called into being as the need arose simply by an appeal for justice by either the plaintiff or the defendant in a dispute. Such an appeal transformed interested observers into a "court" of law (cf. Jer 26; for further details, see Boecker, *Law and the Administration of Justice in the OT,* 30–40, or Köhler, "Justice in the Gate," 149–65). The place where such an appeal was made and the legal assembly convened was most often, as here, the gate of the city. Thus the prophets inveigh against those who "ensnare the arbitrator in the gate" (Isa 29:21) or "hate the arbitrator in the gate" (Amos 5:12); or they urge Israel to "make justice prevail in the gate" (Amos 5:15; cf. also Job 5:4; Deut 21:19; 22:15; 25:7). Rather than the gate itself, whose chambers would have been much too small for such a meeting, the exact locale would doubtless have been the plaza or square inside the gate. (On the archaeological evidence for such a physical setting, see the excellent discussion and illustrations of Campbell, 154–55.)

In the light of the preceding discussion, it would seem that the specific statement that Boaz procured ten of the town's elders is intended to stress the care that he took to ensure that a duly constituted legal forum would be present to notarize and legitimate the civil proceedings he wished to set in motion.

3 חֶלְקַת הַשָּׂדֶה אֲשֶׁר לְאָחִינוּ לֶאֱלִימֶלֶךְ, "the field of our brother Elimelech." This whole phrase constitutes the object of the sentence and stands first. It is most unlikely that this position in the sentence places emphasis on this clause, for this order seems to be normative in spoken Hebrew. Note the same order in Ruth's words in 3:17, and see *Comment* and *Bibliography* there. The same order is to be found in 3:5, 11. Since the most natural nonemphatic order in English is to place the subject first, the order of the Hebrew sentence should be reversed.

The word אָח, "brother," is almost certainly to be understood here in the general sense of "(male) relative," as is often the case in the OT; cf. 2 Kgs 10:13 where the word is used to refer to the forty-two relatives of Ahaziah king of Judah put to death by Jehu. The relationship of Boaz to the family of Elimelech has been described in the preceding narrative in only the most general of terms, i.e., with קרוב לנו, "a relative of ours," in 2:20 and with the closely related but unfortunately quite enigmatic terms מודע and מודעת in 2:1; 3:2 (see *Comments* there). Consequently, we do not know how close that relationship was, and speculation on what it might have been (e.g., "cousins," Joüon, 80; Levine, "Legal Themes," 102) amounts to sheer guesswork. The whole tenor of the story strongly suggests that the relationship was a relatively distant one. Hence, the view adopted by some rabbinic commentators (see the references in Sasson, 108, or Campbell, 143) and revived most recently by Lipiński (*VT* 26 [1978] 126–27) that אח, "brother," is to be taken literally and that Elimelech, Boaz, and the nearer redeemer were therefore sons of the same father is most improbable.

The Hebrew expression here should simply be translated "the field of our brother Elimelech" rather than either "the field belonging to . . ." or "the field which belongs/belonged to . . ." for the simple reason that this is the usual way in cases like this that the relationship of possession is expressed in Hebrew, since the construct phrase חלקת השדה is a compound noun expressing a single idea, namely, that portion of the שׂדה, the "fields" of Bethlehem, owned by a single individual. (See *Comment* on the similar expression חלקת השדה לבעז in 2:3; cf. GKC § 129d). In particular, the translation "the field which belonged to . . ." (used by almost all the modern translations) should be avoided since in English the past tense "belonged" could imply that the field was no longer regarded as belonging to Elimelech now that he is deceased, whereas in the ancient Hebrew conception of family solidarity exactly the opposite was true, as the meaning of the phrase "the plot [lit. 'portion of the field'] of our brother Elimelech" makes clear.

מָכְרָה נָעֳמִי הַשָּׁבָה מִשְּׂדֵה מוֹאָב, "Naomi, who has returned from the territory of Moab, is hereby surrendering her right." The existence of a field belonging to Elimelech, about which not a hint has thus far been given in the story, is surprising enough. But that Naomi has some kind of rights to "sell," or to "have sold," such property, together with the question of how this fact fits coherently and credibly into what has preceded and what follows, constitutes without doubt the most baffling and difficult development in a narrative replete with such enigmas. In order to deal in a logical and coherent manner with the considerable number of ambiguities, uncertainties, and unknowns that exist in connection with this remarkable turn of events, together with the vast number of hypotheses and proposals that various scholars have presented as a solution, in whole or in part, I shall proceed as follows. I shall first elucidate as far as possible the grammatical and lexical facts and possibilities presented by the exegetical evidence of the text of vv 3–5a itself, together with the pertinent legal and social background raised by the data therein, limiting myself to the questions specifically raised here, namely, the field, Naomi's rights to it, and its redemption, leaving the matter of levirate marriage until that issue becomes pertinent in the interpretation of v 5b. To do this, it will be necessary to carry the exegetical investigation down through 5a, the first clause of v 5 (ending with מיד נעמי, "from Naomi"). Then in *Excursus: The Nature of the Transaction Proposed by Boaz in vv 3–5a,* I shall recount those suggested solutions and proposals that fit these exegetical and socio-legal data and delineate what in my opinion constitutes the most plausible solution.

For the purposes of discussion, the uncertainties that are involved in the interpretation of v 3 can be subsumed under three interrelated questions. One is lexical: What is the meaning of the verb מכר in this context? The second is grammatical: How is the verb form מָכְרָה to be understood and translated? The third is socio-juridical: If Naomi has "sold" or is "selling" the field of Elimelech, she must have some right to do so. What rights does she as the widow have to the field of Elimelech, and how did she come into possession of the same when there is no direct evidence in the OT that a widow could inherit her husband's land? Let us deal with these questions in the order raised.

(1) *The meaning of* מָכַר. The verb מכר bears at least two closely related, yet quite distinct, meanings. In a number of contexts, it means "to sell movable goods outright," i.e., in the normal sense of English "to sell"; that is, the sale includes the transfer of the unconditional right of ownership and disposition of the object sold as well as its possession and use. In this sense, the verb occurs in reference to such items as merchandise in general (Neh 10:32; 13:20), meat (Deut 14:21), oil (2 Kgs 4:7), garments (Prov 31:24), or even the sale of a human being into slavery (Gen 37:27, 28, 36; Deut 21:14). On the other hand, in a significant number of passages in which the object of the action is land, the verb does not mean "to sell outright" in the sense delineated above. Instead, it refers to a transaction in which only the usufruct of the land is transferred for a stipulated value for a stipulated period of time (cf. Lev 25:14–16). See in this regard the excellent study of Lipiński, *SGKAO* 15 (1982) 173–78 (cf. also id., *THAT* 2:869–75; *VT* 26 [1978] 124–27). This situation existed because one ancient and persistent type of land tenure in Israel was that in which ownership was vested in the extended family or clan, not in the

individual. It is generally considered that in this type of land tenure a family's ancestral heritage was inalienable; i.e., it could not be sold permanently (Lev 25:23; cf. 1 Kgs 2:3). It is true that under the monarchy this system came to be in competition with a more commercially oriented view that assumed that the right of ownership included the right of alienation (cf. the study of Dearman, *Property Rights*, 62–74). However, the earlier conservative, agrarian viewpoint that sought to keep immovable property as a family heritage continued to play an important role in the society, as is evidenced by the sharp critique of the accumulation of property in the hands of individuals in the eighth-century prophets (e.g., Mic 2:1–2, 8–9; Isa 5:8; cf. Dearman, *Property Rights,* 74–77). Given such an agrarian-oriented land tenure, only the usufruct of the land was "sold." Further, such a transfer of usufruct was subject either to the right of "pre-emption" by a relative (e.g., Jer 32:6–10) or to the right of "redemption," i.e., repurchase by a relative or the owner himself (Lev 25:24–27), or else it reverted to the owner in the Jubilee year (Lev 25:28); see the discussion on "redemption" in *Comment* on v 4 below. It is not insignificant in this regard that in the case of Abraham's purchase of the cave of Machpelah (Gen 23) and Ahab's proposed purchase of Naboth's vineyard (1 Kgs 2), where the outright sale of property is involved, the verb for "to sell" is נתן rather than מכר (Gen 23:4, 9, 13; 1 Kgs 21:2, 3, 6). Note also that in Deut 21:14; Amos 2:6, where the writer wishes to make it clear that an outright sale is involved, the expression used is מכר בכסף, "to deliver over for money." The same usage is found with נתן (cf. *THAT* 2:3, 701f). Hence, Lipiński concludes (*THAT* 2:875):

> The root *mkr* is used most frequently alongside *ntn* to denote transactions which imply the handing over or making over of moveable and immovable goods. Its semantic range encompasses "to hand over, to consign, to transfer, to deliver." The result of such a transaction was normally legal possession or ownership according to the wording and legal form of the contract. In early Hebrew sources *mkr,* however, refers mostly to the simple transfer of possession, whereas *ntn* is used in stipulations, it should be stressed, that denote a transfer of land, a conveyance, for ever (Gen 14:15, 17:8, 48:4). . . . *mkr* means then a transfer of possession or full conveyance with a gradual shift of meaning to the latter. *mkr* characterizes thus the form of the transaction, but does not specify its substance.

Clearly, just such a transfer of usufruct is involved in the "sale" of the field of Elimelech, for the next verse will indicate that this "sale," whether concluded in the past or now proposed (see the following), is subject to the right of redemption.

Thus, at the very least, to translate מכר here by "to sell," or in the verses that follow to translate קנה with "to buy," is to use verbs that carry "the semantic components of 'commercial transaction' or 'change of ownership'" involving "a complementary set of meanings, of the conversive type buy/sell usually associated with a financial operation involving the use of money" (Schneider, *BT* 33 [1982] 304). But, even if Naomi, as the widow of the deceased, had the usufruct of her deceased husband's estate and had the right to dispose of the same, both of which are highly problematic postulates (see the discussion below), the transaction involved is simply not a commercial "cash transaction" of the nature implied by "buy/sell" (contra Campbell, 145). How is such a transaction to be rendered in English? Lipiński (*THAT* 2:871) argues that the translation "sell" is suitable in none of these passages, including Ruth 4:3, for just these reasons; hence, he would adopt "transfer, assign" (*übertragen, übergeben*). Rudolph (64) also argues that מכר here can "denote no true sale, but is to be translated with 'to dispose of'" (*veraussern*). However, if the translation "to sell" implies too much, such English verbs as "transfer" or "assign" would imply too little. Such renderings would not connote the conveyance of the right of possession and usufruct, while "dispose of" by itself could be understood in this context in the same unconditional sense as "to sell." In order to convey a sense that best fits the context, I have chosen to translate מכר here by the expression "to surrender the right to," leaving unstated what Naomi's rights to the field were, since these remain uncertain. On this question, see the discussion below. Gordis' view ("Love, Marriage, and Business," 255–58) that the verb מכר here bears the technical sense "to transfer the obligation-right of redemption" (as well as the similar views of Brichto and Westbrook) will also be discussed therein.

(2) *The translation of the verb form* מכרה. In form מָכְרָה is perfectly clear: it is qal perfect, third person feminine singular. This form can be understood in this context in several senses, however. (a) As a perfect, it can most obviously be rendered simply as a past tense, i.e., "(she) 'sold,' has 'sold'"; (b) it can also, however, be understood to belong to a category of uses of the perfect that "can be correlated with *present-time reference* as it is understood in English" (*IBHS* § 30.5.1c). With verbs of declaring, swearing, etc. (so-called *verba dicendi*), the perfect often expresses what is called the "instantaneous present," expressing the coincidence of the declaration and execution of the action (*IBHS* § 30.5.1d; *HebS* § 164; GKC § 106i). In this case, the form would be translated "(she) is 'selling.'" Another closely related and often overlapping use is the "performative perfect," in which "not only are speaking and acting simultaneous, they are identical" (*IBHS* § 30.5.1d), often rendered unambiguously in English by the use of "hereby, herewith" (Campbell, 143–44, so understands our passage). It seems less likely that this is applicable here since all the examples that have been cited for Hebrew are first person. Waltke-O'Conner (*IBHS* § 30.5.1d; cf. Driver, *Treatise* § 13) suggest a "perfective of resolve," i.e., "(she) is going to 'sell,'" and include the Ruth passage in their examples. However, the existence of this category is quite uncertain since the other two examples cited by Waltke-O'Conner can just as easily be understood as either the instantaneous or the performative perfect.

A large number of scholars (for a representative list, see Rudolph, 59), rejecting for a variety of reasons the interpretations just given, opt to emend the MT pointing to indicate the participle מֹכֵר, requiring the translation "is 'selling'" or "is about to 'sell.'" The question of which of these interpretations is ultimately preferable depends upon how one understands what is transpiring in this "sale." Hence, we shall postpone that decision until this issue has been discussed below in *Excursus: The Nature of the Transaction Proposed by Boaz in vv 3–5a.*

(3) *Naomi's rights to the field of her deceased husband Elimelech.* Whatever translation is adopted for מכר—"to sell," "to transfer, assign," or "to surrender the right to"—and whether the verb form is a past or present form, it is clearly implied that Naomi has the right so to do. But the legal codes preserved in the OT give no indication that a widow could inherit the property of her husband, so how could Naomi come into the possession of such rights? Is there any evidence that a widow could inherit the usufruct or possession of her husband's land, or the right to dispose of the same?

There are no laws governing inheritance in general in the OT legal codes. Only Deut 21:15–17; Num 27:1–11 (supplemented by 36:6–9) deal with the subject, and these passages refer to particular cases. Further information on inheritance from OT narratives (such as Ruth 4) is difficult to interpret since such materials give such limited data that they are almost invariably open to more than one interpretation (cf. the remarks of Boecker, *Law and the Administration of Justice,* 118–19). Hence, no general statement about the regulations governing inheritance in the OT can be made. Nevertheless, it seems clear that the normal practice was for sons to inherit (Deut 21:15–17). In the absence of sons, daughters would inherit (Num 27:7–8), but they were then subject to the limitation that they must marry within "the clan of the tribe of their father" (Num 36:6) so that the family patrimony would remain within the tribal holdings (vv 7–9). If, on the other hand, a man died without progeny, his property passed first to his brother, then to his father's brothers, and finally to "the closest relative [lit. 'flesh'] of his clan" (Num 27:9–11). These last two provisions demonstrate that the central concern of the system of inheritance in the OT was that the property should remain within the extended family to which it originally belonged, the same concern that lay behind the right of redemption (Lev 25:23–30; see the discussion above) and the prohibition against the sale of land in fee simple. Any unconditional right of inheritance on the part of the widow would mean that the property would be alienated from the clan when she remarried. In fact, as Westbrook notes (*ILR* 6 [1971] 372), it is not clear in the OT that women could own property at all, the few references being problematical indeed (Judg 17:2–4; 2 Sam 14:5–11; 2 Kgs 8:1–6); in any case, these references involve women with sons. Note also that the regular inclusion of the widow with the resident alien and the orphan as those whom the community must especially care for, presumably because they were without means or power, certainly implies that the widow normally was not one of the heirs to her husband's estate.

Assuming that these provisions for inheritance apply in the OT categorically and that they must govern the circumstances in the Ruth story, so that Naomi could not have *inherited* the field, some scholars have contended that the land must have been *Naomi's* originally, either coming to her from her father and held in trust by Elimelech during his lifetime (see Leggett, *The Levirate,* 212; Rowley, "The Marriage of Ruth," 184 n. 2) or else constituting her dowry (cf. Beattie, *VT* 24 [1974] 254–55). Or, since inheritance on the part of widows was not normative, some have suggested that Elimelech must have specifically willed or gifted Naomi a share in or the whole of his inheritance (cf. Leggett, *The Levirate,* 217; Rowley, "The Marriage of Ruth," 184 n. 2; Thompson and Thompson, *VT* 18 [1968] 97). However, besides being at odds with 4:3, 9, which stipulate that the field was specifically Elimelech's, all such proposals are rendered impossible as credible explanations of the situation by the principle of "sufficiency of narrative information." If Naomi came into possession of the land by any such extra-normal (albeit "legal") channels, it would have been incumbent upon the narrator to have so informed his readers or they would have been as mystified as we are about Naomi's possession of land.

Indeed, if it is maintained that the legal stipulations of Deuteronomy and Leviticus categorically apply, it is logical to conclude that, in keeping with Num 27:9–11, Elimelech's field upon his death would have passed to Mahlon and

Chilion, and upon their deaths to the brothers of Elimelech. Since it appears that Elimelech had no brothers (see the *Comment* on אח in 4:3 above), the field would have passed, it would seem, to the "nearer redeemer," since one would presume that this identity (3:12) would mean that he would thereby also be "the closest relative of the clan" (Num 27:11) of Elimelech (cf. Pedersen, *Israel I–II,* 92). However, all such explanations ignore the nature of Israelite casuistic law (as discussed in the *Comment* on 3:9) and assume that the OT codes of law were intended to be complete and comprehensive and that their formulations applied in ancient Israel at all times and places. But, as we have noted, it is increasingly being recognized that customary law in OT times was formulated by precedent within local contexts and therefore must have varied with both location and time. Hence, it is quite improper to conclude on the basis of the codes as we have them that a widow in ancient Israel could not under certain conditions have inherited certain rights to or the usufruct of the property of her husband (contra Levine, "Legal Themes," 102).

Consequently, the majority of scholars have proposed that Naomi must have inherited rights to the field of Elimelech. For example, Rowley concludes, "that she had a title to an unspecified amount of property is quite clear" ("Marriage of Ruth," 184; cf. the remarks of Hubbard, 54–55). Some such right seems suggested by Prov 15:25, "He [Yahweh] keeps the widow's boundaries intact." However, proprietary rights to land in the OT were vested in the clan, while the individual held only the right of possession and usufruct, and the central concern of the OT system of inheritance was that ownership of property should remain with the clan to which it originally belonged (see above). Hence, one must conclude with Lipiński (*VT* 26 [1978] 125–26) that the widow held only usufructuary rights to her husband's property and that she did so only until she married again or died in her turn, at which time such rights reverted to her husband's clan in the normal order of inheritance. For an example of just this custom among the Tsonga people of southeast Africa, whose culture seems similar to that of ancient Israel in many respects, see Schneider, *BT* 33 (1982) 303, and for a similar situation among the Jews of Assuan, Egypt, in the fifth century B.C., see Epstein, *The Jewish Marriage Contract,* 176. Granted that the rights Naomi would have inherited are understood in this manner, one must surely allow that the author of Ruth assumes that his readers will not regard it as strange that a widow without sons or daughters would inherit her husband's property—at least in the sense of the usufructuary rights and possession and the right to transfer or assign the same within the clan (cf. Burrows, *JBL* 59 [1940] 448; Beattie, *VT* 24 [1974] 256).

4 וַאֲנִי אָמַרְתִּי אֶגְלֶה אָזְנְךָ לֵאמֹר, "And I thought I should inform you of it and say." It is difficult to decide with confidence the exact nuance of this expression. The problems are threefold: (1) The breadth of meaning of אמר is very diverse and its nuances of meaning richly varied (see Wagner, *TDOT* 1:329–35). Among the many possibilities, what specific sense is required by the context here? (2) What is the force of its perfect tense form? (3) What is the meaning in this context of the idiom גלה אזן, lit. "to uncover the ear"? First, let us consider the first two interrelated questions. If the perfect form is understood to imply the past tense, then אמר could be understood in the nuance "to promise" (cf. BDB, 3, p. 56; *HALOT,* 5, p. 66). This is the sense in which it is taken by NEB and at one point by Campbell (144), who comments, "It is as though Boaz were quoting a promise actually made earlier, so that we cannot entirely dismiss the possibility of a conversation between Boaz and Naomi, presumably falling between the events at the end of chapter 3 and those at the beginning of chapter 4." Campbell demurs at such a proposal, and, in my opinion, the sequence of events implied by the story (particularly the implications of Naomi's response to Boaz's gift of grain in the concluding scene to the previous chapter; see *Explanation* thereto) makes such an understanding most unlikely, if not impossible. Boaz is not speaking of some promise or agreement made with Naomi that he would broach the matter of the "sale" with the nearer redeemer, for the story rather clearly implies that nothing whatever has transpired between Boaz and Naomi in the interim between the events of chaps. 3 and 4. Taking quite a different direction, Joüon (81) opts for the translation "I have resolved, decided," in which he is followed in detail by Campbell (144; in spite of his comments noted above). In the first place, it is quite problematic whether the verb bears the meaning "resolve, decide" in the passage cited by Joüon and Campbell as the basis for their rendering. However, quite apart from the question of meaning, the syntax of this and other examples, in which the verb either takes a nominal direct object or is followed by the infinitive, is clearly different from the passage in Ruth (as noted by Campbell, 144), because here the verb is followed by direct discourse.

The great majority of modern translations (e.g., JB, NAB, NASV, NIV, RSV, TEV) and commentators (e.g., Gerleman, Haller, Rudolph, Würthwein) adopt the meaning "to say to oneself, to think," a meaning usually carried by the idiom אמר בלב, "to say in the heart," but also borne by אמר without לב (BDB, 2, p. 56; *HALOT*, 4, p. 66; cf. *TDOT* II.4., 1:333). In these passages we find exactly the syntax exhibited in the Ruth passage, for in all the examples in which אמר bears the meaning "to think," the verb is followed by direct discourse. It is also particularly striking that in the majority of such passages the verb occurs in the perfect, first person singular form, אמרתי, as in Ruth 4:4 (e.g., Gen 20:11; 26:9; 2 Sam 12:22; 2 Kgs 5:11). With this sense of אמר, it would fit very nicely either to understand the following verb, אגלה (see below), to be imperfect indicative and so to render "I thought I would inform" or to understand it to be the cohortative and so to render "I thought I should inform."

Sasson (115–16; followed by Hubbard, 239) has suggested another approach: "I think it to be another example of the perfect used in a legal context to speak of an act that is unravelling in the present," i.e., an example of the "instantaneous present" (cf. the discussion of מכרה in v 3 above). Such a usage does occur in a number of passages to make solemn, often public statements (note esp. 2 Sam 19:30; Isa 36:5; cf. also Judg 2:3; Isa 22:4; Job 32:10). Again in the syntax of these utterances the verb is followed by direct discourse. The passage would then mean "I declare: I am informing you" (if אגלה is understood to be imperfect indicative) or "I declare: let me inform you" (if אגלה is cohortative). Such a usage would be particularly appropriate to introduce a formal statement in a legal forum.

Which of these two interpretations best fits the context depends upon how one understands the third problem, the meaning and syntax of the clause אגלה אזנך לאמר. The meaning of the idiom גלה און, lit. "to uncover the ear," admits of no doubt: with "man" as subject in 1 Sam 2:2, 12, 13; 22:8, 17 and with "God" as subject in 1 Sam 9:15; 2 Sam 7:27, it means "to inform, tell" (see *TDOT* II.2.b, 2:480), whereas in Job 33:6; 36:10, 15, where it occurs with the content of the message left totally unexpressed, it means something like "to instruct." That the idiom involves some "element of secrecy," as postulated by Campbell (144), is simply not substantiated by the passages he cites. However, although the meaning of the verbal expression is quite clear, it is not immediately obvious what its object is. What is it that is being communicated? Since the idiom גלה אזן, "to uncover the ear," is an expression that is complete in itself, several different syntactic constructions are used to set forth the information communicated. Only two of these need concern us here: (1) In 1 Sam 20:2, 12, 13; 22:17, the information communicated is presented in an independent sentence that precedes the sentence involving the idiom in question, e.g., 1 Sam 22:17, ". . . they knew that he was fleeing, and they did not inform me" (lit. "uncover my ear"). Since the object is clear from the context, it is not stated again. (2) On the other hand, in 1 Sam 9:15; 2 Sam 7:27, the information communicated follows the idiom "to uncover the ear" and consists of a direct quote introduced by the infinitive לאמר, "saying," e.g., 2 Sam 7:27, "you told your servant [lit. 'uncovered the ear of your servant'], saying, 'I will build you a house.'" In this construction, the infinitive לאמר, "saying," functions virtually as a colon introducing the direct discourse (see *TDOT* II.5, 1:334). In the Ruth passage, since Boaz has just told the nearer redeemer about the "sale" of Elimelech's field, it seems rather natural to take this as the information communicated and to understand the syntactical construction to be that of example (1) above. On the other hand, a direct quote introduced by לאמר, "saying," follows the idiom, suggesting that this may be the information communicated and that it is an example of syntactical construction (2). In my opinion, the context strongly favors the former alternative, for the simple reason that only Boaz's previous statement constitutes information that he has communicated to the nearer redeemer. The content of the clause that follows לאמר, "saying," here is not information but a command from Boaz, a challenge to the nearer redeemer to carry out his obligations vis-à-vis Elimelech's field. As such, it is semantically inappropriate as the object of an idiom meaning "to inform" (contra Hubbard, 240). Hence, Sasson (103) translates the expression אגלה אזנך, "Let me publicly enjoin you," even though there is no parallel at all for the sense "command, order, enjoin." In understanding the expression as an example of syntactic construction (1), the infinitive לאמר must be understood as introducing a further consequence or purpose of the informing and be translated "and say" or "and suggest" or the like; on this use of לאמר, see the discussion in *TDOT* II.5, 1:334.

It seems best then to understand the expression in the sense "I thought I should inform you of it and say . . ." (cf. NJPS). In context it seems preferable to understand אגלה as cohortative rather than independent (in ל״ה verbs, the cohortative and indicative fall together as the indicative form; see GKC § 75l).

Finally, it is quite unlikely that the independent pronoun אני before the inflected verb is emphatic here (as it is understood by Campbell, Haller, Rudolph, Sasson, Würthwein), for this construction occurs regularly in spoken Hebrew in contexts where emphasis is most unlikely (see the discussion by McDonald, *BO* 32 [1975] 166–67). The context calls for no stress on the first person subject in the clause.

קְנֵה, "Acquire (it)." Whatever the tense of מכרה, the transaction under discussion is not a purchase in the absolute, unrestricted sense but a transfer of Naomi's rights in the field. If Naomi has the right of possession and usufruct of the field acquired from Elimelech as his heir (see the discussion on מכר above), then it is this right that Naomi is "selling." Since English "to buy" would connote in ordinary usage the unconditional transfer of the right of ownership, including possession and disposition of the object bought, it is preferable here to use the more general term "acquire." The object to be acquired is left unexpressed since it has just been mentioned in the context. In such cases in Hebrew, when the object of the verb would naturally be expressed by a pronominal suffix, it is omitted (see *HebS* § 588; *GBH* § 146i[2]).

נֶגֶד הַיֹּשְׁבִים וְנֶגֶד זִקְנֵי עַמִּי, lit. "before those sitting (here) and before the elders of my people." Does this mean two different groups of men (as most of the translations imply), or is the second phrase epexegetical; i.e., does the waw mean something like "namely" and the second phrase indicate specifically who is meant (as it is taken by Joüon and NEB)? The conjunction ו, "and," can introduce an epexegetical phrase (cf. 1 Chron 5:26; GKC § 154a n. 1[b]; *HebS* § 434; and esp. Baker, *VT* 30 [1980] 129–36). Campbell (145) is incorrect when he decides that "the Hebrew is as explicit as it can be that there are two groups alluded to, by reusing the preposition *neged* before each group." The preposition may or may not be repeated when several items governed logically by the same preposition are listed (see *HebS* § 238). Further, in cases of strict apposition (i.e., without ו, "and"), the preposition is often repeated (cf. GKC § 131h; *GBH* § 132g). On the basis that only these ten elders of all the elders of Bethlehem have heretofore been mentioned as sitting in the gate, Campbell decides that "those sitting (here)" must mean these ten elders, while "the elders of my people" would refer by extension to the larger group of elders of the city of which the ten "sitters" are representative. It seems clear, however, that the group Boaz has assembled to legitimate and notarize the transaction he is instigating consists of the ten elders whom he has summoned along with the rest of the eligible male citizens who happen to have gathered at the gate; on this point, see the remarks in *Comment* on the ten elders in v 2 above. Given this fact about the normal constitution of the legal assembly, it seems rather clear that "those sitting here" corresponds to "all the people" of vv 9, 11 (so Rudolph, 59); hence, the compound expression refers to the legal assembly at large. This also renders unlikely the view of Brichto (*The Problem of Curse,* 160–61) that it here means "councillors" or "magistrates" on the basis of the usage in 1 Kgs 21:8, 11 (adopted also by Sasson, 117). It also seems unlikely that in this context it bears the meaning "rulers, authorities" established in a number of contexts by Gottwald (*Tribes of Israel,* 512–32).

The expression "the elders of *my* people" rather than "the elders of *our* people" (as would sound more natural to us) probably has no significance but is simply a way of speaking that is culturally determined. Boaz no more intends to exclude the nearer redeemer than Naomi intends to omit herself when in 3:18 she says, "until *you* learn how" instead of "until *we* learn how" (Joüon, 82).

אִם־תִּגְאַל גְּאָל, lit. "If you will redeem, redeem." This clause explicates the preceding and makes clear that, whether the transaction involves Naomi, who has the possession or right of possession of the field, or a third party to whom the possession and usufruct was previously sold, it is not a transfer of full legal ownership but the assignment of the right of usufruct, which is subject to the right of "redemption" on the part of the seller or his family. (For the use of the imperfect to express a desiderative mood, i.e., "if you want to redeem," cf. *HebS* § 171; *GBH* § 113n.)

The right of redemption in ancient Israel sprang from the theological principle that all land belonged to Yahweh and therefore could not be sold permanently (Lev 25:23). It also found its roots in the ancient Israelite concept of family solidarity. The family was so central to ancient Israel's world view that land could not be alienated from the family to whom it ultimately belonged (cf. 1 Kgs 21:3). Brichto (*HUCA* 44 [1973] 9) sums up the principle insightfully by speaking of

> the vertical and horizontal aspects of land ownership. Vertically it is the property of the family in time past and future; it belongs to the dead ancestors and to their unborn descendants. . . . Horizontally it is the property of the family as the living generation; each individual possesses his land subject to the overriding ownership of the family as a whole.

Given such conceptions, the only circumstance envisaged under which land may be "sold" is the pressure of poverty (Lev 25:25a), and any such sale is made subject to the right of redemption (Lev 25:24); i.e., in the language of English common law, no land is ever sold in fee simple. In noting that a very similar, if not identical, type of land ownership prevailed at the northwest Mesopotamian site of Mari, Malamat refers to such land tenure as "a kind of lease" (*JAOS* 82 [1962] 152). On the one hand, such a term would have the advantage that it implies no transfer of ownership, but, on the other hand, it implies regular periodic payment, which was quite apparently not the case in the Israelite transaction, as the stipulations of Lev 25:14–16 and the example of Jer 32 (for which, see below) reveal. The law in Lev 25 enumerates three different conditions under which land subject to such a sale reverts to the original owner—or at least to the original owner's family: (1) the seller's "nearer/nearest redeemer" (הקרוב אליו) must come and "redeem the 'sale' [ממכר] of his 'brother'" (Lev 25:25b); (2) if the seller has no גאל, "redeemer," but recovers sufficient means, he may repurchase the land himself (Lev 25:26–27); or (3) if neither of these is possible, in the year of the Jubilee the land reverts to the seller without payment (Lev 25:28). In addition, most scholars conclude that the order of the redeemers listed in Lev 25:48b–49a for the case of the redemption of a relative from slavery also applied to the redemption of land: "one of his brothers . . . , or his (paternal) uncle, or his cousin . . . , or one of the blood relatives [lit. 'the rest of his flesh'] of his clan."

When one seeks to apply these regulations, a number of ambiguities and uncertainties arise, two of which are of concern for understanding the transaction taking place in Ruth 4. The first of these involves the question of the "pre-emption" of the sale of the land to someone outside the family through its purchase by the redeemer. Is such a practice covered by the law of redemption, or is it a separate, albeit obviously related, matter? At first glance, "pre-emption" does not appear to be included in the redemption regulations of Lev 25, although, as we shall see, it may be implied therein. It arises specifically, however, in the narrative account in Jer 32:6–10. Here Jeremiah's cousin Hanamel requests that Jeremiah purchase his field in Anathoth since Jeremiah has the "right of redemption" so to do (v 7). Jeremiah formally purchases the field by signing the deed and weighing out the purchase price before witnesses, vv 9–10. Since this is clearly a case of pre-emption rather than redemption, some scholars have posited that such a transaction is not part of the redemption obligation. Gordis ("Love, Marriage, and Business," 253) argues that only the procedures prescribed in Lev 25 "are, properly speaking, instances of redemption, that is to say, the restoration to its original owner of land sold to an outsider." The procedure described in Jer 32, he argues, "which does not involve either the removal of the land from the possession of an alien purchaser or its restoration to its original owner, is not an instance of redemption, and is therefore not included in the laws of *geʾullah* in Leviticus." Indeed, if Gordis' view could be sustained, our interpretational problems in Ruth 4 would be considerably simplified, for the second of the two scenarios that we shall outline below would thereby be eliminated (as Gordis indeed does, "Love, Marriage, and Business," 254). But such a view cannot be sustained, for it is excluded by the fact that Hanamel specifically grounds his request in Jeremiah's redemption obligation. He asks Jeremiah to acquire the field "because the right of redemption to acquire is yours" (כי לך משפט הגאלה לקנות), Jer 32:7, and "the right of inheritance and the redemption obligation is yours" (כי־לך משפט הירשה ולך הגאלה), Jer 32:8. Note especially the language of v 7, where Hanamel gives as the reason for his appeal Jeremiah's "right of redemption (so) *to acquire.*" In this light, it is far more likely that the causal clause means that the redemption obligation included the right of pre-emption than that it simply means, as Gordis argues ("Love, Marriage, and Business," 254), that Jeremiah had a vested interest in the field as its potential redeemer and heir (cf. also the remarks of Levine, "Legal Themes," 100). It seems clear then that "pre-emption" is also included in the practice of גאלה, "redemption." Indeed, pre-emption may be covered in Lev 25:25 if one concludes with Rudolph (63) that the term ממכר in the stipulation "his nearest redeemer shall come and redeem the 'sale' [ממכר] of his brother" means "what is for sale" as well as "what has been sold." In my opinion, Rudolph's proposal that the language is deliberately vague so as to include both possibilities is most probable.

It is immediately clear that, of the four procedures noted above, only two can possibly be involved in seeking to understand what is transpiring in Ruth 4: (1) the repurchase by the redeemer of land already sold (Lev 25:25) and (2) the pre-emption of the sale of land to someone outside the family through the redeemer's purchase of the same (Jer 32; perhaps implied in Lev 25:25).

The second ambiguity in the redemption laws pertinent to the transaction in Ruth 4 is in the stipulation covering redemption of the land by the redeemer, Lev 25:25, which leaves quite unclear who has the possession and usufruct of the land after it has been repurchased, the redeemer or the impoverished original owner. Since, however, this question is pertinent to the problem of the nearer redeemer's change of mind in v 6, we shall consider it in the comment on that verse.

וְאִם לֹא יִגְאַל, "But if you do not wish to exercise your right of redemption" (cf. *Note* 4:4.c.). Almost all modern translations and commentaries read the *second* person here, following a number of Hebrew MSS and all the ancient versions. The emendation, demanded by the context, must be made, even though no cogent explanation for the third-person reading can be offered (see Barthélemy et al., *Preliminary and Interim Report* 2:141). Rudolph's explanation (59), that the verb was originally a marginal comment since the verb itself is unnecessary to the syntax, simply pushes the enigma one step further back, for it is equally inexplicable that a scribe should add a marginal comment in the incorrect person. Two attempts to interpret the original text do not commend themselves. NEB translates "but if not, someone must do it," but this is not an acceptable rendering of the Hebrew. Sasson (108, 118) attempts to explain the third-person form as original by averring that it "is purposely used in order to attribute to Boaz a series of realistic movements, as he briefly turns to address the assembled elders in between harangues aimed at the next of kin." Not only does this not present us a series of realistic movements, but it is a forced and unlikely interpretation, as evidenced from the fact that Sasson (103) must add to his translation of the phrase the bracketed comment "[added Boaz as he addressed the elders before turning back to the redeemer]" in order to render the abrupt change of persons acceptable.

הַגִּידָה לִּי וְאֵדַע כִּי . . ., "Tell me, so that I may know, for . . ." Almost all commentators and translators have taken the first three words as a separate clause, consisting of the imperative plus imperfect/cohortative to express purpose/result (cf. GKC § 108d; *IBH* § 107[c]), yielding the translation "Tell me so that I may know," or the like. The following כי then bears its regular causal meaning, "for, because," and introduces a subordinate clause of reason (e.g., Campbell, Rudolph, Sasson). Hubbard (237 n. 7), however, divides the clauses after לי, "to me," on the grounds that the disjunctive MT accent *(rebiaʿ)* thereon so dictates. This requires adopting the imperfect ואדע (K) rather than the cohortative (Q; see *Note* 4.d.) and understanding that כי then introduces a noun clause, object of ואדע, the resulting translation reading, "tell me, for I know that. . ." However, that the Masoretes did not so intend the disjunctive accent is rather clearly indicated by the Q reading, in which, by adding ה to the verb following the accent, *they* demonstrate that they understood the verb to be cohortative, expressing purpose/result. Further, nothing in the context then suggests the nuance "for," with which Hubbard begins the second clause, and it is more likely that the present tense would be expressed by אני יודע, participle + independent pronoun, than by the imperfect (cf. Gen 3:5; see *IBHS* § 37.6b).

אֵין זוּלָתְךָ לִגְאוֹל וְאָנֹכִי אַחֲרֶיךָ, lit. "there is no one but you to redeem and I after you." Campbell, reasoning that the expression is "odd, because the Hebrew *zūlat,* 'apart from, except' is always used elsewhere to designate the *only* exception" (145), does not recognize that the preposition does indeed designate the only exception here, namely, "you and I." This is simply an example of the failure to repeat the preposition when it logically governs two (or more) items (see *HebS* § 238). The clause causes confusion partly because the normal order would be to place the infinitive לגאול immediately following the negative particle אין, i.e., אין לגאול זולתך. The order of the text places emphasis upon זולתך, "but you." It may well be that there is also stress placed upon the independent pronoun אנכי, "I," by using it instead of the repetition of the preposition plus pronominal suffix.

אָנֹכִי אֶגְאָל, "I am willing to redeem it." As Joüon (83) notes, the redeemer avoids the perfect גאלתי, which would imply a formal declaration by which the matter is settled: "I hereby exercise my right" (see the discussion of the performative perfect above; cf. קניתי, vv 9, 10). On the contrary, he simply expresses his willingness or intention so to do, leaving the way open for any further proposals from Boaz. Again the independent pronoun before the inflected verb is not emphatic (contra, e.g., Morris, 303; see the remarks on ואני אמרתי at the beginning of the verse).

5a מִיַּד נָעֳמִי, "from Naomi." There is no particular significance to the idiom מיד, lit. "from the hand of," for several different prepositions are used to designate the one from whom something is bought, including simple מן, "from" (Lev 25:44, 45), and the compound prepositions מעם (2 Sam 24:21) and מאת (e.g., Lev 27:24) as well as מיד (Gen 33:19; 39:1; Lev 25:14), all of which in such a context simply mean "from."

With this last piece of evidence, we have elucidated as far as possible the different grammatical and lexical possibilities connected with the sudden appearance of the field of Elimelech, together with some of the pertinent legal and social background. Let us now seek to elucidate the most plausible understanding of the situation presumed thus far in the text.

Excursus: The Nature of the Transaction Proposed by Boaz in vv 3–5a

Here so many ambiguities, uncertainties, and unknowns confront us that any final solution to the problems involved will doubtless permanently escape us. Nevertheless, in spite of these difficulties and uncertainties, I shall adopt as my working hypothesis the view that most of these uncertainties arise from our lack of knowledge of the socio-legal customs and institutions that regulated such real estate transactions and family obligations in ancient Israel rather than from our narrator's ignorance, ineptitude, or deliberate (albeit "artful") manipulation of legal principles and formulations for the purpose of constructing a "good" story (contra Levine, "Legal Themes," 96). The narrator has thus far shown himself to be such a skillful and well-informed storyteller that the only reasonable working hypothesis is the assumption that he and his ancient readers shared sufficient knowledge of the social and legal customs and obligations to comprehend what was going on. As Campbell has observed, "the civil issues at stake here were not as confusing to the ancient audience as they are to us. . . . [P]eople provided the explanation out of their knowledge of common practice, and probably gave it barely a second thought." With this as my working hypothesis, I shall attempt in the following discussion first to set forth the various options that the facts seem to demand and second to delineate what seems to me to be the most plausible solution. In doing so, I shall perforce be guided by (1) the principles of coherence, sufficiency, and credibility that must guide a narrator if his story is to function effectively as a story and (2) the implications of the nature of Israelite casuistic law, both of which were explained above in *Comment* on 3:9.

First, let us note that we cannot take the verb מכרה here (v 3) in its most obvious meaning (as a past tense) and suppose that Naomi "sold" the field some time in the past. She could hardly have done so from Moab during the ten years after her husband's death, and the principle of credibility precludes the possibility that she could have done so since her return, for she and Ruth have been living as paupers (see below). This very problem is one of the major difficulties with Beattie's treatment (*VT* 24 [1974] 251–67). Although he (*VT* 24 [1974] 256; cf. id., *JSOT* 5 [1978] 39–40) appeals so clearly to the principle of coherence and credibility to establish that it was normative for childless widows to inherit their husband's estate, in the matter of the sale of the field he simply baldly states (*VT* 24 [1974] 266),

> Boaz tells the redeemer that Naomi has sold the field and asks him if he wishes to redeem it. It would probably be more correct, legally speaking, for him to have said "Ruth has sold the field," but the narrator makes Boaz refrain for the moment from any mention of Ruth; to introduce her name here would destroy the drama of Boaz's second speech.

Nowhere does Beattie even raise the question of when such a sale could have taken place nor how the story can meet the principle of credibility if Naomi or Ruth had rights to such land as heirs and sold it and yet have been forced heretofore to live as paupers and glean in the fields. On the contrary, the principle of credibility precludes the possibility that מכרה can be translated as past tense. It must be understood, then, in one of the present senses discussed above.

This being the case, there are, in point of fact, only two broad scenarios possible in understanding this situation. (1) In the first scenario, Elimelech sold the usufruct of his land (sale in fee simple not being possible to him; see the discussion on מכר above) before emigrating to Moab, and the field since then has been in the possession of others. Now Naomi through Boaz is calling upon the nearer redeemer to repurchase the field from its present possessor. The transaction then is a case of *redemption* such as is described in Lev 25:25. (2) In the second scenario, Elimelech did not sell the usufruct of his field prior to emigrating, and Naomi now has the usufructuary rights to the field. Naomi through Boaz is calling upon the nearer redeemer to acquire these rights from her. The transaction then is a case of *pre-emption* such as is related in Jer 32 (and probably implied in Lev 25:25).

The difficulty that faces the interpreter is that each of these possible scenarios fits coherently with some of the story and with some of the exegetical and socio-legal data that must govern the situation (some of which has been elucidated above) but does not seem to fit at all with other such data. Let us examine the implications of each of these two possible scenarios in turn and then decide on a most probable case.

(1) *The first scenario, that the transaction is a case of redemption.* As a number of commentators have noted (e.g., Brichto, *HUCA* 44 [1973] 15; Campbell, 156; Gordis, 254; Rudolph, 66), Naomi and Ruth returned from Moab destitute. In 1:21 Naomi bitterly complains, "Full was I when I went away, but empty has Yahweh brought me back," and subsequent events demonstrate that she is not referring simply to the loss of husband and sons, for in order to gain sustenance for the two of them, Ruth must stoop to the vocation of the poverty stricken and glean in the fields as a pauper (chap. 2). Hence, the coherence and credibility of the story require that Elimelech must have sold the usufruct of his field before leaving for Moab, for Naomi and Ruth very obviously have had no access to it or its produce. If that is the case, what sense do we make of v 3, which clearly states that *Naomi* is "selling" the field, or of v 5a, which states that the nearer redeemer is to acquire the field *from Naomi?*

Several attempts have been made to deal with these apparent contradictions. Westbrook (*ILR* 6 [1971] 373–74) argues that, though the text says "Naomi," it really was Elimelech who sold the field. Since it would be tedious for the narrator of Ruth to explain the full details of the original sale by Elimelech and since Naomi is now the last link to the ancestral land and the narrator throughout emphasizes her role, we must understand the statement that she sold the land as a "technique of narrative" whose "mistake would be obvious." Although such narrative techniques are certainly not unknown, especially when the incorrect attribution would be quite obvious (see, e.g., the example cited by Westbrook, *ILR* 6 [1971] 374 n. 34), there hardly seems to be any need for such a technique here. The narrator could have been quite specific about who actually made the sale without including any more "tedious details" than he did in stating that Naomi sold the land. He could have said something like, "Our brother Elimelech, the husband of Naomi who has returned from the territory of Moab, sold the field which belongs to him," and he still would have left totally to the surmise of the audience the same details about when, to whom, and under what circumstances the sale was made as he did by stating that Naomi sold the field.

In like vein, Brichto (*HUCA* 44 [1973] 15) argues that Elimelech sold the land before emigrating to Moab, and he deals with the apparent contradiction of v 3 with the sole statement that "The active perfect is to be rendered as past and passive (the latter being far from unprecedented in biblical Hebrew: cf. Gen. 29:34; 31:48)." Whatever one may conclude about the correctness of rendering the active perfect as past and passive (qal passive or the impersonal use of the third person singular?), such an understanding is simply not possible in Ruth 4:3 without performing radical surgery on the text, for the sentence includes both subject ("Naomi") and object ("the field of . . ."); cf. also the remarks of Sasson, 110.

By far the most coherent and attractive attempt to deal with these data is that of Gordis ("Love, Marriage, and Business," 252–59), who proposes that what Naomi possesses as the heir of Elimelech is the right to redeem the alienated property of her husband by repurchasing it from its buyers. Since she has no means whatsoever to do so, she transfers (מכר) this obligation-right to her nearest kinsman. Boaz calls upon the nearer redeemer to acquire (קנה) this obligation-right and redeem the field (v 4). When this man ultimately declines (v 6), the obligation-right is taken over by Boaz through the symbolism of the shoe transfer (vv 7–8). In Gordis' view, the only transaction actually described in Ruth 4 in regard to the field is the transfer of the right of redemption from the nearer redeemer to Boaz. Boaz's subsequent redemption of the land itself from the person who acquired it from Elimelech is not described in the book (because Ruth is the focus of interest). To sustain this view, Gordis must assume that the verbs מכר, "to deliver over, to sell," and קנה, "to acquire, to buy," carry in this context the special nuance "to transfer the obligation-right of redemption" and "to acquire the obligation-right of redemption," respectively. The studies of Westbrook (*ILR* 6 [1971] 375) and Brichto (*HUCA* 44 [1973] 15) imply a similar understanding of the transaction. Now, if the only meanings accorded to מכר and קנה are "sell" and "buy," respectively (e.g., Campbell, 145), and these are understood in the limited modern sense of a commercial "cash" transaction (e.g., Sasson, 117), then such a meaning for these verbs seems difficult to maintain. But, as has been noted above, Lipiński has demonstrated that the semantic range of מכר encompasses "to hand over, to consign, to transfer, to deliver," most often used of the conveyance of the usufruct of movable and immovable goods, and concludes that מכר "characterizes the form of the transaction, but does not specify its substance" (*THAT* 2:875; see *Comment* on v 3 above). When such a range of meaning is recognized, it does not seem beyond the range of probability at all that, in the context of a widow's right of usufruct of her husband's estate, these verbs have shed their component of compensation and mean "to dispose of, surrender (the rights to)" and "acquire, accept (the rights to)," with the context making clear what rights are meant. See the helpful discussion of Schneider (*BT* 33 [1982] 304–5), set against the background of the similar culture of the Tsonga people of southeast Africa (although I do not agree with his conclusion that מכר and קנה here are synonyms of the verb גאל). It is important to stress in this regard that no proper "sale" of any kind takes place between Boaz and Naomi in Ruth 4. No amount is negotiated, and Naomi is not even present; see the discussion below.

(2) *The second scenario, that the transaction is a case of pre-emption.* This seems to be the clear implication of the language of v 3, which states that *Naomi* is "selling" the usufruct of the field of Elimelech, and of v 5a, which states that the field is to be acquired *from Naomi.* Plainly, it is argued, Elimelech did not sell his field before leaving for Moab, and Naomi as the widow possesses the usufructuary rights to the field of her deceased husband, which she now through Boaz offers for sale. This, however, seems to make nonsense of the story! Naomi and Ruth have been living throughout the story as paupers dependent on the largesse of Boaz, as was noted above. Surely the coherence and credibility of the story preclude the possibility that Naomi had either the right to or the actual possession and usufruct of such land.

Various scholars have suggested a number of expedients to solve this conundrum. Most have argued that, contrary to views such as those of Gordis and Westbrook noted above, it is unlikely that Elimelech would have sold his land before emigrating to Moab. Sasson (113) argues that he would not have intended to find permanent shelter in a foreign land but would have expected to return as soon as the famine was over. Rudolph (66–67) contends that he would have been unable to dispose of the field in haste before he left Bethlehem since in the general famine none of his "redeemers" would have had the means to exercise their obligation of pre-emption. Further, since agricultural land is far too valuable and essential to the ongoing life of the community for such land to lie abandoned or fallow while its owner was absent for an extended period, we must assume that Elimelech would have left the plot in the care of family or friends (Sasson, 113), or someone else had silently appropriated the abandoned property (cf. Hubbard, 53). A number of commentators have argued (e.g., Burrows, *JBL* 59 [1940] 448; Campbell, 157; Rudolph, 66) that such a scenario was not only possible but probable on the basis of the account in 2 Kgs 8:1–6, concerning the Shunammite woman whose son was brought back to life by Elisha (2 Kgs 4:8–37). She went to live in the land of the Philistines for seven years because of a famine (vv 1–2). When she returned at the end of this time, she had to appeal to the king for the return of her home and her field (v 3). Although the narrative does not so state, it is reasonable to suppose that she was then a widow, and, although the parallel with the situation in Ruth is not exact for she was apparently administering the property on behalf of her minor son (v 2 states that she "and her household" left the land), the account illustrates that property abandoned under such circumstances could well end up in the hands of others. To account for the silence of our narrator about such matters, Rudolph (66) follows Gunkel in plausibly arguing that such an occurrence was apparently so common that neither the narrator of 2 Kgs 8:1–6 (note v 3!) nor the narrator of the book of Ruth thought it necessary to report specifically the irregular seizure. Further, Sasson plausibly argues that in the absence of OT information, we might assume that the standing of women in the legal forum of rabbinic times obtained in earlier periods, that is, that the rights of women during judicial proceedings, especially in matters of property transfer, were severely restricted. Hence, Naomi on her own could not have legally convened a group of elders in order to initiate proceedings concerning her husband's land. For this she needed a sponsor, who turned out to be Boaz. It is perhaps also pertinent in this regard to note that the Shunammite woman in 2 Kgs 8 does not seek redress through the normal channels of the legal assembly of her town but appeals to the king (cf., however, the remarks of Boecker, *Law and the Administration of Justice*, 51–52).

(3) *The most probable case.* Obviously, many assumptions and presumptions must be made in seeking to spell out the implications and variant possibilities attendant upon each of the two major scenarios described above. In such a maze of uncertainties and unknowns, it would seem difficult indeed to delineate a most plausible or probable case. However, there is one further aspect of the whole transaction that, in my opinion, makes the first scenario, despite its difficulties of language, much more probable and plausible. The second scenario understands that the transaction involved is a case of pre-emption. Naomi has the right of possession and usufruct of Elimelech's field as his heir, and she, through Boaz, requests the nearer redeemer to "purchase" this possession and usufruct from her, analogous to Jeremiah's "purchase" of his cousin Hanamel's field (Jer 32). When the nearer redeemer relinquishes his right to do so, Boaz then does so, v 9. However, if this is the case, the transaction would conform to no other such "purchase" of land in the OT, neither a purchase in which outright ownership is conveyed (e.g., Gen 23:4–18; 33:19; 2 Sam 24:24; 1 Kgs 16:24) nor a transfer in which possession and usufruct are conveyed as in Jer 32. As Westbrook (*ILR* 6 [1971] 373) notes, the seller, Naomi, is not present at all, and there is no mention of the price, a point about which the other narratives relating a purchase of land seem to be extremely particular. The parallel case of pre-emption in Jer 32 is most revealing in this regard. Since Jeremiah wishes to emphasize the certainty of the future restoration of the land of Judah (cf. v 44), he seeks to stress that the transaction is legally valid and complete, so the purchase price, the deed of purchase, and the witnesses are all specifically mentioned. Now Boaz likewise, for quite different reasons, obviously does everything necessary to ensure the legal validity of the transaction involved in Ruth 4 by convening the legal assembly as witnesses and publicly invoking their notarial function and power

(vv 9–10; see the discussion below). How then could a *sale* of land or of rights to land of any kind be effected if the seller is not present and the determination and delivery of the purchase price, without which the transaction cannot be legally binding, are omitted? (Compare the involved and improbable hypothesis of Rudolph [64], who can account for the striking anomaly of the omission of the legally necessary payment only by assuming that the obligation of the purchaser to care for the widow, who presumably goes along with the field, stands in place of the purchase price.) On the contrary, the absence of the seller and the failure to mention any payment or its amount render it most difficult, if not impossible, to regard the transaction involved as a pre-emptive sale, or sale of any kind, of the field of Elimelech to Boaz by Naomi. In addition, as we shall see below, the nearer redeemer's change of mind also makes it virtually impossible to understand the transaction as a pre-emption; see *Comment* on v 6.

Hence, the most plausible interpretation of the situation is that provided by Gordis' proposal described in the first scenario above. Naomi as the wife of the deceased has the right to the usufruct of the field of Elimelech and, hence, the right to redeem it, i.e., to buy it back from whoever now is in possession of it. It is these rights that Boaz states she is offering to transfer to Elimelech's nearest relative, since she as a woman has little or no legal standing in the matter (see Sasson's view noted above), nor the means to redeem the field. Therefore, Boaz calls on the nearer redeemer to exercise his rights in the matter and redeem the field. In the dénouement in vv 9–10, the solemn declaration by Boaz before a duly constituted legal assembly and the solemn affirmation of that legal assembly as witnesses conclude and notarize in a legally binding manner the only transaction involving the field that clearly and unmistakably has transpired, the transfer of the right and obligation to redeem the field from the nearer redeemer to Boaz. The actual redemption of the field is not related—it takes place offstage, so to speak. We must conclude then that the verbs מכר and קנה in vv 3–4 bear the meaning, unattested elsewhere, "to dispose of (the rights to)" and "to acquire (the rights to)," respectively, and the context makes it clear that the rights involved are the usufruct of the field of Elimelech and its redemption.

Finally, in the light of this, the verb form מכרה in v 3 is best taken as an "instantaneous perfect," i.e., "Naomi is (now) disposing of her right." It could be either a "performative perfect," i.e., "Naomi is hereby disposing of her right," or a "perfect of resolve," i.e., "Naomi is going (intends) to dispose of her right," but these seem less likely for the reasons noted in *Comment* on v 3.

I have now elucidated the grammatical and lexical facts and possibilities presented by the exegetical evidence of vv 3–5a, together with the legal and social background raised therein, and I have delineated the most plausible scenario involved in making sense of this sudden appearance of Elimelech's field, Naomi's rights to it, and the nature of its redemption. Having done so, we can now proceed to consider the meaning of Boaz's next statement in v 5b, in which he informs the nearer redeemer not only that the matter involves the right to redeem the field of Elimelech but also that it involves marriage to Ruth the Moabitess, the wife of the deceased. Two critical issues must be addressed here. First, does Boaz propose that the nearer redeemer must marry Ruth, or does he announce that he will do so? Second, in what way, if at all, is this proposed marriage related to the practice of levirate marriage that appears elsewhere in the OT? Let us deal with these issues as they are raised by the exegetical data of the text of v 5b.

5b וּמֵאֵת רוּת הַמּוֹאֲבִיָּה אֵשֶׁת־הַמֵּת קָנִיתָ, "you acquire Ruth the Moabitess, the wife of the deceased." There are three major problems that must be dealt with in this clause in order to give a coherent interpretation of the passage: (1) What is the object, expressed or implied, of the verb קניתי? (2) If the object of קניתי is taken to be Ruth, what is the meaning and significance of the verb קנה, "buy, acquire," when used in regard to taking a wife? (3) Which is the correct reading of MT קָנִיתָ? K קָנִיתִי, "I acquire," or Q קָנִיתָה, "you acquire." Let us deal with these in the order mentioned.

(1) *The object of the verb* קניתי. The syntax of the verse as it stands seems to be problematic. First, no object for the verb קנה is expressed, and although the verb can be used without an object expressed when that object is clearly implied in the context (contra Vriezen, *OTS* 5 [1948] 81; cf. Lev 25:14, 15; Ruth 4:4), the object intended here is wholly unclear. The clumsy attempt of NIV to take as the object the phrase "wife of the deceased," pointed in MT as in apposition to "Ruth the Moabitess," does not in the least commend itself, because it leaves the referent of the phrase wholly ambiguous (cf. Gow, *TB* 41 [1990] 302–3) and only Naomi is mentioned in v 4. Surely there can hardly have been two persons with the right to dispose of the field. In an attempt to interpret the verse as it stands as "fairly regular Hebrew," Sasson (121) takes the object implied in the context as the field itself. The translation that results is, however, semantically inappropriate. In meaning, the resulting sentence simply states the purpose for which the field is acquired, and in such a semantic setting the temporal clause verges on the tautological: "when you acquire the field . . . , you acquire the field in order to . . ." Further, this is contradicted by vv 9–10, which, as Rudolph (59) notes, form the proper commentary on v 5, for in vv 9–10 Boaz publicly assumes the obligations that he proposes in v 5. And he does not say in vv 9–10 that he acquires the field from Naomi and Ruth in order to raise an heir for Elimelech, but he assumes two separate obligations: one with regard to the field, the other with regard to Ruth. Taking a different tack, Gow (*TB* 41 [1990] 310–11) interprets the Q reading קניתה as קָנִיתָהּ, "you acquire *her*," citing the LXX rendering. This yields the translation, "On the day you acquire the field from the hand of Naomi and from Ruth the Moabitess, the widow of the deceased, you acquire her in order to . . ." This proposal meets with the objection that only Naomi is mentioned in v 4 and there can hardly have been two persons with the right to dispose of the field; it also clumsily leaves the referent of the pronoun "her" ambiguous.

Second, it is highly unusual and syntactically suspect in the sentence as it stands (contra Sasson, 120) that the logical governing of two nouns in the prepositional phrase "from Naomi and Ruth" is accomplished not by the repetition of the same preposition (see *Comment* on נגד . . . ונגד in v 4 above) but by the use of two different (though synonymous) prepositions: מיד נעמי ומאת רות. Gow's proposal (*TB* 41 [1990] 309) that the change in prepositions is intentional, מיד (governing Naomi) "signifying that she is the one authorizing the transaction and giving up possession" but מאת (governing Ruth) signifying "that Ruth also has a *legal interest* in the transaction," does not in the least commend itself. Given the lack of an appropriate and suitable object for קנה, and especially given that Boaz refers to two quite different actions with respect to Naomi and Ruth when he assumes in vv 9–10 the obligations he proposes here, the syntactically suspect and inappropriate change of prepositions from מיד to מאת strongly suggests that the locus of the problem lies here.

In this light, then, most commentators have opted to emend ומאת either to גם את־ (so *BHK/BHS*, followed by most commentators; see Leggett, 224 n. 53) or to וגם את (so, e.g., Gray, *NCBC*, 380; Gerleman, 35; Hubbard, 243 n. 8). However, emendation may no longer be necessary if it is accepted that ומאת consists of the conjunction ו plus enclitic mem prefixed to the direct object particle את. The same combination can be interpreted as the conjunction plus enclitic mem in other passages in the OT; see Andersen, *Hebrew Verbless Clause,* 48, 124 n. 13. Note also the corroboratory evidence now elucidated from the possibly distantly related language from ancient Ebla; see Gordon, "*WM-* 'and,'" 29; and Rendsburg, "Eblaite *U-MA,*" 33–34.

Finally, least satisfactory of all is the attempt of Barthélemy et al., *Preliminary and Interim Report* 2:142, to maintain the MT by proposing that מאת here means "'on behalf of' and is somewhat parallel to מיד 'in the name of,'" yielding the translation "and the day you buy the rights to the field in the name of Naomi, you will buy (it) also on behalf of Ruth." However, מאת (used 9x elsewhere) and מיד (used 3x elsewhere) are the regular prepositions used with קנה to express the nuance "to acquire *from* (someone)," and there is nothing in the semantic content of this clause to indicate that they are being used here in some other sense than that which they bear in the normal idiom. Further, an extensive examination of the uses of the prepositions מאת and מיד has turned up no single context where they bear the meanings suggested.

(2) *The meaning of* קנה. This verse and the parallel passage in v 10 are the only passages in the OT in which the verb קנה, "to acquire, buy," is used to refer to taking a wife in marriage. When the meaning of קנה is restricted to the translation "to purchase," the usage here has been invoked to establish the specialized meaning of "to purchase to be one's wife" (i.e., through the payment of the bride-price [Heb. מהר]; cf. KB[1], 843; Ges.-Buhl, 717). Many have attempted to substantiate this view by contending that it reflects "marriage by purchase," a view of marriage in the ancient Near East and the OT first expressed for Babylonian society by Koschaker (see Westbrook, *Old Babylonian Marriage Laws,* 53–54; in regard to Ruth, see Bewer, *AJSL* 19 [1902–3] 146; Neufeld, *Marriage Laws,* 94–95). However, Schmidt is certainly correct when he observes that, on the basis of the usage here, קנה לאשה can hardly be taken in the narrow sense to mean "to purchase (through the payment of the bride-price)" but must be understood more broadly to mean "to acquire (as wife)" (*THAT* 2:653). In the first place, it is highly doubtful whether a conception of marriage by purchase, in which the woman was acquired in a manner analogous to a commercial transaction of buying and selling, was known to either the OT or any ancient Near Eastern society (see esp. the criticisms of Koschaker's views by Westbrook, *Old Babylonian Marriage Laws,* 54–58; in regard to the OT, see Mace, *Hebrew Marriage,* 169–72; for further bibliography, see Leggett, *The Levirate,* 225–29). Even though in most ancient Near Eastern societies, including the OT, the act by which a woman formally and legally became the wife of a man consisted of the payment of the "marriage-money" (Heb. מהר; cf. Lipiński, *THAT* 4:372–74) by the bridegroom or his father to the family or father of the bride, such a payment in actuality constituted nothing more than the legal form for contracting the marriage (see Boecker, *Law and the Administration of Justice,* 101). As Boecker notes, to designate such a proceeding "marriage by purchase" is misleading for modern Western readers because, since we purchase only objects, it treats the woman as if she were a piece of property purchased by the man, a view disparaging to the woman. In Oriental thinking, however, exactly the opposite was true: the amount of the "marriage-money" was an indication of the esteem in which the man held his

bride-to-be. (See further the remarks of Schneider, *BT* 33 [1982] 306–7.) Hence, the customary translation "bride-price" for this payment (Heb. מהר) is unfortunate and misleading. That this means of contracting the marriage was not conceived of as a commercial transaction in the OT is supported by avoidance of the terminology of purchase in favor of the piel stem of ארש, customarily translated "to betroth" (but better rendered "to acquire [someone] as a wife"; see Wolff, *Hosea,* 52, on Hos 2:21). For a similar avoidance of commercial terminology by the Babylonians in describing the act by which a marriage was contracted, see Boecker, *Law and the Administration of Justice,* 101.

Further, Weiss has argued (*HTR* 57 [1964] 244–48) that the reason for the choice of קנה here is exclusively contextual or stylistic. It does not imply the general use of קנה as a technical term for marriage. Weiss notes several passages in mishnaic Hebrew in which the idiom "to take a wife" occurs in contexts involving other transactions for which the use of the verb קנה is normative, such as levirate marriage or the purchase of slaves. In these passages, the verb is then also used for acquiring a wife, though it is never used elsewhere with such a meaning. Weiss proposes that such a usage is for purposes of stylistic uniformity. Likewise in Ruth 4, the verb קנה in reference to the "purchase" of the field in vv 5a, 9 triggers in both cases the use of קנה in the immediately following phrase to express "to acquire a wife." However, in 4:3, where such conditions do not apply, the verb used is the customary one, לקח, "to take." If the transaction involved here is such that the verb קנה in vv 5a, 9 is being used to mean "to acquire the rights to," then Weiss's argument is compelling.

Finally, Sasson (136) interprets the meaning of קנה here as "to purchase, to buy" and then (123–25) suggests what he terms the "speculative but by no means implausible" proposal that Ruth's relationship to Naomi was some type of "promise" or "(unwritten) contract" (125) such that "to obtain Ruth's release from the bonds that tied her to Naomi, Boaz may have had to buy her outright or at least to compensate Naomi for the loss of a valuable helper," but this "purchase price" was nevertheless not a bride price (124). Later he speaks of an "indentured" Ruth and of a "sale" by Naomi (136). But surely such an understanding of the relationship of these two women flies in the face of those numerous passages that depict the relationship as one of loving loyalty (e.g., 1:16–17; 2:11–12; 3:10; 4:15) and reduces it at best to the level of indentured slavery and at worst to that of a commercial transaction. That Ruth regards herself as under Naomi's authority seems clear (cf. the comments of Thompson and Thompson, *VT* 18 [1968] 96), but that authority is surely the moral authority of the older family member over the younger, the mother-in-law over the daughter-in-law, willingly received, and not a status that would demand the literal purchase of her by a prospective husband!

(3) *The correct reading of* קָנִיתָ֯י. One must read, of course, either K קניתי, undoubtedly to be pointed קָנִיתִי, "*I* acquire, have acquired," or Q קניתה, which is almost invariably interpreted as קָנִיתָה, the "long" form of the perfect second masculine singular (i.e., with the final vowel marked by ה, a form that often occurs with ל״ה verbs; cf. esp. *GBH* § 42f; GKC § 44g), "*you* acquire, have acquired." Indeed, the long form may have been deliberately used here to mark unmistakably the second person. All the ancient versions and virtually every modern translation and commentary have read Q, "you acquire." This has almost invariably been done on the basis of the traditional view of the book, that Ruth in 3:9 calls upon Boaz to carry out the legal obligation of levirate marriage by grounding her request for marriage

in Boaz's identity as a גאל, "redeemer" (see the *Comment* on 3:9). Based on this view, it has seemed *prima facie* evident to almost all commentators that Boaz calls on the nearer redeemer to take on this legal responsibility, and hence Q is necessarily the correct reading. However, as we have argued in interpreting 3:9 above, no reference to a legal obligation for anyone to enter into a levirate marriage with Ruth has thus far surfaced in the book, since Ruth did not use גאל in 3:9 in that technical sense. Rather, she appealed to Boaz as גאל in the general sense of the one responsible to come to the aid of family members in need, in this case to remove the reproach and destitution of her widowhood by marrying her (see *Comment* on 3:9). However, a responsibility at the very least similar to levirate marriage is introduced in the clause immediately following the K-Q form קָנִיתָי, and this fact forms the most significant piece of evidence on which the decision must be based regarding whether the K or the Q form is the correct reading. Therefore, it is logically necessary first to set forth the exegetical data involved in the following clause and to discuss the socio-legal background of the custom raised therein. Then it will be possible to return to the question of the correct reading of קָנִיתָי.

לְהָקִים שֵׁם־הַמֵּת עַל־נַחֲלָתוֹ, lit. "to raise up the name of the deceased on his inherited property." This clause, introduced by the preposition ל plus the infinitive, expresses the purpose for which Ruth is to be acquired. Since this purpose is very similar, even in language (cf. also v 10), to the purpose of levirate marriage as expressed in Deut 25:6, it has been the conclusion of almost all interpreters of the book of Ruth that this identifies the marriage here proposed as a levirate marriage, very similar if not identical to that described in Deut 25:5–10 (see also *Comment* on 3:9). To deal with this issue, I shall proceed as follows: (1) I shall first ascertain the meaning of this clause in the light of the use of similar expressions in the OT. (2) Since this investigation will show that this clause means "to produce descendants for the deceased," a meaning that clearly suggests that the purpose of this marriage is, at the very least, similar to that of levirate marriage, I shall consider the nature of levirate marriage in the OT, excluding the book of Ruth, in an excursus. (3) Against this background I shall then examine the nature of the marriage responsibility assumed in the book of Ruth. (4) Having determined the meaning of this clause and examined the nature of the obligation involved therein, I shall then determine the correct reading of K-Q קָנִיתָי.

(1) *The meaning of the clause "to raise up the name of the deceased on his inherited property."* The exact force of this idiom is not easy to ascertain. The specific idiom occurs only here and in 4:10, but three expressions that are close and clearly parallel in meaning occur in two other passages in the OT: (a) Deut 25:5–10, the passage in the law code of Deuteronomy that delineates the obligation of the levirate, and (b) Gen 38:6–26, the narrative of Judah and Tamar, within which the levirate obligation figures prominently. Deut 25:5–10 specifies that when a man died without leaving a son, the brother of the deceased would take the wife of the deceased as his wife, and the first son of that union would "be accounted to" (יקום על־שם, lit. "rise/stand upon the name of") the deceased brother (vv 5–6). If the man refused, the wife of the deceased might charge the man before the elders at the gate by saying "my husband's brother has refused 'to raise up a name for his brother' [להקים לאחיו שם] in Israel" (v 7). The text goes on to relate that, if the husband's brother persists in spite of the elders' remonstrances (v 8), then (v 9) the wife of the deceased shall "go up to him in the presence of the elders, pull the sandal off

his foot, spit in his face, and declare, 'Thus shall be done to the man who will not build up his brother's house'" (לא יבנה את־בית אחיו). Similarly, in Gen 38 when Er, Judah's oldest son, dies (v 7), Judah tells Onan, his second son, to have sexual relations with Tamar, the wife of Er, and to perform the duty of a husband's brother for her and "raise up descendants [lit. 'seed'] for your brother" (הקם זרע לאחיך, v 8).

It seems rather clear, as a number of scholars have noted, that the word שׁם, "name," in these passages is not being used in its literal sense but rather in that dynamic sense in which it is the embodiment of the deeds and achievements, the substance (property, goods, assets), and the renown, honor, and reputation of a person (cf. van der Woude, *THAT* 2:947). "Name" in this sense in the OT can be used as the virtual equivalent of "descendants, posterity" (cf. Isa 66:22). (On this use and meaning of "name," see BDB, 2.c, p. 1028; and esp. Thompson and Thompson, *VT* 18 [1968] 84–88; Leggett, *The Levirate*, 48–54.) Thus, יקום על־שׁם, Deut 25:6, "to stand for the 'name' of," means "to represent the person of," and להקים שׁם, Deut 25:7, means "to produce descendants," as the parallel expressions in those passages, "to build up the house of" (Deut. 25:9) and להקים זרע, "to raise up descendants" (Gen 38:8), clearly reveal. Note how "name" is virtually equivalent to "person" in passages such as Num 1:2; 26:53, and note especially the remarks of Burrows, *JBL* 59 (1940) 31. Hence, these idioms do not mean that the son to be born will literally bear the name of the deceased. First, there is an idiom that specifically means "to be called by the name of": להקרא על־שׁם or להקרא בשׁם (cf., e.g., Gen 48:6, 16). Second, as has often been pointed out, the sons born to Judah and Tamar and to Boaz and Ruth use as their patronymics the names of their true fathers, rather than the names of those whose lines and families they continue. It ought to be noted, however, that this argument assumes that both Tamar's relationship with Judah and the marriage of Boaz and Ruth are examples of the performance of the levirate obligation. This is by no means certain (see the discussion below).

Levine ("Legal Themes," 105–6) has argued that להקים in vv 5b, 10 "means 'to fulfill, confirm,' the opposite of *hēp̄ēr* [הפר] 'to annul, void,'" and hence the phrase means "to confirm the title of the deceased over his estate." Therefore, its sense here differs from its meaning in the parallel passages dealing with the levirate (cited above). To establish this sense, Levine appeals to the meaning of הקים in legal passages and cites its use in Num 30:14–15. These passages, however, exhibit specific, technical meanings for both קום and הקים that are in no way parallel to the meanings required by the context of Ruth 4. Thus, throughout Num 30 the verb קום is used as the predicate of nouns such as נדר, "vow," in the technical sense "to be valid" (e.g., vv 5, 6, 13, 14), and the hiphil הקים is used to govern such nouns as נדר, "vow," as object to mean "to validate, affirm the validity of." Such a meaning in no way fits the meaning required in Ruth 4. If one granted that שׁם, "name," here bears the sense "title" (a meaning Levine nowhere substantiates), it makes little sense in Ruth 4 that the nearer redeemer (or Boaz) is to marry Ruth "in order to affirm the validity of the title of the deceased over his estate." The question is not the validity of the title but the existence of an heir. Further, the additional reason given in v 10, "that the name of the deceased may not perish from among his brothers," shows very clearly that the idiom bears a meaning close to that which it has in Deut 25, where a similar expression occurs, "and his name will not be extinguished from Israel" (v 6b). I must conclude, then, that להקים שׁם־המת here means "to produce descendants for the deceased," "name" being used as the virtual equivalent of "person."

(2) *Excursus: Levirate Marriage in the Old Testament*

From the preceding discussion of the meaning of לְהָקִים שֵׁם־הַמֵּת, "to produce descendants for the deceased," it is patently clear that the purpose of the marriage proposed by Boaz is very similar to that of the levirate marriage prescribed in Deut 25:5–10 and to the conjugal duties incumbent upon the sons of Judah in Gen 38. When it is further noted that the principle characters of Gen 38, Judah, Tamar, and Perez, are invoked in the blessing of the elders in v 12, it is not surprising that almost all commentators have concluded that the marriage here proposed is either a levirate marriage or a custom very closely related. Thus, in his classic treatment of the question Rowley observes "all probability is against those who differentiate Ruth's marriage from levirate marriage in kind and not merely in the degree of relationship between Ruth and Boaz" ("Marriage of Ruth," 174–75).

Nevertheless, there are very significant differences among these three passages, Deut 25:5–10, Gen 38, and Ruth 4, in the nature of the requirements and in the way that these function—so much so that a very considerable literature has arisen in the attempt to deal with the problem. The older literature through ca. 1964 is discussed in detail in Rowley, "The Marriage of Ruth," passim; see also the bibliography in Rudolph, 60–61. The literature up to ca. 1973 is surveyed and discussed in Leggett, *The Levirate,* 9–62. The more significant discussions since Leggett are those of Anderson, *JSS* 23 (1978) 171–83; Beattie, *VT* 24 (1974) 251–67; Davies, *VT* 31 (1981) 138–44, 257–68; Gordis, "Love, Marriage, and Business," 241–64; Thompson and Thompson, *VT* 18 (1968) 79–99; and Sasson, 125–29, 143–46. It is not my purpose here to survey in detail this literature or to solve the difficult problems it entails. We must, however, delve into the complexities involved in a manner sufficient to ascertain the nature of the obligation involved in Boaz's statement to the nearer redeemer.

In the legal provisions for the levirate obligation set forth in Deut 25:5–10, not only is the custom limited to the brother of the deceased, presumably the eldest (cf. Gen 38), but the circumstances under which it is operative are described by the enigmatic phrase "When brothers dwell together" (v 5a). Whatever is meant by this provision, no other relative more distant than a brother is mentioned and in fact, if the (elder?) brother is unwilling, there is no provision for the transfer of the obligation to another brother, let alone a more distant relative. As Anderson notes (*JSS* 23 [1978] 177), it would certainly seem unfair that the reluctant brother-in-law should be so publicly humiliated and ostracized if another brother or more distant relative had been able to perform the same duty with the same effect. Further, the levirate as conceived here is a serious legal obligation. True, it could be refused by the brother-in-law without fine or imprisonment or worse. But, in the event of such refusal, the widow of the deceased was allowed the right of public legal action. She could take her complaint to the elders at the gate, the legal assembly of her place of residence, and there publicly charge her recusant brother-in-law with his refusal to perform his obligation (v 7) and, if he persisted in his refusal, publicly humiliate him (vv 9–10). This was a considerable right in a culture that accorded women little, if any, legal standing (see Boecker, *Law and the Administration of Justice,* 32; de Vaux, *Ancient Israel,* 39–40; and esp. Trible, *IDBSup,* 964). Note that this was not a legal action whose primary purpose was to provide a means by which the brother-in-law could formally renounce his duty (contra Neufeld, *Marriage Laws,* 42; Davies, *VT* 31 [1981] 260; see also the insightful comments of Morgenstern, *HUCA* 7 [1930] 166–67; Leggett, *The Levirate,* 55–57), however much it came to be so used in later rabbinic interpretation. Rather, it was a means by which the widow could bring to bear upon her reluctant brother-in-law all the coercion that custom and precedent would allow. It was probably also a means by which she could acquire her freedom from the authority of her brother-in-law, i.e., the freedom to dispose of herself as she chose, to "be married outside the family to a stranger," v 5d (if this is the correct meaning of the symbolic action of drawing off the brother-in-law's shoe; cf. the remarks of Morgenstern, *HUCA* 7[1930] 168–69; Thompson and Thompson, *VT* 18 [1968] 92–93; and below). This legal right accorded the widow was of the utmost importance to her. True, the charge she brings against her recusant brother-in-law in the presence of the public legal forum is stated in terms of the dominant concerns of the patriarchal culture of which she is a part (viz. he has "refused to produce descendants for his brother," v 7, and he "will not build up his brother's house," v 9). But, she "is not to be married outside the family to a stranger," v 5d; hence, she belongs through marriage to her deceased husband's family. That a marriage is intended is unmistakable from the next clauses in v 5: "her brother-in-law shall enter to her [i.e., have intercourse with her] and take her as his wife"; i.e., the marriage is effected by its consummation; no ceremony is necessary. Hence, the widow not only has obligations but rights—the right to the security and status that only marriage could give a woman in that patriarchal culture (cf. the remarks of McKane, *TGUOS* 19 [1961–62] 29–30; esp. Niditch, *HTR* 72 [1979] 146).

In Gen 38 the obligation is likewise incumbent upon the brother, in this case clearly the older brother, and would appear to be stringent indeed, since Onan resorts to a particularly offensive subterfuge by which he ostensibly meets the obligation but yet avoids "producing offspring for his brother" (38:9). Second, that Tamar, the wife of the deceased, has the right to such a marriage is confirmed by her actions, which are unmistakably based on such a premise. Further, the narrator indicates this even more clearly when in Gen 38:14 he gives as the reason for her stratagem to obtain a child through Judah: "for she saw that Shelah was grown up, but she had not been given to him as a wife" (הִוא לֹא־נִתְּנָה לוֹ לְאִשָּׁה; cf. also Judah's words in Gen 38:26). It is not unequivocally clear that this is a legal obligation, but the words of Judah in 38:26 and the parallel with Deut 25 make this the most likely understanding. Here we see the purpose of levirate marriage from the woman's perspective. It provided her with the protection and security that husband and progeny alone could give (cf. מנוח, Ruth 3:1). This very specific language speaks conclusively against Coats' view (*CBQ* 34 [1972] 461–66) that the widow had the right to expect from her brother-in-law only the conception of a child but not actual marriage (see also Davies, *VT* 31 [1981] 143). That this much can be deduced from Gen 38 about the nature of the levirate obligation seems reasonably certain.

A number of scholars, however, have attempted to draw two further conclusions from this narrative: (a) that the levirate obligation reflected therein was more binding than that described in Deut 25 and (b) that this obligation extended beyond brothers, specifically to the father-in-law. Thus, it is argued that the levirate in Gen 38 is "obligatory and brooks of no exception" (Gordis, "Love, Marriage, and Business," 249) or "would have to be regarded as an unavoidable obligation" (Davies, *VT* 31 [1981] 261; cf. also Anderson, *JSS* 23 [1978] 177; Morgenstern, *HUCA* 7 [1930] 165; Rudolph, 62–63). Others, however, have concluded from the same data that there is little if any difference between the two texts in the binding nature of the obligation (e.g., Thompson and Thompson, *VT* 18 [1968] 93–94; Rowley, "Marriage of Ruth," 181). Similarly, some have concluded from Tamar's stratagem to obtain conception from her father-in-law, Judah, that the levirate duty therein did (e.g., Rowley, "Marriage of Ruth," 176, with further bibliography, n. 1; Thompson and Thompson, *VT* 18 [1968] 94–95; Gordis, "Love, Marriage, and Business," 249) or did not (Beattie, *VT* 24 [1974] 260–61; Anderson, *JSS* 23 [1978] 175–76) extend to the father-in-law, contrary to the situation in Deuteronomy, where the obligation is limited to "brothers dwelling together." In my opinion, most such attempts press the conclusions that can be drawn from this story far beyond what may be legitimately concluded from the actions and conversations related. The narrator tells us what his characters did and said and leaves in the main ambiguous what they *could* have done or not done, legally or otherwise. Consequently, such conclusions must be regarded as too hypothetical and uncertain to be of value.

Nevertheless, from the discussion above, some reasonably certain conclusions can be drawn about the nature and extent of the obligation set forth in Deut 25:5–10 and exemplified in Gen 38. (a) In both passages, the obligation described is with certainty incumbent upon the brothers of the deceased, and there is no clear evidence that it extended any further. That it extended to the father-in-law (and hence, by implication, to more distant kinsman) cannot be determined from Gen 38 with any certainty at all. (b) The obligation is a stringent one that not only had the force of law behind it but involved the penalty of public humiliation when violated (which, though it did not extend to fine or imprisonment, was nonetheless severe). (c) In the event of its refusal, this legal standing accorded to the widow the very considerable right to initiate public legal action before the proper legal forum, which in turn would bring to bear upon the recusant brother-in-law all the coercion that custom and precedent would allow. (d) The purpose of this custom was threefold. It functioned (i) to "produce descendants for the deceased," (ii) to provide for the protection and security of the widow (cf. also the remarks of Sasson, 132–33), and (iii) to provide the legal heir of the deceased and so keep the נחלה, "inherited property" of the family, within that family line, since the son born of this union is considered by a legal fiction to be the descendant of the deceased. This seems an almost necessary concomitant purpose of the levirate obligation. As evidence for this, the case of the daughters of Zelophehad in Num 27:1–11 is usually cited. Since their father had died without sons, the daughters appealed to Moses for the right to inherit their father's property, stating their case as follows: "Why should the name of our father be taken away from his family because he has no son? Give us landed property [אחזה] among our father's relatives" (v 4). Although in my opinion to conclude that "name" here means "estate" (Neufeld, *Marriage Laws*, 47) or "property and inheritance" (Thompson and Thompson, *VT* 18 [1968] 87) is mistaken (something like "personal remembrance" or "personal existence [through descendants]" would be closer to the meaning intended), it is nonetheless clear that the passage implies that the "name" of a man was preserved through the inheritance of his land by his descendants. Although this last purpose, to prevent the alienation of the family estate, is not explicitly stated anywhere in the language employed in either Deut 25:5–10 or Gen 38, it is implied.

(3) *The nature of the "levirate-type" marriage responsibility of Ruth 4.* From the conclusions about the nature of the levirate that have just been elucidated above, it can immediately be seen that significant differences indeed exist between this custom and that assumed by the situation in Ruth. Three differences can be established without cavil.

(a) First and most important, the custom in Ruth does not in any way have the binding character of a legal formulation. To begin with, as Rudolph (62) notes, Boaz, who is throughout depicted as a man of exemplary character and honor, has not made a single move up to this point in the story that would indicate that he is in any way subject to such a legal obligation. Further, the levirate obligation not only served as a significant vehicle of protection and security for the widow; it also accorded her the right to initiate legal action in the event that her right to a levirate marriage was refused or ignored. Neither Naomi nor Ruth has acted in a manner that would suggest that they had any such legal right. Rather than pressing any such legal action, they have been living in straitened circumstances, depending upon Ruth's gleaning for sustenance. Instead of availing themselves of some legal recourse to bring about a marriage to the nearest redeemer, which the existence of a levirate law would presuppose, they have had to resort to the risky and dangerous stratagem of Ruth's nocturnal excursion to the threshing floor. Further, the levirate not only accorded the widow the legal right to redress; it also imposed on her legal obligations (cf. Deut 25:5; Gen 38:11). But, Boaz's statement in 3:10, praising Ruth for "not going after the young men, rich or poor," reveals that she was a free agent when it came to marriage and hence was under no legal obligation to enter into a levirate marriage with any relative of her deceased husband. See *Comments* on 3:1, 9, 10 above. In addition, as Beattie (*VT* 24 [1974] 262–63) and Sasson (128–30) have noted, if there was a legal obligation for levirate marriage extant, which Boaz invokes in 4:5, then it is very difficult to explain the nearer redeemer's sudden change of mind in v 6. It is obvious that the nearer redeemer was well aware of his prior claim in law to redeem the field of Elimelech, and, when Boaz brings the matter up, he immediately declares his intention to do so (v 4). Yet Boaz's second statement must have contained a requirement that he did not anticipate when he agreed to redeem the field, for he immediately recants. This requirement can hardly have been the legal obligation of levirate marriage, for it is not reasonable to suppose that the nearer redeemer was any less cognizant of his legal responsibilities than Boaz was.

(b) Second, the levirate obligation can be substantiated only for the brother of the deceased husband, and there is no certain indication in Deut 25 or Gen 38 that any more distant relative could serve in his place if he refused (cf. Anderson, *JSS* 23 [1978] 175–77). The exact relationship of the nearer redeemer and Boaz to the family of Elimelech is unknown, hidden from us by our imprecise knowledge of the meaning of the enigmatic term מודע (2:1), but it is clear that they are not brothers of Elimelech (see *Comment* on אח in 4:3), let alone of Mahlon or Chilion. In all probability they belonged to collateral kinship lines related to Elimelech's father, perhaps cousins (so Levine, "Legal Themes," 102). Hence, neither the verb יבם, "to perform the brother-in-law's duty," nor the noun יבמה, "brother-in-law," occurs in relation to the marriage of Ruth (see *Comment* on יבמתך in 1:15).

(c) Third, since in both Deut 25 and Gen 38 the levirate is a binding obligation, there is a humiliating social stigma attached to its refusal (Deut 25:9–10), whereas no such stigma is attached to the nearer redeemer in Ruth 4 when he renounces his right in favor of Boaz.

These very significant differences between Deut 25:5–10/Gen 38 and Ruth have usually been handled in discussions of levirate marriage in the OT by seeking to establish a chronological evolution and development of the regulations and customs governing the practice. These attempts have almost invariably pressed the data of the narrative of Gen 38 in such a way as to conclude that the levirate obligation reflected therein is significantly different from Deut 25:5–10, usually in regard to its binding character and the extent of its applicability (see *Excursus: Levirate Marriage in the OT*). Taking Ruth a priori to represent an example of the levirate, these discussions have attempted to place the form of the levirate custom therein at a stage in the development of the practice appropriate to the nature of the levirate assumed and the line of development posited. These attempts differ radically in their conclusions (cf. Leggett, *The Levirate,* 271–93). For example, Bewer maintains that Ruth is the earliest, then Gen 38, then Deut 25 (*AJSL* 19 [1902–3] 143–44); Davies that Gen 38 is the earliest, then Deut 25, then Ruth

(*VT* 31 [1981] 267); and Gordis that Gen 38 is the earliest, then Deut 25, then the prohibitions of Lev 18:16, 20:21, and that Ruth exhibits no levirate custom at all ("Love, Marriage, and Business," 248–50). In my opinion, these attempts press the data of the narrative of Gen 38 beyond what may be legitimately drawn therefrom, and they have not adequately taken into account the radical differences outlined above between the nature of the levirate in Deut 25 and Gen 38 and that of the obligation presumed in the book of Ruth. Hence, conclusions based on such methodology are too hypothetical and uncertain to carry their case (cf. the remarks of Hubbard, 50).

Rather, the levirate as it appears in Deut 25 and Gen 38 is (a) a legal obligation and (b) restricted to brothers of the deceased (as the name "levirate," from Latin *levir,* "brother-in-law," implies), (c) which accords to the widow both legal obligations and the substantial prerogative of legal action in order to effect her rights in the matter and (d) whose refusal incurred the penalty of a serious social stigma. None of these conditions applies to the obligation presumed in the book of Ruth. Therefore, it seems to me that clarity and lack of confusion can be brought to the question not by defining levirate marriage so broadly as to unite the disparate customs of Deut 25/Gen 38 and Ruth in a single institution (contra Brichto, *HUCA* 44 [1973] 12 n. 16) but by reserving the name "levirate marriage" exclusively for the legal obligation of brother-in-law marriage depicted in Deut 25 and Gen 38. Several studies have given serious attention to these irreconcilable differences and have also come to the conclusion that the marriage proposed in Ruth 4:5, 10 is not a levirate marriage (see Beattie, *VT* 24 [1974] 251–67; Gordis, "Love, Marriage, and Business," 246–52; Sasson, 125–29, 143–46).

Nevertheless, there are features of the obligation presumed in Ruth 4:5, 10 that are markedly similar to the levirate institution of Deut 25 and Gen 38. Even though the obligation presumed had no legal standing and accorded no legal rights to the parties involved and its refusal carried no appreciable social stigma, Ruth 4:5d clearly implies that a communally recognized *moral* obligation, a family responsibility, on the part of the next of kin *did* exist. This responsibility was to acquire "the wife of the deceased in order to produce descendants for the deceased on his inheritance" (v 5). Note how Ruth's identity has significantly changed in Ruth 4:5, 10. Previously in the story she is simply "Ruth" (1:4, 14, 16), or "Ruth the Moabitess" (1:22; 2:2, 21), or "daughter-in-law (of Naomi)" (1:22; 2:22). The overseer identified her to Boaz in 2:6 as simply "a Moabite young woman who came back with Naomi." When she identifies herself to Boaz, it is simply as a "foreigner" in 2:10, and, most significantly, on the threshing floor in 3:9, she is "Ruth, your handmaid" (see *Comment* thereto). Clearly, neither her identity in the community at large nor the status she accords herself at moments of significance is "wife of Mahlon." But in 4:5, 10 her identity is dramatically different. In this public legal assembly, Boaz now invokes her identity and her status, and hence her *moral* responsibilities, as "Ruth, the Moabitess, *wife of the deceased* [אשת־המת]"; cf. v 10a. Further, she is to be married in this capacity in order to "produce descendants for the deceased *on his inheritance* [על־נחלתו]." Here Boaz specifically and overtly enunciates the dual responsibility to continue the family line and thereby to prevent the alienation of the family estate. The threefold purpose of this marriage is identical to that of levirate marriage: to provide descendants for the deceased, to prevent the alienation of the family estate, and, concomitantly, to provide for the protection and security of the widow (although, with her identity as "wife of the deceased," this last has fallen quite into the background).

The studies mentioned above that have marshaled arguments to deny that the marriage of Ruth and Boaz was a levirate marriage have done so by denying not only that there was an obligation *in law* but also that there was an obligation *in custom* for Boaz or the nearer redeemer to marry Ruth. In my opinion, this badly overstates the case. I agree that there was no legal obligation, but I would insist that there was a customary obligation, which, though voluntary, was an acknowledged family obligation recognized by the community. Note that, when these studies turn to the discussion of 4:5, they have perforce been obliged to recognize that customary obligations are involved in that marriage that are similar in nature to those of the levirate. Thus, Gordis ("Love, Marriage, and Business," 256–59) notes the differences between the levirate custom and the marriage of Ruth and then attempts to establish a chronological development of the levirate in which its exercise is increasingly limited until it is totally proscribed and in which the custom as seen in Ruth can find no place. Nevertheless, when he interprets Ruth 4, he must assume that, when Boaz informs the nearer redeemer that Naomi is disposing of the obligation-right to redeem the land of Elimelech (4:3) and calls upon him to acquire this obligation-right (4:4), Boaz also informs him "that the obligation will also include the marriage and support of Ruth, with the probability that she will bear children, who will then claim the land that had originally belonged to Elimelech" (256). Gordis does not enlighten us regarding the source of such an obligation, but clearly it can only derive from a custom that called upon the גאל, "redeemer," to undertake a marriage whose purposes were very similar to those of levirate marriage, i.e., "to perpetuate his brother's name in Israel" (Gordis, 248). Likewise Beattie (*VT* 24 [1974] 264–67) concludes that the marriage of Ruth and Boaz was not a levirate marriage, primarily on the grounds that the levirate was restricted to the brother-in-law (265). However, having concluded that a childless widow would customarily inherit her husband's estate (252–56) and that one of the purposes of the levirate law was that a childless widow who is heiress to her husband's estate must marry within her husband's family in order that the property may be preserved within the family, Beattie then avers that the same purpose attaches to the marriage of Boaz and Ruth (265). Hence, according to Beattie, Boaz in 4:5 announces to the redeemer: "'I am going to marry Ruth,' he says, 'and raise an heir to the field'" (266). Such a proviso could have been publicly announced by Boaz and been perceived as a threat to the nearer redeemer only if there was a custom in which it was incumbent upon a relative to marry the widow for the purpose of producing descendants for the deceased to keep the family property intact. Likewise Sasson, after having marshaled arguments at length to deny that levirate marriage was an issue in Ruth (125–32), nonetheless notes that "*one* of the two major *goals* of this institution—that of producing a male child who will continue the 'name' of the deceased" (132; italics in the original)—*was* involved in the marriage of Boaz and Ruth. Hence, in order to persuade the redeemer that there would be no profit for him in the purchase of Elimelech's property, Sasson asserts, "Boaz announced before a duly organized legislative body his intention to pledge the first born son of Ruth as Mahlon's heir, the future owner of Elimelech's land" (135). Again, Boaz could have made no such public announcement in such circumstances and could have made no threat to the redeemer thereby if there had not been a custom that dictated that it was incumbent upon a relative to marry the widow for purposes very similar to those of levirate marriage. As Houston puts it, "Unless there was some recognition in custom that Boaz's marriage could produce seed for Mahlon (could a man make his offspring his relative's by mere fiat?), there was no cause for the first *gôʾēl* to change his mind" (*JSOT* 16 [1980] 70).

Consequently, it is my conclusion that, to avoid confusion, the name "levirate law" should be restricted to the legally required social custom prescribed in Deut 25:5–10 and evidenced in the narrative of Gen 38. However, the book of Ruth does assume a family responsibility, moral not legal in nature, i.e., voluntary, in which it was incumbent upon the next of kin to marry the wife of a deceased relative and produce descendants for the deceased who will inherit his property. Such an obligation could appropriately be termed a "levirate-type responsibility" since its purposes are very similar to those of levirate marriage proper, and the differences in the two obligations in regard to their legal standing, the legal rights of the parties involved, whether the obligation devolved upon brothers of the deceased or more distant kin, and the social stigma attached to its refusal can all logically be understood to result from the fact that the obligation was less pressing the more distant the kin relationship. To adopt such a term as "redeemer-marriage" (cf. Epstein, *Marriage Laws in the Bible*, 84–88) accords such a moral responsibility a more formal standing and observance than is warranted, for doubtless its performance was rare indeed, representing a remarkably benevolent act on the part of any more distant relation than a brother.

(4) *The correct reading of the K-Q* קָנִיתָ. Having examined, then, the exegetical data involved in the last clause of 4:5 and having ascertained the nature of the obligation involved therein, let us return to the question of the correct reading of MT's K-Q קָנִיתָ. Is Boaz informing the nearer redeemer that when he acquires the field *he*, the nearer redeemer, must also marry Ruth for the purpose ascertained above, or is he informing him that *he, Boaz*, is going to marry Ruth? As noted above, all the ancient versions, every modern translation known to me except REB, and almost every modern commentary have adopted the former alternative and read the Q, "you acquire." In my opinion, the Q reading is necessitated by the combined data and interpretation of Ruth 3:9–13; 4:3–5 set forth above. That this is so is clearly to be seen in 3:13. In 3:11 Boaz agreed to do what Ruth had requested, to marry her, i.e., to fulfill his responsibility as a גאל, "one who was responsible to come to the aid of family members in need"; see *Comment* on 3:9. However, 3:13 indicates that there was a hierarchy of those upon whom such responsibilities *and rights* were incumbent and that there was a closer relative who had the prior right, as well as obligation, to "redeem" Ruth. This point is made clearly and emphatically by the three separate clauses in that verse in which "Ruth" appears, twice explicitly and once implicitly, as the direct object of the verb "to redeem," which in this context is used to mean "marry the widow of a relative"; see *Comment* on 3:13. Hence, chap. 3 unequivocally demonstrates that the nearer redeemer had the prior right to marry the widow. Therefore, in chap. 4, when Boaz, having convened the legal assembly, now publicly announces that the marriage to the widow is not simply for her protection and support but has as its major purpose the raising of descendants to the deceased to keep the family property intact, *he can only be referring to a further family responsibility incumbent on the* גאל *who has prior rights in regard to family*

responsibilities. However, both Beattie (in *VT* 21 [1971] 490–94; *VT* 24 [1974] 261–64) and Sasson (129–135) have argued at length in favor of K קָנִיתִי, "I am buying" (cf. also Gordon, *Forgotten Scripts,* 169–71). Beattie, followed by Sasson, has based his argument against Q on the grounds that the nearer redeemer could not have been ignorant of a legal obligation to contract a levirate marriage, for it is not reasonable to suppose that the nearer redeemer was any less cognizant of his legal responsibilities than Boaz was. Nor could he have been any more ignorant of Ruth's existence than Boaz was (cf. 2:11). With both of these points of view I agree. The change of mind of the nearer redeemer cannot be explained on the basis of assuming he was ignorant of his legal obligations or of his family relationships. (For my view of the reason for his change of mind, see *Comment* on the following verse.) Both Beattie and Sasson argue that the only fact about which the nearer redeemer was ignorant was Boaz's agreement and promise to marry Ruth, made the previous night on the threshing floor. Therefore, it was Boaz's announcement that *he* was marrying Ruth *and* that the purpose of this marriage was to raise up an heir for the property of the deceased that caused the nearer redeemer to change his mind. However, as I have shown, and as both Sasson and Beattie assume in their analysis of the situation, no such pledge and purpose could have been publicly announced by Boaz that would have threatened the nearer redeemer's prior right to redeem the land, if there had not also been a publicly acknowledged moral obligation on the next of kin to marry the widow of the deceased for this express purpose. *And,* as I have shown, 3:12–13 demonstrates that there was a hierarchy of rights in regard to the marriage of the widow as well as in regard to the redemption of the field; see *Comment* there. Beattie observes that Boaz's words about the purpose of the marriage to Ruth (4:5d) imply "that he intends to lay claim to the land on behalf of his and Ruth's children" (*VT* 21 [1971] 493; cf. also id., *JSOT* 5 [1978] 46). The right to redeem the land, a legal right that carried with it in the absence of an heir substantial economic advantage, is a right and duty that devolves upon near relatives in a fixed order of priority (4:4). Beattie and Sasson's adoption of the K reading, meaning that Boaz announces that he is marrying Ruth, means that there was no order of preference according to which family members were called upon to take on the moral responsibility to marry the widow of the deceased and "raise up descendants for the deceased on his inheritance." But it is just as reasonable to suppose that a *moral* obligation that carried with it substantial economic *disadvantage* (viz. the support of the widow and the providing of an heir for property, which without an heir one would oneself inherit) would devolve upon near relatives in a fixed order of priority as it is to suppose that a *legal* obligation that carried with it substantial economic *advantage* (viz. the redemption of the field) would do so. In point of fact, however, whether reasonable or unreasonable, 3:12–13 demonstrates that such a moral obligation indeed existed.

Finally, Vriezen's attempt (*OTS* 5 [1948] 80–88) to solve the difficulties of 4:5 by adopting the K reading קניתי and reinterpreting both its meaning and that of the preposition מאת is most improbable. (See discussion of the object of the verb קניתי above.) Not only does it attribute to the words involved meanings that they bear nowhere else in the OT (cf. Rudolph, 59), but the meaning thus derived cannot square with the fact that 3:12–13 shows clearly that the nearer redeemer has the prior right to marry Ruth (cf. also Rowley, "Marriage of Ruth," 193 n. 1; Leggett, *The Levirate,* 233–37).

In light of these considerations, it is clear that only Q קָנִיתָה, "you must acquire," meets the facts of the case.

6 לֹא אוּכַל לִגְאוֹל־לִי, lit. "I cannot redeem for myself." The preposition לְ plus pronominal suffix, first person singular, is an example of the so-called ethical dative, in which the person of the pronominal suffix must always agree with that of the verb and which is used "to give emphasis to the significance of the occurrence in question *for* a particular subject" (GKC § 119s). No object is expressed, as in v 4 (see the *Comment* there). The object most immediately in view is "Ruth" since Boaz has called upon the nearer redeemer to exercise his family responsibility and marry Ruth to produce descendants for the deceased. But (contra Joüon, 84), the nearer redeemer has in mind principally the right to "redeem" the field of Elimelech as well as his right to marry Ruth. The verb גאל here makes precise the obligations, legal in the matter of the field, voluntary in regard to Ruth, the rights to which he has been called upon to accept (קנה, vv 4, 5).

פֶּן־אַשְׁחִית אֶת־נַחֲלָתִי, "lest I bring ruin upon my own inheritance." The verb שחת in a context such as this means either "to destroy" (e.g., Gen 6:13; 18:28, 31) or "to ruin, despoil, (seriously) damage" (e.g., Judg 6:4; 1 Sam 6:5). No matter which of the two meanings is intended here, the nearer redeemer clearly envisages being brought to such a condition of impoverishment that his own family inheritance would be endangered.

This necessarily raises the question of how the nearer redeemer's estate could have been threatened by Boaz's announcement of the nearer redeemer's responsibility to marry Ruth. To begin with, let us dismiss as improbable those attempts to explain the nearer redeemer's change of mind by assuming that he was ignorant of the existence of Ruth, as do Leggett (*The Levirate,* 231–32) and Davies (*VT* 33 [1983] 233–34). Beattie (*VT* 21 [1971] 492 n. 3) is surely correct in observing that "Boaz knew all about Ruth before he met her (2:11), while the whole town apparently witnessed her arrival (1:19) and knew all about her too (3:11)." As Leggett himself notes (*The Levirate,* 231 n. 73), of all people the relatives of Naomi must have been aware of the circumstances. We can no more assume that the nearer redeemer was less aware than Boaz of family members and family ties and responsibilities than we can assume that he was less aware than Boaz of his legal duties (see the discussion of this latter point in *Excursus: Levirate Marriage in the OT* following *Comment* on v 5d above).

On the contrary, since the reason for the nearer redeemer's refusal to redeem Ruth and the field is that it will endanger his own family inheritance, it necessarily follows that the type of redemption involved in Ruth 4 gave the nearer redeemer *neither an unconditional nor a reimbursable right to the possession and usufruct of the redeemed land.* If he had possession of the land and it could not be taken from him in any way, or if it could be taken from him only by reimbursing him for his purchase of it (which we are calling a "reimbursable right of possession"), then there is no conceivable way that his estate could be seriously threatened by the transaction. Therefore, to understand what is here transpiring we need to examine the pertinent redemption regulations to determine which party to the transaction these regulations vested with possession and usufruct of the land redeemed.

In *Comment* on v 4 above, I noted that only two of the four different procedures involved in the redemption obligations that are prescribed in Lev 25 and that form the legal background for Jer 32 were relevant to the understanding of the transaction involved in Ruth 4. These two procedures are: (1) The repurchase by the redeemer of land previously sold to someone outside the clan. This type of redemption was involved in the understanding of the transaction involved in Ruth 4 that I termed "the first scenario" in *Excursus: The Nature of the Transaction Proposed by Boaz in vv 3–5a.* (2) The pre-emption of the sale of land to someone outside the clan by the redeemer's purchase of the same. This type of "redemption" was involved in the understanding of the transaction involved in Ruth 4 that I termed "the second scenario" above.

In procedure (2), pre-emption, there can be no doubt whatsoever that the purchase of the field by the redeemer from his impoverished relative gave to the redeemer what we have called above the reimbursable right to the possession of the property. That, having delivered to his impoverished relative the price of the field, he should then be required to return the field to him without reimbursement (before the Jubilee year, at least) is simply incredible. Indeed, it is just such a scenario that is envisioned by Sasson (139) to explain the nearer redeemer's change of mind. Sasson maintains that, although neither Lev 25:25 nor the prototype found in Jer 32 quite fits the situation in Ruth because of the very different circumstances obtaining therein, nevertheless, the nearer redeemer's "redemption" of Elimelech's land would be "similar to the situation of Jeremiah." Then, Sasson suggests, since Boaz has "pledged the first male child of Ruth as Mahlon's heir," the nearer redeemer "might have to return the land to her in her capacity as trustee of this offspring." But on what grounds? Simply because there is now an heir? Is it conceivable that Jeremiah would have had to turn over the field he purchased from Hanamel to Hanamel's heir without being reimbursed? Surely not! To compound the improbabilities, Sasson then envisions that, Naomi and her infant "son" now being impoverished kinfolk (even though the child is the son of Boaz?), they could now sell the land once more and the nearer redeemer would again be called upon to act as the גאל, "redeemer"! Surely such a scenario taxes the bounds of credulity beyond belief! On the other hand, it does seem highly probable that the original possessor did retain the right, if he subsequently gained the means, to repurchase the field from the redeemer, i.e., to "redeem" it himself, exactly as he did when the field was sold to someone outside the clan, Lev 25:26–27. But that simply reinforces the point: the field could only return to the original possessor if he reimbursed the redeemer for his purchase. If this is the case, then there is no conceivable way that the transaction envisaged in Ruth 4:3–4 could be any kind of *pre-emption* of the sale of Elimelech's field by offering it to the nearer redeemer. For, whether Naomi has inherited the full rights of possession and usufruct of the field from her husband and hence acts *in loco conjugis* or she holds such rights in trust and, as widow of the deceased, acts only as representative of the prospective heir or she acts in any other conceivable capacity, if the transaction involved is a pre-emption, then the right of possession acquired by the nearer redeemer would be reimbursable and no voluntary responsibility to raise up an heir for the estate could have threatened his financial situation. Indeed, if the tragedy of death and deprivation in Moab had never occurred and Elimelech himself had returned along with Naomi and Mahlon the heir, and had been forced by poverty to pre-empt the sale of his land outside the family by offering it himself to the nearer redeemer, exactly the same circumstances surely would apply. Having purchased the field, the redeemer would not then simply turn it over to Elimelech. If either Elimelech or Mahlon gained the necessary means, they would have had to repurchase the land from the nearer redeemer to gain possession of it, i.e., to "redeem" it themselves, doubtless in a manner exactly analogous to the situation described in Lev 25:26–27. If such conditions would have been binding upon Elimelech had he lived, they certainly also would have been binding upon Naomi if she is acting in any way *in loco conjugis.*

In procedure (1) (noted above), the repurchase by the redeemer of land previously sold to someone outside the clan, i.e., redemption proper, our difficulties unfortunately are compounded by the fact that the law in Lev 25:25 leaves unstated who obtains the possession and usufruct of the field when it has been repurchased by the redeemer from the third party. The law simply states, "If your brother becomes poor and sells part of his (inherited) property, his nearest redeemer shall come to him and redeem what his brother has sold" (Lev 25:25). As Beattie puts it, this law "does not deal in such precise concepts as titles of ownership" (*VT* 24 [1974] 257). Its purpose was to maintain property within the possession of the family and does not state which member of the family received the right of possession. Only two possible options present themselves, of course, and both have been argued by interpreters. In the first, the redeemer retains the right of possession and usufruct on the grounds that the purpose of the law is to keep the land within the extended family, with whom the right of ownership proper resides. If the original possessor did not have the strength and ability to maintain possession of the land, then he must lose it; but the extended family, as family, loses nothing (so Pedersen, *Israel I–II,* 84; cf. also Westbrook, *ILR* 6 [1971] 369–70, who argues on the basis of a parallel with the redemption of slaves that the land probably remained the property of the redeemer). In the second option, the redeemer redeems the land not simply in order to keep it within the extended family but in order to restore its possession and usufruct to his impoverished relative (so Daube, *Studies in Biblical Law,* 44–45; Gordis, "Love, Marriage, and Business," 253–54). In this case, the law operates in the interest of the individual family, not the whole clan (so Levine, "Legal Themes," 100–101). In the light of this analysis, it becomes very clear that the nearer redeemer's change of mind can only be explained if the law of redemption governing the repurchase of the land in Ruth 4 functioned according to this second option, however the law may have functioned at other places and at other times. In my opinion, Beattie's argument (*VT* 24 [1974] 258) is, at this point, incontrovertible:

> If the principles on which this study is based—that credibility be granted to the legal situations represented by the story-teller—be granted validity, it must be concluded that, after a property had been sold and redeemed by a member of the seller's family, the original seller and his heirs retained some rights to the property.

In my opinion, the "some rights" must have been the rights of possession and usufruct, for, if the redeemer acquired either an unconditional right of possession and usufruct or a reimbursable right to the same, then the prospect of an heir to the line of Elimelech could never have so threatened his own estate as to induce him to change his mind about redeeming the field.

On this basis, the type of redemption involved in Ruth 4 must be redemption proper, i.e., the repurchase of the land of Elimelech from a third party to whom the land was previously sold. Since it makes nonsense of the story if Naomi was the heir to the land of Elimelech and has previously sold it, then it must be assumed that Elimelech sold the land before emigrating to Moab and that the original hearers of the story would have surmised such a state of affairs as soon as the question of redeeming Elimelech's land was raised (v 4d). In addition, this further line of evidence strongly corroborates the view, argued above on other grounds, that the verbs מכר (v 3) and קנה (vv 4–5) bear the meaning "transfer, surrender the rights to" and "acquire, accept the rights to," respectively.

If these considerations are cogent, then we must understand the nearer redeemer's change of mind as follows: Boaz convenes the legal assembly (vv 1–2) and informs the nearer redeemer that Naomi is surrendering her right to the field of Elimelech (v 3). As the widow of the deceased, she has the right to the usufruct of the field as long as she lives, but since the field stands in need of redemption and she has neither the means nor the legal standing to redeem it, she is surrendering her rights to the nearer redeemer, who is also the eventual heir since Elimelech and Mahlon have died childless. Since there is no possibility of the levirate law being invoked, there being no brothers of the deceased extant, and since the nearer redeemer could doubtless quietly ignore the voluntary family responsibility to marry Ruth, the only nubile widow involved, and raise a descendent to the deceased, he gives his assent to redeeming the field (v 4). Without a descendant of the line of Elimelech, the amount he must expend to redeem the field and care for the widow involved is more than offset by the value and produce of the field itself, a field that, in the absence of any heir to the line of Elimelech, will simply become part of his own family inheritance. Boaz then publicly calls upon the nearer redeemer to take on the voluntary family responsibility of marrying the nubile widow Ruth and of producing descendants for the deceased on his inheritance (v 5). The nearer redeemer is now publicly caught in an ethical and economic dilemma. There are certainly at least three courses of action open to him. (1) He can agree to redeem the field and marry Ruth and so raise up an heir to inherit the family property of Elimelech that he has redeemed. If he does so, he will incur the cost of redeeming the field, presumably a substantial one (v 6c), only to see it become the property of the heir he must raise for the line of Elimelech. (2) If, on the other hand, he agrees, subsequently redeems the field, but then ignores his pledge to marry Ruth, he will not only have revoked his public pledge but have cast himself in an unfavorable and niggardly light as one who was willing to meet family obligations that accrue to his benefit but not those that cost him something. (3) If he is unwilling to take either of these courses of action for obvious reasons, he could cede his rights as redeemer in both matters to Boaz. It is barely possible that a fourth option was open to him: He perhaps could have chosen to exercise his right as redeemer in the matter of the redemption of the field but cede his right to marry the widow to Boaz (although in my opinion such a selective exercising of one's rights as redeemer would have been most unlikely). Not only would this have also cast him in an unfavorable and niggardly light before the whole community, but it doubtless would also have meant that Boaz, as the next redeemer in line, could marry the widow and raise an heir to the line of Elimelech who would inherit the field the nearer redeemer had repurchased. Hence, caught in this economic and ethical dilemma and unwilling either to bear the cost of taking on both responsibilities or the dishonor of the other courses of action, he chooses to cede his right of redemption in both matters to Boaz.

גְּאַל־לְךָ אַתָּה אֶת־גְּאֻלָּתִי, lit. "redeem for yourself, you, my redemption-right." The ethical dative לך, "for yourself," is contrasted with the first-person ethical dative in the first clause and hence is emphatic. The independent pronoun אתה in apposition to the pronominal suffix adds even greater emphasis (GKC §§ 135d–g; *HebS* § 107), an overall effect difficult to convey in translation. I have attempted to do so by rendering "you then take on." As Joüon (84) points out, the verb גאל with the cognate accusative noun bears the meaning "to exercise, perform (the *ge*ʾ*ullāh*)"; cf. with a different verb, בקנאו את־קנאתי, "by his exercising my zeal," Num 25:11. גאלה here bears the nuance "right (or duty) of redemption," as in Jer 32:8 (cf. 32:7).

7 וְזֹאת לְפָנִים בְּיִשְׂרָאֵל, lit. "and this formerly in Israel." The use of waw plus a nonverbal element to introduce a clause is not infrequently disjunctive and parenthetical (cf. *IBHS* § 39.2.3c), hence "*Now* this was." זאת, "this," in a neuter sense referring to an act, event, or announcement is not infrequent in Hebrew (cf. BDB, 1.a, p. 260; *HALOT,* 4, p. 264), the referent here being the clause beginning "a man took off his sandal." What is a little unusual is the implied sense "this formerly was *the manner of/the custom of.*" Since the LXX reads καὶ τοῦτο τὸ δικαίωμα, "and this was the justice/justification," and Syr, Tg, and Vg all read "this was the custom/usage," Joüon (85) supposes an original וזה המשפט, "And this was the custom," the LXX translator having taken משפט in its more common meaning of "justice, right" and so translated it by δικαίωμα. However, the demonstrative pronoun זאת is feminine, not the masculine required for such a reading, so it is far preferable to understand the versions as having given a requisite paraphrase of the Hebrew of the MT rather than as having translated a different Hebrew original (Campbell, Rudolph). The LXX does then remain an enigma, for δικαίωμα in Greek does not mean "custom, mode" as the context requires. Of course, the same enigma exists if the original Hebrew read וזה המשפט!

As Campbell (147) documents, the adverb לפנים, "formerly, in former times," can refer to a previous time period of a generation or less (Job 42:11; Judg 3:2), a long period (1 Chron 9:20, several hundred years), or primeval antiquity (Ps 102:26). The time here is simply long enough that the symbolic action of removing the sandal is no longer in use, and its meaning has been forgotten. How long a time that might have been can only be conjectured, but it need not have been many generations as is sometimes assumed (see Campbell, 148).

עַל־הַגְּאוּלָּה וְעַל־הַתְּמוּרָה, lit. "concerning redemption and exchange." The preposition על, bearing the meaning "concerning, with regard to" (see BDB, 1.f[h], p. 754; *HALOT,* 3, p. 826), is here repeated with each noun governed, as is usually the case; see the remarks on נגד in v 4 above. Although the meaning of גאלה, "redemption(-responsibility)" is clear, the exact meaning of תמורה is not so easily attained, partly because of its paucity of usage. The word is used only five times outside the book of Ruth. In four of those passages, it means "that which is exchanged," i.e., "substitute, replacement," referring to the substitution or exchange of animals in Lev 27:10, 33, and to vessels of fine gold as a substitute for wisdom in Job 28:17. In Job 15:31 its meaning seems closer to "recompense" than "substitute, replacement." In Job 20:18, however, it means "the act of exchanging" and in that context probably refers to barter (cf. the remarks of Gordis, *JQR* 61 [1970] 102). Therefore, given the context here where the transaction involved is the transfer (or exchange) of rights from one redeemer to the next (see below), it is clear that the word means "act of exchanging, transferring." Supporting this conclusion is the fact that the verb מור in the hiphil means "exchange, replace" (see Andersen-Freedman, *Hosea,* 355–58). Sasson's attempt (141–42) to define תמורה rather precisely as "a commercial transaction in which monetary values are ultimately at stake," in contrast to גאלה, which refers to "social transactions," is not at all borne out by the usages noted above. The meaning "exchanging, transferring" quite fits this context for, as Brichto points out, the only transaction taking place here is the transfer of the right to redeem the field from the nearer redeemer to Boaz (*HUCA* 44 [1973] 18). Brichto goes on to propose that גאלה here means "right of redemption" (as it does in the immediately preceding verse) and that hence הגאלה והתמורה, "the redemption-right and the exchanging," is a hendiadys meaning "the transfer of the right of redemption" (cf. also Andersen-Freedman, *Hosea,* 357; contra Sasson, 142; Hubbard, 249, who understand the combination as a merism meaning all forms of transactions). In my opinion, his arguments are compelling.

לְקַיֵּם כָּל־דָּבָר, lit. "to effectuate any matter." As Sasson (142) notes, the zaqep-qaton on דבר shows that the Masoretes understood this phrase to go with the preceding. In my opinion, this is most probable (see also Brichto, *HUCA* 44 [1973] 18). Hence, the symbolic act of the shoe transfer confirms not all transactions (contra Sasson, 142, who maintains this in order to corroborate his suggestion that גאלה and תמורה form a merism) but merely the particular transaction here—the transfer of the redemption responsibility from one גאל, "redeemer," to the next (cf. the remarks of Andersen-Freedman, *Hosea,* 357). This understanding is important for the task of interpreting the meaning of this symbolic act. Even if one understands the proposed transaction between Naomi and the nearer redeemer as the outright purchase of the field of Elimelech, that is not what is being confirmed here. As Rowley put it ("Marriage of Ruth," 182),

> The drawing off of the shoe did not signify the purchase or sale of any property, for the kinsman neither bought nor sold anything . . . . The drawing off of the shoe here signified the abandonment of the obligation resting on the kinsman in respect of the property and in respect of Ruth.

שָׁלַף אִישׁ נַעֲלוֹ וְנָתַן לְרֵעֵהוּ, lit. "a man drew off his sandal and gave it to his fellow." Only here and in v 8 is שלף used in reference to the drawing off of sandals. However, since it most frequently refers to the action of drawing the sword from its scabbard (cf. Judg 8:20), there is no doubt of its meaning here. Elsewhere the verbs נשל (Exod 3:5; Josh 5:15) and חלץ (Deut 25:9, 10; Isa 20:2) are used to refer to the drawing off of the sandal. (For evidence that this is a calque in Hebrew based upon Aramaic usage and for its implications for the date of Ruth, see *Date* in *Introduction* to Ruth.) Since the singular נעל is used as often as the dual to refer to the two sandals normally worn (cf. Isa 20:2; 1 Kgs 2:5; compare esp. Josh 5:15 with Exod 3:15), this is doubtless the case here (as also in Deut 25:9, 10; cf. the comments of Joüon, 86).

It is clear in this clause that the one drawing off the sandals draws off his own and not those of the other party, for the pronominal suffix "his" on נעלו can only refer to the subject of the verb שלף, namely, איש, "man." However, there are a number of other ambiguities and grammatical difficulties in the clause. First, the text simply leaves ambiguous who takes his sandals off and gives them to the other party, the one transferring the redemption responsibility or the one to whom the right is transferred. Hence, the symbolic act can be understood in two different and opposite ways. It can be argued that, since this is a transfer of the *right* to redeem the field and marry Ruth for which no payment is made, there is no material transfer per se, no *quid pro quo,* and therefore the transfer of the sandal is a symbol of the transfer of the right itself—it *makes concrete* what is otherwise nebulous and tenuous (so Brichto, *HUCA* 44 [1973] 18). In this case, the one transferring the right removes his sandals and gives them to the other party. On the other hand, it can be argued that, though there is no material transfer per se, there is a transfer of rights, and such a transfer demands a *quid pro quo.* To *legitimate* the transfer, a symbolic payment must be made—hence, the transfer of the sandals. In this case, the one receiving the right removes his sandals and gives them to the other party. V 8 is equally ambiguous in this regard, for it reads, "Then the (nearer redeemer) said to Boaz, 'Acquire the right yourself,' and he drew off his sandals." Since the nearer redeemer and Boaz have been explicitly mentioned in the first clause, it is not clear which is the subject of the verb שׁלף, "he drew off," in the last clause. Indeed, as Campbell (148) has argued at some length, the idiom in v 7, . . . איש לרעהו, "a man . . . to his counterpart," often bears a reciprocal force, expressing that the parties do something "to one another" (cf. 1 Sam 20:41). As far as the syntax of v 7 is concerned, it could bear such a meaning here: "each took off his sandals and gave them to the other." However, Sasson (142) is surely correct when he observes that v 8 makes it clear that only one person transferred his sandals to the other (contra Campbell, 150; Andersen-Freedman, *Hosea,* 357).

In the light of such ambiguity, scholars have turned, not surprisingly, to possible examples of such a symbolic act in extrabiblical literature. Speiser (*BASOR* 77 [1940] 151–56) draws upon certain transactions in the Nuzi texts to suggest that shoes and garments were "token payments to validate special transactions by lending them the appearance of normal business practice" (154). If Speiser's interpretation of the Nuzi texts is correct, such a practice would suggest that Boaz transferred his sandals to the nearer redeemer as a token payment for the right to act as גאל, "redeemer," which the nearer redeemer ceded him. However, the interpretation of the Nuzi texts is notoriously difficult, and these transferred articles may well be actual payments or gifts or pledges rather than symbolic actions (cf. the remarks of Thompson and Thompson, *VT* 18 [1968] 90–92). It is precarious indeed to base our interpretation of the Ruth passage on material of such uncertain interpretation. Similarly, Lachemann (*JBL* 56 [1937] 53–54), drawing likewise on the Nuzi texts, refers to a practice involving the transfer of real property in various types of transactions in which, in order to make the transfer of property valid, a man would "lift up his foot from his property" and "place the foot of the other man in it" (53). However, this symbolic act, lifting up and placing down the foot, is palpably different from the action in Ruth, and it symbolizes the transfer of ownership and possession of real property, a transaction patently not involved in the Ruth passage (see the observations above). Hence, such a symbolic act throws no light on the interpretation of vv 7–8.

Consequently, it must remain uncertain who removed his sandals and gave them to the other and whether the act made concrete a transfer of rights or legitimated the same by a symbolic payment. However, the most natural interpretation of v 8 is to understand that the subject of the first verb, ויאמר הגאל, "the redeemer said," is also the subject of the following verb, וישלף, "and he drew off," and therefore it was the redeemer who took off his sandals and gave them to Boaz (cf. Hubbard, 250). The act then symbolizes and makes concrete the transfer of rights from the one גאל, "redeemer," to the next. The same is strongly suggested by the parallelism; see *Form/Structure/Setting*. A point in favor of this understanding is that it then permits a coherent interpretation of the similar act in Deut 25:9 in connection with the levirate law. Since the brother-in-law, who stands to inherit the estate from his deceased brother, has refused to do his duty and, by marrying the widow, both care for her and raise a descendant for his deceased brother's estate, the widow symbolizes the taking of the right to her own person and freedom (and perhaps even the right to her husband's estate, which he would then have forfeited; cf. the remarks of Thompson and Thompson, *VT* 18 [1968] 92–93; Sasson, 145–46; contra Davies, *VT* 31 [1981] 262–63) by removing his sandals. Fortunately, however, this uncertainty as to the exact nature of the act and its meaning is in no way crucial to the interpretation of the subsequent narrative.

The second difficulty is a grammatical one. In a passage that describes a customary action in past time, the use of the perfect tense שָׁלַף, "he drew off," is deemed by most interpreters to be rather surprising and problematical. One would expect rather a form of the verb that more commonly expresses the habitual or frequentative "he would draw off, used to draw off," such as the imperfect ישלף. Further, this verb is followed by "and gave," an action that is temporally sequential, and it is highly problematic for such a sequence to be expressed with the perfect plus waw, ונתן; the normal and regular form would be the imperfect plus waw consecutive ויתן. (For the implications of this unusual usage for the date of Ruth, see *Date* in *Introduction* to Ruth.) A number of suggestions have been made to resolve the difficulty, none of which are very satisfying. Rudolph (60) proposes to read the infinitive absolute שָׁלֹף (and also וְנָתֹן?), but such a use of the infinitive absolute is quite out of character with its use elsewhere when it functions as a substitute for the finite verb (cf. GKC §§ 113y–ff) and hence is highly questionable. Joüon's argument (85–86) for the reading יִשְׁלֹף, based on the LXX, entails such an involved line of reasoning as to be most improbable. Despite the reservations of most scholars, the perfect is not unexampled in a passage requiring a habitual or frequentative force, although it most often then carries the waw prefix (cf. GKC § 112dd; Brockelmann, *Syntax* § 41a). Thus, in 1 Sam 9:9, a passage very similar to Ruth 4:7 since it also cites a usage no longer in vogue, the perfect is used: "In former times in Israel a man *spoke* [אָמַר] as follows when he went to inquire of God." With these examples, and the inchoate state of our knowledge of the use of tenses in Hebrew, it seems best to leave the text as it is.

וְזֹאת הַתְּעוּדָה בְּיִשְׂרָאֵל, "And this was the form of ratification in Israel." Again the task of interpretation is hindered by the paucity of usage. Outside of this passage, תעודה occurs only in Isa 8:16, 20, two difficult contexts where the meaning of the word is also very unclear. The word is usually understood to be from the root עוד, which is used most frequently in the hiphil with two ranges of meanings: (1) "to warn, admonish, solemnly enjoin," (2) "to bear witness, call as witness." In Isa 8:16, 20, where the word is used in parallel with תורה, "instruction," the meaning "attestation, testimony" makes tolerably good sense, referring to Isaiah's solemn declarations in support of his oracles of admonition and judgment in the surrounding text. The meaning "testimony" or "attestation," i.e., a solemn declaration in support of a fact, simply does not make tolerable sense in Ruth 4:7, however. As the repeated וזאת, "and this," shows, the word must refer to or designate the symbolic action of removing the sandals (not the transactions of "redeeming" and "exchanging" mentioned earlier, contra Campbell, 149). Since this symbolic act was the means of visibly and tangibly making concrete or legitimating a transfer of rights (see the discussion above), it makes sense that תעודה here moves in the same range of meaning as לקים, "to effectuate, confirm," and some such meaning as "ratification, validation" makes sense in context. Tucker, however (*CBQ* 28 [1966] 44, followed by Sasson, 146–47), accepting the meaning "attestation, witnessing," avers that therefore two archaic practices are being referred to: (1) "confirming" and (2) "attesting." The first refers to the ceremonial act of handing over the shoe, but the second "refers to the means of validating, or proving that the transaction . . . had in fact taken place," and "therefore . . . refers to the witnessing formulae in the oral contract" (i.e., vv 9–11a). However, it is quite impossible (in spite of Sasson's arguments, 147, concerning the position of וזאת in relation to its referent) for the second וזאת to refer to the formal act of witnessing by the elders and the people in the gate, for the whole procedure to which the narrator refers in his digression, i.e., the editorial comment of v 7, is brought to a close by the narrative statement of v 8, precluding the possibility that the second וזאת could refer to the witnessing role of the elders that Boaz calls upon in vv 9–10 (cf. Hubbard, 252). Hence, the context demands some such meaning as "ratification, validation" for תעודה.

8 קְנֵה־לָךְ, lit. "acquire (the right) for yourself." Here the redeemer succinctly recapitulates his previous statement in v 6 in which he ceded his rights to Boaz (see *Comment* above). Only here he uses the verb קנה rather than גאל. This may well be a fixed formula in such transactions (note the repeated use of the phrase at the beginning and at the end of Hanamel's words in Jer 32:8; cf. Boeker, *Redeformen des Rechtslebens,* 168). *Since no "purchase" is taking place, this is the clearest possible evidence that the verb* קנה *in this passage bears the meaning "acquire the right to."* As in v 4 the object is understood from context. Hence, there is no need, contra Joüon (87), to follow the LXX (see *Note*) and provide the object את־גאלתי. Since this is a different verb from that used in v 6, we are doubtless to understand that this was a further statement of the redeemer, which he accompanied with the symbolic act of removing his sandals, rather than simply a statement of the narrator in which he recapitulates the redeemer's words of v 6. On the question of who removed his sandals, see *Comment* on the preceding verse

9 עֵדִים אַתֶּם הַיּוֹם כִּי קָנִיתִי, "You are witnesses this day that I am hereby acquiring." The purpose for which Boaz convoked the legal assembly in the gate he now invokes. In the words of Boecker (*Redeformen des Rechtslebens,* 160):

> The function of the Hebrew legal forum assembled in the gate was not restricted to the settlement and conclusion of disputes of various kinds. In proceedings involving rights of inheritance, family, and movable property, an official ratification was often necessary for the proper settlement of a legal transaction. As the official representative of the inhabitants of the locality, the legal forum also had to observe a notarial function.

As Boecker goes on to show, only when the nearer redeemer has assented to the transfer of his rights to redeem the field and marry Ruth is the legal forum called upon to take action. Since the matter has already been settled between the two parties to their mutual satisfaction, "a notarial function falls upon the court: it merely has to ratify the agreement" (*Redeformen des Rechtslebens,* 161). It is to this function that Boaz calls the legal forum with his summons "You are witnesses this day that . . ." Tucker has pointed out that this is a strictly oral transaction (*CBQ* 28 [1966] 42–44). The legal assembly does not perform its notarial function by means of a written document, but the transaction is no less formalized than if written, and no less valid. Boaz's formal and public calling upon the legal assembly to bear witness and their public affirmation and declaration of that role (v 11) certify and attest the performance and validity of the transaction as fully as did, in a later more literate era, the reducing of the transaction to writing, the recording of the names of the witnesses, and the application of a seal (cf. Jer 32:10). (For the similar invoking of witnesses to attest to the legality and performance of certain legal facts and transactions, cf. Josh 24:22; 1 Sam 12:3–5.) Tucker also proposes that the twice-repeated היום, "this day," when compared with the "date" formulae of Akkadian legal documents, can be seen to signify "that the act had intervened at a definite moment and was—without stipulation to the contrary—valid forever . . . . [T]he formula in Israelite legal affairs indicated the consummation and perpetual validity of a transaction" (*CBQ* 28 [1966] 44–45). (On the use of the perfect tense in קניתי to designate the coincidence between the declaration and the execution of the action, the so-called performative, see the discussion of מכרה in v 3 above.)

וְאֵת כָּל־אֲשֶׁר לְכִלְיוֹן וּמַחְלוֹן, "and all that belongs to Chilion and Mahlon." Although the order of the sons of Elimelech given here is the opposite of the order in which they are stated in 1:2, 5, there is little of significance to be drawn from the fact. Rudolph's suggestion that this represents an alphabetic ordering needed for legal purposes seems most unlikely, while Campbell's proposal that the change in order results from chiastic considerations seems most difficult given the great amount of material separating the two contexts. The most plausible suggestion may be Sasson's view that the more important person is named second, as with Ruth in 1:4, 14.

10 וְגַם אֶת־רוּת הַמֹּאֲבִיָּה אֵשֶׁת מַחְלוֹן, lit. "and also Ruth the Moabitess, the wife of Mahlon." The position of the object here before the verb קניתי, opposite to the order of the previous clause, lays stress upon it (rather than some emphatic force inhering in וגם, contra Campbell, 151; cf. Sasson, 150). On the significance of Ruth's identity as אשת מחלון, "wife of Mahlon," see *Comment* in v 5 above.

Both here and in v 5c Ruth is identified by her full name "Ruth the Moabitess," as is appropriate in the public setting of the legal assembly, where full identification is necessary. Such identification is particularly important here in v 10, where Boaz's statement is intended to be legally binding and so his obligation is spelled out in as detailed a form as possible (see *Explanation*). For "Ruth the Moabitess" as Ruth's full name, see *Comment* on 2:21.

לְהָקִים שֵׁם־הַמֵּת עַל־נַחֲלָתוֹ, "in order to raise up descendants for the deceased on his inheritance." On the meaning of this phrase, see *Comment* on v 5 above.

וְלֹא־יִכָּרֵת שֵׁם־הַמֵּת מֵעִם אֶחָיו וּמִשַּׁעַר מְקוֹמוֹ, "so that the memory of the deceased may not perish from among his brothers and from the gate of his town." The syntax of this sentence is not that of a negative final clause (GKC §§ 109g, 165a) used as a quotation from a body of oral or written law to justify Boaz's actions (Sasson, 134–35). Rather it is simply an example of the regular way in which "constructions of the infinitive with a preposition . . . are . . . continued in the further course of the narrative by means of the *finite verb*, . . . not by a co-ordinate infinitive" (GKC § 114r). Hence, it expresses a second purpose or result (cf. the remarks of Hubbard, 253 n. 7). As Campbell notes (151), the use of מקום, literally "place," to mean "place of residence; town, city" is not uncommon in the OT (see 2 Kgs 18:25; cf. BDB, 3.a, p. 880). Compare Deut 21:19 and note the expression in 3:11 (see *Comment* there).

עֵדִים אַתֶּם הַיּוֹם, "you are witnesses this day." Since the intervening transaction and purpose statements have been so long and detailed, Boaz repeats the summons to the legal forum to bear witness to the performance and legality of his assumption of the right to redeem the land and marry Ruth, ceded to him by the nearer redeemer. Such repetition is also solemn and emphatic.

11 וַיֹּאמְרוּ כָּל־הָעָם אֲשֶׁר־בַּשַּׁעַר וְהַזְּקֵנִים עֵדִים, "And all the people who were in the gate and the elders said, 'We are witnesses!'" The identification of the respondents to Boaz's summons is stated in the opposite order to that in which they were given when Boaz addressed them in 4:9. Given this fact, it is most improbable that the LXX preserves an original reading with "all the people who were in the gate" as the subject of the affirmation "we are witnesses" and "the elders" as subject of a second verb "said" with the following blessing as its object (contra Joüon, JB, NJB; cf. Campbell, Gerleman, Rudolph). Both in 4:4 and in 4:9 the legal assembly comprises two groups (see *Comment* on הישבים in v 4) who act in concert (Campbell, 152); it is most probably the same here. Compare the parallelism of the narrative statements introducing the two halves of the dialogue in this episode (see *Form/Structure/Setting*). Joüon alleges (89) that it is difficult if the blessing, in such poetic style, with such clever allusions to Rachel and Leah, to Perez and Tamar, should be spoken by the people (because of its length?), but in narrative style it would be quite appropriate to assign such a blessing to "all the people in the gate," understanding it to have been spoken by one of them as representative of the whole while the rest gave willing and glad assent. The affirmation עדים, "witnesses," rather than being "laconic" (Sasson, 151), constitutes the normative response by which the legal assembly notarizes the performance and legality of the transfer of rights from the nearer redeemer to Boaz (see the previous *Comment*). This is not only Hebrew legal style (Campbell, 152) but the regular way in which an affirmative response is given to a question or a statement (cf. GKC § 150 n.). Since biblical Hebrew, like Latin, possesses no word equivalent to "yes," it must repeat the critical word or phrase of the question to form a positive response.

יִתֵּן יְהוָה אֶת־הָאִשָּׁה הַבָּאָה אֶל־בֵּיתֶךָ כְּרָחֵל וּכְלֵאָה, "May Yahweh make the woman who is entering your house like Rachel and Leah." With its attestation "We are witnesses," the legal assembly has formally concluded its task of certification, for which it was convoked by Boaz, but its role in the story is not concluded. Having performed its notarial function, it winds up its role with a threefold blessing on Boaz, the theme of which is a prayer that the purpose of this marriage, "to raise up descendents for the deceased," may be fully and abundantly met. The blessing opens with a prayer beseeching fecundity for the bride. She is spoken of as האשה הבאה אל־ביתך, "the אשה who is coming (going to come) into your house." Since אשה can mean either "woman" or "wife," we must decide which sense was intended, and "heard," in a passage such as this. In my opinion, the sense "woman" is more probable (contra Hubbard, 258; note הנערה, "the young woman," in v 12), since Boaz has not yet married Ruth and the language הבאה אל־ביתך, "who is coming into your house," reflects the formal procession to the groom's home in the marriage ceremony (the *traditio puellae;* cf. Mace, *Hebrew Marriage,* 173–74, 180–81; de Vaux, *Ancient Israel,* 33–34), after which the bride "entered his house" (cf. Gen. 24:67; Deut 20:7). In this context, the participle באה expresses the nearer future (cf. GKC § 116d; *GBH* § 121i). The order "Rachel and Leah" has, rather surprisingly, been cause for much comment (Campbell, 152; Rudolph, 69); Sasson (154) may well be correct in surmising that the second position is the more important (see *Comment* above on "Chilion and Mahlon," v 9) and is accorded to Leah since she was the mother of Judah and since the third member of the blessing (v 12) concerns her descendants.

אֲשֶׁר בָּנוּ שְׁתֵּיהֶם אֶת־בֵּית יִשְׂרָאֵל, lit. "the two of whom built up the house of Israel." Since the twelve sons of Jacob were born to Leah and Rachel and their handmaids Zilpah and Bilhah, whom they gave to Jacob as surrogates, it is no overstatement to say that the two of them "built up the house of Israel." (On this idiom, see Deut 25:9; cf. Gen 16:2; 30:3.) The apparent attachment of the masculine suffix "them" to the feminine form of the numeral "two" probably reflects a further example of the homophonous dual suffix (see *Comment* on עמכם in 1:8). The first blessing, then, wishes for Ruth the same fecundity as that of the two renowned mothers of Israel, Rachel and Leah.

וַעֲשֵׂה־חַיִל בְּאֶפְרָתָה וּקְרָא־שֵׁם בְּבֵית לָחֶם, "so that you may flourish in Ephrathah and gain renown in Bethlehem." The second portion of the threefold blessing is a poetic bicolon, the syllables and stresses of the two members of which are fully and perfectly balanced, so that it reads in Hebrew with striking, iterative beauty. Unfortunately, however, its meaning is as problematic as its cadence is pleasing, and no scholarly consensus as to its sense has yet emerged. The first phrase, עשה־חיל, carries a wide range of meanings, while the usual meaning of the second, קרא־שם, "to give a name," does not seem to fit the context. The range of possible meanings for עשה־חיל has resulted in a wide variety of translations. Since חיל can mean "power, strength," עשה־חיל can mean "to perform valiantly; exercise power, might; do great deeds" (e.g., Num 24:18; 1 Sam 14:48; Ps 60:12), a meaning that has often been adopted (e.g., JB, NEB, Gerleman, Hertzberg, Rudolph). Since חיל can mean "worth, ability," עשה־חיל can mean "to do worthily" (e.g., Prov 31:29), as a number of translations render it here (e.g., KJV, ASV, NAB, NEB). חיל can also mean "wealth, possessions," so that עשה חיל can mean "achieve wealth, gain riches" (e.g., Deut 8:17, 18), a translation frequently adopted in the Ruth passage (e.g., NASV, NJPS, RSV, Joüon, Moffatt, Smith-Goodspeed).

Labuschagne (*ZAW* 79 [1967] 364–67) has proposed a new interpretation of the phrase, arguing that the range of meaning of the middle member of the threefold blessing must be consistent with that of the first and third. Since both of these relate to fertility and offspring, so must the second. "There is no reason to suppose," he avers, "that Boaz's well-wishers expressed the hope that his bride may be productive of offspring, and then, turning to him personally, wished him to be wealthy, or brave, or famous (as if he had no part to play in making the marriage fruitful!), and went on to express the hope that his offspring may be like the progeny of Judah and Tamar" (365; cf. also Parker, *JBL* 95 [1976] 23–24). In this light, Labuschagne appeals to certain passages in the OT, Job 21:7–8; Joel 2:22; Prov 31:3, where he finds that חיל bears the meaning "procreative power," "the ability to produce offspring"; hence, he proposes that עשה חיל in Ruth 4:11 means "engender procreative power." "The elders' wish for Boaz personally was that he may be virile and potent enough to beget a child" (*ZAW* 79 [1967] 366). This understanding of the phrase has been accepted by Campbell (153–54) and Sasson (155). However, there are serious problems with Labuschagne's interpretation (cf. also Witzenrath, 56 n. 29). In none of the passages he cites does חיל clearly mean "procreative power." In Prov 31:3, the clearest passage that he adduces, חיל means "sexual capability, prowess," *not* "the ability to produce offspring." In Joel 2:22; Job 21:7, the meaning suggested is most improbable. Furthermore, it may be unlikely that the ancient world knew the concept of male virility or sterility. The ability or inability to have children was invariably connected with the woman (cf. Mace, *Hebrew Marriage*, 203–4). Hence, the evidence from other passages that עשׂה חיל can bear the meaning "engender procreative power" is tenuous, to say the least.

But further, the very premise with which Labuschagne begins his study, that both the first and third members of the blessing deal with the issue of fertility and offspring, is highly questionable. That the first member does so by beseeching fecundity for the bride is beyond doubt, but Labuschagne misstates the third and avows without discussion that it too takes as its point of comparison the number of offspring. But v 12 does not "express the hope that his [Boaz's] offspring may be like the progeny of Judah and Tamar" (*ZAW* 79 [1967] 365). To be specific, it wishes that Boaz's house, i.e., his family line, may be like the house, i.e., the family line, of Perez. Nothing is said in the passage regarding in what capacity or respect the comparison is being made (as there so clearly is in the first member). The passage does express the means through which this similarity will be expressed—"through the offspring that the Lord will give you by this young woman"—but this clause also leaves quite open the specific character of each family line that is being compared. It could only clearly mean the multitude of offspring if זרע, "seed, offspring," had been modified by some such adjective as רב, "many." Thus, the point of comparison must be that for which the line of Perez was most well known. There is nothing in the OT to suggest that the line of Perez was particularly large or fruitful, but a plausible case can be made from the narrative of the birth of Perez in Gen 38:27–30 and from the other references to him in the Pentateuch (Gen 46:12; Num 26:20–21) that the Perezites were the most important clan in Judah. There is no doubt of this in later times for from this line sprang David. That this is the view of the book, at least in its present form (since the genealogy in 4:18–22 may not be original), can clearly be seen from the fact that the genealogy of David, 4:18–22, begins with Perez, rather than Judah. It is true, of course, that at the time of the story itself this could not have been the reason for the importance of the line of Perez, for the birth of David is yet three generations in the future. But the story is being told after the time of David certainly (cf. 4:17d), most likely long after, and such historical anachronisms, if even thought of, would have been of no concern to the storyteller at all. Therefore, in my opinion, we must understand the third member of the blessing to mean "May your line be like the line of Perez (the most important of the clans of Judah)" (cf. also Hubbard, 261; Sasson, 155–56). In this light, then, there is nothing incongruous at all for the blessing to turn from wishing success for Boaz by wishing fecundity for his bride (where such issues in ancient thought properly belonged), v 11b, to the wish for worth, prowess, might, or prosperity for the groom, v 11c, to the wish for honor and importance for his family line, v 12. That it does indeed follow such a progression is strongly suggested by the parallels noted by Parker (*JBL* 95 [1976] 23–30) between the "marriage-blessing" here in Ruth

4:11b–12 and the blessing that El, the head of the Ugaritic pantheon, pronounced upon King Krt on the occasion of his marriage to the Lady Ḥry, daughter of the King of Udm (*Krt*B[= *CTA* 15/*KTU* 15/*UT* 128] ii.11–iii.16; see Ginsberg, *ANET*^{3}, 146; cf. also the translation of Gibson, *Canaanite Myths,* 91–92). Parker is able to show that this text also begins by wishing fecundity for the bride whom Krt is taking (ii.19–28) and climaxes in a twice-repeated wish for greatness for Krt himself (iii.2–4, 13–15). In comparing the two texts, Parker observes (*JBL* 95 [1976] 28):

> Both blessings have the same form insofar as they are addressed to the groom, but speak immediately of the bride, who serves only to introduce the main subject of progeny. But in both passages this is the mode of expressing the real concern of the text: the greatness of the bridegroom, treated directly in the middle section of the Ruth-blessing, and in the refrain of the *Krt*-blessing.

This clear parallelism shows, at the very least, that there is nothing implausible, as Labuschagne maintains (*ZAW* 79 [1967] 365), in the elders blessing Boaz by using the wish for fecundity for his bride as the grounds for wishing worth, powers, or prosperity for Boaz himself and greatness for his family line. We must conclude that the strained attempt to understand עשׂה חיל and קרא שׁם as expressions that must relate specifically to Boaz's progeny or virility is erroneous and that these phrases must bear in this context one of their regularly attested meanings.

As numerous examples in the OT attest, the imperative with waw following a jussive or cohortative expresses result or purpose (cf. GKC § 110i; *GBH* §§ 116f, 120; *HebS* § 519). Hence, the two imperatival clauses of the middle member of the blessing are best taken as the consequence of the first member (so also Rudolph, 59; Sasson, 155; Parker, *JBL* 95 [1976] 23–24; surprisingly, not so Joüon, 90–91). Since, then, עשׂה חיל expresses the consequence of the fecundity wished for the bride and since its range of meanings encompasses "to do great things, show prowess; to act worthily; to gain wealth, prosper," some such translation as "to flourish" seems most adequate because it connotes the achieving of honor and greatness as well as wealth, as does the Hebrew expression.

The meaning of the second imperatival clause is equally troublesome, for שׁם as the object of the verb קרא, "call, proclaim, summon," is elsewhere regularly used in idioms meaning "to call the name of someone or something X," with the name regularly expressed (cf. BDB, קרא, 6.a, p. 896; KB^3, קרא, A.2, p. 1028; note discussion in *Comment* on 4:17). In the light of the above discussion, this meaning makes no sense in the context (contra Labuschagne, *ZAW* 79 [1967] 366). Further, in no other context is the idiom קרא שׁם used without stating at least the person named, and usually also the name itself. שׁם is used in the OT in the sense "fame, reputation," a meaning that admirably fits the context here, but the idiom "to make a name, gain fame for oneself" is either עשׂה שׁם ל׳ or שׂם שׁם ל׳. Consequently, commentators have suggested a number of solutions. The most common is to emend the text either to וְנִקְרָא שִׁמְךָ (cf. *BHK*^{3}; Gray, *NCBC,* 379) or to וְיִקָּרֵא שִׁמְךָ (Rudolph, 60), both meaning "may your name/fame be proclaimed." Rudolph appeals to v 14b as evidence for the niphal stem and suggests that the kaph on שׁמך elided before the following beth (cf. also Würthwein, 20). Joüon (90–91) emends עשׂה to קנה, "acquire (a name)." Richter (*ZAW* 95 [1983] 123–24) proposes that the waws in ועשׂה and וקרא are mistaken readings for yodhs, yielding the translation (according to Richter) "May an increase be made in Ephrathah! May a name continue to be mentioned in Bethlehem!" However, there is neither manuscript nor versional support for any such readings, and the first two destroy the perfect syllabic and tonal balance of the bicolon, while all four require, as Campbell (154) notes, "emendation from a more difficult reading to a reading which, if original, should have been protected by the context." Richter's proposal, in addition, would present the unusual phenomenon of three coordinate jussive clauses in sequence without any conjunction. Consequently, I infer from context that the expression קרא שם is a synonym of שׂם/עשׂה שם and means "to acquire a name, gain fame" (cf. Sasson, 156; esp. Hubbard, 260). DeWaard-Nida (74) note that such blessings are still in use in the Middle East. Is the synonymous expression קרא שם chosen here to avoid the repetition of עשׂה (cf. Joüon, 91)?

12 וִיהִי בֵיתְךָ כְּבֵית פֶּרֶץ, lit. "May your house be like the house of Perez." A jussive joined with waw to a preceding imperative may express simple coordination (e.g., Gen 20:7; Ps 27:14). More frequently, however, it is logically subordinate, expressing purpose or result (e.g., Gen 20:3; 2 Kgs 6:17; see GKC §§ 109f, 165a[j]; *GBH* § 116d; *IBH* § 107[c]). Only the context, i.e., the semantic content of the two clauses, determines which relationship is intended, and at times the relationship intended is quite ambiguous (e.g., Gen 24:51; 31:37). In my opinion, this clause is best taken as coordinate to the preceding since it includes the agency through which Boaz's family line may be like that of Perez: "through the offspring that Yahweh will give you by this young woman." This makes it most improbable that this is a further result clause dependent on the fecundity wished for his bride (contra Parker, *JBL* 95 [1976] 24; cf. Hubbard, 254 n. 13).

Explanation

Progress in the resolution of the death and emptiness that had afflicted the lives of Ruth and Naomi now depends upon Boaz. At the beginning of chap. 2, initiative for progress in the story had devolved upon Ruth, since Naomi was wrapped up in the silence of her bitter despair. At the beginning of chap. 3, the initiative passed to Naomi, who had come to life again upon hearing the name of Boaz. Here the initiative devolves upon Boaz, who has been challenged to act upon his responsibility as a redeemer by Ruth's execution of Naomi's daring plan. True to his promise to Ruth (3:13) and consonant with his symbolic pledge to Naomi expressed by the gift of grain and the words reported by Ruth about not returning "empty" (see *Explanation* to the previous scene), Boaz acts immediately. And—having signaled that our story now rushes irrevocably toward resolution by closing the previous scene not with a narrative summary, as with the first two scenes, but with Naomi's confident words that Boaz will not rest this day until the matter is settled—our narrator wastes no words. The issue that Boaz's promise in the preceding scene (3:12–13) has raised involves the matter of the prior right of the nearer redeemer in the matter of "redeeming" Ruth, i.e., marrying her. Hence, Boaz convenes the legal assembly of the town, whose task was not only to sit in judgment in the matter of criminal cases but also to exercise a notarial function in the matter of such transactions as the transfer of rights in civil matters. By this means in a largely nonliterate society, such transactions were orally "recorded" and preserved for posterity in the event of subsequent dispute in the matter (on the nature and function of the legal assembly, see *Comment* on v 2). Consequently,

Boaz proceeds straightway to the plaza of the city gate, the place where business and legal matters were normally conducted. There he convenes the legal assembly by summoning the other party involved and procuring ten of the elders of the town. The convening of the assembly is related in three short parallel sentences (vv 1–2), with the presence of each necessary party signaled by the conclusion "he/they sat down" (see *Form/Structure/Setting*). Here our narrator has Boaz summon the nearer redeemer in a surprising way. He does not just leave him anonymous but underscores his namelessness by having Boaz address him as "So-and-So," using the characteristic wordplay in Hebrew employed when a name is unknown or avoided. Since a name or word of address is not required by the sentence structure (see *Comment* on v 1), such a device can only raise our eyebrows and make us wonder proleptically about the role this man will play in the proceedings about to take place. (One wonders indeed if the Hebrew expression we have translated "So-and-So" was also used euphemistically in place of a stronger epithet, as the English expression is!)

Having convened the legal assembly, Boaz immediately opens the negotiation with a statement to the nearer redeemer (v 3). This first statement introduces a totally new development and complication in the story, a complication that creates consternation and incredulity for modern readers, consequent upon the great temporal and cultural distance that separates us from the customs involved (see the discussion in *Excursus: The Nature of the Transaction Proposed by Boaz in vv 3–5a* following *Comment* on v 5a). This complication, however, would have created a stir of knowing and enjoyable surprise on the part of the original hearers of the story, for suddenly the patrimony, the ancestral land, of the line of Elimelech has surfaced, as they must have felt it would. For the people of that culture, the question of what could have happened—and would happen—to the family patrimony of a substantial citizen like Elimelech must have been one that was constantly in the background of their thoughts and concerns as they heard this story. So, without a single word previously on the subject, our narrator has Boaz inform the nearer redeemer that Naomi is surrendering her rights to the usufruct of Elimelech's land, rights that she enjoys as the widow of the deceased (v 3). He then solemnly calls upon the nearer redeemer to accept these rights (v 4a–c) and to redeem the field (v 4d–l), i.e., to repurchase it from the unnamed third party to whom, since it stands in need of redemption, Elimelech must have sold it. (For a discussion and defense of this interpretation of the proceedings taking place, see *Comment* on vv 4–8, and especially *Excursus: The Nature of the Transaction Proposed by Boaz in vv 3–5a* following *Comment* on v 5a.) There are no brothers of the deceased men of the family extant, so there is no possibility of the levirate law being invoked. If he even thought of it, the nearer redeemer could doubtless plan on quietly ignoring the voluntary family responsibility to marry Ruth, the only nubile widow involved, and to raise a descendant to the deceased, a course of action that any *ordinary* heir presumptive who had his own interests at heart would follow. Without a descendant of the line of Elimelech, the field will simply become part of his own family inheritance, and the amount he must spend to redeem it (and probably care for the elderly widow involved) would be offset by the value and produce of the field itself. Consequently, he readily gives his assent to redeeming the field, v 4k–l (see *Form/Structure/Setting*).

With this, the nearer redeemer may well have thought that the negotiations were concluded, although he may have wondered why Boaz bothered to convene the legal assembly to present a course of action so simple and so obviously advantageous to himself. The readers of the story, however, wait in anticipation for a further statement from Boaz, for he has not yet broached the responsibility to which he has committed himself to Ruth and Naomi—the marriage of Ruth. To this question Boaz immediately turns in the second half of the negotiation, vv 5–8 (see *Form/Structure/Setting*). Here he plays his trump card, so to speak. He publicly calls upon the nearer redeemer to take on the voluntary family responsibility of marrying the nubile widow Ruth and so raise up an heir for the deceased to inherit the field (v 5; for the discussion of the difficulties entailed in the K-Q here see *Comment*). The nearer redeemer is now publicly caught in an ethical and economic dilemma (for details, see the discussion in *Comment* on v 6c). He has publicly declared his willingness to assume the legal requirement of redemption, which in and of itself functions to his advantage. To now publicly declare his willingness to take on the voluntary family responsibility of marrying the widow and raising an heir to the field, which functions to his disadvantage, and then subsequently to ignore this pledge and duty is to cast himself in an unfavorable and niggardly light before the whole community. It would reveal that his willingness to redeem the property sprang from motives of personal gain, the acquisition of property, rather than family restoration and succor. Indeed, this, in my opinion, explains why Boaz chose to conduct a proceeding involving intrafamily obligations and rights in such a public forum. The whole legal assembly convened in the gate is surely not necessary in order to ratify such a proceeding. Could not Boaz have accomplished the purpose of such a ratification in a matter concerning intrafamily obligations in front of a few of the elders in a much less public setting? But the highly public forum chosen (most of the men of the city would have passed through the gate in the morning on their way to work the fields) is the setting Boaz needs to compel the nearer redeemer to face the full obligations, both legal and voluntary, that are his in his role as the nearer redeemer. So the nearer redeemer is faced with the choice of either exercising his rights and taking on both obligations or refusing to do so, thereby transferring his rights as redeemer to Boaz. (For the question regarding whether he had the option of exercising one right and refusing the other and the possible attendant consequences, see *Comment* on v 6c.)

The nearer redeemer *could* agree to take on both responsibilities. If he does so, Boaz's promise to Ruth and Naomi made in the preceding scene in word (3:13) and gift (3:17; see *Explanation*) will be met. He will have provided a home and husband for Ruth and a descendant for the line of Elimelech who will inherit Elimelech's patrimony and so be Naomi's redeemer by "restoring her life and sustaining her in her old age" (v 15). Given such a possibility, a brief moment of suspense and surprise is created, for the whole story heretofore, both explicitly and by implication, has led its readers to believe that it is the magnanimous and honorable Boaz who will provide the solution to our heroines' desperate plight. Just for an instant we entertain the thought—most unsatisfying—will it turn out differently than had been anticipated and assumed? But our disappointment at the possibility of such an infelicitous resolution is no sooner aroused than relieved. The very first words of the nearer redeemer in response reveal that he has neither the motives nor the character to rise to this occasion: "Then I for my part cannot redeem it lest I bring ruin upon my own estate" (v 6). Although our almost total ignorance of the costs incurred and the advantages gained from such family obligations prevents any demonstration of the fact, the general tenor both of this man's acts and our narrator's treatment of him (see below) strongly suggests that this statement of the effects attendant upon his taking up his responsibilities rather badly overstates the case. However that may be, his words clearly express concern only for his own patrimony and interests; they show no concern for Ruth and the line of Elimelech at all. Thus, unwilling to shoulder his full responsibilities as the redeemer with the prior right, he summons Boaz to acquire his rights (v 8a) and expresses the transfer symbolically by the physical act that customarily accompanied such a transfer: he removed his sandals and gave them to Boaz (v 8b). This symbolic act is so outmoded at the time of the story that our narrator must explain its significance to his readers in an explanatory comment (v 7). With this act, the nearer redeemer "fades from the story. As a foil to Boaz, he is finished, and he finishes as he began, without a name" (Trible, 190). Now we see the reason that the narrator not only left the nearer redeemer anonymous but had Boaz address him pejoratively as "So-and-so" (see above). "Since he refused to 'restore the name of the dead to his inheritance,' he himself has no name. Anonymity implies judgment" (Trible, 190).

With the negotiations between himself and the nearer redeemer successfully concluded by the redeemer's ceding him his rights, Boaz turns to the legal assembly (vv 9–10). He calls upon them to carry out their notarial function—to certify the transfer of rights—by their formal declaration that they are witnesses, thus orally "recording" the transaction and preserving both its existence and its legality for posterity (see *Comment* on v 9). To this summons to witness, the assembly responds with the affirmation "we are witnesses" (v 11a–b). Since the transfer that the assembly attests is to be legally binding, Boaz formally repeats in as full and detailed a form as possible the twofold obligation that the nearer redeemer has ceded him. Thus, "the field belonging to our brother Elimelech," v 5a, becomes "all that belongs to Elimelech and all that belongs to Chilion and Mahlon," v 9c; Ruth is given her full and formal name, "Ruth the Moabitess, wife of Mahlon," v 10a, rather than "Ruth the Moabitess, wife of the deceased" in 5c; and the purpose of the marriage to Ruth, "to raise up descendants for the deceased on his inheritance," v 5e, is given added importance by being expanded with a second statement, "so that the memory of the deceased may not perish from among his brothers and from the gate of his town," v 10c. This expansion rings with associations, for the memory of the deceased will not perish from the gate of his town when he has a descendant who will occupy his rightful position in the legal assembly that convenes in "the gate of the town," the very place and circumstances where Boaz now makes his affirmation. As Trible (191) insightfully observes, in Boaz's solemn and emphatic statement the whole family that sojourned from Judah to Moab is once again named for the first time since the opening scene (1:2). Indeed, of all the characters of that opening act, only Orpah is missing, for obvious reasons. Her role, however, as a foil for Ruth has been taken by the nearer redeemer as a foil for Boaz.

> But substitution means dissimilarity. Orpah had both name and speech (1:10). She decided to die to the story by returning to her own people, and the judgment upon her is favorable (1:15). The unnamed redeemer chooses to die to the story by returning to his own inheritance, and the judgment upon him is adverse. After all, he is not a foreign woman but the nearest male kin. Thus he passes away with the infamy of anonymity. (Trible, 191)

In contrast to the penurious self-interest of this man, the selfless generosity of Boaz expressed in the fullness and detail of this formal announcement stands in bold relief.

In recognition of this, the legal assembly concludes its testimony with a threefold blessing (vv 11c–12) that is a fitting conclusion to the scene, for it narrowly and specifically devotes its attention to Boaz. It is true that the blessing begins and ends with a reference to the woman he has pledged himself to marry. But she is not named, and the blessing upon her in the first frame asks for fecundity only so that Boaz may have a family commensurate in size with that of the patriarch Israel. She is mentioned in the last frame only as the means through which Boaz may have a family line as significant as that of Perez. The emphasis of the chiastic structure (see *Form/Structure/Setting*) is on the central blessing, which asks that, through this family, Boaz may flourish and gain renown in Bethlehem. It is important to note that the protagonists of the story themselves (as well as the genealogy at the end) recognize that the offspring of Boaz's union with Ruth not only will belong to Naomi (v 17), and so continue the family line of Elimelech, but will in a genuine sense also belong to Boaz.

With the legal assembly's threefold blessing of Boaz, the scene draws to a close. Through its carefully structured negotiations, the major complication of the story has been overcome. Before we look at this in more detail, however, it is important for the nature and purpose of the narrative as a whole that we note the very different agenda and purposes of this scene from that of previous scenes. In the male world of the legal assembly in the city gate, the protagonists see the persons, events, and needs wholly from within the perspective of the male side of their patriarchal world (cf. Trible, 192–93). Illustrative of this is the striking change in Ruth's identity—it is markedly different from that which she has in the rest of the story. In the scene on the harvest field, Boaz's overseer identified her to him as "a Moabite young woman who came back with Naomi" (2:6). Clearly her identity in the community at large (even when one man identified her to another) was not "wife of Mahlon." Most important, when she identified herself to Boaz on the threshing floor in 3:9, preparatory to requesting that he marry her, she is simply "Ruth, your handmaid," not "wife of Mahlon." This is patently in keeping with the purpose of both Naomi and Ruth in concocting and carrying out this daring scheme—to secure home and husband for Ruth—not to preserve the family line of Elimelech (see further *Explanation* to 3:1–5). And it was not only women who recognized the legitimacy of this female agenda. In the privacy of their meeting on the threshing floor, Boaz made Ruth's welfare the sole object of his concern. Gratified and delighted at her choice of him (3:10), he responds solely to the agenda there addressed—security for Ruth through marriage to him (3:11, 14)—and, as an earnest of his intention to provide security for both women, sends Ruth home with a magnanimous gift of grain for Naomi. But in the male world of the legal assembly at the city gate, not only does the matter of the family land of Elimelech and its redemption surface, but the identity of these women and Boaz's marriage to Ruth are also viewed from a different perspective and must meet another agenda. In that patriarchal world, the family line must be preserved on the family inheritance, and so (1) Naomi surrenders her right of usufruct so that the family land may be redeemed, (2) Ruth's identity now becomes "wife of the deceased," and (3) the purpose of Ruth's marriage is now to provide a son to continue the family line by inheriting the family property. It has not only taken the faithfulness of Naomi and Ruth to one another, together with their willingness to call Boaz to be faithful to his responsibilities toward them, but it has also taken Boaz's faithfulness to and skillful use of the concerns and institutions of his own male world to overcome the obstacle represented by the prior rights of the nearer redeemer and so make possible the transformation of the death and emptiness of Naomi's world into the life and fullness the next scene will depict.

It is entirely appropriate that this scene should conclude with the legal assembly's threefold blessing of Boaz, for, as noted above, initiative for progress in the story had devolved upon him, and he has indeed been equal to the task. Without him, the joyous conclusion to the story of Naomi about to unfold could not have taken place. Naomi's daring scheme at the beginning of the previous act (3:1–4) sprang from her loving concern for Ruth (3:1) and had as its limited objective the end of the destitution and reproach of Ruth's widowhood. In carrying out this scheme, Ruth put the symbolic actions Naomi ordered her to perform into words (3:9), grounding her request for marriage in Boaz's responsibility as a גאל, "redeemer," to come to the aid of family members in need. In so doing, she opened to Boaz a course of action in which he could *both* redeem the field *and* end the destitution and reproach of Ruth's widowhood and provide an heir to the line of Elimelech (and Naomi!—v 17) to inherit the redeemed family land and so end the death and emptiness afflicting Naomi's life as well. The legal assembly's words of praise and blessing are thus a fitting encomium upon him.

Having faithfully fulfilled his obligations to these two distantly related female relatives who had stumbled into his life when chance—that code word for the divine (see 2:3)—brought Ruth to glean in his field, he passes from the story. Apart from the narrative statement opening the next scene, which introduces him solely to relate that he faithfully fulfilled his word and married Ruth from which union a son was born, his name will appear only in the genealogical epilogue (v 21) as one link in the patronymics that lead from Perez to David. The joyous resolution of death and emptiness in the next scene is a story not about Boaz but about Naomi.

Although this scene does not relate the dénouement of our story, Rauber (*JBL* 89 [1970] 34–36) surely underestimates its role when he deems it an "interlude" and concludes that it is "relatively unimportant, . . . indeed a deliberate descent into the ordinary with the rhetorical purpose of setting off and separating two scenes of great importance." On the contrary, the scene is fascinating and powerfully drawn. Although its role in the plot development is secondary, it is nonetheless an important one. In it Boaz has overcome the major complication in the story line—the existence of Mr. "So-and-So" who had prior rights both in the matter of the legal obligation to redeem Elimelech's land and in the family responsibility of marrying Mahlon's widow. By challenging this man in the public forum provided by the legal assembly at the city gate to take on both these obligations, Boaz has succeeded in securing the nearer redeemer's voluntary withdrawal and the transfer of his rights in these matters to himself, both of which actions have been duly notarized by the legal assembly. With this major hurdle cleared, the way is open for the final resolution of the childlessness and widowhood—the death and emptiness—that have afflicted the lives of Naomi and Ruth.

Scene 2
A Son Is Born to Ruth and Boaz: Naomi Is Restored to Life and Fullness (4:13–17)

Bibliography

Bettan, I. *The Five Scrolls: A Commentary on the Song of Songs, Ruth, Lamentations, Ecclesiastes, Esther.* Cincinnati: Union of American Hebrew Congregations, 1950. 49–72. **Bewer, J.** "The *Goël* in Ruth 4:14,15." *AJSL* 20 (1903–4) 202–6. **Bush, F. W.** "Ruth 4:17, A Semantic Wordplay." In *Go to the Land That I Will Show You.* FS D. W. Young, ed. J. Coleson and V. Matthews. Winona Lake, IN: Eisenbrauns, 1996. 3–14. **Eissfeldt, O.** *The Old Testament: An Introduction.* Tr. P. Ackroyd. New York: Harper and Row, 1965. 477–83. ———. "Sohnespflichten im Alten Orient." *Syria* 43 (1966) 39–47. ———. "Wahrheit und Dichtung in der Ruth-Erzählung." *SSAW* 110 (1965) 23–28. **Gunkel, H.** "Ruth." In *Reden und Aufsätze.* Göttingen: Vandenhoeck & Ruprecht, 1913. 65–92. **Holladay, W.** *The Root Šûbh in the Old Testament.* Leiden: Brill, 1958. **Hubbard, R.** "Ruth IV:17: A New Solution." *VT* 38 (1988) 293–301. **Key, A.** "The Giving of Proper Names in the Old Testament." *JBL* 83 (1964) 55–59. **Köhler, L.** "Die Adoptionsform von Ruth 4,16." *ZAW* 29 (1909) 312–14. **Long, B.** *The Problem of Etiological Narrative in the Old Testament.* BZAW 108. Berlin: Töpelmann, 1968. **Loretz, O.** "Das Verhältnis zwischen Rut-Story und David-Genealogie im Rut-Buch." *ZAW* 89 (1977) 124–26. **Mace, D.** *Hebrew Marriage: A Sociological Study.* London: Epworth, 1953. **Parker, S. B.** "The Birth Announcement." In *Ascribe to the Lord.* FS P. C. Craigie, ed. L. Eslinger and G. Taylor. JSOTSup 67. Sheffield: JSOT, 1988. 133–49. **Porten, B.** "The Scroll of Ruth: A Rhetorical Study." *GCA* 7 (1978) 23–49. **Rauber, D.** "Literary Values in the Bible: The Book of Ruth." *JBL* 89 (1970) 27–37. **Richter, H.-F.** "Zum Levirat im Buch Ruth." *ZAW* 95 (1983) 123–26. **Vaux, R. de.** *Ancient Israel: Its Life and Institutions.* Tr. J. McHugh. New York: McGraw-Hill, 1961.

Translation

[13]*So Boaz took Ruth, and she became his wife. And when they came together,*[a] *Yahweh caused her to conceive,*[b] *and she gave birth to a son.* [14]*And the women said to Naomi, "Blessed be Yahweh, who has not left you today without*[a] *a redeemer! May his name be renowned*[b] *in Israel!* [15]*He shall become the one who restores your life*[a] *and provides for your old age, for your daughter-in-law who loves you*[b] *has given him birth*[c]*—she who is more to you than seven sons!"* [16]*And Naomi took the boy and held him to*[a] *her breast and became the one who took care of him.*[b] [17]*And the women of the neighborhood gave him a name, saying, "A son has been born to Naomi," so they called him Obed—he is the father of Jesse, the father of David.*

Notes

13.a. Lit. "And he went unto her."
13.b. Lit. "Yahweh gave to her conception/pregnancy."
14.a. Lit. "caused to be lacking to you."
14.b. Lit. "be proclaimed."
15.a. Lit. "a restorer of life to you."

15.b. Many MSS have the correct pointing אֲהֵבָתֶךְ, i.e., בָ rather than the בַ of L; cf. *BHS* n. 15a; GKC § 59g.

15.c. The form here, יְלָדַתּוּ, has arisen through the regressive assimilation of the heh of the 3rd masc sg suff *-hû* to the taw of the suffixal form of the pf 3rd fem sg verb יָלְדָה; i.e., *yĕladat-hû* > *yĕladattû* (cf. GKC § 59g and note the remarks on the similar form in *Note* 3:6.b.). In pause, the assimilation does not take place; cf. אֲהֵבַתְהוּ in 1 Sam 18:28.

16.a. Lit. "placed him on."

16.b. Lit. "became a nurse to him."

Form/Structure/Setting

Despite its brevity in comparison with the preceding, this scene forms the high point and culmination of the fourth act, indeed of the whole book, for it resolves the death and emptiness that have afflicted the life of Naomi. For the general characteristics that determine this division and the parallelism with chap. 1, see the discussion of the form and structure of the whole chapter given above in describing the structure of the opening scene.

The boundaries of the scene are marked by the inclusio formed by ותלד בן, "and she bore a son," in 13e and ילד בן, "a son has been born," in 17b (see the table). The scene itself divides into two episodes, each of which comprises a narrative statement (A, v 13; A′, v 16) followed by a resultant action on the part of the women of the city (B, vv 14–15; B′, v 17a–c). It is clear that each of the actions of the women, the first a speech, vv 14–15, the second a name-giving, v 17a–c, constitutes a response to the important events related in the preceding narrative statements. Both structure and content unite to confirm this. Even though the events of v 13 are glad and joyous and constitute the fulfillment of preceding plans and promises (see *Explanation*), they are nonetheless related in a series of five rapid-fire, staccato clauses, the longest of which comprises but four words! This very brevity signals that this is not the high point of the scene. Rather, in keeping with the pattern set by all the preceding scenes, the high point is provided by the speech of the participants—in this case that of the women of Bethlehem. Their threefold speech provides the commentary on and the meaning of the events just related in such brief compass. And this speech devotes itself almost exclusively to describing Naomi's restoration to life and fullness. Likewise in v 16, the touching and tender scene of an old woman's joy in and care for the child—a woman so long bereaved and bereft of husband and sons—triggers the glad cry of the neighboring women that at last a son has been born to Naomi; this in turn forms the circumstances that suggest his name, עובד, *ʿôbēd*, lit. "server, worker," but in context "guardian, provider," he who will care for and sustain her in her old age (see *Comment*).

These two episodes exhibit strictly synonymous parallelism (see the table). Thus, the narrative statements A (13a–e) and A´ (16a–c) are parallel in both form and content, in form in that each consists of a series of short, temporally sequential clauses and in content in that each begins with a clause of identical syntactic structure using לקח, "to take" (13a, 16a), and each contains a clause of identical syntactic structure using the idiom ותהי לו ל״, "And she became to him" (13b, 16c). The resultant actions B (14a–15b) and B´ (17a–c) are also parallel in form and content in that each involves a statement made by the women of the city (הנשים, 14a; השכנות, 17a); both center their whole attention on the relationship between the newborn child (גאל, "a redeemer," 14b; עובד/בן, "a son, Obed," 17b–c) and Naomi

The Structure of Ruth 13–17

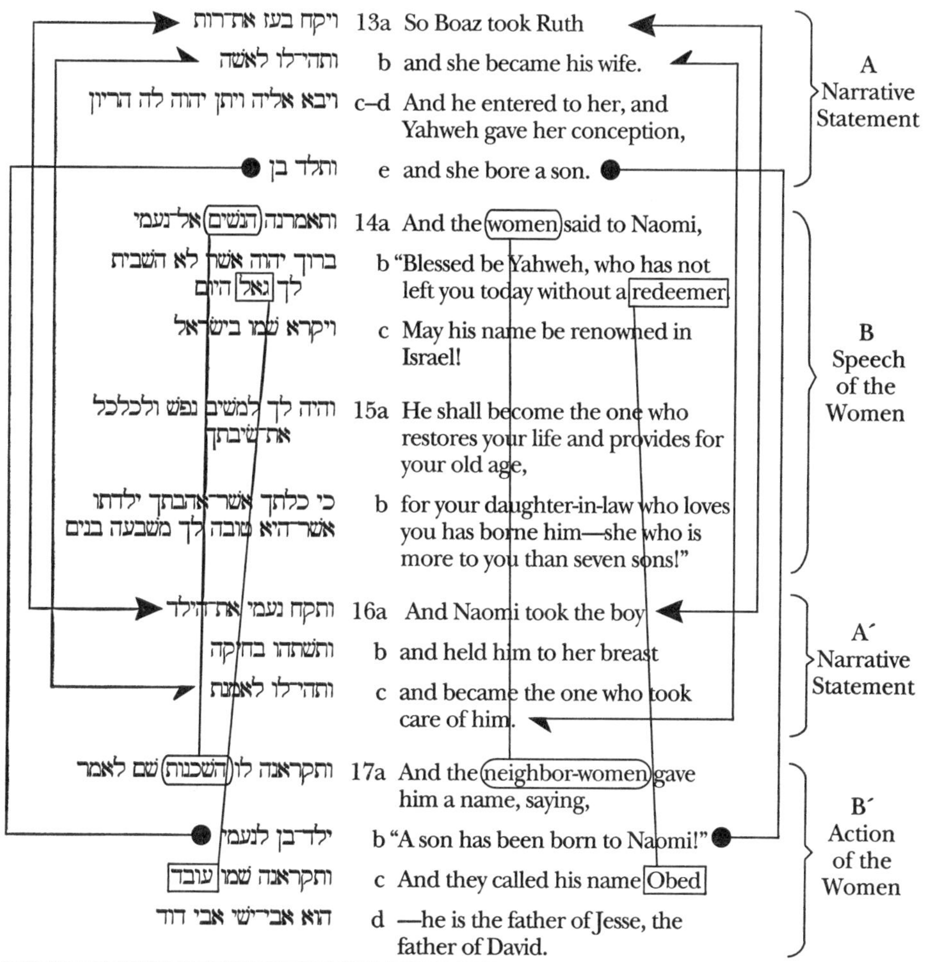

ויקח בעז את־רות	13a	So Boaz took Ruth	A Narrative Statement
ותהי־לו לאשה	b	and she became his wife.	
ויבא אליה ויתן יהוה לה הריון	c–d	And he entered to her, and Yahweh gave her conception,	
ותלד בן	e	and she bore a son.	
ותאמרנה הנשים אל־נעמי	14a	And the women said to Naomi,	B Speech of the Women
ברוך יהוה אשר לא השבית לך גאל היום	b	"Blessed be Yahweh, who has not left you today without a redeemer.	
ויקרא שמו בישראל	c	May his name be renowned in Israel!	
והיה לך למשיב נפש ולכלכל את־שיבתך	15a	He shall become the one who restores your life and provides for your old age,	
כי כלתך אשר־אהבתך ילדתו אשר־היא טובה לך משבעה בנים	b	for your daughter-in-law who loves you has borne him—she who is more to you than seven sons!"	
ותקח נעמי את־הילד	16a	And Naomi took the boy	A′ Narrative Statement
ותשתהו בחיקה	b	and held him to her breast	
ותהי־לו לאמנת	c	and became the one who took care of him.	
ותקראנה לו השכנות שם לאמר	17a	And the neighbor-women gave him a name, saying,	B′ Action of the Women
ילד־בן לנעמי	b	"A son has been born to Naomi!"	
ותקראנה שמו עובד	c	And they called his name Obed	
הוא אבי־ישי אבי דוד	d	—he is the father of Jesse, the father of David.	

(14a, 17b); and each contains the idiom קרא שם, "call his name." Indeed, the appended and important appositive in 17d, "he is the father of Jesse, the father of David," provides the fulfillment of the prayer of the women for the newborn infant in 14c, "May his name be renowned in Israel." The expanded length and fullness of the first statement of the women, B (14a–15b), signals that here is the most important part of the scene. And even though it has the form of words of praise to Yahweh, which is important in its own right (see *Explanation*), the women's praise centers all its attention on Naomi. The narrative introduction (14a) notes that it is addressed to her, and the second person feminine singular pronominal suffix, referring to Naomi, reverberates six times throughout the women's speech. A fourfold parasonantic wordplay (cf. Sasson, *IDBSup*, 969) involving the consonants שׂ/שׁ, ב (*ś/š, b*) and the vowel **i* (see the table; cf. Porten, *GCA* 7 [1978] 47) highlights and unites the progress of Naomi's restoration: "God has not 'let cease' [השבית *hS̱Byt*] a redeemer for her, one who will 'restore' [למשיב *lm<u>ŠYB</u>*] her soul and support her 'old age' [שׂיבתך *<u>ŚYB</u>tk*], one brought forth by her daughter-in-law who is better to her than 'seven' [משבעה *m<u>ŠB</u>ʿh*] sons" (Porten, *GCA* 7 [1978] 47). A further parasonantic wordplay punctuates the importance of the scene in the assonance between לכלכל *lklkl,* "to support," and כלתך *kltk,* "your daughter-in-law" (Porten, *GCA* 7 [1978] 47).

This structure reveals how completely this scene, representing the culmination and resolution of the narrative, centers all its attention on Naomi and her restoration to life and fullness, even though it does not completely ignore Ruth and her relationship to Naomi (see *Explanation*). This exclusive attention to Naomi in the culminating scene creates problems for those who postulate that the major figure in the book is Ruth and its major theme the way in which her faithfulness to her obligations to her dead husband have successfully produced an heir to the line of Elimelech. Rudolph (70) identifies v 13 as the culmination of the whole (cf. also Campbell, 167), for in it the blessing of Boaz in 2:12 is fulfilled: "the motherhood heretofore denied is Ruth's 'full recompense.'" He emends v 17 to read "so that the neighbor-women called out about him 'A son has been born to Naomi'" and thereby contends that it forms the "crowning event of the whole" since it affirms that *Ruth* became the ancestress of David. He then concludes, "With v 13 and 17b the story could therefore come to an end." Consequently, he must treat vv 14–16 as an afterthought: "The narrator, however, has something yet on his mind concerning Naomi." In like vein, he understands the neighbor-women's proclamation in v 17 that a son has been born to Naomi as "good-natured mockery." But surely such treatment utterly misconstrues the force and meaning of the scene! V 13 is but a short summary of the events whose very brevity shows that it is not the culmination, as the structure shown above reveals. On the other hand, Gerleman (37) correctly notes that the concluding scene concentrates its attention not on Ruth but on Naomi. However, in order to explain this, he avers that it was not sufficient to the narrator just to incorporate Ruth into the Jewish nation (having previously concluded that the major purpose of the book was to "Judaize" Ruth, whom tradition bequeathed to the author as the ancestress of David). On the contrary, in vv 13–17 the author "goes to great trouble to give the newborn a true Jewish mother by an act of adoption." Gerleman sees this "act of adoption" in Naomi's gesture of taking the child to her bosom. But such an interpretation, besides misconstruing the meaning of Naomi's act of taking the child in her arms (see *Comment* on v 16), also totally misses the point of the scene. Morris (313) takes another tack in order to explain why Naomi is featured in the closing scene. He "psychologizes" the narrative by postulating that the women come to Naomi now "possibly because they know her so much better, possibly because she is the one with the greater need of companionship."

All such interpretations of the scene, however, miss its significance. As the structure reveals, the central point of the scene is to describe Naomi's restoration to life and fullness through the child of Ruth and Boaz who is hers both by a legal fiction and by virtue of the fact that he has been born to the daughter-in-law who loves her and is more to her than seven sons. Such a culmination, balancing as it does the poignant scene of death and emptiness portrayed in 1:19b–23, shows indeed that Naomi is "the person whose 'trial' holds the whole story together" (Campbell, 168).

Comment

13 וַיִּקַּח בֹּעַז אֶת־רוּת וַתְּהִי־לוֹ לְאִשָּׁה, lit. "Boaz took Ruth, and she became his wife." The language of this idiom is culture specific in that the verb "to take" doubtless carries the connotation "to take home" (cf. Deut 20:7), reflecting the formal procession to the bridegroom's home in the marriage ritual (cf. Gen 24:67; see *Comment* on v 11b above). It is the reflex from the bridegroom's perspective of the language in the blessing of the elders, who spoke of "the woman who is coming into your house" (v 11). The whole expression, then, is culturally equivalent to "So Boaz married Ruth."

וַיָּבֹא אֵלֶיהָ, lit. "He went to her." This is the common OT euphemism for sexual intercourse (e.g., Gen 16:2; 29:21, 23; 2 Sam 16:21). The euphemism originates from the action of the husband entering the tent or room of his wife (as is conclusively demonstrated by such passages as Gen 39:14; Judg 15:1; 2 Sam 12:24; Prov 2:19; it can also be used of a woman entering a man's room for the same purpose; cf. Gen 19:34; 2 Sam 11:4). The literal translation "he went to her" (NIV) simply has no such connotation in English usage, while such translations as "he went in to her" (NASV, RSV, Moffatt) are unfortunate in that they are doubtless understood by English speakers to refer to the act of coitus itself, hence, hardly a euphemism! As an expression with approximately the same meaning in English, we have chosen to render it "When they came together."

וַיִּתֵּן יְהוָה לָהּ הֵרָיוֹן, lit. "Yahweh gave to her pregnancy." As Joüon notes, הריון is more properly "pregnancy" than "conception."

14 אֲשֶׁר לֹא הִשְׁבִּית לָךְ גֹּאֵל הַיּוֹם, lit. "who has not caused to be lacking for you a redeemer this day." This usage of השבית is rather unusual. When used with the preposition מן, it can mean "to remove from" (e.g., "yeast from houses," Exod 12:15) or "to let (something) be lacking from" (e.g., "salt from grain offering," Lev 2:13) or "to stop (someone) from doing (something)" (e.g., "people from working," Exod 5:5). Without the prepositional phrase, it can mean simply "to remove" (e.g., "pagan priests," 2 Kgs 23:5) or "to put an end to" (e.g., "the kingdom of Israel," Hos 1:4). With this clear semantic range, the positive statement here would mean "he has put an end to/caused to be lacking a redeemer for you this day." When the phrase is negated, such a meaning could be conveyed in English with a positive statement: "He has provided a redeemer for you" (cf. TEV), but the common translation "he has not left you without a redeemer" is perhaps preferable, in that it has the same sense and preserves the negative connotation of the Hebrew.

The "redeemer" must be the newborn child. This is the most natural implication of the היום, "this day" (v 14b), and the statement in v 15b that it is Ruth who has borne him makes this mandatory, especially since it is clearly the "redeemer" who is the unexpressed subject of the preceding clause (15a). The word גאל, "redeemer," is not used here in any of its technical senses but in the general sense in which he is described in v 15a, i.e., the one who restores Naomi's life and sustains her old age (cf. the comments of Leggett, *The Levirate,* 259). This is the way the women of the story have used גאל previously; see *Comments* on 2:20; 3:9. There is nothing improper in applying such a general sense to a child who is the son of Naomi by a legal fiction (contra Sasson, 163–64).

A number of scholars, however, have argued that the redeemer referred to here is Boaz (e.g., Bewer, *AJSL* 20 [1903–4] 202–23; cf. the bibliography in Leggett, *The Levirate,* 255 n. 2). This conclusion is grounded in the view that גאל, "redeemer," is being used here in a technical sense, i.e., the one who is called upon to perform the levirate marriage and so to provide an heir to the family line of Elimelech. This almost invariably goes along with the view that this is the major purpose of both Naomi's scheme to prevail upon Boaz to marry Ruth and the legal proceedings instituted by Boaz at the city gate. Thus, Bettan states, "The reference is to Boaz, who fulfilled the obligation of a near kinsman; and this very day, having secured an heir for Mahlon, has given full effect to his office" (*The Five Scrolls,* 71). In a similar vein, Sasson (163) argues "the women were glorifying God not so much for his *positive act* in which a *gôʾēl* is created to care for Naomi's needs, but for his *intervention to* prevent *the end of Elimelech's line.*" Joüon (93) carries this view to the extreme by arguing that the term "redeemer" here refers to the newborn child and is "very nearly equivalent to (legal) heir, but with the nuance *who redeems* or *delivers* the name of the grandfather from oblivion." Since the following phrase, ויקרא שמו בישראל, expresses result, "so that his name may be pronounced in Israel," the name so pronounced must then be that of Elimelech. Consequently, according to Joüon, there is lack of harmony between the two clauses: he has not caused a גאל, "redeemer," to be lacking for *you,* so that *his* name may be pronounced in Israel. Hence לך, "for you," must not be authentic, and it must be emended to למת, "for the deceased," "the alteration of which to לָךְ," he avers, "could easily happen with a scribe swept along by the thought of Naomi whom the women are addressing!" But it is not some ancient scribe who has been swept along by the thought of Naomi and so read her into the text, but Joüon himself who has been swept along (as have others, including JB) by the view that redemption here can only refer to the responsibility of providing an heir for the line of Elimelech, and so read that concern into the text. It is exactly the same predilection that leads Richter (*ZAW* 95 [1983] 125) to conclude that the text of vv 14–15 is not in order ("for the child, not Boaz, is said to care for Naomi in her old age"). He feels that a "major conjecture" is in order and so posits that the word בית fell out of the text after השבית by haplography, subsequent to which some later scribe inserted לך גאל in order to supply the missing words! Changes must then also be made in v 15 so that the text can be made to present the women as praising Yahweh for maintaining the family line of Elimelech rather than for restoring Naomi to life and fullness. But surely such drastic emendation of a felicitous clause that is syntactically and semantically correct as it stands reveals that Richter is reading into the passage his hypothesis that "the true intent of the book is . . . to praise the faithfulness of a wife to her deceased husband and his family" (125). I must emphatically demur from such conclusions and unsupported emendations and insist that it is women and women's concerns that occupy center stage here and that there is not a shred of evidence that their interest in this child relates *primarily* to the fact that Boaz has voluntarily pledged him as the heir of the patrimony of Elimelech in order to continue his family line. On the contrary, the neighbor-women are solely interested in the child because he will resolve the emptiness of Naomi's life. This is unmistakably clear in the succeeding verses, for the function of the child as a redeemer is to become for Naomi "one who will restore your life and sustain you in your old age" (v 15a).

And the reason given that this child can so redeem Naomi totally reflects women's concerns and relationships. It is not expressed in terms that relate to his role of continuing by a legal fiction the family line of the deceased (such as יקום על־שם המת . . . , Deut 25:6), but, on the contrary, *it is because of his maternity.* It is because of Ruth's proven commitment and fidelity that Naomi can count on this child to redeem her old age: "for your daughter-in-law who loves you has given him birth—she who is more to you than seven sons" (v 15b)!

וְיִקָּרֵא שְׁמוֹ בְּיִשְׂרָאֵל, "May his name be renowned in Israel." The exact nuance of this expression is difficult. Its meaning depends on the answers to two questions: (1) What is the antecedent of the pronominal suffix "his" on "his name"? (2) What is the meaning of the idiom נקרא שמו? As far as the first question is concerned, "his" can refer to either the redeemer or Yahweh, both of whom have been mentioned in the previous clause. It is impossible that it can refer to the deceased (either Elimelech or Mahlon; contra NEB; cf. REB), for he has not been mentioned or referred to in any way since v 10. Concerning the second question, it is rather clear that the idiom is not being used in the literal sense of "his name shall be called N," an idiom that occurs in Gen 17:5; 35:10; Deut 25:10; Ezek 20:29; Dan 10:1 (and possibly 2 Sam 6:2 = 1 Chron 13:6). This latter idiom is the passive form of the active construction "he will call his name N," e.g., in Gen 5:2, 3; 16:15 (see form § 2a in the analysis of the syntactic structures of name-giving formulas in Bush, "Ruth 4:17," 8). Not only does this literal idiom make no sense in this context, but the idiom here is syntactically different at one critical point—no object of the verbal expression יקרא שמו, "his name is called," is given; i.e., no name is expressed.

Loretz (*ZAW* 89 [1977] 125), however, does take the phrase as a name-giving formula. He concludes that the story must find its conclusion at 4:16 on the tenuous grounds that the point and purpose of the story are "the events concerning levirate marriage and the birth of the male child." Hence, he proposes that the phrase here in v 14 must have originally read PN ויקרא שמו and the personal name was changed to בישראל when the names of Boaz and Obed were secondarily introduced into the narrative. However, apart from the utterly speculative nature of such views and the tenuous nature of the grounds upon which they are based, a name-giving formula cannot possibly fit the context of the final clause of v 14, where the women are praising Yahweh for providing a גאל, "redeemer," who will restore Naomi's life and provide for her old age.

Sasson (164–66) also notes the fact that the name is missing. But, observing that all the occurrences of the above idiom apart from our passage in Ruth have a proper name following, he argues that the same is likely here. Therefore the passage "may have originally included the personal name of the child who was to become Naomi's *gôʾēl*" (166). Sasson uses this argument to buttress his hypothesis that 4:13–17 comprises two—not one—separate birth episodes. The first, to be found in vv 13–15, which he terms the "*Gôʾēl*" episode, describes a son born to Ruth and Boaz who is legally theirs and becomes Naomi's גאל, "redeemer," taking over the function from Boaz. The second, to be found in vv 16–17, which he terms the "Son" episode, describes a second son born to Ruth and Boaz, who is Naomi's son and heir, fulfilling Boaz's pledge to raise an heir to the line of Elimelech (158–61). But Sasson's attempt to understand vv 13–15 as a birth and naming episode separate from vv 16–17 cannot be sustained. To do so, he seeks to understand vv 13–15 as an example of the "mixed" type of birth and name-giving etiology suggested by Long in *The Problem of Etiological Narrative.* In Sasson's analysis of the text from this point of view (159), v 13 comprises the "Setting" and vv 14–15 the "Report of birth" (and the naming). However, the report of the birth surely occurs in 13c–d: "And when they came together, Yahweh caused her to conceive, and she gave birth to a son," for which 13a–b is surely the setting: "So Boaz took Ruth, and she became his wife." Further, v 14a–b cannot be interpreted as "An announcement by *nāšîm* of the *gôʾēl*'s birth" (159). In the first place, the birth has already been reported in 13c–d, and second, the women's statement does not have the form of an announcement. Rather, it is a word of praise to Yahweh for providing her with a גאל, "redeemer," i.e., one who will care for family members in need (as the language of v 15 makes patently clear). Such a context precludes taking the meaning of the idiom יקרא שמו in the literal sense of giving a name (and Sasson does not so translate it!). The women here are not making an announcement of the birth of the גאל, "redeemer"; they are praising Yahweh for restoring life and fullness to Naomi, a setting within which the naming of the child (by Ruth or Boaz?) has no meaningful place. Finally and decisively, Sasson's hypothesis reinterprets a pericope in which our author depicts with great power and touching humanity Naomi's transformation from death and emptiness to life and fullness into a concern with meeting legal niceties, one son to continue the line of Elimelech and another to be the גאל, "redeemer," that, in Sasson's interpretation, Ruth requested from Boaz in 3:9.

Consequently, since the one critical, syntactical element necessary to understand the idiom נקרא שם as a name-giving formula is missing, namely, the object, the name, the idiom must be employed in another sense. It is not without point to note that we have already seen this absolute use of the idiom employed in the active mood in this very chapter (4:11). The idiom does occur in two other passages in the OT, Gen 48:16; Jer 44:26, but in both of these passages the meaning is not pertinent to the usage here. Since there are no other uses of the verb קרא in the niphal stem (i.e., the passive) with שם, "name," as the subject with which to compare our passage, it will be necessary to turn to the active use of the verb for which our idiom could be the passive reflex, i.e., the use of the qal stem of קרא with שם plus pronominal suffix (or plus *nomen rectum*) as the *single* object. Here we have a number of uses in which the idiom קרא שם means "to call out the name of" Yahweh, either in supplication (e.g., Lam 3:55) or in praise or celebration, i.e., "to proclaim his name" in the sense of "to extol, to celebrate his name" (see esp. Deut 32:3; Ps 99:6, and note the helpful comments of Campbell, 163). Since all the examples of this active use of the idiom have Yahweh as the subject, it may be that the passive form of the idiom here in Ruth 4:14 should be understood the same way, so that Yahweh would be the antecedent of the pronoun "his" in "his name" and the phrase would be virtually equivalent to "may his name be praised" (so NJB), which could fit this context since the women began by praising Yahweh. However, the subject of both the preceding clause, 14a, and the following clause, 15a, is the newborn child. Since there is no indication of any change of subject here, it seems more natural to see the newborn child as the subject of this clause also. It is not impossible that such an idiom could be used of a human being, especially if "name" is used here in the sense of "fame, reputation" (see BDB, 2.b, p. 1028). I conclude then that the idiom as used here means "May his name be proclaimed [i.e., in the sense 'renowned'] in Israel" (cf. BDB, 2.a, p. 896; KB³, 2.b, p. 1055). Finally, the term "Israel" here refers to the whole covenanted people of God, so that "the scope here has been greatly broadened, beyond local realities like Bethlehem and Ephrathah in 4:11, or political units like Judah and Israel as the southern and northern kingdoms" (Campbell, 163).

15 וְהָיָה לָךְ לְמֵשִׁיב נֶפֶשׁ וּלְכַלְכֵּל אֶת־שֵׂיבָתֵךְ, lit. "And he shall become for you a restorer of life and the support of your old age." The literal force of השיב נפש is "to restore life," as in Job 33:30. As such it is the transitive (or causitive) reflex of the idiom ישוב נפש, "life returns, is restored," as in 1 Kgs 17:21, 22 (cf. Holladay, *The Root Šubh,* 75, 97). More frequently, however, it is used in a figurative sense, "to revive/restore someone's spirit, courage, or strength" in the sense of restoring a normal, full state of being (cf. Westermann, *THAT* 2:79). In Lam 1:11, 19 the idiom is used to describe what food does for the starving man, while in Lam 1:16 it describes the reviving of spirit provided by one who consoles and comforts in the midst of great tragedy. One context, Prov 25:13, provides a rich and expressive imagery: "To those who send him, a trustworthy messenger is like the coolness of snow in the heat of the harvest: he refreshes the soul of his master [נפש אדניו ישיב]." Given these parallel uses of the idiom, it is clear in the context of the story of Ruth that the phrase is used in a figurative sense, "to restore to fullness of life." Here our author creates an inclusio that provides artistic closure for the whole story, for it was a hiphil of שׁוב that he placed in the mouth of Naomi in 1:21 when she expressed most poignantly the death and emptiness that are here resolved: "full was I when I went away, but empty has Yahweh *brought me back*" (השיבני). Given this significance of the phrase in this context, it captures Naomi's restoration in a rich and expressive metaphor (contra Morris, 313–14).

The meaning of the second expression used to describe the function of this child is quite clear. כלכל means specifically "to sustain, to provide the necessities for" (cf. Gen 45:11; 1 Kgs 4:7). Its syntax, however, is striking, for it is the infinitive construct plus ל, whereas one would expect the participle מכלכל to balance משיב. One other comparable example has been noted in the OT (so Rudolph, 69), and this should caution us against overhasty emendation (cf. Sasson, 167).

אֲשֶׁר־הִיא טוֹבָה לָךְ מִשִּׁבְעָה בָּנִים, "She who is more to you than seven sons." The idiom טוב ל means literally "to be/do good to/for"; cf. 1 Sam 25:15. Here it is used figuratively: "she is better to you" (NJPS) in the sense "she means more, is worth more to you" (cf. Joüon, 94; Campbell, 164). The reference is not so much to the past (contra NEB, TEV) as to the present. The expression well captures all that Ruth means to Naomi, for "seven" is the ideal number of sons in the biblical conception (cf. 1 Sam 2:5; Job 1:2; 42:13; 2 Macc 7; Acts 19:14–17). Elkanah's affirmation to Hannah that he is worth more to her than ten sons (1 Sam 1:8) is probably intended to outdo the conventional expression.

16 וַתְּשִׁתֵהוּ בְחֵיקָהּ, lit. "she placed him in her bosom." חיק refers to that portion of the body where one holds and carries infants (Num 11:12) or holds a spouse or lover (a man of a woman, 1 Kgs 1:2; a woman of a man, Deut 28:56). It can also refer by metonymy to the clothing of this portion of the body, in which one can place hands (Exod 4:6, 7) or objects (Prov 17:23). In one passage it is the virtual equivalent of "lap" (Prov 16:33), but in all other passages it is the equivalent of "breast, chest." It never refers to the female breast at which an infant is nursed. The verbal expressions most frequently used with it when it bears the sense "breast" are נשׂא ב, "to carry on/in," and השׁכיב/שׁכב ב, "to lay/lie on." Only here does it occur with the verbal expression שׁית ב, "to place in/on."

This passage devotes its whole attention to depicting Naomi's restoration to life and fullness from the death and emptiness that afflicted her in chap. 1 (see *Form/Structure/Setting* and *Explanation*). This restoration is effected through the birth of the child of Ruth and Boaz whom Boaz has pledged as the heir of the line of Elimelech, hence, Naomi's grandson by a legal fiction. It is because of this relationship that he can be designated a גאל, "redeemer," who will become the one who restores her life and provides for her old age (v 15). When this is recognized, it is very clear that this expression "she laid him on her bosom" is intended to denote an act of tenderness and love that depicts the completeness of Naomi's restoration to life and fullness in terms every woman can understand. As Gunkel expressed it, vv 16–17 present a "tender picture" ("Ruth," 84; cf. Rauber, *JBL* 89 [1970] 34–35). It is indeed a misunderstanding of the scene to judge that "such an understanding would ill-fit the denouement of a well-told story" and to designate such an expressive and poignant picture of Naomi's full restoration as engaging in "flabby and purposeless sentimentalities" (Sasson, 171–72).

Often, however, it has been argued that Naomi's act of placing the child in her bosom is a symbolic act of adoption (Gerleman, 37–38; Würthwein, 23; see esp. Köhler, *ZAW* 29 [1909] 312–14; Leggett, *The Levirate,* 260–63), but it is highly doubtful that adoption in the proper sense was known or practiced in the OT at all (cf. Mace, *Hebrew Marriage,* 116–17, 212–13; de Vaux, *Ancient Israel,* 51–52). De Vaux compares Naomi's action with the custom of bearing a child on another's "knees" (see Gen 30:3; 48:12; 50:23) and concludes that these are not adoptions in the full sense, for they take place within the family and in the direct line and "the legal consequences of such an adoption are therefore not far-reaching" (*Ancient Israel,* 51). But, the two actions involved are distinctly different: the Genesis passages involve the knees, whereas חיק is properly "bosom," not "lap" (cf. Köhler, *ZAW* 29 [1909] 312). Further, rather than an act of adoption, the Genesis practice can better be understood as a rite whereby the children born on or placed between the "knees" of the patriarch or matriarch are acknowledged as their own by their taking part in the birth process (so Köhler, *ZAW* 29 [1909] 312; cf. Sasson, 171). Since, as we have shown above in *The nature of the "levirate-type" marriage responsibility of Ruth 4* in the *Comment* on 4:5b, the first child of the union of Ruth and Boaz continues the family line and becomes heir to the property of Elimelech by a legal fiction, Naomi has no need to adopt the infant; he is already hers (cf. Joüon, 94). Quite apart from the highly tenuous nature of these parallels and their interpretation as adoptions, it is above all the nature of this passage as a depiction of Naomi's full restoration to life and felicity that renders most improbable the interpretation of this act as a legal proceeding. Naomi's action is "an act of love and not of law" (Rudolph, 71).

וַתְּהִי־לוֹ לְאֹמֶנֶת, lit. "and became a nurse to him." The qal stem of אמן occurs with the meaning "to rear, take care of children" only in the participial form. It is used once in a verbal construction (Esth 2:7); elsewhere it functions as a noun. The masculine form, surprisingly, is used to refer to a person who takes care of an infant (ינק, Num 11:12), as well as to designate the "guardians" who are "rearing" (מגדלים) Ahab's seventy sons (2 Kgs 10:1, 5; cf. Isa 49:23). The feminine form occurs in one passage (other than Ruth 4:16) to refer to the "nurse" of the five-year-old Mephibosheth (2 Sam 4:4). Hence, it is quite clear that the word is used to mean "nurse" in the sense of the one who takes care of or looks after a child. It does *not* mean "wet-nurse" (contra deWaard-Nida, 79). That meaning is expressed by מינקת, the hiphil participle from the root ינק, "to suck" (note that even this term can be used in the sense of "guardian, governess": it is used to refer to the woman who takes care of the full-grown Rebekah, Gen 24:59; 35:8). It is best in our opinion to avoid the English term "nurse" since it is ambiguous and could be taken to mean "wet-nurse."

That חיק means "bosom, chest," while Hebrew uses other terms to refer to the female breast at which infants are suckled, that אמנת means "the one who looks after" a child and never "wet-nurse," and that Naomi is far too old to fulfill such a function (cf. Sasson, 172)—these remove from the bounds of probability Sasson's attempt (235–37) to suggest that the language here is intended to be reminiscent of those references in ancient Near Eastern literature in which a royal infant is said to have been suckled at the breasts of various goddesses. Since this is the tender picture of a grandmother cradling her grandson, with no reference to the suckling of infants, there simply is no "vestigial motif" (237) present with which to compare the passages cited by Sasson.

17 הַשְּׁכֵנוֹת, "women of the neighbohood." The feminine form of שָׁכֵן, "neighbor, inhabitant," occurs elsewhere only in Exod 3:22, in the singular, where it clearly means "(female-)neighbor." However, the masculine form can mean both "neighbor" and "inhabitant" (e.g., Isa 33:24; Hos 10:5). Hence, it is possible that השכנות here refers to the female inhabitants of Bethlehem in general (cf. NIV). However, since the women so designated play an intimate role in reference to the child and to Naomi, i.e., they name him on the basis of his relationship to her (see below), it seems far more probable that the term here means "(female-)neighbors" rather than "(female-)inhabitants."

וַתִּקְרֶאנָה לוֹ הַשְּׁכֵנוֹת שֵׁם לֵאמֹר יֻלַּד־בֵּן לְנָעֳמִי וַתִּקְרֶאנָה שְׁמוֹ עוֹבֵד, "And the women of the neighborhood gave him a name, saying, 'A son has been born to Naomi,' so they called him Obed." The complex name-giving here is so unusual in both form and content that it has often been concluded that it cannot be understood in the straightforward sense given in the translation above. Two main objections have been advanced to taking the text as it stands: (1) The idiom ותקראנה לו . . . שם in 17a cannot be taken in its straightforward sense to mean "And . . . gave him a name," so some other meaning must be intended. (2) The original text of the sentence was a standard name-giving but has been altered by later editors, and so various changes must be made in order to put the text in order, such as restoring the original name (see below). The arguments usually advanced to justify such conclusions are the following: (1) The neighbor-women not only make the statement that ostensibly explains the name (17a–b), but they also name the child (17c). There are no other examples in the OT of anyone other than the mother, or occasionally the father, naming the child. The possible parallel in 2 Sam 12:25 is not valid, for there it is the matter of Yahweh giving Solomon a symbolic name through the agency of the prophet Nathan, not the giving of the child's personal name (cf. Witzenrath, 23). Luke 1:59 is also not pertinent, for there it is a matter of a suggestion of the neighbors, which the parents decline (so Rudolph, 70; cf. the remarks of Sasson, 273–74). (2) The speech of the neighbor-women in 17b does not contain a phonetic allusion to, or suggestion of, the name of the child given by them in 17c, as is overwhelmingly the case in OT accounts of name-giving (see the discussion below). (3) Since 17a contains the expression קרא לו שם and is followed by what appears to be an explanation of a name introduced by לאמר, "saying," it appears to be a defective etiological name-giving, and hence, the verse contains two such namings (cf. Ap-Thomas, *ET* 79 [1967–68] 370–71; Campbell, 166; Eissfeldt, *Introduction,* 479; Joüon, 95; Witzenrath, 24–25). However, in a recent article (see Bush, "Ruth 4:17," 3–14), I have argued that the text can be given a coherent interpretation as it stands if one takes into account (1) the literary character and meaning of the scene that it concludes (see *Form/Structure/Setting* above) and (2) a correct understanding of the syntactic structures of name-giving extant in the OT. First, it can be shown that, in structure at least, v 17 is a perfectly regular example of an etiological name-giving. The explanation for the name, consisting of a direct speech of one of the principals, precedes, and the name-giving itself has the very frequent structure קרא (waw consecutive) + שם + pronominal suffix + personal name (see syntactic structure § 3a in Bush, "Ruth 4:17," and esp. the explanation, p. 10):

Explanation: v 17a–b
וַתִּקְרֶאנָה לוֹ הַשְּׁכֵנוֹת שֵׁם לֵאמֹר יֻלַּד בֵּן לְנָעֳמִי
And the neighbor-women gave him a name, saying,
"A son has been born to Naomi."
Name-giving: v17c
וַתִּקְרֶאנָה שְׁמוֹ עוֹבֵד
And they called his name Obed.

Second, the phrase "the neighbor-women gave him a name" in the explanation is not a defective name-giving so that it must be emended (e.g., by supplying the missing name, so Eissfeldt, *Introduction,* 479–80; Würthwein, 2–3, 24; or by some other procedure, so Rudolph, 69–70; Joüon, 45). Nor is it necessary to assume some other meaning for it ad hoc (e.g., R. Hubbard, *VT* 38 [1988] 299–301; Campbell, 165–66; Sasson, 168; cf. Bush, "Ruth 4:17," 11). On the contrary, there is nothing defective about the form or the meaning at all. It is simply an example of the well-attested "generic" statement of name-giving (e.g., Gen 2:20; 26:18; Isa 65:15; see syntactic structure § 1 in Bush, "Ruth 4:17," 7).

Finally, although in the etiological forms of name-giving the explanation of the name usually depends on parasonancy (see Sasson, *IDBSup,* 969), i.e., it contains a phonetic allusion to or suggestion of the name (see Bush, "Ruth 4:17," 9–10), there is a variant of this type of wordplay that is directly relevant to the passage here. Occasionally the explanation of the name does not depend on parasonancy, on *phonetic* allusion, but on a play on *meaning* (cf. Witzenrath, 24). For example, in Gen 35:18b the name that Rebecca gives to Benjamin, Ben-Oni, "Son of my sorrow," is explained by the circumstance related in v 18a, that her difficult labor resulted in her death. Similarly, in Gen 38:30 the name זרח *zeraḥ,* "Zerah" (as if from זרח, "sunrise"; cf. 2 Kgs 3:22) is explained by a semantic play on שני *šānî,* "scarlet thread" (cf. also 2 Sam 12:24–25; Gen 22:14; 26:21; 1 Sam 23:24–28). As these examples show, this semantic play can be based on allusions that seem obscure and remote (at least to our way of thinking), as is also occasionally the case in parasonancy. This interpretation has been cogently argued by

Eissfeldt in two articles (*SSAW* 110 [1965] 23–28; *Syria* 43 [1966] 39–47) in which he reversed the view he had espoused in *The Old Testament,* 479–80, regarding the lack of historical connection between the story of Ruth and the family line of David. In the later articles Eissfeldt argues (see "Wahrheit," 27–28) that tradition gave the names of Boaz, Ruth, and Obed to the author of Ruth as historical celebrities, as ancestors of David, and this fact explains the unevennesses that led him and others to emend v 17. Since Obed was known to the narrator as the name of the son of Ruth, he could make no wordplay based on parasonancy between "Obed" and "Naomi" (the usual emendation assumes such a play; see Eissfeldt, *The Old Testament,* 479; id., "Wahrheit," 26). But, more to the point, in the context here the emphasis is on "son," not on "Naomi" (*Syria* 43 [1966] 47; contra Parker, "Birth Announcement," 138 n. 13). Hence, the narrator intends a *semantic* wordplay: the "son born to Naomi" receives the name "Obed/server," understood here in the sense of "provider, guardian" (cf. Mal 3:17), since he will show the kindness incumbent on a son for his grandmother. The context for this play on meaning is set by the relationship between Naomi and this "son" already stated with unmistakable clarity in vv 14–15. The women congratulate Naomi because Yahweh has given her a "redeemer," which carries approximately the same meaning here as Obed, i.e., one who "will restore her life and provide for her in her old age" (v 15). Since the context has already made this clear, the play on meaning between "A son has been born to Naomi" and the name Obed, otherwise somewhat strained and remote, is feasible enough. The fact that "Obed" is in all probability a hypocoristic or diminutive for a theophoric name (cf. עבדיה/עבדיהו, a name borne by twelve different men in the OT) does not speak against this view (contra Witzenwrath, 282 n. 143; cf. Rudolph, 70), for such a semantic play totally ignores scientific etymology.

When this is seen and when the literary character and meaning of the scene are taken into account, the other problems of content usually alleged against the passage as it stands can be given a coherent interpretation that fits the context. The fact that it is the women-neighbors who name the child is "literally appropriate" (so Hubbard, *VT* 38 [1988] 294). As the analysis of the structure of the scene has revealed (see *Form/Structure/Setting*), the author has used this "female chorus" already in vv 14–15 as the fitting vehicle to express with a sense of wonder and joy what the birth of this child means in restoring Naomi to life and fullness. Hence, in v 17 he has them continue that same theme in their joyful exclamation "A son has been born to Naomi!" Here our narrator uses his "poetic license." He does not expect us to take him literally and to believe that it was these neighbor-women who actually formally named the child. What he means by his blatant statement "they [fem pl] named him," so utterly in conflict with the fact known to all that the parents (usually the mother) named the child, is that these women "named" him by providing the explanation for his name with their glad cry "A son is born to Naomi." An analogous situation is provided by the naming of Perez in Gen 38:27–29. There, as the infant is born, the midwife exclaims, "What a breach you have made!" (v 27c), and the narrator then relates that the child was named Perez, "breach" (v 27d). If it had been literally appropriate in this setting, the narrator could just as well have said, "The midwife gave him a name, saying 'What a breach you have made,'" for it is this statement that provides the explanation for the name.

Further illumination that buttresses this understanding has been provided by Hubbard (*VT* 38 [1988] 295–99) and Parker ("Birth Announcement," 133–49), who have independently drawn attention to the significance for the Ruth passage of the evidence for a "birth announcement formula" in the OT (Jer 20:15; Isa 9:5; Hubbard; Parker) and in the *Aqht* text from Ugarit (*KTU* 1.17, II.14–15; Parker). Parker carefully examines the language of these four texts (including the Ruth passage, "Birth Announcement," 139; cf. R. Hubbard, *VT* 38 [1988] 295) and concludes that they

> come from two different languages and literatures; from poetry and prose; from lament, poetic narrative, prophetic proclamation and prose narrative. Yet all share several formal features: a third masculine singular passive form of the verb *yld,* the noun *bn* as subject, and a prepositional phrase consisting of the preposition *l* with a following pronominal suffix or personal name. It is reasonable to conclude that this is a traditional fixed saying, used to convey news of a birth.

The form of the saying in Ruth is the same as in the other passages except for the substitution of a personal name for the pronominal suffix following the preposition ל (Parker, "Birth Announcement," 139).

> But this corresponds exactly to the situation in which it is uttered. The announcement is addressed to the larger community outside the family, which is invited, not to claim the child for itself, as in the Isaiah passage, but to appreciate what this means for Naomi. Hence, Naomi, as the primary beneficiary of the birth, is cited as the one to whom the child is born.

Doubtless, R. Hubbard (*VT* 38 [1988] 296) is correct in contending that the saying in its original setting was made to the father who waits nearby to hear the news. He would have received the news as more than a simple statement of fact. It was an exclamation of joy, intended to gladden and delight (cf. esp. Jer 20:15 and the context of the *Aqht* passage; see Parker, "Birth Announcement," 144–45; R. Hubbard, *VT* 38 [1988] 298). Given this background and setting for the saying, its use is then most appropriate to the scene in Ruth (R. Hubbard, *VT* 38 [1988] 298–99). Exercising his literary license, our author underscores the happy significance of this child for Naomi—she who was childless now has a son—by applying to her the very language of the joyous birth announcement that commonly comes to the waiting father.

The recognition noted above (see Bush, "Ruth 4:17," 7) that the idiom קרא שׁם ל- is the generic name-giving formula (contra Sasson, 165) means that it is to be translated "gave him a name." It cannot, then, be translated "established his reputation" (contra Sasson, 158, 233), a meaning apparently based on Sasson's interpretation of the expression קרא שׁם (103, 156), an expression significantly different syntactically (see Bush, "Ruth 4:17," 11 n. 16). This removes the grounds for Sasson's attempt (233–35) to see here vestigial motifs ". . . strongly reminiscent of divine acts and utterances used in the ancient Near East as metaphors for the legitimacy of royal figures," indicating that the book of Ruth was used as "a vehicle to support David's claim to the throne of Saul" (Sasson, 240).

Explanation

As we noted in the concluding remarks to the *Explanation* section of the last scene, Boaz has successfully overcome the major complication of the story—the existence of Mr. "So-and-So," the redeemer with prior rights. He has accomplished this by acquiring from him, through his skillful negotiations before the legal assembly of Bethlehem, the right both to redeem Elimelech's land and to marry Mahlon's widow and raise an heir to inherit that patrimony (4:9–10). With this hurdle cleared away—and indeed with the sound of the legal assembly's blessing of the astute and selfless Boaz still ringing in our ears—our author turns immediately to a brief but powerful scene that provides a full resolution of the death and emptiness with which his tale commenced.

He begins with a succinct summary that states in five short clauses (see *Form/Structure/Setting*) the fulfillment of the expectations, plans, and promises set forth in the whole series of scenes from 2:1, where he first suggestively introduced Boaz in a digression, to 4:11–12, where the legal assembly pronounced their blessings upon him. In Boaz's marriage to Ruth, Naomi's daring plan to secure home and husband for Ruth (3:1–4) has come to fruition, and Boaz's private pledge to Ruth on the threshing floor (3:11) and his public proclamation to the legal assembly in the city gate (4:10) are fulfilled. In the statement that it was Yahweh who enabled Ruth to conceive and that she bore a son, we find a dramatic fulfillment of Boaz's petition to Yahweh on behalf of Ruth in 2:11–12, for in the realization of home, husband, and child is surely to be seen both her "full recompense" (v 12) and her repayment for the good deed of leaving father, mother, and homeland for Naomi (v 11). Indeed, the young woman who "reversed sexual allegiance" and "committed herself to the life of an old woman rather than the search for a husband . . . in a world where life depends upon men" (Trible, 173; cf. *Explanation* to 1:7–19a) has now seen restored all that she gave up—and more, for the instant fertility that Yahweh provides stands in stark contrast to the ten years of barrenness in Moab. In this same terse statement the conception granted by Yahweh marks the immediate fulfillment of the prayer of the legal assembly for fruitfulness for Boaz's bride, and the birth of the child constitutes the beginning of the fulfillment of their wish for an abundance of descendants for Boaz (4:11b–12).

All of this, however true, is left wholly unformulated by our narrator, for he alludes to such fulfillment in no way whatsoever. It is not, indeed, that "Events move quickly" (Trible, 193). The actual events of v 13 tell of a marriage, its consummation, the intervention of Yahweh to transform Ruth's former barrenness into instant fertility, and the birth of the child, all of which must have taken nearly a year—a period of time probably considerably longer than that required for the whole of the preceding narrative. Rather, it is the narration itself that moves both rapidly and without a word to spare. In fact, given the brevity and terseness of his statement, it is almost as if our author presents these events with a sense of "Of course, what would you expect?" It is not the events themselves to which he wishes to draw our attention but their meaning and significance for the life of Naomi. In keeping with the pattern set in all the preceding scenes, he depicts this through speech—once again that of the women of Bethlehem, who comprise a sort of "female chorus" (Porten, *GCA* 7 [1978] 30, 47), whose speech, vv 14–15, is devoted almost exclusively to describing the significance of the birth of this child for Naomi. They describe the child's meaning for her first of all by designating him her "redeemer." Here they use the term in the same sense with which it has been used throughout the rest of the book (except for the technical force it carried during the legal negotiations at the gate in 4:1–12), namely, the one responsible to deliver a relative from evil (see *Comment* on 2:20). And we are not left to wonder about the evil from which Naomi needs deliverance, for the women go on, v 15, to describe the redeemer in terms that lack nothing in clarity. He is to be to her both the "one who restores her life" and the "support and stay of her old age." The resolution is perfect. Our story has come full circle. Death and emptiness (1:3–5, 21) have given way to life and fullness, and the vehicle our author uses to describe this transformation is appropriate in every way. The women of Bethlehem were those whose delighted cry of recognition triggered Naomi's bitter lament, "Full was I when I went away but empty has Yahweh *brought me back*" (1:19). Now they are the ones who describe in jubilant chorus the complete reversal of her tragic state and encapsulate her restoration in their happy description of the child as the "one who *brings back* life" (see *Comment* on v 15).

This is in striking contrast to the male personnel and concerns that occupied center stage in the previous scene, for this scene is completely dominated by women and by their concerns. Yahweh is celebrated by the female chorus not because he has not left the line of Elimelech without a descendant but because he has not left Naomi without a redeemer to care for her in her need. And the female chorus sees the meaning of this child not in his identity as the heir of Elimelech and all his property but in his role as the restorer of Naomi to life who will support her in her old age. They do not celebrate his identity by crying "A son has been born to Elimelech" but by declaring "A son has been born to Naomi" (v 17).

Though the significance of the events of v 13, expressed in the speech of this female chorus in vv 14–15, centers its attention upon Naomi's restoration to life and fullness, Ruth and the child are not passed by in silence. Their reference to Ruth is both touching and powerfully expressive. The female chorus exudes a happy confidence that the child will be to Naomi all that they affirm. Is such a confidence grounded in wishful thinking, since children do not always fulfill the hopes that are cherished for them? No, for the women ground their prediction in past realities. "He shall become the one who gives you new life and provides for your old age," they say, "because your daughter-in-law who loves you has borne him—she who is more to you than seven sons!" The love they speak of has been demonstrated by Ruth both in words (1:16–17) and in the deeds that matched them (2:11). So there is no doubt in the minds of these women that the child of Ruth will also exhibit such character and so live up to their confident expectation of him. Rudolph (70) does not go too far when he states that Ruth's "own love for Naomi will be bequeathed to him." These words also enshrine "the story's ultimate evaluation of Ruth" (Campbell, 168) by stating that she has meant more to Naomi than seven sons—the ideal number in the OT conception (see *Comment*). Such an estimate is particularly telling in a context in which the acquisition finally of but one son (17b) is seen to mean so much. For the newborn himself they wish a reputation that outshines that of his father, in that his name will be renowned not only in Bethlehem and Ephrathah (v 11) but throughout all Israel (v 14c; cf. Rudolph, 70).

Having portrayed Naomi's return to life and fullness in such expressive speech, our author now depicts the same by painting for us a tender and moving scene (v 16). Naomi, the woman who "was left alone without her two *boys* [ילדים]" (1:5), now takes the *boy* (ילד), holds him to her bosom, and becomes the one who cares for him. In turn this scene also triggers a response, not this time from the women at large but from Naomi's neighbors. Exercising his poetic license (see *Comment*), our author once again sums up this child's relationship to Naomi by having these women name him, basing their name on the semantic wordplay between who the child is—expressed in their delighted cry, "A son has been born to Naomi"—and the meaning of the name Obed, "guardian, provider" (cf. *Comment*), i.e., one who will take care of her with all the solicitude incumbent upon a man for his grandmother (cf. Mal 3:17).

Only with the final clause appended to the name Obed does our author leave the women, the female chorus, and their joyous celebration of Naomi's return to life and fullness to describe the significance of this child in his own male world. This significance does not inhere in some valorous exploit or some quality of his person but in a surprise identification: "He is the father of Jesse, the father of David." This surprise is all the more delightful because the narrator had at the very beginning of his story already subtly hinted at some such connection by his identification of this family born to trouble as "Ephrathites from Bethlehem in Judah" (1:2), the very clan and city used to give David's patronymic when he is introduced to the narrative in 1 Sam 17:12 (see *Explanation* to 1:1–6). For the implications of this surprising identification, see the *Explanation* to the genealogy that follows.

Scene 3
Epilogue: A Judean Family Restored: The Line of David (4:18–22)

Bibliography

Curtis, E. L. *A Critical and Exegetical Commentary on the Books of Chronicles.* ICC. Edinburgh: T. & T. Clark, 1910. **Flanagan, J. W.** "Chiefs in Israel." *JSOT* 20 (1981) 47–73. **Leggett, D.** *The Levirate and Goel Institutions in the Old Testament.* Cherry Hill, NJ: Mack, 1974. **Porten, B.** "The Scroll of Ruth: A Rhetorical Study." *GCA* 7 (1978) 23–49. **Wilson, R.** *Genealogy and History in the Biblical World.* New Haven: Yale UP, 1977.

Translation

[18]*Now these are the descendants*[a] *of Perez: Perez fathered Hezron;* [19]*Hezron, Ram;*[a] *Ram, Amminadab;* [20]*Amminadab, Nahshon; Nahshon, Salmon;*[a] [21]*Salmon, Boaz; Boaz, Obed;* [22]*Obed, Jesse; and Jesse, David.*

Notes

18.a. Lit. "generations."
19.a. Lit. "Hezron fathered Ram" and so through v 22.
20.a. The Heb. reads שלמה here, but in the clause immediately following שלמון. See *Comment.*

Form/Structure/Setting

For the characteristics of form and content that determine the division into three "scenes," see the discussion of the structure of the whole chapter given above for the opening scene. The very form of this third section of the fourth act, a genealogy, unmistakably sets it apart. It is linked to the preceding by the personal name Perez and by the skillful use of the numeral seven, as noted by Porten (*GCA* 7 [1978] 48):

> Ruth is said to be better to Naomi than "seven" sons (4:15). The descendant of Perez who married Ruth appeared in the *seventh* generation (4:21). The young widow Ruth, worth more to the old widow Naomi than seven sons, married the seventh generation Boaz. The elders had blessed Boaz that his house be like the house of Perez (4:12). The reader is now shown what the house of Perez meant—seven generations to Boaz (4:18–21) and ten to David.

The formula . . . ואלה תולדות, "Now these are the 'generations' of . . . ," is the standard formula in the Pentateuch for introducing a descending genealogy (cf., e.g., Gen 6:9; 10:1; 11:1; Num 3:1). This expression is usually regarded as characteristic of the putative priestly source of the Pentateuch (cf., e.g., Campbell, 170; Joüon, 96; for further bibliography, see Leggett, *The Levirate,* 265 n. 44). Since the question of the relationship of this genealogy to that in 1 Chron 2 is important (as Campbell notes, 170), it is noteworthy that the author of 1 Chronicles uses quite different formulae, most commonly either "The sons of X were PN_1, PN_2, . . ." (e.g., 1 Chron 1:5, 6) or "These are the sons of X, PN_1, PN_2, . . ." (e.g., 1 Chron 2:1; 3:1).

For a detailed discussion, relating to such matters as whether the genealogy is original or a later addition, or whether it contradicts the rest of the story in making Obed a son of Boaz instead of Mahlon, see the section *Unity* in the *Introduction.*

Comment

18 חֶצְרוֹן, "Hezron." The LXX, OL, and Vg show "Hezrom" rather than "Hezron," followed by the NT in Matt 1:3; Luke 3:33. Since, however, two other Hebrew personal names know variant endings in *-n* and *-m* (*Gershōn/m* and *Zēytān/m*), it is possible that these are genuine variant forms of the one name (Campbell, 170).

19 רָם, "Ram." The versions unanimously fail to support the reading Ram here, with the majority of LXX MSS, Vg, and Syr reading Aram (so also Matt 1:3–4). In the parallel passage in 1 Chron 2:9–10, MT agrees with Ruth, but the versions diverge widely, with the majority of the LXX MSS giving both a Ram and an Aram as sons of Hezron but making Aram the father of Amminadab. Given the divergence in the LXX tradition, however, and the persistence in the other versions of the name Ram in 1 Chron 2:9, notably in Syr (for a full discussion see Campbell, 171), there seems insufficient warrant for emending MT Ram to Aram with *BHS*. Further, since the OT elsewhere knows no other genealogy of the line of Judah that goes back to a Ram son of Hezron (see Curtis, *Chronicles*, 87), the appearance of the name Ram in the MT of both Ruth and 1 Chron 9 strongly suggests an interdependence of these two genealogies (cf. also Sasson, 187–88).

עַמִּינָדָב, "Amminadab." The Amminadab who fathers Nahshon here is usually identified with the father of Elisheba, the wife of Aaron, who is identified as the sister of Nahshon (Exod 6:23).

20 נַחְשׁוֹן, "Nahshon." The identification of Amminadab with the father-in-law of Aaron is strengthened by the appearance of Nahshon son of Amminadab as the leader of the tribe of Judah in the wilderness era (Num 2:3; 7:12, 17; 10:14) and as one of those who assisted Moses with the census (Num 1:7).

20–21 שַׂלְמוֹן/שַׂלְמָה. The difficulty of the variant forms of this name in Ruth, *Śalmāh* in v 20 and *Śalmôn* in v 21, is compounded by the further variant form *Śalmaʾ* consistently used in 1 Chron 2:10–11. Sasson's view (189–90), that all three forms are variants of the same name with different hypocoristic suffixes attached, is plausible. However, the phenomenon may simply result from the fluidity that is characteristic of genealogies, particularly in regard to the names in the middle of the list, a characteristic known as "telescoping." See the comments in the section *Unity* in the *Introduction*.

Explanation

This third "scene" of the fourth act provides an epilogue to the story as a whole. As such, it balances chiastically the prologue in 1:1–6 (see the discourse structure of the book set forth in the *Introduction*), for it documents implicitly ten generations of birth in Israel parallel to the ten years of death in Moab (1:1–6; see Porten, *GCA* 7 [1978] 23–24, 48). This is also signaled by the subtle allusion to the origins of David mentioned in the prologue in the identification of the male members of this family as "Ephrathites from Bethlehem in Judah" (1:2; cf. 1 Sam 17:12; *Explanation* to 1:1–6). The subtle suggestion created by the foregrounding of such origin in the prologue is now happily concluded by this explicit citing of the family line of David.

Indeed, this genealogy provides a striking and fitting epilogue to the resolution of the story (vv 13–17) rather than a contradictory and clumsy secondary appendage as it is often interpreted (see discussion in the section *Unity* in the *Introduction*). It does this in two ways. First, in the *Explanation* to the first scene of this act, 4:1–12, it was noted that the blessing of the legal assembly in vv 11–12 specifically devoted its attention to Boaz. The assembled elders and people importuned Yahweh to make Boaz flourish and to give him renown in Bethlehem through a family line whose size would be as great as that of the patriarch Israel and whose significance would match that of Perez, the premier clan of Judah. This genealogy, which leads from Perez through Boaz to David, bears eloquent testimony to the fulfillment of the blessing of the legal assembly of Bethlehem.

Second, the genealogy provides a fitting epilogue to the story because it adds a striking significance to the story's resolution—Naomi's return to life and fullness. As recent studies of the use of genealogy in kinship-based societies have documented (see, e.g., Flanagan, *JSOT* 20 [1981] 58–65), linear genealogies normally function to legitimate the political, juridical, or religious role of the last person named by connecting him with the stream of individuals who stand above him, leading finally and most importantly to the lineage founder. However, the implications both of the parallelism of prologue and epilogue just elucidated and of the resolution so powerfully and poignantly portrayed in the preceding scene (4:13–17) mean that our storyteller stands that function on its head, so to speak. As used here, the genealogy of the line of David is not being used to legitimate David by providing his kinship qualifications. Rather, our narrator intends to portray the significance of the resolution of his story, for that resolution has meaning not only by virtue of all that the *Explanation* to the last scene set forth but also by virtue of the fact that it provided an integral link in the family line that led two generations later to David.

Indeed, the loving commitment and obedience of Ruth the Moabitess to her mother-in-law, which transcended the claims of national origin and national religion (2:16); the sagacity of Boaz and his faithfulness to his family responsibilities to both Ruth and Naomi, which transcended the claims of self-interest; the concern and care of Naomi for the welfare of her daughter-in-law, which prompted the risky scheme on the threshing floor; and Yahweh's gracious provision of fruitfulness for field and womb—all have afforded home and husband for Ruth, the restoration of life and fullness for Naomi, and, now we learn, inestimable benefit for all Israel. For the son that has resulted from such faithfulness on the part of man and God was to be the grandfather of the great King David *and*—as the genealogy at the beginning of Matthew (1:5–6) notes—the distant ancestor of great David's greater Son. In this way the original point of the narrative is extended beyond showing God's providence and care in the life of one family. It now concerns the life of the entire nation, for in the son born to Naomi the history of God's rule through David has begun. By concluding with this "coda" (see for this term the discussion of Berlin, *Poetics,* 107–10, esp. 110), the book is brought into relationship with the Bible's main theme of redemptive history (cf. Childs, *Introduction,* 566).

Esther

Main Bibliography

COMMENTARIES
(referred to in text by authors' names only)

Anderson, B. W. *The Book of Esther: Introduction and Exegesis.* IB 3. New York: Abingdon, 1954. 820–74. **Baldwin, J. G.** *Esther: An Introduction and Commentary.* Downers Grove, IL: InterVarsity, 1984. **Bardtke, H.** *Das Buch Esther.* KAT 17/5. Gütersloh: Mohn, 1963. **Barucq, A.** *Judith Esther.* La Sainte Bible. 2nd ed. Paris: Cerf, 1959. **Bettan, I.** *The Five Scrolls: A Commentary on the Song of Songs, Ruth, Lamentations, Ecclesiastes, Esther.* Cincinnati: Union of American Hebrew Congregations, 1940. **Brockington, L. H.** *Ezra, Nehemiah and Esther.* CB. London: Nelson, 1969. **Clines, D. J. A.** *Ezra, Nehemiah, Esther.* NCBC. Grand Rapids, MI: Eerdmans, 1984. **Dommershausen, W.** *Ester.* Die neue Echter Bible. Würzburg: Echter, 1980. **Fox, M. V.** *Character and Ideology in the Book of Esther.* Columbia, SC: University of South Carolina, 1991. **Gerleman, G.** *Esther.* BKAT 21. Neukirchen: Neukirchener, 1982. **Gordis, R.** *Megillat Esther.* New York: Ktav, 1974. **Haller, M.** *Die Fünf Megilloth.* HAT 18. Tübingen: Mohr, 1940. **Keil, C. F.** *The Books of Ezra, Nehemiah, and Esther.* Biblical Commentary on the Old Testament. Tr. S. Taylor. Repr. Grand Rapids, MI: Eerdmans, 1950. **Meinhold, A.** *Das Buch Esther.* ZBAT 13. Zurich: Theologischer, 1983. **Moore, C. A.** *Esther.* AB 7B. Garden City, NY: Doubleday, 1971. **Paton, L. B.** *The Book of Esther.* ICC. Edinburgh: T. & T. Clark, 1908. **Re'emi, S. P.** *The Faithfulness of God: A Commentary on the Book of Esther.* In Coggins, R. J. *Israel among the Nations.* ITC 34. Grand Rapids, MI: Eerdmans, 1985. 103–40. **Ringgren, H.** *Das Buch Esther.* ATD 16. Göttingen: Vandenhoeck & Ruprecht, 1967. **Roberts, M.** *Ezra, Nehemiah, Esther.* The Communicator's Commentary. Dallas: Word, 1993. **Streane, A. W.** *The Book of Esther.* Cambridge Bible for Schools and Colleges. Cambridge: Cambridge UP, 1907. **Würthwein, E.** *Die Fünf Megilloth.* HAT 18, 2nd ed. Tübingen: Mohr/Siebeck, 1969.

OTHER STUDIES

Albright, W. "The Lachish Cosmetic Burner and Esther 2:12." In *A Light unto My Path.* FS J. M. Myers, ed. H. Bream, R. Heim, and C. Moore. Philadelphia: 1974. 25–32 (= Moore, *Studies,* 361–68). **Anderson, B. W.** "The Place of the Book of Esther in the Christian Bible." *JR* 30 (1950) 32–43. **Bardtke, H.** "Neuere Arbeiten zum Estherbuch." *EOL* 19 (1965–66) 519–49. **Ben-Chorin, S.** *Kritik des Esterbuches: Eine theologische Streitschrift.* Jerusalem, 1938. **Berg, S.** *The Book of Esther: Motifs, Themes and Structure.* SBLDS 44. Missoula, MT: Scholars, 1979. **Bergey, R. L.** "The Book of Esther—Its Place in the Linguistic Milieu of Post-exilic Biblical Hebrew Prose: A Study in Late Biblical Hebrew." Diss., Dropsie College, 1983. ———. "Late Linguistic Features in Esther." *JQR* 75 (1984) 66–78. ———. "Post-exilic Hebrew Linguistic Developments in Esther: A Diachronic Approach." *JETS* 31 (1988) 161–68. **Bickerman, E. J.** *Four Strange Books of the Bible.* New York: Schocken, 1967. **Botterweck, G. J.** "Die Gattung des Buches Esther im Spektrum neuerer Publikationen." *BibLeb* 5 (1964) 274–92. **Cazelles, H.** "Note sur la composition du rouleau d'Esther." In *Lex tua veritas.* FS H. Junker, ed. H. Gross and F. Mussner. Trier: Paulinus, 1961. 17–29 (= Moore, *Studies,* 424–36). **Clines, D. J. A.** *The Esther Scroll: The Story of the Story.* JSOTSup 30. Sheffield: JSOT, 1984. ———. "In Quest of the Historical Mordecai." *VT* 41 (1991) 130–36. **Cohen, A. D.** "'Hu Ha-goral': The Religious Significance of Esther." *Judaism* 23 (1974) 87–94. **Condamin, A.** "Notes critiques sur le texte biblique: II. La disgrace d'Aman (Esth. VII, 8)." *RB* 7 (1898) 253–61. **Cook, H. J.** "The A-text of the Greek Versions of the Book of Esther." *ZAW* 81 (1969) 369–76. **Craig, K.** *Reading Esther: A Case for the Literary Carnivalesque.* Louisville:

Westminster/John Knox, 1995. **Darr, K. P.** "More than Just a Pretty Face: Critical, Rabbinical, and Feminist Perspectives on Esther." In *Far More Precious Than Jewels: Perspectives on Biblical Women.* Louisville: Westminster/John Knox, 1991. 164–202. **Daube, D.** "The Last Chapter of Esther." *JQR* 37 (1946–47) 139–47. **Dommershausen, W.** *Die Estherrolle: Stil und Ziel einer alttestamentlicher Schrift.* SBM 6. Stuttgart: Katholisches Bibelwerk, 1968. **Dorothy, C. V.** "The Books of Esther: Structure, Genre, and Textual Integrity." Diss., Claremont, 1989. **Duchesne-Guillemin, J.** "Les noms des eunuques d'Assuérus." *Mus* 66 (1953) 105–8 (= Moore, *Studies,* 273–76). **Ehrlich, A. B.** *Randglossen zur hebräischen Bibel: Textkritisches, Sprachliches und Sachliches.* VII. 1914. Repr. Hildesheim: Georg Olms, 1968. 107–25. **Fox, M. V.** *The Redaction of the Books of Esther.* SBLMS 40. Atlanta: Scholars, 1991. ———. "The Structure of the Book of Esther." In *Isac Leo Seligmann Volume: Essays on the Bible and the Ancient World,* ed. A. Rofé and Y. Zakovitch. Jerusalem: Rubinstein, 1983. 3:291–303. **Gehman, H. S.** "Notes on the Persian Words in Esther." *JBL* 43 (1924) 321–28 (= Moore, *Studies,* 235–42). **Gerleman, G.** *Studien zu Esther: Stoff-Struktur-Stil-Sinn.* BS 48. Neukirchen: Neukirchener, 1966. **Goldman, S.** "Narrative and Ethical Ironies in Esther." *JSOT* 47 (1990) 15–31. **Gordis, R.** "Religion, Wisdom and History in the Book of Esther: A New Solution to an Ancient Crux." *JBL* 100 (1981) 359–88. ———. "Studies in the Esther Narrative." *JBL* 95 (1976) 43–58. **Hallo, W. W.** "The First Purim." *BA* 46 (1983) 19–26. **Harris, M.** "Purim: The Celebration of Dis-Order." *Judaism* 26 (1977) 161–70. **Haupt, P.** "Critical Notes on Esther." *AJSL* 24 (1907–8) 97–186 (= Moore, *Studies,* 1–79). **Heltzer, M.** "The Book of Esther." *BR* 8 (1992) 24–30, 41. **Herrmann, W.** *Esther im Streit der Meinungen.* Beiträge zur Erforschung des AT und des antiken Judentums. Frankfurt am Main: Peter Lang, 1986. **Herst, R.** "The Purim Connection." *USQR* 28 (1972–73) 139–45. **Horbury, W.** "The Name Mardochaeus in a Ptolemaic Inscription." *VT* 41 (1991) 220–26. **Hoschander, J.** *The Book of Esther in the Light of History.* Philadelphia: Dropsie College, 1923. **Humphreys, W. L.** "A Life-style for Diaspora: A Study of the Tales of Esther and Daniel." *JBL* 92 (1973) 211–23. ———. "The Story of Esther and Mordecai: An Early Jewish Novella." In *Saga, Legend, Tale, Novella, Fable: Narrative Forms in Old Testament Literature,* ed. G. Coats. JSOTSup 35. Sheffield: JSOT, 1985. 97–113. **Jacob, B.** "Das Buch Esther bei den LXX." *ZAW* 10 (1890) 241–98. **Jones, B. W.** "The So-called Appendix to the Book of Esther." *Semantics* 6 (1978) 36–43. **Klingbeil, G. A.** "רכש and Esther 8,10. 14: A Semantic Note." *ZAW* 107 (1995) 301–3. **Lebram, J. C. H.** "Purimfest und Estherbuch." *VT* 22 (1972) 208–22 (= Moore, *Studies,* 205–19). **Levenson, J. D.** "The Scroll of Esther in Ecumenical Perspective." *JES* 13 (1976) 440–51. **Lewy, J.** "The Feast of the 14th Day of Adar." *HUCA* 14 (1939) 127–51. **Limosín, R.** "Estudios filológicos-derásicos acerca de Ester y el Iran antiguo: II. El nombre Mŏrdekay." *Aula Orientalis* 1 (1983) 209–13. **Loader, J. A.** "Esther as a Novel with Different Levels of Meaning." *ZAW* 90 (1978) 417–21. **Loewenstamm, S. E.** "Esther 9:29–32: The Genesis of a Late Addition." *HUCA* 42 (1971) 117–24 (= Moore, *Studies,* 227–234). **McKane, W.** "A Note on Esther IX and 1 Samuel XV." *JTS* 12 (1961) 260–61. **Meinhold, A.** "Die Gattung der Josephgeschichte und des Estherbuches: Diasporanovelle I." *ZAW* 87 (1975) 306–24. ———. "Die Gattung der Josephgeschichte und des Estherbuches: Diasporanovelle II." *ZAW* 88 (1976) 72–93. ———. "Theologische Erwägungen zum Buch Esther." *ZAW* 34 (1978) 321–33. ———. "Zu Aufbau und Mitte des Estherbuches." *VT* 33 (1983) 435–45. **Millard, A. R.** "The Persian Names in Esther and the Reliability of the Hebrew Text." *JBL* 96 (1977) 481–88. **Moore, C. A.** *Daniel, Esther, and Jeremiah: The Additions.* AB 44. Garden City, NY: Doubleday, 1977. ———. "Esther Revisited: An Examination of Esther Studies over the Past Decade." In *Biblical and Related Studies Presented to Samuel Iwry,* ed. A. Kort and S. Morschauser. Winona Lake, IN: Eisenbrauns, 1985. 163–72. ———. *The Greek Text of Esther.* Ann Arbor, MI: University Microfilms, 1965. ———. "A Greek Witness to a Different Hebrew Text of Esther." *ZAW* 79 (1969) 351–58 (= Moore, *Studies,* 521–28). ———. *Studies in the Book of Esther.* New York: Ktav, 1982. **Morris, A. E.** "The Purpose of the Book of Esther." *ExpTim* 42 (1930–31) 124–28. **Murphy, R. E.** *Wisdom Literature: Job, Proverbs, Ruth, Canticles, Ecclesiastes, and Esther.* FOTL 13. Grand Rapids, MI: Eerdmans, 1981. **Radday, Y. T.** "Esther with Humour." In *On Humour and the Comic in the Hebrew Bible,* ed. Y. T. Radday and A. Brenner. Sheffield: Almond, 1990. 295–313. **Ringgren, H.** "Esther and Purim." *SEÅ* 20 (1956) 5–24 (= Moore, *Studies,* 185–204). **Rosenthal, L. A.** "Die Josephgeschichte mit den Buchern Ester und Daniel verglichen." *ZAW* 15 (1895) 278–84 (= Moore, *Studies,* 277–83). **Rudolph, W.** "Textkritisches zum Estherbuch." *VT* 4 (1954) 89–90. **Shea, W.** "Esther and History." *AUSS* 14 (1976) 227–46. **Stiehl, R.** "Das Buch Esther." *WZKM* 53 (1957) 4–22. **Striedl, H.** "Untersuchung zur Syntax und Stilistik des hebräischen Buches Esther." *ZAW* 14 (1937) 73–108. **Talmon, S.** "'Wisdom' in the Book of Esther." *VT* 13 (1963) 419–55. **Torrey, C. C.** "The Older Book of Esther." *HTR* 37 (1944) 1–40. **Tov, E.** "The 'Lucianic' Text of the Canonical and Apocryphal Sections of Esther: A Rewritten Biblical Book." *Textus* 10 (1982) 1–25. **Wehr, H.** "Das Tor des Königs in Buche Esther und verwandte Ausdrücke." *Der Islam* 39 (1964) 247–60. **White, S. A.** "Esther: A Feminine Model for Jewish Diaspora." In *Gender and Difference in Ancient Israel,* ed. P. Day. Minneapolis: Fortress, 1989. 161–77. **Wiebe, J. M.** "Esther 4:14: 'Will Relief and Deliverance Arise for the Jews from Another Place?'" *CBQ* 53 (1991) 409–15. **Wright, J. S.** "The Historicity of the Book of Esther." In *New Perspectives on the Old Testament,* ed. J. B. Payne. Waco, TX: Word, 1970. 37–47. **Yahuda, A. S.** "The Meaning of the Name Esther." *JRAS* (1946) 174–78. **Yamauchi, E.** "The Archaeological Background of Esther." *BSac* 137 (1980) 99–117. ———. "Mordecai, The Persepolis Tablets, and the Susa Excavations." *VT* 42 (1992) 272–75. **Zadok, R.** "Notes on Esther." *ZAW* 98 (1986) 105–10. ———. "On the Historical Background of the Book of Esther." *BN* 24 (1984) 18–23. **Zimmern, H.** "Zur Frage nach dem Ursprunge des Purimfestes." *ZAW* 11 (1891) 157–69 (= Moore, *Studies,* 147–59).

Introduction

Canonical Status and Position

Bibliography

Anderson, B. W. "The Place of the Book of Esther in the Christian Bible." *JR* 30 (1950) 32–43. **Bardtke, H.** "Neuere Arbeiten zum Estherbuch." *EOL* 19 (1965–66) 519–49. **Beckwith, R.** *The Old Testament Canon of the New Testament Church.* Grand Rapids, MI: Eerdmans, 1985. **Ben-Chorin, S.** *Kritik des Esterbuches: Eine theologische Streitschrift.* Jerusalem, 1938. **Bickerman, E. J.** "The Colophon of the Greek Book of Esther." *JBL* 63 (1944) 339–62. **Clines, D. J. A.** *The Esther Scroll: The Story of the Story.* JSOTSup 30. Sheffield: JSOT, 1984. **Eissfeldt, O.** *The Old Testament: An Introduction.* Tr. P. Ackroyd. New York: Harper and Row, 1965. **Finkel, J.** "The Author of the Genesis Apocryphon Knew the Book of Esther." (Heb.) In *Essays on the Dead Sea Scrolls.* FS E. L. Sukenik, ed. C. Rabin and Y. Yadin. Jerusalem: Hekhal Ha-sefer, 1961. **Jacob, B.** "Das Buch Esther bei dem LXX." *ZAW* 10 (1890) 241–98. **Leiman, S. Z.** *The Canonization of Hebrew Scripture: The Talmudic and Mishnaic Evidence.* Hamden, CT: Archon, 1976. **Lewis, J. P.** "What Do We Mean by Jabneh?" *JBR* 32 (1964) 125–34. **McDonald, L. M.** *The Formation of the Christian Biblical Canon.* Nashville: Abingdon, 1988. **Moore, C. A.** *Daniel, Esther, and Jeremiah: The Additions.* AB 44. Garden City, NY: Doubleday, 1977. ———. "Esther." *ABD* 2:633–43. **Neusner, J.** *The Talmud of the Land of Israel: Vol. 19. Megilla.* Chicago: University of Chicago Press, 1987. **Orlinsky, H. M.** *Essays in Biblical Culture and Bible Translation.* New York: Ktav, 1974. **Sanders, J. A.** "Canon, Hebrew Bible." *ABD* 1:837–52. ———. *From Sacred Story to Sacred Text.* Philadelphia: Fortress, 1987. **Sandmel, S.** *The Enjoyment of Scripture: The Law, the Prophets, and the Writings.* New York: Oxford UP, 1972.

CANONICAL STATUS

The determination of the date when the canonicity of the book of Esther was finally fixed is most difficult, for both the evidence and its interpretation are matters of considerable uncertainty and debate. First, as might be expected, evidence prior to the second century A.D. comes from Jewish sources, the earliest being that from the Essene community at Qumran (ca. 150 B.C. to A.D. 70) and Josephus (ca. A.D. 90). Unfortunately, however, the significance of this evidence is difficult to assess. As far as the first is concerned, the evidence suffers from the ambiguity of silence, for Esther is the only OT book not found among the texts used by the Essenes. Though this may be the result of chance or the vagaries of manuscript preservation, this seems most improbable. (Beckwith, *Canon,* 291, notes the contrast with the scrolls from the Cairo Genizah, where fragments from Esther are far more numerous than those of any other book outside the Pentateuch.) It seems far more likely that Esther was not found at Qumran because the community did not include Purim in its liturgical calendar. Beckwith (*Canon,* 291–94) argues plausibly that 14 Adar, one of the dates established by the book of Esther for the celebration of Purim, conflicted with the liturgical calendar in use at Qumran, in which that date was a sabbath. If that is so, Esther may have been included in the general Jewish canon of the era but either repudiated or ignored by the Qumran sect. Consequently, it is not clear what the absence of Esther at Qumran implies about its status in the canon of the Qumran community or about its status in other Jewish circles (cf. Sanders, *ABD* 1:842). (For the view of Finkel, "Author," that the Qumran community knew the book of Esther, see Bardtke, *EOL* 19 [1965–66] 523–24.)

It is likewise unclear what the testimony of Josephus implies about the canonicity of Esther. In *Against Apion* 1.7–8, he gives the number of the books of the Jewish canon as twenty-two but, unfortunately, does not name them. Concerning the post-Mosaic books, he writes, "From the death of Moses until Artaxerxes who succeeded Xerxes as king of Persia, the prophets . . . wrote the history . . . in thirteen books. The remaining four books contain hymns to God and precepts for life." No consensus exists among scholars regarding the identity of Josephus' thirteen books. Some scholars (e.g., Beckwith, *Canon,* 79–80; Leiman, *Canonization,* 153 n. 160; Moore, xxiii) argue that Esther must certainly have been included among them. This is claimed on the grounds that in his enumeration he would have adopted the Jewish practice attested much later by Origen, Epiphanius, and Jerome (cf. Beckwith, *Canon,* 185–87, 188–90, 119–21), numbering Ruth with Judges and Lamentations with Jeremiah (Beckwith, *Canon,* 253; Leiman, *Canonization,* 32, 152 n. 154), and on the grounds that he mentions Artaxerxes whom he elsewhere identified with the Persian king in the book of Esther. Others, however, exclude Esther (e.g., Orlinsky, *Essays,* 272–72).

The earliest clear evidence for the book is that of *Midr. Esth. Rab.* 2.7, which includes a short quotation in Greek from Aquila's translation, made ca. A.D. 128–29, demonstrating that Esther was included in the Hebrew text used by him (Beckwith, *Canon,* 277). Finally, the Talmud bears witness that Esther was accepted as scripture by the Jews in the first two centuries A.D. Thus, *b. B. Bat.* 14b quotes a *baraita* (i.e., a quote from the Tannaim, the rabbinic scholars who lived in the first two centuries A.D.) on the order of books of the Prophets and the Writings that includes Esther (Beckwith, *Canon,* 122; Eissfeldt, *Introduction,* 563); the Mishnah devotes a whole tractate (Megilla) to regulations for the proper reading of the book at the festival of Purim; and other tannaitic literature cites the book as authoritative scripture (cf. Beckwith, *Canon,* 328 n. 50).

Besides this positive evidence, however, there is clear evidence that the book of Esther was among the five books whose status as scripture was questioned in various rabbinic circles (the other four books being Ezekiel, Proverbs, Ecclesiastes, and Song of Songs). First, the secularity of the book of Esther (one of the two main grounds on the basis of which the rabbis disputed the scriptural status of the five books; cf. Beckwith, *Canon,* 283–87) may have created a difficulty from the earliest times. The Greek translation of the Septuagint (probably made either ca. 114 B.C., see Jacob, *ZAW* 10 [1890] 278–79; or ca. 78–77 B.C., see Bickerman, *JBL* 63 [1944] 346–47) added to the narrative substantive religious content and motivations in the noncanonical Additions to the Hebrew version, particularly Additions A, C, and F, and overt references to God and to religious practices in the canonical sections (for examples, see Moore, *Additions,* 158; Clines, *Esther Scroll,* 171). This strongly suggests that the secularity of the book was felt to be a difficulty that needed to be corrected. Whatever the purpose of these changes, this "transformation of its canonical shape had the effect of affirming its canonical status" (Clines, *Esther Scroll,* 174). Further evidence is the statement in *y. Meg.* 1.5 that, when Mordecai and Esther wrote to the Jews to establish the festival of Purim, there was resistance on the grounds that (1) its celebration would bring upon them the same troubles that Haman did (see Neusner, *Talmud of the Land of Israel,* 32, II.A), and (2) nothing new should be added to the Mosaic Law (see Neusner, III.A, B; cf. Beckwith, *Canon,* 289). Though attributed to rabbis from the third and fourth centuries A.D., the statement indicates their belief that questions had been raised about the book from the earliest times. However that may be, several statements in the Babylonian Talmud make it clear that the canonical status of the book was being challenged at least as early as the second century A.D. The earliest such challenge appears to be the reference in *b. Meg.* 7a to a rabbinical debate on the canonicity of Esther dating to the beginning of the second century, occasioned by the claim that Purim was an addition to the festivals prescribed in the Pentateuch (noted by Beckwith, *Canon,* 289, 315, 327 n. 45). Two later texts, dating to the middle of the second century A.D., also reported in *b. Meg.* 7a (for the text of both, see Leiman, *Canonization,* 106; cf. also Beckwith, *Canon,* 279), record the statements of certain rabbis questioning the canonical status of Esther (on the meaning of the highly unusual term involved, "to make the hands unclean" = "to be canonical," see Leiman, *Canonization,* 102–20; and esp. Beckwith, *Canon,* 278–81). In the first text it is stated that ". . . [all agreed that] Ruth, Song of Songs, and Esther make the hands unclean," the necessity for stating which clearly indicates that questions had already been raised. In the second the explicit statement is made that Esther "does not make the hands unclean." The discussion seems to have dragged on at least until the end of the third century, from which period comes an opinion that the scroll of Esther did not need a scroll mantle, implying that it did not make the hands unclean, i.e., was not canonical (*b. Sanh.* 100a; see Leiman, *Canonization;* Beckwith, *Canon,* 290).

As far as Christian sources are concerned, there is little clear evidence for the canonicity of Esther prior to the end of the second century. Beckwith (*Canon,* 295–97) surveys the evidence prior to this and concludes that it is likely, though not certain, that the book was always regarded as canonical in the Western Church (cf. also Moore, xxv–xxviii). The situation was much different in the East, however, where the book was frequently denied canonical status. Thus, in the second half of the second century, Melito, Bishop of Sardis (whose sources, though from Palestine, were very likely Christian, rather than Jewish; so Beckwith, *Canon,* 183–85), omits Esther from his list of the books of the canon. Among the numerous Eastern Fathers who rejected Esther were Athanasius, Gregory of Nazianzus, and Theodore of Mopsuestia, all dating to the fourth century (cf. Beckwith, *Canon,* 297; Moore, xxv–xxviii). Its canonicity was finally affirmed by the Church Councils of Hippo (A.D. 393) and Carthage (A.D. 397).

The confusion of this evidence for the canonicity of Esther is further compounded by the present uncertainty as to the date when the Jewish canon became fixed. Prior to the last few decades of the present century, there was a widespread consensus regarding this question. The contents of the Pentateuch were considered to have been fixed by ca. 400 B.C., that of the Prophets by ca. 200 B.C., and it was generally concluded that the contents of the Writings (or Hagiographa) remained open until the so-called Council of Jamnia (Jabneh) ca. A.D. 90, at which it was closed (for a representative discussion, see Eissfeldt, *Introduction,* 564–68). With the studies of Lewis and Leiman (cf. also the succinct discussion of Beckwith, *Canon,* 276–77), it is now recognized that the gathering of rabbinic scholars at Jabneh was not an authoritative council (after the analogy of later church councils), nor is there any record of discussion of the canonicity of any books except Song of Songs and Ecclesiastes (and their canonicity continued to be debated in the succeeding centuries). Further, with the discovery and study of the Qumran literature and the other texts from the area of the Dead Sea, the debate concerning the nature of the process of canonization and the dates at which the limits of the canon became fixed has been reopened (cf. Sanders, *ABD* 1:839–43). On the one hand, it is claimed that the canon was closed as much as two centuries earlier than the first century A.D. (Beckwith, *Canon;* Leiman, *Canonization*), and, therefore, the discussion in the rabbinic sources regards the possible exclusion of books that have already been canonized (cf. for Esther, Beckwith, *Canon,* 288–91). On the other hand, it is claimed that socio-political (not conciliar or official) factors brought about the closure of the canon during the first two centuries A.D. (e.g., McDonald, *Formation,* 60–66; Sanders, *Sacred Story,* 11–13), so the rabbinic discussion of the five disputed books records a genuine debate about their canonicity.

The preponderence of the evidence, in my opinion, is in favor of the former understanding, in which case Esther would have achieved canonicity sometime in the second century B.C. Beckwith (*Canon,* 312) postulates that this occurred when Judas Maccabeus made a collection of the Scriptures after the Antiochene persecution (reported in 2 Macc 2:14; cf. also Leiman, *Canonization,* 201 n. 634). If this is the case, the disputes dealt with the exclusion of a book already canonical. In favor of this view is the fact that the rabbinical opinions questioning the books are clearly a minority view and are quoted in order to be refuted. On the other hand, if the second interpretation of the evidence is the correct one (and the evidence for the first view is far from compelling), then Esther did not achieve full canonicity in Judaism until the end of the rabbinical debates in the third century A.D., and in Christianity in general not until a century or more later.

The canonicity of the book of Esther has rarely been questioned in the Jewish community after the rabbinical debates of the first four centuries A.D. On the contrary, it became one of the most important books of the Jewish canon outside the Pentateuch, since the festival of Purim, which it established and at which it is regularly read, became one of the most important festivals of the Jewish liturgical year (see the discussion of Purim in *Theology* below).

The opposite has been the case, however, in the Christian world. Not only did none of the Church Fathers write a commentary on the book, but references to it in their writings are rare (for representative citations, see Bardtke, *EOL* 19 [1965–66] 258–60). Further, in those references that do occur, it is the religiously oriented Additions of the Septuagint that are given precedence throughout and that set the tone by which other statements in the book are given religious meaning (cf.

Bardtke, *EOL* 19 [1965–66] 260). Not until the early Middle Ages was a commentary devoted to it: that of Rhabanus Maurus, Archbishop of Mainz in the ninth century. Further, even though it has been officially recognized as part of the Christian canon since the middle of the first millennium A.D., it has frequently been given a very negative evaluation in the Christian world, and its canonical status and worth have been seriously questioned. The failure of the book to mention God or allude to his presence in the world except in the most veiled and indirect manner necessarily raises questions about its theological meaning. Most of this negative evaluation, however, springs from a misreading of the intents and purposes of the book as a whole, as well as certain passages in it (see the discussion of Purim in the *Theology* below).

Canonical Position

With the invention of printing in the modern era, the book of Esther has come to have a stable, almost invariable, position in both the Jewish and Christian canons. By the time of the Tiberian Masoretes in the tenth century A.D., all five of the Festal Scrolls (Song of Songs, Ruth, Lamentations, Ecclesiastes, and Esther) had come to be read at the five major festivals of the Jewish liturgical year (see *Canonical Position* in the *Introduction* to Ruth). As a consequence of this development, these five books were grouped together as a collection, termed the "Megilloth" (the "Scrolls"), and regularly placed after Proverbs and before Daniel, Ezra-Nehemiah, and Chronicles at the end of the Jewish canonical order. In both the chronological and the historical order of the Megilloth (see *Canonical Position* in the *Introduction* to Ruth), Esther occupies the last position immediately before Daniel.

With the revision of the Jewish canonical order by the Christian Church, Esther has been considered to belong to the category of "historical" books, the second of the four divisions of the Christian canon. Since the order of these books is chronological, Esther occupies the last position after Ezra-Nehemiah, immediately preceding Job, the first of the books of the poetical and wisdom corpus.

Prior to the modern period, however, the order of the books of the canon, apart from the Pentateuch, was extremely variable. In the Jewish lists of the books of the canon that stem from the period prior to the development of the collection of Festal Scrolls (from the sixth to the tenth centuries A.D.) and in Jewish manuscripts that do not use a liturgical order (i.e., do not group the five Festal Scrolls together, for which see the full listing in Beckwith, *Canon,* 452–57), Esther is regularly grouped at the end of the canon along with Daniel, Ezra-Nehemiah, and Chronicles. Indeed, in three of the four earliest lists that clearly are dependent upon Jewish sources, that of Origen, Epiphanius, and Jerome (see Beckwith, *Canon,* 185–87, 188–90, 119–21), Esther is listed at the very end of the Writings, suggesting that it may have been the last book to have been added to the canon. It would be possible to add to this evidence that of the earliest Jewish list, the *baraita* in *b. B. Bat.* 14b, if Beckwith's explanation (*Canon,* 159–60) is correct, namely, that the order of the last books of the Writings therein, Daniel, Esther, Ezra/Nehemiah, Chronicles, is a mistaken attempt to arrange the books chronologically based on an incorrect knowledge of the chronology of the period.

Text

Bibliography

Jacob, B. "Das Buch Esther bei dem LXX." *ZAW* 10 (1890) 241–98. **Moore, C.** *Daniel, Esther and Jeremiah: The Additions.* Garden City, NY: Doubleday, 1977. **Torrey, C. C.** "The Older Book of Esther." *HTR* 37 (1944) 1–40.

As with the book of Ruth, the text upon which this translation and commentary are based is that of the *Codex Leningradensis* as published in *BHS* (for further data on this text, see *Text* in the *Introduction* to Ruth). As was the case with the book of Ruth, the text of Esther has been very well preserved. This is indeed most fortunate, because evidence for the text of Esther from the ancient versions is limited. Not only does the LXX include several pericopes that are unmistakably additions to the Hebrew narrative (see *Unity and Redaction* below), but its translation of the MT is very free and paraphrastic, rather than literal (cf. Fox, 10). Moore, who has done the most recent work on the Greek version of Esther, states that "there is scarcely a verse where the LXX^B does not omit a word, phrase, or clause of the MT" (Moore, *Additions,* 162). As an evidence of this, one has only to note how frequently the siglum > G* ("lacking in the LXX") appears in the apparatus of *BHS.* Indeed, so free and paraphrastic is the translation that B. Jacob concluded that it is "more or less worthless as a critical witness of the original Hebrew text" (*ZAW* 10 [1890] 270, as cited in Moore, *Additions,* 162 n. 22); and C. C. Torrey could write, "Why is there no Greek translation of the Hebrew text? Every other book of the Hebrew Bible . . . has its faithful rendering . . . in Greek. For the canonical Esther, on the contrary, no such version is extant" (*HTR* 37 [1944] 1, as cited in Moore, *Additions,* 162 n. 18). My own study of the text has corroborated the judgment that the LXX translation is so free and paraphrastic as to be of very limited use as a witness to the original Hebrew. Hence, I have not felt it expedient to deal with every Septuagintal textual plus or minus that has been culled from the many possible by F. Maass in the apparatus of *BHS.* Only Syr and Vg present fairly literal renderings of the Hebrew, the other ancient versions being translations of the LXX.

In my opinion, of all the numerous variant readings from the versions and from the conjectural emendations proposed in the scholarly literature noted in the apparatus of *BHS,* only two readings are preferable to the text of the MT. First, in 3:7 the text of MT lacks by homoeoteleuton a clause that can be supplied with reasonable assurance from the LXX; see *Comment* thereto. Second, in 9:29, 31 (in which verses the LXX translation is literally incoherent; see Fox, 286–87) I have felt it necessary to adopt three widely accepted conjectural emendations on the basis of internal coherence; see *Additional Note on vv 29–32* in the *Notes* section thereto.

Finally, a number of variant readings are possible on the basis of other Hebrew MSS or the K/Q readings of the MT. Four of these are relatively insignificant since they consist of variant or synonymous grammatical morphologies (the Q כאמרים vs. the K באמרים in 3:4; the Q וַתְּבוֹאנָה vs. the K וַתְּבוֹאֶינָה in 4:4; the Q יְהוּדִים vs. the K יְהוּדִיִּים in 4:7; 8:1, 7, 13; 9:15, 18; and the Q עֲתִידִים vs. the K עֲתוּדִים in 8:13). In four cases, however, the Q represents a superior reading to that of the

K. In 1:16 מְמוּכָן is preferable to מימכן; in 9:19 הַפְּרָזִים is preferable to הפרוזים; in 9:27 וְקִבְּלוּ is preferable to וקבל; and in 10:1 אֲחַשְׁוֵרוֹשׁ is preferable to אחשרוש. (See the discussion of each in loco.)

Unity and Redaction

Bibliography

Berg, S. B. *The Book of Esther: Motifs, Themes and Structure.* Missoula, MT: Scholars, 1979. **Bickerman, E. J.** *Four Strange Books of the Bible.* New York: Schocken, 1967. **Brooke, A. E., McLean, N.,** and **Thackeray, H. St. J.** *The Old Testament in Greek.* Vol. 3/1. London: Cambridge UP, 1940. 32–42. **Cazelles, H.** "Note sur la composition du rouleau d'Esther." In *Lex tua veritas.* FS H. Junker, ed. H. Gross and F. Mussner. Trier: Paulinus, 1961. 17–29 (= Moore, *Studies,* 424–36). **Clines, D. J. A.** *The Esther Scroll: The Story of the Story.* JSOTSup 30. Sheffield: JSOT, 1984. **Cook, H. J.** "The A-text of the Greek Versions of the Book of Esther." *ZAW* 81 (1969) 369–76. **Eisenmann, R.,** and **Wise, M.** "Stories from the Persian Court." In *The Dead Sea Scrolls Uncovered.* Rockport, ME: Element, 1992. 99–103. **Fox, M. V.** *The Redaction of the Books of Esther.* Atlanta: Scholars, 1991. **Gan, M.** "The Scroll of Esther in the Light of the Story of Joseph in Egypt." (Heb.) *Tarbiz* 31 (1961–62) 144–49. **Gerleman, G.** *Studien zu Esther: Stoff-Struktur-Stil-Sinn.* BS 48. Neukirchen: Neukirchener, 1966. 1–48. **Hanhart, R.** *Septuaginta: Vetus Testamentum Graecum Auctoritate Academiae Scientiarum Gottingensis editum.* 2nd ed. Vol. 7/3. Göttingen: Vandenhoeck & Ruprecht, 1983. **Lagarde, P. de.** *Librorum Veteris Testamenti Canonicorum Pars Prior Graece.* Göttingen, 1883. **Lebram, J. C. H.** "Purimfest und Estherbuch." *VT* 22 (1972) 208–22 (= Moore, *Studies,* 205–19). **Martin, R.** *Syntactical Evidence of Semitic Sources in Greek Documents.* SBLSCS 3. Cambridge: Cambridge UP, 1974. ———. "Syntax Criticism of the LXX Additions to the Book of Esther." *JBL* 94 (1974) 65–72 (= Moore, *Studies,* 595–602). **Milik, J. T.** "Les modèles araméens du livre d'Esther dans la grotte 4 de Qumrân." *RevQ* 15–16 (1992–93) 321–99. **Moore, C. A.** *Daniel, Esther and Jeremiah: The Additions.* AB 44. Garden City, NY: Doubleday, 1977. ———. *The Greek Text of Esther.* Ann Arbor, MI: University Microfilms, 1965. ———. "A Greek Witness to a Different Hebrew Text of Esther." *ZAW* 79 (1969) 351–58 (= Moore, *Studies,* 521–28). **Rosenthal, L. A.** "Die Josephgeschichte, mit den Büchern Ester und Daniel verglichen." *ZAW* 15 (1895) 278–84 (= Moore, *Studies,* 277–83). **Tov, E.** "The 'Lucianic' Text of the Canonical and Apocryphal Sections of Esther: A Rewritten Biblical Book." *Textus* 10 (1982) 1–25. **Watson, W. G. E.** "Aramaic Proto-Esther." In *Dead Sea Scrolls Translated.* Brill: Leiden, 1992. 291–92.

In contradistinction to the book of Ruth, which we have argued is a unity on the grounds that there is little, if any, evidence for composite origin (see *Introduction* to Ruth), the book of Esther presents such striking incongruities, repetitions, and changes in literary style and diction that there has been a strong consensus of opinion among scholars that it is a composite work. Theories in this regard have focused on two different sections of the book. On the one hand, a number of scholars have posited that earlier sources and traditions have been used in constructing the basic narrative, i.e., chaps. 1–8, usually predicating earlier "Esther" and "Mordecai" stories that have been combined to produce the present narrative. On the other hand, it has been posited since early in the critical study of the text (for views dating to the eighteenth and nineteenth centuries, see Paton, 57) that the concluding pericopes of the book, usually 9:20–10:3, contain layers of additions and glosses.

A. *The view that the basic narrative, chaps. 1–8, is composite.* Theories that the narrative as a whole is derived from earlier stories or traditions have been based, on the one hand, upon the view that the author is consciously adapting earlier biblical narratives, and, on the other, upon the view that he is drawing upon extrabiblical traditions.

1. *The view that the author is consciously dependent upon and adapting earlier biblical narratives.* Two different views have been advanced in this regard. First, Gerleman (11–23; *Studien,* 1–48), though maintaining that the book is a unity, has argued that it is a conscious imitation and adaptation of the plot and characterizations of the Exodus narrative, including "the foreign court, the deadly threat, the deliverance, the revenge, the triumph and the institution of a festival" (11). Though undoubtedly the Exodus tradition has influenced the author of Esther, probably both consciously and unconciously, the comparisons and parallels Gerleman cites are simply too general or problematic to prove his case. A number of them seem much more likely to be simply the results of "the demands of effective story-telling technique" (Moore, "Esther Revisited," 166) rather than indications of the influence of Exodus on Esther. Further, some parallels are simply not as close as Gerleman alleges, while other features of the two works are markedly different (cf. also the critiques of Berg, *Book of Esther,* 6–8; Z. Jacques, *Bib* 47 [1966] 463). Second, Meinhold has argued that chaps. 1–8 of Esther are a conscious adaptation of the Joseph narrative, not only in overall plot development but in individual structural elements (though with significant differences), written as a "diaspora novella" for the very different theological outlook of the secularized diaspora world, to which adaptation the final chapters dealing with Purim have been secondarily added (14–17; *ZAW* 87 [1975] 306–24; *ZAW* 88 [1976] 72–93). But, Berg (*Book of Esther,* 133–36) has shown that the structural elements and sequences are not so similar as Meinhold maintains, and, hence, though the author of Esther was doubtless familiar with the Joseph narrative, "no individual comparison of texts decisively indicates direct borrowing" (*Book of Esther,* 141). Nevertheless, the studies of both Meinhold and Berg (*Book of Esther,* 123–42; esp. 174–79) have shown that the author of Esther undoubtedly drew, consciously or unconsciously, upon the language, and even minor episodes, of the Joseph story, as has long been recognized (see Rosenthal, *ZAW* 15 [1895] 278–84; Gan, *Tarbiz* 31 [1961–62] 144–49).

2. *The view that the author is consciously drawing upon extrabiblical narratives.* Some scholars have averred that the book is derived from extrabiblical stories or traditions, based upon criteria such as the following: (i) certain supposed "inconsistencies" in the narrative development; (ii) the existence of two protagonists, Esther and Mordecai, both of whom make major contributions to the resolution of the crisis that sets the story in motion; (iii) the twofold focus of Haman's anger and plot, against Mordecai on the one hand and against the whole Jewish people on the other; (iv) the significant number of "doublets" in the story, e.g., the king's two banquets (chap. 1); Esther's two banquets (chaps. 5, 7); two lists of seven Persian officials (1:10, 14); two letters in chap. 9, one written by Mordecai and one by Esther; two gatherings of the maidens (2:8, 19). On such grounds Cazelles ("Note") presented the most detailed analysis and argument for two sources, one of a "liturgical" nature involving Esther and a plot against the Jews centered in the provinces, the other of a more "political" nature involving Mordecai and his contest with Haman centered in Susa (for a succinct summary and critique, see Clines, *Esther Scroll,*

115–21). Based on similar criteria, Bardtke (248–52), Bickerman (*Four Strange Books,* 172–200), Lebram (*VT* 22 [1972] 208–22), and Ringgren (374–76), though differing considerably from one another in many respects, also assumed the existence of separate original stories, one involving Esther and the other Mordecai (Bardtke and Ringgren also postulate a separate "Vashti" source lying behind chap. 1). It is not necessary to examine any of these hypotheses here, for Clines has summarized and evaluated them, effectively demonstrating that they are seriously deficient in making their case (*Esther Scroll,* 130–38).

However, building on these views, particularly those of Cazelles, Clines has plausibly extrapolated two separate sources from the narrative of chaps. 2–8: (i) a "Mordecai" story that is "a tale of the conflict of two courtiers that revolves about the question of their relative rank, and issues in a dramatic reversal of their standing at the Persian court," and (ii) an "Esther" tale that is a success story in which Esther, by a "combination of charm, courage, rhetoric, and strategy" (*Esther Scroll,* 145), removes Haman's plot to destroy the Jews by devising his personal destruction (*Esther Scroll,* 115–26). But, even though the two sources that Clines deduces are plausible, this does not constitute proof that such sources ever actually existed. Indeed, Clines himself notes: "I cannot say with any conviction that I believe that the existence of the two stories . . . is very probable" (*Esther Scroll,* 138). Fox (*Redaction,* § 2, 97–99) presents strong arguments against the validity of all the proposed variants of the two-source theory, including Clines'. First, the existence of the doublets upon which the theory is based and the delineation of coherent narrative sequences within the larger story fall short of constituting evidence for sources, for the doublets are not contradictory and the narrative strands evidence no differences in style or conception. Hence, they can comprise no more than two thematic developments within the overall plot. Second, the weakness of the theory is exposed by the facts that both the sources reflect throughout parallels in phraseology and formal-structural features with the story of Joseph and each is influenced by different parts thereof (*Redaction,* 98–99). Finally, Fox cogently argues that, even if we had independent evidence that such stories did exist, they have been so transformed and creatively used in the resulting narrative that the transformation and use constitute authorship, not redaction. The sources are so distant from the final text as to be of no value for its interpretation. This being the case, we shall neither assume nor refer to any such putative sources in seeking to interpret the book.

B. *The view that the ending of the book, chaps. 9–10, is a later addition.* When one turns to the concluding pericopes of the book, however, the situation is quite the opposite. Here, recent critical investigation has presented evidence for redactional layers. This evidence depends in the first place on inner criteria, those criteria that one must usually depend upon to determine the putative sources of a supposedly composite text, such as incongruities, apparent contradictions, repetitions, and changes in literary style. Though such evidence is always subtle and necessarily speculative, it is particularly strong for the ending of Esther. But, in this case we may not be dependent only upon the evidence presented by such inner criteria. On the contrary, it may be supported by the fact that a collateral version of the narrative of Esther exists. This is the so-called Alpha-text, or A-text (hereafter AT), a Greek text that Clines and Fox have recently argued contains a form of the Esther story translated from a Hebrew text that is quite different from the

Hebrew text of MT Esther (see Clines, *Esther Scroll,* 71–92; esp. Fox, *Redaction,* 10–95). The view that is accepted here, following Clines and Fox, is that the book of Esther is the product of two redactional stages in which an author-redactor creatively adapted and supplemented an earlier narrative to create a marked literary and thematic unity that functions as the etiology of the festival of Purim. One important piece of evidence for these redactional stages may be an earlier version of the Esther story (to be described below and termed the "proto-AT") now enshrined in the A-text.

1. *The nature and character of the A-text: A Greek translation of a variant Hebrew version of the story of Esther—the proto-AT.* The A-text of Esther is extant in five MSS dating from the tenth to the thirteenth centuries A.D. The text is presently available in two editions: (i) the 1883 edition of P. de Lagarde is published in the Larger Cambridge Septuagint, following the regular LXX text of Esther (see Brooke et al., *The Old Testament in Greek*), and (ii) in the Göttingen Septuagint, a new critical edition is published at the foot of the page beneath the LXX text (see Hanhart, *Septuaginta*). The Greek text of the Larger Cambridge Septuagint edition has also been published by both Clines (*Esther Scroll,* 215–48) and Fox (*Redaction,* Appendix B, 156–67). Clines very helpfully includes a fairly literal English translation.

The AT had been largely ignored until recent decades, since it was regarded as a part of the Lucianic revision of the LXX, but in 1965 C. A. Moore demonstrated that this was not the case (*The Greek Text,* 133–39; see also id., *ZAW* 79 [1969] 352–53; *Additions,* 163–65), a conclusion that has now met with almost universal agreement (cf., e.g., Hanhart, *Septuaginta,* 92; and esp. the concise discussion of Fox, *Redaction,* § 1.2, 14–17). In these studies Moore presented some evidence that the AT, except for the six noncanonical additions to Esther that the AT has in common with the LXX, is a translation of a Hebrew text that is significantly different from the MT version (see Moore, *ZAW* 79 [1969] 355–58; *Additions,* 165). This evidence has been further developed by Clines (*Esther Scroll*) in three ways. (i) He refuted the view of Tov (*Textus* 10 [1982] 1–25) that the AT is a recension of the LXX that underwent revision toward a Hebrew (or Aramaic) version different from the MT (*Esther Scroll,* 85–92; see also the refutation by Fox, *Redaction,* § 1.2, 14–15). (ii) He presented some additional evidence that the text of the AT that roughly corresponds to canonical Esther (i.e., excluding the six noncanonical Additions) was a translation of a Hebrew *Vorlage* different from the MT (*Esther Scroll,* 87–92). (iii) Building on the work of Torrey (*HTR* 37 [1944] 14–15) and in interaction with the work of Cook (*ZAW* 81 [1969] 369–76), he argued that, in addition to the six noncanonical Additions, the ending of the AT, which he identified as 8:17–21, 33–52 and which consists of material that parallels in part MT 8:5–10:3, is also dependent on the LXX. (AT 8:22–32 and 53–59 are omitted because the first comprises the noncanonical Addition E, and the second Addition F; the verse enumeration used here is that of the Cambridge Septuagint, followed also by Clines and Fox.) To establish this he cited two lines of evidence: (a) five examples from the ending of the AT cited by Tov that demonstrate dependence on the LXX (*Esther Scroll,* 86–87) and (b) a detailed examination of the narrative coherence of the ending of the AT in which he argued on literary grounds that it was secondary (*Esther Scroll,* 78–84).

Clines' work has been significantly expanded and advanced by Fox (*Redaction*), who has given the matter of redactional layers in Esther a detailed examination. Fox corroborates Clines' main conclusions by presenting arguments for two related hypotheses: (a) The AT contains two distinct compositional levels, one a redactional level consisting of material taken from the Septuagint, and the second a level consisting of material not related to the LXX. (b) This second level is a translation of a Hebrew *Vorlage* (which Fox, following Clines, calls the "proto-AT") that tells a story that, though similar, differs from the narrative of Esther preserved in the MT and the LXX (excluding the Additions); see *Redaction,* § 2, 17–34.

Fox establishes hypothesis (a) by a detailed statistical analysis of the vocabulary correspondences between the AT and the LXX (which he terms "matches," for a definition of which, with examples, see *Redaction* § 2.7, 19–22). His analysis reveals that the AT contains, on the one hand, material that has so many matches with the text of the LXX that it is clearly dependent upon the LXX and, on the other hand, material where there are only vague, incidental vocabulary correspondences between the two, such as one would expect from two texts that relate a similar story. Except for a few isolated, short passages, the material that evidences dependence upon the LXX clusters densely in eight contiguous passages of the AT. These are as follows. First, there are the six noncanonical Additions, A to F (for these, see Moore, *Additions*). Second, there is the ending of the AT (hereafter AT-end, whose exact beginning Fox places at a different point than does Clines; see below). And third, there is a short section, AT 6:13–18, which Fox calls D+ (so termed because it follows directly on from Addition D). Since D+ is clearly dependent upon the text of LXX 5:3–8, Fox very plausibly argues that it is a passage where the redactor overwrote his *Vorlage* (i.e., the text of the AT to which he was adding material from the LXX; see *Redaction* § 6.1, 42–43). Finally, Fox presents evidence that, apart from these contiguous sections, the following isolated verses also show dependence on the LXX: AT 2:1a (= LXX 1:1a); 2:5b–8 (= LXX 1:5b–8); 4:2 (= LXX 3:2); 4:9b–11–10a (= LXX 3:9b–11; AT transposes order of the verses); 5:4b–5 (= LXX 4:8b); 5:9b–10 (= LXX 4:14b); 6:21ab (= LXX 5:10ab); and 7:1 (= LXX 6:1a); see *Redaction* § 6.2 (43–47).

The rest of the text of the AT demonstrates so few "matches" with the LXX text that it cannot be derived from the LXX (see esp. Fox's tables, *Redaction* § 7, 47–50). Fox, following Clines, terms this material the "proto-AT."

Fox establishes hypothesis (b) by applying the syntactical criteria developed by Martin (*Syntactical Evidence*) for determining whether a Greek text is an original Greek composition or a translation of a Semitic (Hebrew or Aramaic) original. Applying Martin's criteria to fifty-seven lines from the proto-AT, he shows that it is a translation of a Hebrew or Aramaic original (cf. also Martin, *JBL* 94 [1975] 65–72). Indeed, it has a radically more pronounced translational character than LXX-Esther (which, of course, is a translation of MT-Esther; see *Redaction* § 2.10, 30–34). Finally, he convincingly shows that the language of the *Vorlage* of proto-AT is Hebrew, not Aramaic (see *Redaction* §§ 2.9.5, 2.9.6, 26–28).

With these investigations, Fox and Clines have demonstrated that in the proto-AT we possess a Greek variant of the Esther story that is a translation of a Hebrew version, and one that they argue differs from the MT narrative. This presents us with the very intriguing and important possibility that here we have a collateral version of the Esther narrative, through which, by means of comparison with the MT version, we may gain greater insight into the redactional history of the book and, in particular, come to some greater certainty about the questions that have been raised regarding the origin of chaps. 9–10 and their relationship to the earlier narrative. Though our task here is not to investigate the redactional history of the various versions of the Esther story but to understand and interpret MT-Esther, nevertheless, the fact that a text has a redactional history that can perhaps be extrapolated is an important factor in its interpretation (on this score, see the remarks of Fox, *Redaction,* chap. 5, 142–54).

2. *The original ending of the proto-AT.* Before we can make such comparisons, however, we must address ourselves to the important question of precisely where in the AT the proto-AT ends and the AT-end (i.e., the redactional ending taken over from the LXX) begins. Clines, as was noted above, argued that the proto-AT concluded at AT 8:17, the point at which the king responds to Mordecai's request to annul Haman's edict (which point in the AT story roughly approximates that of MT 8:7, where the king responds to Esther's request to revoke Haman's edict). He based this conclusion partly on the evidence of Cook (who argued for a change in the character of the AT after AT 8:16) but primarily on literary grounds, i.e., on a detailed analysis of the narrative coherence of the AT-end, in which he attempted to show that it is "a poorly written narrative, almost unintelligible in places, that cannot be attributed to the same author or level of redaction as the principal part of the book, but can only be regarded as secondary to it" (*Esther Scroll,* 84). However, Clines himself was forced to note that AT 8:17 as it stands is not a suitable conclusion to the book, and so he must assume that something has been omitted (*Esther Scroll,* 189 n. 25). Fox has also addressed this question (*Redaction* § 5, 38–42). In an extended interaction with the view of Clines, he has argued that the proto-AT did not end at 8:17 but that AT 8:18–21, 33–38 (i.e., excluding vv 22–32, which constitute Addition E taken over from the LXX) are also to be included. Fox's argument here is not dependent only upon the subtleties of literary interpretation, as was Clines'. Rather, on the basis of the comparison he has made of matches between the vocabulary of the AT and the LXX, he shows that, of the material after AT 8:17, these verses alone are not dependent upon the LXX (see his detailed discussion of the work of the redactor in §§ 8.1–8.8, 52–70). Finally, he attempts to refute most of the literary arguments advanced by Clines for the secondary character of these verses, in the course of which he is able to show that, at the very least, whatever stylistic or literary flaws may be detected could just as well come from an author as a redactor. In my opinion Fox's arguments here are more compelling than Clines', and the proto-AT should include AT 8:18–21, 33–38. In addition, however, it seems to me possible that the proto-AT should be extended to include vv 39–40, rather than ending with v 38. Vv 34–38 relate that Mordecai sent out a letter to inform the whole populace of Haman's death and, by implication (so Fox, Redaction, 41), of the annulment of the decree. This surely can hardly be said to be "an appropriate . . . conclusion to the proto-AT" (Fox, *Redaction,* 39). It seems much more fitting that the tale should end with Mordecai leaving the court dressed in the accoutrements of royalty at which the city of Susa rejoices (vv 39–40a), and in particular with the celebration of the Jews (v 40b). The objection to this, of course, is that these verses have a number of vocabulary correspondences (Fox's "matches") with the

LXX. The AT has here one synonym substitution in v 15a (ἐσθῆτα for στολήν); it omits v 15b (MT ועטרת זהב גדלה = LXX καὶ στέφανον ἔχων χρυσοῦν) and has a plus in v 16 (πότος). But, in addition, there is a further long omission that may be significant. AT omits the clause that stipulates "in every province and every city wherever the king's command and edict reached" (v 17a, present in both MT and LXX; see the chart below) there was joy and celebration for the Jews. This could very well be an addition made by the redactor of the MT and occasioned by the long and detailed account of the counteredict that has just been decribed in MT 8:9–14, which immediately precedes. This, perhaps, indicates that these verses are indeed part of the proto-AT, for which such a specific reference would be less appropriate, because what precedes in the proto-AT is a letter from Mordecai informing the whole populace of the annulment of Haman's edict. However, the agreement with the LXX in clauses 15a, c, d, and 16a, would then have to be accidental. But, the AT redactor (i.e., the redactor who is supplementing the proto-AT with the LXX) has periodically taken over a verse or two from the LXX (see above), and this may perhaps be another such case. Since this is the end of the proto-AT and he will henceforth be dependent on the LXX alone to complete his redaction, he may well have begun his use of the LXX before these last two verses of the proto-AT.

3. *The relationship of the proto-AT and the MT versions of Esther.* If this, then, is the scope of the proto-AT narrative, the question that must be addressed is, what is the relationship between it and the MT version? To establish this, it is necessary to compare and contrast the two versions.

a. *A comparison of the proto-AT and MT stories.* Since both Clines (*Esther Scroll,* chap. 8, 93–114) and Fox (*Redaction,* chap. 2, 96–126) have given this comparison a detailed examination, it can be done for our purposes in a concise manner by examining the endings of the two versions. For, though the basic plot line of the proto-AT is in some passages much more succinct, it is in the main very similar to that of MT-Esther up through the end of MT chap. 7, at which point Haman's plot has been exposed and he has been put to death. After this point, however, the two versions diverge arrestingly. This is best seen by a comparison of the two arranged in parallel columns. (See the chart on the following pages.)

Comparison of the Ending of MT and Proto-AT

In the arrangement, elements in the two versions that are equivalent, closely parallel, or play a similar role, are placed directly opposite one another. Elements that have no parallel in the immediate context of the other version stand alone. The MT material from chap. 9, which is thematically parallel to this, has been inserted in the chart (in parentheses and italics) opposite the proto-AT material to which it corresponds. However, the function of this parallel material in the narrative of the proto-AT is significantly different from its function in MT chap. 9 (see below). The MT column is my literal translation, the proto-AT that of Clines.

MT	proto-AT
8:1 That day King Ahasuerus gave to Queen Esther the property of Haman, the enemy of the Jews,	

and Mordecai came into the king's
presence, for Esther had informed him
of all that he was to her.

[8:15]And the king called Mordecai

[2]Then the king took off his signet ring,
which he had taken away from Haman,
and gave it to Mordecai,
and Esther placed him in charge of
Haman's property.

and bestowed upon him all that was
Haman's.

[16]And he said to him, "What do you want?
I shall do it for you."

[3]Then Esther again spoke to the king.

She fell down at his feet and wept, and
implored him to get rid of the wicked
scheme of Haman the Agagite which
he had devised against the Jews.
[4]The king held out to Esther the gold
scepter, and she rose and stood before
the king.
[5]She said, "If it pleases the king, and if
I have found favor with him, and if he
considers the proposal proper and if I
am pleasing in his eyes,
let an order be given to revoke the
dispatches—the scheme of Haman son
of Hammedatha, the Agagite—which he
has written in order to destroy the Jews
who are in all the king's provinces.

Mordecai said, "That you should revoke
the letter of Haman."

[6]For how could I bear to see the disaster
which would fall upon my people? And
how could I bear to see the destruction
of all my relatives?"

[7]Then King Ahasuerus said to Queen
Esther and to Mordecai the Jew, "Look,
I have given Haman's property to Esther,
and he has been hanged on the gallows
because he lifted his hand against the Jews.

[17]And the king put into his hands the
affairs of the kingdom.

*[[9:1–5]The Jews triumph over their
enemies and inflict upon them slaughter
and destruction.]*
*[[9:13]Esther said, "If it please the king, let
it be granted to the Jews in Susa tomorrow
also to do according to today's decree,*

[18]Moreover Esther said to the king,
"Grant me permission to punish my
enemies with slaughter."

and let the ten sons of Haman be hanged on the gallows.]
[9:14 And the king commanded that it be done.]

[9:16 the Jews kill 75,000 in the provinces.]

[9:6, 16 in Susa the Jews kill 500 men on the first day and 300 on the second.]

8 So you write concerning the Jews as you please in the king's name and seal it with the king's signet ring, for a decree written in the king's name and sealed with the king's signet ring cannot be revoked."

9 And so the royal scribes were summoned at that time, on the twenty-third day of the third month, the month of Sivan.
And an edict was written, exactly as Mordecai directed, to the Jews, and to the satraps, the governors, and the rulers of the provinces—the one hundred and twenty-seven provinces which stretched from India to Ethiopia—to each province in its own script and to each people in their own language, and to the Jews in their script and in their language.
10 It was written in the name of King Ahasuerus and sealed with his signet ring.

[9:20–22 Mordecai writes to obligate the Jews to celebrate a festival commemorating their celebration of their deliverance.]

And Mordecai sent dispatches

19 And Esther the queen took counsel with the king also against the sons of Haman, that they also should die together with their father. And the king said, "So be it."

20 And she smote the enemies in great numbers.
21 And in Susa the king made an agreement with the queen to slay men, and he said, "Behold, I give them to you to hang." And it was so.

[Addition E, vv 22–32]

33 And a decree comprising these matters was set out also in Susa,

and the king gave permission to Mordecai to write whatever he wished.

34 And Mordecai sent orders in writing,

and sealed them with the king's signet ring,

that his people should remain each in his own place and should keep festival to God.

35 And the letter which Mordecai sent was as follows:
36 "Haman has sent to you letters as follows: 'Hasten with all speed to send to destruction on my behalf the disobedient race of the Jews.'

37But I, Mordecai, advise you that the
man who did this has been hung at the
gates of Susa, and his family has
been slain.
38For he planned to kill us

by means of mounted couriers riding
post-horses from the state sevice, bred from
the royal stud,
11to the effect that the king granted
permission to the Jews in each and every
city to assemble, to defend themselves, to
destroy, slay, and annihilate the forces of
any people or province attacking them,

women and children included, and to
seize their goods as plunder,

12on one day, the thirteenth day of the
twelfth month, the month of Adar,
throughout all the provinces of King
Ahasuerus.

on the thirteenth day of the month
which is Adar."

13Also a copy of the edict was to be
promulgated as law in every single
province, being publicly displayed to
all peoples, so that the Jews might be
ready for this day, to take vengeance on
their enemies.
14As the couriers went forth, mounted
on post-horses, from the state service
and hastened and spurred by the king's
command, the edict was issued in the
Citadel of Susa.

15Mordecai went forth from the king
in royal clothing of blue and white,
and a large, gold turban,
and a cloak of white and purple linen.
And the city of Susa rejoiced and was glad.
16For the Jews all was light, joy, gladness,
and honor.

[39And Mordecai went forth
clothed in royal garments,
and with a headdress of linen edged with
purple.]
[40And when those in Susa saw him,
they rejoiced. And the Jews had light, and
drinking,

17And in each and every province and
each and every city, wherever the king's
command and edict reached, there was joy
and gladness for the Jews, and a banquet
and celebration.

and a banquet.]

And many of the peoples of the land
professed to be Jews, because fear of
Mordecai had fallen upon them.

[lacking]

9:1–5: The Jews are victorious; they put all their enemies to the sword.	[lacking]
9:6–19: The events that occasion the celebration of Purim over two days.	[lacking]
9:20–32: Mordecai, Esther, and the Jews set the dates of Purim and commit themselves to its perpetual celebration.	[lacking]
10:1–3: An encomium upon Mordecai.	[lacking]

Note: Vv 39–40 are in brackets because it is not certain that they are part of the proto-AT (see the discussion above).

As the chart reveals, MT-Esther contains v 8:17c and chaps. 9–10, which the proto-AT did not contain. This material the redactor of the AT covered by incorporating passages from the LXX. It is, however, important to note that the ending of the proto-AT contains material that is at least thematically parallel to material in MT chap. 9. Thus, AT 8:18–21 presents an account of the slaughter of the enemies of the Jews, and 8:34c relates that Mordecai wrote to the Jews that they should keep a festival to God.

b. *The differences between the proto-AT and the MT versions.* A careful examination of these divergent endings of the MT and the proto-AT will reveal the following differences:

(i) First, it is readily apparent, even by an examination of only this concluding section of the proto-AT, that it knows nothing of the conception of the inalterability of Persian law. Though this is stated explicitly in the MT in only two passages (1:19; 8:8), it is assumed throughout the MT version. Because of this different conception, two very different plot developments result, which are apparent in the comparison above. In the proto-AT, which is fully coherent and consistent in this regard, once Haman's plot has been exposed at Esther's banquet and he has been hanged in 8:1–14 (immediately prior to the text above), the terrible threat of his edict can be removed very easily. The king simply asks Mordecai what he wants, and he replies, "That you should revoke the letter of Haman" (AT 8:16). The revocation is effectively implied by the following statement that the king put into Mordecai's hands the affairs of the kingdom (AT 8:17). The situation is very different, however, in the MT. With the assusmption of the inalterability of Persian law, Haman's edict cannot simply be revoked. The whole plot development is now loaded with tension as protagonists and reader face the problem of how to revoke an irrevocable decree. Since Esther, more than Mordecai, now stands in the king's good graces in the MT version, she importunes him to revoke Haman's decree (MT 8:3–6; parallel to Mordecai's request in the proto-AT, 8:16b). The king's response turns the whole problem over to Esther and Mordecai, since no decree sealed with the king's ring can be revoked (8:7–8). Hence, Mordecai must issue a decree that will effectively counter Haman's edict by virtue of its identical provisions and subtle additions (8:9–14; see *Form/Structure/Setting* to act 7). Further, the narrator then must continue in MT 9:1–5 and tell the result for the Jews of the conflict of these two irreconcilable decrees (contra Clines, who argues that the MT narrative once concluded with 8:15–17, the glorification of Mordecai and the joy and celebration of the Jews that follow the proclamation of the second decree; see the discussion in the *Comment* on 9:1–5).

(ii) Second, the proto-AT ends very differently than MT-Esther in regard to the reports of the Jews' slaughter of their enemies. This theme functions very differently in the MT from the way that it does in the proto-AT (cf. Fox, *Redaction,* § 6.2, 119). In the proto-AT Haman's edict has been annulled (8:16–17), so the Jews are in no danger of attack. Esther requests simply that the king grant permission to "punish" (*κολάσαι*) their enemies (8:18). In the MT, however, Haman's decree has not been annulled but only countered with an almost identical decree granting them the right of self-defense (MT 8:9–14). This requires an account of the "life-and-death matter of Jewish self-defense" (Fox), which occurred when the time came for the two irreconcilable decrees to be carried out (MT 9:1–5).

(iii) Even more strikingly, the Jews' slaughter of their enemies in Susa (AT 8:21) has a radically different function in the MT. It is greatly expanded in MT 9:6–19 and spread over two days of fighting, and it has nothing to do with the "punishment" of the enemies of the Jews. Rather, it has a literary purpose. It functions to explain the two different days of celebration of the festival of Purim (see the discussion in the *Comment* and *Explanation* to 9:6–19; cf. Fox, *Redaction,* § 6.4, 120). There is not a hint in the proto-AT either of two days of fighting in Susa or of two days of celebration, let alone of the use of this element for determining the dates of a festival.

(iv) Undoubtedly most significant of all is the fact that the proto-AT knows nothing of the use of the Esther story as an etiology for the festival of Purim. The proto-AT does relate that Haman cast lots to determine the day (identified as "the thirteenth of Adar-Nisan," a most puzzling month designation that occurs also in AT 1:1; for discussion see Fox, *Redaction,* 60–61) for the extermination of the Jews (AT 4:7). However, not only does this lot-casting come after Haman has secured the king's permission to annihilate the Jews (rather than immediately prior as in the MT), but the lot is not called "pur" as it is in MT 3:7. There is nothing in the proto-AT equivalent to the days of celebration after the battles in Susa (MT 9:18) and in the provinces (MT 9:17, 19), and there is nothing about Mordecai having written to obligate the Jews to a two-day perpetual annual commemoration of these days of celebration (MT 9:20–23) or about the Jews having obligated themselves to such a festival (MT 9:26b–28). Nor is there a word about a festival named "Purim" (MT 9:26a). The proto-AT knows only the statement that Mordecai wrote to the Jews that they were to "stay each in their own place and celebrate a festival [*ἑορτάζειν*] to God" (AT 8:34). This is very much a passing reference (there is no reference to such a festival in the quotation of the letter that follows, AT 8:36–38), and it is unmistakably a reference to a one-time celebration of their deliverance, rather than to a perpetual annual celebration. This festival is not related in any way to the dates of the Purim celebration of the MT. Mordecai does mention 13 Adar in AT 8:38, but this refers exclusively to the date that Haman determined by lot for the extermination of the Jews (AT 4:7). Indeed, it is quite clear in the proto-AT, despite its paucity of dates, that all these events, i.e., the permission to annul Haman's decree (8:16–17), the punishment of the enemies of the Jews (8:18–21), and Mordecai's letter informing the populace of this fact (8:34–38), took place well before 13 Adar (cf. Fox, *Redaction,* § 9.8, 80–83).

(v) The proto-AT has nothing comparable to the encomium upon Mordecai in MT 10:1–3. If AT 8:39–40 does constitute the closing verses of the proto-AT (as we have suggested above), the verses do contain a vague hint of Mordecai's new stature with their depiction of his going forth in royal dress to the joy of the residents of Susa. Hence, it could have provided the instigation for the MT redactor to add such an encomium.

(vi) The proto-AT does not have the account of Mordecai's deliverance of the king from the eunuch's plot (MT 2:21–23). Though Clines argues forcefully that this was not in proto-Esther and was added by the MT redactor from the hint of such a plot in AT 7:3 (= MT 6:2; see *Esther Scroll,* 104–5), it could just as easily have been omitted by the redactor of the Greek proto-AT, since it became redundant as soon as he added Addition A from the LXX, which mentions the eunuch's plot (so Fox, *Redaction,* § 6.7, 121).

(vii) The proto-AT has one intriguing plus vis-à-vis the MT, namely, references to God or religious practices. In 5:9; 8:2 reference is made to God's actions on behalf of the protagonists or their people; in 5:11; 7:17 reference is made to prayer and supplication to God; and in 8:34 there is reference to celebrating a festival to God. In 4:7; 6:23 references to pagan gods are made by Haman and his wife. (In 5:5; 7:1; and probably 7:22, there are references to God that were taken from the LXX by the redactor of the AT [since their language, as Fox, *Redaction,* § 6.6, 120, has shown, is virtually identical to that of the LXX, it is most improbable that they were in the proto-AT].) In contrast to this, MT-Esther never mentions either God or religious practices explicitly directed to God. (The only religious practice mentioned by the MT is fasting [4:3, 16; 9:31], but it is never specifically stated that their purpose is the supplication of God.) The significance of this plus in the proto-AT is most difficult to ascertain. Either one must postulate that, if these references were present in proto-Esther, the redactor of the MT systematically removed them (as Clines at first cautiously suggested, *Esther Scroll,* 107–12, and then affirmed, 152). Or one must postulate that no such references were present in proto-Esther (a characteristic then maintained by the redactor of the MT), and the references in the proto-AT were added later (preferred by Fox, *Redaction,* § 6.6, 120). Though one might object to the idea that a Jewish author would have composed proto-Esther without any such references, the existence of MT-Esther demonstrates that, however it arose, such a composition was possible, at least in the Jewish diaspora of the period. In this light, it seems more likely that they were not present in proto-Esther and were added during the AT redaction.

c. *Conclusion: The relationship between the proto-AT and the MT versions.* In their examination of the MT and the proto-AT, Clines (*Esther Scroll,* 93–114) and Fox (*Redaction,* 96–126) both concur that the proto-AT is not only not a recension of MT-Esther but must have been composed prior to that version; i.e., it enshrines a form of the story much closer to proto-Esther, the original story from which both were derived. An examination of the five minuses of the proto-AT vis-à-vis the MT described above (paragraphs [i] through [v]), reinforces that conclusion.

Thus, in regard to difference (i) above, as Clines observes (and then demonstrates with an insightful analysis of the two narratives, 94–104), "the conflict between the two decrees is so valuable a source of narrative tension that it is difficult to imagine any reviser of the story writing it out of the record" (*Esther Scroll*, 94). It is indeed far more probable that proto-Esther did not contain this feature and that it is thus an addition to the story by the redactor of the MT. As Clines likewise notes (95), the source of this narrative development in the Jewish world in the era to which Esther dates (see the discussion of date below) is not hard to imagine, since this same tradition plays an important role in Dan 6 but is simply unknown elsewhere. (Fox's suggestion, *Redaction,* § 6.1, 118–19, that the idea came from the king's words to Haman in AT 4:10 seems to me to be far less likely.)

As regards the four MT pluses vis-à-vis the proto-AT described in differences (ii) through (v) above, all of them in the MT relate directly and only to the character and establishment of the festival of Purim. Surely, as central and important to Jewish life and practice as the subsequent popularity and history of that festival reveals it to be, it is hardly conceivable that the redactor of the proto-AT would have written these elements out of his narrative, if they had been present in proto-Esther (cf. Fox, *Redaction,* § 4.2, 113–14). The only possible conclusion is that these pluses in the MT have been added to proto-Esther by the redactor of MT-Esther.

4. *The redaction of the MT version.* The question that now needs to be addressed is whether all these elements were added to proto-Esther to form the present MT at one time by the same hand or they were added in stages. In *The Esther Scroll,* chaps. 1 (27–30), 3 (39–49), 8 (93–114), and 10 (15–68), Clines has vigorously argued for the development of the MT in a series of stages. In the first stage an author (a) added to proto-Esther (which Clines basically equates with the proto-AT) the theme of the irrevocability of Persian law; (b) added the conspiracy of the eunuchs (2:21–23); and (c) removed all references to God and religious practices. The introduction of (a), the theme of irrevocability, then required that Mordecai and Esther draft a decree to counter Haman's decree. Arguing on literary grounds, Clines contends (27–28) that this second decree so "denatures" the first decree that the resolution of the story is thereby effected. The outcome is stalemate, and, with the glorification of Mordecai and the joy and celebration of the Jews in 8:15–17, the principle threads of the plot were drawn together and an effective ending to the story produced (64–68). The result of this redaction is a second Esther story that Clines dubs the "proto-MT." Subsequently, later redactors, possessed of far inferior narratival and logical skills than the author of the proto-MT, added first 9:1–19, out of a conviction that the earlier story needed to be translated into action in order to tell what actually happened on 13 Adar and to introduce the theme of the joyous celebration of the deliverance (158–62). Then, they added 9:20–32 in order more clearly to connect the celebration with the institution of the festival of Purim (162–67). Finally, they added 10:1–3, the encomium upon Mordecai (167–68).

As was noted above, Clines bases this reconstruction on the logical narrative weaknesses and contradictions between the contents of these appendixes, particularly 9:1–19, and the previous narrative, his "proto-MT." (Many interpreters have made the same argument about 9:20–10:3.) Some of the differences that Clines alleges have merit, strongly suggesting that this material does indeed have a different literary pre-history than chaps. 1–8, as the redactional investigation above has made most probable. Nevertheless, the major literary differences and contradictions between the two passages postulated by Clines are not sufficient in my opinion to sustain his view. In contrast to Clines, Fox has presented a strong case for the literary unity of chaps. 9–10 of the MT narrative (*Redaction,* § 3, 99–109; a case that I find compelling), in contradistinction to those who, like Clines, consider them to be a series of later appendages on the grounds that they exhibit literary incongruities and redundancies with the preceding narrative. Having established the literary unity of chaps. 9–10, Fox then presents evidence that there is considerably more literary congruity than Clines perceives between his putative "proto-MT" (chaps. 1–8) and the conclusion to the book (chaps. 9–10). They are indeed the natural and necessary continuation of the previous narrative. For a detailed discussion presenting the grounds for this conclusion, see the *Comment* on 9:1–5 below and especially Fox, *Redaction,* §§ 4–4.1.4, 110–13, to which my discussion there is heavily indebted.

5. *Conclusions.* If the above arguments are cogent, the following conclusions may be drawn. The MT redactor added to proto-Esther (which must have been fairly close to the proto-AT) the theme of the inalterability of Persian law. This in turn required the considerable expansion of chap. 8, in which Mordecai finally solves the conundrum of revoking an irrevocable decree by issuing a counteredict granting the Jews the right of self-defense. This requires, in turn, the account of the Jewish victory over their enemies related in 9:1–5. This story the redactor then uses as the etiology of Purim by composing in 9:6–32 an ending that institutes the perpetual annual observance of that festival. As Fox has succinctly put it, the book of Esther is (*Redaction,* 115)

> indeed a unity, but one compounded of two stages in the history of the text. A single redactor shaped the entire MT by adapting and supplementing the Hebrew proto-AT, or—to be cautious—proto-Esther, their common forerunner. In chs. 1–7 this author-redactor is closely reworking an older story, most of it ready to hand. In ch. 8 he continues the narrative, but now treats his source much more expansively. In ch. 9 he is composing a new ending with a liturgical purpose, building upon only a few hints supplied by his source. The MT is a unity insofar as a single redactor has imposed his will and his intentions on an earlier text.

This investigation of the redactional history of the book of Esther is very important for the interpretation of the book. First, it provides a redactional explanation for the sharp differences in both the literary characteristics and the intents and purposes of the narrative that biblical scholarship has almost from its beginning perceived to exist between the first eight chapters of the book and the last two. Second, it provides strong redactional evidence, in addition to the literary evidence, that, whatever may have been the genre of the original story, the genre of the book in the final form we have is that of a "festival etiology" (see the discussion of genre below).

Finally, recently published texts from Qumran may provide some background that renders more plausible the view that MT Esther originated through the redaction of an earlier form of the story whose basic contents are now preserved in the proto-AT. These materials consist of some six badly broken Aramaic texts from

Qumran (4Q550, given the siglum 4QProto Esther[a-f] by Milik, *RevQ* 15–16 [1992–93] 321). Milik's ingenious attempt (*RevQ* 15–16 [1992–93] 321–99) to interpret these texts as containing a series of stories of Jews at the Persian court that specifically formed the precursers to and sources of the narratives of Esther is most unconvincing, since it involves so many conjectural emendations and highly debatable readings. Nevertheless, these texts, badly broken though they are, do preserve fragments of stories of Jews at the Persian court who suffer various vicissitudes and fates, including vindication (for Eng. translations, see Watson, "Aramaic Proto-Esther," 291–92; Eisenmann and Wise, "Stories from the Persian Court," 99–103, esp. the brief description of the contents in the latter). They do, then, provide further evidence for the existence in Jewish circles of narratives dealing with themes reminiscent of some of those of the proto-AT and MT forms of Esther, which at least removes the isolation of the proto-AT story.

In conclusion, it is important to stress that the author-redactor of the final form of the book radically transformed the character of the proto-AT narrative by the changes that he made in that story. He also transformed the genre and purposes of the whole by the additions that he made, above all the final pericopes relating to the establishment of the festival of Purim (which I have argued, following Fox, are a literary and authorial unity). By his alterations, the author-redactor has created a work with marked literary and thematic unity.

Authorship and Date

Bibliography

Berg, S. B. *The Book of Esther: Motifs, Themes and Structures.* Missoula, MT: Scholars, 1979. **Bergey, R. L.** "The Book of Esther—Its Place in the Linguistic Milieu of Post-exilic Biblical Hebrew Prose: A Study in Late Biblical Hebrew." Diss., Dropsie College, 1983. ———. "Late Linguistic Features in Esther." *JQR* 75 (1984) 66–78. ———. "Post-exilic Hebrew Linguistic Developments in Esther: A Diachronic Approach." *JETS* 31 (1988) 161–68. **Bickerman, E. J.** "The Colophon of the Greek Book of Esther." *JBL* 63 (1964) 339–62. **Clines, D. J. A.** *The Esther Scroll: The Story of the Story.* JSOTSup 30. Sheffield: JSOT, 1984. **Fox, M.** *The Redaction of the Books of Esther: On Reading Composite Texts.* Atlanta: Scholars, 1991. **Jacob, B.** "Das Buch Esther bei dem Septuagint." *ZAW* 10 (1890) 241–98. **Moore, C. A.** *Daniel, Esther and Jeremiah: The Additions.* AB 44. Garden City, NY: Doubleday, 1977. ———. "Esther, Book of." *ABD* 2:633–43. **Morris, A. E.** "The Purpose of the Book of Esther." *ExpTim* 42 (1930–31) 124–28. **Pfeiffer, R. H.** *Introduction to the Old Testament.* New York: Harper, 1948. **Rowley, H. H.** *The Growth of the Old Testament.* 3rd ed. rev. London: Hutchinson, 1967.

AUTHORSHIP

As was the case with the book of Ruth, the writer of the book of Esther provides no indications of authorship, an anonymity characteristic of OT narrative (on this question, see the comments in the discussion of the authorship of the book of Ruth). The author of Esther never refers to himself in any way whatsoever and so gives us not the slightest hint, directly or indirectly, of his identity as a historical person. However, the fact that the book specifically and narrowly has to do with the life and concerns of Jews in the diaspora (see the discussion of its "diaspora agenda" in *Theme and Purpose* below) renders diaspora authorship a virtual certainty, and the wealth of accurate knowledge the author evidences about the Persian world and court strongly suggests that he was a member of the eastern diaspora. Fox (140) suggests, as others have before him, that his evident knowledge of Susan geography and his interest in the Susan date of the festival of Purim (9:18–19) indicate that he was a resident of Susa itself. Though this is highly probable, the author's knowledge of Persian affairs does not necessitate an eastern provenance (as Fox notes), for at least two works written in this general period and giving great detail about the Persian world, Herodotus' *History* and Berossus' *Babylonica,* could have supplied such information.

Granted the validity of the redactional history of the book that was argued in *Unity and Redaction* above, there appear to be two authors involved, the author of the original story, which was probably close to the present form of the proto-AT, and the author-redactor of the MT version. It is proper in my opinion to refer to this redactor as an "author" (on the question of "redactors" as "authors," see the succinct but helpful comments of Fox, *Redaction,* 1–3, 142–43), given the manner in which his changes to the proto-AT narrative have so radically transformed the character of that narrative and the way that his additions, especially the final pericopes relating to the festival of Purim in chaps. 9–10, have significantly transformed the story's genre and purposes. Clines has provided brilliant insight into both the significance of the changes made by the MT author-redactor and the dramatic and narrative skill with which he performed his task. See his discussion of the implications of the addition of the concept of the inalterability of Persian law to the proto-AT (*Esther Scroll,* 94–104). One can surely attribute authorship to a redactor who

> . . . though in one sense . . . did no more than plump out the thinner story-line of his predecessor, in another quite transformed his *Vorlage* with a fresh, ingenious dramatic twist (the need for a second decree), and in yet another amply maintained the stylish demands of the original story. (103)

However, none of this permits us, as with Ruth, to say anything about the author(s) of Esther as historical person(s).

DATE

In contrast to the book of Ruth, for which the dates proposed have ranged over a major portion of the whole OT era (from the Davidic period to the late post-exilic; see *Ruth*), the limits of the period within which the date of Esther must be set are prescribed by the facts of the case. It must, obviously, have been written after the reign of Ahasuerus (Xerxes I, 486–65 B.C.), and probably some considerable time thereafter, for references such as 1:1, 13–14; 4:11; 8:8; 10:2 would seem to imply several generations at least (though they can hardly be said to imply that the Persian empire was "but a dim memory," Pfeiffer, *Introduction,* 741; cf. Anderson, 827; Paton, 61). The certain *terminus ad quem* is determined by Josephus' full use of the story in his *Jewish Antiquities* (11.184–296) written ca. A.D. 90, although the colophon to the LXX version of Esther most probably establishes an earlier terminus (since there seems little reason to doubt the veracity of the information given therein; cf. Moore, *Additions,* 251). It states that "in the fourth year of the reign of Ptolemy and Cleopatra, Dositheus . . . and his son Ptolemy brought the above book of Purim" to Alexandria presumably (the colophon does not state the destination). This provides evidence that the LXX translation must have been made some time before either 114 B.C., the fourth year of Ptolemy VIII (so Bickerman, *JBL* 63 [1944] 347) or 77 B.C., the fourth year of Ptolemy XII (so Jacob, *ZAW* 10 [1890] 279–80), these being the most likely of the several Ptolemies who had a wife named Cleopatra and ruled more than four years (see Moore, *Additions,* 250). Hence, the Hebrew *Vorlage* must be earlier than the first century B.C. by the amount of time sufficient for it to circulate and become well enough known to warrant a translation into Greek.

However, the data for narrowing the range of possibilities within these limits (the fourth to the second centuries) do not permit much precision. The most helpful data are the following. First (contrary to the views of some interpreters), the book does not evidence a negative attitude toward the Jews on the part of both the Persian government and the majority of the non-Jewish population. True, there clearly must have been a sufficient element of the population willing to act on Haman's decree to make it a significant threat. Nevertheless, the enemies of the Jews do not constitute either the Persian government or the majority of the polyglot Persian population. They consist only of those who "hoped to triumph over them," "sought to do them harm," "hated them" (9:1–5). Ahasuerus is malleable and criminally culpable in assenting to the annihilation of the Jews, but his action does not spring from animus toward them. He is merely indifferent, for he has no idea who the people he is assigning to oblivion are (see *Explanation* to act 2, scene 2, 3:7–11). And the Persian world is epitomized by its ruler. Though it evidences a precarious instability, it too is not inherently inimical to the Jews (see *Theme and Purpose* below). This is clearly demonstrated by passages such as 3:15d (see the *Comment* thereto) and 8:15b and the overall tenor of the book. Second, the corollary is equally true. The book displays antagonism on the part of the Jews only toward those who seek to harm the Jewish community (contra Pfeiffer, *Introduction,* 741; cf. the well-taken remarks of Berg, *Esther,* 170). As Clines (272) and others (e.g., Moore, *ABD* 2:641) have observed, such a generally amicable attitude is more likely to have been adopted by an author who lived in the late Persian or early Hellenistic era (i.e., late fourth to early third centuries B.C.). In particular, it makes it highly improbable that it reflects the circumstances of the Maccabean period (as was advocated by earlier scholars, e.g., Morris, *ExpTim* 42 [1930–31] 125–28; Pfeiffer, *Introduction,* 741–42; Rowley, *Growth,* 155), when antagonism between Jews and their rulers ran high.

The evidence of the language of the book, though it cannot give us any greater precision within the period, does corroborate the era suggested above. In his full investigation of the linguistic data of the book ("Book of Esther"; cf. also id., *JETS* 31 [1988] 161–68; *JQR* 75 [1984] 66–78), Bergey has been able to show that some seventeen of the fifty-eight features that he determined to be pertinent for dating do not occur in the other LBH prose compositions, but they are found in MH (see "Book of Esther," 182–83). (In order to give a sense of this evidence, thirteen of these linguistic features are commented on in the *Notes;* see *Notes* 1:8.a., 11.a., 15.b.; 2:1.b.; 3:8.b., 12.a.; 4:11.b., 11.c.; 6:6.a.; 7:4.a.; 8:5.b., 15.a.; 9:26.b.)

Conversely, in the case of some eleven of the late language features that appear in both Esther and MH, the other LBH prose compositions use only their SBH equivalents. Given this significant evidence for the lateness of a significant number of the linguistic features of Esther, Bergey comes to the following tentative conclusion: Though "a more definite conclusion concerning Esther's linguistic position among other LBH prose sources awaits diachronic and synchronic analyses of all the linguistic features of all the LBH sources," nevertheless, "the Book of Esther's place in the linguistic milieu of post-exilic BH prose appears to be closer to the latter part of the post-exilic literary spectrum than to the earlier" ("Book of Esther," 185). This makes a dating earlier than the last half of the fourth century B.C. unlikely.

These considerations render the late Persian to early Hellenistic period, i.e., approximately the fourth century B.C., the most probable date for the redactional process that produced MT Esther, with the preponderance of the evidence being slightly in favor of the latter half of the period.

Genre

Bibliography

Alter, R. *The Art of Biblical Narrative.* New York: Basic, 1981. **Beekman, J., Callow J.,** and **Kopesec, M.** *The Semantic Structure of Written Communication.* Dallas: Summer Institute of Linguistics, 1981. **Berg, S. B.** *The Book of Esther: Motifs, Themes and Structure.* Missoula, MT: Scholars, 1979. **Berlin, A.** *Poetics and Interpretation of Biblical Narrative.* Sheffield: Almond, 1983. **Botterweck, G. J.** "Die Gattung des Buches Esther im Spektrum neuerer Publikationen." *BibLeb* 5 (1964) 274–92. **Childs, B.** *Introduction to the Old Testament as Scripture.* Philadelphia: Fortress, 1979. **Clines, D. J. A.** *The Esther Scroll: The Story of the Story.* JSOTSup 30. Sheffield: JSOT, 1984. **Coats, G.,** ed. *Saga, Legend, Tale, Novella, Fable: Narrative Forms in Old Testament Literature.* JSOTSup 35. Sheffield: JSOT, 1985. ———. "Tale." In *Saga, Legend, Tale, Novella, Fable: Narrative Forms in Old Testament Literature,* ed. G. Coats. JSOTSup 35. Sheffield: JSOT, 1985. 82–96. **Crenshaw, J. L.** "Method in Determining Wisdom Influence upon 'Historical' Literature." *JBL* 88 (1969) 129–42. **Dorothy, C. V.** "The Books of Esther: Structure, Genre, and Textual Integrity." Diss., Claremont, 1989. **Driver, S. R.** *Introduction to the Literature of the Old Testament.* Edinburgh: T. & T. Clark, 1913. **Eissfeldt, O.** *The Old Testament: An Introduction.* New York: Harper and Rowe, 1965. **Gerleman, G.** "Studien zu Esther: Stoff-Struktur-Stil-Sinn." *BS* 48 (1966) 1–48. **Gordis, R.** "Religion, Wisdom, and History in the Book of Esther—A New Solution to an Ancient Crux." *JBL* 100 (1981) 359–88. **Herst, R.** "The Purim Connection." *USQR* 28 (1972–73) 139–45. **Humphreys, W. L.** "A Life-style for Diaspora: A Study of the Tales of Esther and Daniel." *JBL* 92 (1973) 211–23. ———. "Novella." In *Saga, Legend, Tale, Novella, Fable: Narrative Forms in Old Testament Literature,* ed. G. Coats. JSOTSup 35. Sheffield: JSOT, 1985. 82–96. ———. "The Story of Esther and Mordecai: An Early Jewish Novella." In *Saga, Legend, Tale, Novella, Fable: Narrative Forms in Old Testament Literature,* ed. G. Coats. JSOTSup 35. Sheffield: JSOT, 1985. 97–113. **Jensen, P.** "Elamitische Eigennamen: Ein Beitrag zur Erklärung der elamitischen Inschriften." *WZKM* 6 (1892) 47–70, 209–26. **Long, B.** "Introduction to Historical Literature." In *1 Kings with an Introduction to Historical Literature.* FOTL 9. Grand Rapids, MI: Eerdmans, 1984. 1–8. **Meinhold, A.** "Die Gattung der Josephgeschichte und des Estherbuches: Diasporanovelle I." *ZAW* 87 (1975) 306–24. ———. "Die Gattung der

Josephgeschichte und des Estherbuches: Diasporanovelle II." *ZAW* 88 (1976) 72–93. **Moore, C. A.** "Esther, Book of." *ABD* 2:633–43. ———. "Esther Revisited: An Examination of Esther Studies over the Past Decade." In *Biblical and Related Studies Presented to Samuel Iwry,* ed. A. Kort and S. Morschauser. Winona Lake, IN: Eisenbrauns, 1985. 163–72. **Stiehl, R.** "Das Buch Esther." *WZKM* 53 (1957) 4–22. **Talmon, S.** "'Wisdom' in the Book of Esther." *VT* 13 (1963) 419–55. **Zimmern, H.** "Zur Frage nach dem Ursprunge des Purimfestes." *ZAW* 11 (1891) 157–69 (= Moore, *Studies,* 147–59).

For a general discussion of the concept of genre and its importance for OT narrative, see the section *Genre* in the *Introduction* to Ruth. It was observed in that discussion that the determination of the genre of Ruth has been seriously troubled by methodological problems. The same is true for the determination of the genre of Esther (for an overview of many of the differing views of the genre of the book adopted by scholars prior to 1964, see Botterweck, *BibLeb* 5 [1964] 274–92). A century ago, in the heyday of "pan-Babylonianism," Jensen (*WZKM* 6 [1892] 47–70, 209–26) and Zimmern (*ZAW* 11 [1891] 157–69) advanced the opinion that the book was the historicization of Babylonian type myths in which the Elamite gods Human/Haman and Mashti/Vashti were defeated by the Babylonian gods Marduk/Mordecai and Ishtar/Esther (for details of such views, see Paton, 87–94). Apart from the question of whether the OT contains such "historicized myths," the narrative contains no mythical features whatsoever (beyond the similarity of these names, which in the case of Esther is probably fortuitous; see *Comment* on 2:7). In particular, the book knows no association of Haman and Vashti in a confrontation with Mordecai and Esther (Berg, *Book of Esther,* 22 n. 27; cf. also Eissfeldt, *Introduction,* 507–8). The view has, unfortunately, been resurrected by Herst (*USQR* 28 [1972–73] 139–45) in an attempt to interpret the book as an adaptation of such a myth by John Hyrcanus (ca. 125 B.C.) in order to substitute the festival of Purim for the "Day of Nicanor" (for which see 1 Macc 7:48–49; 2 Macc 15:36).

Stiehl (*WZKM* 53 [1957] 5, 7), Eissfeldt (*Introduction,* 507), and others have designated the book a "historical novel." This not only draws on extrabiblical analogues without adequately justifying the comparison but utterly misses the fact that the most important and obvious function of the book is to institute and regulate the festival of Purim (see below).

Also adverting to analogues outside the OT, Gordis has advanced the hypothesis that the genre of the book is that of a "Persian court chronicle" (*JBL* 100 [1981] 359–88). Gordis suggests that the book was composed in the form of such a chronicle by a Jew of the eastern diaspora and written as if by a gentile scribe. In this way he seeks to explain the total absence of both the name of God and Jewish religious motifs, as well as several other features that, he opines, thereby receive "a simple and unforced explanation" (375). However, there are no Achaemenid historical chronicles, royal or otherwise, extant (as Gordis himself notes, 375 n. 50) with which one might make comparisons, either for the purpose of understanding the book or for the purpose of confirming or disputing the hypothesis (cf. Fox, 144). The Letter of Aristeas, though it establishes the possibility of the attribution of a pseudepigraphic Hellenistic Jewish work to a member of a gentile (Egyptian) court, is so different from Esther that it very effectively undermines the hypothesis (see Fox, 144), rather than supporting it, as Gordis postulates.

Equally problematical, though it draws upon OT analogues, is the view of Talmon (*VT* 13 [1963] 419–55) that Esther is a "historicized wisdom-tale." It is "an enactment of standard 'Wisdom' motifs . . . which are present also in other biblical narratives of a similar nature, and which biblical literature has in common with Ancient Near Eastern Wisdom literature" (426). Talmon bases his case not on formal literary parallels and vocabulary but upon similarities in the general situations and conceptions in Esther and wisdom literature, such as the concept of an unspecified and remote deity, the absence of Jewish religious concepts, the anthropocentrism and individualistic slant of the book, its interest in the details and atmosphere of the royal court, and its presentation of its protagonists as three couples who exemplify the traditional wisdom triangle: the powerful, but witless dupe (Ahasuerus and Vashti), the righteous wise (Esther and Mordecai), the conniving schemer (Haman and Zeresh). However, as a number of scholars have pointed out (e.g., Bardtke, *EOL* 19 [1965–66] 115–17; Crenshaw, *JBL* 88 [1969] 140–42; Fox, 142–43), not only can a number of these feature be found in literature other than wisdom, but the theory misunderstands both wisdom categories and the book of Esther. Thus, for example, the conception that the nonspecific references to deity in Ecclesiastes or Job, such as *Elohîm, Elôah,* or *El-Shadday,* can explain the absence of references to God in Esther is simply a non sequitur. These are unmistakable references to God, in utter contrast to Esther. Further, in other OT examples of wisdom such as Proverbs, God is intimately involved in the lives of human beings, rather than being unspecific and remote (Fox, 143). And the view that the book of Esther depends upon a nonhistorical and non-national wisdom ideology because it misrepresents internal Jewish issues, such as Jewish history, identity, or destiny, fails to recognize that these issues are central to the purpose and teaching of the book (Fox, 143), even though the book does not specifically mention Palestinian geography or institutions (see *Purpose* below). Nor can the protagonists be understood as wisdom stereotypes. Mordecai does not typify the wise man in any characteristic or action, nor is the king a type of the witless dupe in power (Crenshaw, *JBL* 88 [1969] 141).

In an entirely different direction, Gerleman (11–23 and passim; cf. also id., *Studien,* 1–48) argues that the book is neither the historicization of a myth nor a folk tale (or a composite of such) but a conscious imitation and adaptation of the plot and characterizations of the Exodus narrative. As such, it is "a deliberate and conscious desacrilization and detheologization of a central, salvation [*heilsgeschichtlichen*] tradition" (23). Apart from the fact that the parallels and comparisons Gerleman alleges do not prove his case (see discussion in *Unity and Redaction* above), the book of Esther makes such a definite theological statement, however implicit it may be (see *Purpose and Theme* below), that it is hard indeed to conceive of it as a deliberate "detheologizing" of the Exodus tradition (see Clines, *Esther Scroll,* 156).

Finally, Humphreys (*JBL* 92 [1973] 211–23; "Story of Esther"), Meinhold (succinctly, 14–17; in greater detail, *ZAW* 87 [1975] 306–24; *ZAW* 88 [1976] 72–93), and Fox (145–48) posit that the story of Esther and Mordecai (i.e., excluding the connection with Purim) belongs to a genre of "diaspora novella," which genre intends to set forth for Jews living under foreign rule in the diaspora a style of life that will enable them to meet the threats to their existence that arise in this dangerous, yet tolerable, world. Humphreys bases his elucidation of such a genre upon the motif of the "wise courtier in the foreign court," which he finds common to Esther, Dan 1–6, and the Joseph story (cf. the perceptive critique of Berg, *Book of Esther,* 129–33), while Meinhold adduces the supposed detailed literary structures that are common to Esther and the Joseph story (see the discussion in *Unity and Redaction* above), and Fox appeals in general terms to the intent of Esther, Dan 1–6, and Tobit to teach a way of life for Jews in the diaspora. Since this genre designation intentionally excludes the pericopes dealing with the institution of Purim and hence treats only the first part of the book, the "story of Esther and Mordecai," it cannot be the genre of the whole text. However, as the discussion below will attempt to demonstrate, it does deal with a genuine aspect of the complex genre of the whole work, to the elucidation of which I shall now turn.

In the discussion of the genre of Ruth, I argued that it is possible to elucidate the genre of such narratives as Ruth and Esther given the discussion of the general interpretation of narrative in Beekman, Callow, and Kopesec, *Semantic Structure,* and the discussion of some of the specific OT narrative genres pertinent to texts such as Ruth and Esther in Coats, *Saga, Legend, Tale, Novella, Fable.* In the light of these discussions, it is clear that Esther as well as Ruth does not belong to that category of narratives whose main purpose is to present in some detail a sequence of events in which the cause-effect relationship is dominant and whose primary intention is objectively to report events in their proper order (cf. Long, "Introduction"; Coats, "Tale," 63). On the contrary, the narrative of Esther, like Ruth, is controlled by the "problem-based plot" structure described by Beekman, Callow, and Kopesec (*Semantic Structure* § 4.2.4), the pattern of whose discourse roles consists of the following: (a) setting, (b) problem, (c) complicating incident(s), (d) resolving incident(s), (e) resolution, (f) dénouement, and (g) conclusion/coda. For a succinct definition and discussion of these structural elements of the problem-based plot, including the three causal relationships that may exist between them and between their constituent parts, see the *Genre* section of the *Introduction* to Ruth.

Using these structural/discourse roles and their relationships, the plot of the book of Esther may be analyzed as in the chart of the discourse structure on the following pages (for the structure and roles of the underlying scenes and episodes, see the *Form/Structure/Setting* sections in the following commentary). Chaps. 1–2 constitute the setting or exposition; the problem, Haman's edict to annihilate the Jews, is depicted in chap. 3; chaps. 4–7 constitute a series of complicating and resolving incidents; and the problem is resolved in the dual resolutions of 8:1–9:5. The dénouement follows in the account of the institution of Purim in 9:6–32. Finally, the encomium upon Mordecai in 10:1–3 constitutes the conclusion/coda.

From this analysis of the discourse roles of the narrative, the genres of the story may be deduced. They are at least threefold. Two are set by the character of the dénouement and one by that of the problem-based plot that precedes.

A. *The genres set by the dénouement.* 1. *Festival etiology.* First it must be noted that, when the discourse roles of these elements of the structure are carefully examined, the dénouement, act 9, 9:6–32, is markedly incongruous. The dénouement of a problem-based plot is normally the response to the "problem-resolution" pair.

The Discourse Structure of Esther

Discourse Role	Relationship		Verses	Contents
SETTING (The protagonists are introduced and the events necessary to set the scene are related.)	occasion		1:1–1:9	King Ahasuerus gives two lavish banquets for: (1) his nobles and (2) the men of the Citadel of Susa.
	outcome	occasion	1:10–1:22	Queen Vashti is deposed since she refuses to be displayed before the men of the Citadel of Susa.
	stimulus	outcome	2:1–2:4	Ahasuerus decides to seek a new queen by finding the beautiful young woman who pleases him.
	response	occasion	2:5–2:11	Mordecai and Esther introduced. Along with all the young women, Esther is taken to the royal harem.
		outcome	2:12–2:18	Of all the young women, Esther wins the king's favor and is chosen queen.
	DIGRESSION		2:19–2:23	Mordecai uncovers a plot on the life of the king and informs the king through Esther.
PROBLEM STATED / stimulus		stimulus	3:1–3:6	Haman is promoted and obeisance to him ordered. Mordecai refuses to bow, so Haman decides to annihilate the Jews.
	stimulus	response	3:7–3:11	With lies and innuendo, Haman obtains the king's permission to annihilate the Jews.
	response	stimulus	3:12–3:15	Haman issues an edict to the whole empire, ordering the annihilation of the Jews.
response / RESOLVING INCIDENT / stimulus	occasion	response	4:1–4:3	Mordecai and all the Jews lament. Mordecai goes to the entrance of the royal court in sackcloth.
	outcome	stimulus	4:4	Mordecai refuses to accept the clothing that Esther sends him.
	stimulus	response	4:5–4:9	Esther asks why, and Mordecai tells her of Haman's edict and orders her to plead with the king on behalf of her people.
	COMPLICATION; response	stimulus	4:10–4:17	Esther consents to appeal to the king at the risk of her life. She orders Mordecai and the Jews to fast for three days for her.

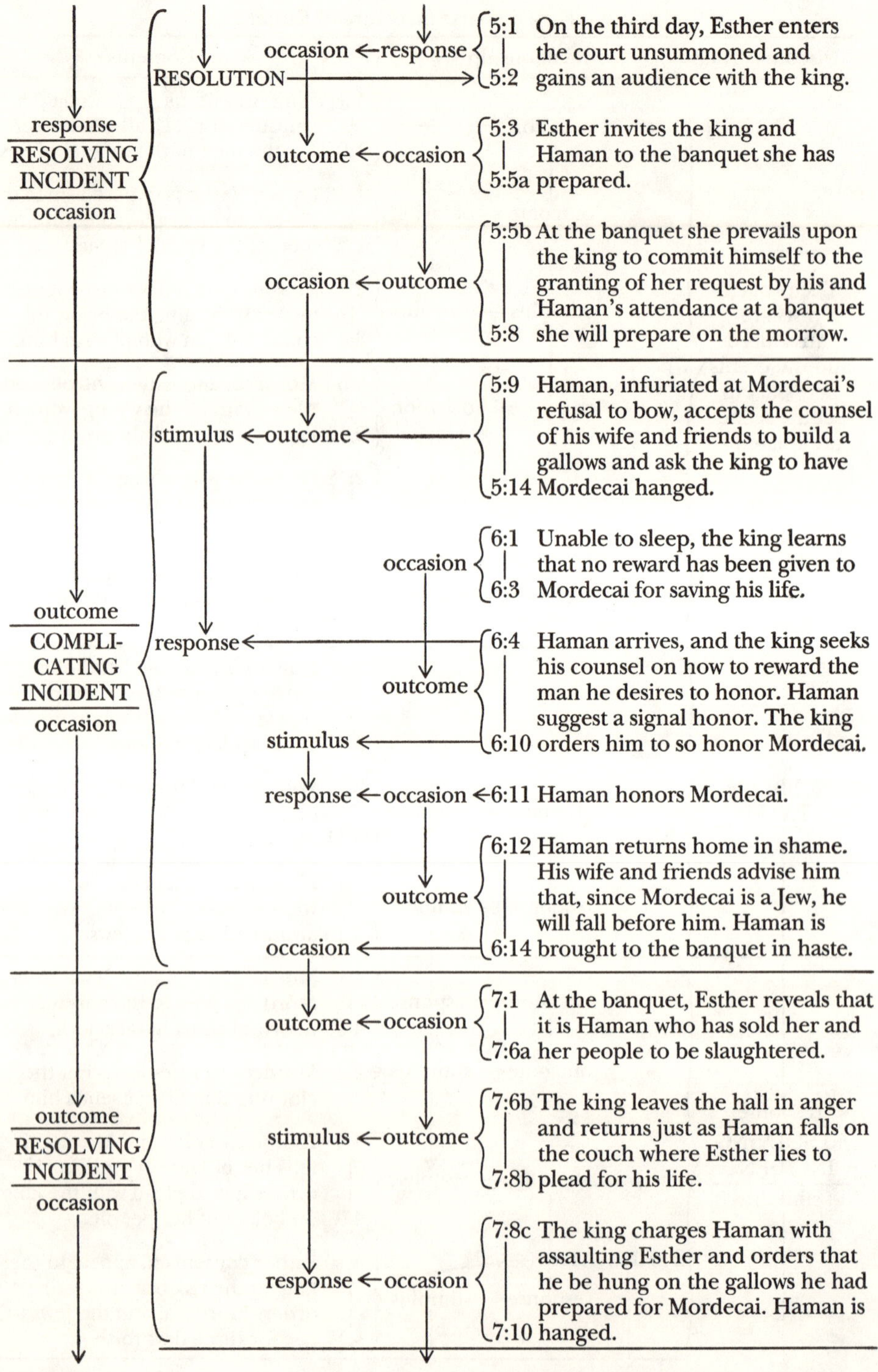
response
RESOLVING INCIDENT
occasion
RESOLUTION
occasion ← response
5:1–5:2 On the third day, Esther enters the court unsummoned and gains an audience with the king.
outcome ← occasion
5:3–5:5a Esther invites the king and Haman to the banquet she has prepared.
occasion ← outcome
5:5b–5:8 At the banquet she prevails upon the king to commit himself to the granting of her request by his and Haman's attendance at a banquet she will prepare on the morrow.
outcome
COMPLI-CATING INCIDENT
occasion
stimulus ← outcome
5:9–5:14 Haman, infuriated at Mordecai's refusal to bow, accepts the counsel of his wife and friends to build a gallows and ask the king to have Mordecai hanged.
occasion
6:1–6:3 Unable to sleep, the king learns that no reward has been given to Mordecai for saving his life.
response
outcome
stimulus
6:4–6:10 Haman arrives, and the king seeks his counsel on how to reward the man he desires to honor. Haman suggest a signal honor. The king orders him to so honor Mordecai.
response ← occasion
6:11 Haman honors Mordecai.
outcome
occasion
6:12–6:14 Haman returns home in shame. His wife and friends advise him that, since Mordecai is a Jew, he will fall before him. Haman is brought to the banquet in haste.
outcome
RESOLVING INCIDENT
occasion
outcome ← occasion
7:1–7:6a At the banquet, Esther reveals that it is Haman who has sold her and her people to be slaughtered.
stimulus ← outcome
7:6b–7:8b The king leaves the hall in anger and returns just as Haman falls on the couch where Esther lies to plead for his life.
response ← occasion
7:8c–7:10 The king charges Haman with assaulting Esther and orders that he be hung on the gallows he had prepared for Mordecai. Haman is hanged.

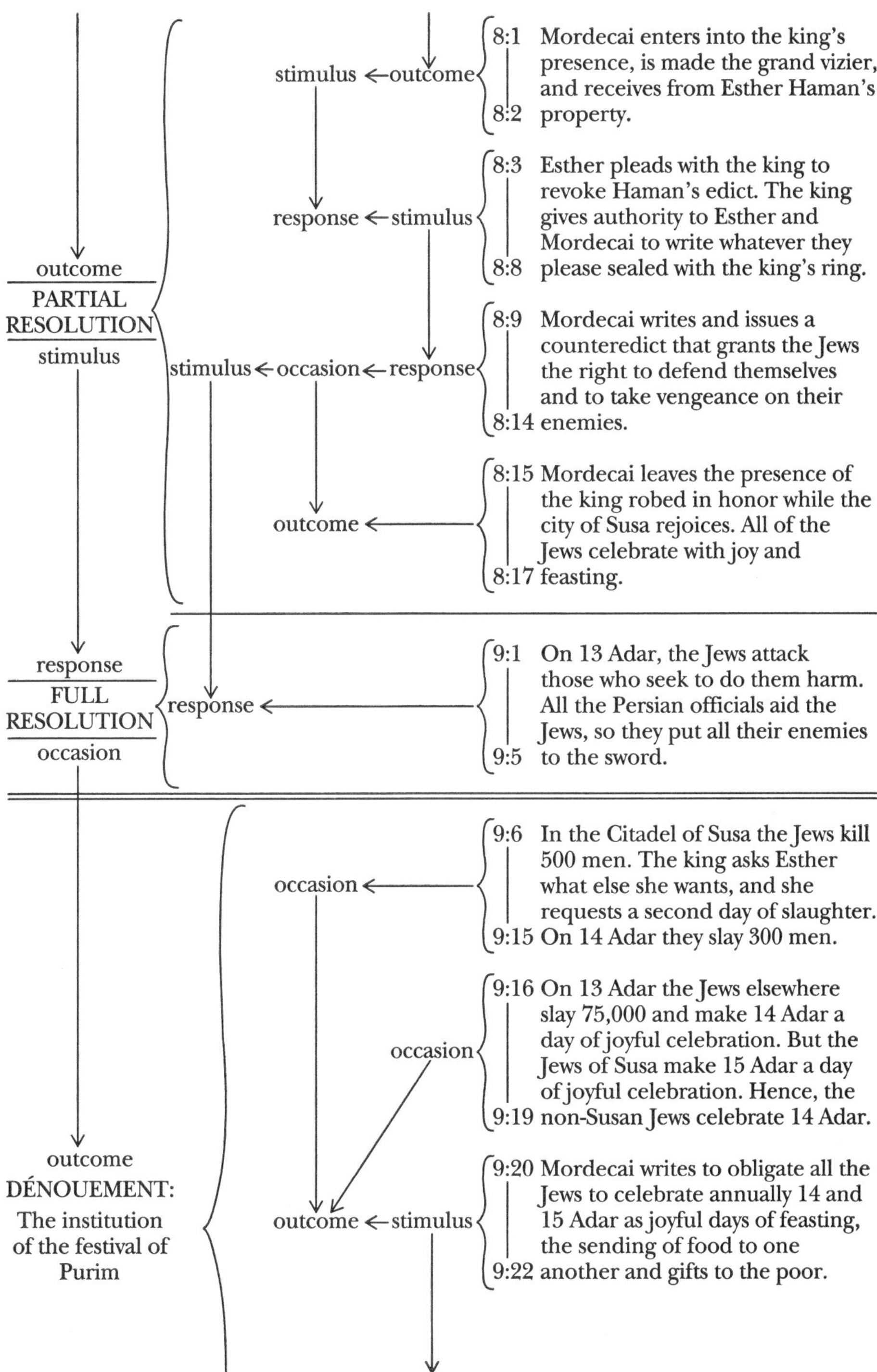
outcome
PARTIAL RESOLUTION
stimulus
stimulus ← outcome
response ← stimulus
stimulus ← occasion ← response
outcome ←
8:1–8:2 Mordecai enters into the king's presence, is made the grand vizier, and receives from Esther Haman's property.
8:3–8:8 Esther pleads with the king to revoke Haman's edict. The king gives authority to Esther and Mordecai to write whatever they please sealed with the king's ring.
8:9–8:14 Mordecai writes and issues a counteredict that grants the Jews the right to defend themselves and to take vengeance on their enemies.
8:15–8:17 Mordecai leaves the presence of the king robed in honor while the city of Susa rejoices. All of the Jews celebrate with joy and feasting.
response
FULL RESOLUTION
occasion
response ←
9:1–9:5 On 13 Adar, the Jews attack those who seek to do them harm. All the Persian officials aid the Jews, so they put all their enemies to the sword.
outcome
DÉNOUEMENT:
The institution of the festival of Purim
occasion ←
occasion
outcome ← stimulus
9:6–9:15 In the Citadel of Susa the Jews kill 500 men. The king asks Esther what else she wants, and she requests a second day of slaughter. On 14 Adar they slay 300 men.
9:16–9:19 On 13 Adar the Jews elsewhere slay 75,000 and make 14 Adar a day of joyful celebration. But the Jews of Susa make 15 Adar a day of joyful celebration. Hence, the non-Susan Jews celebrate 14 Adar.
9:20–9:22 Mordecai writes to obligate all the Jews to celebrate annually 14 and 15 Adar as joyful days of feasting, the sending of food to one another and gifts to the poor.

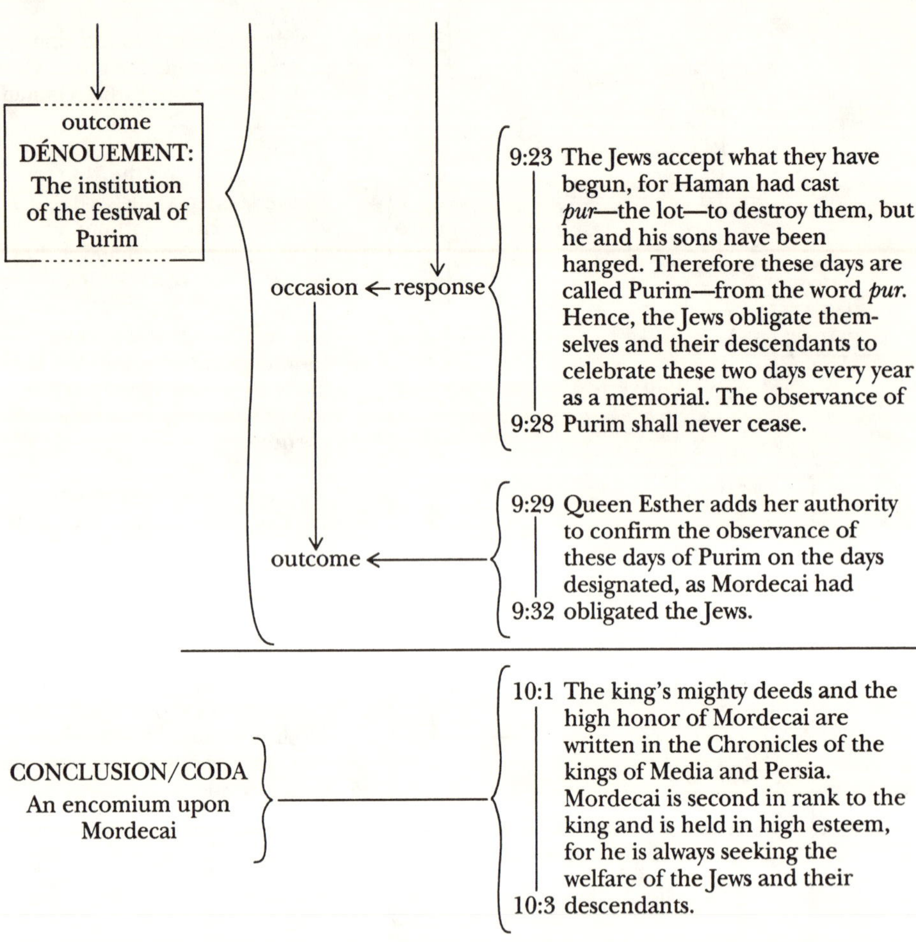

outcome
DÉNOUEMENT:
The institution of the festival of Purim
occasion
response
9:23 The Jews accept what they have begun, for Haman had cast *pur*—the lot—to destroy them, but he and his sons have been hanged. Therefore these days are called Purim—from the word *pur*. Hence, the Jews obligate themselves and their descendants to celebrate these two days every year as a memorial. The observance of
9:28 Purim shall never cease.
outcome
9:29 Queen Esther adds her authority to confirm the observance of these days of Purim on the days designated, as Mordecai had
9:32 obligated the Jews.
CONCLUSION/CODA
An encomium upon Mordecai
10:1 The king's mighty deeds and the high honor of Mordecai are written in the Chronicles of the kings of Media and Persia. Mordecai is second in rank to the king and is held in high esteem, for he is always seeking the welfare of the Jews and their
10:3 descendants.

It should express the consequences of the resolution, the difference that it makes for the principal characters (see the *Introduction* to Ruth and the discussion of the dénouement of Ruth in the *Purpose* section thereto). However, this is not the function of the dénouement in Esther, as our examination of this pericope in the commentary below reveals. The discussion there documents that the contents and purposes of 9:6–32 are significantly different from those of both the narrative that has preceded and the conclusion/coda that follows (see *Form/Structure/Setting* and *Explanation* to act 9, 9:26–32; cf. Fox, *Redaction,* § 4.3, 114–15). The pericope certainly does not simply enumerate the consequences of the resolution for Esther, Mordecai, and the Jews. It neither fills in the details of the Jewish victory, nor does it simply relate how the celebration of Purim came to be. As Fox notes, it "is analytical rather than narrational, more interested in explaining events than in reporting them" (*Redaction,* 115). Its purpose is not narrational but legislative, setting forth the dates, purposes, and character of Purim and obligating the Jewish community to its perpetual celebration (see the first paragraph of *Explanation* to 9:26–32). This can be corroborated by the fact that even the narrative style undergoes a dramatic change. The previous story has been told with great narrative skill and sensitive characterization, but the narrative here falls apart. Particularly inept are the king's renewal of his offer to Esther to fulfill whatever she asks (v 12c) and Esther's subsequent request for another day of fighting (v 13). Neither are motivated by anything in the preceding narrative; they are motivated solely by the need for two days of fighting in Susa, in contrast to what happened elsewhere, in order to explain the different days of celebration of the festival in the different parts of the Jewish community (see *Explanation* to 9:6–15). This can be further corroborated by the striking contrast between this dénouement and that of the proto-AT (see the analysis and comparison of the proto-AT with MT-Esther in *Unity and Redaction* above). There, after the resolution of the crisis is effected when Mordecai requests that the king revoke Haman's edict and the king gives him control over the affairs of the kingdom, AT 8:16–17, the dénouement consists of the following: (1) the punishment of the enemies of the Jews and the ten sons of Haman at Esther's request, AT 8:18–21; (2) Mordecai's letter, which orders the Jews to remain quiet and hold a festival and advises the empire of the resolution of the crisis, AT 8:34–38; and (3) probably also the facts that Mordecai went out clothed in royal apparel, Susa rejoiced, and the Jews celebrated, AT 8:39–40. This does indeed recount the consequences of the resolution for the protagonists of the story.

Finally, the dénouement contrasts also with the conclusion/coda in 10:1–3, for the conclusion does not relate in the slightest way to the celebration of Purim. It would do so if, for example, it related that the Jewish community did indeed institute the festival and have continued to celebrate it "to this day" (or the like). On the contrary, the narrator leaves the legislative concerns of Purim and returns to the concerns of the previous narrative by completing the discourse with an encomium upon Mordecai. In fact, it is quite striking how fully the narrative of 10:1–3 continues the emphasis upon the status and impact of Mordecai, which had been set in the resolution (cf. 8:15; 9:3–4).

Thus it is clear that the first part of the book of Esther, 1:1–9:5, and its conclusion, 10:1–3, fulfill the functions of the "setting" through "resolution" and "conclusion/coda" discourse roles of a problem-based plot; the first part does so with dramatic and narratival skill combined with sensitivity to characterization. However, the narrative style of the dénouement, 9:6–32, is dramatically different, and its discourse role takes an entirely new direction. The explanation for this can be found in the evidence for redaction of the present book in *Unity and Redaction* above. There it was argued that an original story ("proto-Esther") was modified by the addition of the theme of the inalterability of Persian law, the drafting and issuance of the counteredict in chap. 8, rendered necessary thereby, and the ultimate victory of the Jews in the conflict in 9:1–5, required by the irreconcilable edicts. Indeed, it is striking that this presents us with three independent lines of evidence for the composite character of the book, for the subtle but unmistakable incompatibility in (1) narrative style and (2) discourse roles between the first two parts of the book dovetails almost perfectly with (3) its redactional structure, corroborating the hypothesis that an original story has been adapted to the purposes of the institution of the festival of Purim.

The result of all this as far as genre is concerned requires the recognition that the purpose of the book has a dual character. The genre of its final form is unmistakably that of a "festival etiology"; i.e., the narrative as a whole not only explains the origin of the festival of Purim but inculcates its observance (see esp. Fox, 151). A number of commentators have specifically designated its genre as "festival legend" (e.g., Bardtke, 251–52; Gerleman, 23; Haller, 114; Ringgren, 375), while many others have recognized that this is the purpose (or function) at least of the final form of the book (e.g., Driver, *Introduction,* 481; Childs, *Introduction,* 603–5; Clines, 262; id., *Esther Scroll,* 158–67; Moore, liii; id., *ABD* 2:634; Paton, 54–56). At one level, then, the genre of Esther is that of *a festival etiology.*

2. *Festival lection.* A careful reading of the institution of Purim will also show, however, that the genre of the book at the level of function is *festival lection* (see Fox, 152). In 9:26 the phrases "because of all that was written in this letter, and what they had experienced in this regard and what had happened to them," which constitute the reason that the Jews have obligated themselves to the celebration of Purim (v 26b), clearly refer to the whole story of the deliverance from the crisis occasioned by Haman's edict of extermination. V 28 stipulates that these days of Purim "are going to be celebrated as a memorial [lit. 'remembered and performed,' a hendiadys; see *Comment*] throughout all generations" and "their *commemoration* shall not come to an end among their descendants." Clearly, to commemorate the joy of this deliverance requires retelling the story. To celebrate the ancestor's experience requires retelling what that experience was. It is an essential part, then, of the celebration of Purim to hear the story. Therefore the function of the story in the context of Purim means that its genre is also that of *festival lection.*

B. *The genre set by the problem-based plot of 1:1–9:5: a short story that reveals the quality of a situation.* As the discussion above shows, the closely related genre designations elucidated there deal only with the final form of the book. In determining its genre, the earlier part of the narrative and its conclusion, which comprise such a large part of the whole, must be taken into account. The discourse roles and function of these sections, elucidated in the analysis of the structure above, suggest that Humphreys' attempt ("Novella") to define a genre of "novella" in the OT and to apply this designation to the book of Esther ("Story of Esther and Mordecai") is a helpful starting point. Humphreys distinguishes between a genre of "short story" and "novella" on the grounds of length and complexity. The novella in general will be longer; it will have more characters, a more complex plot structure, and a more extended time frame ("Novella," 85). Most helpful in my opinion is Humphreys' observation (drawing on the distinction made by James Joyce between the modern short story and the novel) that the short story has an "epiphany quality," i.e., it *reveals* the nature of a character or a situation, while the novel *develops* characters or situations (for a more detailed treatment, see the discussion in the *Genre* section of the *Introduction* to Ruth). Given this analysis, Humphreys interprets the story of Esther as a novella (see his article "The Story of Esther and Mordecai"), not only on the grounds of the length and complexity of its plot but also because it *develops* the quality of its *characters.*

However, this seems to me to be a significant misunderstanding of the point and purpose of these chapters. First, and most important, in these chapters the author is primarily interested in the quality of a *situation* rather than in the quality of his *characters.* (In the *Purpose and Theme* section to follow, it will be argued that the specific situation that the author of Esther wishes to characterize is the quality of life for Jews in the diaspora.) The author's interest in the quality of a situation can be seen first in the fact that the book's stance is far to one side of the spectrum of OT narrative in the matter of what Alter has helpfully and insightfully called the OT's "narration-through-dialogue" (*Art*, 69; cf. also Berlin, *Poetics*, 33–42); i.e., in most OT narration the plot, as well as the characterization of the protagonists, is advanced primarily through dialogue. Thus, Alter notes, "the primacy of dialogue is so pronounced that many pieces of third-person narration prove on inspection to be dialogue-bound, verbally mirroring elements of dialogue which precede them or which they introduce. Narration is thus often relegated to the role of confirming assertions made in dialogue . . . ." (*Art*, 65). Through such narration-through-dialogue "what is significant about a character, at least for a particular narrative juncture, can be manifested almost entirely in a character's speech" (*Art*, 70). This is the narrative style of Ruth, in which the author characterizes his three protagonists in such a way as to present them as models for his readers to emulate and advances the plot itself primarily through dialogue (see the discussion in the *Genre* section of the *Introduction* to Ruth). However, this is far removed from the narrative style of Esther. This can be revealed by such a coarse measure as the percent of each narrative that the speeches of the protagonists constitute. Of the words of the book of Ruth, 738 out of 1,392 are uttered by the characters, constituting 53.0 percent. Of the words of the book of Esther, however, only 718 out of 3,044 are direct discourse, constituting 23.6 percent, significantly less than half that of Ruth. (The total number of words for Esther is taken from Dorothy, "Books of Esther," 1; the other figures are my own count, obtained by ignoring maqqeph and counting את.)

Much more revealing, however, than a simple word count is the *distribution* and *use* of dialogue (or direct discourse) in Esther. In contrast to the author of Ruth, the narrator of Esther primarily advances his plot through straight narration, either without dialogue at all or by the use of indirect discourse. Thus, OT narration is very sparing in what Alter calls the "expository information" that introduces a narrative (*Art*, 80–81), and especially in the physical description of either characters or scenes. Thus, in the book of Ruth the exposition is set forth in the spare narrative of 1:1–6, and it knows no physical description of any sort. In contrast, the exposition of Esther comprises the long and detailed opening two chapters, 1:1–2:23, all of which is narration but for the brief dialogue between the king and his counselors over what to do about Vashti's disobedience (1:15–20) and the very brief monologue with which the king's personal attendants make their proposal for replacing her (2:2b–4). One will look almost in vain in the rest of the OT for a detailed description of a scene such as the depiction of the opulence, extravagance, and excesses of the setting and circumstances of Ahasuerus' second banquet in 1:5–8. The "problem" section (3:1–15) and the "resolution" section (8:1–9:5) of the discourse structure are developed with straight narration but for Haman's appeal to the king in 3:8–11 and Esther's in 8:5–8. In fact, the important parts of both sections (Haman's edict to annihilate the Jews, 3:12–15, and Mordecai's counteredict granting them the right of self-defense and retribution upon their enemies, 8:9–14) are presented not only totally in indirect discourse but also in the passive voice, an effect that dramatically conveys the inexorable and impersonal machinery of the Persian bureaucracy. Only in the critical central section of the narrative, acts 3–6, 5:1–7:10, in which Esther is first recruited by Mordecai and then skillfully appeals to the king for the life of her people in her two banquets, does the narrator carry the plot primarily through dialogue. (Note the artful shift from indirect discourse to direct discourse in the introduction to this critical section in 4:5–17; see the *Form/Structure/Setting* section thereto.) Finally, the whole of the dénouement, which depicts the institution of the festival of Purim, is in straight narration or indirect discourse but for the brief dialogue between the king and Esther over the second day of slaughter in Susa (9:12–14). This emphasis on narrative focuses the reader's attention on the quality of the situation.

The same conclusion results from comparing *characterization* in the two books. In the book of Ruth, two of the major protagonists, Ruth and Boaz, are characterized not only by their words and actions but repeatedly by "embedded evaluation," i.e., through the words of other characters (e.g., Ruth by Boaz in 2:11; 3:10, 11; Boaz by Naomi in 3:17–19), and by the use of character contrasts (Orpah for Ruth and the unnamed "redeemer" for Boaz; see Berlin, *Poetics,* 40–41, 104–6). In one striking case, the narrator gives his own (omniscient) evaluation (Boaz in 2:1). (See the detailed discussion in the *Genre* section of the *Introduction* to Ruth). There is virtually none of this in Esther. None of the characters give any embedded evaluation, and there are no character contrasts. Indeed, speech is only marginally used in characterization. The extreme nature of the disparity between the two books can be seen in that in the whole book of Esther the narrator gives to Mordecai, one of the most important characters in the book, but one short speech of thirty-one words (4:13b–14)! The evil of Haman is primarily depicted not by what he says but by the narrator's (omniscient) disclosure of his thoughts and feelings (see *Theme and Purpose* below). Indeed, not just these general aspects of characterization in Esther, but in particular a detailed investigation of the characterization of the protagonists of the narrative (the king and the world he rules, Haman, Mordecai, Esther, and the Jews, as well as the role of God in the story) shows unmistakably that the narrator intends to reveal the quality of a situation rather than the quality of his characters. Because of its pertinence for determining what that situation is, however, this investigation of the characterization of the protagonists will be presented in the discussion of the theme of 1:1–9:5 (see *Theme, Purpose, and Theology* below). All of this makes it clear that the author primarily describes not the quality of his characters but the quality of a situation (for the identification of which see *Theme and Purpose* below).

Finally, in my opinion it is clear that the narrator does *not* intend to *develop* the quality of this situation; instead, he wishes to *reveal* it. That is, it partakes of the "epiphany quality" of the short story, not the developmental quality of the novella. Humphreys designates Esther a "novella" on the grounds that the story's four principal characters, though they "seem more stereotypical" in contrast to those of the Joseph narrative, nevertheless "all . . . appear to evolve" ("Story of Esther and Mordecai," 105). On the contrary, of the four main protagonists, only Esther changes or develops (see the discussion in *Theme* below). Humphreys alleges ("Story of Esther and Mordecai," 106) that Mordecai becomes more passive as Esther becomes more active. It is true, as Humphreys notes, that Mordecai is very much in the background in the two resolving incidents and in the complication in the central section (5:1–7:10), but this is entirely because of the necessities of the plot development and hence has little to do with the characterization of Mordecai. His role in the latter part of the book can hardly be termed passive. In the resolution of the crisis (8:1–9:5), it is Mordecai who drafts and issues in the king's name the counteredict that effects the Jews' deliverance, and he unquestionably plays the major role in the dénouement (9:6–32), writing the letter that obligates the Jews to the celebration of Purim (9:20–22, 23b, 26b; cf. Fox, 185). Humphreys' own discussion of the characterization of Haman and Ahasuerus (107–8) evidences no change or development at all. Haman is unmitigated evil from beginning to end, and Ahasuerus remains malleable, unstable, impulsive, and self-willed throughout. Clearly, evolution of the central characters can hardly be said to be a quality of Esther.

The same is true for the quality of the situation it portrays. The possibility, yet risk and uncertainty, of life for Jews in the diaspora (for which see *Theme and Purpose* below) does not significantly change or develop throughout the course of the story. Thus, for example, the character of the terrible threat to the Jews does not either improve or worsen as the plot develops but rather remains as heinous in the end as it is in the beginning. This can clearly be seen by the way that the crisis of the story is introduced in act 2, scene 1 (3:1–6). When Haman is informed of Mordecai's refusal to do obeisance to him, he does not decide to take some action against Mordecai himself, but rather, having been told who Mordecai's people are, he seeks a way to destroy all the Jews. Not only does the character of this terrible crisis remain the same throughout, but the narrator does not introduce development by, for example, increasingly raising doubt as to its resolution. True, some slight doubt briefly appears when Esther raises the issue of the risk she faces in going to the king unsummoned (4:10–11). But this concern is quickly resolved when the narrator immediately relates the account of Esther's two banquets (5:1–8; 7:1–10), in which the inexorable progress toward Haman's demise is slowed only by the interlude of his attempt to hang Mordecai (5:9–6:14). This interlude, though it increases suspense, raises no doubts whatsoever about Haman's fate. Rather, it dramatically signals its certainty by presaging his downfall through two complete reversals: his hope of honor (6:6) turns into utter humiliation (6:10–11), and the counsel of his wife and friends is transformed from happy prospects (5:14) to the somber announcement of his doom (6:13). Finally, that the conflict between the two irrevocable edicts, one prescribing the Jews annihilation and the other the right of self-defense and retribution upon their enemies, will inevitably result in the success of the latter is unmistakably indicated by the account of Mordecai's royal robes, the joyous cheers of the city of Susa, the celebrations of the Jews, and the conversion of many non-Jews that the narrator describes as the immediate upshot of Mordecai's counteredict (8:15–17). The genre of the narrative of the Jews' deliverance from Haman's edict of annihilation is a "short story," not a "novella," for it reveals the quality of a situation; it does not develop it. (For a further argument that "short story" designates the genre of Esther better than "novella" on the grounds of the meaning and length of the genre designation "novella" in the literary tradition from which it was borrowed, see Fox, 146 n. 15.)

On these grounds, then, the genre of the narrative of Esther is at least threefold. At one level, in its final form, it functions as *the etiology for the festival of Purim* and as its *festival lection.* At a second level, however, its genre is *a short story that reveals the quality of a situation.*

Theme, Purpose, and Theology

Bibliography

Alter, R. *The Art of Biblical Narrative.* New York: Basic, 1981. **Anderson, B. W.** "The Place of the Book of Esther in the Christian Bible." *JR* 30 (1950) 32–43. **Bandstra, B. L.** *Reading the Old Testament: An Introduction to the Hebrew Bible.* Belmont, CA: Wadsworth, 1995. **Baumgarten, A. I.** "Scroll of Esther." *EncJud* 14:1047–57. **Ben-Chorin, S.** *Kritik des Esterbuches: Eine theologische Streitschrift.* Jerusalem, 1938. **Berg, S. B.** *The Book of Esther: Motifs, Themes and Structure.* Missoula, MT: Scholars, 1979. **Berlin, A.** *Poetics and Interpretation of Biblical Narrative.* Sheffield: Almond, 1983. **Bettan, I.** *The Five Scrolls.* Cincinnati: Union of American Hebrew Congregations, 1950. **Bewer, J. A.** *The Literature of the Old Testament.* Rev. ed. New York: Columbia UP, 1933. **Brenner, A.** "On the Semantic Field of Humour, Laughter and the Comic in the Old Testament." In *On Humour and the Comic in the Hebrew Bible,* ed. Y. T. Radday and A. Brenner. Sheffield: Almond, 1990. 39–58. **Childs, B.** *Introduction to the Old Testament as Scripture.* Philadelphia: Fortress, 1979. **Clines, D. J. A.** *The Esther Scroll: The Story of the Story.* JSOTSup 30. Sheffield: JSOT, 1984. ———. Review of W. Hermann, *Esther im Streit der Meinungen.* Society for Old Testament Study Book List, 1988. 78. **Cornill, C. H.** *Introduction to the Canonical Books of the Old Testament.* Tr. G. Box. New York: Williams and Norgate, 1907. **Darr, K. P.** "More than Just a Pretty Face: Critical, Rabbinical, and Feminist Perspectives on Esther." In *Far More Precious Than Jewels: Perspectives on Biblical Women.* Louisville: Westminster/John Knox, 1991. 164–202. **Dillard, R. B.,** and **Longman, T. III.** *An Introduction to the Old Testament.* Grand Rapids, MI: Zondervan, 1994. **Driver, S. R.** *Introduction to the Literature of the Old Testament.* 9th ed. Edinburgh: T & T Clark, 1913. **Eissfeldt, O.** *The Old Testament: An Introduction.* Tr. P. Ackroyd. New York: Harper and Row, 1965. **Fohrer, G.** *Introduction to the Old Testament.* Tr. D. Green. Nashville: Abingdon, 1968. **Fox, M.** "The Structure of the Book of Esther." In *Isac Leo Seligmann Volume: Essays on the Bible and the Ancient World,* ed. A. Rofe and Y. Zakovitch. Jerusalem: Rubinstein, 1983. 3:291–303. **Gaster, T. H.** *Purim and Hanukkah in Custom and Tradition.* New York: Henry Schuman, 1950. **Gordis, R.** *Megillat Esther: The Masoretic Hebrew Text with Introduction, New Translation and Commentary.* New York: Rabbinical Assembly, 1972. **Harris, M.** "Purim: The Celebration of Dis-Order." *Judaism* 26 (1977) 161–70. **Herrmann, W.** *Esther im Streit der Meinungen.* Beiträge zur Erforschung des AT und des antiken Judentums. Frankfurt am Main, 1986. **Humphreys, W. L.** "A Life-style for Diaspora: A Study of the Tales of Esther and Daniel." *JBL* 92 (1973) 211–23. ———. "The Story of Esther and Mordecai: An Early Jewish Novella." In *Saga, Legend, Tale, Novella, Fable: Narrative Forms in Old Testament Literature,* ed. G. Coats. JSOTSup 35. Sheffield: JSOT, 1985. 97–113. **Ironside, H. A.** *Joshua, Ezra, Nehemiah, Esther.* Neptune, NJ: Loiseaux Brothers, 1983. **Jacob, L.** "Purim." *EncJud* 13:1390–95. **LaSor, W. S., Hubbard, D. A.,** and **Bush, F. W.** *Old Testament Survey: The Message, Form, and Background of the Old Testament.* Rev. ed. Grand Rapids, MI: Eerdmans, 1996. **Levenson, J. D.** "The Scroll of Esther in Ecumenical Perspective." *JES* 13 (1976) 440–51. **Lewy, J.** "The Feast of the 14th Day of Adar." *HUCA* 14 (1939) 127–51. **Loader, J. A.** "Esther as a Novel with Different Levels of Meaning." *ZAW* 90 (1978) 417–21. **Moore, C. A.** "Esther, Book of." *ABD* 2:633–43. **Radday, Y. T.** "Esther with Humour." In *On Humour and the Comic in the Hebrew Bible,* ed. Y. T. Radday and A. Brenner. Sheffield: Almond, 1990. 295–313. **Ringgren, H.** "Esther and Purim." *SEÅ* 20 (1956) 5–24 (= Moore, *Studies,* 185–204). **Sandmel, S.** *The Enjoyment of Scripture.* New York: Oxford UP, 1972. **Shmeruk, C.** "Purim-shpil." *EncJud* 13:1396–1404. **Sternberg, M.** *The Poetics of Biblical Narrative: Ideological Literature and the Drama of Reading.* Bloomington: Indiana UP, 1985. **Weiser, A.** *Introduction to the Old Testament.* Tr. D. Barton. London: Darton, Longman and Todd, 1961. **White, S. A.** "Esther: A Feminine Model for Jewish Diaspora." In *Gender and Difference in Ancient Israel,* ed. P. Day. Minneapolis: Fortress, 1989. 161–77.

THEME AND PURPOSE

In the remarks in the *Theme and Purpose* section of the *Introduction* to the book of Ruth, it was deduced that in the narrative genre the discourse elements of *resolution* and *dénouement* have the greatest importance, since the dominant relationship between the discourse roles in narrative is that of cause-effect (either stimulus-response or occasion-outcome), and effects are naturally more prominent than causes. Hence, it is these discourse elements that will be the most significant in determining the theme and purpose of the work (i.e., the statement of its plot with an emphasis on conceptualized meaning, the central and dominating idea).

Since this is the case, it is immediately apparent that the theme and purpose of Esther will be twofold, as its genre was twofold, since there is a marked incongruity between the "problem-resolution" discourse elements and the "dénouement" that follows. The dénouement does not simply describe the consequences of the "problem-resolution" sequence for the participants; rather it describes the dates, purposes, and character of the festival of Purim and seeks to obligate the Jewish community to its perpetual observance (see the discussion in *Genre*). However, despite this incongruity with the problem-based plot that precedes, the dénouement depends upon the story as the etiology for the festival it prescribes. Hence, it is necessary first to deduce the theme and purpose of the story. Then it will be possible to turn to the purpose and theme of the dénouement.

A. *The theme and purpose of the "problem-based plot" of Esther 1:1–9:5; 10:1–3.*

1. *General considerations.* It will be argued here that the portrayal of the quality of a situation (see the discussion of the genre of 1:1–9:5 in *Genre* above), namely, the dangerous and uncertain character of life for Jews in the diaspora, is a significant element in its theme. This can be seen at every level of the narrative.

a. *The significance of the narrative's non-speech narration.* Let us begin by noting that non-speech narration carries the primary freight in this story in both plot development and characterization. Here again, as with the determination of genre, comparison between Ruth and Esther is instructive. In the book of Ruth, the narrator advances his plot primarily through dialogue, through which he reveals the quality of life of the protagonists of his story. It is as much the quality of their character as their actions that moves the story forward (see the *Theme and Purpose* section of the *Introduction* to Ruth). But the opposite is the case in Esther. The author here primarily uses narration rather than dialogue to advance his plot. Consequently, the plot structure and development play a role equal to, if not more important than, that of characterization in determining the theme and purpose of the book.

b. *The significance of the narrative's "domain."* Second, let us note the important, even though obvious, domain of our story. The contrast with the book of Ruth is again striking. The setting in Ruth is rural and agricultural (the harvest field, the threshing floor, the village gate), and all its major characters are ordinary people. Every scene of Esther, except the two brief episodes in Haman's home (5:9–14; 6:12–14) and the brief account of the final Jewish victory (9:1–5), takes place in the royal court of Persia, and some take place in the throne room and the king's private quarters. Three of the major characters in Esther are the most important members of the royal court (the king, the queen, and the grand vizier), and the fourth begins as a member of the court (see *Comment* on 2:19) and eventually replaces the grand vizier. The pomp and pageantry with which so much of the story is vested is nicely caught by the statistics given by Radday, who notes that, of the 3,270 words of the book as a whole (his enumeration), "no fewer than 439 belong to the semantic field of staff, etiquette and wealth" ("Esther with Humour," 329; cf. his list there). The story, then, is completely set in the centers of power that control and dominate its world.

2. *The "world" of the story: the Jewish diaspora.* Within the larger domain noted above, the narrower world of the story is that of the Jews of the diaspora. Two elements of the story establish this with dramatic clarity: (a) the significance of Mordecai's epithet היהודי, "the Jew," and (b) the story's diaspora agenda.

a. *The significance of Mordecai's epithet* היהודי, *"the Jew."* When Mordecai is introduced in the story's exposition, he is identified by the epithet איש יהודי, "a *Jewish* man" (for the argument that the epithet should be understood as "Jewish" and not "Judean" or "Judahite," see *Explanation* to 2:5), and his primary identity throughout the rest of the book is "Mordecai the Jew" (5:13; 6:10; 8:7; 9:31; 10:3). Epithets in scripture are seldom incidental identifiers (Fox, 186; cf. Sternberg, *Poetics,* 328–31). Sternberg observes, "A biblical epithet serves at least two functions, one bearing directly on the character it qualifies and the other bearing indirectly on the plot where he figures as agent or patient" (*Poetics,* 337–38). The epithet, then, characterizes Mordecai's role in the story in a most important way. (Its meaning for the characterization of Mordecai himself will be noted below.) Its significance is indicated by the fact that this is the only time in the whole OT that a native member of the community of Israel is named and identified by a gentilic. In the OT a member of Israel is regularly identified by a patronymic (i.e., the male line of descent), even though his place of origin in Israel may also be given. Only foreigners who are domiciled in Israel as resident aliens are regularly identified only by their country or region of origin. Thus, contrast the foreigner "Uriah the Hittite" (1 Sam 11, passim; 23:29) with "Uriah son of Shemaiah from Kiriath-jearim" (Jer 26:20–23), or the Philistine "Ittai the Gittite" (2 Sam 15:19–22; 18:2–12) with "Ittai son of Ribai from Gibeah of Benjamin" (2 Sam 23:29), and note the use of "Ruth the Moabitess" as Ruth's full name in the book of Ruth (see esp. *Comment* on Ruth 2:21). Thus, the use of this gentilic as the only identification of Mordecai signals a conscious recognition of the foreign, the diaspora, status of both Mordecai and the Jewish community throughout the book. Mordecai is "Mordecai the Jew" and never "Mordecai son of Jair" or even "Mordecai the Benjaminite" because he and all his fellow "Jews" are living as foreigners, "resident aliens," in a foreign land. It is true, then, that "the ideal typified by Mordecai . . . is of the representative Jew, a man identified first and foremost by his Jewishness" (Fox, 186), as long as one understands that in the book of Esther "Jew" specifically identifies him as a member of the diaspora and that "Jewishness" is synonymous with "diaspora existence."

b. *The narrative's "diaspora agenda."* Levenson (*JES* 13 [1976] 444–51) has pointed out a most important feature of the book of Esther, a feature that corroborates the significance of Mordecai's epithet, "the Jew." In the course of arguing that the book is intended specifically to provide for the diaspora "an example of God's salvation" in "the great pattern of redemption history" (448–49), Levenson insightfully observes that all the rest of Israel's literature from the exilic and post-exilic periods (2 and 3 Isaiah, Haggai, Zechariah, Obadiah, Ezra-Nehemiah, Daniel) have one single-minded agenda. These works are narrowly and specifically concerned with the return of the exiled leaders of the Judean community to the ancient land of Israel and the re-establishment of the city of Jerusalem and the temple "as the perfect type of divine deliverance and the first sign of ultimate redemption" (445). From the perspective of this agenda, the theological estimate of the exile was "overwhelmingly negative, . . . a barren interlude valuable only as propaedeutic to the return" (446). Whether those who remained in exile were considered by their Palestinian compatriots to be under a curse and hence presumably outside the community of faith (Levenson, 446, 448) is hard to establish, for outside of the books of Esther and Daniel there is hardly a word at all about those who remained in exile.

The operative word here is "remained." Humphreys has argued that Jeremiah's words to the exiles (Jer 29:4–7) suggest "a remarkable style of life for the exile: one that was quite open to the possibilities of an enriched life in, and contact with, the foreign culture of the new situation" (*JBL* 92 [1973] 211). But, in this statement Jeremiah is not intending to set a permanent agenda for the diaspora. Rather, he unmistakably intends to establish the certainty of the exile (to last for some seventy years) as a measure of the reality of judgment (as vv 8–14 demonstrate), not the establishment of a permanent and viable diaspora existence. This tradition, along with other Jeremiah traditions, *possibly* could have been "preserved and developed within Jewish communities" of the diaspora (as well as within the Palestinian Jewish community) and "would quite possibly receive considerable notice" in the attempt to "rebuild and construct anew a style of life and theological self-understanding" for the diaspora (Humphreys, *JBL* 92 [1973] 212), but there is no evidence in the OT for this. It is certainly true, at least, that those who remained in exile are simply never taken into consideration in any meaningful way in the rest of the post-exilic literature.

The difference between the agenda of Judeans of the diaspora reported in Palestinian post-exilic literature and that of the book of Esther is dramatic. Levenson (*JES* 13 [1976] 447) notes three relevant examples, ranging from Persian to Hellenistic times. (i) Nehemiah, like Mordecai, is a high official in the Persian court in Susa. His whole attention, concern, and actions, however, center on the restoration of Jerusalem (Neh 1–2), to which he returns (2:5). When he is introduced (in Susa), he is identified as Nehemiah son of Hacaliah (1:1), and in Jerusalem his identifying epithet is "Nehemiah the governor" (8:9; 10:1; 12:26). His example, then, can hardly be used, as Humphreys does (*JBL* 92 [1973] 212), as evidence for a concern to construct a life style for the diaspora. Not only is Nehemiah's heart still in Zion (Levenson, *JES* 13 [1976] 447); so is that of the narrator of the book of Nehemiah. (ii) Daniel also serves in the Persian court, but the concern of the book of Daniel is the future of the Judean community in Palestine: Daniel himself faces Jerusalem when he prays (Dan 6:10–11), agonizes in prayer over the seventy years prophesied for the devastation of Jerusalem, and receives a prophecy of its future (Dan 9). (iii) When Zerubbabel, Darius' personal bodyguard, is promised whatever he wishes, he requests the rebuilding of Jerusalem and the temple, and the restoration of the temple vessels (1 Esdr 4:42–46).

The agenda of the book of Esther contrasts sharply with this. Esther and Mordecai not only do not ever voice any concerns about Jerusalem and the temple and its cultus; they do not address even a single word to the Palestinian community (once the threat of Haman's edict has been countered and all the enemies have been slaughtered—they could hardly be concerned about Palestine until that was effected). They have but one agenda, the institution of the festival celebrating the joy of deliverance *in the diaspora* (see for Mordecai, 9:20–22, and for Esther, 9:29–32). In the encomium upon Mordecai, "the Jew," it is "among the Jews" (i.e., the diaspora) that he is held in high esteem, and it is their welfare and that of their descendants that he is said to be constantly seeking (10:3). In contradistinction, then, to the rest of Israel's post-exilic literature, the book of Esther is specifically and narrowly concerned with the life and concerns of Jews in the diaspora (cf. Fox, 228). The narrower focus of our story, then, is the world of the Jewish diaspora, and our narrator characterizes that world as a dangerous and uncertain place.

3. *The narrator's characterization of the protagonists of his story.* As was noted in the discussion in *Genre* above, the clearest indication that the narrator intends to reveal the quality of a situation is to be found in the way in which he does so by the characterization of his protagonists. This can be seen in his characterization of each of them.

a. *The characterization of the king and the world he rules.* That the theme of the story includes the dangerous and uncertain character and quality of life for Jews in the diaspora can be seen primarily, however, by the characterization of the world of the story. This is set first and foremost in the opening two chapters, the story's "setting" or "exposition." In most OT narration, the exposition (what Alter calls "expository information") consists of "a few brief statements" and is "pretemporal, statically enumerating data that are not bound to a specific moment in time: they are facts that stand before the time of the story proper" (*Art,* 80). From this, the setting of the book of Esther diverges dramatically. It does, of course, introduce to us three of the four major characters of the story (Ahasuerus, Esther, and Mordecai), and the events it relates do stand before the time of the story proper. But it is not brief, and it does not statically enumerate data. The basic facts presented, necessary to provide the information to understand the story to come, could actually have been stated (in narrative form, of course) in brief compass indeed: because of an offense against the king's royal dignity, the queen is deposed; when candidates are gathered to replace her, Esther, the cousin of Mordecai, a Jewish man who is an official in the court, is included and becomes the queen of Persia; Mordecai through Esther informs the king of an attempt on his life, which good deed is recorded in the daily court record. By expanding these facts into the detailed and embellished narrative we have, our narrator has accomplished much more than the telling of a good story. He has portrayed with satire and parody the world in which his story will be set.

This is particularly the case in the opening scene, 1:1–22 (see the *Explanation* and Clines, *Esther Scroll,* 9–11, 31–33). Here we see depicted an ordered world that is ruled inexorably by law (see the insightful analysis of Fox, 248–53), but it is not a law that can bring much assurance of stability or justice to those who stand under its mandates. It is irrevocable (1:19), but its source is the will and whim of an all-powerful king (he rules the known world, 1:1) who is portrayed in the first episode, 1:1–9, spending his time throwing lavish banquets. The first of these is described with mocking hyperbole as lasting for six months(!) and has the purpose of showing off "the riches and glory of his empire and the pomp and splendor of his majesty" (1:4). The description of the rich and lavish scenery (a rarity in OT narrative) of the second banquet, depicted with wonder and amazement, and the emphasis on the abundance of king's wine, which flowed without restraint (vv 5–8), continues the portrayal of the opulence and extravagance of the king and his court (see *Explanation*). In the second episode, 1:10–22, the king is described with delicious and satirical humor as losing a contest of wills with his wife, Vashti, when he orders her to appear before him in order to parade her beauty, adorned with her royal crown, before the tipsy common crowd. Vashti evidences the only element of decorum and decency in this world of opulence and excess, and refuses. Not knowing how to remedy the situation, the king turns helplessly to his privy council, whose long list of comically sounding names would have seemed ludicrous to the Hebrew ear and who are laughingly called "the sages who understand the times . . . who know law and legal process" (1:13). These pompous worthies promulgate a ridiculous (and irrevocable!) law mandating that "all women, high and low alike, will give honor to their husbands" (1:20) and that "every man should be ruler in his own household" (1:22). Consequently, in the opening scene the king is portrayed as a proud and ostentatious despot who is obsessed with honor, acts upon whim, and is dependent upon his privy council even to decide how to deal with an affair of family honor. By the contrast between this male world and the sense of decorum and self-respect that Vashti reveals in refusing to be shown off like a common courtesan before the drunken crowd at the second banquet, the narrator heaps further scorn upon the world in which his story will be set.

The opening scene of our story does recount some of the basic facts necessary to tell the tale, but the narrator uses it satirically to characterize the world within which the story will be set. This type of humor is "tendentious," a "rhetorical means of exposure" (Brenner, "Semantic Field," 39–40), whose satire, because it is the world in which diaspora Jews must live, intends not just to ridicule but also to instruct.

The same tone of mockery and satire is continued in the second act (2:1–18). In relating the basic facts of Esther's ascent to the queenship, the story also caricatures the blatant and carnal self-indulgence of this world (see *Explanation*). Thus, it is the king's young body-servants who suggest what he should do to assuage his pathetic regret upon remembering Vashti and her banishment (2:1–2a). Their advice (perhaps befitting their age and experience) is not that he should make an alliance through marriage with one of the powerful and noble families of the regime and so increase the stability of his realm but rather that he should gather beautiful young women from all the provinces of his empire and let the one "who pleases the king be queen in place of Vashti" (2:4). The first criterion for pleasing the king is described with extravagant and derisive hyperbole: their intensive beauty treatment goes on for a full year (2:12)! The second criterion for pleasing him, though told with exquisite reserve, is also transparently clear: "In the evening she would go in, and in the morning she would return again to the harem, but now to the custody of Shaashgaz, the king's eunuch in charge of the concubines. She would not go again to the king unless he took pleasure in her and she was summoned by name" (2:14). Surely to imply so subtly and yet so expressively that the only criteria the king and his courtiers have for the woman who will be queen over a vast and powerful empire is her beauty and her sexual prowess is to cast a sardonic and jaundiced eye on the Persian monarch and his court. After having held up to ridicule the king's gaudy ostentation and extravagance in 1:1–9 and the buffoonery of king and court scrambling to buttress by law their power and right to be lord and master in their own households in 1:10–22, he now depicts them as shallow and jaded men whose only measure of the woman who is fit to rule as queen by the king's side is her beauty of figure and face and her performance in his bed!

This characterization of the king as a man given to excess in the self-indulgent satisfaction of his appetites, who is ruled by impulse, obsessed with his own honor (see Fox, 171–77), and can make no decisions on his own, is consistent with his portrayal in the rest of the narrative. For example, in the next act, when Haman presents to the king his incredible proposal to have an unnamed people of his empire annihilated for trivial reasons and the payment of an enormous bribe, it can surely only be the king's irresponsible absorption with his own world of pleasure and privilege that prompts him to give Haman carte blanche without question or comment and to dismiss the whole matter with the offhand remark "Do with the people and the money as you please" (3:11). (See also the discussion of similar characterizations in the *Explanations* to 5:7–8; 6:1–11; 7:8c–10; 8:3–8.)

Thus has the narrator characterized the king and the Persian world that he rules. His pronounced and biting mockery is not only derisive but also judgmental. Such a world is not to be trusted. It is under the rule of a spoiled, self-indulgent despot, who, though he is not inherently evil, is impulsive and malleable, easily swayed by his nobles (1:10–22), his body-servants (2:1–4), his grand vizier (3:7–11), and his queen (5:1–8; 7:1–10). But, the satire has also a sinister side. It reveals a society fraught with danger. Though it is ruled by law, this does not guarantee either security or justice (Fox, 249), for it is easily manipulated by buffoons whose tender egos can marshall the state's whole legislative and administrative machinery for the furthering of selfish causes.

Nevertheless, though this is a dangerous world whose order exists in a state of precarious balance, and though there must have been enough people willing to act on Haman's edict to make its promulgation effective, neither the king nor his world are inherently inimical to the Jews. As the confusion of the people of Susa over the promulgation of Haman's decree in 3:15d (which contrasts with the cold-hearted insouciance of the king and Haman) and their joyous cheers at Mordecai's edict and royal status in 8:15b reveal, the only inveterate enemies of the Jews in the empire are those who "hoped to triumph over them" and those who "sought to do them harm" (9:1–2).

The satirical edge to the exposition has portrayed the story's world as a dangerous and uncertain place for the Jews who must live a diaspora existence within it. As Fox (249) observes, "Such a world is not inherently pernicious . . . but it is fertile ground for terrifying evils." The extent and frightfulness of that evil can be seen in the nature of the crisis that immediately follows. In the past, the Jewish community had known the destruction of capital and temple and the disintegration of expulsion and exile at the hands of the Babylonians, and in the future it would know similar catastrophe under Antiochus Epiphanes as well as the prohibition of keeping the Law, the proscription of circumcision, and the profanation of the temple. Horrible as such events had been and would be, they pale in comparison to the chilling terror of the utter annihilation of the whole people envisioned by Haman and enacted into law by Haman's terrible decree.

However much the narrative indicates in subtle, and not so subtle, ways that the threat will not be carried out, the extreme nature of the threat speaks volumes about the terrible dangers that lurk below the seemingly ordered society of the world of the diaspora.

b. *The characterization of Haman.* The horror of the event itself is indicated not only by the nature of the crisis but also by the unrelenting characterization of Haman, its perpetrator. Haman, like Mordecai, is presented as an ideal figure, the enemy of the Jews par excellence, as his epithet, repeated at crucial junctures in the narrative, reveals (see 3:10; 8:1; cf. also 9:10, 24; see esp. *Explanation* to 3:1–6). But Haman is not characterized primarily by his epithet, nor even by his actions (as is Mordecai; see below). His character is revealed by the narrator's direct statements, especially his report of "inward speech" (cf. Alter, *Art,* 114–30; and see esp. Fox's insightful study, 178–84). As Fox observes, Haman is "allowed no mysteries. His motives, drives, and attitudes are transparent, his twisted soul laid bare to all" (178). Apart from a few statements about the king (his anger, 1:12; 7:7; 2:1; his pleasure at a proposal, 1:21; 2:4; his love of Esther, 2:17), it is only Haman whose feelings and emotions the narrator constantly reveals with such direct statements (e.g., his anger, 3:5; 5:9; his joy, 5:9; his grief and shame, 6:12; his terror, 7:6; see Fox, 178). He even lays bare his thoughts (6:6), deliberations (3:6), and perceptions (7:7). In contrast, the personalities of Mordecai and Esther are revealed almost exclusively by their words and actions. For example, compare the portrayal of Mordecai's grief only by his actions (4:1) with the narrator's direct statement of Haman's grief and shame (6:12).

This portrayal shows that Haman's anti-Semitism is not fueled simply by racial and religious hatred (cf. Fox, 181), even though the author's play on his and Mordecai's origins in their patronymics subtly reveals that such enmity is there. Rather, Haman's evil is fueled principally by the inordinate pride of a "vast but tender ego" (Fox, 179). That this is what drives him is clearly revealed in the first three scenes in which we see him. In 3:1–6 his wounded pride could not be healed by just the destruction of his enemy. Only the annihilation of the whole Jewish people could assuage an anger rooted in his deep feeling of inferiority (see *Explanation*). In 5:9–14 he confesses to his wife and friends that all that should give life meaning becomes meaningless in the face of that one man's existence (see *Explanation*). And in 6:1–11, entranced by the phrase "the man whom the king desires to honor," his swollen pride and ego cause him to conclude that this can only refer to himself and prompt him thus unwittingly to prescribe the honoring of Mordecai. Haman is thus portrayed as irrational evil personified.

The fact that such evil can so easily bend the source and machinery of Persian power to its purposes is what makes this diaspora world such a dangerous and uncertain place. But this is not the theme of our story. It is not simply a story of human courage and sagacity (contra Humphreys' view [*JBL* 92 (1973) 223] that the story presents "a style of life for the diaspora Jew which affirms . . . that . . . the Jew can remain loyal to his heritage and God and yet can live a creative, rewarding, and fulfilled life . . . within a foreign setting"; cf. also Clines' comments, *Esther Scroll,* 157). The theme must take into account the resolution of the story effected by Mordecai and Esther (on the importance of the "prominence" of the resolution in determining theme, see the discussion in the *Theme and Purpose* section of the *Introduction* to Ruth). Let us turn, then, to the narrator's characterization of the roles of Mordecai, Esther, and the Jews.

c. *The characterization of Mordecai.* The threat of Haman's edict is both terrifying and terrifyingly portrayed. The major point of the story, however, is not just the complete reversal of Haman's edict but how this is achieved. The terrible threat is not carried out in part because through Mordecai and Esther the Jews also have access to power.

Though Mordecai is the most important figure in the book (see Fox, 185, and the discussion of the dénouement [9:6–32] and Purim below), he is not the most important factor in the reversal of the edict. That honor goes to Esther (see below). But, he is the instigator of the reversal, and he is the first of the book's heroes to be introduced. As was noted above, his significance for the theme of the book is signaled in 2:5 by the epithet איש יהודי, "a Jewish man," with which he is identified. This epithet, however, not only qualifies his role in the story; it also qualifies Mordecai himself in an important way (cf. the insightful study of Mordecai's character by Fox, 185–95). Its significance is indicated by the fact that it is not really needed in 2:5. Both his patronymic and the attached relative clause giving the historical origins of his family line would unmistakably have identified him. Further, he is called "Mordecai the Jew" in several passages where the identification is important. Thus does Haman identify him as the one whose existence renders his world meaningless (5:13); thus does the king identify him to Haman as the one to whom he must now give the honor Haman relished for himself (6:13); thus is he identified by the narrator when the king gives him the responsibility of countering Haman's edict (8:7); and thus is he identified in the story's encomium upon him (10:3; cf. also 9:31 in the discussion of the dénouement below). It is striking that, apart from relating his actions (and the statement of his role as a courtier, 2:19, 21), the primary way that the narrator characterizes Mordecai, not only in this part but in the whole book, is this epithet. Nor is anyone else in the story so identified. Mordecai, then, is the quintessential Jew. That the narrator so intends to characterize him is further evident in the depiction of his final status of power and authority. He leaves the king's presence robed in royalty (8:15); his position of power and fame both in the court of Susa and in the provinces is a substantial factor in the Jews' victory over their enemies (9:3–4); and in the final encomium upon him, he is second in rank only to the king himself and preeminent among his countrymen (10:3a).

Apart from the epithet "the Jew" and the portrayal of his final status of power and authority, Mordecai is characterized by his actions, and in every one of these he is distinguished by his absolute loyalty and constancy. He is loyal to Esther, his ward (2:7, 10–11), and to the king (2:21–23). Above all he is loyal to the Jewish people. Every action he takes is directed toward their deliverance (e.g., his lamentation in 4:1–3 is specifically directed to bringing Haman's edict to Esther's attention; see *Explanation* to 4:1–3). At his instigation, buttressed by his stern warning of the effects of her inaction, Esther agrees to risk appealing to the king; and he brilliantly solves the conundrum of revoking an irrevocable edict by drawing up and promulgating a second edict that counters Haman's at every point (see *Explanation* to 8:9–14). The capstone is placed upon this characterization of Mordecai in the encomium upon him in 10:3b. He is held in esteem by all because "he was constantly seeking the good of his people and promoting the welfare of all their descendants."

Further, it is striking that the narrator does not even once describe with direct statements Mordecai's feelings, emotions, thoughts, or deliberations, in sharp and striking contrast with the way he so frequently characterizes Haman (see above). Nor does he use dialogue, an avoidance remarkable in the Bible, where dialogue regularly carries the narration (see the discussion in *Genre* above, and cf. the book of Ruth). Mordecai's actual words are quoted only once, as he persuades Esther to intercede with the king (4:13–14). (Indeed, it is remarkable how the significance of these words is signaled by the use of indirect discourse in relating Mordecai's communication with Esther up to this point; see *Form/Structure/Setting* and *Explanation* to 4:4–17.) As a result, Mordecai's motives are an enigma. We have no idea what moves him. Most perplexing is his refusal to bow to Haman. The only hint the narrator gives us is the possibility of long-standing tribal enmity (see *Explanation* to 3:1–6), which is not only very subtly expressed but only moves the mysterious nature of his motives back one step. For Mordecai the narrator only gives us "a sense of ambiguous depths in character" (Alter, *Art*, 115; cf. Fox's perceptive remarks, 191–95).

Mordecai's character, then, is built around a single quality or trait, his utter loyalty to the Jewish people. He is what Berlin (*Poetics*, 23–32) calls a flat character or "type"; that is, he stereotypically represents what the ideal diaspora Jew should be.

d. *The characterization of Esther.* Though Mordecai is the first of the heroes of the tale to be introduced and is the instigator of the reversal of Haman's edict, the most important figure in effecting the reversal is Esther (see Fox, 196–205). Hence, she is the focus of the interest point of view in the story (for the concept of point of view, see Berlin, *Poetics*, 43–82, esp. 47–48, 84). She is also the only full-fledged character in the book (on types of characters, see Berlin, *Poetics*, 23–31, 85; and the *Genre* and *Theme and Purpose* sections of the *Introduction* to Ruth), for the narrator does not build her character around a single trait, as he has done with the king, with Haman, and to a great extent with Mordecai. Rather, she is portrayed with some depth and complexity, accomplished to a large extent by the fact that her character develops, in contrast to the static portrayal of the other three. Yet this is not accomplished by direct statements revealing her feelings or her thoughts and motives as the narrator has done with Haman. (Only once does he do so, reporting her great distress at the lamentation and actions of Mordecai and the Jewish community, 4:1–4, indicating that she knew some great tragedy had transpired. His statement about her great beauty, 2:7, is required by the plot, foreshadowing that she will be swept up in the king's net; see *Explanation* to 2:5–11.) Rather, she is characterized through her actions and her speech.

The narrator begins his characterization of her quite indirectly, for she is not given an independent introduction in the story but is presented as Mordecai's ward, a role the narrator maintains for her even when she becomes queen (as the repeated note in 2:10, 20 that she continued to obey Mordecai indicates). This continues in the tight series of three passive verbs ("the king's edict was proclaimed . . . many young women were gathered . . . Esther too was taken"), which depict her arrival in the king's harem as an ineluctable fate (see *Explanation* to 2:5–11). In the account of her choice as queen, however, he begins to present a favorable picture of her. She instantly won the favor of Hegai (2:9) and "all who saw her" (2:15), and even though she is the passive object of Hegai's actions (2:9) and advice (2:15), the narrator's choice of language (she "earned" or "won" favor, 2:9, 15, 17; see *Comment* on 2:9) subtly suggests her active involvement in what is transpiring. He avoids any negative portrayal of her by his presentation of her entry to the king devoid of the sensuous implications of the general description of the young women's journey from the seraglio to the king's bedroom (see *Explanation* to 2:5–11).

This is dramatically changed, however, in the exchange with Mordecai (4:4–17; cf. Clines, *Esther Scroll,* 33–36). In one moving and surprising dialogue she is transformed from the pretty young thing who has been more object than agent, and the dutiful ward who is always obedient, into Queen Esther, one of the two leaders of the Jewish community. The whole exchange is presented to us from the point of view of Esther, not Mordecai (note that she initiates the dialogue, 4:4–5, and it is her intermediary who carries it on, 4:6–10; cf. Fox, 198). Further, the narrator uses direct speech only at the high point of the exchange, beginning with Esther's response to Mordecai's order to appeal to the king (4:10–16; see *Explanation* to 4:10–17). She begins this response with an objection based on her doubt about the efficacy of her appeal to the king: she has not been summoned to him for thirty days (see *Explanation*). Mordecai's reply first reminds her that her own life is at stake in the matter, and then he counters her doubts about the efficacy of her appeal by pointing out, with the blunt power of an emphatic rhetorical question, that she is the only possible source of deliverance for the Jews (see *Comment* on 4:14). He concludes by reminding her of the possibility that there is providential purpose behind her present position: perhaps it is for just such an occasion as this that she has become queen. Esther makes no further objection, but she immediately assumes command, giving orders for a three-day fast for her as preparation for her appeal to the king. Her response demonstrates that she has not merely been cowed into submission by Mordecai's authority (Fox, 63), for it is not one of resigned acceptance but one of firm conviction. She has been completely convinced by Mordecai's reasoning. The only hope for the deliverance of the Jews from Haman's edict, as well as her own, is in her appeal to the king on their behalf, and this she is now determined to do. Her final words, "If I perish, I perish," are not, then, a despairing expression of resignation to the inevitable (Paton, 226) but courageous determination (Clines, 303).

This is a decisive turning point in Esther's development. Heretofore, though queen, she was nevertheless fully under Mordecai's authority as his ward. Now she is the one who sets the conditions and gives the commands. Indeed, in his closing narrative summary, 4:17, the narrator sets up a striking contrast. In v 8 it was Mordecai who *ordered* Esther to go to the king in order to plead with him on behalf of her people. Here he reports "Mordecai did exactly as Esther had *ordered* him."

The transformation of Esther is dramatically continued in the account of her appeal to the king in chaps. 5 and 7 (cf. Fox, 200–202). Once having been accepted into the king's presence (which, taking her courage in hand, she pursued without vacillation or delay), she is completely in command. The banquet strategy is entirely her own stratagem, and she pursues it with courage, consummate skill, and commendable shrewdness, particularly in the way she cleverly tricks the king into publicly committing himself to grant her unstated request in advance by his attendance at the second banquet (see *Comment* and *Explanation* to 5:7–8). When at the second banquet the king again asks what her request is, her reply is both shrewd and tactful: shrewd in that she avoids any reference to the king's complicity by putting the matter in the passive voice, and tactful in that she apologizes for raising an issue that could distress and trouble the king (see *Explanation* to 7:1–6a). The image of Haman falling upon her couch to plead for his life nicely depicts that she is now indeed "a force to be reckoned with in her own right" (Fox, 202). This is also clear from her final role in this narrative (8:1–8). First, she succeeds in having Haman's power and property given to Mordecai (8:1–2). Then, with skill and great tact, in which she unabashedly plays upon the king's obvious affection for her, she makes her final appeal to the king, this time to revoke Haman's edict. Once again she is successful, and the king grants permission for her and Mordecai to write to this end whatever they please in his name (see *Explanation* to 8:3–8).

Esther, too, is an ideal, a model, but a far more lively and "real" one than Mordecai. She begins as a nonentity, valued in that courtly world only for her good looks and her body, but she resolutely accepts Mordecai's challenge to use her position as queen to act for the salvation of her people (with but one brief objection). In one decisive moment she becomes a force to be reckoned with. Mordecai's loyalty is a key factor in the Jews' deliverance. However, it is Esther, with her courage, cunning, ingenuity, and diplomacy—a woman in a world that was not only ruled by men but devalued women—who is the main agent in effecting their deliverance. (For a feminist perspective on Esther that views her role in the world of the diaspora positively, see White, "Esther"; for a sensitive look at several feminist perspectives on Esther, see Darr, "More than Just a Pretty Face"; for a critique of more extreme feminist views, see Fox, 205–11.)

e. *The characterization of the Jews.* The Jews as a people (see the insightful study of Fox, 212–34, to which this discussion is much indebted) are an ever-present reality in the book. They are given no introduction in the exposition (chaps. 1–2), although Mordecai's identity as איש יהודי, "a Jewish man," could imply that there was a Jewish people. In the rest of the narrative, the narrator does not characterize them with even a single direct statement (in contrast, for example, to Haman), but he lets us see them (irony of ironies!) through the eyes of Haman son of Hammedatha, the Agagite, the enemy of the Jews! (On "embedded evaluation," see Berlin, *Poetics,* 105; cf. the discussion in the *Genre* section of the *Introduction* to Ruth.) They are "scattered," "unassimilated," and "their laws are different," Haman tells us, the first indicating that they are spread throughout the empire and the last two doubtless indicating that their social and religious customs were different from others, a phenomenon true of all people groups (see *Explanation* to 3:7–11). His last statement, that they do not obey the king's law is a blatant lie, refuted by their actions throughout the book (cf. Fox, 215). Throughout the crisis, right up to the moment of its final resolution, they are a single, undifferentiated entity whose role in the story is a passive one. Thus, they make their first appearance simply as an ethnic entity, "the Jews" (twice designated "the people of Mordecai," 3:6, 7), whom Haman decides to annihilate, because attacking Mordecai alone will not assuage his anger. Up until the resolution, they act only twice. At the news of Haman's edict, they mourn and fast (4:3), and at the news of Mordecai's counteredict, they celebrate and feast (8:17). These events are reported with impersonal, passive constructions (cf. Fox, 213) and function in the plot as one of the dramatic reversals that depict the significance of their deliverance. In between, they "can do nothing but wait while others shape their fate in ways they are unaware of" (Fox, 214). Their passivity ends, however, with the final resolution of the crisis (9:1–5), for they act independently to save themselves, described with a series of active, not passive, verbs. Here, since this is the fulfillment of Mordecai's counteredict, they are acting according to the law of the land. Further, the action is presented in only the most brief and summary of statements, not only omitting all the gory details but also signaling that the most important part of the resolution is the preceding, detailed account in which Esther and Mordecai gain the king's permission and issue the counteredict (cf. Fox, 215). They also act independently in the institution of Purim (9:23–28). In assessing the way the Jews are characterized by these functions and actions, it is extremely important to note that there is nothing that suggests that the Jews are in any way hostile to either the Persian court or the Persian world in general. The only hostilities the narrator describes are between the Jews and "those who hate them" (9:1, 5) and "those who sought to do them harm" (9:2; see *Comment* and *Explanation*). Nor is there any evidence of any inherent hostility toward the Jews on the part of either the court or the Persian world in general, as 3:15b and 8:15d make transparently clear (see the discussion of the characterization of the Persian world above, and esp. Fox, 217–20).

Nevertheless, though the Jewish people are not depicted as hostile to their world and they do not engage in senseless slaughter, the actions of Mordecai and Esther on three occasions are morally indefensible. First, the motive for Mordecai's refusal to bow down to Haman (which action precipitates Haman's deranged response) the narrator portrays as ethnic pride by the subtle use of patronymics (see *Explanation* to 3:1–6). Mordecai's motives are of no importance for understanding our story, for the narrator does not address that question in any meaningful way. He merely states his refusal without characterizing it at all. Hence, he draws no attention whatsoever to his pride (indeed, we have to read between the lines to recognize it as pride). Since his characterization of Mordecai is unfailingly positive throughout, it is unmistakable that the narrator takes for granted Mordecai's national pride and his faithfulness to Israel's ancient traditions and considers them wholly acceptable. These aspects of Mordecai's character are simply presented as data of the story (Clines, 294). The ethnic pride, then, is the narrator's, and for that he may be faulted. Second, Mordecai's edict does include women and children in the permission granted the Jews to destroy those who attack them (8:11; the attempt to remove this by re-interpreting the syntax of the verse cannot be sustained; see *Comment*), and, third, Esther does request from the king and carry out a second day of slaughter in Susa (9:13–15). It is important to note, however, that both of these are used by the narrator to provide literary functions in the plot development. The first results from the narrator's verbatim use of the wording of Haman's edict in Mordecai's counteredict as an expression of the total reversal effected thereby (see *Form/Structure/Setting* to 8:1–17), and the second functions in the narrative solely to explain the two different dates of the Jews' celebration (see *Explanation* to 9:6–15). The moral failure, then, lies far more with the narrator than with the characters of his story, but they must be acknowledged as moral failure (cf. the remarks of Fox, 224–26). They are insufficient, however, to characterize the characters or the story as bloodthirsty and full of hatred as is often done (see *Theology* below).

4. *The role of God in the story.* As was the case in the book of Ruth, God is not one of the characters in the narrative, and it is not possible to speak in any way of a "characterization" of him. Yet, in my opinion God (or at least his providence) is present in the story in (a) the series of unlikely circumstances and extraordinary coincidences with which the book abounds and (b) the remarkable series of reversals that characterize the plot.

a. *The unlikely circumstances and extraordinary coincidences.* The deliverance of the Jews from Haman's edict is just as much a consequence of these factors as it is a result of the loyalty of Mordecai and the sagacity and cunning of Esther. On the one hand, they involve, as Clines observes, *Esther Scroll,* 155 (his quotes are from W. Beet, *Exp* 22 [1921–22] 298–99),

> the overall shape of the plot. . . . [W]hether it is the vacancy for a queen at the Persian court, the accession of a Jewish queen, Mordecai's discovery of the plot, Esther's favorable reception by the king, the king's insomnia, Haman's early arrival at the palace or even his reckless plea for mercy at Esther's feet, the chance occurrences have a cumulative effect. "Each of these incidents regarded by itself might well appear to be the result of chance, and to have no bearing whatever upon the success or otherwise of the great plot. But *taken together, the element of chance disappears;* they all converge upon one point; one supplements the other." The whole course of events is shaped by "the guiding hand of the Great Unnamed."

On the other hand, these factors also extend to the critical details of the plot itself. This can be most clearly seen in the event that constitutes the decisive turning point in the course of Haman's confident plans to exterminate the Jews, his decision to ask the king to have Mordecai hanged (act 5, 5:9–6:14). There, five coincidences occur of such an extraordinary nature that they can hardly be anything but the narrator's cipher for "divinely arranged" (see *Explanation* to 6:1–11).

b. *The remarkable series of reversals.* Equally striking is the remarkable series of reversals that characterizes the plot. This principle is explicitly articulated by the author himself when he observes that, "on the day in which the Jews' enemies hoped to triumph over them, *that was overturned,* in that the Jews triumphed over those who hated them" (9:1; see *Comment* and *Explanation*). Fox helpfully terms this "peripety" ("Structure," 296, drawing on terminology from Aristotle), i.e., the principle that an action or event intended or expected to produce a certain result actually produces its direct opposite. These "reversals" are remarkable not just for their number. The careful reader cannot help but note that the narrator in a number of instances consciously draws attention to the reversals by using identical, or nearly identical, phraseology in both the event and its opposite (cf. Berg, *Book of Esther,* 106). This is most fully and consciously employed in the high point of the resolution, in which the report of the drafting, promulgation, and wording of Mordecai's counteredict in 8:9–16 repeats in detail the language of the report of the drafting, promulgation, and wording of Haman's edict in 3:12–15 (see the chart in the *Form/Structure/Setting* and the discussion in the *Explanation* sections). The identity of language is also striking in a number of the other cases as well, as the following table reveals (identical phrases are in bold type; cf. Berg, *Book of Esther,* 106–7; Fox, "Structure," 294–96):

Event/Action	Reversal
3:1–2 King Ahasuerus promoted Haman son of Hammedatha, the Agagite. He advanced him in rank and gave him precedence over all his other nobles. And all the king's officials at court bowed down and did obeisance to Haman, for so the king had commanded.	9:3–4 [Mordecai] had come to occupy a position of great power in the palace, while his fame was spreading through all the provinces. . . . Mordecai was growing more and more powerful. 10:3 Mordecai the Jew was second in rank only to King Ahasuerus himself and was preeminent among the Jews.
3:10 **Then the king took his signet ring** from his hand **and gave it to Haman son of Hammedatha, the enemy of the Jews**.	8:2a **Then the king took off his signet ring** which he had taken from Haman **and gave it to Mordecai.**
4:1 Mordecai . . . tore his clothes, put on sackcloth and ashes, **went out into the city,** and raised a loud and bitter cry.	8:15a Then Mordecai **went out from the king** clad in a royal robe of violet and white, wearing a large gold turban and a purple cloak of fine linen.
4:3 **And in every single province to which the command and edict of the king came, there was** great mourning **among the Jews, with** fasting weeping, and lamentation, **while many** made their beds on sackcloth and ashes.	8:17a **And in every single province** and every single city **to which the command and edict of the king came, there was** joy and gladness **among the Jews, with** feasting and celebration, **while many** of the peoples of the land professed to be Jews.
5:14 And his wife Zeresh and all his friends said to him, "Have a gallows erected, fifty cubits high, and in the morning speak to the king and have Mordecai hanged upon it. Then go with the king to the banquet full of joy."	6:13b–14 Then his advisers and Zeresh his wife said to him, "Since Mordecai, who has already begun to defeat you, belongs to the Jewish race, you will not get the better of him, but will most certainly fall before him." While they were still talking with Haman, the king's eunuchs arrived and brought him in haste to the banquet.
5:14 And his wife Zeresh and all his friends said to him, "Have **a gallows erected, fifty cubits high,** and in the morning speak to the king and **have Mordecai hanged upon it."**	7:9–10 Then Harbonah . . . said, "Look, the **gallows which Haman erected** for Mordecai, whose report benefited the king, is standing at Haman's house, **fifty cubits high."** "Hang him on it!" said the king. **So they hanged Haman on the gallows** he had prepared for Mordecai.
6:6–9 Haman thought, "Now, whom would **the king desire to honor** more than me?" So he said, ". . . let **royal robes** be brought which the king has worn and **a horse** which the king has ridden, with a royal diadem upon its head. **Let the robes and the horse** be given to a noble and **let him robe the man whom the king desires to honor and lead him through the city square and proclaim before him, "This is what is done for the man the king desires to honor!"**	6:11–12 So Haman got **the robes and the horse.** He **robed Mordecai and led him through the city square** mounted on the horse. **And he proclaimed before him, "This is what is done for the man whom the king desires to honor!"** . . . and Haman hurried home mourning and in shame.

In this respect, the book of Esther differs from the book of Ruth. Since the author of Ruth primarily portrays the quality of his characters rather than that of a situation, the providence of God primarily acts through the quality of life of the characters; God acts in the acts of חסד *ḥesed,* "kindness, graciousness, and loyalty," of Ruth and Boaz. But here the narrator is portraying the quality of a situation, and hence the providence of God acts through the coincidences and the remarkable reversals that advance the plot.

However, remarkable coincidences and dramatic reversals do not in and of themselves demonstrate that God is behind them (cf. the comments of Clines, *Esther Scroll,* 155). Indeed, Fox (235–47), forsaking the position he took in his article on structure (see *Structure*), argues that the evidence of the book implies that God is totally veiled. Hence, the author intends to convey total uncertainty about the presence of God. "By refusing to exclude either possibility, the author conveys his belief that there can be no definitive knowledge of the working of God's hand in history" (247). Fox does not equate this view with skepticism. Rather, "the willingness to face history with an openness to the possibility of providence . . . is a stance of profound faith" (247).

However, I do not believe the context permits us to read the author this way. The meaning of a discourse at all levels, up to and including genre, just like the meanings of its words, depends upon context (as Fox himself notes, 238). The context in this book is decidedly in favor of reading all of these elements as a statement about divine providence. First, the author himself hints in two places that his context is indeed the OT's world of faith. In 4:3 he depicts the Jews as fasting at the news of Haman's edict, and in 4:15–17 Esther orders (and Mordecai carries out) a three-day, twenty-four-hour fast "for me," i.e., in preparation for her entry to the king. Even though the name of God is not mentioned, "what purpose do these acts serve if not to affect God's will?" (Fox, "Structure," 297). Likewise, in the context of the strong statement that Mordecai has just made to Esther in 4:14 that there is no other source besides her who can effect deliverance for the Jews, the hope that she occupies the queenship for just such a time as this (see *Comment*) is surely a statement that is intended to affirm divine providence, not one that denies it. Second, the theme of peripety, in which God acts to effect the reversal on behalf of his people is a dominant one in the OT (see the examples cited by Fox, "Structure," 299–303; Loader, *ZAW* 90 [1978] 419). In this context the function of peripety has more than aesthetic value. It "points to divine direction of human events" and so "mirrors the author's world-view and at the same time communicates that view to the reader" (Fox, "Structure," 296, 299). Third, that the book echoes in its conceptions and in some cases its language both the Joseph and the Exodus narratives (see the discussion in *Unity and Redaction* above) and hence draws consciously on one of the central themes of the OT, the deliverance of Israel, further indicates that the author writes in a religious rather than a secular context, and specifically he evokes a context of OT faith. This background is surely also made clear in a subtle but unmistakable manner by the way in which the three-day, twenty-four-hour fast that Esther requires of the Jews of Susa, 4:15–17 (which is a continuation of the fast already begun by the Jewish community in general, 4:3), commencing as it did on the thirteenth day of the first month (3:12; see *Comment* on 4:16), would have canceled the celebration of Passover.

Indeed, in such a context "the storyteller is no theological sophisticate promoting a 'religionless Judaism,' but an Old Believer whose ultimate act of faith is to take the protective providence of God for granted" (Clines, *Esther Scroll,* 155–56). Finally, I agree with Clines (269), contra Berg (*Book of Esther,* 178) and Loader (*ZAW* 90 [1978] 418), that "there is nothing *hidden* or *veiled* about the causality of the events of the Esther story: it is indeed *unexpressed* but it is unmistakable, given the context within which the story is set" (*Esther Scroll,* 156).

5. *Conclusion: The theme of Esther 1:1–9:5; 10:1–3.* On the grounds of this study of the characterization of the plot and its characters, the theme of the story can be stated as follows. In the dangerous world of the diaspora with its opulence, excess, uncertainty, and evil, the loyalty of Mordecai to the Jewish people and the king, the courage, shrewdness, and sagacity of Esther, both of whom willingly accepted roles of leadership in that world, and the reliable providence of God delivered the diaspora Jewish community from the terrible threat of annihilation, demonstrating that a viable life for diaspora Jews is possible even in the face of such propensity for evil.

B. *The theme and purpose of the dénouement, Esther 9:6–32.* The theme of the dénouement is immediately clear from the fact that it does not simply portray the consequences of the problem-based plot that precedes. Its purpose, rather, is to obligate the Jewish community to institute an annual celebration whose purpose is to memorialize the days of celebration and joy that occurred after the dramatic deliverance on 13 Adar (see the discussion in the *Explanation* to this pericope and in the *Genre* section above).

Thus, the contents of the first scene, vv 6–19, are primarily devoted to accounting for the two different dates on which different parts of the Jewish community celebrate the festival. In so accounting for these dates, the narrator introduces the new theme of the days of rest and celebration that took place on the days following the victory in battle (see the discussion in *Explanation*). In the original circumstances, these festivities could only have been a spontaneous celebration of the victory that took place on the preceding day, and it seems highly probable that the continuing celebration described in v 19 would have had largely the same character. This theme of celebration is picked up in the directives of Esther and Mordecai set forth in the following scene, but the character of the celebration is transformed in a most significant way.

In the second scene of the dénouement, vv 20–32, Mordecai writes to obligate the Jewish community to turn this spontaneous celebration into a perpetual, annual festival (see *Explanation* and esp. the *Theology* section below). He sets its character by establishing the festival not as a commemoration of the days of military victory but as a commemoration of the days of rest and joyful feasting that followed the days of fighting and bloodshed: "the days in which they had rest from their enemies and the month which was transformed for them from sadness to joy and from mourning to a holiday" (v 22). Hence, he establishes its dates as 14 and 15 Adar, the days immediately following the battles. The author then relates that the Jewish community corroborated what Mordecai had written by obligating themselves to both the dates and the character of the festival. Finally, Esther also wrote, adding her authority as queen to the establishment of Purim.

The theme of the book of Esther must combine the themes of both its redactional sections. The theme of the whole then is: The festival of Purim, to be held on 14 and 15 Adar and established by the joint leadership and action of Mordecai, Esther, and the Jewish community itself, is to consist of joyful days of feasting and the sending of presents of food to one another and gifts to the poor as a perpetual, annual commemoration of the transformation from sadness to joy and from mourning to a holiday that marked the days following their deliverance from the terrible edict with which Haman sought to annihilate them. This deliverance from the threat of annihilation in the dangerous world of the diaspora, with its uncertainty and propensity for evil, was effected by the loyalty of Mordecai to both the Jewish people and the king, the courage, shrewdness, and sagacity of Esther, both of whom willingly accepted roles of leadership in that world, and the reliable providence of God, demonstrating that a viable life for diaspora Jews is possible even in the face of such propensity for evil.

THEOLOGY

Blessed are you, LORD our God, King of the universe, who has hallowed us with his laws and commanded us to read the Scroll.	בָּרוּךְ אַתָּה יְיָ. אֱלֹהֵינוּ מֶלֶךְ הָעוֹלָם. אֲשֶׁר קִדְּשָׁנוּ בְּמִצְוֹתָיו. וְצִוָּנוּ עַל־מִקְרָא מְגִלָּה:
Blessed are you, LORD our God, King of the universe, who wrought miracles for our fathers in days of old at this season.	בָּרוּךְ אַתָּה יְיָ. אֱלֹהֵינוּ מֶלֶךְ הָעוֹלָם. שֶׁעָשָׂה נִסִּים לַאֲבוֹתֵינוּ בַּיָּמִים הָהֵם. בַּזְּמַן הַזֶּה:
Blessed are you, LORD our God, King of the universe, who has kept us in life and sustained us and brought us to this sacred season.	בָּרוּךְ אַתָּה יְיָ אֱלֹהֵינוּ מֶלֶךְ הָעוֹלָם. שֶׁהֶחֱיָנוּ. וְקִיְּמָנוּ. וְהִגִּיעָנוּ לַזְּמַן הַזֶּה:
Blessings recited before the reading of the Scroll of Esther in the Purim Maᶜariv Service. (Gordis, *Megillat Esther*, 93)	ברכות מתפלת מעריב לפורים

From this analysis of the genres, themes, and purposes of the book of Esther, the major theological emphases flow, however subtly they are expressed in such a literary vehicle. And since, in the final shape of the book, its genres and themes are twofold, so are the theological emphases that inform it. They spring from the "dénouement" of the book (9:6–32), the institution and nature of Purim, on the one hand, and, on the other hand, from the "problem-based plot" (1:1–9:5, 10:1–3), the story of the deliverance from Haman's edict effected by the loyalty of Mordecai, the courage and cunning of Esther, and the providence of God (see *Theme and Purpose* above).

A. *The theological emphases of the "dénouement," 9:6–32.* Since the primary theme is the institution of the festival of Purim as a commemoration of the "joy of deliverance" from the terrible evil of Haman's edict of annihilation, this theme sets the book's primary theological agenda. The meaning of this festival must come from the character it is given in the book itself, for though it is clear that some form of the festival was already being celebrated at the time of the writing of the book's final form, the author leaves that origin buried in the traditions of the past (see *Explanation* to 9:20–32). A number of suggestions for a non-Jewish origin have been made over the years, such as Lewy's appeal to the Persian festival of Farvardīgān (*HUCA* 14 [1939] 127–51) or Ringgren's attempt to derive it from some form of Persian new year festivities (*SEÅ* 20 [1956] 5–24). Some of these suggestions are more plausible than others (see the helpful discussions in Clines, 263–66; Moore, xlvi–xlix; for detailed discussion of the views extant at the beginning of this century, see Paton, 77–94), but, since they are based on no firm evidence within the story itself and do not contribute in any way to understanding the nature of Purim, they will not be discussed here.

In assessing the character of the festival, several features need to be stressed. First, the authority the narrator uses to establish it is twofold (see Clines, *Esther Scroll*, 165–66; esp. Fox, 226–28). (a) As the head of the diaspora community, Mordecai writes to obligate the community to its institution and observance. He does not write as a law-giver and "order" or "command" its observance; rather, he "requires" this of them (see *Comment* on 9:21 and *Explanation* to 9:20–22), grounding the obligation in the whole story of the crisis recapitulated in the retrospective drawn from his letter (9:24–25; see *Explanation*). (b) The Jewish community also acts to take this obligation upon themselves (see *Explanation* to 9:23–28). The authority to establish the new festival lies not only in the leader of the community but also in the independent actions of the community itself, first in spontaneously beginning the celebration and then in its decision to make that celebration permanent.

Second, the narrative establishes the cultic significance of Purim. Its observance is obligatory (cf. the significance of לקים על, "to require of, impose upon"; see *Comment* on 9:21), and its perpetuity and comprehensiveness are stressed. It is to be celebrated "annually" (v 21), "throughout all generations and in every family, province and city" and is "never to be repealed"; its observance "shall never cease among the Jews" nor "come to an end among their descendants" (vv 27–28; cf. Childs, *Introduction*, 603).

Third, Mordecai directs that the festival is to commemorate the days of rest and joyful festivities that followed the battles. The character of the celebration, then, is transformed from what it was originally in a most significant way (cf. Childs, *Introduction*, 603–4; Clines, *Esther Scroll*, 160–62). It is not, like the original, a spontaneous celebration of military victory and the slaughter of the enemy. Though fighting took place in Susa on 14 Adar, the contrast drawn in 9:17–18 makes it clear that this is included only to explain the two different days of celebration. On this day the Jews in the provinces were not fighting but were engaging in a day of joyful celebration. Hence, the festival does not celebrate victory in battle, and the joy prescribed is not malicious glee over the slaughter of their enemies. The festival commemorates, rather, the fact that they "gained relief from their enemies" and that life was "transformed for them from sadness to joy and from mourning to a holiday" (v 22). It is, then, a celebration of relief from persecution, a commemoration of the joy of deliverance from the terrible threat to their existence. This is especially obvious in the brief retrospective of the story in 9:24–25, which moves the Jewish community solemnly to commit to this annual observance (vv 26b, 23a), for there is no mention whatsoever in this account of either the battles or the victory (Clines, *Esther Scroll*, 164). The reference is exclusively to deliverance from Haman's plot. The same emphasis is also clearly indicated by the name of the festival itself, Purim, which is understood to be a reference to פור *pur*, the lot cast by Haman in 3:7 for the extermination of the Jews (as the etiology of v 26a specifically states; cf. Clines, *Esther Scroll*, 164). Thus, both the story that instigated their decision to observe the festival and the very name of the festival itself bring to mind neither military victory nor the slaughter of enemies, but Haman's plot and their subsequent deliverance from evil and disaster.

Of equal importance is Esther's word that Purim is to be observed in the same manner as the Jewish community has already taken upon themselves, in their religious traditions, the observance of fasting and mourning (9:31). This also serves to stress that the festival is a celebration not of military prowess but of deliverance from danger and disaster. Their joy is to be tempered by what occasioned it. The festival celebrates a "month which was transformed for them from sadness to joy and from mourning to celebration" (v 22). Hence, "it provides a context for the season of joy. . . . The joy is not just a licensed release of high spirits but is participated in consciously as reversal of grief, deliverance from mourning" (Clines, *Esther Scroll*, 167).

Finally, in the discussion of genre above, it was demonstrated that the criteria for the institution of Purim in vv 26–28 required the retelling of the story, since to celebrate the ancestors' experience requires the retelling of that experience. Hearing the story of crisis and deliverance is essential to recapturing the experience of joy that the festival commemorates. Hence, in terms of its function, the genre of the book is that of festival lection.

From this analysis of the character of Purim, it is clear that the festival called upon the Jews of the diaspora to a celebration of the joy of deliverance even in the face of unmitigated and unthinkable evil. For all the disturbing and troubling character of such a call (especially for Jews), the Jewish community has responded to it with alacrity and enthusiasm. The celebration of Purim must have begun very soon after the appearance of the book of Esther, since the reference to the "day of Mordecai" in 2 Macc 15:36 demonstrates that the festival was in existence sometime in the first half of the first century B.C. Its early celebration is also attested by Josephus' statement in the first century A.D. that "the Jews still keep the forementioned days, and call them days of Phurim" (*Ant.* 11.6.13) and by a whole tractate of the Mishnah (dating to the first two centuries A.D.), entitled Megillah, "The Scroll," which is devoted to prescriptions for the dates of Purim, regulations for the reading of the scroll, and haggadic expositions of the text. It is still one of the most important and popular festivals of the Jewish liturgical year. The book itself is the only one of the OT outside of the Torah (the Pentateuch) to have a second targum devoted to its exposition, and the number of midrashim and other Jewish commentaries on it exceed those written for any other book of the OT (Paton, 97; for a summary, see 101–7). Its esteem in the Jewish community is often estimated by quoting the saying of the famous Jewish scholar Maimonides that, when the Prophets and the Writings pass away when the Messiah comes, only Esther and the Torah will remain. Its significance can further be seen in the fact that the second commandment of the decalogue had been interpreted in Jewish circles to prohibit all forms of representation of the human figure by the time of the Middle Ages, but this prohibition was not applied to the decoration of the Scroll of Esther. The impressive and artistic illustrations with which Jews have adorned the scroll throughout the centuries (for examples, see Baumgarten, *EncJud* 14:1049–53) give eloquent expression to the affectionate regard in which they have held the book. Indeed, the illumination of Esther manuscripts has preserved some of the finest examples of medieval Jewish art (Gordis, *Megillat Esther,* 15). (On the impact of Esther on Jewish art in general, see *EncJud* 6:908–12.) So overwhelming is its popularity and acceptance that the tendency on the part of Christian scholars, when discussing problems with the book of Esther, to quote the exceedingly rare occasions when Jewish scholars have questioned its canonicity (e.g., Anderson's quote of the views of Ben-Chorin, *Kritik,* 5, in *JR* 30 [1950] 33–34, 39; or Moore's quote of the statement of Sandmel, *Enjoyment,* 44, in *ABD* 2:635) is utterly misleading.

The joy of deliverance that the prescriptions of the book set as the primary character of the festival (see above) has been well caught by the Jewish observance of Purim, for it is a boisterous celebration, full of merriment and high spirits (see Jacob, *EncJud* 13:1392–95; Harris, *Judaism* 26 [1977] 161–70). That this also began very early is attested in the well-known statement by the Babylonian teacher Raba in the Mishnah (*m. Meg.* 7b) that a man is obliged to drink so much wine on Purim that he cannot distinguish between "Blessed be Mordecai" and "Cursed be Haman." A festive meal is eaten on the evening of 14 Adar, often lasting late into the night; gifts of food are sent to friends (among the most popular being *hamantaschen,* lit. "Haman's pockets," three-cornered pies often called "Haman's ears" from the Hebrew expression אזן המן *ʾozen Haman*); and money is donated to the poor. Children often rattle hand-held noisemakers or hiss and boo whenever the name of Haman occurs during the reading of the scroll. The four "verses of redemption" (2:5; 8:15, 16; 10:3) are read much louder than the rest of the text. Mummeries and masquerades involving role reversals, often quite extreme, mark the festival (Harris, *Judaism* 26 [1977] 163–66). Children dress up in garish costumes and solicit gifts from neighbors (cf. Gaster, *Purim,* 59). In modern times a carnival parade, called *Adloyada* ("until one does not know," alluding to the statement of Raba), is held yearly on the streets of Tel Aviv, attended by thousands. From the Middle Ages until the Holocaust put an end to them, there developed in European Jewish communities the practice of presenting satirical and comic monologues or group performances called Purim-shpils ("plays") at the festive family meal. This practice eventually evolved in the nineteenth and twentieth centuries into well-developed plays on biblical themes and stories, reflecting many of the trends of the European theater in its literary style, choice of subject, and scenic design (see Shmeruk, *EncJud* 13:1396–1406). In the talmudic academies of Eastern Europe, until the Holocaust wiped them out, a "Purim Rabbi" would often be elected from among the students who would be granted the license to parody his teachers and even frivolously to manipulate sacred texts (Gordis, *Megillat Esther,* 16). In all of this, ordinary conventions of decorum and deportment are held in abeyance and a spirit of satire and fun is given full sway, fully in keeping with the satirical spirit of the book of Esther itself.

To ask why the book of Esther and the festival of Purim it has engendered have so entered into and marked the Jewish soul (cf. Bettan, 200–201) is perhaps to belabor the obvious, but in a post-Holocaust world it bears repeating. First, as we have noted above, the book of Esther is the only book in the OT that is exclusively concerned with a *Jewish = diaspora* agenda. And ever since the destruction of Jewish life in Judea by the Romans in the first and second Jewish revolts, the *Jews* have known only a *diaspora existence,* at least until the establishment of the state of Israel. Second, one of the two major themes of the book is to show how the leadership of Mordecai and Esther and the providence of God delivered Jews of the diaspora world from the worst of all the evils that world contains, the threat of annihilation. Throughout their existence, but especially in the last one hundred years in the Western world, the Jews have known and experienced the propensity for evil resident in their diaspora world, extending from discrimination, subtle and blatant, through persecution of various kinds, to pogroms that have involved the extensive loss of property and life. For all the joy, satire, and carnival atmosphere of regular Purim observance, Jewish custom reveals a significant awareness of Purim as the celebration of deliverance in the practice of establishing "Special Purims." These are Purim-like celebrations of escape from destruction involving rituals similar to those of Purim, often including festive meals, charity to the poor, and the reading from a scroll in the synagogue an account of the specific deliverance, accompanied by special prayers of thanksgiving. These "Special Purims" were inaugurated by an individual community or family and hence are known as "the Purim of . . ." (followed by the name of the place or family). See *EncJud* 13:1396–98, where a representative (and long) list of those known is given, dating from the twelfth through the twentieth century. The list of deliverances it celebrates is sober and chilling reading. For Jews, the book of Esther *is* true. As a community, they have lived it.

One who stands outside the Jewish community of faith can only imagine what a disturbing and troubling summons the call of Purim to a perpetual commemoration of the joy of deliverance from evil and disaster must be for the Jewish community, for their experience has all too often been the opposite of that of the book of Esther. For far too many Jewish families and communities over the centuries, their experience has been the mirror image of the story. The pogroms have all too often been successful. This culminated in the unmitigated and unthinkable horror of Haman's spiritual descendants, Hitler and his Nazi minions, who, unlike Haman, succeeded in the Holocaust in annihilating six million of the seven million Jews of Europe and virtually exterminating European Jewish culture. For them, there was no Mordecai; for them, there was no Esther; for them there was no deliverance; and faith hardly knows how to hang on to the providence of God in such circumstances—but it must. Perhaps, at the risk of making easy judgments, an outsider who has not lived through such horror, either personally or through community identity, might venture the judgment (and the hope) that the message of the book of Esther and Purim should continue to live, and indeed loom even larger, in a post-Holocaust world, since it summons the community to exercise its faith and hold on to its hope in the very face of that diabolical element in the character of the world whose horror and irrationality the story of Esther has captured so frighteningly and so well in Haman and his evil plot. Indeed, Purim celebrates the fact that the Holocaust, for all its tragedy and horror, has meant neither the end of Judaism nor the end of the Jews!

In the light of the Holocaust, what Esther and the celebratory joy of the festival of Purim mean to the Jewish world is best left to Jews to express:

> Purim is play time in Jewish tradition. It has an important function. . . . Nietzsche . . . wrote, "I know of no other way of coping with great tasks, than play." This is what Purim accomplishes; it enables the Jew to cope with a great task: coming to grips with exile. (Harris, *Judaism* 26 [1977] 166)

> These artistic and informal modes of Purim observance point up a remarkable aspect of the Jewish spirit. The subject matter of the book of Esther is deadly serious—nothing less than an attempt, which fortunately proved abortive, to execute a total pogrom and thus bring about the annihilation of the Jewish people. Moreover, Haman's plot was not an isolated episode in Jewish experience. It was reenacted time and again in the intervening centuries, until our own day, when Hitler undertook the most colossal and all-but-successful effort at genocide. Jews rarely, if ever, were able to afford the luxury of regarding the book of Esther as ancient history; for them it was almost always current events. Living perpetually in the shadow of immanent catastrophe, the Jew was threatened not only physically but psychologically. Walking in the shadow of death was as perilous as dying. That the Jew was able to survive and preserve his sanity was due to an extraordinary gift, his capacity to laugh at his oppressors. (Gordis, *Megillat Esther,* 16)

One might only add that among the major sources of that gift of play and laughing at oppressors unmistakably are the book of Esther and the festival of Purim that it has engendered.

It is not surprising, of course, nor a matter for concern, that, when the Bible of the Jews, the "Tanakh" (from *T*orah = Law; *N*ebîʾîm = Prophets, *K*etûbîm = Writings), was taken over as the OT by the Christian church as part of its canon, the church did not take up the call of the book of Esther to a commemoration of the joy of deliverance from evil by celebrating the festival of Purim. The Church fully celebrates the joy of deliverance in other ways, since with the coming of the Messiah almost all the OT expressions of redemption and faith evolved into new forms. But, though the Church did not embrace the festival of Purim, it did embrace, with the rest of the Jewish canon, the book of Esther. For the most part, however, it has been a cold embrace indeed. Representative are Martin Luther's oft-cited remark, "I am so hostile to this book (2 Macc) and Esther that I could wish that they did not exist at all, for they judaize too greatly and have much pagan impropriety," and Eissfeldt's comment, ". . . Christianity . . . has neither occasion nor justification for holding on to it. For Christianity Luther's remark should be determinative" (*Introduction,* 511–12). Nor is the festival of Purim spared. Ironside dismisses it with scorn on the grounds that it "has degenerated into a season of godless merrymaking, and is more patriotic than devotional in character" (*Esther,* 115). Much of this negative assessment of Esther, particularly in the century prior to World War II and the Holocaust, has doubtless been influenced by the subtle and latent anti-Semitism that has so perniciously influenced the Western world. Cornill could write, "All the worst and most unpleasing features of Judaism are here displayed without disguise; and only in Alexandria was it felt absolutely necessary to cover up the ugliest bare places with a few religious patches"

(*Introduction,* 257). For further examples, see the overview of the interpretation of Esther by Herrmann (*Esther im Streit der Meinungen,* 19–29), whose "catalogue of anti-Semitic sentiments that have been voiced under the guise of interpretation of Esther makes depressing reading" (Clines, Review of *Esther im Streit der Meinungen*).

However that may be, many of the specifics upon which this assessment is based spring from misreadings of the book. The Jews' response in 9:1–5 to those who sought to put into effect the pogrom licensed by Haman's edict is interpreted as "a massacre of defenceless Gentiles" (Pfeiffer, *Introduction,* 741). It is claimed by many that the book espouses an intense nationalistic spirit and virulent hostility to Gentiles. It is "inspired by a fierce nationalism and unblushing vindictiveness," "a witness to the fact that Israel, in pride, . . . made nationalism a religion" (Anderson, *JR* 30 [1950] 32, 40); "the product of a nationalistic spirit, seeking revenge upon those who persecute the Jews, which has lost all understanding of the demands and obligations of Yahwism" (Fohrer, *Introduction,* 253); "a memorial to the nationalist spirit of Judaism which had become fanatical" (Weiser, *Introduction,* 312; cf. also Bewer, *Literature,* 306–7; Driver, *Introduction,* 486–87; Eissfeldt, *Introduction,* 511; Pfeiffer, *Introduction,* 743–44). Nor are the characters spared. Anderson writes, "The story unveils the dark passions of the human heart: envy, hatred, fear, anger, vindictiveness, pride," and ventures the opinion that "If a Christian minister is faithful to the context, he will not take his text from Esther" (*JR* 30 [1950] 39, 42), while Paton opines, "There is not one noble character in the book," and avers that the author "gloats over the wealth and the triumph of his heroes and is oblivious to their moral shortcomings" (96).

But, the close reading of the book that has been argued throughout this commentary demonstrates that these points of view are in error. For the view that the Jewish military action is basically defensive, see the discussions in *Comment* and *Explanation* for 9:1–5. Both the discussion of the characterization of the Jewish people (see *Theme and Purpose*) and the determination of the genre of the book as a diaspora short story whose theme is the deliverance of the diaspora Jewish community from the terrible threat of annihilation (see *Genre* and *Theme and Purpose*) have shown that the book simply cannot be read as a nationalist diatribe. The characterization of Mordecai and Esther (see *Theme and Purpose*) documents that the views expressed above, and others like them, are a highly tendentious reading. Though no paragons of virtue, they are no worse than (and better than some of) the very human characters, the עם קשה ערף, "stubbornly sinful people" (lit. "stiff-necked," Exod 32:9; 33:3, 5; 34:9), who grace(?) the pages of the Bible, OT and NT. On the contrary, as the exposition presented here has shown, I believe, the book of Esther does not portray an unethical and narrow racial and nationalist agenda but calls the community of faith to a commemoration of the joy of deliverance from evil and disaster. Fortunately, more recent commentaries on the book in the Christian world, such as those of Baldwin, Bardtke, Gerleman, Meinhold, Moore, Roberts, and especially Clines, have accorded it a much more sensitive and positive treatment (cf. also such introductions as Bandstra, *Reading,* 459–64; Dillard-Longman, *Introduction,* 189–97; LaSor et al., *OT Survey,* rev. ed., 532–41).

Indeed, rather than producing negative and unsympathetic readings, the book of Esther should prick the Christian conscience, especially in a post-Holocaust world. "Esther says to the Christian that anti-Jewish hostility is not God's will, and he cannot tolerate it" (Lasor et al., *OT Survey,* 629). Indeed, given the fact that the vast majority of the evils that the Jews in the Western world have experienced in the last two centuries (not to mention the preceding millennium), culminating in the Holocaust, have been at the hands of nominally Christian nations and communities and that this has all too often been met by silence and passivity on the part of the Church, the story of the book of Esther above all else should drive us in the Christian community to our knees in repentance and contrition, and with the prayer and the resolve (in keeping with the synergism of Esther!) that the future will be different from the past.

But the function of the book of Esther as a festival lection, the story read to provide the context for and especially the character of the festival (as described above), makes it clear that the book has a word to speak to the NT as well as the OT community of faith. Christians have also lived in a dangerous and unfriendly "diaspora world," marked by hatred and persecution (e.g., the Roman world of the early Church and the Communist regimes of the present century, to mention the most obvious), and will again (see John 15:18–21). In the modern Western world, the community of faith now lives in an increasingly technological and secular world that is more and more indifferent, if not unfriendly, to the issues of faith. The deliverance of the story of Esther holds out to all such communities the hope that "relief and deliverance" may indeed be effected by the combination of human effort and the providence of God. The festival of Purim calls the community to celebrate the joy of deliverance even in the face of unmitigated and unthinkable evil.

B. *The theological emphases of the "problem-based plot," 1:1–9:5; 10:1–3.* The story of the loyalty of Mordecai, the courage and cunning of Esther, and the providence of God makes a strong statement about the complementarity, the synergism, of divine and human action in effecting the deliverance of the people of God. In discussing the role of God in the book of Ruth, it was observed that the narrator's portrayal of the presence of God in the story places the book far to one side of the OT's representation of the divine causality. For, though his name is frequently on the lips of the protagonists in blessing and thanksgiving and though the narrator himself explicitly affirms that God's causality lies behind two of the (minor!) events of the story, his providence is more implicit than explicit (see the *Genre* and *Theology* sections of the *Introduction* to Ruth). This is far more the case in the book of Esther. The author does not once mention God, nor does he make a single statement to the effect that God's causality lies behind any of the events of the narrative. Yet God's providence is present in the story, expressed in the remarkable coincidences and dramatic reversals that move the plot forward (see the "role of God" section in *Theme and Purpose*). Far more than in the book of Ruth, the providence of God is utterly and completely implicit in the book of Esther. But it is there.

However, the deliverance of the Jews from Haman's edict of annihilation is as dependent on the loyalty of Mordecai and the courage, shrewdness, and sagacity of Esther as on the remarkable coincidences and dramatic reversals that portray the providence of God (cf. Clines, 270–71; id., *Esther Scroll,* 156–58; Berg, *Book of Esther,* 178–79). Further, in the book of Esther, God is not portrayed as acting primarily through the characters in the story, as he is in the book of Ruth. Rather, both divine providence and human initiative are necessary to deliverance from Haman's evil edict. They are complementary. "Without the craft and courage of the Jewish characters the divinely inspired coincidences would have fallen to the ground; and without the coincidences, all the wit in the world would not have saved the Jewish people" (Clines, 271). Indeed, by the manner in which the author portrays implicitly God's providence, but very explicitly the loyalty, shrewdness, and sagacity of the human protagonists in effecting deliverance for the Jews, he lays all the stress on the human contribution to the divine-human synergism. This is far different from the way that the divine causality is expressed in the rest of the OT, in which God's action not only is explicit but is also frequently depicted as directly effecting events, sometimes setting aside the laws that govern the natural world, and often leaving little, if any, role for human efficacy (cf. Clines, 271). As in so many other things, the Bible has more than one way of conceiving of and portraying the way that God works in the world.

Furthermore, the end to which the providence of God and the loyalty and sagacity of the human characters direct their efforts is also important theologically, for that end is the deliverance of the Jewish people. By placing his own beliefs (very ironically!) in the mouth of Haman's wife Zeresh (6:13; see *Comment* thereon and *Explanation* to 6:12–14), the author expresses his conviction that this people is invincible. This is no ancient form of "manifest destiny" or the like, for both the larger context of the book and the other OT deliverance stories (Joseph and the Exodus) that his theme and language reflect (see *Unity and Redaction* above) place this deliverance fully within the context of the faith of the OT. A central tenet of that faith, maintained throughout the OT, is God's promise to the patriarch Abraham that through him and his descendants all the families of the earth would be blessed (Gen 12:3). Hence, the deliverance of the Jews has implications for more than the people affected. From a Jewish perspective, Gordis has put it this way:

> [T]he preservation of the Jewish people is itself a religious obligation of the first magnitude. This is true because Israel has been the bearer of God's word throughout its history, beginning with the Covenant at Sinai. . . . [A]t Sinai Israel learned that it cannot live for itself alone, being "a kingdom of priests and a holy nation" (Exod. 19:6). . . . Israel's eternal task, imposed upon it both by its tradition and its destiny, is "to open the eyes of the blind, to free the prisoner from the dungeons and from the prison-house, those dwelling in darkness" (Isa. 42:6). As Israel lives, it keeps alive for all men the hope of the Messianic age, when "men will do no evil and work no destruction on all God's holy mountain, for the earth shall be filled with the knowledge of the Lord as the waters cover the sea" (Isa. 11:9). (*Megillat Esther,* 13)

Those who share the faith stance of the NT and affirm that that OT hope of blessing has begun to be actualized in the coming of Jesus, the Jewish Messiah, read this story of the deliverance, then, with special thanks for the grace of God, because the preservation of the Jews (important as that is in its own right) assured the coming of the (Jewish) Savior of the world, making possible the salvation of both Jews and Gentiles.

Outline

Act 1. Introduction and Setting: Esther Becomes Queen of Persia (1:1–2:23)
Scene 1. The deposal of Queen Vashti (1:1–22)
Episode 1. The banquets of King Ahasuerus: Persian pomp and circumstance (1:1–9)
Episode 2. Queen Vashti is deposed: Persian folly and foolishness (1:10–22)
Scene 2. Esther becomes queen (2:1–18)
Episode 1. Ahasuerus decides to seek a new queen (2:1–4)
Episode 2. Esther is taken to the royal harem (2:5–11)
Episode 3. Esther is chosen queen (2:12–18)
Scene 3. Mordecai uncovers a plot (2:19–23)

Act 2. The Crisis: Haman's Plot to Destroy the Jews (3:1–15)
Scene 1. Haman decides to annihilate the Jews (3:1–6)
Scene 2. Haman sets in motion a plot to annihilate the Jews (3:7–15)
Episode 1. Haman obtains the king's permission to annihilate the Jews (3:7–11)
Episode 2. Haman orders the annihilation of the Jews (3:12–15)

Act 3. Mordecai's Stratagem: Esther Must Consent to Appeal to the King (4:1–17)
Scene 1. Mordecai and all the Jews lament over Haman's edict (4:1–3)
Scene 2. At Mordecai's command Esther consents to appeal to the king (4:4–17)
Episode 1. Mordecai refuses the clothing Esther sends him (4:4)
Episode 2. Mordecai orders Esther to appeal to the king (4:5–9)
Episode 3. Esther consents to appeal to the king (4:10–17)

Act 4. Esther Begins Her Appeal: She Invites the King and Haman to a Banquet (5:1–8)
Scene 1. Esther invites the king and Haman to a banquet (5:1–5a)
Episode 1. Esther gains an audience with the king (5:1–2)
Episode 2. Esther invites the king and Haman to a banquet (5:3–5a)
Scene 2. Esther again invites the king and Haman to a banquet (5:5b–8)

Act 5. Haman's Stratagem Backfires: He Is Humiliated and Mordecai Honored (5:9–6:14)
Scene 1. Haman's hubris: his wife and his friends persuade him to ask the king to hang Mordecai (5:9–14)
Scene 2. Haman's humiliation: the king commands him to honor Mordecai (6:1–11)
Episode 1. The king discovers the failure to reward Mordecai (6:1–3)
Episode 2. Haman advises the king how to reward the man he wishes to honor (6:4–10)
Episode 3. Haman so honors Mordecai (6:11)
Scene 3. Haman's end: his wife and his friends predict his downfall (6:12–14)

Act 6. Esther Makes Her Appeal: The Fall of Haman (7:1–10)
Episode 1. Esther pleads with the king for her life (7:1–6a)
Episode 2. Haman attempts to plead with Esther for his life (7:6b–8b)
Episode 3. Haman loses his life (7:8c–10)

Act 7. Esther Appeals Again to the King: She and Mordecai Counter Haman's Plot (8:1–17)
Scene 1. Esther and Mordecai acquire authority to issue a counterdecree (8:1–8)
Episode 1. Mordecai is admitted into the king's presence (8:1–2)

Episode 2. The king grants Esther and Mordecai authority to write an edict on behalf of the Jews (8:3–8)
Scene 2. Mordecai issues the counterdecree (8:9–17)
Episode 1. The counterdecree is written and promulgated (8:9–14)
Episode 2. Mordecai leaves the king's presence with honor and the Jews rejoice (8:15–17)

Act 8. The Jews Are Victorious: They Put All Their Enemies to the Sword (9:1–5)

Act 9. The Festival of Purim Is Instituted: Mordecai, Esther, and the Jewish Community Set Its Dates and Establish Its Character (9:6–32)
Scene 1. The events that occasion the celebration of Purim over two days (9:6–19)
Episode 1. How the fighting in Susa took place on 13 and 14 Adar (9:6–15)
Episode 2. Why the Jews in Susa and the Jews elsewhere celebrate on two different days (9:16–19)
Scene 2. Mordecai, Esther, and the Jewish community set the dates of Purim and commit themselves to its perpetual celebration (9:20–32)
Episode 1. Mordecai writes to the Jews to require them to celebrate annually 14 or 15 Adar as days of joyful festivity (9:20–22)
Episode 2. The Jews commit themselves, their descendants, and all who join them to the perpetual annual observance of the two-day festival of Purim (9:23–28)
Episode 3. Esther writes to confirm the observance of Purim (9:29–32)

Act 10. Epilogue: An Encomium on Mordecai (10:1–3)

Act 1
Introduction and Setting: Esther Becomes Queen of Persia (1:1–2:23)

Scene 1
The Deposal of Queen Vashti (1:1–22)

Bibliography

Barthélemy, D., et al. *Preliminary and Interim Report on the Hebrew Old Testament Text Project.* Vol. 2. New York: United Bible Societies, 1979. **Berg, S. B.** *The Book of Esther: Motifs, Themes and Structure.* SBLDS 44. Missoula, MT: Scholars, 1979. **Bergey, R. L.** "The Book of Esther—Its Place in the Linguistic Milieu of Post-exilic Biblical Hebrew: A Study in Late Biblical Hebrew." Diss., Dropsie College, 1983. **Briant, P.** "Persian Empire." *ABD* 5:236–44. **Cameron, G.** "The Persian Satrapies and Related Matters." *JNES* 32 (1973) 47–56. **Cook, J. M.** "The Rise of the Achaemenids and Establishment of Their Empire." In *The Cambridge History of Iran: Vol. 2. The Median and Achaemenian Periods,* ed. I. Gershevitch. Cambridge: Cambridge UP, 1985. 200–291. **Craig, K.** *Reading Esther: A Case for the Literary Carnivalesque.* Westminster: John Knox, 1995. **De Miroschedji, P.** "Susa." *ABD* 6:242–45. **Dorothy, C. V.** "The Books of Esther: Structure, Genre, and Textual Integrity." Diss., Claremont, 1989. **Driver, G. R.** *Aramaic Documents of the Fifth Century* B.C. Oxford: Clarendon, 1957. ———. "Problems and Solutions." *VT* 4 (1954) 224–45. **Duchesne-Guillemin, J.** "Les noms des eunuques d'Assuérus." *Mus* 66 (1953) 105–8 (= Moore, *Studies,* 273–76). **Gehman, H. S.** "Notes on the Persian Words in Esther." *JBL* 43 (1924) 321–28 (= Moore, *Studies,* 235–42). **Gordis, R.** "Studies in the Esther Narrative." *JBL* 95 (1976) 43–58 (= Moore, *Studies,* 408–23). **Haupt, P.** "Critical Notes on Esther." *AJSL* 24 (1907–8) 97–106 (= Moore, *Studies,* 1–90). **Herzfeld, E.** *The Persian Empire: Studies in the Geography and Ethnography of the Ancient Near East.* Wiesbaden: Steiner, 1968. **Junker, H.** "Konsonantenumstellung als Fehlerquelle und textkritische Hilfsmittel im AT." In *Werden und Wesen des Alten Testaments,* ed. J. Hempel et al. BZAW 66. Berlin: Töpelmann, 1936. 162–74. **Millard, A. R.** "The Persian Names in Esther and the Reliability of the Hebrew Text." *JBL* 96 (1977) 481–88. **Murphy, R. E.** *Wisdom Literature: Job, Proverbs, Ruth, Canticles, Ecclesiastes, and Esther.* FOTL 13. Grand Rapids, MI: Eerdmans, 1981. **Oppenheim, A.** "On Royal Gardens in Mesopotamia." *JNES* 24 (1965) 328–33 (= Moore, *Studies,* 350–55). **Radday, Y. T.** "Esther with Humour." In *On Humour and the Comic in the Hebrew Bible,* ed. Y. T. Radday and A. Brenner. Sheffield: Almond, 1990. 295–313. ———. "Humour in Names." In *On Humour and the Comic in the Hebrew Bible,* ed. Y. T. Radday and A. Brenner. Sheffield: Almond, 1990. 59–97. **Rudolph, W.** "Textkritisches zum Estherbuch." *VT* 4 (1954) 89–90. **Shea, W.** "Esther and History." *AUSS* 14 (1976) 227–46. **Striedl, H.** "Untersuchung zur Syntax und Stilistik des hebräischen Buches Esther." *ZAW* 14 (1937) 73–108. **Stronach, D.** "Pasargadae." In *The Cambridge History of Iran: Vol. 2. The Median and Achaemenian Periods,* ed. I. Gershevitch. Cambridge: Cambridge UP, 1985. 838–55. **Weidner, E. F.** "Hof- und Harems-Erlasse assyrische Könige aus dem 2. Jahrtausend v. Chr." *AfO* 17 (1954–55) 257–93. **Yamauchi, E.** *Persia and the Bible.* Grand Rapids, MI: Baker, 1990. **Zadok, R.** "Notes on Esther." *ZAW* 98 (1986) 105–10.

Translation

Episode 1. The banquets of King Ahasuerus: Persian pomp and circumstance (1:1–9)
Time: year 3 of the reign of Ahasuerus

1It happened[a] in the days of Ahasuerus[b]—the Ahasuerus[c] who ruled over one hundred and twenty-seven[d] provinces stretching from India to Ethiopia.[e] 2In those days,[a] when King Ahasuerus was ruling from the Citadel of Susa[b] 3in the third year of his reign, he gave a banquet for all his nobles and courtiers,[a] both the aristocracy of Persia and Media[b] and the governors of the provinces who were present,[c] 4putting on display the riches and glory[a] of his empire and the pomp and splendor of his majesty for many days,[b] one hundred and eighty in all! 5At the end of this time,[a] the king gave another banquet for all the men[b] who were present in the Citadel of Susa, from the least to the greatest. The banquet lasted for seven days and took place in the court located in the garden of[c] the royal pavilion.[d] 6And, oh, the white and violet hangings of linen and cotton,[a] held by white and purple cords of fine linen[b] on silver rods and alabaster columns; the couches[c] of gold and silver on a mosaic pavement of porphyry, alabaster, shell-marble, and turquoise! 7And, oh, the drinks that were served from golden decanters, each different from the other, while the king's wine flowed in royal style![a] 8By ordinance of the king there were no restraints placed upon the drinking,[a] for the king had instructed every one of his wine stewards to serve each and every man as much as he desired.[b]

9And Queen Vashti also gave a banquet for the women in the royal palace of King Ahasuerus.

Episode 2. Queen Vashti deposed: Persian folly and foolishness (1:10–22)
Time: year 3

10On the seventh day of the banquet, when the king was lightheaded[a] with wine, he commanded Mehuman, Biztha, Harbona, Bigtha, Abagtha, Zethar, and Carcas—the seven eunuchs who personally waited upon him[b]—11to bring Queen Vashti before the king, wearing her royal crown,[a] in order to put her beauty on display before the people and the nobles, for she was a beautiful woman. 12But Queen Vashti refused to come at the king's command conveyed by the eunuchs.[a] At this the king became very angry, and his rage burned within him.

13The king then said to the sages who understood the times[a]—for in this manner did the king consult with[b] all who knew law and legal process 14(those closest to him[a] being Carshena, Shethar, Admatha, Tarshish, Meres, Marsena, and Memucan, the seven nobles of Persia and Media who had immediate access to the king[b] and occupied the highest posts in the realm[c]): 15"According to law,[a] what should be done with Queen Vashti because she has not obeyed the king's command[b] conveyed by the eunuchs?"

16And Memucan[a] said to the king and the nobles, "It is not just the king alone whom Queen Vashti has wronged but all the nobles and all the peoples who are in all the provinces of King Ahasuerus. 17For knowledge of the queen's conduct will spread[a] to[b] all the women so that they will treat their husbands with contempt,[c] saying, 'When King Ahasuerus ordered Queen Vashti to be brought before him, she would not come.' 18And this very day the noble ladies[a] of Persia and Media who will have heard what the queen has said will say the same[b] to the nobles of the king, and there will be no end to the disrespect and anger![c]

[19] *"Therefore, if it please the king, let a royal decree be issued by him,*[a] *and let it be inscribed in the laws of Persia and Media, never to be repealed, that Vashti shall not come again into the presence of King Ahasuerus, and let the king give her place as queen to another woman who is better than she.* [20] *And let the king's proclamation which he will make be heard throughout all his kingdom—how magnificent it is!*[a]*—so that all women, high and low alike, will give honor to their husbands."*

[21] *This proposal pleased the king and the nobles, and the king did as Memucan said.* [22] *He sent letters to all the provinces of the realm, to each and every province in its own script and to each and every people in their own language, that every man should be ruler in his own household and speak the language of his own people.*[a]

Notes

1.a. Esther opens with a clause introduced by the characteristic waw-consec form of the verb היה, "to be," lit. "And it was in the days of Ahasuerus." In SBH this construction is regularly followed by a second verbal clause introduced by an impf + waw-consec form of the verb and the first clause regularly expresses a circumstantial sense (most frequently temporal; cf. *IBHS* § 33.2.4.b; Ruth 1:1). Here, however, the main clause is introduced by the pf (עשׂה, v 3b; contra *IBHS* § 33.2.4.b), in keeping with the marked decrease in the use of the waw-consec forms in LBH (see linguistic feature [2] in the discussion of date in the *Introduction* to Ruth). This in no way implies that the book of Esther is the continuation of some preceding narrative (see the discussion in the *Comment* on Ruth 1:1; cf. the comments of Moore, 3).

1.b. The LXX and Josephus read Ἀρταξέρξης, "Artaxerxes," throughout the story of Esther. AT reads Ἀσσυῆρος, Vg reads *Asuerus*, and Syr reads *ʾḥšyš*, all of which support MT. See *Comment.*

1.c. Syr has "son of Ahasuerus" here, a historically impossible reading that perhaps is intended to imitate the customary royal titulature, which normally included the patronymic (cf. Gerleman, 47).

1.d. Syr reads "one hundred and twenty provinces" (perhaps influenced by Dan 6:1), but cf. 9:30.

1.e. Lit. "who ruled from India to Ethiopia 127 provinces."

2.a. Because of the long appositive clause in v 1 identifying Ahasuerus, the author must begin again with this resumptive temporal clause בימים ההם, "in those days." Though it is possible that in Heb. this implies a new sentence (what the Eng. translation requires is another matter), the circumstantial construction discussed in *Note* 1.a. makes this most unlikely.

2.b. Lit. "as King Ahasuerus sat upon his royal throne, which was in the Citadel of Susa." בִּירָה, here translated "citadel," is a loan word through Aram. from Akk. *birtu*, "fortress, fortified city" (cf. ברתה, Ezra 6:2, referring to the acropolis of another of the Persian capital cities, Ecbatana). On its meaning, see the discussion in *Form/Structure/Setting* and *Comment.*

3.a. Heb. עבדיו, lit. "his servants."

3.b. Lit. "the power of Persia and Media, the nobles." The insertion of "princes of" or "chiefs of" before "power" (cf. *BHS* n.) is to be rejected; see *Comment.*

3.c. Lit. "the nobles of the provinces before him," i.e., the rulers of the provinces of the empire present at court.

4.a. Lit. "the riches of the glory of . . ." Syr reads "the riches *and* the glory of . . . , while LXX omits "glory." MT is to be preferred (contra Bardtke, 275). The versions are an attempt to provide a smoother translation.

4.b. The phrase "for many days" is not to be omitted following LXX. The LXX of Esther is a very free translation with numerous additions and omissions compared to the MT. See the *Introduction* to Esther.

5.a. Lit. "when these days were completed."

5.b. Though the text reads העם, "people," v 9 makes clear that only the men are meant.

5.c. Lit. "the garden of the court of . . ."

5.d. Good Eng. style demands that the long Heb. sentence be broken into two.

6.a. Lit. "white-cloth, linen, and violet-cloth." The emendations often suggested (e.g., *BHS* n.) are unnecessary; see *Comment.*

6.b. Lit. "cords of fine linen and purple-dyed wool."

6.c. The addition of בְּ or וּ to מטות, "couches," on the basis of the Lucianic text of the LXX and Syr (*BHS* n. b) do not attest to a different Heb. text. They are attempts of the translators to smooth out the Heb. syntax (see *Comment*).

7.a. Lit. "the royal wine was copious, according to the king's hand."

8.a. Lit. "The drinking [השׁתיה] was according to the edict: 'let there be no restraint.'" שְׁתִיָּה, "drinking," occurs only here in BH. To name the verbal action (the Eng. "gerund"), SBH uses the inf constr. The lateness of the usage in Esther is indicated by the fact that the noun שתיה occurs elsewhere only in MH and by the fact that the use of its nominal pattern (*qĕtîlah*) to name the verbal action (instead of the inf) is exceedingly rare in BH, if it occurs at all, but is frequent in MH. See Bergey, "Esther," 29–30.

8.b. Lit. "to do according to the desire of each and every man."

10.a. Lit. "when the heart of the king was good." See *Comment.*

10.b. Lit. "who served the face of King Ahasuerus."

11.a. The word כֶּתֶר, "crown" (see *Comment*), occurs in BH only in Esther. In SBH and elsewhere in LBH נזר or עטרה is used. The lateness of the usage in Esther is indicated by the fact that it appears elsewhere only in MH; see Bergey, "Esther," 98–99.

12.a. Lit. "which was through (in the hand of) the eunuchs."

13.a. On the emendation of העתים, "times," to הדתים, "laws," proposed by some scholars, see *Comment.*

13.b. Lit. "for so were the king's affairs before . . ."

14.a. Syr takes והקרב אליו as a second ind obj of the verb in v 13, ויאמר, "and he said," while the LXX tradition throughout reads προσῆλθεν, which would reflect the finite verb והקריבו, "and they drew near." The MT is to be preferred. The verse is a parenthesis and as such stands outside the thread of the narrative (Gerleman, 47). It is also unnecessary to repoint קָרֹב to קָרֵב following 1 Kgs 5:7 (*BHS* n.). This use of the inf abs is acceptable syntax in the LBH idiom of Esther.

14.b. Lit. "who saw the face of the king."

14.c. Lit. "sat first in the kingdom."

15.a. To omit the word כדת as a dittograph of the final consonants (כות) of the last word of the preceding verse (Rudolph, *VT* 4 [1954] 89; *BHS* n. a) is unacceptable. It is most improbable that a waw would be misread as a daleth in either the Old Heb. or the later square Heb. script. It is also unnecessary to move it to the end of the preceding verse (Haupt, *AJSL* 24 [1907–8] 111; Bardtke, 285; *BHS* n. a). Though the word can hardly be said to be "resumptive, . . . after the long parenthetical expression of vss. 13b–14" (Moore, 10), for there is nothing in the text preceding the parenthesis for it to resume, it fits the context. The phrase is fully in keeping with the farcical mood of the scene. See *Comment.*

15.b. The word מַאֲמַר, "command," occurs in BH only in Esther (also 2:20; 9:32). In SBH and elsewhere in LBH the sense "command" in a royal context is expressed by דבר or מצוה. The lateness of the usage in Esther is indicated by the fact that it occurs elsewhere only in MH; see Bergey, "Esther," 100–101.

16.a. Given the form מְמוּכָן in v 14, the K מומכן is doubtless a scribal error.

17.a. Lit. "the affair of the queen will go forth."

17.b. על need not be changed to אל (so Bardtke, 285; cf. *BHS* n. a). These two words are frequently confused in BH in general (cf. *GBH* § 133b) and esp. in LBH (cf. Striedl, *ZAW* 14 [1937] 77). This may well be an influence from Aram., since the use of אל is extremely rare in Aram. and the prep על expresses all the meanings that אל does in Heb. אל and על are frequently interchanged in Esther; see *Notes* 2:14.b., 4:5.b., 7:7.b., 7:8.a. Cf. *BHS* n. 9:23c; *GBH* § 133f.

17.c. Lit. "causing them to despise their husbands in their eyes."

18.a. The Heb. is שׂרות, the fem pl of שׂר, which I have translated "noble."

18.b. The Heb. reads simply "will say," without an obj. For the emendations that have consequently been suggested, see *Comment.*

18.c. The Heb. is cryptic and unclear, reading lit. "according to sufficiency (will be) contempt and wrath."

19.a. Lit. "from his presence."

20.a. The interjection is lacking in the LXX. For its meaning, see *Comment.*

22.a. The Heb. is lit. "speak according to the language of his people." The phrase is lacking in the LXX. For discussion of the various emendations suggested, see *Comment.*

Form/Structure/Setting

The first act of the book of Esther consists of 1:1–2:23. These two chapters form a single act because they constitute the exposition for the story (cf. Dorothy, "Books of Esther," 272–73). In this act our author does two things: (1)

introduces the main characters of the narrative and narrates those events and situations necessary to the development of the plot and (2) establishes the tone and temper of the story (see *Explanation*). Each of the three scenes of this act lays out situations and developments that are crucial for understanding the story to follow (cf. Clines, *Esther Scroll*, 9–10). They introduce three of the four important characters of the narrative, Ahasuerus, Mordecai, and Esther, and begin their characterization. Scene 1 recounts the events that lead to the deposal of Queen Vashti, necessary for Esther's rise to the queenship. Scene 2 depicts the manner in which Esther replaces Vashti as the queen of Persia, necessary for her role in foiling Haman's plot to destroy the Jews. Scene 3 presents the unrewarded service that Mordecai renders to the king, which service is indispensable to the events related in 6:1–13. That scene is symbolically significant, for in it Mordecai is exalted and Haman debased.

The first episode of the opening scene comprises vv 1–9 (cf. Murphy, *Wisdom*, 158). It is introduced by ויהי, the characteristic opening of a new section of narrative (see *Comment* below). The ending of the episode is signaled by the shift in the third independent statement (see below) in v 9 to the sentence order *subject* + *verb* (on the use of such inversions to mark the boundaries of a pericope, see *SBH*, 78, 80–82).

The episode structurally comprises only three main independent statements, each of which contains the verb עשה and predicates the giving of a banquet:

(1) v 3b, "King Ahasuerus gave a banquet for all his nobles and courtiers."
(2) v 5b, "the king gave for all the people . . . a banquet."
(3) v 9a, "Queen Vashti also gave a banquet."

The first and second independent statements are expanded by modifying clauses. It is these expansions that form the vehicle for the author's mockery (see *Explanation*).

In the first independent statement, the main clause (v 3b) is prefaced by three temporal clauses (vv 1ab, 2ab, 3a) and followed by a circumstantial clause (v 4; cf. Dorothy, "Books of Esther," 268–70). The temporal clauses establish the time and place of the story (cf. Dommershausen, *Estherrolle*, 18): ". . . in the days of Ahasuerus," v 1a; ". . . when King Ahasuerus was ruling from the Citadel of Susa," v 2b; "in the third year of his reign," v 3a. The circumstantial clause that follows (v 4) exhibits perfectly balanced parallelism:

בְּהַרְאֹתוֹ אֶת־עֹשֶׁר כְּבוֹד מַלְכוּתוֹ
וְאֶת־יְקָר תִּפְאֶרֶת גְּדוּלָּתוֹ
יָמִים רַבִּים
שְׁמוֹנִים וּמְאַת יוֹם

putting-on-display the-riches-of the-glory-of his-empire
and-the-pomp-of the-splendor-of his-majesty
many days
eighty and-a-hundred days

In my opinion (contra Dorothy, "Books of Esther," 268–71), vv 1–4 do not function as a "frame prologue" to balance 10:1–3, since its theme of banqueting and

Persian power, pomp, and circumstance relates so directly to the two pericopes that follow. Further, along with the king, Mordecai is a major figure in 10:1–3, if not the major figure, and there is no such parallel element here.

The second independent statement (v 5b) is, like the first, modified by three adverbial clauses (vv 5a, 5c, 5d) and followed by circumstantial clauses (vv 6–8), the form and content of which, however, are markedly different from the circumstantial clause in the first statement. Rather than a clause introduced by the infinitive construct, the narrator here uses nominal clauses. V 6, the first set of nominal clauses, is striking in both form and content. It comprises two asyndetic sentences (i.e., no conjunction is used) with highly unusual syntax (see *Comment*). The two sentences are parallel in structure, the first consisting of a nominal phrase modified by a participial phrase and a prepositional phrase, the second consisting of a nominal (construct) phrase modified by a prepositional phrase:

חוּר כַּרְפַּס וּתְכֵלֶת
אָחוּז בְּחַבְלֵי־בוּץ וְאַרְגָּמָן
עַל־גְּלִילֵי כֶסֶף וְעַמּוּדֵי שֵׁשׁ

fine-white-linen, and-violet-colored-cloth
held by-cords-of white-linen and-purple-cloth
on rods-of silver and-columns-of alabaster

מִטּוֹת זָהָב וָכֶסֶף
עַל רִצְפַת בַּהַט־וָשֵׁשׁ וְדַר וְסֹחָרֶת

couches-of gold and-silver
on a-pavement-of porphyry and-alabaster and-shell-marble and-turquoise

Unlike v 6, vv 7–8 exhibit normal syntax, consisting of standard noun clauses (i.e., subject + predicate). As such, however, they too are circumstantial and continue the description of the character of the banquet. Indeed, v 7 consists of such terse noun clauses that it partakes of the same exclamatory and poetic character as v 6.

Finally, the third independent statement (v 9) is short and to the point, setting forth in brief compass and general terms only those for whom the banquet was given and its locale.

V 2, the second of the temporal clauses prefaced to the first main clause of the episode (see above), names not only the time of our story but also its place, "the Citadel of Susa." It is highly probable that the term בירה, "citadel, acropolis," refers to the high mound in the center of the city of Susa where the Persian palace complex was located. This seems clear from the meaning of the term (see *Comment*) as well as from the distinction made in the book of Esther between the citadel and the city itself (see 3:15; 4:1–6; 8:14–15). Virtually all the events of the narrative, certainly all those crucial to its plot, take place in the Citadel of Susa. The city of Susa, the ancient capital of the earlier state of Elam (see the full and excellent treatment by Yamauchi, *Persia*, 279–303), was located on a fertile plain, close to and only a little higher than the valley of the Tigris river, about 150 miles north of the Persian Gulf, at the exits of the main rivers of the central Zagros mountain range. Hence, it was centrally located between Persia proper to the east and south and Mesopotamia and Asia Minor to the west and north, commanding the main routes in both directions (De Miroschedji, *ABD* 6:244), particularly the "royal road" from Susa to Sardis (see Yamauchi, *Persia,* 174–78). The Elamite city was completely destroyed by the Assyrian king Ashurbanipal in 640 B.C. but seems to have undergone a modest restoration late in the neo-Babylonian era and to have known some Persian occupation under Cyrus and Cambyses. However, because of the strategic position it occupied, Darius I made the city both the administrative capital of his empire and his principal residence (so Cook, "Rise of the Achaemenids," 238). To do so he completely rebuilt and greatly expanded the old Elamite acropolis, raising a terrace some fifty feet high and surrounding it with massive fortifications and a canal separating the tell from the rest of the city. On this acropolis, he built his magnificent palace and audience hall (for a description, see Yamauchi, *Persia,* 293–98). Inscriptions of Darius in three languages have been found (for a quote, see Yamauchi, *Persia,* 293–98) that tell of the gold, gems, rare woods, building stone, and artisans that were brought from all over the empire to construct its buildings. Modern excavations have uncovered the plan of the palace, the audience hall to the north, and the magnificent gate on the west, which provided access to the palace complex. Several features of these structures can be correlated with aspects of our narrative, permitting at least the conclusion that the author was familiar with them. Yamauchi (*Persia,* 300) notes the conclusion of Perrot, who excavated the area of the audience hall in the 1970s, that the ". . . detailed description of the interior disposition of the palace of Xerxes is now in excellent accord with archaeological reality." We shall note these correlations at the appropriate points in the discussion below.

The second episode of this, the first scene, comprises 1:10–22, as indicated by both form and content. Formally, its onset is signaled by another circumstantial clause (the previous episode also having closed with such a clause; see the discussion above), which begins with a temporal statement, "on the seventh day of the banquet." Its closure is formally marked by the circumstantial clause with which the next scene begins (v 2:1). In terms of general content, the episode concerns events that take place during the second of the banquets that have been described in the first episode. In terms of specific content, it involves new personae: the queen, whose deposal will prepare for the events to come, and Memucan, one of the king's closest advisors, whose counsel effects the queen's deposal.

Structurally, the episode comprises two succinct narrative summaries, vv 10–12 and 21–22, enclosing a much longer dialogue, vv 13–20 (cf. Murphy, *Wisdom,* 158–59). As is standard in OT narrative, the dialogue carries the freight of the episode. It is significant that both the opening narrative summary and the dialogue are expanded by long and detailed identifications, both by name and function, of the secondary personages who carry out the king's wishes. In a long and involved parenthetical comment at the beginning of the dialogue, the narrator gives (1) the names of the "sages who understood the times," (2) their identity as "those who had immediate access to the king and occupied the highest posts in the realm," and (3) the fact that in such a manner the king would customarily consult with "all those who knew law and justice." Such detailed information about these secondary characters adds markedly to the pomposity and pretentiousness of the scene, an effect clearly contributing to the farcical nature of the whole (see *Explanation*).

Comment

1 אֲחַשְׁוֵרוֹשׁ *ʾăḥašwērôš*, "Ahasuerus." It has been clear since early in this century that this name must be the Hebrew form of the Old Persian *Xšayāršān*, the traditional English form of which is "Xerxes," from the Greek *Χερξης*. That the Hebrew name does not represent Old Persian *Artaxšaça*, "Artaxerxes," is now certain on linguistic grounds alone. The names Xerxes and Artaxerxes are both now attested in seven of the ancient languages of the period (Akkadian, Aramaic, Egyptian, Elamite, Greek, Hebrew, and Old Persian), and the latter name is always spelled with a "t" (Shea, *AUSS* 14 [1976] 228). Clearly, the author meant the first Persian king to bear that name, the fourth king of the Persian empire, Xerxes I, who ruled from 485 to 465 B.C. (see esp. Yamauchi, *Persia*, 187–239; Paton, 41–45; Moore, xxxv–xli; contra Reʾemi, 116–17).

הוּא אֲחַשְׁוֵרוֹשׁ הַמֹּלֵךְ . . . וּמֵאָה מְדִינָה, "The Ahasuerus who ruled over one hundred and twenty-seven provinces stretching from India to Ethiopia." This long appositive, which gives further information about the character just named, can hardly be intended to give a careful designation of which Persian king is meant, for the Persian empire had reached this extent under Ahasuerus' predecessors (so Clines, 275). Nor does it seem a particularly apropos identification to distinguish this Ahasuerus from another of the same name. The narrator surely understands that his readers will know who this king is, so he characterizes him solely by reference to the vastness of the realm that he rules. It is often alleged that the reference here to "one hundred and twenty-seven provinces" is either historical error (Paton, 71–72) or literary license (Brockington, 224). The matter is far from clear. According to Herodotus (3.89), it was Darius I (522–486 B.C.), Xerxes' father, who organized the Persian empire into only twenty "satrapies" governed by "satraps" (Old Persian *xšaçapāvan*, "protector of the kingdom/kingship"). Though the number and nature of these administrative divisions varied over time, later sources never mention more than thirty-one. However, the text here uses the word מדינה, "province," which, as Bardtke (278) states, could well refer to the administrative subdivisions that were ruled by officials subordinate to the satraps. Indeed, Cameron's study (*JNES* 32 [1973] 47–56) has made it highly probable that the several lists that occur in Achaemenid texts are lists of various groups of peoples, rather than lists of the satrapies themselves as some have contended (cf. also the comments of Briant, *ABD* 5:239; Yamauchi, *Persia*, 178–80). Herzfeld notes (*Persian Empire*, 288, as cited in Yamauchi, *Persia*, 179) that the total of the names of national groups cited in both the Greek and Persian sources amounts to eighty and, he concludes, "the books of Esther (1:1) and Daniel (6:1) speak of 127 (and 120) nations, and the original lists, kept in the offices of the tax collectors, may have contained that number." Hence, one should not too readily reject the Esther datum as historically unreliable (cf. Clines, 275). However all that may be, the decision to enumerate the administrative subdivisions of the empire has a purpose in the narrative that has largely been missed in the controversy about historicity. By the choice of the larger number, the pomp and glory of the empire is magnified, contributing to the sardonic picture presented in this whole chapter (cf. Radday, "Humour," 296; Craig, *Reading Esther*, 54; and see the discussion below). So much power and such a cumbersome administration seem intended primarily to indulge the king's festive excesses depicted in six-month banquets. Whatever horrible edicts this administration will later be called upon to effect, it is first depicted by our narrator as functioning to effect such puerile causes as legislation buttressing male domestic authority (see vv 10–22 below). Finally, the conjecture of Dommershausen (*Estherrolle,* 18; cf. also Meinhold, 23) that the number 127 is a symbolic number comprising 12 x 10 + 7 as numbers of completion and perfection is suggested by nothing in the text.

2 כְּשֶׁבֶת הַמֶּלֶךְ אֲחַשְׁוֵרוֹשׁ עַל כִּסֵּא מַלְכוּתוֹ, lit. "as King Ahasuerus was sitting on his royal throne." Many ancient (see reference in Paton, 124) and modern interpreters (e.g., Bardtke, 278; Dommershausen, 13; Meinhold, 24) have understood this phrase to mean "sat *securely,*" i.e., "firmly in power," referring to the fact that Xerxes had to put down rebellions in Egypt and Babylon during the first three years of his rule. However, as Fox (16) observes, the expression in and of itself simply does not carry such a connotation. It seems far more probable, since this pericope provides the exposition for the story, that the phrase is intended to set its location in the citadel and city of Susa (cf. Clines, 275; Fox, 16; on the setting, see *Form/Structure/Setting* above).

בְּשׁוּשַׁן הַבִּירָה, lit. "in Susa, the Citadel." It is highly probable that this expression refers to the high mound in the middle of the city where Darius built his huge palatial complex (see *Notes* and *Form/Structure/Setting;* cf. Berg, *Esther,* 49 n. 5). To avoid possible confusion, we have used the term "citadel," not "acropolis," in translating בירה, since today only a part of the modern site is called the "acropolis," and this part is not the mound upon which Darius' palace complex stood. For a more detailed description of the city and citadel of Susa, see *Form/Structure/Setting* above.

3 עָשָׂה מִשְׁתֶּה, "He gave/put on a *mištêh.*" The term *mištêh* bears the same meaning as the English words "banquet" or "feast" (e.g., Gen 19:1–3; 26:30–31; cf. also Esth 5:4–9). In vv 5, 9 the affair lasted for 7 days, a time span that would be possible for a "reception," or "festival" (cf. Clines, 276, who notes the LXX translation *δοχή*), which people attended at various times during the days that it lasted (cf. the wedding *mištêh,* "feast," which lasted for 7 days; Gen 29:21–28; Judg 17:10–17). But that cannot be the case here where the "banquet" lasts for 180 days, almost six months! Clearly the narrator is engaging in sardonic hyperbole.

לְכָל־שָׂרָיו וַעֲבָדָיו חֵיל פָּרַס וּמָדַי הַפַּרְתְּמִים וְשָׂרֵי הַמְּדִינוֹת לְפָנָיו, lit. "for all his officials and his servants the power of Persia and Media the nobles and the officials of the provinces before him." It is unclear how many different groups are intended here. The ambiguity is caused by (1) the lack of any waw connective before both the construct phrase חיל פרס ומדי, "the power of Persia and Media," and the noun הפרתמים, "the nobles," making it unclear whether they are appositives or separate entities, and (2) the exact connotation of the word חיל, "power." The first is ambiguous simply because the use of the waw connective on the individual items of a nominal series is highly variable (see *IBHS* § 39.2.1.b), not least in the book of Esther. It is usually found on each item in a series (e.g., Esth 9:6–9, the list of the ten sons of Haman; cf. also 4:3; 8:9; 9:3); sometimes it is found only on the last item (e.g., the first three words of Esth 1:6); rarely is it irregularly distributed (e.g., Esth 1:10, the list of the seven attendants of the king); and still more rarely is it omitted altogether (e.g., Esth 1:14, the list of the seven prominent nobles of the kingdom). Hence, the two entities without waw connective may be separate items in the list, or they may both be in apposition to the preceding. The decision, then, rests upon the meaning assigned to חיל, "power." The word can hardly bear the frequent meaning "armed force, army," for the king could not possibly have entertained such a number. Yamauchi (*Persia,* 196) estimates the size of the army Xerxes took to Greece to be approximately 150,000 to 200,000! To obviate this difficulty, Moore (5–6, following the view of many scholars; cf. *BHS* n. a) inserts ושרי, "and the chiefs of," before חיל, yielding the translation "and the chiefs of the army of . . ." He bases this on the supposition that the LXX reading καὶ τοῖς λοιποῖς, "and the rest," represents a Hebrew reading ושאר, which could be a corruption of ושרי. This is highly conjectural, and it is probable that the LXX expands the text here for clarity, as frequently (Fox, 276). It seems much preferable to take the lack of waw connective to imply that the last three expressions are in apposition to the first two and further define who these groups are (so also Bardtke, 278). In this case חיל, "army," could refer by metonymy to the officer corps (Bardtke, 278–79; Dommershausen, *Estherrolle,* 19). However, in my opinion, it makes best sense in the context to take חיל here in the sense of "nobility, aristocracy, upper classes" (Gerleman, 54–55, followed by Clines, 276; cf. *HALOT,* 4, p. 311), a meaning it has in another post-exilic text, Neh 4:2 (MT 3:34); cf. also 1 Kgs 10:2. In this case שרי המדינות, "the officials of the provinces," would refer to the governors of the provinces outside of the Persian and Median heartland (so Gerleman, 54).

5 בַּחֲצַר גִּנַּת בִּיתַן הַמֶּלֶךְ, lit. "in the court of the garden of the pavilion of the king." As Oppenheim (*JNES* 24 [1965] 328–33) has convincingly shown, the word ביתן is a loan word through Aramaic from Akkadian and refers to a small building interior to the palace complex, a kind of open, columned "pavilion" or "kiosk." The banquet took place outdoors in a paved (v 6) court or patio located in the garden associated with this pavilion. The pavilion and garden are also the scene of the climax of the story in chap. 7. The Persians were famous in antiquity for gardens and parks connected with and surrounding their palaces (cf. Yamauchi, *Persia,* 332–33; for a description of the palace garden at Pasargadae, see Stronach, "Pasargadae," 846–47).

6 This verse exhibits highly unusual syntax. It consists of two asyndetic, incomplete sentences. They are incomplete in that each of the two nominal phrases stands independently, lacking a predicate. Driver's view (*VT* 4 [1954] 235) that the text is in disorder because "these words hang in the air" and because the ancient versions imply something like "and the hall was adorned with . . . linen" does not commend itself. It is much more likely that the ancient versions were trying to smooth out the unusual syntax involved. Further, Striedl (*ZAW* 14 [1937] 86) and others (e.g., Dommershausen, *Estherrolle,* 22) have quite satisfactorily interpreted the unusual syntax as intentional on the part of the narrator—as terse, exclamatory sentence-equivalents, poetic in character, intended to express wonder and amazement at such luxury and magnificence (see *Explanation*). Following Fox (274), I have attempted to express this exclamatory sense of amazement (which is also present in v 7) with the translation, "And, oh, the . . . !"

The meanings of a number of the terms used are quite uncertain, and several appear only here. חוּר, occurring elsewhere only in Esth 8:15, is otherwise unknown. However, since it comes from a Semitic root meaning "white" (cf. Isa 29:22) and the meanings of כרפס, "linen," and תכלת, "purple cloth," are known, it is usually taken to be a type of white cotton or linen cloth. On this basis, חור כרפס ותכלת may be three different types of fabric (so Gerleman, 58). But, the parallelism of this phrase with the one in the second sentence (see *Form/Structure/Setting*) rather strongly suggests that חור כרפס is instead a compound term expressing one idea, "white linen/cotton." The term שׁשׁ, the material from which the columns were made and one of the four materials that formed the mosaic floor, is probably a loan word from Egyptian, for which the meaning "alabaster" is highly probable. (Clines, 277, notes that this is a true marble, not the English or Italian alabaster, which is a variety of gypsum.) In the final clause, then, the terms בהט, דר, and סחרת, which are coordinate with שׁשׁ, must be other materials suitable for use in a mosaic floor, but their meanings are quite uncertain. בהט may be a loan word from an Egyptian term that may have the meaning "porphyry." דר may be related to Arabic *durrun*, "pearl" (also suggested by the LXX rendering πίννινος λίθος, "pearl stone"), hence the frequent translation "mother-of-pearl." However, as Clines (277) notes, mother-of-pearl is hardly suitable as tesserae for a mosaic pavement. Thus, I have adopted the suggestion of Haupt (*AJSL* 24 [1907–8] 106) to render the term "shell-marble" (a marble containing fossil shells). The meaning of סחרת is completely uncertain. It can hardly mean "precious/costly stones" (so, e.g., JB, NIV, RSV), since such materials are also unsuitable as tesserae in a pavement. My translation, "turquoise" (so NEB, REB), is a sheer guess.

7 וְהַשְׁקוֹת בִּכְלֵי זָהָב וְכֵלִים מִכֵּלִים שׁוֹנִים, lit. "and the serving of drinks was from vessels of gold and vessels differing from vessels." השקות means "to serve a drink to, to give a drink to" (cf. Gen 19:32; 21:19) and the word כלי, "vessel," when used in connection with liquids, refers almost exclusively to the vessel in which liquids were stored or served but rarely, if ever, to the container from which one drank. The statement, then, is very general, referring to the cups and goblets from which the wine was drunk as well as to the decanters and vessels from which it was served. The point is not only the quality of the vessels but also their quantity and diversity; "vessels differing from vessels" can only mean "each different from the other." Xenophon (*Cyropaedeia* 8.8.18) mentions the Persians' great pride in having as many drinking cups as possible. The description, then, highlights the royal ostentation (Clines, 277).

כְּיַד הַמֶּלֶךְ, "according to the king's hand." The exact meaning of the idiom is not clear. In keeping with its usage elsewhere (particularly in Esth 2:18; cf. also 1 Kgs 10:13; Neh 2:8) and the context of this verse, the sense is either "liberally, generously" (Bardtke, 282; Dommershausen, 14; cf. most of the modern translations) or "as befits a king" (Moore, 7; NEB).

8 וְהַשְּׁתִיָּה כַדָּת אֵין אֹנֵס, "And the drinking was according to the rule: let there be no restraining." As Haupt pointed out long ago, from its use in the Talmud (*AJSL* 24 [1907–8] 106) the verb אנס, "to constrain" (used only here in the OT), has both a positive sense, "to urge to action," and a negative sense, "to restrain from action." From the context here, in which the king's stewards were "to do according to the desire of each and every man," the meaning must be "to restrain," and the mood must be precative, "let there be." Moore (7–8) adopts the view that the first clause, "the drinking was according to rule," reflects the custom mentioned by some ancient authorities (e.g., Herodotus, 1.33; Josephus, *Ant.* 11.188) that, whenever the king drank at Persian banquets, all the guests drank. If this is the meaning, it is clearly in conflict with the following clause, "let there be no constraining." To obviate this difficulty he adopts the reading of the LXX, which inserts a negative in the first clause. But, if this is the original text of the first clause, what could possibly have occasioned the loss of the negative from the whole Hebrew MS tradition? Rather, it seems much more probable that the LXX reading arose in an attempt to solve just such an apparent contradiction. It is much more natural to understand that the clause refers to a special royal ruling for this banquet. Such a view fits with the evident irony of the narrative: even the absence of a rule requires a decree (Clines, 278; cf. also Berg, *Book of Esther,* 36)! It also contributes to the depiction of the king's liberality and excess and helps explain why Vashti would refuse to be displayed before the common crowd, who have been drinking without restraint.

9 גַּם וַשְׁתִּי הַמַּלְכָּה . . ., "Queen Vashti also . . ." For a possible Elamite etymology for the name Vashti, see Zadok, *ZAW* 98 [1986] 109–10 (cf. Moore, 9; Clines, 278). For bibliography, see *Comment* on the names in v 10 below.

10 כְּטוֹב לֵב־הַמֶּלֶךְ בַּיָּיִן, lit. "when the king's heart was good with wine." According to Hebrew anthropology, the "heart" is the seat of the will and of thought. The expression "good of heart" in and of itself simply means to be in an expansive and happy mood (cf. 1 Kgs 8:66; esp. Prov 15:15, where it expresses the mood opposite to that of the עני, "oppressed"). When the condition is brought on by alcohol, however, it also implies the impairment of judgment (cf. Judg 16:25; esp. 1 Sam 25:36). The translation here (adopted from Fox, 18) seeks to capture that nuance. The reference to the king's intoxication serves to continue the stress upon the frivolity and excess of the event that have been so pointedly noted in the preceding description.

מְהוּמָן . . . וְכַרְכַּס שִׁבְעַת הַסָּרִיסִים הַמְשָׁרְתִים אֶת־פְּנֵי הַמֶּלֶךְ, lit. "Mehuman . . . and Carcas—the seven eunuchs who serve the face of King Ahasuerus" (for a similar expression in a much different context, see 1 Sam 2:11, 18). Though the term סריס can refer simply to an official of the court, here it perhaps has the technical sense of "eunuch," since it refers to the king's most personal attendants, who had access to the harem. (For similar functionaries in the Assyrian court, see Weidner, *AfO* 17 [1954–55]; yet for evidence that not all Assyrian pages and bodyguards who had access to the harem were eunuchs, see Yamauchi, *Persia,* 262–63.) The names of the seven eunuchs are composed of onomastic elements that, for the most part, have been given reasonable etymologies from the Persian or Median family of languages, even though they have not, at the present time, all been documented in known Persian/Median names (see Gehman, *JBL* 43 [1924] 321–28; Duchesne-Guillemin, *Mus* 66 [1953] 105–8; Millard, *JBL* 96 [1977] 481–88; Zadok, *ZAW* 98 [1986] 105–10). The author's purpose in listing them in detail is probably not to give historical verisimilitude to his story (contra Bardtke; Fox) but to add to the solemnity and pomposity of the occasion (in Clines' words, the story's "decorative handling"). Note the repeated reference to them by the use of the expression "conveyed by the eunuchs" in vv 12, 15. The queen is to appear with the full escort of the king's most personal attendants. In my opinion, Fox (20) has captured their significance: ". . . it is a phony ritual created for the nonce, to show that in this court, everything, even an invitation to the queen, is thick with pomp and circumstance." For the suggestion that these foreign-sounding names were meant to sound ludicrous, see *Comment* on v 14.

11 בְּכֶתֶר מַלְכוּת, lit. "in/with a royal 'crown.'" The term כתר is a rare word used in BH only in the book of Esther (see *Note* 11.a.). Here and in 2:17 it refers to the headdress worn by the Persian queen, and in 6:8 (see *Comment*) it is used for the adornment on the head of the king's horse. Here it doubtless refers not to a "crown" in the European sense but to the Persian "turban" (Moore, 9), i.e., the "tall stiff cap, with jewels inset, that is depicted on the monuments" (Clines, 279).

13 לַחֲכָמִים יֹדְעֵי הָעִתִּים, "to the sages who understood the times." According to Moore (9) and others, the expression suggests the court astrologers, the presence of which functionaries is documented for the Persian court by Herodotus (cf. 1.107; 7.19). On the grounds that this is incompatible with the immediately following explanation that these men are "those who know law and the legal process" (דת ודין; see the next entry), Moore follows the lead of Haller and others and emends עתים, "times," to דתים, "laws," a correction followed unfortunately by JB, NAB, NJB, and NRSV. For similar reasons Brockington (226 n. 13) connects עת with the Arabic root *ʿnt,* "to cause trouble," rendering it "trouble, crime," a correction followed unhappily by NEB. The emendation is to be rejected (cf. Barthélemy et al., *Preliminary and Interim Report* 2:547). The context prohibits taking the phrase to mean the court astrologers (cf. Bardtke, 287; Clines, 280; Gerleman, 64). Nothing in their reply hinges upon technical astrological lore (Clines), and the narrator himself makes clear, with his parenthetical explanation that "in this manner did the king consult with all who knew law and the legal process," that the phrase refers not to astrologers and diviners but to "all-around experts" (Fox, 21; cf. also the helpful discussion of Gerleman, 64–65). Further, the fact that virtually the same phrase occurs in 1 Chron 12:33 (Eng. v 32), where a reference to astrologers is totally out of place, points strongly in the same direction (Clines, 280; Fox, 21).

כָּל־יֹדְעֵי דָּת וָדִין, "all who know law and legal process." As a verb דין means "to plead a cause, to execute judgement," while elsewhere the noun דין means "legal claim; legal contest, case" (see *HALOT*, 1, p. 220). In this light it most likely here means "judgment" in the sense of the legal process, which fits the context.

14 כַּרְשְׁנָא . . . מְמוּכָן שִׁבְעַת שָׂרֵי פָּרַס וּמָדַי רֹאֵי פְּנֵי הַמֶּלֶךְ, lit. "Carshena . . . Memucan, the seven nobles of Persia and Media who saw the face of the king." As with the names of the king's personal attendants in v 10 above, some of the names of the seven nobles have been given reasonable etymologies from the Persian/Median onomasticon (for bibliography, see *Comment* on v 10 above). Seven counselors of Artaxerxes are also mentioned in Ezra 7:14, and other ancient sources mention groups of noble advisors and confidants who had immediate access to the king (see esp. Herodotus 3.31, 84, 118; Xenophon, *Anabasis,* 1.6.4). For a full and reasoned discussion, which casts serious doubt on the continued existence of a formal "Council of Seven," see Cook, "The Rise of the Achaemenids," 232–35. The naming in full of all these worthies, those who "know law and legal process," enhances the irony of the situation: a domestic squabble is turned into a cause célèbre (cf. Radday, "Esther with Humour," 297). Radday suggests that the very sound of these foreign names would have been ludicrous to Hebrew ears, and so the list is intended to be satirical, giving "the impression of a dumb chorus in an opera bouffe" ("Humour in Names," 71–72). Given the mockery of the whole scene, the suggestion is most attractive.

15 כְּדָת, "according to law." The expression, of course, cannot imply that some regulation was already in existence legislating penalties for queenly disobedience! "Law" here must be taken more in the sense of "legal precedent" or "proper established procedure" (Fox, 20). Even so, the qualification is intended to be farcical and humorous—not knowing how to handle his recalcitrant wife, the king turns the affair into a matter of state. In addition, his request for legal precedent avoids any admission of his inadequacy to handle the situation (Baldwin, 61). As has often been noted, neither law nor legal precedent plays any role in Memucan's reply; it is purely pragmatic advice (Clines, 281).

18 וְהַיּוֹם הַזֶּה תֹּאמַרְנָה שָׂרוֹת פָּרַס־וּמָדַי אֲשֶׁר שָׁמְעוּ אֶת־דְּבַר הַמַּלְכָּה לְכֹל שָׂרֵי הַמֶּלֶךְ, "and this very day the noble ladies of Persia and Media who will have heard about the queen's reply will say the same to all the nobles of the king." The syntax is difficult since there seems to be no object for the verb תאמרנה, "will say." Consequently, a number of scholars (e.g., Bardtke, Haller, Moore; see *BHS* n. a) emend the verb to תִּמְרֶינָה, "will be obstinate, rebellious," or תַּמְרֶינָה, "will rebel," a translation adopted by NAB and NRSV. NEB and REB take the temporal expression "this very day" as the object, a most improbable expedient (as Clines, 281, observes). Clines, on the other hand, follows Gordis (*JBL* 95 [1976] 45–46) in taking the relative particle אשר, "which," as the equivalent of כי, "that." It is not, then, introducing a relative clause modifying "the noble ladies of Persia and Media," but a noun clause, object of the verb תאמרנה, "will say" (so NJB). Though this usage of the relative particle is one that is particularly frequent in LBH, it is a strained interpretation here, apparently sensed by Clines, for he emends the text by introducing the sign of the definite object את before the relative particle. The interpretation has, moreover, further problems. Gordis (*JBL* 95 [1976] 46) must then understand the following adverbial clause, לכל שׂרי המלך, in the sense "in the presence of the king's nobles," a most improbable sense in this context after the verb אמר, "to say." Clines seeks to avoid this by taking את־דבר המלכה, "the queen's reply," not as the direct object of שמעו, "have heard," but as an epexegetical apposition: "the ladies . . . will say [or 'are saying'] what they have heard, namely, the reply [*dābār*] of the queen." Given the context, this is an equally forced interpretation. None of this is necessary if one recognizes that the ellipsis of the direct object is regular in BH whenever the object is clear in the context, a situation that arises most often when it has been mentioned in the immediately preceding context, as here (cf. Fox, 274–75).

19 וּמַלְכוּתָהּ יִתֵּן הַמֶּלֶךְ, "and that the king will give her place as queen." In my opinion this clause is coordinate with the immediately preceding clause, and hence governed by the relative particle אשר, rather than being coordinate with the jussives at the beginning of the verse.

20 וְנִשְׁמַע פִּתְגָם הַמֶּלֶךְ, "and let the king's proclamation be heard." Since this clause begins with a perfect plus waw consecutive and continues directly (i.e., without an intervening clause) the series of jussive clauses at the beginning of v 19, it too must be jussive in force and not a simple future as most translations render it.

כִּי רַבָּה הִיא, "how magnificent it is!" The interjection, jarring in its context, has been taken as a gloss since it is lacking in the LXX (see Moore, 11; omitted by NEB and REB). To make sense of it, most commentators take the particle כי in an adversative/concessive sense and translate "vast as it is" or the like (so Gerleman, 69; NIV, NASV, RSV, NRSV). However, in my opinion the context is highly in favor of Fox's interpretation (275) that כי is used here in its affirmative-emphatic sense (as in Gen 18:20). The phrase, then, is "an incidental courtly interjection" (Fox), a "flattering parenthetical remark" (Paton, 158), which clearly reveals the derision in which the narrator holds these pompous sycophants!

22 אֶל־מְדִינָה וּמְדִינָה כִּכְתָבָהּ וְאֶל־עַם וָעָם כִּלְשׁוֹנוֹ, "to each province in its own script and to each people in their own language." According to Herodotus, the Persian system of royal roads and communication was efficient and well maintained (see Herodotus 5.52–53; 8.98; also Xenophon, *Cyropaedeia* 8.6.17; see esp. the description of the "Royal Road" from Susa to Sardis in Yamauchi, *Persia,* 174–78), a reality reflected in the language here. It is, however, consciously hyperbolic (contra Paton, 160–61), "intended to display the super-efficiency of the Persian administrative machine to do everything—except ensure that a man be master in his own house!" (Clines, 283).

לִהְיוֹת כָּל־אִישׁ שֹׂרֵר בְּבֵיתוֹ וּמְדַבֵּר כִּלְשׁוֹן עַמּוֹ, lit. "each man to be the ruler in his own house and the one speaking according to the language of his people." To begin with, it should be noted that this, the contents of the edict to be circulated throughout the realm (and in the script and language of each indigenous people!), is quite different from the edict proposed by Memucan in v 19. That edict dealt very specifically with what should be done with the queen and presumably was issued in and for the court and its environs. Its execution is reported in the summary statement of v 21b. This edict deals with the Memucan's second concern (v 20), that the king's proclamation should be heard throughout all the kingdom "so that all women, high and low alike, will give honor to their husbands."

In this context the meaning of the second clause, "and the one speaking according to the language of his people," has seemed problematic to many, leading to numerous and varied emendations (cf. *BHS* n.). Since the clause is lacking in the LXX, a number of translations omit the phrase as a gloss (e.g., JB, NAB, NJB, NRSV). Others follow one of the two most common conjectural emendations, reading either ומדבר כל־שוה עמו, "and speak whatever suited him" (proposed by Hitzig over a century ago; see Haupt, *AJSL* 24 [1907–8] 17; so Meinhold, 22; Moore, 11–12) or וּמַדְבִּיר כָּל־נָשָׁיו עִמּוֹ, which is taken to mean "and keep all his wives in subjection" (proposed by H. Junker, "Konsonantenumstellung," 173; so NEB, Bardtke, 284; Brockington, 227). But, as has often been noted (Fox, 275; Clines, 283), apart from their totally conjectural nature, neither of these emendations is acceptable Hebrew. The first would require לו rather than עמו (see the use of שוה in 3:8; 5:13) and would properly mean "what is fitting, proper for him," implying a restriction on the man's actions (Haupt, *AJSL* 24 [1907–8] 17; Fox, 275). In the second, the meaning of הדביר, "to subdue, overwhelm" in a military sense (cf. Fox, 275), is inappropriate to such a context as this. Clines' suggestion (283) to read וּמְדֻבָּר בִּלְשׁוֹן נֹעַם, "and be addressed civilly [lit. with a pleasant tongue]," is equally conjectural, while the transposition of the clause prior to "that every man should be ruler in his own household" (so NIV, REB) is not merely conjectural; the meanings proposed simply cannot be obtained from the Hebrew. If, however, one takes into full account that this is a story told *for* the post-exilic Jewish diaspora *by* a member of that community, then the interpretation of the older commentators is fully appropriate (so Gordis, *JBL* 95 [1976] 53; cf. Barthélemy et al., *Preliminary and Interim Report* 2:547). It simply affirms that in a racially mixed household (a situation probably all too common in the Jewish diaspora, contra Clines), the man would, or should, want to speak his national language (cf. Neh 13:23–28). As Fox (23) puts it, "Whether or not other peoples in the Persian empire actually shared that feeling, the phrase is indeed a reflex of a Jewish concern for preserving Hebrew as the Jewish vernacular."

Explanation

Episode 1. The banquets of King Ahasuerus: Persian pomp and circumstance (1:1–9). In this the opening episode, the narrator begins to set forth the circumstances that provide the setting, the backdrop so to speak, for his story. In terms of the facts involved, these circumstances can be stated in very short compass indeed: Who? Ahasuerus. When? In the third year of his reign. Where? In the Citadel of Susa. What happened? He gave two banquets. The first one was for all the high-ranking nobles and officials of his court and lasted for 180 days. The second one was for all the people (meaning men) of his capital, the Citadel of Susa, and lasted for 7 days. At the same time Queen Vashti put on a banquet for the women. Indeed the very structure of this episode signals that these are the basic facts, for it formally comprises but three main independent statements, each of which predicates the giving of a banquet (see *Form/Structure/Setting*).

In actuality, of course, the narrator does very much more than state these basic facts. In the rest of the content, which consists of modifying and descriptive clauses appended to the first two independent statements, he skillfully begins to set the tone and temper of his story. Thus, the first of the temporal clauses (v 1) prefaced to the first main statement of the episode (v 3b; see *Form/Structure/Setting*) not only gives us the name of one of the principal characters of the narrative, Ahasuerus, but also defines who this character is by appending a long appositional clause that identifies him by the vast extent of the realm he rules: "one hundred and twenty-seven provinces stretching from India to Ethiopia," i.e., the whole known world. What can such an identifying clause suggest but absolute and unlimited power? Such an identification is in keeping with the far from subtle way in which the narrator in the rest of the modifying clauses of the scene satirically portrays the festivities of the Persian court as grandiose and lavishly excessive. And we do not have to wait long for such a characterization. The circumstantial clause (v 4a–b) that immediately follows the first main statement depicts explicitly and forcefully the showy grandeur and prideful ostentation of the Persian monarch: "putting on display the riches and glory of his empire and the pomp and splendor of his majesty" (v 4a). Then the temporal phrase that concludes this clause (v 4b), expressing the duration of these glorious festivities, presents us with an obvious and extravagant hyperbole—the banquet lasted for 180 days! Since lunar months are all either 29 or 30 days in length, this is virtually the equivalent of six months. As Bardtke (279) notes, in the context of the previous clause this is another extravagant exhibition of the royal opulence.

It is, however, in the highly circumstantial noun clauses (vv 6–8) appended to the giving of the second banquet (v 5b) that the depiction of the opulence and extravagance of the royal court are primarily portrayed. The terse, exclamatory sentence-equivalents of v 6, poetic in character, exquisitely express the wonder and amazement the narrator wishes us to feel at such magnificence and luxury (see Fox, 16–17). Fox nicely captures the feeling portrayed: "The exclamatory listing creates a mass of images that overwhelm the sensory imagination and suggest both a sybaritic delight in opulence and an awareness of its excess." Vv 7, 8 underscore the extravagance of the serving vessels, the copiousness of the royal wine, and the freedom of the guests to drink as much as they pleased.

Finally, the third independent statement (v 9) is markedly different. Brief and to the point, it is not expanded by circumstantial clauses like the first two, signaling a wholly different tone and temper. Here there are no statements expressing extravagance or opulence, no descriptions of pomp and circumstance, gaudy hangings, and rich accoutrements, no portrayal of royal wine being freely imbibed in copious amounts. Whatever may actually have been the case for a banquet for women in ancient Persia, the narrator clearly intends to present a sober and striking contrast between the ostentation and excesses of the banquets of the king and his male subjects and the modest celebration of Vashti and her female companions (see esp. Fox, 167–69). The second episode of the scene will portray the difference with even more stark and unrelenting satire.

It is indeed a derisive eye that our narrator has cast upon the royal court he describes: A king who rules the whole known world spends his time giving lavish banquets! The first of these lasts for six months for all the king's high-ranking nobles and courtiers and is for the express and single purpose of displaying the riches and glory of his empire. The second, given for all the residents of his capital city, takes place in a setting that reeks of wealth, from the luxurious fabric of the canopy overhead to the exotic mosaic floor of the king's own garden court beneath, from the golden couches upon which the guests recline to the multivaried vessels of gold from which the royal wine flowed without restraint. He closes the episode with the simple statement, completely without any such embellishment, that the queen too gave a banquet for the women. With such a sharp contrast between the festivities of the queen and those of the king, he has subtly and mockingly set the scene for the comedy that is about to transpire.

Episode 2. The deposal of Queen Vashti: Persian folly and foolishness (1:10–22). In this the second episode, the narrator continues to set forth the preliminary events and circumstances that provide the backdrop for the crisis that will set his story in motion. As in the first episode, the actual events necessary to understand this crisis are really very few and could have been presented in short compass indeed: Because of Queen Vashti's public disobedience, the king issued an edict that deposed her and ordained that another, more worthy woman, should be found to take her place. These are all the facts necessary to set the stage for telling how Esther could rise to a position where she could affect the course of events.

What, then, does our narrator accomplish by embellishing his account in the way that he has? (1) In his expanded treatment of this episode, the derisive eye that he cast upon the Persian court in the opening one is unrelentingly continued. From the satirical depiction of the grandiose and lavishly excessive lifestyle of the Persian court, our narrator turns to undisguised farce: the king who rules the whole world cannot bend his own wife to his will! Deprived by wine of all propriety, he blunders into a contest of wills with her and loses when she refuses to be shown off to the drunken (vv 7–8) and common crowd (v 5) as a beautiful object, an adornment for his richly appointed pavilion (v 6). Force her he could; control her will he cannot!

Vashti's refusal to be shown off like a common concubine (cf. the comments of Fox, 168) before the tipsy hoi polloi of the Citadel of Susa reveals a sense of decorum and self-respect that places her outside of the mocking characterization that the narrator has given the rest of the royal court. She is evaluated positively. The contrast markedly sharpens the scorn with which the narrator views the courtly and royal world within which his story will be set (cf. Fox, 167–69).

To hide his inadequacy to handle this situation, the king invokes standard court procedure (v 13b). He appeals to his closest and most important counselors—and thereby raises a domestic squabble to the level of a matter of state. These worthies, described in pretentious detail (v 14), demonstrate that they are not "sages" who "understand the times" (v 13a). Rather, they lose all their common sense and decorum in the hysterical assumption that Vashti's disobedience will spark not only conjugal disrespect in general (v 17) but also rebellion in their own households (v 18; Clines, *The Esther Scroll,* 32)! Their solution is ironic. They decree for Vashti what she has already decided: she "shall not come again into the presence of King Ahasuerus" (v 19). Their decision to demand honor from their wives by an empire-wide edict would have actually achieved, of course, the dissemination of the very rumors about Vashti's actions and the king's embarrassment that they feared and sought to quash (cf. Fox, 24; Clines, *The Esther Scroll,* 33).

(2) Our narrator's expanded treatment sharply underlines that the Persian empire is ruled inexorably by law, but it is not a law that can bring much assurance of stability or justice to those who stand under its mandates. It is, on the one hand, irrevocable (v 19), but, on the other hand, its source is the will and whim of a weak and unstable despot who seems to care about little other than his own pride and pleasure.

So the opening scene of our story sets a satirical tone that prepares us for more of the same:

> [T]he opening chapter has set a tone that cannot be forgotten, conditioning the reader not to take the king, his princes, or his law at their face value, and alerting the reader to keep his eyes open for ironies that will doubtless be implicit in the story that is yet to unfold. Without the rather obvious satire of the first chapter we might well be in more doubt over the propriety of ironic readings in the body of the book. Chapter 1 licenses a hermeneutic of suspicion. (Clines, *The Esther Scroll,* 33)

But its mockery has also a sinister side. It reveals a society fraught with danger, for it is ruled by the pride and pomposity of buffoons whose tender egos can marshal the state's legislative and administrative machinery for the furtherance of selfish and childish causes. Indeed, in such a setting, it will not seem incongruous to find this same machinery of state mobilized to effect the slaughter of one of its own minorities, or to find that this is an end that the king can both blissfully contemplate and cavalierly condone.

Scene 2
Esther Becomes Queen (2:1–18)

Bibliography

Albright, W. "The Lachish Cosmetic Burner and Esther 2:12." In *A Light unto My Path.* FS J. M. Myers, ed. H. Bream, R. Heim, and C. Moore. Philadelphia: 1974. 25–32 (= Moore,

Studies, 361–68). **Berg, S. B.** *The Book of Esther: Motifs, Themes and Structure.* Missoula: Scholars, 1979. **Bergey, R. L.** "The Book of Esther—Its Place in the Linguistic Milieu of Post-exilic Biblical Hebrew: A Study in Late Biblical Hebrew." Diss., Dropsie College, 1983. **Cameron, G. G.** *Persepolis Treasury Tablets.* Chicago: University of Chicago Press, 1948. **Clines, D. J. A.** *The Esther Scroll: The Story of the Story.* JSOTSup 30. Sheffield: JSOT, 1984. ———. "In Quest of the Historical Mordecai." *VT* 41 (1991) 130–36. ———. "Mordecai." *ABD* 4:902–4. **Delaporte, L.** *Épigraphes araméens.* Paris: Librairie Paul Geuthner, 1912. **Driver, G. R.** *Aramaic Documents of the Fifth Century B.C.* Oxford: Clarendon, 1957. **Edelman, D. V.** "Kish." *ABD* 4:85–87. **Gordis, R.** "Studies in the Esther Narrative." *JBL* 95 (1976) 43–58 (= Moore, *Studies,* 408–23). **Haupt, P.** "Critical Notes on Esther." *AJSL* 24 (1907–8) 97–106 (= Moore, *Studies,* 1–90). **Horbury, W.** "The Name Mardochaeus in a Ptolemaic Inscription." *VT* 41 (1991) 220–26. **Knobloch, F. W.** "Adoption." *ABD* 1:76–79. **LaSor, W. S.** *Handbook of Biblical Hebrew.* 2 vols. Grand Rapids, MI: Eerdmans, 1978. **Levenson, J. D.** "The Scroll of Esther in Ecumenical Perspective." *JES* 13 (1976) 440–51. **Lewy, J.** "The Feast of the 14th Day of Adar." *HUCA* 14 (1939) 127–51. **Limosín, R.** "Estudios filológicos-derásicos acerca de Ester y el Iran antiguo: II. El nombre Mŏrdeḵay." *Aula Orientalis* 1 (1983) 209–13. **Murphy, R. E.** *Wisdom Literature: Job, Proverbs, Ruth, Canticles, Ecclesiastes, and Esther.* FOTL 13. Grand Rapids, MI: Eerdmans, 1981. **Paul, S.** "Adoption Formulae: A Study of Cuneiform and Biblical Legal Clauses." *Maarav* 2 (1979–80) 173–85. **Shea, W. H.** "Esther and History." *AUSS* 14 (1976) 227–46. **Stolper, M. W.** *Entrepreneurs and Empire: The Murašû Archive, the Murašû Firm, and Persian Rule in Babylonia.* Leiden: Nederlands Historisch-Archaeologisch Instituut te Istanbul, 1985. ———. "Murashû, Archive of." *ABD* 4:927–28. **Talmon, S.** "The Ancient Hebrew Alphabet and Biblical Text Criticism." In *Mélanges Dominique Barthélemy,* ed. P. Casetti et al. Göttingen: Vandenhoeck & Ruprecht, 1981. 497–530. **Vanderkam, J. C.** "Calendars, Ancient Israelite and Early Jewish." *ABD* 1:814–20. **Wenham, G. J.** "*Bᵉtûlāh,* 'A Girl of Marriageable Age.'" *VT* 22 (1972) 326–48. **Wright, J. S.** "The Historicity of the Book of Esther." In *New Perspectives on the Old Testament,* ed. J. B. Payne. Waco, TX: Word, 1970. 37–47. **Yahuda, A. S.** "The Meaning of the Name Esther." *JRAS* (1946) 174–78. **Yamauchi, E.** "The Archaeological Background of Esther." *BSac* 137 (1980) 99–117. ———. "Mordecai, the Persepolis Tablets, and the Susa Excavations." *VT* 42 (1992) 272–75. **Zadok, R.** "Notes on Esther." *ZAW* 98 (1986) 105–10.

Translation

Episode 1. Ahasuerus decides to seek a new queen (2:1–4)
Time: some time after year 3

[1]*Some time later,*[a] *when the anger of King Ahasuerus had subsided, he remembered Vashti and what she had done and the measures that had been taken*[b] *against her.* [2]*So the king's personal attendants suggested,*[a] *"Let a search be made*[b] *for beautiful young women for the king.* [3]*And let the king appoint officials in all the provinces of his kingdom to bring*[a] *each of these beautiful young women to the harem*[b] *in the Citadel of Susa. Let them be put into the custody*[c] *of Hegai,*[d] *the king's eunuch in charge of the women, and let him provide them*[e] *the cosmetics they will need.*[f] [4]*And let the young woman who pleases the king*[a] *be queen in place of Vashti."*

The idea pleased the king,[b] *and he did as his attendants suggested.*[c]

Episode 2. Esther is taken to the royal harem (2:5–11)
Time: some time after year 3

[5]*Now there was a Jew in the Citadel of Susa whose name was Mordecai, son of Jair,*
son of Shimei, son of Kish, a Benjaminite [6]*who had been deported from Jerusalem among*

those whom Nebuchadnezzar king of Babylon had carried off with Jeconiah king of Judah.[a]
7He was raising Hadassah (also known as Esther[a]*), his cousin,*[b] *since she had neither*
father nor mother. She was a very beautiful young woman,[c] *and Mordecai had adopted*
her[d] *as his own daughter when her father and mother died.*
8So when the king's command and edict were proclaimed and many young women
were gathered into the Citadel of Susa into the custody of Hegai, Esther too was taken to
the palace and put in the care of Hegai,[a] *who was in charge of the women. 9And the*
young woman pleased him[a] *and won his favor. So he promptly supplied her with*[b] *her*
cosmetics and her allowance of food. And he also gave her the seven specially chosen
maids from the palace and transferred her and her maids to the best part of the harem.
10Esther did not make known her nationality or her parentage, for Mordecai had
commanded her not to do so. 11And every day Mordecai would walk back and forth in
front of the court of the harem in order to find out how Esther was and what was hap-
pening to her.

Episode 3. Esther is chosen queen 2:12–18
Time: month 10, year 7

12Now when each young woman's turn came to go to King Ahasuerus, after having
completed the twelve-month period[a] *prescribed for the women*[b] *(for the required period of*
their beauty treatment was fulfilled as follows: six months in oil of myrrh and six months
in perfumes and other cosmetics used by women), 13she would go to the king in the follow-
ing manner: everything that she requested[a] *to take with her from the harem to the king's*
quarters was given to her. 14In the evening she would go in, and in the morning she
would return again to the harem,[a] *but now to*[b] *the custody of Shaashgaz, the king's*
eunuch in charge of the concubines. She would not go again to the king unless he took
pleasure in her[c] *and she was summoned by name.*
15But when it came the turn of Esther the daughter of Abihail, the uncle of Mordecai
(who had adopted her as his daughter),[a] *to go to the king, she requested nothing except*
what Hegai, the king's eunuch in charge of the women, advised, and she won the favor
of all who saw her. 16So Esther was taken to King Ahasuerus in his royal quarters[a] *in*
the tenth month, the month of Tebeth,[b] *in the seventh*[c] *year of his reign. 17And the king*
loved Esther more than all the women, and she won his favor and approval more than
all the girls. He placed a royal crown on her head and made her queen instead of Vashti.
18And the king gave a great banquet in Esther's honor for all his nobles and courtiers,[a]
and he proclaimed a remission of taxes[b] *for the provinces and distributed gifts in royal*
style.[c]

Notes

1.a. Lit. "after these things/events."

1.b. Lit. "what had been decreed." The idiom גזר על, "to decree," occurs in prose texts in BH only here. In SBH the idiom is צוה על. The lateness of the usage in Esther is indicated by the fact that it occurs elsewhere only in MH; see Bergey, *Esther*, 109–10.

2.a. Lit. "the attendants [lit. 'youths'] of the king who served him said."

2.b. Heb. uses the 3 m pl without antecedent, the equivalent of the pass in Eng. (cf. *GBH* § 155b).

3.a. "to bring . . . into . . . ," lit. "and let them gather . . . to."

3.b. The phrase is lit. "the house/quarters of the women," referring to that portion of the king's private residence in the palace where his wives and concubines were domiciled.

3.c. Good Eng. style demands that the long Heb. sentence here be broken into two.

3.d. The name in the text here is הֵגֶא, *Hēgeʾ*, but הֵגַי, *Hēgay*, in vv 8, 15.

3.e. The clause begins with the inf abs with waw, ונתון, functioning in place of a finite verb. This usage is more common in LBH than in SBH (see the discussion in *IBHS* § 35.5.2.b; *GBH* § 123x, esp n. [1]). The verb is subordinate (i.e., sequential in time or logic) to the preceding verb, which determines its person and tense/aspect (cf. *IBHS* § 35.5.2.d).

3.f. Lit. "their cosmetics."

4.a. Lit. "is pleasing in the king's eyes."

4.b. Lit. "was pleasing in the king's eyes."

4. c. Lit. "thus/so."

6.a. Lit. "with the exiles who were exiled with Jeconiah king of Judah, whom Nebuchadnezzar king of Babylon had exiled." The narrator uses the alternate form of the name of Jehoiachin (cf. Jer 24:1; 27:20; 1 Chron 3:16), who was taken into exile in 597 B.C.

7.a. Lit. "that is, Esther."

7.b. Lit. "daughter of his uncle." The LXX reads "daughter of Aminadab, his uncle," the same name that the LXX gives to Esther's father in 2:15; 9:29. The OL and Vg make Esther Mordecai's niece.

7.c. Lit. "fair of figure and lovely of appearance."

7.d. Or "took her to him for a daughter"; see *Comment.* The LXX reads ἐπαίδευσεν αὐτὴν ἑαυτῷ εἰς γυναῖκα, "he raised her as a wife for himself." This probably means that he had not yet married her (contra Moore, 21), for the next verse reports that she was taken to the palace with all the other unmarried young women gathered for the king. Haupt's suggestion (*AJSL* 24 [1907–8] 116) that the LXX read לבת as לבית, "for a wife," following the Talmudic sense of "wife" for בית, "house," though ingenious, is most unlikely. It is highly improbable that the word bore this meaning as early as the translation of the LXX.

8.a. Lit. "taken to the palace to the custody of Hegai."

9.a. Lit. "was pleasing in his eyes."

9.b. Lit. "hastened to give her."

12.a. Syr reads "days" instead of "months" throughout the verse. This is most probably a deliberate change occasioned by the ludicrously extended period (for the significance of which see *Explanation*), rather than evidence for a different Heb. text.

12.b. Lit. "at the end of her being according to the regimen of the women twelve months." The clause "her being according to the regimen of the women" is lacking in the LXX, doubtless another example of free translation rather than evidence for a different Heb. text.

13.a. As happens with some frequency, the direct obj marker את here marks the subject of the pass verb ינתן, "was given"; see *IBHS* §§ 10.3.b, c; 10.3.2.b.

14.a. Or "return to the second harem"; see *Comment.*

14.b. אל־יד is not to be changed to על־יד (Haller, 122; cf. *BHS* n. b); see *Note* 1:17.c.

14.c. The phrase "he took pleasure in her," lacking in the LXX, is not to be deleted (*BHS* n.). This is another example of free translation rather than evidence for a different Heb. text.

15.a. Moore (16) posits that the parenthetical phrase, which is lacking in the LXX, is a later gloss from v 7. Since the LXX is a very free translation and includes a large number of pluses and minuses vis-à-vis the Heb. text, it is more likely that the phrase was omitted by the LXX translator.

16.a. Lit. "to his royal quarters." The phrase, lacking in the LXX, is not to be deleted. That it is original in the Heb. is shown by its unusual form, for discussion of which see *Comment.*

16.b. The LXX reads "in the twelfth month, which is Adar."

16.c. Syr reads "fourth," doubtless regarding the four years since the deposing of Vashti as too long a time. Those who argue for the historicity of the story note that Xerxes spent two of those four years away on his campaign against Greece (e.g., Shea, *AUSS* 14 [1976] 233–35).

18.a. Lit. "a great banquet for all his nobles and courtiers—a banquet for Esther." For the translation "nobles and courtiers" for שׂריו ועבדיו, see the *Comment* on the phrase in 1:3.

18.b. הֲנָחָה, lit. "causing rest, relief, alleviation," is an LBH form built after the pattern of the Aramaic haphel inf (see *GBH* §§ 88L, b; BL § 61jϵ). The meaning "remission of taxes" is uncertain (see *HALOT*, 252; cf. Clines, *Esther Scroll,* 184 n. 41). Other meanings suggested have been "holiday," "amnesty," "release from forced labor," or "exemption from military service."

18.c. Lit. "according to the king's hand." On the meaning, see *Comment* on 1:7. The whole last clause is lacking in the LXX.

Form/Structure/Setting

In both content and form this, the second scene of the exposition, divides into three episodes. As regards content, they are distinguished as separate stages by both chronology and plot development (cf. Murphy, *Wisdom,* 159–60). The first episode, vv 1–4, relates the king's decision to replace Vashti and how he will do so. The second episode, vv 5–11, chronologically later, relates the circumstances of Esther's arrival in the king's harem. Therefore, the narrator must begin the episode by introducing Esther, which necessarily entails introducing Mordecai and describing his relationship to her. The third episode then relates the events and circumstances of Esther's choice as the queen who will replace Vashti.

The division into episodes is also formally marked. The first episode is introduced by the general temporal expression "after these things," an opening frequently used in Hebrew narrative to begin a new section. Its closure is indicated not only by the summary statement of v 4c but also by the nonsequential sentence that marks the onset of the second episode: איש יהודי היה בשושן הבירה..., "Now there was a Jew in the Citadel of Susa . . ." (v 5). The closure of the whole scene is marked by a clear inclusio: וימליכה תחת ושתי, "and he made her queen in place of Vashti," in the third episode (v 17d), for it brings us full circle from the words of the king's attendants, תמלך תחת ושתי, "let her be queen in place of Vashti," in the first episode (v 4). It is also highlighted by the long circumstantial clauses, vv 19–20, with which the next scene opens. Formally, the division between episodes 2 and 3 is less clearly marked. However, that the boundary lies between vv 11 and 12, rather than between vv 14 and 15, is indicated by the parallelism of the structure of vv 12–13 and v 15, which alerts us to their unity:

vv 12–13	ובהגיע תר נערה ונערה לבוא אל־המלך	When each young woman's turn came to go to the king . . . ,	A
	... את כל־אשר תאמר ינתן לה	everything she requested was given to her.	B
v 15	ובהגיע תר־אסתר . . . לבוא אל־המלך	When Esther's turn . . . came to go to the king	A´
	לא בקשה דבר כי אם את־אשר יאמר הגי	she asked for nothing except what Hegai advised.	B´

It is also indicated by the significant change in subject between vv 11 and 12 and the lack of the same between vv 14 and 15.

Finally, the unity of the whole scene is indicated by the coherence of its content (see the diagram on the following page). This is primarily established by a series of leitmotifs (repeated expressions) that are skillfully woven into the text in a striking and parallel pattern that binds the whole together. As the diagram reveals, one leitmotif, C, dealing with the women's cosmetics, is present in all three episodes. But it is episode 2 that ties the whole together. Six of the leitmotifs in episode 2 form two sets of three leitmotifs each. One set, A, B, and D, is common to episodes 1 and 2 only. The other set, F, G, and H, is common to episodes 2 and 3 only. This arrangement artfully ties all three episodes together. Leitmotif E, common to episodes 1 and 3, sounds the central motif of the scene and thus provides an inclusio that creates closure for the whole.

The Coherence of Scene 2

Episode 1, vv 1–4:

v 2b	let them seek *beautiful young women*	A
v 3b	each *beautiful young woman*	
v 3b	let them gather to the Citadel of Susa into the custody of Hegai, the king's eunuch in charge of the women	B
v 3c	and let him give them their cosmetics	C
v 4a	**let the young woman who pleases the king**	D
v 4a	*be queen in place of Vashti*	E

Episode 2, vv 5–11:

v 7b	she was a *beautiful young woman*	A
v 7c	*Mordecai adopted her as his daughter*	F
v 8b-c	were gathered to the Citadel of Susa into the custody of Hegai, . . . into the care of Hegai, who was in charge of the women,	B
v 8d	*Esther was taken to the house of the king*	G
v 9a	**And the young woman pleased him**	D
v 9b	and she won his favor ותשׂא חסד לפניו	H
v 9c	and he promptly gave her her cosmetics	C

Episode 3, vv 12–18:

v 12c	. . . the days of their cosmetic treatment	C
v 12d	. . . six months in women's cosmetics	
v 15a	. . . *who adopted her as his daughter*	F
v 15c	and Esther won the approval of all who saw her ותהי אסתר נשׂאת חן בעיני כל־ראיה	H
v 17b	and she won his favor and approval more than all the girls ותשׂא־חן וחסד לפניו מכל־הבתולת	
v 16a	*Esther was taken to King Ahauerus to the royal house*	G
v 17d	*he made her queen in place of Vashti*	E

Comment

2 נְעָרוֹת בְּתוּלוֹת טוֹבוֹת מַרְאֶה, lit. "young women of marriageable age, beautiful in appearance." The term בתולה does not mean "virgin" in the technical sense of the English use of the term. It means "a young woman of marriageable age" (see M. Tsevat, בתולה, *TDOT* 2:341–43; esp. Wenham, *VT* 22 [1972] 343–44). As Wenham points out, that the term bears the general sense in this passage is clearly indicated by its use in v 17, where it cannot mean "virgin." Thus there is no emphasis here on virginity per se, although, particularly in that patriarchal world, the expectation would be that a young woman of marriageable age would have had no sexual experience.

3 אֶת־כָּל־נַעֲרָה־בְתוּלָה טוֹבַת מַרְאֶה, lit. "each beautiful young woman." The Hebrew at first glance seems problematic. It is prefixed with the particle את, which is rarely used in prose with the *indefinite* direct object (normally it marks the *definite* direct object). However, constructions with את plus כל, "all," or numerals are logically determinate (so *IBHS* § 10.3.1.a; p. 180; cf. GKC § 117d), especially when the indefinite class, here "beautiful young women," has been mentioned in the previous verse. One must avoid, then, the rendering "every beautiful young woman" (so NASV; Moore, 18; Fox, 26–27), as if the king's attendants now speak hyperbolically.

5 אִישׁ יְהוּדִי הָיָה, lit. "A Jewish man (there) was." Since the term יהודי refers here to a man who was exiled from Judah with Jeconiah (or whose ancestor Kish was; see the discussion below), it could be rendered "Judean" (or even "Judahite"). But "Judean" (or "Judahite") properly refers to a member of the independent state of Judah, or in the period of the setting of our story to a member of the geographical area known by the same name, which was an administrative entity (perhaps something like a "sub-province"; cf. the books of Ezra-Nehemiah) of the Persian empire. But the epithet is used of Mordecai here and in five other passages (5:13; 6:10; 8:7; 9:31; 10:3; in my opinion the use in 9:29 is not original; see *Additional Note on vv 29–32* in *Notes* to 9:6–32), and he is emphatically not a member of the Palestinian "Judean" community but rather one of the Judean/Judahite "diaspora," i.e., those who have not taken part in the restoration of the Judean community around Jerusalem but who live as expatriates in various localities in the Persian empire. This is transparent from the use of the denominative verb מתיהדים, lit. "became Jews" (8:17), which "signifies . . . something one can become without changing one's residence" (Levenson, *JES* 13 [1976] 450). The story is not about "Judeans" but about "Jews," i.e., members of the expatriate Jewish community dispersed throughout (2:8) the Persian empire. Hence, the epithet can only be rendered "Jew." The distinction is of the utmost importance for understanding the purpose and meaning of the whole narrative (see the discussion in *Theme and Purpose* in the *Introduction* to Esther).

וּשְׁמוֹ מָרְדֳּכַי בֶּן יָאִיר בֶּן־שִׁמְעִי בֶּן־קִישׁ אִישׁ יְמִינִי, "whose name was Mordecai, son of Jair, son of Shimei, son of Kish, a Benjaminite." There is no longer any doubt that the name Mordecai is a genuine personal name in use in the period. It appears in the fifth century B.C. in a number of different texts in both Aramaic alphabetic writing and in cuneiform syllabic script. For example, it occurs in Aramaic: (1) in a letter found in Egypt written *mrdk,* the name of an official probably located in northern

Mesopotamia (Driver, *Aramaic Documents,* 27–28, 56); (2) written *mrdkʾ* on the reverse of a text (which is otherwise written in Babylonian cuneiform; Delaporte, *Épigraphes,* 59). It occurs in cuneiform script: (1) in the form *marduka* in the Murashû archive (Stolper, *Entrepreneurs,* 294); (2) in some thirty Elamite texts in the Persepolis Treasury Tablets and the Persepolis Fortification Texts in the form *marduka* or *marduku,* perhaps referring to as many as four individuals (see Yamauchi, *VT* 42 [1992] 273); (3) as a theophoric element in compound names in the same texts (cf. Cameron, *Persepolis Treasury Tablets,* 84); and (4) in a tablet apparently from Borsippa near Babylon, containing a list of payments made to Persian officials, in the form *marduka,* the name of a "scribe" or "administrative functionary" (for the meaning, see Clines, *VT* 41 [1991] 134) of the satrap of the province of Babylon and Beyond the River (Abar Nahara). In most of these cases, the bearer appears to be some kind of official in the Persian administration. In none is there any evidence that he is Jewish.

There is also clear evidence that the name was adopted by Jews of the same general period. Thus, apart from its use in Esther, it occurs (1) as the name of one of the exiles who returned with Zerubbabel (Ezra 2:2; Neh 7:7; 1 Esdr 5:8); and (2) it has recently been noted in the Greek form *μαρδοχαῖος Mardochaios* in a funerary inscription on the portal of a Jewish burial in Alexandria, Egypt, dating to the mid-Ptolemaic period, ca. 200–150 B.C. (see Horbury, *VT* 41 [1991] 220–26). With high probability the name is derived from the name Marduk, the chief god of the Babylonian pantheon, probably originally as a theophoric element (though Clines, *ABD* 4:902, notes Limosín's recent suggestion that it was Hurrian or Elamite, meaning "the man *par excellence*"). It was apparently not uncommon in this period for Jews in the eastern diaspora to have Babylonian names. This is strongly suggested by the biblical names Sheshbazzar and Zerubbabel and the Babylonian names of Daniel and his three companions (Dan 1:6–7) and by the tendency of Jewish residents of Babylonia to give Babylonian names to their children (see Stolper, *ABD* 4:928). Possibly Mordecai had a Hebrew name as well as the Babylonian one (Clines, 286) as did Esther ("Hadassah," v 7) and Daniel and his friends. If so, it seems strange that the narrator would not have so indicated, as he did for Esther.

5–6 Given the attached series of three relative clauses of v 6, the meaning and intention of Mordecai's genealogy in v 5 has been much debated. On the one hand, the names Shimei and Kish may be distant ancestors in Mordecai's Benjaminite family line, since Kish was the father of Saul (1 Sam 1:9) and Shimei is the name of a member of the "clan" (Heb. *mišpāḥāh*) to which Saul's family (lit. *bêt,* "house") belonged who was a rebel against David (2 Sam 16:5–13). It is hypothesized (so Paton, 167–68; Moore, 19–20, 35; Bardtke, 299) that the narrator carries Mordecai's ancestry back to Kish, the father of Saul, in order (1) to explain both Mordecai's refusal to bow to Haman and the resulting implacable enmity between the two and/or (2) to emphasize the significance of Mordecai eliminating Haman the Agagite, since Saul failed to eliminate his ancestor Agag, king of the Amalekites (1 Sam 15; see *Comment* on 3:1 below). If, however, these are distant ancestors dating to the time of Saul, then it can only be Mordecai himself to whom the series of relative clauses in v 6 refers. Consequently, it is he who was taken into exile with Jehoiachin (see *Note* 6.a. above) in 597 B.C. This would create the highly improbable situation that he would have been about 120 years old at the time of our story, and

Esther (who is chosen as one of the נערות בתולות טובת מראה, "beautiful young women," v 7) would have been only slightly younger. It may simply be that the narrator was confused chronologically (so Fox, 29; Moore, 27). But it seems at least implausible that a narrator who shows himself at every level to be so fully cognizant of the setting and circumstances of the Persian world of his story would be unaware of the general chronology of the period (contra Bardtke, 299). As Clines (286) notes, it is improbable that the narrator would not have been aware that only the oldest members of the community among those who returned from exile at the time of the first Persian king could remember the Solomonic temple (Ezra 3:12). Further, Kish and Shimei clearly do not belong to the same genealogical line (see above), and it seems unlikely that such a knowledgeable narrator would invent an impossible genealogy (yet see Berg, *Book of Esther,* 64–66).

On the other hand, the three members of the genealogy can be taken as Mordecai's immediate ancestors. In that case, in order to avoid the improbabilities noted above, one must conclude that the series of relative clauses in v 6 refer not to Mordecai but either to Kish, the last member of the genealogy (so, e.g., Edelman, *ABD* 4:86; Yamauchi, *BSac* 137 [1980] 107; Wright, "Historicity," 38), or to the genealogical line collectively (so Gerleman, 77; Bardtke, 299). Although this is certainly not the most natural interpretation of the syntax, it is by no means excluded (Clines, 287). In favor of this is the fact that the tribal appositive איש ימיני, "a Benjaminite man," may well be in apposition to "Kish" rather than "Mordecai" since Mordecai has been identified at the beginning of the sentence with the ethnicon יהודי, "Jew," and hence needs no further ethnic identification (so Edelman, *ABD* 4:86).

Nevertheless, even if the members of this genealogy are taken to be Mordecai's immediate ancestors, this patronymic identifies him as a descendant of a Benjaminite Kish, inevitably connecting him with a line related to, or at least reminiscent of, that of Saul, the inveterate enemy of Agag and the Amalekites, preparing the way for the bitter enmity and antagonism between him and Haman the Agagite (see *Explanation* to 3:1–15). Finally, the fact that Mordecai's great-grandfather was taken into exile with Jehoiachin clearly implies that his family belonged to the nobility, or at least the upper classes of Judahite society, since it was primarily this group that was exiled in this, the first deportation, in 597 B.C.

7 אֶת־הֲדַסָּה הִיא אֶסְתֵּר, lit. "Hadassah, that is, Esther." After the analogy of the examples cited above in the discussion of the name Mordecai, the addition of the epexegetical phrase, "that is, Esther," is best taken to mean that Esther had both a Hebrew and a non-Hebrew name. "Hadassah," then, could be understood as a feminine form of Hebrew הדס, "myrtle." If this is the case, the older views that saw the name as derived from Akkadian *ḫadašatu,* "bride," an epithet of the goddess Ishtar (Lewy, *HUCA* 14 [1939] 128–29), are erroneous (cf. Fox, 275). As for the name "Esther," determining its etymology adds nothing to the meaning of our story, though the subject has been much written about. It now seems most improbable that the name is a form of the Babylonian goddess Ishtar (cf. Clines, 287), given the graphic and onomastic evidence to the contrary expressed by Zadok (*ZAW* 98 [1986] 107). The other etymology most frequently suggested is the Persian word *stâra,* "star" (see Zadok; for the view that the name is a form of a Persian word for "myrtle," see Yahuda, *JRAS* [1946] 174–78).

לְקָחָהּ מָרְדֳּכַי לוֹ לְבַת, lit. "Mordecai took her to him for a daughter." Since legal adoption is unknown in OT law, there is no technical Hebrew terminology for it. Hence, this phraseology may simply mean a family arrangement rather than a formal legal action. However, formal legal adoption was widespread in Mesopotamia, and it seems highly probable that Jews of the Babylonian diaspora would have conformed to local legal requirements, especially in the delicate situation of an unmarried woman of Esther's age living in an older cousin's household (cf. Knobloch, *ABD* 1:78). That the Hebrew expression is virtually a calque (a literal rendering of a foreign idiom) of the Babylonian phrase *ana mārūtim leqū*, "to take for son/daughtership" (see the remarks of Paul, *Maarav* 2 [1979–80] 182), supports this interpretation.

9 וַתִּשָּׂא חֶסֶד לְפָנָיו, lit. "she lifted up/took favor before him." Both Bardtke (303) and Moore (21) observe that the idiom *nāśā*ʾ + *ḥesed* and its synonym *nāśā*ʾ + *ḥēn*, "to *lift up/ carry/ take* favor /grace," used only in Esther, have the more active sense of "winning" or "earning" favor, rather than the more passive sense of the idiom *māṣā*ʾ + *ḥēn*, "to *find/ obtain* favor." The observation is supported by the fact that in the three instances where Esther, following court protocol, prefaces her requests with the conditional use of the idiom (5:8; 7:3; 8:5), it is appropriately the more passive *māṣā*ʾ + *ḥēn* that is used.

וַיְבַהֵל אֶת־תַּמְרוּקֶיהָ וְאֶת־מָנוֹתֶהָ לָתֵת לָהּ וְאֵת שֶׁבַע הַנְּעָרוֹת הָרְאֻיוֹת לָתֶת־לָהּ מִבֵּית הַמֶּלֶךְ, lit. "he hastened to give her her cosmetics and her allowance of food and to give her from the palace the seven specially chosen maids." Paton (175) interprets the article on שבע הנערות הראיות, "the seven specially chosen maids," to mean that "this was the prescribed number allotted to every one of the candidates for royal favour," whereas "the addition of *picked* shows that Esther's seven were better than those assigned to the other beauties" (cf. also Fox, 32). This is most unlikely. First, these two quite different conceptions can hardly be communicated by this one single expression. Second, the interpretation misunderstands the force of the definite article here. On one hand, the article may be used with its *generic* force, i.e., that use which "marks out . . . a class of persons, things, or qualities that are unique and determined in themselves" (*IBHS* § 13.5.1.f; cf. also *GBH* § 137n). These maids are unique and determined by virtue of the fact that they are ראיות, "picked/specially chosen." On the other hand, the article may simply indicate that "these seven girls were something special, possibly attendants deliberately reserved by Hegai for the most likely successor to Vashti" (Moore, 22). This last interpretation is supported by the statement that these maids are designated as "from the palace" (which probably means that they were maintained at the king's expense, so Clines, 288). Further indication that these particular maids were given to Esther alone is the lack of the pronoun "her" (note how "*her* cosmetics" and "*her* allowance of food" specify those that belonged to Esther in distinction from those given to the other candidates) and the fact that their being given is stated separately from the preceding through the repetition of לתת־לה, "to give to her." (The fact that the phrase לתת־לה, "to give to her," stands between ראיות, "specially chosen," and מבית המלך, "from the palace," precludes NIV's translation "selected from the king's palace.") Since all the women had to go through the same twelve-month-long regimen of beauty treatments (v 12), the statement "he *hastened* to give her [see *Note* b] her cosmetics . . ." probably means that Hegai started her on the process earlier than the other women (Fox, 31–32).

12 וּבְהַגִּיעַ תֹּר נַעֲרָה וְנַעֲרָה לָבוֹא אֶל־הַמֶּלֶךְ אֲחַשְׁוֵרוֹשׁ, lit. "when the turn of each young woman came to enter to King Ahasuerus." It is striking that the idiom בוא אל, "to go to," is used four times in vv 12–14 (12a, 13a, 14a, 14c), the detailed description of the manner in which each of the young women vied for the queenship. Given this frequency, the idiom may well be used with a double entendre. The passage is loaded with sensual implications, and this Hebrew idiom is a frequently used OT euphemism for sexual intercourse, used either of a man (e.g., Gen 16:2; 29:21, 23; 2 Sam 16:21, 22; Ruth 4:13; see esp. the *Comment* on Ruth 4:13) or a woman (e.g., 2 Sam 11:4).

שִׁשָּׁה חֳדָשִׁים בְּשֶׁמֶן הַמֹּר וְשִׁשָּׁה חֳדָשִׁים בַּבְּשָׂמִים וּבְתַמְרוּקֵי הַנָּשִׁים, "six months in oil of myrrh and six months in perfumes and other cosmetics used by women." Albright's explanation ("Lachish Cosmetic Burner") that this refers to the impregnation of a woman's clothes and skin with the fumes of cosmetics burnt in a type of stand may perhaps explain the process. However, Clines' caveat (289) that the explanation is weakened by depending upon parallels from Ethiopian customs of the nineteenth century is well taken.

13 וּבָזֶה הַנַּעֲרָה בָּאָה אֶל־הַמֶּלֶךְ, lit. "and in this the young woman would enter to the king." V 13 must provide the main clause, to which the extended temporal clause and parenthesis of v 12 have been prefaced. It begins with an opening adverbial phrase, ובזה, lit. "and in/with this." What the phrase refers to, however, is quite unclear. On the one hand, Moore (23; so also Paton, 181) gives it temporal force, so that this clause resumes the sentence after the parenthesis by restating the opening temporal clause of v 12 (so NJB, NRSV). But the parenthesis is hardly long enough to require the redundant restatement of that whole clause. On the other hand, the expression may be taken as an adverbial phrase expressing manner or mode, "and in this (manner, condition)." In this sense it can be taken to refer to the state of beautification that has just been described (so RSV). However, given the lack of any conjunctive waw connecting this clause with what follows, the manner of her entering is best taken to be expressed by the clause that follows (so NIV, NASV; Fox, 34–35).

מִבֵּית הַנָּשִׁים עַד־בֵּית הַמֶּלֶךְ, lit. "from the house of the women to the house of the king." Here בית המלך, "house of the king," cannot mean "the palace complex," as it did in vv 8, 9, since the harem could only have been located in that part of the palace reserved for the king's own private use (cf. Paton, 179; Moore, 21; esp. Fox, 276). Therefore, the translation "from the harem to the palace" or the like, used by almost all the modern versions except NJB (so at least JB, NAB, NASV, NEB, NIV, NRSV, REB, and RSV), is incorrect, inasmuch as it would probably imply to most English speakers two separate locales (if not, indeed, two separate buildings).

14 הִיא שָׁבָה אֶל־בֵּית הַנָּשִׁים שֵׁנִי, lit. "she would return to the house of the women, second/again." Whether שֵׁנִי, "second," modifies the noun phrase preceding, i.e., "the second harem," or the verb, i.e., "returns again," is hard to determine. In either case the form is problematic. In the first case, השני must be read since the noun phrase is definite. In the second case, the expected form is feminine, שֵׁנִית. In my opinion, the first interpretation is less likely. On the one hand, it is hard to explain the loss of the definite article, and on the other, the phrase would literally mean "the second harem," not the second part of the harem, and such a separate locale in the palace seems most unlikely (so Gordis, *JBL* 95 [1976] 53). The second interpretation is also problematical, but the form may simply be an alternate form of the adverb (Fox, 276), or it may have lost the taw either by haplography with following aleph (whose form was very similar in the paleo-Hebrew script; cf. Talmon, "The Ancient Hebrew Alphabet," 513) or by deliberate abbreviation (Gordis, *JBL* 95 [1976] 54). The expression "returned again," redundant in English, is no difficulty; exactly the same expression occurs in 1 Kgs 9:7.

16 אֶל־בֵּית מַלְכוּתוֹ, lit. "to the house of his royalty/kingship." This expression must clearly be a synonym of בית המלך, lit. "house of the king," in 2:13 (see the discussion there), probably chosen here to avoid the repetition of the word "king," which occurs in the previous phrase (Moore, 24). Compare also the different use of the term in 5:1.

בַּחֹדֶשׁ הָעֲשִׂירִי הוּא חֹדֶשׁ טֵבֵת בִּשְׁנַת־שֶׁבַע לְמַלְכוּתוֹ, "in the tenth month, the month of Tebeth, in the seventh year of his reign." The post-exilic community adopted the Babylonian names of the months of the lunar calendar (see Vanderkam, *ABD* 1:816). Tebeth, used only here in the OT, corresponds to our December-January. Our narrator gives not a single hint why four years have elapsed since Vashti's deposal (see 1:3)—or what else might have transpired in the kingdom of Ahasuerus in this interval. Hence, the dating only suggests that Esther's victory came after a lengthy competition.

17 וַיֶּאֱהַב הַמֶּלֶךְ אֶת־אֶסְתֵּר מִכָּל־הַנָּשִׁים, "and the king loved Esther more than all the women." The use of the word אהב, "loved," here is doubtless intended to contrast with the king's "taking pleasure" (Heb. חפץ) in the other women (v 14), and so goes "a stage beyond liking" (Fox, 37). Nevertheless, it expresses neither the deep emotional bonds nor the romantic feelings that are usually associated with the English term. Indeed, given the criteria on which the king's choice of the woman to replace Vashti is based, namely, her beauty and her ability to please the king sexually (see the *Comment* on vv 12–14 above), it is doubtless true that Ahasuerus' feelings for Esther "could hardly amount to more than pride of possession plus sexual arousal" (Fox, 38).

Explanation

This, the second scene, continues the exposition of the story (see the *Form/Structure/Setting* section of scene 1) by relating the events and circumstances by which Esther replaces Vashti as the queen of Persia, a situation necessary for her role in foiling the plot with which Haman seeks to destroy the Jews. As with the first scene, the narrator fleshes out and embellishes his account (the basic facts could have been presented very briefly indeed). In so doing he accomplishes two things. First, he continues to set the tone and temper that he established in the first scene (see *Explanation* thereto). Second, he begins the characterization of the new personae that the scene introduces, particularly that of Esther. The scene divides into three episodes (see *Form/Structure/Setting* above).

Episode 1. Ahasuerus decides to seek a new queen (2:1–4). The first episode relates the circumstances that set this process in motion: the king's decision to replace Vashti and how he will do so. It opens with a statement that expresses in narrative form Ahasuerus' thoughts (v 1). The detail of his recall, that "he remembered Vashti and what she had done and the measures that had been taken against her," and the content of the immediate response of his personal attendants imply that he wistfully expressed regret over the whole affair, and particularly the hasty action that had been taken (cf. Clines, 284–85). Further, the passive verb used to refer to her banishment implies that he accepted little personal blame in the matter (so Fox, 26), continuing our narrator's characterization of the Persian monarch and his world (see *Explanation* to the previous scene). Ahasuerus may be king of a vast empire, but he is prisoner of his own laws! In addition, he takes no personal responsibility for what those laws effect.

Episode 2. Esther is taken to the royal harem (2:5–11). This episode relates the circumstances of Esther's arrival at the king's palace along with all the other young women who are to be candidates to replace Vashti. The narrator must break off his story line to introduce her to us (vv 5–7), which also entails introducing Mordecai, for not only is he involved in her circumstances in the harem (v 10), but both he and their relationship will play a critical role in the events to follow. Since these are the two most important characters in the book and their relationship is of the greatest importance for his story, he provides them a considerably more extended introduction than is usually accorded characters in biblical narrative (cf. the introduction of Boaz in Ruth 2:1). In so doing, he also begins their characterization. Mordecai's identity as איש יהודי, "a Jewish man," is of the utmost importance in establishing the diaspora setting of the story (see *Comment* and the *Theme and Purpose* section of the *Introduction* to Esther). As part of this introduction, he also gives us Mordecai's patronymics, names that will be important for his story. Whether these names identify immediate or distant ancestors (see *Comment*), they will loom large in explaining the enmity that will instantly surface between Mordecai and Haman (see below). In a ponderous and detailed clause he informs us that Mordecai's family (or perhaps Mordecai himself; see *Comment*) was taken into exile with Jehoiachin, probably implying that the family belonged to the nobility, or at least the upper classes of Judahite society (see *Comment*). He also informs us of the relationship between Mordecai and Esther: though she was his cousin, he had adopted her as his own daughter. This is important for the story to follow, for even as queen she remained under his familial authority (v 10, and esp. v 20 below).

Finally, Esther is described as "a very beautiful young woman"; i.e., she fits the description of those who will be taken to the harem as candidates to replace Vashti. Indeed, by his description of Esther, the narrator clearly foreshadows what will happen, for Esther's beauty quite exceeds the criterion given for the candidates for queenship. They must be "young women, lovely of appearance" (vv 2–3). But Esther is described as "a young woman, beautiful of figure and lovely of appearance" (hence the translation "*very* beautiful young woman"), surely making it inevitable that she should be swept up in the king's net.

The account of Esther's being taken to the palace (v 8) is told succinctly and with the barest of detail. Yet, both the language and the form used eloquently indicate that the principals just introduced had no choice whatsoever in what transpired. By the sudden invoking of the unalterable (see 1:19) royal command and edict (v 8a), the narrator intends to characterize the taking of Esther into the king's harem as an ineluctable fate that neither he nor Esther can resist. Further, their passivity in the matter is effected by the tight series of three passive verbs in v 8, ". . . was proclaimed, . . . were gathered, . . . was taken," which portray an irresistible series of events. In this way, contrary to the views of many commentators (e.g., Paton,

173), "the narrator effortlessly forecloses any criticism of Mordecai" (Clines, 288; cf. also Bardtke, 301).

In his description in v 9 of the manner in which Hegai, the king's eunuch in charge, reacts to Esther, the narrator begins his characterization of her as one who is actively involved in what takes place. First, the affirmation that "the young woman was pleasing in the eyes of" Hegai implies that she may well be the one to fulfill the suggestion of the king's attendants that it should be "the young woman who is pleasing in the eyes of" the king who should "be queen in place of Vashti" (v 4). The implications of the subtle repetition of this expression is continued in the circumstances that follow. The idiom that the narrator uses to describe the impression she makes upon Hegai implies that she plays an active role in it, for the idiom has an active sense "to win or earn favor" (see *Comment*). The statement that Hegai "promptly" (lit. "made haste") gave her her cosmetics and her allotment of food (see *Comment*), together with the "specially chosen maids" that he provides her and "the best part of the harem" (v 9d) to which he transfers them all, clearly indicate that she has gained from him a special interest in her. "Esther is a success even before Ahasuerus sees her" (Clines, 288).

The episode continues with further characterizations of Mordecai. First, the narrator reveals that the relationship beween Mordecai and Esther is still that of parent and protégée: he notes that Esther kept her racial identity hidden at Mordecai's command (v 10a). But he gives us not the slightest hint why Mordecai might have so instructed her. Though it might seem obvious to surmise that Mordecai feared in the king's palace the same kind of prejudice against Esther that he would experience from Haman, no such prejudice has surfaced in the story thus far. Rather, the fact that neither Mordecai nor the narrator gives us the slightest reason for Mordecai's command prompts a vague dread that public disclosure of Esther's nationality would be dangerous in the extreme, thus preparing us for the events to come. The episode closes by revealing to us Mordecai's solicitous concern for Esther's welfare: daily he paced back and forth in front of the court of the harem to find out "how she was and what was happening to her" (v 11).

Episode 3. Esther is chosen queen (2:12–18). The opening of episode 3 consists of one long, complex temporal clause (v 12). To the main temporal statement, "when each young woman's turn came" (v 12a), is appended a second temporal clause, giving the timing of each woman's turn (v 12b). Here the narrator indulges in extravagant hyperbole: the candidates' beauty treatment goes on for a year! Further, he emphasizes this statement by adding an extended parenthesis involving further hyperbole: "six months in oil of myrrh and six months in perfumes and other cosmetics used by women" (v 12c)! Clearly he does not expect us to take him literally. Rather, in this almost ludicrous exaggeration our narrator continues his biting satire on the silly artificiality and the frivolous extravagance of the Persian court (Clines, 289).

In the first subsection of episode 3, vv 12–14, the narrator gives a brief description of what happened with each of the young women who were candidates for the queenship. In so doing he continues his satirical depiction of the king and his court, for the account is loaded with sensual implications. Unmistakably, there are two criteria by which the king will decide which of the young women will please him and so take Vashti's place as queen: (1) her beauty and (2) her ability to please him sexually. The first is not only explicitly stated but also emphasized by the repetition of the "giving of cosmetics" motif in all three episodes (see leitmotif C in *Form/Structure/Setting*), a motif that reaches a crescendo here in the satirical hyperbole of the year-long "beauty treatment" (see above). The second criterion is more implicit, but nonetheless transparent. After "entering to" the king in the evening, each young woman would return to the harem in the morning, but now to the custody of Shaashgaz, the king's eunuch in charge of the concubines, not be summoned again unless the king "took pleasure in her" and she was "summoned by name" (v 14). Clearly, the grounds on which the king took pleasure in her do not need to be stated. "With exquisite reserve the story is fully told—yet devoid of sensual details" (LaSor, *Handbook* 1:62). Indeed, the story *is* told with reserve, and indeed, it *is* devoid of sensual details, but it is nonetheless charged with sensuality. This extends to the choice of vocabulary. In such a context the sexually charged idiom "to go to," used four times, constitutes a double entendre (see *Comment*). Fox observes, "The patient dwelling on the details of the harem, the preparation of the beauties, their visit to the king and their subsequent return to the seraglio where their life will be devoted to preparing and hoping for a new invitation—all this is scarcely justified by the demands of plot alone." But it is not "sensuality primarily for its own sake" (Fox, 36). On the contrary, it derisively depicts the sensual and sexual excess of the story's world by caricaturing the carnal self-indulgence of its ruler. The only criteria he and his courtiers have for the woman who will be queen are her beauty (enhanced with a year-long treatment with cosmetics) and her sexual prowess (see further in the *Theme and Purpose* section of the *Introduction* to Esther). Contrast the criterion, thrice set forth by Herodotus (1.135; 3.84; 7.61), that the king could only marry a woman from one of the seven noble families of Persia (which surely implies that the choice was in actuality dictated by the demands of politics and the balance of power, as both history and common sense attest).

Only when he has completed this brief account of what happened in general when each of the young women went to the king does the narrator then turn to tell us about Esther (vv 15–18). By dividing his narrative into these two subsections, he avoids having to state in connection with Esther the sensuous details (however restrained they may be) that he has just related in regard to the other young women, thus avoiding, or at least softening, a negative characterization of her. Indeed, on the contrary, he gives a positive characterization of her by opposing her actions to theirs, for the opening statements of these two sections, vv 12–13 and v 15, are synonymously parallel in form but contrast in content (see *Form/Structure/Setting*). In opposition to the "everything" that they had requested to take with them to the king's quarters, emphasized by virtue of its initial position in the sentence (v 13b), Esther "requested nothing but what Hegai . . . advised" (v 15). The contrast implies a garish extravagance in dress and adornment on the part of the other young women but an unpretentious and perceptive willingness on Esther's part to dress prudently and in good taste according to the advice of Hegai, who, after all, "knew better than anyone else the king's taste in women" (Moore, 27). Further, whatever other activities her acceptance of her role in these events may have required of her that were contrary to the mores of the post-exilic Jewish world (such as the dietary rules), she evidences here a refusal of pagan luxury that is in keeping with the actions and attitude of other figures in the diaspora world (cf. Dan 1:8–15; Tob 1:10–11).

Given the subtle expectations of Esther's superiority and success already raised by the narrative (see above), it is not surprising that "the king loved Esther more than all the women" (v 17a). And indeed, the king's reaction to her reaches a crescendo in episode 3 through the use of the motif of "winning favor" (see the discussion of episode 2 in *Explanation* above). Not only is there a double statement of the motif here (vv 15c, 17b), but the second statement of the motif combines the two previous idioms, "she won his *favor*" (v 9b) and "(she) won (their) *approval*" (v 15c), into the emphatic "she won (the king's) *favor and approval* more than all the girls" (v 17b; see the table in *Form/Structure/Setting*). With the statement "he made her queen in place of Vashti," the scene has come full circle (see v 4).

Finally, the statements "he placed a royal crown upon her head" (v 17c) and "he gave a great banquet in Esther's honor for all his nobles and courtiers" (v 18a) link scenes 1 and 2 and provide closure for both. Esther now wears the royal crown that Vashti refused (v 11), and the "great banquet for all his nobles and his courtiers" in her honor takes us back to the first banquet Ahasuerus gave "for all his nobles and his courtiers" (1:3), while it contrasts with the banquet that Vashti gave (1:9).

Scene 3
Mordecai Uncovers a Plot (2:19–23)

Bibliography

Brockington, L. H. *The Hebrew Text of the Old Testament: The Readings Adopted by the Translators of the New English Bible.* Oxford: Oxford UP, 1973. **Driver, G. R.** "Problems and Solutions." *VT* 4 (1954) 224–45. **Ehrlich, A. B.** *Randglossen zur hebräischen Bibel: Textkritisches, Sprachliches und Sachliches.* VII. 1914. Repr. Hildesheim: Georg Olms, 1968. **Gordis, R.** "Studies in the Esther Narrative." *JBL* 95 (1976) 43–58. **Heltzer, M.** "The Book of Esther." *BR* 8 (1992) 24–30, 41. **Loretz, O.** "*šʿr hmlk*—'Das Tor des Königs.'" *WO* 4 (1967) 104–8. **Murphy, R. E.** *Wisdom Literature: Job, Proverbs, Ruth, Canticles, Ecclesiastes, and Esther.* FOTL 13. Grand Rapids, MI: Eerdmans, 1981. **Rudolph, W.** "Textkritisches zum Estherbuch." *VT* 4 (1954) 89–90. **Rüger, H. P.** "'Das Tor des Königs'—der königliche Hof." *Bib* 50 (1969) 247–50. **Thornton, T.** "The Crucifixion of Haman and the Scandal of the Cross." *JTS* 37 (1986) 419–26. **Wehr, H.** "Das Tor des Königs in Buche Esther und verwandte Ausdrücke." *Der Islam* 39 (1964) 247–60. **Yamauchi, E. M.** "Mordecai, the Persepolis Tablets, and the Susa Excavations." *VT* 42 (1992) 272–75.

Translation

Time: year 7

19 *Now, while young women were being gathered a second time,*[a] *Mordecai was serving as an official in the court.*[b]
20 *(Esther continued to keep secret her parentage and her*

nationality,[a] *as Mordecai had instructed her. She continued to do*[b] *what Mordecai told her, as she had done when she was under his care.*[c]*)* 21 *At that time, when Mordecai was serving as an official,*[a] *Bigthan and Teresh, two of the eunuchs who guarded the entrance to the king's quarters,*[b] *became angry at King Ahasuerus and sought to assassinate*[c] *him.* 22 *The affair became known to Mordecai, who told Queen Esther, and she told the king, giving credit to Mordecai.*[a] 23 *When the plot was investigated, it was found to be true, and the two men were hung on the gallows. All this was recorded in the daily court record*[a] *in the presence of the king.*

Notes

19.a. The clause, whose sense is most difficult, is lacking in the LXX. For discussion, see *Comment.*
19.b. The Heb. expression is lit. "sitting in the king's gate." On the meaning, see *Comment.*
20.a. Lit. "was not making known."
20.b. Lit. "she was doing."
20.c. More lit. "during her upbringing with him" or "when being raised by him." The Heb. אמנה is taken by *HALOT* as a noun meaning "care, guardianship," hence the translation "was his ward" (NEB, REB), but the Heb. syntax is very awkward if the word is understood as a noun. Much to be preferred is the view of Driver (*VT* 4 [1954] 235), who understands the form to be inf constr + 3 f sg pron suff (repointing the final ה with mappiq, ָהּ, or taking ָה to be the 3 f sg suff without mappiq, GKC § 91f; cf. Fox, 277; *BHS* n.), yielding the literal translation given above.
21.a. See *Note* 19.b.
21.b. Lit. "from those who guard the threshold."
21.c. Lit. "to send a hand against."
22.a. Lit. "in the name of Mordecai."
23.a. The Heb. expression is "the document of the events of the days."

Form/Structure/Setting

Both form and content signal that we have here a separate scene, albeit a short one. Formally, the onset of a new section is indicated by the marked circumstantial nature of vv 19–20, including a long parenthesis (v 20). The matter is not clear-cut, however. The circumstantial nature of these clauses could also signal that they are functioning to close the second scene rather than open the third (so Bardtke, 291–93, 309; Fox, 26, 36–41; Murphy, *Wisdom,* 159–60), but their content requires that these verses form the beginning of the third scene. The opening temporal phrase, "when the young women were gathered a second time" (if properly so understood; see *Comment*), places these events some time after those preceding. The note that Mordecai was serving as an official in the palace (on the meaning, see *Comment*) provides both the opportunity and the means for the part that he will play in the following events. (The narrator states this fact again in v 21 because of the long parenthesis in v 20.) Quite in contrast to the previous two scenes, the events are related with staccato brevity (especially apparent in the Heb. sentence structure of vv 21–23) without any of the embellishments that have characterized those scenes.

Comment

19 וּבְהִקָּבֵץ בְּתוּלוֹת שֵׁנִית, "When young women were gathered a second time." Though the meaning of the words is clear enough, the interpretation of the clause in this context is most problematic. Since Esther has been chosen queen, there hardly seems to be any need for a further collection of young women. Numerous expedients have been adopted (for older suggestions, see Paton, 186–87). NEB and REB follow the LXX and omit the clause (Brockington, *Hebrew Text,* 100; so also TEV), but the LXX is too free a translation to inspire much confidence that its omission here attests to a Hebrew text without the clause. Moore (30) and others follow Ehrlich (*Randglossen,* 114) and emend שֵׁנִית, "second," to שׁוֹנוֹת, "various," which understands the clause to refer to the previous collection of young women reported in vv 8–10. Gerleman (83, followed apparently by NAB), seeks to interpret שֵׁנִית, "second," not as modifying the infinitive ובהקבץ, "and when were gathered," but in a logical sense: "regarding the gathering of the young women, a second thing (is to be said)," clearly also understanding the clause as a reference to the previous gathering of young women. Neither of these expedients, however, makes sense in the context. First, the word בתולות, "young women," is indefinite, making it most difficult to see it as a reference to the previous collection of young women. Second, as v 22b shows, Esther is already queen at this time, so this gathering cannot refer to the previous one in which she was brought to the harem (cf. Fox, 277). Others attempt to understand the clause as a reference to the return of the women to the "second house of the women," reported in v 14. Fox (277) seeks to interpret the clause as it stands in this sense, whereas *BHS,* n. 19a-a, simply emends the clause to give this sense (reading בהקבל הבתולות אל־בית הנשים משנה, "when the young women were taken into the second house of the women"); cf. also NEB, REB. But, the action reported in v 14 took place repeatedly, each evening and morning, and hence can hardly function as a meaningful temporal clause. Further, the reference here is to בתולות, "young, unmarried women," and the lack of the definite article creates difficulties for this interpretation also. Most importantly, the women who returned to this part of the harem returned to the care of Shaashgaz, who was in charge of הפילגשים, "the concubines," and hence they no longer belonged to the category of בתולות, "young, unmarried women." Finally, Rudolph (*VT* 4 [1954] 89–90; cf. *BHS* n.) argues that the whole of v 19 originated as a marginal comment on v 20 (which verse, because of v 22b, is necessary to the context). In his view, someone first added שֵׁנִית, "(for the) second (time)," since v 20 repeats v 10. Subsequently, the rest of v 19 was added in order to identify (since there were then no verse numbers) the two occasions upon which Esther kept her nationality secret, namely, "when the young women were gathered" (v 8) and "while Mordecai was sitting in the king's gate" (v 21). When this marginal comment was later incorporated into the text, שֵׁנִית was moved to an incorrect position. The suggestion is ingenious but far too hypothetical to be given credence. The coherence of the text without v 19 precludes the need for either the creation of such marginal glosses or their incorporation into the text. Though it leaves much to be supplied from the context, we interpret the clause as it stands to be a further sarcastic depiction of king and court by implying that the king continued his gathering of concubines even after the choice of queen had been made.

וּמָרְדֳּכַי יֹשֵׁב בְּשַׁעַר־הַמֶּלֶךְ, lit. "Mordecai was sitting at the king's gate." The phrase might be taken literally, meaning that Mordecai was resorting to the palace area in order to hear further news of Esther's welfare (Clines, 281; cf. v 10). Most interpreters, however, understand the phrase in a figurative sense. Since the gate area was the place in the ancient Near East where the legal assembly met (see, e.g.,

Ruth 4) and business was conducted, the "king's gate" has come to mean "the royal court in general" (see Rüger, *Bib* 50 (1969) 247–50). This is made considerably more probable by the discovery of a monumental gate building comprising almost 13,000 square feet and situated some ninety yards east of the palace, unearthed by the French excavations of the 1970s (for a brief description with bibliography, see Yamauchi, *VT* 42 [1992] 274). Wehr (*Der Islam* 39 [1964] 247–60) has presented evidence from Herodotus and Xenophon as well as Assyrian and Babylonian royal inscriptions that such buildings housed the administrative and supply functions for the royal palace (for a brief description, see Heltzer, *BR* 8 [1992] 29; and for a more detailed treatment see Loretz, *WO* 4 [1967] 104–8). On the basis of this evidence, the expression "sitting in the king's gate" probably means "to hold an office in the palace administration" (see Loretz, *WO* 4 [1967] 104–8; Gordis, *JBL* 95 [1976] 47–48; Gordis' view, however, that the phrase refers specifically to a magistrate or judge seems too narrow an interpretation). This meaning of the term gives a better reason for the narrator's insertion of the following parenthesis (v 20) than does the literal understanding (note the significance of the reversal of the order of the phrase "parentage and nationality" from that in v 10). The literal rendering makes him virtually "an idler in the king's gate" (so Paton, 188). The reason for the mentioning of his position here is clear: his presence in the palace both gives him opportunity to discover the plot against the king and permits him access to Esther to report it.

23 וַיִּתָּלוּ שְׁנֵיהֶם עַל־עֵץ, "And the two of them were hung on the gallows." The LXX translation quite clearly understood the Hebrew idiom תלה על עץ, lit. "to hang on a 'wood,'" to refer to crucifixion (cf. Thornton, *JTS* 37 [1986] 421). This is a natural interpretation in the light of the prevalence of this type of execution of criminals in an era influenced by Rome, but it is quite uncertain whether the idiom meant "impalement" or "crucifixion" in the period and area under Persian domination. It probably does not refer to execution by hanging, for references to hanging in the ancient world most likely refer not to execution but to the public exposure of the body after death (contra Thornton, *JTS* 37 [1986] 421).

Explanation

This scene concludes the exposition, that is, the setting and circumstances of the story (cf. the discussion of the content of the first act in the *Form/Structure/Setting* section of scene 1). It does so by relating the unrewarded service that Mordecai rendered the king necessary to the events of 6:1–13. When this has been related, the narrator will turn immediately to the crisis that will set his story in motion.

The scene opens with a temporal clause that sets the time of these events as later than what has gone before and subtly alludes to the lascivious characterization of the king presented in the last scene (if this is its correct understanding; see *Comment*). It then continues with the fact (to be emphatically restated in v 21) that Mordecai held an office in the palace administration (lit. "sat in the king's gate"; see *Comment*). Whether this has always been his post or is a result of Esther's new position as queen (so Gordis, *JBL* 95 [1976] 47–48; accomplished presumably without revealing their relationship; see below), the narrator gives us not the slightest clue, in keeping with the brevity of his narrative in this scene. His purpose in relating the fact is clear. It enables us to understand how Mordecai was in a position to learn of the plot against the king and to communicate the same to Esther.

Our narrator then informs us again (cf. v 10) that Esther has continued to keep secret both her relationship to Mordecai and her nationality. The repetition of this fact signals its importance. It will enable us to understand two circumstances in the ensuing narrative that otherwise hardly make sense. First, and most important, it renders comprehensible that the king will exhibit utter ignorance of the queen's nationality both when Haman presents to him his plot to annihilate the Jews (3:8–11) and particularly when Esther unmasks him as the perpetrator of the same (7:3–5). Second, the order "parentage" and "nationality" here, the reverse of the order in 2:10, enables us to understand why Mordecai, though the adoptive father of the queen of Persia, still continues as a minor official in the palace administration, a position important to the conflict between him and Haman that is about to erupt. The narrator further informs us that Esther continued to obey Mordecai as she had done when under his care (v 20b). This explicit statement, remarkable in a scene marked otherwise by such brevity, signals that the Jews have a not inconsiderable entrée to the Persian court, one open to pressing Jewish concerns. The importance of such an entrée will be transparently clear in the next act when the crisis that sets our story into motion is revealed (see *Explanation* thereto).

The actual events of this scene are related in the briefest terms possible. We know nothing about what prompted the proposed attack upon the king or about how Mordecai learned of it. That his conduit to inform the king about it was his adopted daughter, now the queen, seems most natural indeed, and that she should have informed the king "giving credit to Mordecai" (lit. "in the name of Mordecai") is crucial, of course, to the events of 6:1–13, for which this scene is preparatory. Likewise crucial to these later events is the fact that they were recorded in "the daily court record before the king." That it was recorded in the king's presence clearly implies that he was fully aware of it (whatever the exact meaning of the phrase). As a number of commentators have noted (cf. esp. Clines, 293; Fox, 40), Herodotus portrays Persian kings as particularly diligent in rewarding such acts, speaking even of a list of "King's Benefactors." In that light, King Ahasuerus' failure to reward Mordecai at the time is a serious omission on his part (though the narrator does not bring it to our attention in any way). This prepares the way for his willingness to rectify the omission in 6:1–3, a "pleasingly dramatic turn" (Clines, *Esther Scroll*, 105) that will significantly move the plot forward in chap. 6. Finally, Mordecai's unrewarded deed contrasts sharply with the unexplained advancement of Haman related in the very next verse.

With this short scene, the narrator brings to a conclusion the setting and circumstances necessary for the telling of his story. He has introduced to us three of the four main characters of the narrative and begun their characterization, and he has recounted the most important circumstance that will make the resolution of the crisis of his story possible: Esther has won the king's favor and become the queen of Persia. With this information given and the tone and temper set, the narrator turns immediately to the crisis that will set the plot of his story in motion.

Act 2
The Crisis: Haman's Plot to Destroy the Jews (3:1–15)

Bibliography

Alter, R. *The Art of Biblical Narrative.* New York: Basic, 1981. **Barthélemy, D.,** et al. *Preliminary and Interim Report on the Hebrew Old Testament Text Project.* Vol. 2. New York: United Bible Societies, 1979. **Bergey, R. L.** "The Book of Esther—Its Place in the Linguistic Milieu of Post-exilic Biblical Hebrew: A Study in Late Biblical Hebrew." Diss., Dropsie College, 1983. ———. "Late Linguistic Features in Esther." *JQR* 75 (1984) 66–78. **Bivar, A. D. H.** "Achaemenid Coins, Weights and Measures." In *The Cambridge History of Iran: Vol. 2. The Median and Achaemenian Periods,* ed. I. Gershevitch. Cambridge: Cambridge UP, 1985. 610–39. **Brockington, L. H.** *The Hebrew Text of the Old Testament: The Readings Adopted by the Translators of the New English Bible.* Oxford: Oxford UP, 1973. **Clines, D. J. A.** *The Esther Scroll: The Story of the Story.* JSOTSup 30. Sheffield: JSOT, 1984. **Daube, D.** "The Last Chapter of Esther." *JQR* 37 (1946–47) 139–47. **Dommershausen, W.** *Die Estherrolle.* Stuttgart: Katholisches Bibelwerk, 1968. **Dorothy, C. V.** "The Books of Esther: Structure, Genre, and Textual Integrity." Diss., Claremont, 1989. **Fretz, M. R.** "Agagite." *ABD* 1:89–90. **Hallo, W. W.** "The First Purim." *BA* 46 (1983) 19–26. **Haupt, P.** "Critical Notes on Esther." *AJSL* 24 (1907–8) 97–186 (= Moore, *Studies,* 1–90). **Jones, B. W.** "The So-called Appendix to the Book of Esther." *Semantics* 6 (1978) 36–43. **Kutscher, E. Y.** *A History of the Hebrew Language.* Leiden: Brill, 1982. **Lewy, J.** "Old Assyrian *puru'um* and *pûrum.*" *RHA* 5 (1939) 116–24. **Mattingly, G.** "Amalek." *ABD* 1:169–71. **Millard, A. R.** "The Persian Names in Esther and the Reliability of the Hebrew Text." *JBL* 96 (1977) 481–88. **Murphy, R. E.** *Wisdom Literature: Job, Proverbs, Ruth, Canticles, Ecclesiastes, and Esther.* FOTL 13. Grand Rapids, MI: Eerdmans, 1981. **Olmstead, A. T.** *History of the Persian Empire.* Chicago: University of Chicago Press, 1948. **Qimron, E.** *The Hebrew of the Dead Sea Scrolls.* Atlanta: Scholars, 1986. **Zadok, R.** "Notes on Esther." *ZAW* 98 (1986) 105–10. ———. "On the Historical Background of the Book of Esther." *BN* 24 (1984) 18–23.

Translation

SCENE 1. HAMAN DECIDES TO ANNIHILATE THE JEWS (3:1–6)
Time: late in year 11

1 *Some time later,*[a] *King Ahasuerus promoted Haman son of Hammedatha, the Agagite.*
He advanced him in rank and gave him precedence[b] *over all his other nobles.*
2 *And all the king's officials at the court*[a] *bowed down and did obeisance to Haman, for so the*
king had commanded. But Mordecai would not bow down, and he would not do obeisance.
3 *So the king's officials said to Mordecai, "How come*[a] *you're disobeying the king's*
order?"
4 *And when*[a] *they challenged*[b] *him day after day and he paid them no heed, they*
informed Haman to see whether Mordecai's explanation[c] *would stand up,*[d] *for he had*
told them that he was a Jew.
5 *And when Haman saw that Mordecai would not bow*
down or do obeisance to him, he was furious.[a]
6 *But, since they had told him who Mordecai's*
people were, he thought it beneath him[a] *to lay hands on him alone.*[b] *So he sought for a*

way to destroy all the people of Mordecai,[c] *the Jews, who were in the whole empire of Ahasuerus.*

SCENE 2. HAMAN SETS IN MOTION A PLOT TO ANNIHILATE THE JEWS (3:7–15)

Episode 1. Haman obtains the king's permission to annihilate the Jews (3:7–11)
Time: month 1, year 12

7 *In the first month, the month of Nisan, in the twelfth year of King Ahasuerus,* pur [a]—*that is, the lot—was cast* [b] *in Haman's presence* [c]*for the day and the month to annihilate the people of Mordecai in one day; and the lot fell on the thirteenth day of*[c] *the twelfth month, the month of Adar.* 8 *Then Haman said to King Ahasuerus, "There is one people scattered among the peoples in all the provinces of your realm, yet who keep themselves separate.*[a] *Their laws are different* [b] *from those of every other people, and the king's laws they do not obey. Hence it is not in keeping with the king's interests to let them be.* 9 *So, if it please the king, let an edict be drawn up* [a] *for their destruction, and ten thousand talents of silver I will pay* [b] *to the king's officials* [c] *to deposit in the royal treasury."* 10 *Then the king took his signet ring from his hand and gave it to Haman son of Hammedatha, the enemy of the Jews.*[a] 11 *And he said, "The money and the people are yours;*[a] *do with them as you please."*

Episode 2. Haman orders the annihilation of the Jews (3:12–15)
Time: 1/13, year 12

12 *And so the royal scribes were summoned on the thirteenth day of the first month,*[a] *and an edict was written,*[b] *exactly as* [c] *Haman directed, to the royal satraps, to the governors who were in charge of each province, and to the rulers of each people, to each province in its own script and to each people in their own language. It was written in the name of King Ahasuerus and sealed with his signet ring.* 13 *And dispatches were sent* [a] *by means of couriers to all the provinces of the king, giving the order* [b] *to destroy, slay, and annihilate all the Jews, young and old, women and children included, on one day, the thirteenth day of the twelfth month, the month of Adar, and to seize their goods as plunder.* 14 *Also a copy of the edict was to be promulgated* [a] *as law in every province, being publicly displayed* [b] *to all peoples so that they might be ready for this day.* 15 *As the couriers went forth spurred by the king's command, the edict was issued in the Citadel of Susa. Then the king and Haman sat down to a banquet,*[a] *but the city of Susa was confused and in tumult.*[b]

Notes

1.a. Lit. "after these events."
1.b. Lit. "placed his seat above."
2.a. Lit. "the kings servants who were in the king's gate." On the meaning of the latter, see the *Comment* on 2:19.
3.a. מדוע in most contexts means simply "why?" In this context it is much more a challenge than simply a question; see v 4.
4.a. Q reads כאמרם instead of באמרם, which is inexplicable, since the two forms are virtual synonyms (contra Moore, 33; cf. *IBHS* § 36.2.2.b).
4.b. Lit. "spoke to."
4.c. Lit. "words/matters."
4.d. The idiom is עמד דברי מרדכי; see *Comment.*
5.a. Lit. "was filled with rage."

6.a. Lit. "he scorned in his eyes." The emendation to the niphal stem, וַיִּבָּז, "it was despised" (*BHS* n. b), is unnecessary.

6.b. This whole sentence is lacking in the LXX, another example of free translation rather than evidence for a different Heb. text. The omission leaves out the very effective intensification of Haman's decision (Bardtke, 315).

6.c. In the Heb. sentence structure, this appositive, עם מרדכי, "the people of Mordecai," is separated from its referent, "all the Jews," by the relative clause "who were in the whole empire of Ahasuerus." On the grounds that the clause is "syntactically unrelated to the rest of the clause" and is "semantically less appropriate," Moore (37) follows Gunkel and numerous others (e.g., Brockington, *Hebrew Text,* 100; cf. NEB, REB) in repointing עַם, "people," as עִם, "with." However, neither reason is sufficient for repointing the MT. For the appositive to be separated from its referent is not contrary to BH syntax, though the separation here is unusually great (which undoubtedly explains why it is lacking in the LXX; cf. *BHS* n. d-d), as it is with the appositive "words of peace and truth" in 9:30 (Fox, 278). Further, in my opinion, it is the meaning of the repointed text that is less appropriate semantically, for it implies that Haman's strategy will be primarily an attack on Mordecai that will implicate all the Jews, whereas it is just the opposite.

7.a. The foreign word *pûr,* which the narrator defines as equivalent to Heb. *gôrāl,* "lot," is an Akk. word meaning "lot" (cf. the Akk. idiom *pûra karāru,* "to cast a lot," the exact equivalent of Heb. הפיל פור; KB[3] 3:870); see Lewy, *RHA* 5 (1939) 116–24. Either the word was actually a borrowed term in Old Persian or it was so considered by the narrator.

7.b. The Heb. reads "he cast," which must be taken as indefinite subject, although such a subject is usually pl in Heb. This is best expressed as a pass in Eng.

7.c-c. The Heb. reads lit. "from day to day and from month to month twelfth, that is, the month of Adar," an expression that does not make sense as it stands. The addition is based on the LXX; see the *Comment.*

8.a. Lit. ". . . one people scattered and unassimilated"; see *Comment.*

8.b. The idiom שנה מן, "differing from," occurs in BH only here. In SBH the same idea is expressed with אחר. The lateness of the usage in Esther is indicated by the fact that שנה מן occurs elsewhere only in MH; see Bergey, "Book of Esther," 115.

9.a. Lit. "let it be written."

9.b. Lit. "I will weigh out into the hands of."

9.c. The expression עשי המלאכה, lit. "the doers of the work," in SBH means "skilled artisans" (cf., e.g., Exod 36:8; 2 Kgs 12:12, 15, 16). In Esther it seems to be more a term for officials in the king's administration in general; cf. 9:3. Here, of course, it refers to officials involved with the collection and recording of revenue.

10.a. Haman's patronymic, "son of Hammedatha," and the phrase in apposition, "the enemy of the Jews," is lacking in the LXX, which adds instead *σφραγίσαι κατὰ τῶν γεγραμμένων κατὰ τῶν Ἰουδαίων,* "in order to seal the decrees against the Jews," an obvious explanatory addition.

11.a. Lit. "The money is given to you, and the people, ..." The textual emendation suggested in *BHS* nn. a, b is unnecessary; see *Comment.*

12.a. In the calendar formula used here, the addition of the referential prep phrase בו, "in it" (lit. "in the first month, on the 13th day *in it*"), occurs in BH only in Esther (see also 8:9; 9:1, 17, 18[3x], 21). SBH omits the prep phrase or else substitutes לחדש, "of the month." The lateness of the usage in Esther is indicated by the fact that it occurs elsewhere in the DSS and is characteristic of MH; see Bergey, *JQR* 75 (1984) 72; more fully in id., "Book of Esther," 73–74.

12.b. Lit. "it was written."

12.c. Lit. "according to all that . . ."

13.a. For this use of the inf abs with waw, ונשלוח, see *Note* 2:3.e.

13.b. The Heb. reads simply "to destroy, slaughter, and annihilate." The infinitives doubtless express not just the purpose of the sending of dispatches but also their content.

14.a. The structure of this clause makes clear that this is a part of the orders sent out; see *Comment.*

14.b. This seems more likely the sense of גלוי, "being revealed, disclosed, made known" (so NIV, REB, TEV), rather than the sense of "being published" (so JB, NAB, NASV, NEB, NJB).

15.a. In a context such as this, the inf לשתות, from the verb שתה, lit. "to drink," probably refers not to drinking only but by metonymy to a full meal (cf. Fox, 280; Paton, 211), as does the noun משתה in 1:1, 5 and regularly elsewhere (see *Comment* on 1:1; cf. Job 1:4). Strongly in favor of this interpretation is the fact that the fuller expression משתה היין, lit. "banquet of wine," must be used in Esth 5:4; 7:2 to specify the part of the meal where only drinking took place.

15.b. On the suggestion that 4:3 should be transposed here, see the *Note* to that verse.

Form/Structure/Setting

Both form and content signal that this is a new act. Formally, the beginning of the new act is set by the opening temporal clause, "some time later," which establishes a chronological gap between the events about to be related and those that have preceded. Its closure is indicated by the circumstantial nature of its concluding sentences in v 15. Content demonstrates that we have a new act in several ways. First, we are introduced immediately to a new character, Haman son of Hammedatha, the Agagite, the last of the four main protagonists of the narrative. Second, and most important, the events now related constitute the "problem" of the story (i.e., the crisis that will set the story into motion; see the discourse structure in the *Genre* section of the *Introduction* to Esther), namely, Haman's plot to annihilate the Jews. Finally, we have a new venue. From the harem and its concerns we move to the court, its personnel, and its machinations.

The act divides into two scenes: (1) vv 1–6, in which Haman makes the decision to destroy all the Jews, and (2) vv 7–15, in which the scheme he devises to effect this end is related. The division between the two scenes is not easy to determine. Clines (293), Dommershausen (*Estherrolle,* 58–61), and Murphy (*Wisdom,* 161) include v 7 with the first scene rather than the second. However, this verse intends to establish the propitious date for the annihilation of the Jews (see *Comment*), inextricably linking it to the second scene. The fact that it is appropriate to see it as a note concerning the day determined by Haman before he has recourse to the king (Bardtke, 318; cf. Murphy, *Wisdom,* 161) specifically joins it with vv 8–15 rather than vv 1–6. Dorothy's decision (*Books of Esther,* 279–80) to link v 6 with vv 7–15 on the grounds that v 6 presents the conception of the plot and the following verses its preparation, proposal, and execution may describe the logical relationship of these sentences, but it does not fit the scenic structure.

Fox (41) divides the second scene into two different scenes: (1) vv 7–11, entitled "Haman gets permission to exterminate the Jews," and (2) vv 12–15, entitled "Haman's decree is issued." However, vv 12–15 do not really portray new persona or a new venue. They but describe the implementation of the decree the king has granted Haman to issue in vv 7–11. These two pericopes are different episodes of one scene. They are tied together both by the decree and by the fact that the date set for the annihilation of the Jews in the second episode (v 13) is the date that is determined by lot at the beginning of the first (v 7). Yet, though they are not separate scenes, they are separate episodes of one scene, whose division into episodes is indicated by the difference in content. The first episode consists almost entirely of the brief dialogue between Haman and the king. The second one relates in brief compass the dissemination of the edict and concludes with a note regarding its immediate effect, namely, that confusion reigned in the city of Susa (v 15d).

Comment

1 אֶת־הָמָן בֶּן־הַמְּדָתָא הָאֲגָגִי, "Haman son of Hammedatha, the Agagite." The etymology and meaning of the names "Haman" and "Hammedatha" are far from certain, though they are usually considered to be Persian (on "Hammedatha," see Millard, *JBL* 96 [1977] 484; Zadok, *ZAW* 98 [1986] 107). (The doubts expressed by Moore [xliv] regarding the reliability of the Hebrew transcription of the names in Esther have been effectively answered by Millard.) Since the author makes no play on the meaning of these two names, the question is of little import for the meaning of his story. The same is not true, however, for the ethnicon "the Agagite." It could possibly originally designate a Persian or Elamite lineage unknown to us (see Ringgren, 387; Zadok, *BN* 24 [1984] 21; for other possible origins, see Moore, 35). As it now appears in the story, however, there is little doubt that it is intended to reflect the name of Agag, king of the Amalekites, for the significance of which, see *Explanation*.

2 וּמָרְדֳּכַי לֹא יִכְרַע, "Mordecai would not bow down." The narrator gives no explicit motive for Mordecai refusing to do obeisance to Haman. The only reason we have is the fact that he is a Jew, which the narrator seems to take for granted, for he does not mention it here, instead stating it in the following narrative (vv 4c, 6a). But why as a Jew would Mordecai refuse to do obeisance? Brockington (231) dubs it "a virtual breaking of the first and second commandments," and the addition in the LXX attributes it to his unwillingness to give to a human the homage due to God alone. But, as many interpreters have noted, his refusal can hardly relate to his religious obligations, for Jews regularly did obeisance to kings (e.g., 1 Sam 24:8) and other superiors (e.g., Gen 23:7; cf. Moore, 36). Other suggestions are even less likely. Paton (197) attributes it simply to Mordecai's arrogance. However, as Fox (43) notes, this cannot have been the author's attitude, for it is quite in opposition to his positive characterization of Mordecai throughout. The explanations of the Targumim and Midrashim, e.g., that Haman claimed the status of divinity or that he had a divine image embroidered on the chest or sleeve of his garment, are simply ad hoc speculation (see Fox, 43–44). Both the way in which the narrator takes for granted that it relates to Mordecai's Jewishness (see above) and the absence of any other reasonable explanation gives great credence to the view that the narrator assumed his readers would recognize the tribal and racial enmity implied by the patronymics of the two men (see *Explanation*).

4 וַיַּגִּידוּ לְהָמָן לִרְאוֹת הֲיַעַמְדוּ דִּבְרֵי מָרְדֳּכַי כִּי־הִגִּיד לָהֶם אֲשֶׁר־הוּא יְהוּדִי, "they informed Haman to see whether Mordecai's explanation [lit. 'words'] would stand up for he had told them that he was a Jew." Fox (277–78) notes that the idiom עמד דבר, "a statement to be valid," used only here, is the LBH equivalent of קום דבר (since עמד was replacing קום in LBH, a process virtually complete in MH; cf. also Kutscher, *History*, 84), and its meaning here is close to that of the latter idiom in Deut 19:15, "a charge/claim to be valid."

The sentence consists of a main clause, "they informed Haman," followed by a purpose clause, "in order to see if Mordecai's explanation would stand up," followed in turn by a motive clause, "for he had told them that he was a Jew." This structure raises the interesting question whether the motive clause is intended as the reason for the action reported in the main clause or for that reported in the purpose clause. Fox (45–46) makes a very plausible case against the former. He bases his conclusion on three grounds. (1) If the motive clause was intended as the reason that they informed Haman, the formulation of the reason would have been "for he was a Jew," not "for he had informed them that he was a Jew." Or, alternatively, to make the point clearer, the formulation of the purpose clause would have been "in order to see whether Mordecai would prevail," not "to see whether his explanation would prevail." (2) The interpretation implies that they would not have informed Haman of the same behavior on the part of a non-Jew, yet they challenged Mordecai before they knew his nationality. (3) The interpretation implies anti-Semitic motives on the part of the king's officials, yet the fact that they do not immediately exploit his act in order to bring down upon him the wrath of Haman and the law, but instead challenge him day by day, implies that they are not basically hostile to him. Rather, argues Fox, the motive clause gives the reason for their desire to see if Mordecai's explanation, namely, that he was a Jew, would stand. In my opinion, Fox's arguments are cogent (cf. also Clines, *Esther Scroll,* 44–45). Fox goes on to argue, however, that the motives of Mordecai's fellow officials would have been an uninvolved and objective interest in whether such a reason would prove valid, but this hardly seems likely. It seems far more plausible that they were much less disinterested than this. That is, they were offended by Mordecai's flouting of the king's edict and by his motives (convinced of the principle that "pride goeth before a fall"). They would have had, in my opinion, little question whether his explanation would stand up or not. But, in keeping with his subtle reticence in this whole scene, our narrator leaves us to read between the lines!

7 הִפִּיל פּוּר הוּא הַגּוֹרָל לִפְנֵי הָמָן, lit. "he cast *pur,* that is, the lot, in the presence of Haman." Ever since the work of Lewy (*RHA* 5 [1939] 116–24), it has been clear that, whatever may be the origin of the festival of Purim, the Hebrew word פור means "lot," the precise equivalent of Hebrew גורל. The casting of lots among the Persians is mentioned by Herodotus (3.128) and Xenophon (*Cyropaedeia* 1.6.46; 4.5.55; so Clines, 295). For evidence for the use of lots in the ancient Near East and their significance for the story of Esther, see Hallo, *BA* 46 (1983) 19–26.

מִיּוֹם לְיוֹם וּמֵחֹדֶשׁ לְחֹדֶשׁ שְׁנֵים־עָשָׂר, lit. "from day to day and from month to month twelfth." Clearly the meaning is incomplete and something is missing after לחדש, "to month." Context limits the possible meanings intended. First, the expression cannot mean that the lot was cast each day from the first to the twelfth month (as NASV and RSV imply) to determine if that particular day was the propitious one, for the date has already been set by the thirteenth day of the first month (see v 12). Second, Paton (201–2) posits that the lot is being cast for the most propitious day for Haman to present his petition to the king, not for the day to destroy the Jews. But this is unacceptable (nor in the context is it really ambiguous; so Fox, *Redaction,* 12 n. 4), for, as incomplete as the MT text is, it unmistakably indicates that this process involved the twelfth month, whereas v 12 shows that Haman had already presented his petition to the king by the thirteenth day of the first month. Clearly, the context demands that (1) the statement that "the lot was cast in Haman's presence from day to day and from month to month" means that the lot was cast during one particular day for each month and day in succession in order to determine the most propitious day of the year (even though, as Paton, 202, notes, this is not the most natural interpretation of the words "the lot was cast . . . from day to day"), and (2) the day so chosen was to be the one on which to annihilate the Jews. To restore the text to order the simplest solution is to assume haplography of לחדש and so read ומחדש לחדש לחדש שנים־עשר, giving the translation, "for the day and for the month until the twelfth month (was taken)" (so JB, NJB). However, this does not fit the context well, for not only does the language of this verse clearly imply that the day as well as the month was being sought (see above), but the thirteenth day of the twelfth month is specified in Haman's decree in v 13. Hence, it is logical to expect that date to be mentioned here.

After “from month to month” the LXX adds *ὥστε ἀπολέσαι ἐν μιᾷ ἡμέρᾳ τὸ γένος Μαρδοχαίου, καὶ ἔπεσεν ὁ κλῆρος εἰς τὴν τεσσαρεσκαιδεκάτην τοῦ μηνός*, “so as to annihilate in one day the people of Mordecai and the lot fell on the fourteenth of the month.” The date here, the fourteenth of the month, does not fit this context. It may well be, however, an inner Greek corruption under the influence of 9:17–19 (so Clines, 295), particularly since the A-Text reads “thirteenth” in a similar passage (for which see Clines, *Esther Scroll*, 225). If the LXX reading represents the original text, the additional words could well have fallen out of the MT by homoeoteleuton, giving the reading: . . . מחדש לחדש להשמיד עם מרדכי ביום אחד ויפל הגורל על שלשה עשר יום לחדש שנים־עשר, “from month to month in order to destroy the people of Mordecai on one day, and the lot fell on the thirteenth day of the twelfth month.” On the other hand, this might be an addition to the text by the LXX translator according to context. But, the Hebrew is faulty and the context demands something similar at least; therefore, we have adopted the full LXX addition with the correction to “thirteenth” (so NEB, NIV, NRSV, REB; Fox, 278–79; cf. also Barthélemy et al., *Preliminary and Interim Report* 2:548–49). The whole verse is often considered to be secondary (cf. Clines, 294–95; Moore, 37–38), since it interrupts the flow of thought between v 6 and v 8. But, since the date of the attack is almost a year in the future, some explanation of the choice of such a date seems called for, and the proleptic placement of its determination fits the subtle and reticent style of our narrator in this passage.

8 עַם־אֶחָד, “one people.” The numeral אחד, “one,” here may simply have the force of the English indefinite article, “*a* people” (GKC § 125b). In this context, however, the numeral has the implication of “insignificant,” one among the many (Clines, 295). As Fox (48) expressively puts it, “Haman chooses phraseology that insinuates: Your empire has many peoples. One of them (just one; no big deal) is peculiar and dangerous.” In context this seems preferable to the commonly adopted sense of “certain,” i.e., “particular, but not specified.”

מְפֻזָּר וּמְפֹרָד, “scattered and unassimilated.” Though the meaning of מפזר is unambiguous, “to be scattered, dispersed, strewn” (for the active meaning, see Joel 4:2[Eng. 3:2]), the meaning of מפרד is problematic. The root פרד occurs nowhere else in the pual stem, and in the piel it occurs only in Hos 14:4 in a figurative usage in which the meaning is quite unclear. It may be but a synonym for פזר, “to be scattered” (so NASV, NIV, NRSV, REB, RSV, TEV). However, in the niphal stem it means “to be divided, be separate, be separated,” and in the hiphil, “to separate” (cf. Ruth 1:17). Given that range of meanings, it seems much more likely that the meaning intended by the pual stem here is “to be separated (from), isolated (i.e., from other peoples), unassimilated,” referring to the religious and ethnic customs that the Jews maintained rather than adopting those of the diaspora world (so JB, NAB, NEB, NJB).

9 וַעֲשֶׂרֶת אֲלָפִים כִּכַּר־כֶּסֶף, “ten thousand talents of silver.” This is doubtless intended to represent a monetary sum, since there is considerable evidence that the main circulating medium of exchange in the eastern part of the Achaemenid empire (the Levant, Babylonia, and Iran) was bulk silver, usually in the form of bars and slabs (Bivar, “Achaemenid Coins,” 2:612–13). The weight of the Babylonian standard talent in use in the Achaemenid empire after the reform of Darius I is 30.240 kilograms or 66.67 pounds (a figure widely accepted by modern investigators; see Bivar, 2:621–25). On this basis Haman’s payment would amount to a little over 333 tons (or 302 metric tons) of silver, an enormous sum. As Clines (296) cogently observes, such a sum is truly meaningful only when compared with contemporary revenues. The most pertinent information is the list of annual tribute paid by the various satrapies in the time of Artaxerxes reported by Herodotus (3.89–95; cf. Olmstead, *History,* 291–99). Here we learn (1) that the annual taxes paid by most satrapies was of the order of 200 to 700 "Euboic" talents (it is generally assumed that by "Euboic" Herodotus meant the Athenian standard of his own day; see Bivar, "Achaemenid Coins," 623), (2) that the largest annual tributes paid by any of the satrapies were those of India, 4,680 talents, and Babylon, 1,000 talents, and (3) that the total annual revenue of the whole Persian empire was 14,560 talents (3.95; see Olmstead, *History,* 297–98). Since the Babylonian talent was equivalent to 1.3 Euboic talents (Herodotus 3.89; cf. Bivar, "Achaemenid Coins," 623), this equals 10,920 Babylonian talents. Hence, the figure offered by Haman is almost equal to the total annual tribute paid by the whole Persian empire, an utterly fantastic sum! Bardtke (322) takes the sum at face value and understands the text to imply that the money would come from the booty to be gained from plundering the Jews, alluding to v 13. However, there is nothing whatsoever in the context of v 9 that suggests this. The plunder mentioned in v 13 is probably intended as an attractive inducement for those who attack the Jews ("all peoples," v 14) to carry out the order for the pogrom (contra Daube, *JQR* 37 [1946–47] 141; cf. Clines, 296–97). In support of this is the fact that 8:11; 9:15 clearly imply that the Jews were to be the recipients of the spoil of their enemies (cf. Paton, 206). Hence, in my opinion, the narrator continues to engage in extravagant hyperbole, once again holding up to ridicule Persian greed and avidity.

10 טַבַּעַת, "signet ring," refers to a "signet," a seal in the form of a ring used as a signature in marking documents as official. As often noted, the language here is very close to that of Gen 41:42.

11 הַכֶּסֶף נָתוּן לָךְ, lit. "the silver is given to you." At first glance this can be taken to mean that the king is refusing the offer and telling Haman "keep the money" (so the LXX translates, followed by NAB, NIV, NJB, JB, REB). The example of Xerxes' refusal of the even larger amount offered by Pythius, the Lydian, for Xerxes' war effort is often cited in support of this literal understanding of the words (see Moore, 40). However, the ensuing narrative makes it clear that this is not what the narrator meant by the phrase. Thus, in his report of Mordecai's communication of the facts to Esther in 4:7, he states that Haman would pay this sum to the king's treasury for the annihilation of the Jews, and in 7:4 Esther claims that she and her people had been "sold." Consequently, the language here is frequently regarded as the beginning of a polite round of bargaining such as that carried on in Gen 23 between Abraham and Ephron the Hittite (see esp. Daube, *JQR* 37 [1946–47] 142–43; cf. Fox, 52). Since not only the silver but also the people are said to be "given" to Haman, the expression is "a courtly form of accepting the money" (Clines, 297) and means that both are at Haman's disposal.

12 אֶל אֲחַשְׁדַּרְפְּנֵי־הַמֶּלֶךְ וְאֶל־הַפַּחוֹת ... וְאֶל־שָׂרֵי עַם וָעָם, "to the royal satraps and the governors . . . and the rulers of each people." Those officials to whom Haman's orders were sent were the major administrative officials of the empire: a "satrap" governed a "satrapy," the major administrative division of the empire (see the discussion of the term "province" in *Comment* on 1:1); "governors" ruled the provinces or city states within a satrapy; and the "rulers [lit. 'princes'] of each people" were the heads of less formally constituted entities, such as ethnic and tribal groups. The list is thus intended to be all-inclusive.

14 פַּתְשֶׁגֶן הַכְּתָב לְהִנָּתֵן דָּת, lit. "a copy of the writ was to be promulgated as law." The structure of this clause, consisting of subject, "a copy of the writ," plus infinitive predicate, "to be promulgated [lit. 'given']," expresses a modal or precative sense (see *IBHS* § 36.2.3.f; this usage is much more common in LBH and DSS Hebrew than in SBH; see *HDSS*, 70–71). Hence, this is part of the order sent by the couriers to all the provinces of the king.

15 וְהָעִיר שׁוּשָׁן נָבוֹכָה. The implications of the meaning of the niphal stem of בוך, "bewildered," in this context are not clear. It can be taken to mean simply a state of uncertainty, or even grief (so Paton, 211, who then avers that the narrator ascribes his own emotions to the residents of Susa), but the word refers to a highly agitated, bewildered, and tumultuous state. Thus, in Exod 14:3 it refers to the agitated and bewildered state that Pharoah attributes to the Israelites after the escape from Egypt when the desert "hemmed them in." In Joel 1:18 it refers to the agitated condition of cattle who have no pasture because of drought (the parallel clauses speak of the animals "moaning" and "suffering"). Hence, here it refers to a tumultuous and agitated state brought on by the enormity of what Haman's edict proposed. Since the narrator intends the description to point up the utter callousness of Haman and Ahasuerus, who coolly and calmly feast as the terrible order goes out, it undoubtedly implies empathy with the situation of the Jewish community on the part of the inhabitants of Susa.

Explanation

This, the second act, portrays the crisis that will set our story proper into motion, namely Haman's plot and edict to exterminate all the Jews in the whole empire of Ahasuerus. Having set at some length the tone and temper of his story in the preceding exposition by the way that he there has fleshed out and embellished his account, our narrator engages in little of the same here. Indeed, his narrative is not only brief but so spare and reticent that we must often read between the lines.

Scene 1. Haman Decides to Annihilate the Jews (3:1–6)

This, the first of two scenes (see *Form/Structure/Setting* above), relates the reason for Haman's plot, namely, the enmity between Haman the Agagite and Mordecai the Jew, and in particular the bitter hatred and ill will that Haman bears for Mordecai. He begins by introducing to us the fourth and last major character of his story, Haman son of Hammedatha, the Agagite. His spare narrative introduces this new character in the course of telling us that the king promoted him by advancing him in rank and giving him precedence over all his other nobles (v 1). The narrator gives absolutely no hint about the reason for this advancement, for his real purpose is to relate that the king had commanded that all his officials at the court should bow down and do obeisance to Haman (v 2a).

In introducing Haman, he gives us his patronymic and ethnicon in a manner very similar to the way in which he introduced Mordecai in the previous act. Such information is not given for the other two major characters, Esther and King Ahasuerus, simply because patronymics are not pertinent to their identification and characterization. Whatever its origin and original sense may have been (see *Comment*), the term Agagite is here intended as a most significant ethnic identification (cf. Clines, *Esther Scroll,* 14). Agag was the king of the Amalekites defeated by Saul and put to death by Samuel (1 Sam 15), and the OT tradition univocally stressed the bitter and unrelenting enmity that existed between the two peoples. Amalek is presented as the pre-eminent enemy of Israel (see Mattingly, *ABD* 1:169–71). Thus, the conclusion of the story of the attack of the Amalekites upon Israel in the wilderness (Exod 17:8–16) notes, "Yahweh will have war with Amalek from generation to generation," and the book of Deuteronomy avows, ". . . you shall blot out the memory of Amalek from under heaven; you must not forget" (25:19; cf. also 1 Sam 15:2–3). Further, not only were the Amalekites Israel's ancient and inveterate enemies, but Agag himself is so portrayed in Num 24:7. This ethnic identity of Haman is doubtless also intended by the narrator to be connected with that of Mordecai, for Mordecai's patronymic (see the *Comment* on 2:5) identifies him as a descendant of the Benjaminite Kish, and Saul, another direct descendant of Kish, defeated Agag, king of the Amalekites. The patronymics of these two protagonists, then, subtly indicate that both men are heirs to a long-standing and bitter tradition of ethnic enmity and antagonism. Indeed, the manner in which Haman is identified in the book signals him to be the pre-eminent enemy of the Jews (see Jones, *Semantics* 6 [1978] 36–43; and Fretz, *ABD* 1:89–90). This is done in a sequence that is most revealing:

3:10	Haman son of Hammedatha, the Agagite, the enemy of the Jews
8:1	Haman, the enemy of the Jews
8:3	Haman, the Agagite
8:5	Haman son of Hammedatha, the Agagite
9:10	Haman son of Hammedatha, the enemy of the Jews
9:24	Haman son of Hammedatha, the Agagite, the enemy of all the Jews

There is a chiastic sequence in the use of the two appellatives. The most complete identification of Haman, using both appellatives, forms an inclusio (and one with a climax, achieved by the addition of the word "all"). Sandwiched between them are abbreviated forms, omitting one or the other of the appellatives, also in a chiastic pattern: in 8:1 and 9:10 he is identified as "the enemy of the Jews," whereas in 8:3 and 8:5 he is simply "the Agagite." These variant identifications in such a structure clearly make "Agagite" virtually synonymous with "the enemy of the Jews" (cf. Fretz, *ABD* 1:89–90). This is further strengthened by the fact that the most ancient interpreters also so understood the term. Thus, Josephus calls Haman "the Amalekite," and the Targumim add to "Agagite" the appositive *br ᶜmlq,* "descendant of Amalek." The LXX replaces Agagite with *bougaion* (meaning uncertain) in 3:1, but *makedôn,* "Macedonian" in 9:24, both of which can be understood as pejorative terms in the Greek period (see Haupt, *AJSL* 24 [1907–8] 123–24). That is, the Greek translator is "up-dating" the text, using terms for a "hated enemy" contemporary with, and hence meaningful for, his Greek-reading Jewish contemporaries (Moore, 36).

Having set the stage by telling us of Haman's exalted position and his right to obeisance from all his fellow officials, our narrator comes immediately to his main point: Mordecai would not bow down and do obeisance as the king had commanded (v 2b). Here our narrator is as indirect and subtle as he is with the use of patronymics, for he gives us no explicit motive for his refusal. Since a good narrator must supply the information necessary to understand his story, clearly he must have felt that no explanation was needed, at least for his original readers. Indeed, he must have believed that they would have immediately recognized that the motive relates to the fact that Mordecai is a Jew, for he only relates that fact (1) as an explanation of why Mordecai's fellow officials informed Haman of his actions, v 4b, and (2) as the reason that Haman thought it beneath him to attack Mordecai alone, v 6b, not in connection with Mordecai's failure to do obeisance. But, why would the fact that Mordecai was a Jew be sufficient reason for either Mordecai's refusal or Haman's monstrous pride? Clearly, the former cannot relate to Mordecai's religion or temperament (see *Comment*), and that the latter results from Haman's ethnic hatred is made clear by the reason the narrator gives ("they had told him who Mordecai's people were"). The only thing in the context that makes both these reactions reasonable is the subtle allusion to the ancient tribal enmity between Jews and Amalekites (cf. Fox, 42–45). Mordecai's action is one of ethnic pride. He simply would not bow down to a descendant of the Amalekites (cf. Deut 25:17–19). Haman's reaction is unmistakably motivated by racial hatred so callous and senseless (see below) that, beside it, Mordecai's pride pales to insignificance. Whatever else might have motivated Mordecai the narrator leaves hidden behind the opaqueness with which he characterizes him throughout. He gives us for Mordecai only "a sense of ambiguous depths of character" (Alter, *Art,* 115; see *Theme and Purpose* in the *Introduction* to Esther).

In his overweening conceit (Bardtke, 317), Haman was oblivious to Mordecai's refusal to do obeisance (v 5a), but Mordecai's fellow officials were not. They challenged him day after day to explain his reason for flouting the king's edict (vv 3–4a). Finally, motivated by a desire to see whether Mordecai's explanation for his refusal would stand up (v 4b), and doubtless piqued at his violation of the king's law and his ethnic pride (see *Comment*), they informed Haman of his actions.

Whatever Haman's reaction might have been had he privately observed Mordecai's refusal to give him the honor prescribed by the king, now that the matter was public, his reaction was predictable: he was enraged (v 5). In actuality, Mordecai's action in refusing to bow to Haman represents both a matter of civil disobedience and personal affront. Haman's reaction, however, springs exclusively from the latter, for here the narrator does not leave us guessing but states the reason explicitly, "since they had told him who Mordecai's people were" (v 6a). Tribal and ethnic hatred motivate him, but the virulence of his reaction arises from more than tribal enmity, for "he thought it beneath him" to lay hands on Mordecai alone (v 6b). He could have either forced Mordecai's overt compliance or, having charged him with violating the king's order, simply eliminated him, but to do so would reveal that what Mordecai did mattered to him, that the actions of his enemy had touched him in a vulnerable spot. This reveals him as a man of overweening pride and vanity, as his later characterization will emphatically stress (cf. esp. 5:11–13). So he pretends indifference, indicated by his delay in doing anything directly about Mordecai's flagrant violation and insult until much later (cf. 5:9). Instead, he resolves to dispose of Mordecai indirectly: he seeks a way to exterminate the whole Jewish people. And the blunt and almost casual way in which the narrator relates the decision (v 6b) suggests it was made without hesitation or a twinge of conscience. Eventually even this will not be enough, and he will decide to eliminate Mordecai himself (5:9–14), but for now he casually opts for genocide as the way to eliminate his enemy. Haman, then, is moved by power alone, without mercy or compassion. He is the epitome of callous, obdurate, and senseless evil.

SCENE 2. HAMAN SETS IN MOTION A PLOT TO ANNIHILATE THE JEWS (3:7–15)

Episode 1. Haman obtains the king's permission to annihilate the Jews (3:7–11). Having laconically informed us of Haman's insane decision to get at his enemy by exterminating the whole race to which he belongs, the narrator proceeds with an utterly spare and unembellished account. First, he wastes no words at all in telling us how Haman effected his decision. Without a single detail about the setting and circumstances of the two changes of scene the narrative implies, he relates both the choice of the day, v 7, and the gaining of the king's assent, vv 8–11, the latter without the slightest allusion to the difficulty of attaining such an audience, a matter that the narrative later reveals was fraught with the most dire of consequences (4:11; cf. Dommershausen, 63)! Second, he continues the subtly reticent and indirect style of the whole act. Not until the second episode does he give us any information about the exact means by which Haman proposes to accomplish this horrendous goal, and indeed he reveals it there only indirectly in the course of relating the dissemination of the order that will effect it (vv 12–14). Instead, he gives us a chronologically based account of Haman's actions.

He begins by relating the casting of lots to determine the most propitious day for the annihilation of the Jews (for this interpretation of v 7, see *Comment*). Though determined by lot, the day chosen seems maliciously ironical. The number 13 was considered unlucky by the Persians and the Babylonians, while the thirteenth day of the first month, the day on which the edict decreeing the Jews' destruction was dispatched (v 12), is the day preceding Passover, the commemoration of the deliverance from slavery in Egypt.

With this accomplished, the narrator then relates, without a word of transition, Haman's proposal to the king. Here Haman reveals himself as a shrewd, clever, and malignant slanderer. He begins by suppressing the identity of the people, speaking simply of "one people," a usage that insinuates that this people (or the issue of their annihilation) is insignificant (see *Comment*). Yet they are "scattered and unassimilated among the peoples in *all* the provinces" of the empire. "Scattered . . . in *all* the provinces" is not only hyperbole (Clines, 295) but is made into an accusation by the addition of the word "unassimilated, separate," referring to their different social and religious customs (see *Comment*); i.e., they are everywhere, a different, sinister, and ubiquitous presence. From innuendo and half-truth he moves to outright, yet blatantly false, accusation (8c–d). Here our understanding in reading the text in English is beset with problems of translation, for Haman uses the same word, the borrowed Persian term *dât,* in both clauses (8c, d) of the accusation. Since *dât* can mean "custom, regulation" (e.g., Esth 2:12) as well as "order" (e.g., Esth 1:8) and "law" (e.g., Esth 3:14, 4:11), Haman is able to slide from the charge that the Jews' *dâtîm,* "laws/edicts," i.e., their religious and social regulations/customs, are different to the charge that they do not obey the king's *dâtîm.* The first is true, but also true about every other people group in the empire, a diversity upon which the Persians prided themselves. The second, as a generality, is a blatant lie, for the actions of the Jews as a people throughout the book are thoroughly law-abiding (cf. Fox, 215). By using the same word, Haman implies that the first provides the grounds for the second. Haman then appeals to the king's racial superiority and fear, "It is not in the king's interest to let them be," implying that their very existence is detrimental to the king's honor and welfare. Thus, with a series of innuendos, half-truths, and outright lies, Haman has made the case that this unnamed people is omnipresent and lawless, and hence constitute an insidious threat to the king's welfare. Finally, before the king can even conjecture whether it really *is* not in his interest to let this people continue to exist, he learns that it will be immensely in his interest to have them destroyed. Haman blatantly appeals to the king's venality and greed with an enormous bribe: if the king will issue a decree for their destruction, he will pay ten thousand talents to the royal treasury (indeed, a figure so large that it can only be satiric hyperbole; see *Comment*).

Ahasuerus does not respond to this incredible proposal with even a question or a comment, let alone an objection. He simply gives Haman his signet, which empowers him to act fully in his name and authority, with the casual and offhand comment "Do with the people and the money as you please." This response reveals that he doesn't care whether this people is destroyed or not. The whole matter is too insignificant a concern to occupy his time or attention. Haman is unmitigated evil, but the king is dangerous indifference personified.

Episode 2. Haman orders the annihilation of the Jews (3:12–15). Having gained the king's permission to destroy the Jews, Haman wastes no time in implementing the genocide. The story is told in the passive voice: "It was written" (12a, b), "it was sealed" (12c), "dispatches were sent" (13), "a copy of the order is to be promulgated . . . being publicly displayed" (14), conveying an impression of the cold, relentless, and impersonal nature of the process. Further, the destination of the dispatches is all-inclusive: the edict, written in the king's name and sealed with his signet, i.e., with the king's express authority, is sent to the heads of all three major divisions of the imperial administration (v 12; see *Comment*). The edict is an order for the destruction, slaughter, and annihilation of all the Jews, young and old, women and children, and the plundering of their property on one day, the thirteenth of the twelfth month (v 13). But to discover the agency of this extermination we must read between the lines, for it is presented only indirectly through the command that the edict is "to be promulgated as law in every province and publicly displayed to all peoples, so that they might be ready for this day" (v 14). With this, the invidious and horrific extent of Haman's evil plan finally becomes clear. He will use the general background of human tribal and racial enmity, dislike, and suspicion, prompted by the specific motivation of greed in the prospect of plunder and booty, to set the whole general populace to the task of exterminating the whole Jewish race. Furthermore, the genocide will not take place for eleven months. This will both prolong the agony of the Jews (there is no possibility of escape within the Persian empire, for it effectively comprises the known world [Bardtke, 325]) and permit ample time for the intensifying of anti-Jewish feeling (Clines, 298) and preparations for the attack (v 14c).

The act concludes with four brief but expressive pictures. The first two relate to the promulgation of the decree: as the couriers hasten forth on the king's business, the edict is issued in the Citadel of Susa, i.e., to the court and its environs (hence Mordecai is immediately aware of it, 4:1). The second two relate to its effects: the king and Haman sit down to a banquet, but the city of Susa (i.e., the residents of the city itself, not the acropolis) is agitated and in tumult. The stark contrast that this represents to the actions of the king and Haman clearly implies that the local residents respond in empathy with the Jewish community, but that is not the narrator's main purpose in the depiction. Rather the narrator uses the contrast to depict eloquently the enormity of the callous indifference of the king and Haman: they calmly and coolly sit down to a banquet, but the citizens of the city are in tumultuous confusion.

So the "problem," to whose resolution the rest of the story will be dedicated (see the discourse outline in the *Genre* section of the *Introduction* to Esther), is before us. Haman son of Hammedatha, the Agagite, the enemy of the Jews, has written into Persian law the edict that all the peoples of the empire are to be ready to destroy, slay, and annihilate all the Jews, young and old, women and children, and to seize their goods as plunder, on one day, the thirteenth of the twelfth month, the month of Adar. Public violence, murder, and pillage are to be unleashed to provide vengeance for Haman's wounded pride. Given the power of Haman's position and the irrevocability of Persian law, the doom of the Jews seems sealed.

Or is it? One of the major characters of our story has not appeared in this tragic act by even the most veiled or subtle allusion. Yet, unbeknownst to Haman or the king (but well-known to us!), a member of this seemingly doomed race, now occupies, incognito, the chair of the Queen of Persia. But what can one woman do, however highly placed, in the face of such odds? Perhaps not much, but the narrator has not left us without hope or expectations, however fleeting. He has characterized Esther as one who is actively involved in what happens to her (see *Explanation* to 2:5–11), and he has emphasized by repetition (2:10, 20) that she still obeys Mordecai (see *Explanation* to 2:19–23). Hence, the Jewish community has an entrée into the Persian court, and one that, perhaps, is not to be underestimated. About this our narrator will not leave us to wonder long.

Act 3
Mordecai's Stratagem: Esther Must Consent to Appeal to the King (4:1–17)

Bibliography

Ackroyd, P. R. "Two Hebrew Notes." *ASTI* 5 (1966–67) 82–86. **Bergey, R. L.** "The Book of Esther—Its Place in the Linguistic Milieu of Post-exilic Biblical Hebrew: A Study in Late Biblical Hebrew." Diss., Dropsie College, 1983. **Clines, D. J. A.** *The Esther Scroll.* JSOTSup 30. Sheffield: JSOT, 1984. **Dommershausen, W.** *Die Estherrolle.* Stuttgart: Katholisches Bibelwerk, 1968. **Dorothy, C. V.** "The Books of Esther: Structure, Genre, and Textual Integrity." Diss., Claremont, 1989. **Driver, G. R.** "Affirmation by Exclamatory Negation." *JANES* 5 (1973) 107–14. ———. "Problems and Solutions." *VT* 4 (1954) 224–45. **Gerleman, G.** *Studien zu Esther.* Neukirchen: Neukirchener, 1966. **Hasel, G.** זעק. *TDOT* 4:112–22. **Haupt, P.** "Critical Notes on Esther." *AJSL* 24 (1907–8) 97–186 (= Moore, *Studies,* 1–90). **Hillers, D. R.** "A Convention in Hebrew Literature: The Reaction to Bad News." *ZAW* 77 (1965) 86–90. **Hyman, R. T.** "Questions and the Book of Ruth." *HS* 24 (1983) 17–25. **Murphy, R. E.** *Wisdom Literature: Job, Proverbs, Ruth, Canticles, Ecclesiastes, and Esther.* FOTL 13. Grand Rapids, MI: Eerdmans, 1981. **Talmon, S.** "'Wisdom' in the Book of Esther." *VT* 13 (1963) 419–55. **Wiebe, J. M.** "Esther 4:14: 'Will Relief and Deliverance Arise for the Jews from Another Place?'" *CBQ* 53 (1991) 409–15.

Translation

Scene 1. Mordecai and All the Jews Lament over Haman's Edict (4:1–3)
Time: 1/13 or 1/14, year 12

> 1 *Now Mordecai learned of all that had been done. And he tore his clothes, put on sackcloth and ashes, went out into the city, and raised a loud and bitter outcry.* 2 *He went as far as the entrance*[a] *to the royal court*[b] *because it was forbidden to enter the court dressed in sackcloth.* 3 *And in every single province, which the command and edict of the king reached, there was great mourning among the Jews, with fasting, weeping, and lamentation, while many made their beds on sackcloth and ashes.*[a]

Scene 2. At Mordecai's Command Esther Consents to Appeal to the King (4:4–17)
Time: 1/13 or 1/14, year 12

Episode 1. Mordecai refuses the clothing Esther sends him (4:4)

> 4 *Esther's maids and eunuchs came*[a] *and told her about this, and the queen was greatly distressed.*[b] *So she sent garments for Mordecai to wear instead of sackcloth,*[c] *but he would not accept them.*

Episode 2. Mordecai orders Esther to appeal to the king (4:5–9)

> 5 *So Esther summoned Hathach, one of the king's eunuchs whom he had appointed*[a] *to wait on her, and ordered him to go to*[b] *Mordecai to find out why he was acting in this*

way.[c] [6]*Hathach went out to Mordecai in the city square in front of the royal court.*[a] [7]*And Mordecai told him all that had happened to him and the exact amount of money that Haman had promised to pay into the royal treasury for the destruction of the Jews.* [8]*And he gave him a copy of the text of the edict which had been issued in Susa for their destruction, so that he might show it to Esther, tell her about it, and order her to go to the king to implore his favor and plead with him on behalf of her people.* [9]*So Hathach went and told Esther what*[a] *Mordecai had said.*

Episode 3. Esther consents to appeal to the king (4:10–17)

[10]*Esther then ordered Hathach to reply to Mordecai,*[a] [11]*"The king's courtiers and the people in his provinces alike all know that, for every man or woman who enters into the king's presence in the inner court who has not been summoned, the king has but one law.*[a] *That person is to be put to death, unless the king holds out*[b] *the golden scepter;*[c] *then he or she may live. And thirty days have passed since I have been summoned to come into the king's presence."*[d] [12]*And Mordecai was told*[a] *what*[b] *Esther had said.*

[13]*Mordecai then sent this reply to Esther,*[a] *"Do not imagine that you are any more likely to escape in the king's palace than all the Jews.* [14]*For, if you remain silent at this time, relief and deliverance will not arise for the Jews from any other quarter,*[a] *and you and your father's house will perish. And who knows if it is not for a time like this that you have become queen?"*

[15]*Esther then replied to Mordecai,* [16]*"Go, assemble all the Jews to be found in Susa, and fast on my behalf. For three days eat or drink nothing, day or night. I and my maids will also fast in the same way. After that I will go to the king, even though it is against the law. And if I perish, I perish."*

[17]*So Mordecai left and did exactly as*[a] *Esther had ordered him.*

Notes

2.a. Lit. "up to in front of."

2.b. The expression is lit. "the king's gate," for the meaning of which see the *Comment* on 2:19.

3.a. Lit. "sackcloth and ashes were spread out (as a bed) for most." For the identical language in the active voice, see Isa 58:5. It is alleged that v 3 interrupts the continuity between v 2 and v 4. Hence, since the AT omits the verse and the OL version has something very similar immediately after 3:15, some wish to place the verse there (cf. *BHS* n.). But the order of the MT is doubtless correct. Chronologically, Mordecai would have learned of what had been done long before the couriers could have spread the edict throughout the empire (Fox, 58). Further, the verse literarily enhances the effect of Mordecai's reaction since its function is to make the reaction of the rest of the Jews a mirror image of his (Clines, 299).

4.a. K ותבואינה, to be pointed וַתָּבוֹאֶינָה, is a much rarer form of the impf 3 f pl verb than Q וַתָּבוֹאנָה; see GKC § 76g.

4.b. The hithpalpel stem of חול/חיל occurs only here. The qal stem occurs with the meaning "to writhe (in pain)," and the closely related hithpolel stem occurs in Job 15:20 with the meaning "to writhe in fear" (referring to the wicked), and in Jer 23:19 with the meaning "to whirl" (referring to a gale, windstorm). In its literal sense, then, the word connotes a physical reaction occasioned by the shock of calamity or pain. Here it must bear the figurative meaning "to be deeply distressed."

4.c. Lit. "to clothe Mordecai and to remove his sackcloth from him."

5.a. Driver (*VT* 4 [1954] 235; cf. *BHS* n. b) posits that the MT form העמיד is a conflation of two alternative readings, אשר עָמַד לפניה and הָעוֹמֵד לפניה, on the grounds that the LXX, Syr, and the Second Targum presuppose the qal form of the verb (cf. *BHS* n.) and that this offers a preferable sense. In my opinion, the MT sense is much to be preferred.

5.b. על is not to be changed to אל, "to," here (contra Bardtke, 327; cf. *BHS* n. c). Note the same idiom with אל in v 10, and see *Note* 1:17.c.

5.c. Lit. "to find out what this is and why this is."

6.a. See *Note* 2.b.

9.a. Moore (45, 48) follows the LXX and adds כל, "all," reading "*everything* Mordecai had said" on the grounds that Hathach, as a faithful servant, would have reported all that was said (so also in v 12). But this is probably implied in the Heb. idiom "(he) told Esther *Mordecai's words.*" The addition is exactly the type of expanded text that is characteristic of the LXX translation; cf. *Text* in the *Introduction* to Esther.

10.a. Lit. "Esther spoke to Hathach and commanded him (to go) to Mordecai."

11.a. Lit. "his law is one."

11.b. The verb here, יושיט, "to hold out, extend," occurs in BH only in Esther (see also 5:2; 8:4). In comparable contexts in SBH, נטה and שלח are used. The lateness of the usage in Esther is indicated by the fact that it occurs elsewhere only in MH; see Bergey, "Book of Esther," 123–24.

11.c. This dissimilated form of the word שרביט, "scepter," occurs in BH only in Esther (see also 5:2; 8:4). In SBH the undissimilated form שבט is used (cf. Gen 49:10; Judg 5:14). The lateness of the usage in Esther is indicated by the fact that it occurs elsewhere only in MH; see Bergey, "Book of Esther," 50–51.

11.d. Lit. "As for me, I have not been summoned to come to the king these thirty days."

12.a. Lit. "They told to Mordecai . . ." To emend the verb is unnecessary; see *Comment.*

12.b. Moore (46) again follows the LXX and adds כל, "all." See *Note* 9.a.

13.a. Lit. "Mordecai said to reply to Esther."

14.a. The translation understands the clause as a rhetorical question expressing a strong negation; see *Comment.*

17.a. Syr, Vg, and the LXX render the phrase as the direct obj of the verb, suggesting the reading כל, "all," rather than ככל, "according to all" (cf. *BHS* n.; Bardtke, 328). But, if this were the syntax of the original Heb., it would have required the sign of the definite direct obj את. Hence, the MT reading could not have arisen simply by dittogr. The versions doubtless represent a freer translation.

Form/Structure/Setting

Though the opening of act 3 lacks any temporal transition like that which began the previous act (3:1; cf. also 2:1), its beginning is signaled formally by circumstantial clauses: the staccato fourfold circumstantial sentences of 3:15, which mark the closure of the previous act, and the circumstantial sentence of 4:1, which marks the opening of this scene. The transition to a new act is even more sharply marked by the change in content of these same clauses: from the king and Haman in 3:15c to Mordecai in 4:1, to be joined by Esther in 4:3, the opening sentence of the second scene. The closure of the act is denoted by the summary statement of 4:17.

The act comprises two scenes. Dommershausen (*Estherrolle,* 68–69), separates 4:1–3 as a *Kurzbericht,* but the terminal point of Mordecai's journey into the city, "the entrance to the royal court" (where Esther's maids and eunuchs will surely observe his conduct), reveals clearly that this is a prelude to the next pericope, not a separate scene (cf. Murphy, *Wisdom,* 163). Dorothy ("Books of Esther, 282–87) joins this act with the following one, 5:1–8, on the grounds that the first represents the "plan proposed" and the second the "plan initiated." This clearly expresses how the two are related in the structure of the plot but is scarcely sufficient grounds for regarding them as a single act.

The first scene, vv 1–3, compact and precise, consists of straight narrative. It is distinguished as a separate scene from what follows primarily by its content, which relates the anguish and shock with which Mordecai and all the other Jews reacted to Haman's decree and its promulgation. It provides the setting necessary for the opening of the second scene by relating not only that Mordecai went out into the city but also that he went as far as the entrance to the royal court.

The Structure of Scene 2, vv 4–17

Episode	Style	Verses	Content & Function
Episode 1	Straight narration	4	*Narrative:* Esther learns from her maids and eunuchs of the anguish and sorrow of Mordecai and all the Jews. She sends clothing to replace his sackcloth. He refuses.
Episode 2	Indirect discourse with detailed narrative transitions	5a	*Narrative introduction:* Esther summons Hathach and orders him to go to Mordecai.
		5b	*Indirect discourse included within narration:* Esther sends Hathach to find out what has happened and why Mordecai laments.
		6	*Narrative transition:* Hathach goes out to Mordecai in the plaza before the court.
		7–8	*Indirect discourse:* Mordecai tells Hathach what has happened and tells him to order Esther to go to the king and plead for her people.
		9	*Narrative conclusion:* Hathach tells Esther what Mordecai said.
Episode 3	Direct discourse with minimal narrative transitions	10	*Narrative introduction:* Esther orders Hathach to reply to Mordecai.
		11	*Direct discourse:* Esther objects that to go to the king unsummoned puts her life at risk.
		12	*Narrative transition:* When Mordecai is told Esther's words, he replies.
		13–14	*Direct discourse:* Mordecai's remonstrance: Esther will not escape in the royal palace. Perhaps she has become queen for just such a time as this.
		15	*Narrative transition:* Esther replies to Mordecai.
		16	*Direct discourse:* Mordecai and the Jews in Susa are to fast for three days and nights, along with Esther and her maids. After that she will go the the king, whatever the consequences.
		17	*Narrative conclusion:* Mordecai does exactly as Esther has ordered him.

The second scene, vv 4–17, long and detailed in comparison to the first, consists primarily of a dialogue between Esther and Mordecai (see the table). The beginning of a new scene is indicated by the introduction of a new character, Esther. The scene comprises three episodes. The first episode, v 4, consisting of straight narrative, sets the scene for what follows. Greatly distressed by learning of Mordecai's actions and attire from her servants, Esther attempts to replace his sackcloth with clothing. His refusal leads to the dialogue through intermediaries that follows in the next two episodes.

The last two episodes, vv 5–9 and 10–17, relate the ensuing dialogue between Esther and Mordecai. They are carefully crafted (see the table). Though both report a dialogue, they are strikingly different in style and construction. Episode 2 reports a two-member communication between Esther and Mordecai, vv 5–6 and 7–9. It differs markedly from episode 3 in that it is in *indirect* discourse and it emphasizes the mediate nature of their communication by relating in considerable detail the identity and actions of their intermediary, Hathach (cf. vv 5a, 6, 9). The episode concludes with a summary statement, v 9, to the effect that Hathach communicated to Esther Mordecai's response to her query.

Episode 3 reports a three-part communication between Esther and Mordecai, vv 11, 13–14, 16. It differs from episode 2 in that it is in *direct* discourse and it is marked by increasingly brief narrative transitions, vv 10, 12, 15, the last two of which omit all detail about the intermediary who must convey the messages involved. (The first, v 10, provides more detail since it functions as the opening narrative statement for the episode.) The choice of direct discourse and the spare narrative transitions throw all the emphasis on the content of the speeches, showing that here we reach the climax of the scene. Episode 3, and the whole scene, closes with a narrative summary, v 17.

Comment

1 יָדַע אֶת־כָּל־אֲשֶׁר נַעֲשָׂה. To translate this phrase "learned what had happened" (JB, NJB; cf. NAB) is probably not accurate in that it would most likely be taken to mean that he knew of the contents of the edict. The language chosen here by the narrator, "learned all that had been done," is deliberate and is much more inclusive (cf. Clines, 299; Moore, 46; Fox, 57). It undoubtedly implies the same sources of knowledge about affairs in the court by means of which Mordecai learned of the plot of Bigthan and Teresh on the life of the king (2:19–23). That this is so is indicated by Mordecai's knowledge of the exact amount of money that Haman promised to pay into the royal treasury for the annihilation of the Jews (4:7).

שַׂק וָאֵפֶר, "sackcloth and ashes." שַׂק, "sackcloth," refers to a garment of coarse cloth of goat or camel hair, possibly a loincloth. The ashes were usually sprinkled on one's head. These actions are appropriate for expressing grief, anguish, lament, and humiliation over calamity and bad news of all kinds (e.g., Joseph's disappearance, Gen 37:29; military defeat, 1 Sam 4:12; 2 Sam 1:2; rebellion, 2 Sam 15:32; rape, 2 Sam 13:9; siege and threat of attack, 2 Kgs 18:37; cf. Hillers, *ZAW* 77 [1965] 86–90), as well as mourning for the dead (cf. Gen 37:34 with 37:29).

וַיִּזְעַק זְעָקָה גְדֹלָה וּמָרָה, "And he cried out loudly and bitterly." In most of the uses of the verb זעק, "to call out, cry out," and the cognate noun זעקה, "cry, shout," both have the clear connotation of "plaintive cry," "call for help." Gerleman (104) presses the meaning here to the point of understanding Mordecai's outcry as a formal bringing of a legal action intended to move the king to legal intervention. The only thing in the context that could possibly imply that this outcry is intended as such a symbolic legal action is Mordecai's approach to the entrance to the "king's gate." This, however, is best explained as his way of attracting Esther's attention (see below), which is exactly the result (v 4). On similar grounds, Clines (299) interprets the cry as a gesture of protest against the king, which Mordecai would have attempted to take into the king's very presence except for the rule forbidding someone clothed in sackcloth from entering the king's gate (v 2b). However, nothing in the context suggests such a meaning (see esp. Hasel, *TDOT* זעק III.1, 4:116–19; cf. also Fox, 57). On the contrary, the actions that accompany the outcry, tearing the clothes and putting on sackcloth and ashes, imply something quite different from legal complaint or protest. They express grief, anguish, and lament (see above) and imply clearly that this cry is a "'cry of woe' in the sense of lamentation expressing grief over the imminent destruction of the Jewish people" (Hasel, *TDOT* 4:117).

2 וַיָּבוֹא עַד לִפְנֵי שַׁעַר־הַמֶּלֶךְ, "he went as far as the entrance to the royal court [lit. 'the king's gate']." Commentators have debated the exact intent of Mordecai's actions in vv 1–2, without conclusive results, for the narrator leaves us once again to read between the lines. His actions can hardly, however, be occasioned simply by self-reproach over having provoked Haman (Clines, 299; Fox, 57). Nor is it likely that it is his grief and anguish that is intended to get the queen's attention (Haller, Ringgren, Anderson). This is effected, rather, by the fact that he expresses his grief and anguish not just publicly (v 1) but right up to the entrance to the royal court itself, where it was bound to come to Esther's attention.

4 וַתָּבוֹאינָה נַעֲרוֹת אֶסְתֵּר . . . וַיַּגִּידוּ לָהּ, "Esther's maids . . . told her about this." The Hebrew clause has no object, as is often the case when the object is clear from context. The content of Esther's inquiry, literally "what is this and why is it?" (v 5), and Mordecai's response, which follows (which is to tell her what has happened to him and the amount of Haman's bribe, and to give her a copy of the edict, vv 7–8), make the implied object clear. The information communicated to Esther by her maids and eunuchs must have been limited to Mordecai's actions and attire and those of the Jews of Susa (v 3).

וַתִּתְחַלְחַל הַמַּלְכָּה מְאֹד, "and the queen was greatly distressed." Esther's distress (on the meaning of the verb, see *Notes*) can only be occasioned by the grief and anguish expressed by the actions and attire of Mordecai and the Jews of Susa (see the previous *Comment*). Her distress cannot be occasioned by the coming annihilation of the Jews, for, as the sequel shows, she does not yet know of Haman's terrible decree. Obviously, however, from the force of the verb, she believes that Mordecai's attire and actions mean that something very serious has transpired.

וַתִּשְׁלַח בְּגָדִים לְהַלְבִּישׁ אֶת־מָרְדֳּכַי, lit. "she sent garments to clothe Mordecai." Fox (59–60) voices the opinion that Esther's sending of garments to Mordecai exposes her superficiality. In his view "the meaning and cause of Mordecai's behavior does not seem to have mattered to her. If she could have gotten rid of the unpleasantness, that would have been enough" (59). But this hardly fits with the narrator's positive characterization of her throughout. It seems much more plausible (with Paton, 216; Clines, 300) that her purpose was to make it possible for him to come into the palace and inform her of the reason for his actions and attire, since entry in sackcloth was forbidden. This is strongly suggested by her subsequent action, sending her eunuch Hathach to inquire why Mordecai laments (v 5).

וְלֹא קִבֵּל, "he would not accept them." The narrator leaves us once again to surmise what Mordecai's reason for refusing might have been. A number of commentators (e.g., Clines, Paton) accept Josephus' explanation that it was "because the sad occasion that made him put it on had not yet ceased." Moore (48), however, opts for Anderson's explanation, based on Talmudic Judaism's stress on not making a public display of personal sorrow, that Mordecai refused because it was a matter of dire public calamity, not personal sorrow. But the narrator gives us no clue, and his refusal might well have been caused by both considerations.

8 לְהַרְאוֹת אֶת־אֶסְתֵּר וּלְהַגִּיד לָהּ וּלְצַוּוֹת עָלֶיהָ, "to show Esther, to inform her, and to command her." These three succinct, hence emphatic, infinitival clauses express the purpose/result for which Mordecai gave Hathach a copy of the text of Haman's edict. The object of both the first two infinitives is left unexpressed. This is common in Hebrew when the object intended has just been expressed or is otherwise clear from the context, so the unexpressed object of both infinitives must be Haman's edict. The first two infinitives can hardly imply that Esther was illiterate (as is implied by NAB, NIV, NRSV, and RSV, which render the second verb "to explain"). If she were, there would be no point in *showing* the document to her (Fox, 60), and it is a forced interpretation to infer that the edict was in Persian and that Esther could not read it (suggested by Paton, 218; Clines, 301). The verb להגיד most frequently means "to tell, report, announce" (and only means "to explain" with objects such as "riddle, dream"). Hence, the narrative probably implies that Hathach was to show the edict to Esther to read and also to tell her about the situation, presumably including at least the further background information about which Mordecai had informed him (see v 7; so NEB, REB; Fox, 59). Alternatively, but less likely, the two infinitives could be meant as hendiadys (two words intended to convey a single meaning): "to show Esther for her information" (so JB, NJB).

12 וַיַּגִּידוּ לְמָרְדֳּכָי אֵת דִּבְרֵי אֶסְתֵּר, lit. "they told to Mordecai Esther's words." The plural here is best understood as the narrator's use of the indefinite subject "they" (for which see *IBHS* § 4.4.2; Brockelmann, *Syntax,* § 36c), which is the virtual equivalent of the passive. This is a deliberate change by the narrator, not an error in the textual transmission. At this critical juncture in the development of the scene, the narrator has switched from indirect discourse (episode 2, vv 5–9) to direct discourse (episode 3, vv 10–17; see *Form/Structure/Setting*) in order to foreground the contents of the communication. Thus, he dispenses with the detailed report of the movements of the necessary intermediary (cf. Bardtke, 332) and uses the indefinite subject for that intermediary. In v 15 he omits any reference to such at all. However, a number of commentators (e.g., Paton, 221–22; Moore, 46, 50), puzzled by the plural verb since heretofore the only messenger has been Hathach, opt to follow the LXX and OL and read "he [Hathach] told," or to emend the verb to the passive (cf. *BHS* n.). But, both the change to the passive and the singular reading of the LXX and OL translators are attempts to handle an apparent difficulty, and they miss the literary development of the scene (see *Form/Structure/Setting*).

14 רֶוַח וְהַצָּלָה יַעֲמוֹד לַיְּהוּדִים מִמָּקוֹם אַחֵר, lit. "will relief and deliverance arise for the Jews from any other place?" In my opinion, two problems with the translation and understanding of this clause have precluded a coherent understanding of vv

13–14. (1) The expression מקום אחר, lit. "another place," has been understood by both ancient (e.g., Josephus and the Targums to Esther) and modern (e.g., Gerleman, *Studien zu Esther,* 21–22; Moore, 50; Paton, 22–23) commentators as a surrogate for or veiled allusion to God. Often cited (e.g., by Moore) in favor of this understanding has been the use in Talmudic times of המקום, lit. "the place," as a surrogate for God. Recent discussion, however, has demonstrated that this interpretation can no longer be maintained. Apart from the fact that such late usage cannot be assumed for Esther, taking "place" as a reference to God yields the rendering "from another God," an expression whose implications are utterly inadmissable (Ackroyd, *ASTI* 5 [1966–67] 83). Further, taking the compound expression "another place" as a reference to God (thus, e.g., Haupt, *AJSL* 24 [1907–8] 136; Brockington, 235; Talmon, *VT* 13 [1963] 429) creates implications equally inadmissable, for the stark contrast set up thereby between the divine deliverance and the deliverance that Esther might achieve by her appeal to the king (cf. Clines, 302) necessarily implies that the latter is not from God. This flies in the face of the clear implication of the whole text, and particularly v 14c, that Esther's position and actions are the outworking of divine providence (see the discussion of the role of God in the story in *Theme and Purpose* in the *Introduction* to Esther). Hence, the expression "another place" must refer to some other human source of deliverance (see esp. Ackroyd, *ASTI* 5 [1966–67] 82–84; Fox, 63).

(2) The clause has almost always been understood as a positive statement: "relief and deliverance will arise for the Jews from another place." However, this reading of the text produces several problems most difficult to explain (Wiebe, *CBQ* 53 [1991] 413–15).

(a) Given the facts of the story that the narrator has emphasized, such as the character of the king, the power of Haman's position, the diabolical nature of his edict, and the irrevocability of Persian law, a plausible source for another human agency that could deliver the Jews is hard to imagine. Those suggested, e.g., other Jewish officials, a Jewish armed revolt, or the goodwill of the inhabitants of the empire (so Clines, 302; id., *Esther Scroll,* 42–43), seem lamentably implausible. True, Mordecai's confidence in the existence of such a source can be explained by a trust in divine providence, but there is simply nothing in the story even suggesting that the narrator characterizes Mordecai as a man of such firm faith and piety except the interpretation of this sentence as a statement (cf. the discussion of Fox, 189–91, 244–45). In fact, in the only other place where Mordecai evinces some trust in providence, v 14c, it is stated in a most allusive manner indeed: "Who knows if it is not for a time like this that you have become queen?"

(b) If this first clause of the apodosis (v 14b) is taken as a statement, it is most difficult to make sense of the second clause (v 14c), which states that Esther and her "father's house" will perish (Wiebe, *CBQ* 53 [1991] 412–13). Why would Esther and her whole family perish when the rest of the Jews are delivered? Since the narrative gives us not the slightest hint, the explanations suggested amount to mere guesses. The two most common are the judgment of God (so, e.g., Clines, 302; Fox, 62; Moore, 50; a possibility that is much less plausible since "another place" does not refer to God) and Jewish retribution (so, e.g., Brockington, 235; Fox; Moore). These explanations are even less plausible when it is noted that the expression "your father's house" refers primarily (indeed, as far as we know from the narrative, exclusively) to Mordecai and his family. Apart from the concept of family solidarity (whose operation in this setting and date is at least questionable), why would either divine judgment or Jewish vengeance fall upon Mordecai for Esther's presumed cowardice and failure (see Wiebe, *CBQ* 53 [1991] 412–13)?

(c) The particle כִּי, which introduces v 14, has its causal force, "for, because," implying that what follows gives in some sense the reason for Mordecai's statement in v 13 that Esther will not be any more safe in the palace from Haman's edict than all the rest of the Jews. However, when v 14b is taken as a positive statement, the threat to Esther and her family in 14c is inexplicable (see above). Hence, it does not function at all well as a reason or explanation for Mordecai's statement in v 13.

Because of these difficulties, Wiebe (*CBQ* 53 [1991] 413–15) proposes that the clause is not a statement but a question. The fact that the clause has none of the regular Hebrew interrogative particles is not a serious impediment, since interrogative clauses often are unmarked in BH, doubtless signaled by a rising intonation (in addition to the references for such unmarked questions cited by Wiebe, 414, n. 20, cf. *GBH* § 161a; *IBHS* § 18.1.c n. 1). Indeed, such unmarked questions are more frequent in LBH texts, such as Esther, than in SBH (Wiebe). In context the question is a positive rhetorical question, which intends thereby to make a strong negative statement (on such "questions," see Driver, *JANES* 5 [1973] 107–14; esp. Hyman, *HS* 24 [1983] 17–25). The problems occasioned by taking 14b as a statement (noted above), are completely relieved by recognizing that it is a positive rhetorical question expressing a strong negation. Mordecai is not postulating that deliverance will arise for the Jews from some mysterious, unexpressed source. Rather, by affirming that Esther is the only possible source of deliverance for the Jews, he is attempting to motivate her to act. With this understanding of the text, the reason for the demise of Esther and her family, including Mordecai, is not some unknown cause at which we can only guess. On the contrary, the cause is clear and unequivocal: the threatened annihilation of the Jews. Further, v 14 then functions as a coherent explanation why Esther will not escape destruction in the king's palace any more than other Jews (v 13): when it is learned that she is Jewish, she will perish with the rest of the Jews. Finally, it is much clearer in English in such a context as this to transpose the clause from a question to the negative statement implied (on such transformations, see Hyman, *HS* 24 [1983] 18–19).

וּמִי יוֹדֵעַ אִם־לְעֵת כָּזֹאת הִגַּעַתְּ לַמַּלְכוּת, "And who knows if it is not for a time like this that you have become queen?" Mordecai's statement, made in the form of a rhetorical question, that her appeal is the only hope the Jews have is highly emphatic. Consequently, the "who knows?" of this question does not express doubt or skepticism about the providential purpose of her position as queen, or mere possibility. On the contrary, it expresses a confident hope (cf. Jonah 3:9; Clines, 302; see the role of God in the story in *Theme and Purpose* in the *Introduction* to Esther).

16 וְצוּמוּ עָלַי וְאַל־תֹּאכְלוּ וְאַל־תִּשְׁתּוּ שְׁלֹשֶׁת יָמִים לַיְלָה וָיוֹם, lit. "Fast for me. Do not eat and do not drink for three days, night and day." The Jewish community has already been fasting upon hearing of Haman's edict of annihilation (v 3). This fast is not the fast that accompanies grief and mourning (contra Clines, 302; the crisis lies in the future) but surely the fast of intercession (cf., e.g., 1 Kgs 21:27; Jonah 3:5–8; Neh 9:1). The fast Esther requests is clearly intercessory, for she defines its objective as עָלַי, "on my behalf." As has often been noted (cf. esp Clines, 302; id., *Esther Scroll,*

36), this is an exceptionally severe fast. Fasting normally lasted from morning to night (cf. Judg 20:26; 2 Sam 1:12). There is a significant stress, then, both on intercession with God and on the seriousness of that which occasions it. The order "night and day" probably has no special significance, since in the OT the (twenty-four-hour) day began in the evening (cf. the temporal enumeration of Gen 1). Also, although our narrator makes no allusion to the date here, the date of the drawing up and publication of the decree to annihilate the Jews, given in 3:12, was the day before Passover (see the discussion in the *Explanation* to 3:7–11), the significance of which could hardly have escaped the notice of Jewish readers. Hence, the three-day fast that Esther decrees would also have begun on the eve of Passover and so would have abolished that celebration, despite the law of Exod 12 (Clines, *Esther Scroll*, 36–37).

Explanation

The terrible crisis that faces the Jews of Persia was related in act 2 (see *Explanation* there) without even the most veiled or subtle allusion to Esther. Yet, both the position that, incognito, Esther has attained in the Persian court (act 1) and the narrator's characterization of her (act 2) could not but raise our hopes, however fleeting, that she might provide the means to deliver the Jews from Haman. Having so given us cause to place our hopes in Esther, our narrator wastes no words on alternative scenarios. This, the very next act, depicts the first step in the resolution of the problem of our story, the threatened annihilation of the Jews. It relates how, at Mordecai's express command, Esther assents to plead with the king on behalf of her people.

SCENE 1. MORDECAI AND ALL THE JEWS LAMENT OVER HAMAN'S EDICT (4:1–3)

This brief scene relates the anguish and sorrow with which Mordecai and all the Jews reacted to the king's edict, expressed by characteristic cultural expressions of lamentation and intercession (see *Comment*). It also leads directly to the dialogue between Mordecai and Esther that follows, for Mordecai expresses his grief and anguish neither in private nor simply publicly ("out into the city," v 1). Rather, he continues his loud and bitter lamentation right up to the entrance to the royal court. Presumably he would have entered the court itself and loudly wailed his lamentation "back and forth in front of the court of the harem" (2:11), if it were not forbidden to enter the court in sackcloth (v 2). No lament or sackcloth and ashes must be allowed to disturb the king's merry world of ostentatious pleasure (see act 1 above)! Mordecai's action is undoubtedly intended to bring the horrendous situation to the queen's attention as forcefully as possible (see *Comment*). As the narrator immediately relates, this is exactly what happens (v 4).

SCENE 2. AT MORDECAI'S COMMAND ESTHER CONSENTS TO APPEAL TO THE KING (4:4–17)

The second scene is devoted to the ensuing dialogue between Esther and Mordecai. In this dialogue Mordecai informs Esther of all that has happened and succeeds in gaining her consent to plead with the king for the life of her people, even though such an appeal entails great risk to herself. The scene is developed in three skillfully crafted episodes (see *Form/Structure/Setting*), in each of which the communication between Esther and Mordecai becomes more intense, direct, and detailed (cf. Clines, *Esther Scroll,* 34–35).

Episode 1. Mordecai refuses the clothing Esther sends him (4:4). In the first episode, Esther, greatly distressed at having learned of Mordecai's condition from her maids and eunuchs, attempts to remove his sackcloth by sending him clothing (presumably so that he could then enter the royal court and she could learn more directly what terrible calamity could prompt such actions). His refusal prompts further inquiry.

Episode 2. Mordecai orders Esther to appeal to the king (4:5–9). Episodes 2 and 3, in contrast to the first, report the dialogue between Esther and Mordecai, communicated through an intermediary, since Mordecai must remain outside the royal court. The second episode, reported in indirect discourse, retards the pace of narration by relating in some detail the identity and actions of the intermediary, Hathach (see *Form/Structure/Setting*). This dialogue is twofold, consisting of Esther's query about what was going on and why it had happened (vv 5–6) and Mordecai's response (vv 7–8). In his response, Mordecai tells Hathach "all that had happened to him and the exact amount of money Haman had promised to pay into the royal treasury for the destruction of the Jews." Now it becomes clear what our narrator meant by the statement that "Mordecai learned of all that had been done" (v 1). His sources were such that he could learn even the amount of the bribe that Haman promised to the king for the authority to annihilate the Jews (v 7; cf. 3:21–22). In addition, he has Hathach take her a copy of the edict, both to show it to her and to tell her all about the situation (see *Comment*). Finally, he does not just urge her or plead with her to appeal to the king, as a lowly official in the royal bureaucracy would be expected to do in addressing the queen. Rather, he *commands* her to do so, apparently exercising his authority as her parent/guardian. This is an authority that she accords him, as our narrator has already emphasized by repetition (2:10, 20; see *Explanation* to 2:19–23) and as the sequel demonstrates. The episode closes with the summary statement (v 9) that Hathach conveyed to Esther all that Mordecai had said.

Episode 3. Esther consents to appeal to the king (4:10–17). In the third episode our narrator changes his style. Now using *direct* discourse, he reports the very words that Esther and Mordecai exchange, and he does so with only the barest of allusions to the intermediary involved (see *Form/Structure/Setting*). By so doing, he signals that this is the high point of the scene. The exchange is threefold: (1) Esther's objection to Mordecai's order, v 11; (2) Mordecai's response to her objection, vv 13–14; and (3) her final assent and agreement to appeal to the king, v 16. Esther objects to Mordecai's order by informing him that to go to the king without being summoned can only be done at the risk of her very life. Once again the narrator leaves us to surmise the reason behind Esther's objection (apart from the threat to her life). Her hesitancy should perhaps not be regarded as a sign of cowardice, for crucial to her response is that she has not been called into the king's presence for thirty days, a fact doubtless unknown to Mordecai (Clines, 301). Her hesitancy, then, is not only because she doubts she would survive to make the appeal but also because she questions the efficacy of *her* appeal to the king, since her favor with Ahasuerus is apparently at a very low ebb.

Mordecai's response is blunt and to the point. His first words to her, "Do not imagine that you will escape in the king's palace any more than all the Jews" (v

13), are not to be seen as a reproach, still less as a threat. They simply stress that she is in as mortal danger staying out of the king's presence as entering in (cf. Clines, 301–2). His next words (v 14) constitute an explanation of this fact. If she remains silent, he informs her, deliverance will not arise from anywhere else (formulating his statement as an emphatic rhetorical question, see *Comment*), and she and her whole family will perish (himself included). Finally, as the climax to his appeal, he makes the suggestion (see *Comment*), which she needs to take seriously, that there is providential purpose in her position: perhaps she has become queen for just such a time as this.

Esther not only makes no further objection; she reveals no uncertainty whatsoever as to the course of action that she must take: she immediately issues commands that the local community ("all the Jews to be found in Susa") should join her and her maids in a three-day twenty-four-hour fast, v 16. Clearly, Mordecai's veiled suggestion that divine providence might have brought her to the position of being the queen of Persia has borne fruit. The fast is intercessory ("on my behalf"; see *Comment*), the intercession obviously relating to both the danger she will face and the critical nature of her effort (v 14). Consequently, the fast is distinguished by its severity. It is not only a full twenty-four-hour fast (hence unusually strict), but it will also abolish Passover, the most important festival of the Jewish liturgical year (because of its timing, already set by the date given for the issuance of Haman's decree in 3:12; see *Comment*). The contrast between Jews and Persians is dramatic. Persians feast extravagantly (as the narrator has previously sardonically emphasized at length; cf. 1:4), but Jews must engage in the severest of fasts (Clines, *Esther Scroll*, 36).

Esther's reply is one of firm conviction. Her final words, "If I perish, I perish," are not a despairing expression of resignation to the inevitable (Paton, 226) but courageous determination (Clines, 303). Responsibility for progress in the resolution of the crisis of our story has now devolved upon her.

Hope for the Jews' deliverance from annihilation at the hands of Haman and his edict has emerged. It may seem, indeed, a tenuous hope, lying as it does in the hands of a queen who is currently out of favor and one "whose life hitherto has been devoted to beauty treatments and the royal bed" (Fox, 67). However, the narrator has subtly brought the providence of God into the picture, both by the fast that Esther has ordered for the Jewish community and by Mordecai's suggestion that there may indeed be providential purpose behind her position as queen (v 14d). Furthermore, he has portrayed Esther not as one who has passively accepted all that has transpired but rather as one who has been actively involved in the events surrounding her (see *Explanation* to 2:5–11). May she not, perhaps, be up to the challenge?

Act 4
Esther Begins Her Appeal: She Invites the King and Haman to a Banquet (5:1–8)

Bibliography

Brockington, L. H. *The Hebrew Text of the Old Testament: The Readings Adopted by the Translators of the New English Bible.* Oxford: Oxford UP, 1973. **Clines D. J. A.** *The Esther Scroll: The Story of the Story.* JSOTSup 30. Sheffield: JSOT, 1984. **Dommershausen, W.** *Die Estherrolle.* Stuttgart: Katholisches Bibelwerk, 1968. **Dorothy, C. V.** "The Books of Esther: Structure, Genre, and Textual Integrity." Diss., Claremont, 1989. **Haupt, P.** "Critical Notes on Esther." *AJSL* 24 (1907–8) 97–106 (= Moore, *Studies,* 1–90). **Moore, C. A.** *Daniel, Esther and Jeremiah: The Additions.* AB 44. Garden City, NY: Doubleday, 1977. **Murphy, R. E.** *Wisdom Literature: Job, Proverbs, Ruth, Canticles, Ecclesiastes, and Esther.* FOTL 13. Grand Rapids, MI: Eerdmans, 1981. **Radday, Y. T.** "Esther with Humour." In *On Humour and the Comic in the Hebrew Bible,* ed. Y. T. Radday and A. Brenner. Sheffield: Almond, 1990. 295–313. **Rudolph, W.** "Textkritisches zum Estherbuch." *VT* 4 (1954) 89–90. **Speiser, E. A.** *Genesis.* AB. Garden City: Doubleday, 1974.

Translation

SCENE 1. ESTHER INVITES THE KING AND HAMAN TO A BANQUET (5:1–5a)
Time: 1/16 or 1/17, year 12

Episode 1. Esther gains an audience with the king (5:1–2)

1 *On the third day, Esther donned her royal robes*[a] *and stood in the inner court of the palace*[b] *in front of the king's quarters,*[b] *as the king was sitting on his royal throne in the audience hall*[c] *facing the entrance to the building.*[d] 2 *And when the king saw Queen Esther standing in the court, she won his favor and he extended to her the gold scepter which he was holding. Esther approached and touched the end of the scepter.*

Episode 2. Esther invites the king and Haman to a banquet (5:3–5a)

3 *And the king said to her, "What is it, Queen Esther? What is your request? Even if it's for half of my empire, it shall be granted you!"* 4 *Esther replied, "If it please the king, let the king and Haman come today*[a] *to the banquet which I have prepared for him."*
5a *And the king said, "Quick! Bring Haman so that we may do as Esther has asked."*[a]

SCENE 2. ESTHER AGAIN INVITES THE KING AND HAMAN TO A BANQUET (5:5b–8)
Time: 1/16 or 1/17, year 12

5b *So the king and Haman came to the banquet which Esther had prepared.* 6 *And during the wine course,*[a] *the king said to Esther, "What do you want and what is it that you request? Even if it's for half of my kingdom, it shall be granted and it shall be done."*[b] 7 *And Esther replied, "My wish and my request? . . .* 8 *Well, if I have found favor with the king,*[a] *and if it pleases the king to grant what I ask and to fulfill my request, let the king and Haman come to the banquet which I shall prepare for them,*[b] *and tomorrow I will do as the king has said."*[c]

Notes

1.a. Lit. "clothed herself in royalty [i.e., 'royally']." Rudolph (*VT* 4 [1954] 89, followed by Bardtke; cf. Moore, 55; *BHS* n. a) argues that a word is missing before מלכות, "royalty," but the use of a substantive as an adv acc of manner is acceptable Heb. (cf. *IBHS* § 10.2.2.e). Moore (55) supplies לְבוּשׁ, "clothing," appealing to 6:8; 8:15 and to the LXX and OL, but לְבוּשׁ is semantically required in 6:8; 8:15, contrary to the situation here. The LXX in actuality supports the MT reading, rather than the opposite, for, although the LXX in this clause presents a contrast with ἐξεδύσατο τὰ ἱμάτια τῆς θεραπείας, "she took off the clothing of waiting (upon God)," which immediately precedes, it reads περιεβάλετο τὴν δόξαν αὐτῆς, "she put on her splendor." (Contrast the A-Text, which reads περιεβάλετο τὰ ἱμάτια τῆς δόξης, "she put on her clothing of splendor.")

1.b. Lit. "the house of the king"; see *Comment.*

1.c. Lit. "house of royalty," probably referring to the throne room or audience hall; see *Comment.*

1.d. Lit. הַבַּיִת, "the house"; see *Comment.*

4.a. A few Heb. MSS and Syr omit "today," but, since the next clause makes clear that the same day is meant, it is much more likely to have been an omission in these texts than a later addition to MT.

5.a. Lit. "the word of Esther."

6.a. Lit. "in the banquet of wine."

6.b. Lit. "What is your wish? It shall be granted you. And what is your request up to half of the kingdom? It shall be done."

8.a. Lit. "in the king's eyes."

8.b. It is possible that the word מחר, "tomorrow," should be inserted in this clause either after המן, "Haman" (Brockington, 236; cf. id., *Hebrew Text,* 100; NEB, REB, RSV) or after להם, "for them," at the end of the clause (Bardtke, 336; Haller, 126; Moore, 57). Moore explains its absence in the MT on the grounds that the LXX translation indicates that the latter was its position in the Heb. text, and hence it was omitted by haplogr. But, the LXX translation is a free and natural one which, to quote Moore himself, is "not concerned with preserving the Hebrew word order or with giving consistent, mechanical one-for-one translations of the Hebrew" (*Additions,* 162). Hence (apart from the fact that the adv clause ἐπι τὴν αὔριον, "on the morrow," is *not* placed at the end of the clause by the LXX translator), the LXX can hardly provide evidence for the order of the Heb. original. The MT is to be preferred. The adv "tomorrow" in the next clause makes the time reference clear.

8.c. Lit. "do according to the king's word."

Form/Structure/Setting

The opening of this, the fourth act, is begun by the characteristic use of a temporal clause introduced with ויהי, a construction that frequently introduces a new section of narrative. The temporal phrase used here, "on the third day," not only signals the start of a new act but closely relates it to the previous one, for that act closed with the Jewish community in Susa pledged to a three-day fast. The closure of the act is marked by the contrast between *Esther's* temporal reference to the activity of the *morrow* in v 8d and the narrator's temporal reference to *Haman's* actions on that *same day* in v 9, with which the next scene opens.

The act comprises two scenes, vv 1–5a and 5b–8, joined by a narrative transition, v 5b. Murphy's analysis of the structure into five coordinated sections (*Wisdom,* 163) expresses the sequence of events but does not capture the scenic division, namely, Esther and the king in the audience hall, vv 1–5a, vis-à-vis Esther, the king, *and Haman,* at her banquet, vv 5b–8. Dorothy's division into "Exposition, vv 1–2" and "Dialog: King and Esther, vv 3–8" ("Books of Esther," 285–86) hardly captures the structure of the section, let alone its scenic development.

The first scene, vv 1–5a, consists of two episodes, vv 1–2 and 3–5a. The first episode relates a scene that is filled with suspense: Esther's entry into the king's presence without being summoned. Given the significance of this episode, it is tempting to set it apart as a separate scene. However, since there is no change in venue or personae between vv 1–2 and 3–5a and since vv 1–2 provide the setting for vv 3–5a, it is far preferable to treat them as episodes of one scene.

The second episode involves a dialogue between the king and Esther, in which he asks the reason for her unsummoned appearance, following it with a promise of compliance containing a stereotyped phrase of extreme generosity. In reply she invites him and Haman to a banquet.

The second scene is introduced by a narrative transition, v 5b, which links it closely with the first scene. It is markedly parallel to the second episode of that scene. The king again asks what Esther's request is. He follows this question with another promise of compliance containing the same stereotyped phrase of extreme generosity, and Esther again invites him and Haman to another banquet, this time on the morrow.

The dialogues of both scenes 1 and 2 are closely bound together as one act by their close repetition of content and structure. The dialogue in the second scene, however, is more developed and emphatic in each of its elements than that of the first. Thus, in scene 1, after the king's stereotyped introductory question (v 3b), the king asks but once what her request is, followed by a promise of compliance (vv 3c–d). In scene 2, however, there is a dual question and a dual promise of compliance (vv 6b–c). Similarly, in scene 1 Esther prefaces her invitation to the banquet with only the polite phrase demanded by court protocol, "If it please the king, . . ." (v 4a). In scene 2, however, she considerably increases the courtesy and respect with which she makes her invitation. She begins with a query (v 7) that suggests that she is about to express her actual request, but she leaves the sentence incomplete and begins again (v 8; see *Comment*). When she does so, she prefaces the polite phrase used in her first invitation with a second one, this time consisting of an appeal to the favor of the king: "If I have found favor with the king, . . ." (v 8a; for the implications of such contrastive repetition, see *Explanation*).

Comment

1 וַתַּעֲמֹד, lit. "and she stood." In a context such as this, the verb עמד means not "to stand up" but "to stop, stay, remain standing" (cf. its use in 7:7). See also Haupt, *AJSL* 24 [1907–8] 139, and the discussion of the verb in Ruth 2:7.

בֵּית־הַמֶּלֶךְ, lit. "the house of the king." This term is used in both of the adverbial prepositional phrases that identify where Esther stood waiting: "in the inner court of the 'house of the king' in front of 'the house of the king.'" In the first phrase it means the whole palace complex. In the second the locale meant must be the inner portion of the palace reserved for the king's personal use; see the *Comment* on the expression in 2:13.

בְּבֵית הַמַּלְכוּת, lit. "in the house of royalty/kingship." The spatial arrangements intended here are somewhat obscure because the narrator uses identical terms for apparently different entities. Though in 1:9 this expression is clearly a synonym of בית המלך (lit. "the house of the king") in the sense of "palace (complex)," here it must refer to some portion of the king's private quarters (as it does in 2:16; see *Comment* there). Since the king is seated on his throne, it is most probable that it means "throne room." Whatever the exact spatial arrangement implied by these similar terms, it is clear from v 2 that Esther could be seen by the king seated in this room as she stood in front of the בית המלך, "king's quarters." Hence, the term בית at the end of the verse is best taken to refer to this part of the palace complex.

2 נָשְׂאָה חֵן בְּעֵינָיו, lit. "she lifted up/carried favor in his eyes." Again the narrator uses the active expression "she won his favor" rather than the more passive expression "found favor" (see v 8 below). See the discussion in *Comment* on the expression in 2:9, and note its use in 2:15, 17.

3 מַה־לָּךְ אֶסְתֵּר הַמַּלְכָּה, lit. "What is to/with you, Queen Esther?" Fox (281) argues that this colloquialism (when not part of the idiom מה ל-X מה ל-Y) "always suggests that the listener is disturbed or troubled in some way" and hence should be translated here "What troubles you?" However, besides the meaning that Fox notes, the idiom is used in a number of different contexts with a wide variety of nuances (e.g., "expostulation," Ezek 18:2; Jonah 1:6), including the sense "what do you want/wish?" (e.g., Josh 15:18; Judg 1:14). Note especially the contrast in its sense in Judg 18:3 and Judg 18:23, 24. Hence, the context must determine the nuance. Although the risk Esther has taken surely indicates that her purpose is fraught with danger, the second question that the king asks, "What is your request?" rather strongly implies that the idiom should be understood here as a request for what she desires rather than for what is troubling her.

6 בְּמִשְׁתֵּה הַיַּיִן, lit. "at the banquet of wine." Presumably there was a separate course at Persian banquets for the express purpose of drinking wine (see Fox, 67). It is most likely that this would have taken place at the end of the meal (cf. Fox, 67; Clines, 304). Banquets were the socially appropriate "window-dressing" and protocol for serious petitions and negotiations (see next *Comment*), and such a subject would not have been broached until the amenities had been observed.

7 וַתַּעַן אֶסְתֵּר וַתֹּאמַר שְׁאֵלָתִי וּבַקָּשָׁתִי, lit. "Esther answered and said, "My wish and my request . . ." In my opinion, this is unmistakably anacoluthon; i.e., the sentence begins with "My wish and my request . . ." but then breaks off and begins anew in v 8, without syntactical or logical completion (cf. Bardtke, 339). That the Masoretes so regarded it is evidenced by the verse division. However, all the modern English translations (except JB, NJB, and Moffatt) do not so understand the text. Rather, they interpret the two nouns "my wish and my request" as the subject of a complete sentence, for which the following verse is the predicate. Hence, they combine vv 7 and 8 and translate, "My petition and request is: If I have found favor . . . ," or the like. This translation necessarily implies that Esther's "petition and request" is to ask the king and Haman to come to the banquet that she will prepare on the morrow, but this is patently erroneous, for it is quite clear that this is *not* her request. The king demonstrates his understanding that the invitations to the banquets are but social "window-dressing," for after the meal is over and the wine course is served at each banquet (see *Comment* above), he asks Esther to name her "petition and request" (5:6; 7:2).

How, then, is the incomplete clause to be understood? Moore (56; cf. also Meinhold, 56 n. 14, 58) interprets the words as an affirmative reply, a response that is normally achieved in Hebrew by the repetition of the words of the question to which it is a reply (since BH had no word for "yes"; cf. Gen 18:15; 29:6; see Speiser, *Genesis,* 130). But this interpretation cannot be sustained, for it implies, even more clearly than the attempts to combine vv 7 and 8, that Esther's request is her invitation to the banquet.

Hence, we must conclude that Esther began as if she were going to state her petition but then broke off and instead invited the king and Haman to another banquet on the morrow. Does this imply that she hesitated through fear or indecision (so Haupt, *AJSL* 24 [1907–8] 140; cf. Fox, 71)? Perhaps so. But in my opinion, the clever way in which she induces the king virtually to grant her request before he knows what it is suggests that she knows full well what she is doing (see the next *Comment*), so we have treated these words as a query (cf. JB, NJB, Moffatt).

7–8 The discussion in the previous *Comment,* however, raises the interesting question of the reason for Esther's stratagem of inviting the king to *two* banquets. Why, since the matter of her request was so urgent and critical, did she not make her request known the instant that the king magnanimously indicated that he was willing to grant it, without inviting the king and Haman to even one banquet? The numerous suggestions made (e.g., that she wished to make the king merry with wine, that she perceived that this was not psychologically the right moment; cf. Paton, 234; Moore, 56) are all simply speculation, for they are prompted by nothing in the context.

According to Paton (234) it is "psychologically most improbable" that Esther would delay her request under such circumstances. Hence, with most commentators (e.g., Bardtke; Dommershausen; Moore; Murphy, *Wisdom*), he concludes that the true reason for Esther's delay lies not in any stratagem of hers at all but is purely literary: the author needs the postponement in order to relate the exaltation of Mordecai and the humiliation of Haman in 5:9–6:11 and to create suspense. However, such a need hardly explains the present narrative sequence (Fox, 71). For example, there would have been ample time before the first banquet for Haman's humiliation if the banquet had been set on the following day (as was the second banquet). The sequence certainly does create suspense, but this purpose is also hardly sufficient to explain the extant narrative sequence. Bardtke (339) argues that the author's narrative sequence creates this suspense by bringing in another moment of great risk for Esther (such as her appearing before the king unsummoned). According to Bardtke, this "great risk" is created by such possibilities as the king's changing his mind during the banquets, or Haman's learning that Esther was a Jewess. The author's skill is said to be evident in that Esther's hesitation expressed in the sharp break between v 7 and v 8 insinuates that she was conscious of this danger, but suspense surely could have been created in ways far more direct and evident than this. Indeed, suspense for us, the readers, who have the interests and concerns of Esther and Mordecai at heart, would have been much more effectively created if the postponement were effected by someone other than Esther—for example, if the king had shown reluctance to grant her request (cf. Fox, 71).

Clearly, all such explanations leave Esther's seemingly puzzling behavior unexplained and force us to conclude that a gifted narrator has lost his skill. On the contrary, surely the narrator's consummate skill throughout the book suggests that Esther's delay has purpose behind it and is not a result of the narrator's suddenly clumsy need to make room for Haman's humiliation and to create suspense. In this light, Fox's understanding (71–72) of Esther's purpose makes cogent and compelling sense. We must account for Esther's behavior in terms of *her* world. She is clearly the one who is taking the initiative and determining the course of events (see *Explanation*).

Explanation

SCENE 1. ESTHER INVITES THE KING AND HAMAN TO A BANQUET (5:1–5a)

Episode 1. Esther gains an audience with the king (5:1–2). Esther's firm conviction and resolution, expressed at the end of the last act in the orders she gave to Mordecai for a three-day fast on her behalf (4:16), clearly remained undiminished. On the third day (with the fast apparently still in progress), she donned her royal robes, took her life and her courage in hand—"If I perish, I perish!" (4:16)—and entered the king's presence. Our narrator skillfully retards the report of the results of this critical moment. He relates in great detail both Esther's position and that of the king in such a manner that we cannot doubt that she would be seen by the king: "she stood in the inner court of the palace in front of the king's residence, as the king was sitting on his royal throne in the royal residence in front of the entrance to the building" (v 1). In this way he artfully builds suspense as we wait for the result of Esther's action, the possible dire consequences of which still ring in our ears from her plea to Mordecai (4:11). The narrator further signals the significance of this moment by virtually beginning the act again. In v 2 he introduces the result of Esther's action with a second temporal clause that begins with the same syntactic construction with which he began v 1 (see *Form/Structure/Setting*). As she had done previously (with both Hegai, 2:9, and the king himself, 2:17), Esther wins the king's favor and is accepted into his presence.

Episode 2. Esther invites the king and Haman to a banquet (5:3–5a). That Esther would risk her life with an appearance in the king's presence unbidden obviously indicates a matter of great import, and so the king immediately asks what her request is (v 3a). Then, demonstrating the favor with which she has been received, he adds a promise of extreme generosity: "Even if it's for half my empire, it shall be granted you." Though this is doubtless a stereotyped expression that no one took literally, it contributes further to the depiction of the king's predilection for excess and the quicksilver nature of his temperament. In the only direct quote we have had from him prior to this one (cf. Radday, "Esther with Humour," 305), he consigned a whole people to oblivion with a casual and offhand comment (3:11). Now, without a word from Esther about the meaning of her sudden appearance, she who has not been summoned for thirty days is simply given carte blanche! Esther does not immediately respond to this surprising offer, which is quite the opposite of what she feared might happen (4:16). Instead, in keeping with the polite requirements of protocol and etiquette, she invites the king and Haman to a banquet (v 4). The king immediately commands Haman's attendance (v 5a).

SCENE 2. ESTHER AGAIN INVITES THE KING AND HAMAN TO A BANQUET (5:5b–8)

At the wine course during the banquet, the king again asks Esther what her request is, and again adds the same magnanimous promise of compliance. Esther again responds with an invitation to the king and Haman to attend a banquet, this time on the morrow. This delay in Esther's presenting her request to the king does not result from the literary needs of a clumsy narrator (see *Comment*). Rather, the procedure is part of a shrewd and deliberate plan in which Esther is taking the initiative and determining the course of events, as a close reading of the narrative will clearly show. First, when the king for the second time asks what her request is (v 6), she begins her response with a query, "My request and my petition?" (v 7), suggesting that she is about to express her actual request, but she then breaks off and begins again (v 8; see *Comment*). With this near-revelation of her request, she both indicates the seriousness of its nature and piques the king's curiosity (Fox, 73). Second, she is now even more diplomatic and attentive to ceremonial forms and courtesies than in the first invitation, for here she uses the doubly polite phrase "If I have found favor with the king and if it pleases the king" (see *Form/Structure/Setting*). Third, and most important, she uses the second conditional clause in a manner significantly different from the way she used it before. Its subject is not now the invitation to the banquet, as in scene 2. Rather, its subject here is the infinitival phrase that follows. She says, literally, "If granting what I ask and fulfilling my request pleases the king, let him . . . come to the banquet." Unmistakably, with Esther's subtle restatement of the invitation, the king's future compliance (which he can hardly now refuse) has become virtually a public pledge to grant her unstated request (see *Comment*)! This careful and subtle development in the two dialogues demonstrates that Esther is not stumbling blindly in the dark, inexplicably inviting the king to two unneeded banquets, dangerous because of the time they consume, and it demonstrates that the narrator has not clumsily introduced a development that leaves his readers stumbling blindly in the dark, wondering what is going on. Esther is shrewdly and subtly pursuing a well-designed plan, by which she has maneuvered the king into committing himself in advance.

Finally, the king thus far in the story has made decisions only after seeking the counsel of his advisors. Her unmasking of Haman, then, must permit Haman no time to dissuade the king. So not only must Haman be present at the banquet, but she must accomplish the task in such a way as to prompt the king to immediate action.

The scene and the act end with Esther's affirmation that on the morrow she "will do as the king has said"; i.e., she will make her request known. The subtle power and brilliance of this development could hardly be better caught than by Cline's assessment (*Esther Scroll*, 37):

> And by the end of her speech Esther has been able to represent what *she* wants as a matter of doing 'what the king has said' (v. 8), as though it were she rather than he who was doing the favour. The dialogue of vv 3–7, we see, has all been a delicate play of bargaining in which Esther manages to achieve her goal without ever disclosing the object of the play. The text of the narrative is immensely rich and subtle, evidencing at every point the craftsmanship of the narrator.

With Esther's affirmation at the end of v 8 ringing in our ears that at the morrow's banquet she will make her request known, we turn to the sequel with the confident expectation that our narrator will quickly satisfy our curiosity about the outcome, an outcome of such moment to our protagonists and to us, the readers, both of whom now have so much invested in it. But this he does not do. Instead he breaks off the plot line in mid course, holding us in suspense, and in the next act takes us in a different direction entirely: he turns once again to the relationship between Haman and Mordecai.

Act 5
Haman's Stratagem Backfires: He Is Humiliated and Mordecai Honored (5:9–6:14)

Bibliography

Barthélemy, D., et al. *Preliminary and Interim Report on the Hebrew Old Testament Text Project.* Vol. 2. New York: United Bible Societies, 1979. **Bergey, R. L.** "Late Linguistic Features in Esther." *JQR* 75 (1984) 66–78. **Bivar, A. D. H.** "Achaemenid Coins, Weights and Measures." In *The Cambridge History of Iran: Vol. 2. The Median and Achaemenian Periods,* ed. I. Gershevitch. Cambridge: Cambridge UP, 1985. 610–39. **Brockington, L. H.** *The Hebrew Text of the Old Testament: The Readings Adopted by the Translators of the New English Bible.* Oxford: Oxford UP, 1973. **Clines, D. J. A.** *The Esther Scroll: The Story of the Story.* JSOTSup 30. Sheffield: JSOT, 1984. **Dommershausen, W.** *Die Estherrolle.* Stuttgart: Katholisches Bibelwerk, 1968. **Dorothy, C. V.** "The Books of Esther: Structure, Genre, and Textual Integrity." Diss., Claremont, 1989. **Driver, G. R.** "Problems and Solutions." *VT* 4 (1954) 224–45. **Gordis, R.** "Studies in the Esther Narrative." *JBL* 95 (1976) 43–58. **Haupt, P.** "Critical Notes on Esther." *AJSL* 24(1907–8) 97–106 (= Moore, *Studies,* 1–90). **Humphreys, W. L.** "The Story of Esther and Mordecai: An Early Jewish Novella." In *Saga, Legend, Tale, Novella, Fable: Narrative Forms in Old Testament Literature,* ed. G. Coats. JSOTSup 35. Sheffield: JSOT, 1985. 97–113. **Murphy, R. E.** *Wisdom Literature: Job, Proverbs, Ruth, Canticles, Ecclesiastes, and Esther.* FOTL 13. Grand Rapids, MI: Eerdmans, 1981. **Powell, M. A.** "Weights and Measures." *ABD* 6:897–908. **Radday, Y. T.** "Esther with Humour." In *On Humour and the Comic in the Hebrew Bible,* ed. Y. T. Radday and A. Brenner. Sheffield: Almond, 1990. 295–313. **Wiebe, J.** "Zeresh." *ABD* 6:1083.

Translation

SCENE 1. HAMAN'S HUBRIS: HIS WIFE AND HIS FRIENDS PERSUADE HIM TO ASK THE KING TO HANG MORDECAI (5:9–14)
Time: late morning or early afternoon, 1/16 or 1/17, year 12

9 *So Haman left the banquet*[a] *that day full of joy and light of heart. But, when he saw*
Mordecai in the royal court,[b] *and he did not stand up or show any fear in his presence,*[c]
Haman was filled with rage.
10 *But he kept himself under control and went home.*
Then he sent for[a] *his friends and Zeresh his wife*
11 *and recited to them the splendor of*
his wealth, the great number of his sons, all[a] *the ways in which the king had promoted*
him, and how he had elevated him above his[b] *other nobles and courtiers.*[b]
12 *"Further-*
more," Haman said, "Queen Esther had no one come with the king to the banquet which
she had prepared except me, and tomorrow also I have been summoned to come to her[a]
with the king.
13 *But all of this means nothing to me as long as I see Mordecai the Jew in*
attendance at the king's court."[a]
14 *And his wife Zeresh and all his friends said to him, "Have a gallows erected, fifty*
cubits high, and in the morning speak to the king and have Mordecai hanged upon it.
Then go with the king to the banquet full of joy." This proposal pleased[a] *Haman, and*
so he had the gallows built.

SCENE 2. HAMAN'S HUMILIATION: THE KING COMMANDS HIM TO HONOR MORDECAI (6:1–11)

Episode 1. The king discovers the failure to reward Mordecai (6:1–3)
Time: early morning, 1/17 or 1/18, year 12

6:1 *That night the king could not sleep.*[a] *So he ordered the record of daily court events*[b]
to be brought in; and it was read to him. 2 *And it was found recorded therein that Mordecai*
had provided information about Bigthan[a] *and Teresh, two of the king's eunuchs from*
those who guarded the entrance to the king's quarters,[b] *who had sought to assassinate*[c]
him. 3 *So the king asked, "What honor or distinction has been conferred upon Mordecai*
for this?" And the king's attendants[a] *said, "Nothing has been done for him."*

Episode 2. Haman advises the king how to reward the man whom the king wishes to honor (6:4–10)
Time: early morning, 1/17 or 1/18, year 12

4 *"Who is in the court?" the king asked, just as Haman was entering*[a] *the outer court*
of the king's residence[b] *in order to speak to the king about having Mordecai hung on the*
gallows which he had prepared for him. 5 *The king's attendants answered, "Haman is*
standing there in the court." So the king said, "Have him come in."
6 *When Haman entered, the king said to him, "What should be done for the man*
whom the king desires to honor?" And Haman thought,[a] *"Now, whom would the king*
desire to honor more than me?"[b] 7 *So he answered the king, "The man whom the king*
desires to honor . . . 8 *let royal robes be brought which the king has worn and a horse*
which the king has ridden, one with a royal diadem upon its head.[a] 9 *Then let the robes*
and the horse be handed over[a] *to a member of the nobility.*[b] *Let him see that the man*
whom the king desires to honor is robed[c] *and led*[c] *through the city square mounted on*
the horse. And let there be proclaimed[c] *before him, 'This is what is done for the man*
whom the king desires to honor!'"
10 *Then the king said to Haman, "Quick! Take the robes and the horse, just as you*
have said, and do this for Mordecai the Jew who is an official in the court.[a] *Omit noth-*
ing from all that you have said!"

Episode 3. Haman so honors Mordecai (6:11)
Time: late morning, 1/17 or 1/18, year 12

11 *So Haman got the robes and the horse. He robed Mordecai and led him through the*
city square mounted on the horse. And he proclaimed before him, "This is what is done
for the man whom the king desires to honor!"

SCENE 3. HAMAN'S END: HIS WIFE AND HIS FRIENDS PREDICT HIS DOWNFALL (6:12–14)
Time: early afternoon, 1/17 or 1/18, year 12

12 *Mordecai then returned to the royal court,*[a] *but Haman hurried home mourning*
and in shame.[b] 13 *And he related to Zeresh his wife and all his friends all that had*
happened to him. Then his advisers[a] *and Zeresh his wife said to him, "Since Mordecai,*
who has already begun to defeat you,[b] *belongs to the Jewish race,*[c] *you will not get the*
better of him, but you will most certainly fall before him."

[14]*While they were still talking with Haman, the king's eunuchs arrived and brought Haman in haste to the banquet that Esther had prepared.*

Notes

9.a. Lit. "went forth."

9.b. The lit. expression is "in the king's gate." For the meaning, see the *Comment* on 2:19.

9.c. Lit. "trembled before him." On the meaning, see *Comment.*

10.a. Lit. "sent and brought." The idiom refers to the custom of sending servants to escort guests.

11.a. כל, "all," is not be deleted with *BHS.* It is unusual but acceptable Heb. syntax; see *Comment.*

11.b. A few Heb. MSS add כל, "all," before "his nobles," while Syr adds the word before "courtiers" as well. The addition is clearly influenced by 3:1–2.

12.a. Lit. "summoned to her [or 'by her'?]." The idiom reflects the fact that a royal invitation brooks no refusal.

13.a. Lit. "sitting in the king's gate." For the meaning, see the *Comment* on 2:19.

14.a. Lit. "was pleasing before." A few Heb. MSS and Syr read the far more common idiom בעיני, "in the eyes of," instead of לפני, "before." MT is to be maintained (contra Bardtke, 340).

6:1.a. Lit. "the king's sleep fled." On the basis of the LXX reading, *ὁ κύριος ἀπέστησεν τὸν ὕπνον ἀπὸ τοῦ βασιλέως*, "the Lord removed sleep from the king" (which is followed by all the versions except Vg), Driver suggests that נדדה was read as ה׳ נֹדֵד, in which ה׳ was understood to be an abbreviation for יהוה, "LORD," and נֹדֵד, the polel stem "make to flee away" (*VT* 4 [1954] 238). However the translators of the versions may have read the text, such an intrepretation of the MT author's intentions is contradicted by the consistent avoidance of the name of God in the rest of Esther.

1.b. The Heb. phrase is ספר הזכרנות דברי הימים, lit. "the-book-of-the-records of the-events-of-the-days." Though the meaning of the phrase seems reasonably clear (given that the parallel phrase in 2:23 is the very common ספר דברי הימים, lit. "the book of the events of the days"), how to understand it syntactically is problematic. It cannot be taken as a four-membered constr phrase because of the definite article on הזכרנות. Semantically, it is difficult to understand the second phrase as in apposition to the first, with the meaning "annals/chronicles" (so NASV, NIV, NRSV, JB, NJB, RSV), for that meaning is exclusively expressed in the OT (more than some thirty times) by the full phrase ספר דברי הימים, lit. "the book of the events of the days," as in 2:23. It seems even less likely that זכרנות here means "memorable" or "notable," yielding the rendering "the chronicle of memorable events" or the like (so RSV, NAB, REB). Most likely we must understand the expression as a two-membered constr phrase consisting of fixed expressions (each of which is itself a constr phrase), "the-book-of-memoranda of the-events-of-the-days" (i.e., the record of current events). The first constr phrase, ספר הזכרנות, "the book of memoranda," may well be a calque (borrowed expression) in Heb. based upon the Aram. expression ספר דכרניא, "book of records," Ezra 4:15 (cf. also דכרונה, "memorandum," Ezra 6:2).

2.a. The Heb. reads *Bigṯānâ*, a variant of the name *Bigṯān* in 2:23.

2.b. Lit. "from those who guard the threshold."

2.c. Lit. "to send a hand against."

3.a. Lit. "the servants of the king who attend him."

4.a. To read אל חצר instead of לחצר (cf. *BHS* n.), understanding the loss of א through haplogr, is unnecessary (contra Bardtke).

4.b. Lit. "the house of the king," What must be intended here is not the palace in general but the king's private quarters. See *Comment* on 5:1.

6.a. Lit. "said in his heart."

6.b. This idiom, the comparative יותר מן, "more than," occurs elsewhere in BH only in Eccles 12:12. In SBH and elsewhere in LBH, the comparative is expressed by מן alone, without יותר. The lateness of the usage in Esther is indicated by the fact that it occurs in the DSS and is frequent in MH; see Bergey, *JQR* 75 (1984) 75–76.

8.a. The last clause is lacking in the LXX. For discussion, see *Comment.*

9.a. Lit. "given into the hand of." The verb is inf abs; for the use of this form, see *Note* 2:3.e.

9.b. Lit. "a man from the officials of the king, the nobles."

9.c. Lit. "let them clothe the man . . . and let them lead him . . ." The LXX reads these verbs and the verb "let them proclaim" as sg (cf. *BHS* n.). For discussion of this and the translation, see *Comment.*

10.a. Lit. "who is sitting in the king's gate." For the meaning, see the *Comment* on 2:19.

12.a. Lit. "to the king's gate." For the meaning, see the *Comment* on 2:19.

12.b. Lit. "with his head covered"; see *Comment*.

13.a. The Heb. is חכמיו, lit. "wise men, sages"; cf. 1:13. The word used for these people in 5:10, 14, and earlier in this verse is אהביו, "friends." The change here is doubtless ironic: they are "wise men" after the fact (Moore, 66; cf. Barthélemy et al., *Preliminary and Interim Report*, 549–50)! Hence, the word is not to be emended with Brockington (*Hebrew Text*, 100; cf. NEB, REB, NJB, JB) and Haller (128), following the LXX and Syr (cf. *BHS* n.). The A-text of Esther (7:22) reads *οἱ σοφοὶ αὐτοῦ*, "his wise men" (see Clines, *Esther Scroll*, 236), supporting MT.

13.b. Lit. "before whom you have begun to fall."

13.c. Lit. "is from the seed of the Jews."

Form/Structure/Setting

In opposition to the view of many interpreters, who treat 5:9–14 and 6:1–13/14 as separate pericopes (e.g., Clines, 305–10; Dommershausen, *Estherrolle*, 80–92; Moore, 59–67; Murphy, *Wisdom*, 164–65), in my opinion, the section 5:9–6:14 belongs together as one act (so also Fox, 73–82). True, there is a change of personae and venue between Haman and his wife and friends at home in 5:9–14 and 6:12–14 and the king, his attendants, and Haman at the palace in 6:1–10. However, the contents of all three pericopes are essential to tracing two closely related developments (see the table): first, the complication in the plot created by Haman's decision to have Mordecai hanged (5:9–14) and its resolution (6:11) and, second, two dramatic reversals. These reversals are the transformation of Haman's overweening pride into his utter humiliation through his own unwitting prescription of Mordecai's exaltation, which he then must himself effect, and the transformation (because of these events) of the counsel of his wife and friends to have the king hang Mordecai into their prediction instead of his downfall. Dorothy's decision ("Books of Esther," 287–88) to array 5:9–14 as a third-section coordinate with 4:1–5:8 seems determined by his distinguishing 6:1–5 as a separate pericope that constitutes the "crisis/pivot point" of the whole narrative, but this ignores the fact that 6:1–5 is simply part of the resolution of the complication introduced in 5:9–14 (see the discourse structure in *Theme and Purpose* in the *Introduction* to Esther).

The opening and closing of the act (see the table) is marked by a clear inclusio: in 5:9 Haman *leaves the banquet* that day; in 6:14 the eunuchs *bring him to the banquet* the next day. This makes it clear that 6:14 closes this act rather than opening the following one, contra Bardtke (351), Dorothy ("Books of Esther," 292), Moore (68), and Murphy (*Wisdom*, 165). The coherence of the act is demonstrated by a second inclusio: in both the opening scene, 5:9–14, and the closing scene, 6:12–14, Haman is at home and receives the counsel of his wife and his friends. The act clearly divides, then, into three scenes, 5:9–14, 6:1–11, and 6:12–14, on the basis of both structure and content.

The first scene, 5:9–14, and the third scene, 6:12–14, share the same venue, personae, and content: in each Haman is at home with his wife and his friends, and in each they give him counsel. Also, each is framed by an inclusio: at the beginning of the first scene Haman "left *the banquet . . . full of joy*" (5:9) and at the end he is urged to "go . . . to *the banquet full of joy*" (5:14); at the beginning of the third scene *Haman hastens* home (6:12), and at its end the king's eunuchs *hasten . . . Haman* to the banquet (6:14).

The Structure of Act 5

Scene	Verses	Venue & Personae	Content and Structure
Scene 1	5:9–14	Haman at home with his friends and Zeresh, his wife	5:9 "Haman left *the banquet* . . . *full of joy.*" Haman, at home, tells his wife and friends that his life is meaningless because of Mordecai's attendance at the king's court. They counsel him that he should ask the king to have Mordecai hanged. 5:14 ". . . go . . . to *the banquet full of joy.*"
Scene 2 Episode 1	6:1–3	The king and his attendants in the king's private quarters	The king, unable to sleep, discovers in the daily court record that Mordecai has not been rewarded for saving his life.
Scene 2 Episode 2	6:4–10	The king and Haman in the king's private quarters	Haman enters. The king and Haman discuss what should be done with the man whom the king desires to honor. The king accepts Haman's suggestion that the man should be clothed in the king's robe, paraded through the city on the king's horse, and have proclaimed before him, "This is what is done for the man whom the king desires to honor." He orders Haman to so honor Mordecai.
Scene 2 Episode 3	6:11	Haman and Mordecai in the city of Susa	Haman honors Mordecai exactly as he was ordered by the king.
Scene 3	6:12–14	Haman at home with his friends and Zeresh, his wife	6:12b "*Haman hastened* home . . . in shame." Haman relates to his friends and Zeresh, his wife, what has happened with Mordecai. They counsel him that he cannot get the better of Mordecai but will surely fall before him. 6:14b "(They) *hastened . . . Haman* to the banquet."

The opening of the second scene, 6:1–11, is marked by the temporal phrase "that night," which contrasts with the "that day" of scene 1. It closes with the narrative summary that relates Haman's honoring of Mordecai. The scene, which comprises three episodes, differs from the first and third in venue, personae, and content. The first episode, vv 1–3, takes place in the king's private quarters, involves the king and his attendants, and tells of the discovery of the failure to reward Mordecai. The second episode, vv 4–10, also takes place in the king's private quarters, involves the king and Haman, and relates the dialogue between them about what should be done for the man the king desires to honor. The third episode, v 11, takes place in the city of Susa, involves Haman and Mordecai, and relates in narrative summary Haman's honoring of Mordecai.

Comment

9 וְלֹא זָע מִמֶּנּוּ, lit. "and he did not tremble before him." The verb זוע, though rare, means "to move, shake" (cf. Eccles 12:3). In this context a figurative sense "to show fear" makes excellent sense. Hence, Driver's suggestion (*VT* 4 [1954] 236, followed by Bardtke, 340) that the verb should be taken to mean "moved aside from," drawing upon the Arabic cognate *zaġa,* "to deviate," instead of *zaʿa,* "to shake" (on the dubious grounds that verbs of trembling or writhing seem to prefer מפני rather than מן), is unnecessary.

11 וְאֵת כָּל־אֲשֶׁר גִּדְּלוֹ הַמֶּלֶךְ, lit. "and all which the king had promoted him." Gordis (*JBL* 95 [1976] 54–55) argues that the words את כל are an adverbial expression meaning "with everything" (i.e., together with all this), appealing to supposedly similar usages in Gen 20:16; Job 13:1. However, not only are the passages cited not pertinent to the passage here, but את כל־אשר is simply an expansion of the idiom את אשר used as an accusative of respect or manner, i.e., "the way in which" (see GKC § 157c; Fox, 281).

14 יַעֲשׂוּ־עֵץ גָּבֹהַּ חֲמִשִּׁים אַמָּה, "let them construct a gallows [lit. 'wood, pole'] fifty cubits in height." Since ancient units of measurement were never as precise or standardized as modern units, it is always difficult to attempt to translate them into modern terms. In general terms, however, 1.5 feet is a reasonable approximation for the cubit used in the OT (see Powell, *ABD* 6:899–900), making the height of the "gallows" about 75 feet (or perhaps as much as 85 feet if the cubit meant was that in use in Achaemenid Persia, which seems to have been a little longer; see Bivar, "Achaemenid Coins," 625–30, 637). It is difficult to decide whether this is intended to be taken literally or is another satirical exaggeration. If literal, it could be intended as public humiliation in that the body, impaled or hung upon a single pole or platform of this height, would be visible throughout Susa. Since satire seems out of place here, it seems much more likely that the height is to be taken literally and the display is intended as a public humiliation of Mordecai.

וְיִתְלוּ אֶת־מָרְדֳּכַי עָלָיו, lit. "so that they might hang Mordecai upon it." It is not clear whether תלה, "to hang," refers to impalement or crucifixion (see the *Comment* on תלה על עץ, "to hang on a gallows," in 2:23). Given that the "gallows" is apparently very high or is to be erected on a very high platform (see the previous entry), the verb here may well refer to the public exposure of the body rather than to the method of execution.

6:7 וַיֹּאמֶר הָמָן אֶל־הַמֶּלֶךְ אִישׁ אֲשֶׁר הַמֶּלֶךְ חָפֵץ בִּיקָרוֹ, lit. "Haman said to the king, 'a man whom the king wishes to honor.'" This is best taken as anacoluthon, as the Masoretes most likely understood it (as is evidenced by the verse division; for a similar case see 5:7). This is much preferable to the view of Moore (64), who considers the phrase to be another example of a Hebrew affirmative reply (see *Comment* on 5:7) and renders it "all right." All of the modern English translations smooth out the syntax, either interpreting the phrase as a proleptic dative of advantage, "*For* the man . . ." (e.g., KJV, RSV, NRSV, NEB), as a conditional clause (JB, NJB), or as a nominative absolute, "As for the man . . ." (Moffatt). All of these approaches miss the subtlety of the narrator. By the anacoluthon he implies that Haman is so eager to answer the king (cf. Clines, 308; Moore, 64) that he begins the sentence with that which is foremost in his thoughts, "the man whom the king wishes to honor," since he is so sure that this refers to himself. Then, he must break off the sense and begin again in order to describe the honor he wishes to have. That Haman's false start results from his eagerness is strongly supported by his failure to preface his suggestion with the standard formula of courtesy demanded by court protocol, "If it please the king" or the like (cf. Fox, 76). With his unseemly haste, the narrator again depicts him with subtle irony.

8 יָבִיאוּ לְבוּשׁ מַלְכוּת אֲשֶׁר לָבַשׁ בּוֹ הַמֶּלֶךְ, lit. "let them bring royal robes which the king has worn." The third person masculine plural subject with unexpressed antecedent is best expressed in English with the passive. Wearing the king's own robe seems to have been a mark of special favor and standing in Achaemenid Persia (cf. 1 Sam 18:4). Plutarch (*Artaxerxes* 5) relates that Artaxerxes gave the robe that he was wearing to one of his subjects when he asked him for it but forbade him to wear it (the passage is quoted in full in Moore, 64–65). Persian royal attire may even have been thought to possess the power to confer royalty upon its wearers (according to later Greek writers at least; cf. Fox, 77).

וַאֲשֶׁר נִתַּן כֶּתֶר מַלְכוּת בְּרֹאשׁוֹ, lit. "and upon whose head a royal diadem has been placed." The syntax here is clear and unmistakable: the diadem is to be placed upon the head of the horse. Gerleman alleges (115–16; cf. also Clines, *Esther Scroll,* 192 n. 8) that the placing of such an ornament on the head of a horse is improbable (for similar views among the older commentaries, see Paton, 248), so he reads אשר instead of ואשר and interprets the relative pronoun as temporal, yielding "when a royal crown was placed on his [the king's] head" (cf. also the translation of NAB, which seems to imply that the horse should be the one upon which the king rode on the occasion of his coronation). However, such a meaning for the relative pronoun is forced here, as is the resulting sense. Further, such an ornamentation on the head of a horse is not improbable in the Achaemenid period; see the relief from the east stairway of the *apadana* at Persepolis, which shows horses so adorned (for an example of such, see Moore, plate 2 following p. 22).

9 וְהִלְבִּישׁוּ אֶת־הָאִישׁ . . . וְהִרְכִּיבֻהוּ . . . וְקָרְאוּ, ". . . let them clothe the man . . . and let them lead him mounted . . . and let them proclaim." A number of commentators (e.g., Bardtke, 344; Brockington, 238; Haupt, *AJSL* 24 [1907–8] 144–45; Moore, 63) choose to adopt the LXX reading here, and so emend the number of all three of these verbs to the singular. This is done on the grounds that it is necessary to the sense (Brockington) since in the sequel it is a single representative of the king who carries out the honoring of Mordecai (Bardtke). The change, however, is unnecessary. Haman's suggestion began in v 8 with a third person plural verb with unexpressed antecedent, יביאו, "let them bring," the virtual equivalent of a passive. This syntax is continued in each of the following main clauses, first with the qal infinitive absolute וְנָתוֹן, "and let be given," with which v 9 begins, and then with the three verbs here in question. This construction is highly appropriate in Haman's description of the honor, for what is involved is a matter of grammatical focus. The construction with indefinite subject places the grammatical focus on the object of each clause, that is, the honor being suggested, rather than on the agent of the action, which remains indefinite and hence unimportant. Whether the verb in each clause is translated as a passive, as a plural verb with indefinite subject, or as an active verb with singular subject is purely a matter of English (or Greek!) translation. Further, this object-focus construction in Hebrew, which leaves the agent of the action indefinite, clearly implies that it is the member of the nobility who will oversee the carrying out of the honors specified. In English translation, however, this needs to be made explicit.

10 וַעֲשֵׂה־כֵן לְמָרְדֳּכַי הַיְּהוּדִי הַיּוֹשֵׁב בְּשַׁעַר הַמֶּלֶךְ, "and do this for Mordecai the Jew who is an official in the court." Here the king knows not only Mordecai's official position but also that he is a Jew. Given the information about the assassination attempt conveyed to the king by Esther on Mordecai's behalf in 2:19–23, the king's knowledge of Mordecai's position is not surprising. The king's seemingly sudden knowledge of his racial identity, however, has raised in the minds of commentators a number of questions about the coherence and plausibility of the story (e.g., Moore, 65; Paton, 250). Up to this point in the story only two events have been related where it has been clear that the king knows of Mordecai's existence: (1) Mordecai's report to the king of the assassination attempt conveyed by Esther (referred to above), and (2) our present pericope in which this same event is encountered in the court records. In the first Esther is said to make the report to the king "in the name of Mordecai" (2:22). This does not identify Mordecai as "Mordecai the Jew," but neither does it demonstrate that Mordecai's racial origin was kept secret from the king. Further, after 3:1–6 it is clear that Mordecai's identity as a Jew was widely known in the court. Hence, there is nothing thus far in the story that makes it implausible that the king should know Mordecai's racial identity. If he did not know it previously, he certainly could have been informed by his attendants (cf. Bardtke, 349, who notes the knowledge that Harbonah has of the size and purpose of the gallows on Haman's property, reported in 7:9). The story has made it clear, however, that the king is ignorant of two other important facts: (1) that Esther is Jewish (the story has repeatedly stressed this fact, 2:10, 19); and (2) the relationship between Esther and Mordecai (cf. 8:1). Finally, as Clines (309) observes, there is no contradiction between the king's honoring Mordecai the Jew and the edict to exterminate the Jews, for in the account in 3:8–11 Haman never mentions the name of the people involved. True, the king seems to be the only one unaware of the identity of the people who have been assigned to oblivion, but this is quite in keeping with the satirical way that the narrator has characterized him.

12 אָבֵל וַחֲפוּי רֹאשׁ, lit. "mourning and covered of head." "Mourning" refers here, of course, not to those feelings associated with grieving for the dead but to similar feelings stemming from a shameful humiliation. Likewise, having the head covered must refer here to feelings of shame and despair, even though it is a sign of mourning for the dead elsewhere in the OT (cf. Paton, 255, referring to 2 Sam 15:30; Jer 14:4). Brockington's attempt (238; followed by NEB) to interpret the verb חפוי to mean "uncovered" (also as a sign of mourning), based on an Arabic cognate, does not commend itself (cf. Clines, 309).

13 אִם מִזֶּרַע הַיְּהוּדִים מָרְדֳּכַי . . . לֹא־תוּכַל לוֹ כִּי־נָפוֹל תִּפּוֹל לְפָנָיו, lit. "If Mordecai is of the Jewish race . . . , you will not get the better of him, but you will most certainly fall before him." The first Hebrew clause, formally a conditional clause introduced by the particle אם, "if," cannot be a real condition since Haman has already told his wife and his friends that Mordecai is a Jew (5:13). The clause, then, is really causal in meaning, and it is clearer in English to translate it so. It hardly seems plausible that these sentiments could actually be the conviction of Haman's own wife and friends. It was but the previous evening that they had confidently counseled him to build a gallows and ask the king to have Mordecai the Jew hanged upon it. As numerous commentators have noted (e.g., Clines, *Esther Scroll,* 43; Moore, 66; Wiebe, *ABD* 6:1083), it is more likely that Haman's counselors here reflect the convictions of the narrator and his readers. The OT frequently alludes to the bitter enmity between Israel and Amalek (Exod 17:14–16; 1 Sam 15:2–8; 2 Sam 1:8–16) and implies clearly the ultimate victory of Israel (Num 24:7, 20). To the narrator and his readers it is a foregone conclusion that the house of Saul, with whom Mordecai is allied by his patronymics (see 2:5–6 and *Comment* thereto), will be victorious over the house of Agag the Amalekite, with whom Haman is allied by his patronymic (see 3:1 and *Explanation* thereto).

Explanation

As we observed at the end of the previous act, everything suggested that our narrator was immediately going to tell us about the banquet on the morrow and about Esther's request to the king. Hence, it is a surprising shift when, in the very first verse of this, the fifth act, we hear not about the morrow, the banquet, Esther, Haman, the king, and the request but instead about that same day and Haman and Mordecai. Our narrator, building suspense, leaves us still anticipating what will be the outcome of Esther's request and turns to follow once again the relationship between Haman and Mordecai.

Nevertheless, although the scene does follow this relationship again, and although indeed it also indicates how Mordecai was finally rewarded for saving the king's life, these aspects are but ancillary to its main concern, for it centers all its attention upon Haman. Mordecai, in fact, puts in only brief appearances, in each scene functioning primarily as a foil to presage Haman's complete and utter downfall. In the first scene the narrator completes his characterization of Haman by depicting for us his monstrous obsession with his own position, power, and privilege through his gross overreaction to Mordecai's failure to give him the deference he regards as his due. In the second scene Mordecai is the foil for the dramatic reversal in which Haman arrives to ask the king to hang Mordecai but instead must himself personally lavish upon Mordecai the public honor and recognition that he proposes for himself. In the third scene Mordecai is again the foil for the complete reversal of the counsel of Haman's wife and friends, in which their confident advice in the first scene on how to effect Mordecai's demise becomes their somber prediction that Haman's public humiliation at Mordecai's hands presages his doom.

SCENE 1. HAMAN'S HUBRIS: HE DECIDES TO ASK THE KING TO HANG MORDECAI (5:9–14)

Haman leaves the banquet with the king and Esther full of joy and light of heart (5:9), his pride fed by Esther's invitation to a second banquet with the king and queen alone. But his mood is short-lived, for Mordecai, whom he apparently must pass on his way home, continues to pay him no heed. Here our narrator intends to suggest, it would seem, an even more blatant affront to Haman's dignity on Mordecai's part. He not only refuses to bow down and do obeisance, as he had done in their first confrontation in 3:2–5, but now he neither rises before Haman nor shows any fear in his presence. Haman's response once again springs from overweening pride and vanity. As before, he will not reveal that the actions of his enemy could touch him, and so he feigns indifference: "he kept himself under control and went home" (5:10a). In the first occasion the narrator portrayed Haman's inordinate pride by making us privy to his inner deliberations: "he thought it beneath him to lay hands on Mordecai alone" (3:6). On this occasion, however, in the intimate setting of his own home and the presence of his wife and friends, Haman openly voices the pathetic effects of his prideful obsession with his enemy. All his emoluments, his vast wealth, his many sons, the promotions and advancements with which the king has preferred him, and even the fact that today and again tomorrow the queen herself has invited him alone to a banquet with the king—"all of this," he says, "means nothing to me every time I see Mordecai the Jew in attendance at the king's court" (5:13). Indeed, as this last statement reveals, it is not just that Mordecai will not do obeisance, or even, as today, that he will not rise or show any fear. In the final analysis, Haman cannot stomach his very existence. Haman is a case study in that inordinate pride and arrogance that conceals a "vast and tender ego" (Fox, 179).

Absorbed in his prideful obsession with his enemy, Haman is obviously utterly at a loss to know what to do. So it is his wife Zeresh (and his friends, though the Hebrew order of 5:14 makes her the primary spokesperson) who dictates his course of action. The narrator's irony is subtle indeed (only Radday to my knowledge has caught it ["Esther with Humour," 306]): this feckless image of the grand vizier is a travesty of the masculine dominance that the king and his hysterical privy-council enacted into law (1:20–22)!

Haman's wife and his friends understand that his spite will not be appeased simply by the death of his enemy (Clines, 306), so they advise a public humiliation: his execution must be authorized by the king, and his body must be displayed on a gibbet eighty feet high, hence visible over all of Susa (5:14a). Haman is so pleased with the proposal that he immediately has the gibbet built (5:14d). Clearly he fully anticipates that he will on the morrow gain the king's assent to the hanging of Mordecai and will, as his wife and his friends confidently predict, "go with the king to the banquet full of joy" (5:14c).

SCENE 2. HAMAN'S HUMILIATION: THE KING COMMANDS HIM TO HONOR MORDECAI (6:1–11)

At the end of the last scene, Haman's prospects seemed to have reached their peak. The edict he has promulgated under the king's name has assured the annihilation of the Jews, the people of his enemy. Now there is but one simple step to be taken to wreak vengeance upon Mordecai himself, a step whose success can hardly admit of any doubt. If the king could be manipulated to consent to the annihilation of a people, how difficult should it be to gain his consent to the elimination of one man? But Haman's prospects have actually peaked in a manner that he could never have imagined. His decision to speak to the king in the morning about having Mordecai hanged meets with a set of coincidences so remarkable that they can hardly be anything but the narrator's cipher for "divinely arranged" (Clines, 307). Haman's plans are about to run head on into the providence of God.

Unable to sleep (coincidence 1), the king has the daily court record read, discovers therein that Mordecai had revealed the attempt to assassinate him (coincidence 2), and ascertains from his attendants that Mordecai has received no reward for this (coincidence 3). Though he apparently has decided that this must immediately be rectified, the king makes no decision on his own, as is his wont, but looks for counsel. Hence, the most remarkable of this set of remarkable coincidences occurs. He asks his attendants, "Who is in the court?" just as Haman is entering the outer court of the king's residence to ask the king to have Mordecai hanged on the gallows that he had prepared (coincidence 4). Learning of Haman's presence, the king orders him to be brought in and asks him what he should do to reward Mordecai, without, however, identifying him as the one to be honored (coincidence 5): "What should be done with the man whom the king wishes to honor?" A writer whose world view is that of the OT people of God (as so much else in the story has demonstrated is the case with the author of Esther) could only intend his readers to see the hand of divine providence in a series of events seemingly of such pure chance (see the role of God in the story in *Theme and Purpose* in the *Introduction* to Esther).

But what is Haman doing entering the court in the middle of the night? His wife and his friends had counseled him to go to the king "in the morning" (5:14). Perhaps we are to understand that the king's insomnia occurred in the early morning. Whatever the time may have been, by casually introducing Haman's presence at such an unseemly hour, the narrator surely reflects ironically on the unseemly and eager haste with which he pursues the demise of his enemy (cf. Radday, "Esther with Humour," 306).

It has indeed been a remarkable set of providential circumstances that has brought Haman to this moment, but they have been circumstances that have been utterly outside of his control. It is true that the moment is not a propitious one—the king is looking for the means to reward Haman's enemy, and Haman is the one who is at hand by virtue of his own agenda, which has the opposite goal in view. Nevertheless, these circumstances, however remarkable, have not so far set in motion a course of action that necessarily threatens him. Indeed, it is conceivable that the fact that it is Haman who is to be consulted on how to reward Mordecai could augur ill for Mordecai (Moore, 67). But, before the ramifications of such a possibility can even be entertained by the reader, Haman himself takes a hand in what will transpire. And it is his own swollen pride that entraps him. Without a moment's hesitation he jumps to conclusions: "Whom would the king desire to honor," he reasons to himself, "more than me?" (6:6b). Skillfully does the narrator reveal that it is the phrase "the man whom the king desires to honor" that entrances him (cf. Dommershausen, 88–89). With it he begins his response, eagerly savoring it (6:7). Then, starting the sentence again in order logically to frame his answer (see *Comment*), twice more does he roll the phrase around in his mouth, with the last one concluding his proposal (6:9), and the same theme sounds in the reward that he prescribes. He asks not for wealth or power but for the honor and recognition of being paraded through the city square by one of his fellow nobles, wearing the king's own clothes and mounted on the king's own horse, with the phrase that entrances him reverberating in the air: "This is what is done for the man whom the king desires to honor!" "Honour is his life blood, and the thought of honour will divert him even from his plan against Mordecai" (Clines, 307–8).

Haman's words are barely out of his mouth when the honor that he had so confidently envisioned as his own is transformed in an instant into abject and utter humiliation by one sentence from the king (6:10): "Take the robes and the horse . . . and do this for Mordecai the Jew." The bitter irony of the complete reversal of Haman's fortunes is indicated by the way that the narrator now has the king for the first time designate Mordecai as "Mordecai the Jew" (cf. Clines, 309). The pre-eminent enemy of the Jews (see 3:10 and the *Explanation* thereto) must now give to the Jew the honor he envisaged for himself.

The narrator relates Haman's fulfillment of the king's command with the briefest of summary accounts, reporting in just one verse (6:11) only the bare facts of his compliance. His reticence about Haman's reaction is remarkable in a narrative in which elsewhere he so frequently describes his emotions (see *Theme and Purpose* in the *Introduction* to Esther). Here he is completely silent about the reactions of both of these bitter enemies, wisely leaving it to the reader's imagination (contrast the proto-AT, 7:14–19).

> Only an author with a sure hand and confidence in his reader would allow this climax in the bitter relationship between his two protagonists to pass with so few words and leave so much to the audience. A skilled author knows when not to say too much. (Humphreys, "Story," 103)

Indeed, his silence doubtless speaks eloquently of *their* grim silence as they take part in this black comedy (cf. Fox, 76–78). But he is not completely silent. Though he says nothing about their reactions, he does report that Haman proclaimed before Mordecai the words he himself had prescribed. Thus does he suggest that their grim silence is broken only by the intoning of the phrase that Haman so relished when he thought it was meant for him, but which now must fill his mouth with gall as he proclaims it before Mordecai: "This is what is done for the man whom the king desires to honor!"

SCENE 3. HAMAN'S END: HIS WIFE AND HIS FRIENDS PREDICT HIS DOWNFALL (6:12–14)

Haman arrives home in great despair and shame and seeks the solace of his wife and his friends by describing to them all that has happened to him. Once again they offer him counsel. Only now their confident advice in the first scene on how to effect Mordecai's demise becomes the somber realization of the symbolic value of what has transpired since. Haman's downfall, they predict, is certain. The reason they give, however, is dramatic and surprising. The Jews, they are convinced, are invincible: "Since Mordecai belongs to the Jewish race, you will not get the better of him, but will most certainly fall before him" (on the causal meaning of the conditional clause, see *Comment*). In all likelihood the narrator here places his own convictions in the mouths of Haman's counselors (see *Comment*). However that may be, its placement here signals the certainty of Haman's downfall on the morrow. It also strongly hints that a similar fate awaits his plot to annihilate the Jews.

The conclusion to scene 3 skillfully resumes the previous act, dramatically broken off in mid course, as Esther's invitation to Haman and the king to "come tomorrow to the banquet which I shall prepare" (5:8) becomes "the king's eunuchs brought Haman to the banquet which Esther had prepared" (6:14). It marks a smooth transition to the next act, for the prediction of Haman's wife and his friends that his downfall is utterly certain is still hanging in the air when the king's eunuchs arrive and hasten to escort him to the banquet at which Esther has promised the king she will make her request known (5:8). It also dramatically signals that the reversal of Haman's fortunes, which the scene has so powerfully portrayed, will now inexorably hasten to its conclusion.

Act 6
Esther Makes Her Appeal: The Fall of Haman (7:1–10)

Bibliography

Bergey, R. L. "The Book of Esther—Its Place in the Linguistic Milieu of Post-Exilic Biblical Hebrew Prose: A Study in Late Biblical Hebrew." Diss., Dropsie College, 1983. ———. "Post-exilic Hebrew Linguistic Developments in Esther: A Diachronic Approach." *JETS* 31 (1988) 161–68. **Brockington, L. W.** *The Hebrew Text of the Old Testament: The Readings Adopted by the Translators of the New English Bible.* Oxford: Oxford UP, 1973. **Clines, D. J. A.** *The Esther Story: The Story of the Story.* JSOTSup 30. Sheffield: JSOT, 1984. **Condamin, A.** "Notes critiques sur le texte biblique: II. La disgrace d'Aman (Esth. VII, 8)." *RB* 7 (1898) 253–61. **Dorothy, C. V.** "The Books of Esther: Structure, Genre, and Textual Integrity." Diss., Claremont, 1989. **Ehrlich, A.** *Randglossen zur hebräischen Bibel: Textkritisches, Sprachliches und Sachliches.* VII. 1914. Repr. Hildesheim: Georg Olms, 1968. **Ginsberg, H. L.** "Lexicographical Notes." In *Hebräische Wortforschung.* FS W. Baumgartner. VTSup 16. Leiden: Brill, 1967. 71–82. **Goldingay, J. E.** *Daniel.* WBC 30. Dallas: Word, 1989. **Gordis, R.** "Studies in the Esther Narrative." *JBL* 95 (1976) 43–58. **Greenberg, M.** *Ezekiel I–XX.* AB 22. Garden City, NY: Doubleday, 1983. **Haupt, P.** "Critical Notes on Esther." *AJSL* 24 (1970–8) 97–186 (= Moore, *Studies,* 1–90). **Humphreys, W. L.** "The Story of Esther and Mordecai: An Early Jewish Novella." In *Saga, Legend, Tale, Novella, Fable: Narrative Forms in Old Testament Literature,* ed. G. Coats. JSOTSup 35. Sheffield: JSOT, 1985. 97–113. **Murphy, R. E.** *Wisdom Literature: Job, Proverbs, Ruth, Canticles, Ecclesiastes, and Esther.* FOTL 13. Grand Rapids, MI: Eerdmans, 1981. **Perles, F.** *Analekten zur Textkritik des alten Testaments.* Munich: Theodor Ackermann, 1895. **Rudolph, W.** "Textkritisches zum Estherbuch." *VT* 4 (1954) 89–90. **Striedl, H.** "Untersuchungen zur Syntax und Stilistik des hebräischen Buches Esther." *ZAW* 14 (1937) 73–108. **Wagner, M.** *Die lexikalischen und grammatikalischen Aramaismen im alttestamentlichen Hebräisch.* Berlin: Töpelmann, 1966.

Translation

Episode 1. Esther pleads with the king for her life (7:1–6a)
Time: late afternoon/early evening, 1/17 or 1/18, year 12

1 *So the king and Haman went to dine with Queen Esther.* 2 *And also on this second
day during the wine course, the king said to Esther, "What do you want and what is it
that you request, Queen Esther? Even if it's for half of my kingdom, it shall be granted
and it shall be done."*[a]

3 *Queen Esther replied, "If I have found favor with you,*[a] *O King, and if it please the
king, let my life be granted to me—that is my wish; and that of my people—that is my
request.*[b] 4 *For we have been sold, I and my people, to be destroyed, slaughtered, and annihilated.
Now, if*[a] *we had merely been sold as slaves,*[b] *I would have said nothing, for the
trouble would not be commensurate with this annoyance to the king."*[c]

5 *Then King Ahasuerus answered. And he said to Queen Esther,*[a] *"Who is he? And
where is he*[b]*—the man who has dared*[c] *to do such a thing?"*

6a *Esther replied, "He is a hateful man and an enemy*[a]*—this vile Haman!"*

Episode 2. Haman attempts to plead with Esther for his life (7:6b–8b)
Time: late afternoon or early evening, 1/17 or 1/18, year 12

[6b]*At this, Haman faced the king and the queen in terror.*[b] [7]*The king in a rage rushed from the wine course into the garden of the royal pavilion,*[a] *while Haman, realizing that the king intended to do him*[b] *harm,*[c] *remained behind*[d] *to plead with Queen Esther for his life.* [8a]*Just as he was falling upon*[a] *the couch where Esther was reclining,*[b] *the king returned from the pavilion garden to the banquet room.*[c]

Episode 3. Haman loses his life (7:8c–10)
Time: late afternoon/early evening, 1/17 or 1/18, year 12

[8b]*The king exclaimed, "Is he also going to assault the queen in my very presence?"*[d] *As the king uttered the words, Haman's face was covered.*[e]

[9]*Then Harbonah, one of the eunuchs in attendance on the king, said, "Look, the gallows which Haman had erected*[a] *for Mordecai, whose report benefited the king,*[b] *is standing at Haman's house, fifty cubits high!" "Hang him on it!" said the king.* [10]*So they hanged Haman on the gallows which he had prepared for Mordecai, and the anger of the king subsided.*

Notes

2.a. Lit. "What is your wish, Queen Esther? It shall be granted you. And what is your request up to half of the kingdom? It shall be done."

3.a. Lit. "in your eyes."

3.b. Lit. "let my life be granted me as my wish, and my people as my request."

4.a. This form of the contrary-to-fact conditional particle, אִלּוּ, "if," occurs in BH only here and in Eccles 6:6. In SBH the form is לוּ/לוּא. The lateness of the Esther form is indicated by the fact that it is the sole form in use in MH; see Bergey, *JETS* 31 (1988) 163.

4.b. Lit. "male slaves and female slaves."

4.c. The Heb. is cryptic and its meaning uncertain; see *Comment.*

5.a. The Heb. lit. reads, "Then King Ahasuerus said and he said to Queen Esther." The second verb is lacking in the LXX. For discussion, see *Comment.*

5.b. Lit. "who is this-one and where this-one is who . . ." The response is biting and angry; see the *Comment.*

5.c. Lit. "filled his heart." It is unnecessary to read the piel stem מִלֵּא (Bardtke, 355; cf. *BHS* n.). The qal stem of the verb can take an obj when used in a quasi-stative sense (see *GBH* § 79j). In my opinion, לִבּוֹ, "his heart," is the obj of the verb, not the subject; i.e., the clause means "who has filled his heart," not "whose heart has filled him" (contra Bardtke, 355; Haupt, *AJSL* 24 [1907–8] 149). The use of the proleptic pron suff on the verb (i.e., "who has filled it, his heart") is not uncommon in Heb. (*GBH* § 146e; Brockelmann, *Syntax* § 68b).

6.a. Lit. "A man, an enemy and a foe!" See *Comment.*

6.b. Lit. "Haman was terrified in front of/before the king and queen." Moore (71) argues that the verb means "taken by surprise," rather than "was afraid," appealing to the two other contexts in the OT where it is used in the qal stem, Dan 8:17; 1 Chron 21:30, and alluding to the argument of Haupt, *AJSL* 24 (1907–8) 150. A careful examination of these two OT passages, however, will prove the opposite, particularly 1 Chron 21:30. And Haupt's argument is based solely upon the meaning of the Arab. cognate, which proves nothing about the precise meaning of the word in Heb.

7.a. The Heb. idiom involves a rather dramatic ellipsis: "the king rose up . . . from the banquet . . . to the pavilion garden," thus suggesting both his indecision and the haste of his departure; see *Comment.*

7.b. To change אליו to עליו (Bardtke, 355; cf. *BHS* n.) is unnecessary (Gerleman, 12); see *Note* 1:17.b.

7.c. The Heb. idiom is pass: "harm was intended for him from the king."

7.d. This is the meaning of the verb עמד here (contra Bergey, "Book of Esther," 125). עמד was replacing קום in a variety of the senses that were reserved for קום in LBH, and it is used in these senses in four other passages in Esther (see Bergey, "Book of Esther," 125–28). Nevertheless, the use of the verb elsewhere in Esther in the regular senses that it has in SBH (some six times, e.g., 5:1; cf. esp. . . . ותקם ותעמד, "she rose and stood" in 8:4), and the contrast in meaning clearly intended in this context between קום, "to arise, get up," in reference to the king in the immediately preceding clause, and עמד here in reference to Haman (see the table in *Form/Structure/Setting*) demonstrates that עמד is used here in the sense "remain, stay behind," not "arise, get up" (cf. Haupt, *AJSL* 24 [1907–8] 151).

8.a. The change of על־המטה to אל־המטה (Bardtke, 355; cf. *BHS* n. a) is unnecessary. The idiom נפל על, "fall upon," is particularly appropriate here. See also *Note* 1:17.b.

8.b. Lit. "upon which Esther was."

8.c. Lit. "to the house of the banquet of wine."

8.d. Lit. "with me in the building/place"; cf. 1 Kgs 3:17 (*GBH* § 132a). We do not have here two separate adv expressions (contra RSV, NRSV); cf. the parallel in 1 Kgs 3:17.

8.e. This translation understands חפו, "they covered," as the use of the indefinite subject (equivalent to the pass in Eng.), a construction that occurs with some frequency in Heb. (cf. *IBHS* §§ 4.4.2, 22.7; *GBH* § 155b; *Note* 2:2.b.). It is, then, unnecessary to repoint the verb as a qal pass (Brockington, *Hebrew Text*, 102; cf. Condamin, *RB* 7 [1898] 258–61). Since the sense of the expression is not clear (see *Comment*), a number of emendations have been offered. Neither the emendation to חָפֵרוּ (Perles, *Analekten*, 32, preferred by Fox, 283; cf. also Condamin, *RB* 7 [1898] 253; *BHS* n. b), yielding the idiom פנים חפר, "to be ashamed" (cf. Ps 34:6; Rudolph, *VT* 4 [1954] 90; cf. *BHS* n. b), both based on the LXX translation, are at all convincing. Gordis' proposal (*JBL* 95 [1976] 56) to read חפו as a rare and unusual form of the qal pass ptcp חָפוּי, sg by attraction to the noun "Haman," which immediately precedes, is not only forced but unnecessary. Finally, Gerleman (123–24, followed by Clines, *Esther Scroll*, 195 n. 12) understands the idiom as the Heb. equivalent of an Arab. expression meaning "to faint, lose consciousness," but there is nothing to commend the suggestion. There is not even any verbal correspondence between the two idioms (the Arab. verb *ǵana* does not mean "to cover"; cf. Fox, 283).

9.a. Lit. "had made."

9.b. Lit. "who spoke good for [i.e., 'for the benefit of'] the king." The idiom דבר טוב על elsewhere means lit. "to speak good *about* someone" (see Haupt, *AJSL* 24 [1907–8] 153). Nevertheless, it is hardly necessary to read with Haupt גָּמַל דָּבָר טוב על־המלך (so also Haller, 130; cf. *BHS* n. a-a). In this context the idiom must mean lit. "to speak good *to the benefit of* someone" (cf. also Fox, 284). Clearly the LXX omission of "good" (cf. *BHS* n. b) is erroneous.

Form/Structure/Setting

Act 6 is clearly marked as a separate act in both content and form. It constitutes, however, a single scene. It has a single venue and setting, namely, the banquet Esther has prepared in the king's private pavilion (v 7a; cf. 1:5), and the same protagonists throughout, namely, Esther, Haman, the king, and his attendants. Formally, its unity as a single scene is indicated by the various literary means by which the narrator binds it together (see the discussion below and the table).

Since the scene is tightly bound together by the almost breathless sequence of its events, to break it up into episodes is difficult. Murphy (*Wisdom*, 165) divides the scene into an introduction, 6:14–7:1 (for my argument that 6:14 belongs with the previous act, see *Form/Structure/Setting* there), and four coordinated sections, vv 2–4, 5–7, 8a, and 8b–10, while Fox (88) divides it into three sections: (a) vv 1–6, Esther asks for her life; (b) v 7, Haman asks for his life; (c) vv 8–10, Haman loses his life. But it is surely arbitrary to set up as a single entity one event in such a tight sequence of events as both of these analyses do. In my opinion, it is the narrator's own careful sequencing that divides the scene into three clear episodes (see the table), framed by a narrative introduction, v 1 (X), and a narrative conclusion, v 10 (X´). In form, episodes 1 (A) and 3 (A´) consist of tightly sequential dialogues. In the first episode the king asks two questions (a and a´, vv 2 and 5), to each of which Esther responds (b and b´, vv 3–4 and 6). His second question (v 5) is elicited by her first response (vv 3–4). In the third episode the king's

The Structure of Act 6

Pericope	Style	Verses			Content	Structure	
Introduction	Narrative	1			The king and Haman come to Esther's banquet.		X
Episode 1	Tightly sequential dialogue	2–6a	ויאמר המלך	v 2	**The king asks** Esther what her request is.	a	A
			ותען אסתר	vv 3–4	**Esther replies.** She pleads for her life and for the lives of her people.	b	
			ויאמר המלך	v 5	**The king asks** who has dared to so threaten Esther.	a´	
			ותאמר אסתר	v 6a	**Esther replies** that it is Haman.	b´	
Episode 2	Non-sequential narrative	6b–8b	והמן נבעת	v 6b	**Haman** is terrified as	a	B
			והמלך קם	v 7a	**The king** leaves the hall in anger, while	b	
			והמן עמד	v 7b	**Haman** stays to beg for his life.	c	
			והמלך שׁב	v 8a	**The king** returns to the hall, where	b´	
			והמן נפל	v 8b	**Haman** is falling on Esther's couch.	a´	
Episode 3	Tightly sequential dialogue	8c–9	ויאמר המלך	v 8c	The king charges Haman with assaulting the queen,	a	A´
				v 8d	as Haman's face is covered.		
			ויאמר חרבונה	v 9a	Harbonah reports that the gallows Haman made for Mordecai is standing at Haman's house.	b	
			ויאמר המלך	v 9b	The king commands that Haman be hanged upon it.	a´	
Conclusion	Narrative	10			Haman is hung on the gallows, and the king is mollified.		X´

enraged exclamation at seeing Haman falling upon the queen's couch (a, v 8c) elicits Harbonah's proposal (b, v 9a), which prompts in turn the king's command to hang Haman (a´, v 9b). Each of these two dialogues is bound into a single unbroken sequence of cause and effect by the series of waw-consecutive verbal forms with which each speech is introduced (see the table). Episode 2, however, framed by these dialogues, is dramatically different. In form it consists of straight narrative without a word of dialogue. It depicts a scene in which several events take place virtually simultaneously, dramatically expressed with the highly circumstantial waw + subject + verb clause construction with which each of the main clauses begins (see the table). On these grounds, the scene divides into two temporally sequential *dialogues* (episodes 1 and 3, A and A´) framing a scene of virtually simultaneous *events without dialogue* (episode 2, B). This not only divides the scene into closely correlated episodes but gives it an unrelenting momentum and binds it into a cohesive whole. Dorothy's division of the scene ("Books of Esther," 292–94) into three sections (v 1, exposition; vv 2–8, description; vv 9–10, results) misses the subtlety of the structure by uniting the first two episodes in an undifferentiated group of five coordinated elements (vv 2–8).

Particularly in the second question-and-answer sequence between the king and Esther, vv 5–6 of episode 1, form and content unite with dramatic effect. Here structure and form in both the question and the answer skillfully capture the highly charged feelings with which the words are uttered. In v 5b the king replies to Esther's revelation by asking for the identity and whereabouts of this miscreant. The first part of his reply consists of two perfectly balanced, chiastically ordered nominal clauses:

מִי הוּא זֶה
mî hûʾ zeh
who he this-one?

וְאֵי־זֶה הוּא
wĕʾêy-zeh hûʾ
and-where this he?

This is followed by a relative clause in which the object, "his heart," is proleptically emphasized by the appropriate pronominal suffix on the preceding verb:

אֲשֶׁר מְלָאוֹ לִבּוֹ לַעֲשׂוֹת כֵּן
ʾăšer mĕlāʾô libbô laʿăśôt kēn
who has-filled-it his-heart to-do thus

The staccato syllables of the nominal clauses, together with the three stressed *ô*-vowels in the following relative clause, well express the sudden fury with which the king replies (cf. Dommershausen, 95).

Esther's reply (v 6a) is equally expressive. It also consists of abrupt, biting syllables. She answers both his "who?" and "where?" with a perfectly parallel two-part response. Each part is a nominal phrase with three stresses and consists of a head noun plus two modifiers. The last clause, comprising three two-syllable words, each of which begins with the identical syllable *ha-*, produces a sharp, rhythmic effect:

אִישׁ צַר וְאוֹיֵב
ʾîš ṣar wĕʾôyēḇ
a-man an-enemy and-a-foe

הָמָן הָרָע הַזֶּה
Hāmān hāraʿ hazzêh
Haman the-evil the-this

One can virtually hear both of them biting off each syllable!

Comment

4 כִּי אֵין הַצָּר שֹׁוֶה בְּנֵזֶק הַמֶּלֶךְ, "for the trouble would not be commensurate with the annoyance to the king." The translation of this enigmatic clause is most difficult for two reasons: (1) its brevity greatly increases the ambiguity of its meaning, and (2) three of its words, צר, שוה, and נזק, have meanings that are uncertain. צר may mean either "enemy" or "calamity, distress, trouble." Paton's argument (261) that the word must mean "enemy" because it is never used with the meaning "calamity" in Esther badly overstates the case. In fact, the word צר occurs with the meaning "enemy" elsewhere in Esther only in 7:6. Its synonym צֹרֵר is used to mean "enemy" in Esth 3:10; 8:1; 9:10, 24. Such usage implies little about the meaning of צר in 7:4. It is also not necessary to repoint צָר with patah rather than qames for it to bear the meaning "distress, adversity" (Fox, 282), for both forms of the word can bear either meaning (thus, besides the regular form צָר, "enemy," note צַר in Esth 7:6; Amos 3:11, and besides the regular form צַר, "distress, narrow," note צָר in Num 22:26; Ps 4:2).The second word of uncertain meaning, שֹׁוֶה, qal participle < שוה, "to be like, equal," occurs elsewhere in Esther only in the idiom שֹׁוֶה לְ-, "to be suitable, fitting; of value" (3:8; 5:13). Though the idiom שֹׁוֶה בְּ- does not occur elsewhere, the verbal idiom שָׁוָה בְּ occurs in Prov 3:15; 8:22 with the meaning "to be comparable with." The word could, then, carry a number of nuances in the range of "similar, equivalent, suitable, comparable." The last word of uncertain meaning, נזק, occurs only here in OT Hebrew. It is often argued that the noun means "harm, damage," since it occurs frequently in post-biblical Hebrew and Aramaic with this meaning (cf. Fox, 282, who argues for the meaning "monetary loss" on the grounds of its meaning in MH). Further, the verb occurs in biblical Aramaic in the haphel stem in Ezra 4:13 with the meaning "to harm, injure," and probably also in Ezra 4:15, 22 (though the meaning "trouble, difficulty" is also possible in these passages; cf. Ginsberg, "Lexicographical Notes," 81; Haupt, *AJSL* 24 [1907–8] 147). However, it is used in the qal stem in Dan 6:3 where the meaning "to be troubled, annoyed" fits the context far better than "to be harmed, injured" (cf. Goldingay, *Daniel,* 120; Ginsberg, "Lexicographical Notes," 81; Haupt, *AJSL* 24 [1907–8] 147). Hence, in Esth 7:4 (where it is highly probable that its meaning is influenced at least by Aramaic usage; Wagner, *Die lexikalischen,* no. 186, p. 82, treats it as an Aramaic loan word) the noun may well mean "trouble, difficulty" as well as the stronger sense of "harm, injury" (contra Fox, 282; cf. Haupt, *AJSL* 24 [1907–8] 147, who adduces an Arabic cognate). Finally, in the first part of Esther's response (vv 3–4a), she begins with a request for her life, v 3, which she then follows with a reason, "for we have been sold," v 4a. Hence, on the grounds that the second part of Esther's speech has the same structure (cf. Bardtke, 354), the most natural interpretation of the particle כִּי, "for," is to take it in its causal sense and understand the clause to be stating the reason for the preceding conditional sentence.

With this range of possible meanings and the cryptic nature of the clause, it is not surprising that a number of interpretations have been suggested. Least satisfactory of all is the emendation of הַצָּר שֹׁוֶה to הַצָּלָה שָׁוָה, "the deliverance would not be worth . . ." (Haller, 130; cf. *BHS* n.). Besides the fact that the meaning hardly fits the context at all, reasonable sense can be made of the text without resorting to conjectural emendation. Some have taken צר to mean "enemy" and נזק, "damage, injury," yielding the literal translation "the enemy/adversary is not equivalent/suitable/comparable with the damage to the king," which is interpreted to mean "but no enemy can compensate for [or 'be worth'] this annoyance [or 'damage'] to the king" (Dommershausen, 37; NRSV; cf. also NAB, NJB, JB, NIV margin). However, the interpretation is confronted by two serious difficulties: (1) it must assume an ellipsis between the preceding conditional sentence and this clause, that is, "but since we are to be annihilated" or the like (so JB, "but as things are, . . ."; cf. also NJB), and (2) it must either ignore the particle כי or give it some other meaning than the causal sense. (The adversative sense found in all the translations that adopt this interpretation is grounded solely in the context; it cannot be a rendering of the particle כי, "because," for this particle bears an adversative sense only after a negated clause.)

These difficulties may be relieved, however, and a tolerable sense obtained from the Hebrew, despite its cryptic form, if one takes צר in the sense "calamity, difficulty" and נזק in the sense "trouble, annoyance." This yields the literal translation "for the calamity is not comparable with the trouble to the king," i.e., "for the calamity (of our being sold into slavery) would not be worth/justify the annoyance (which I am now causing) to the king" (cf. Clines, 311; Gordis, *JBL* 95 [1976] 55–56; Moore, 70; so NIV, NASV). This is much preferable to taking נזק in the sense "damage, harm," as do RSV, NEB, REB (understanding it to refer to the loss of taxes from the Jewish community, or the like?—so Fox, 282).

5 וַיֹּאמֶר הַמֶּלֶךְ אֲחַשְׁוֵרוֹשׁ וַיֹּאמֶר לְאֶסְתֵּר הַמַּלְכָּה, lit. "And King Ahasuerus said and he said to Queen Esther." At first glance the text seems overloaded with its repetition of ויאמר, "and he said," between the subject and the indirect object. This apparent infelicity has been handled by commentators in two different ways. Some consider the text erroneous and have sought to resolve the apparent overloading. Most have followed the LXX and deleted the second ויאמר, "and he said" (cf. *BHS* n. b), a solution followed by every modern English translation except JB and NJB. The deletion is justified on such grounds as (1) the word is a "dittography" (Moore, 68; Haupt, *AJSL* 24 [1907–8] 149) or (2) it is "mistaken" (Gerleman, 121) or (3) it is "awkward" (Meinhold, 65). But, it is not at all certain that the LXX is a witness to a different Hebrew *Vorlage*, for the LXX translator may well have smoothed out the text because of these apparent difficulties. Clines (*Esther Scroll*, 113) argues that the repetition is to be explained from the history of the tradition (cf. also Paton, 258). He appeals to the AT text, which has two speeches here on the part of the king. Hence, "MT may be supposed to preserve a small slip on the part of the proto-MT narrator, who had two verbs of speaking before him in his *Vorlage*, but he wishes to preserve only the first speech in his narrative." This is surely most tenuous and speculative. It posits a Hebrew *Vorlage* that is antecedent to both the proto-AT and the proto-MT (i.e., the texts antecedent to the present AT and MT), which had two speeches by the king. The only evidence for this is the AT, which uses indirect speech, avoiding the verb "to say" altogether. Hence "there is no particular connection between AT viii 7 and the two verbs in MT" (Fox, 283). Some (e.g., Haller, 130, apparently following Ehrlich, *Randglossen,* 120; cf. *BHS* n.a) emend the text, reading the first ויאמר as וַיְמַהֵר, "and he hastened (sc. to speak)." Though this makes sense in the context, it is pure conjecture.

On the other hand, others find the repetition intentional and seek to find some meaning for it in the context. Dommershausen (*Estherrolle,* 95) posits that the repetition is intended to express the king's surprise and consternation; he "catches his breath" and begins to speak again (cf. also Striedl, *ZAW* 14 [1937] 106; Meinhold, 65 n. 19). However, the construction can hardly be construed to imply some hesitation on the part of the king (Fox, 283). These are not the king's words but those of the narrator. Similarly, the repetition cannot be construed to imply that the king interrupted Esther (so JB, NJB). Much preferable is the view of Bardtke (356), who takes it to be a retarding device of the narrator, intended to raise the reader's suspense regarding to whom the king will speak, Esther or Haman. Though the structure may well increase suspense, the reader surely knows to whom the king will speak. Esther has not in any way hinted at the agency of the threat she has voiced (nothing in her words has brought Haman into the picture, however much the reader may expect that she is about to do so), and the obviously natural question her words elicit is the one that the king immediately proceeds to address to her: "Who has done this?"

Bardtke is certainly correct, however, in understanding that the repetition slows the pace of the narrative and increases suspense. This understanding of the idiom is strongly supported by the narrator's use of the names of both speaker and addressee (both are hardly needed for clarity at this point in the dialogue) as well as their full titles, "King Ahasuerus . . . Queen Esther." Fox (283) notes the same repetition of ויאמר in Ezek 10:2. It occurs in other OT passages as well, e.g., Gen 22:7; 46:2; 2 Sam 24:17, where it likewise slows the pace and thus adds solemnity to the narration (cf. Greenberg, *Ezekiel,* 180). The solemn retarding of the pace here at this critical moment does not raise the reader's suspense, however, regarding to whom the king will speak. Suspense is raised rather in regard to the larger and more important question of what the king's response will be to Esther's revelation and how Haman will ultimately be unmasked as the perpetrator of this threat. My translation also attempts to slow the pace of the narration and so build suspense.

7 וְהַמֶּלֶךְ קָם בַּחֲמָתוֹ מִמִּשְׁתֵּה הַיַּיִן אֶל־גִּנַּת הַבִּיתָן, lit. "The king arose in his anger from the wine-banquet to the pavilion garden." The narrator, as has been his wont, leaves us again to read between the lines in order to understand why the king left the hall and went into the pavilion garden. Many suggestions have been made (see Paton, 262, for those of earlier scholars), including the view that the king's action simply results from the narrator's need to have him out of the way for the scene depicted in v 8 (so Paton; Moore, 71; Brockington, 239). His removing himself completely from the scene is certainly necessary in order that, returning, he may find Haman falling upon Esther's couch and so find a further reason for dispatching him. Clines interprets his action to mean that the outcome of Esther's unmasking of Haman is totally uncertain. Neither the king nor we know whether the king's anger is against Haman or against Esther; indeed, it seems that only the providential coincidence that the king returns just in time to see Haman falling upon Esther's couch causes him to make up his mind (*Esther Scroll,* 15–16). But this actually is not the case. The narrator allows us to see the king's reaction to Esther's revelation through the eyes of Haman: "for he saw that the king intended to do him harm" (v 7c). Clearly the king's action has left no doubt (in Haman's perception, and hence in ours, since the narrator shares Haman's perception with us) that the king's anger is not against the queen. His indecision, then, must relate to what action to take against Haman (hence Haman's decision to appeal to Esther for his life), and his indecision is fully in keeping with his character. He has heretofore made decisions only after appealing to his advisors among the nobles and sages of the realm (1:13–15; 2:2–4; 6:3–6), a practice the author has informed us was his usual custom (1:13). To whom now, in the setting of this intimate soirée, can he appeal (cf. Clines, *Esther Scroll,* 15–16)? Not knowing what to do in his rage, he bolts into the garden. Indeed, the marked ellipsis in the verse, "the king rose up in his rage *from* the wine-banquet *to* the pavilion garden," suggests strongly that in his anger he was at a loss to know what to do.

8 הֲגַם לִכְבּוֹשׁ אֶת־הַמַּלְכָּה עִמִּי בַּבָּיִת, "Is he also going to assault the queen in my presence, here in the palace?" The expression is terse (but not non sequitur, with Dommershausen, *Estherrolle,* 96), doubtless to express the continued anger of the king. It consists of the predicative use of the infinitive construct to express either a modal (i.e., "does he intend to/want to") or imminent sense (i.e., "is he about to"); cf. *IBHS* § 36.2.3.f, g. The English idiom"is he going to . . ." is particularly appropriate here, for it can have the same two ranges of meaning as does the Hebrew idiom. The verb כבשׁ elsewhere in the OT regularly means "to subdue, bring into subjection" (e.g., Gen 1:28; Jer 34:16). On these grounds, Bardtke (359) argues that the word can hardly be intended by the narrator to imply a deliberate assault on the queen. Rather, it may refer to Haman's violation of the extremely strict rules of court propriety, which prohibited any contact, or even close physical proximity, between courtiers and the women of the harem, rules that are well known from Assyrian court etiquette (for examples, see Bardtke, 358 n. 4), though unattested thus far for Achaemenid Persia. That Haman did not intend either a physical or sexual assault on the queen is unquestionable. However, in my opinion, the two adverbial clauses, "here in the palace, in my presence," strongly suggest that the king intended the word to imply more than the mere violation of the rules of court propriety regarding touching or approaching the queen. If the king intended to charge Haman with violating such harem regulations, surely he would have used some other term than כבשׁ. It is far more probable that the word had the stronger meaning of "assault, violate" in the LBH of the period of Esther.

וּפְנֵי הָמָן חָפוּ, lit. "and they covered Haman's face." The translation of the Hebrew clause is not in doubt. What it means, however, is another matter. It is generally taken to mean that the king's attendants (for the presence of whom see the next verse) covered Haman's face as a sign that he had been condemned to death (see the references in Paton, 264; Moore, 72; full quotations in Bardtke, 359 n. 5). However, not only is such a custom unknown among the Persians, but the references in later Greek and Roman texts are problematical (see Fox's critique, 283; Clines, 313). Since the emendations that have been suggested (see *Note* 3.e.) do not commend themselves, I have adopted the literal translation, in spite of the uncertainty of its meaning.

10 וַיִּתְלוּ אֶת־הָמָן עַל־הָעֵץ, "So they hanged Haman on the gallows." On whether this refers to impalement or crucifixion, see *Comment* on 2:23.

Explanation

Episode 1. Esther pleads with the king for her life (vv 1–6a). "So the king and Haman came to dine with Queen Esther." After the last two acts, this almost laconic introduction to the sixth act is charged with tension and suspense. True, we have no doubt that Haman's demise awaits him or that the end result for Esther and her people will be deliverance, for the narrative has signaled in clear terms the certainty of each. The king has indicated by the very extravagance of his repeated promise to grant Esther as much as half of his empire that he has every intention of looking upon her request with the greatest favor, and through Esther's skillful stratagem, his very presence at this banquet amounts to a public pledge to fulfill her request (see *Explanation* to 5:5b–8). Likewise, Haman's fate has been presaged by the way in which his plans to have Mordecai hanged have been turned into publicly honoring Mordecai, and it has been sealed by the somber prediction of his own wife and friends. Nevertheless, suspense in regard to the fate of each remains, for nothing in the narrative thus far has foreshadowed precisely how either fate will come to pass.

The greatest suspense arises, of course, in regard to the king. Despite his favorable promises and the public pledge that Esther has been able to extract from him, he has shown himself to be a weak and unstable despot who is moved by the whim of the moment and is ruled by pride and ostentation—one who can carelessly consign a whole people to oblivion with an offhand comment. It is most uncertain, then, what his response will be, or whether he will make one at all, when Esther's request pits the most favored of his courtiers against the most favored of his wives.

Having thus built up suspense regarding Esther's appeal to the king, the narrator now wastes no words in resolving it. The scene, carefully crafted and tightly constructed, begins immediately with the king repeating both his question and his magnanimous promise for the third time (v 2). It moves from there speedily and unrelentingly toward Haman's demise (see *Form/Structure/Setting*), with but a single change of pace (v 5a). Esther's reply to the king's question (vv 3–4) reveals that she understands full well the delicate and precarious nature of her position. The threat against her and her people has two perpetrators, Haman and the king, and both are present with her. She must somehow fully expose the culpability of Haman, while at the same time never appearing in any way to be bringing any charges against the king. Hence, her response is extremely well thought out and presented with the utmost tact.

First, she prefaces it with the same twofold polite phrase with which she had invited the king to the banquet (5:8), but with one subtle, but expressive, change. In the first phrase, instead of the third-person address she uses everywhere else, which is normal court protocol in speaking to the king, she subtly uses the much more intimate second person, "If I have found favor with *you,* O king." In so doing, she emphasizes her special relationship to him as his queen.

Second, though she uses the form of the king's question in making her petition, she modifies it in a significantly suggestive way. The king's question had twice been doubly stated, using the two words "wish" and "request" (5:6; 7:2), though clearly intending thereby but a single appeal. Esther's response is likewise doubly stated. In terse, expressive clauses, she uses both these words, implying the single petition the king invited but predicating to each of them a different entity, thereby implying their virtual identity: "Let my *life* be granted me as *my wish,* and my *people* as *my request.*" Thus does she fully identify herself with her people: to threaten one is to threaten the other.

Third, in the clause that follows, she explains her request by using language that is carefully chosen (v 4a). On the one hand, she unmistakably exposes the source of the threat to her life and that of her people by using the specific terms of Haman's edict (see 3:13). On the other hand, she uses an idiom with a double entendre (the expression *māḵar lĕ* can mean not only "delivered over to" but also "sold for") and puts it in the passive voice. Thus, she can subtly allude to the transaction between Haman and the king (3:9–11) but avoid with the passive voice any direct reference to the seller in the transaction, the king himself.

Nevertheless, no matter how shrewd she has been, nor how well thought out her reply, she could not avoid fully revealing her racial identity, and so exposing herself to the greatest danger. What will be the king's reaction when he realizes that his queen belongs to the race of people that he has consigned to destruction? Fully realizing the enormous risk this revelation entails, with great tact she apologizes for raising a matter, even obliquely, that might distress and embarrass the king (v 4b; see *Comment*).

Everything now depends upon the king's reaction to this startling revelation. Hence, in v 5a the narrator slows the pace of his narration by using the full titles of both the king and the queen and by twice solemnly using the verb "said," first with the subject and then with the indirect object (see *Comment*). However, though the pace of narration may be slow, the king's reaction is anything but. The short nominal clauses of the first two sentences of the Hebrew, with their monosyllabic words and chiastic parallelism, and the three accented *o*-sounds of the following relative clause (vv 5b–c; see *Form/Structure/Setting*) produce sharp, staccato utterances that skillfully depict the king's highly charged and enraged response: "Who is he? And where is he—the man who has dared to do such a thing?" One can virtually hear him angrily biting off each short, sharp syllable! Clearly the king is incensed at this threat to the life of his queen. It is also clear that he has no memory whatsoever, at least not at this moment, of Haman's insidious plot against the Jews or of his own part in it. So, with marvelous irony, he asks for both the identity and the whereabouts of the perpetrator, utterly unaware that he is sitting at the table with them.

Esther responds in like vein to the king's angry question. Here also the parallel pair of short, three-membered nominal clauses consisting of words of one and two syllables and particularly the rhythmic structure of the second clause (v 6a; see *Form/Structure/Setting*) well catch the force of her angry and biting accusation: "A hateful man and an enemy! This vile Haman!" One can almost see her emphasizing each sharp word with a stabbing finger pointing at Haman!

Episode 2. Haman attempts to plead with Esther for his life (vv 6b–8b). In the first episode (vv 1–6a), the narrator left totally to our imagination Haman's reaction to the events that were transpiring. Nevertheless, it does not at all tax credulity to imagine that he attended the banquet, if not with the assurance, at least with the hope that such an intimate soirée with the king and the queen would, despite the ominous prediction of his downfall made by his wife and friends, bring healing to his pride (cf. 5:12), so deeply wounded by the humiliating debacle that had resulted from his attempt to have Mordecai hanged. We can well imagine, then, with what initial puzzlement and then fearful comprehension he must have listened to Esther's request. He had not the slightest idea that the queen was Jewish. Hence, he would have heard her plead with the king not only for her life but also for that of her *people* with a mixture of incredulity and anxiety, to be replaced with disbelief and rapidly mounting fear as the implications of her identity and the literal language of his own edict rapidly became clear: "*We, I and my people,* have been *sold* to be *destroyed, slaughtered, and annihilated.*" These reactions must have quickly approached utter panic as the king spit out his angry queries, "Who?" and "Where?"

After Esther's vehement and angry accusation (v 6a), however, the narrator no longer leaves us to imagine Haman's reaction. He is gripped with abject terror, which prompts a course of action that proves fatal. This the narrator graphically portrays for us in a scene without dialogue and almost without the passage of time (see *Form/Structure/Setting*), in which a series of virtually simultaneous events rush breathlessly onward: terror grips Haman (v 6b)—the king bolts from the room in anger (v 7a)—seeing that the king intends to do him harm, Haman stays behind to plead with Esther for his life (v 7b)—the king returns from the garden (v 8a)—just in time to see Haman falling on Esther's couch to make his plea (v 8b).

Finding that the perpetrator of the threat to the life of the queen was the very man who sat at table with him, the king bolted from the banquet into the pavilion garden. In his rage, he is utterly at a loss to know what to do (v 7a; for this understanding of the king's action, see *Comment*). He now suddenly lacks the courtiers whom he has heretofore always depended upon for counsel (Clines, 312; cf. 1:13). Clearly, his anger is directed toward Haman, for the narrator allows us to see it through Haman's eyes: "he saw that the king intended to do him harm" (v 7c). This places the king in a considerable quandary (cf. Fox, 86). Can he punish Haman for a plot to which he gave full concurrence or for an irrevocable edict that has gone forth in his own name? Faced with this dilemma, he returns to the hall just in time to see Haman pleading for his life upon the couch where Esther lay (v 8b).

Episode 3. Haman loses his life (vv 8c–10). Providence resolves the king's dilemma (Clines, *Esther Scroll,* 16). It simply strains credulity to believe that he actually thought that Haman under these circumstances was really attempting to assault the queen. Rather, he chooses so to interpret Haman's action, thereby providing a charge with which to condemn him that relieves the king from raising publicly the true reason for the condemnation, the plot against the Jews. Thus, in keeping with the irresponsibility that has consistently marked Ahasuerus' character, he can leave hidden and unexamined his own complicity in the matter. Another remarkable coincidence has acted in favor of the Jews.

Harbonah (cf. 1:10), sensing that the king's accusation implies a sentence of death, relieves the king once again of having to make an independent decision, or even, on this occasion, of having to seek the counsel of his advisors. Harbonah points out an appropriate means of execution, while he also provides another accusation against Haman, namely, that he knowingly sought to take the life of the man who had saved the life of the king. His decision thus further justified, the king immediately orders Haman's execution. Not only is providential coincidence heaped upon providential coincidence, but irony upon irony: Haman is executed upon the very gallows that he had intended for Mordecai, and he is executed for a crime he did not commit!

The final end of Haman, the Agagite, the enemy of the Jews, is very much downplayed by the narrator. After having told us of Haman's terror at Esther's revelation (v 6b), his realization of the king's inimical intentions (v 7), and his rash attempt to importune the queen (v 8a), the narrator tells us nothing of Haman's reaction to the king's sentence. He does not even report that Haman was led away to the gallows. He only tells us that his face was covered (v 8b), and he reminds us of the final irony, that these were the gallows Haman had prepared for Mordecai. Perhaps in this way the narrator is indeed "asking the reader's own imagination to supply his last bitter taste of irony laced with terror" (Humphreys, "Story," 107).

And what of Esther through all this? As he did with Haman in the first episode, the narrator has left Esther's reaction in these last two episodes totally to our imagination. She doubtless would have been very unsure of the king's response to her charges against Haman. We might presume, then, that her feelings would have ranged from fearful anxiety, as she watched the enraged king bolt from the room, to dramatic relief as he angrily accused Haman of assault. However that may be, the narrator has had her remain totally silent through all that has transpired, both as Haman pled for his life and as he was condemned. Some have interpreted this silence as a negative characterization of Esther (e.g., "callous and indifferent . . . she looks on in cold silence," Anderson, 862; "her character would have been more attractive if she had shown pity," Paton, 264), but this is to misrepresent the entire situation (so Moore, 74; cf. Fox, 87). Haman is a falling, not a fallen, foe. His actions have left no doubt that the terrible threat he represents to Esther, Mordecai, and the whole Jewish community will continue as long as he survives. Whatever feelings of mercy and pity Esther might have felt, prudence and logic would have kept her from making any appeal to the king to stay the sentence against Haman.

As the scene closes, we learn that the king's anger cooled when Haman was summarily executed on the gallows he had prepared for Mordecai (v 10b). It has not been the invidious plot against a whole people that has caused the king's rage. Afterall, he had consigned them to oblivion in the first place with a casual and offhand comment (3:11). Quite apparently it was the affront to his honor in the attack upon his queen that moved him, and to have avenged this has been enough for Ahasuerus. But, though the king may be mollified, the threat to the Jewish community is not over. It lives on in Haman's irrevocable edict issued in the king's name. The task of saving the Jewish people, which Mordecai laid upon Esther as queen, has really only just begun. Esther, and Mordecai, must now face the seemingly impossible task of revoking an irrevocable decree.

Act 7
Esther Appeals Again to the King: She and Mordecai Counter Haman's Plot (8:1–17)

Bibliography

Bergey, R. L. "The Book of Esther—Its Place in the Linguistic Milieu of Post-exilic Biblical Hebrew: A Study in Late Biblical Hebrew." Diss., Dropsie College, 1983. ———. "Post-exilic Hebrew Linguistic Developments in Esther." *JETS* 31 (1988) 161–68. **Clines, D. J. A.** *The Esther Scroll: The Story of the Story.* JSOTSup 30. Sheffield: JSOT, 1984. **Driver, G. R.** *Aramaic Documents of the Fifth Century* B.C. Oxford: Clarendon, 1957. **Dommershausen, W.** *Die Estherrolle.* Stuttgart: Katholisches Bibelwerk, 1968. **Dorothy, C. V.** "The Books of Esther: Structure, Genre, and Textual Integrity." Diss., Claremont, 1989. **Fox, M.** *The Redaction of the Books of Esther: On Reading Composite Texts.* Atlanta: Scholars, 1991. **Gordis, R.** "Studies in the Esther Narrative." *JBL* 95 (1976) 43–58 (= Moore, *Studies,* 408–23). **Haupt, P.** "Critical Notes on Esther." *AJSL* 24 (1907–8) 97–186 (= Moore, *Studies,* 1–90). **Healey, J. P.** "Am Ha'arez." *ABD* 1:168–69. **Klingbeil, G. A.** "רכשׁ and Esther 8,10. 14: A Semantic Note." *ZAW* 107 (1995) 301–3. **Murphy, R. E.** *Wisdom Literature: Job, Proverbs, Ruth, Canticles, Ecclesiastes, and Esther.* FOTL 13. Grand Rapids, MI: Eerdmans, 1981. **Naveh, J.** "The Aramaic Ostraca from Tel Arad." In Y. Aharoni, *Arad Inscriptions.* Jerusalem: Israel Exploration Society, 1981. 153–76. **Williamson, H. G. M.** Review of *The Esther Scroll,* by D. J. A. Clines. *JTS* 37 (1986) 146–52.

Translation

SCENE 1. ESTHER AND MORDECAI ACQUIRE AUTHORITY TO ISSUE A COUNTERDECREE (8:1–8)
Time: evening, 1/17 or 1/18, year 12

Episode 1. Mordecai is admitted into the king's presence (8:1–2)

1 *That very day King Ahasuerus gave to Queen Esther the property of Haman, the enemy of the Jews, and Mordecai was admitted into the king's presence*[a] *because Esther had informed him of all that he was to her.*[b] 2 *Then the king took*[a] *off his signet ring which he had taken away from Haman and gave it to Mordecai, and Esther placed him in charge of Haman's property.*

Episode 2. The king grants Esther and Mordecai authority to write an edict on behalf of the Jews (8:3–8)

3 *Then Esther again spoke to the king. She fell down at his feet and wept, and implored him to get rid of the wicked scheme of Haman the Agagite*[a] *which he had devised against the Jews.* 4 *The king held out to Esther the gold scepter, and she rose and stood before the king.*

5 *She said, "If it pleases the king, and if I have found favor with him,*[a] *and if he considers the proposal proper*[b] *and if I am pleasing in his eyes, let an order be given*[c] *to revoke the dispatches—*[d] *the scheme of Haman son of Hammedatha, the Agagite*[d]*—which he has written in order to destroy the Jews*[e] *who are in all the king's provinces.* 6 *For how*

could I bear to see[a] *the disaster which would fall upon*[b] *my people? And how could I bear to see*[a] *the destruction of all my relatives?"*[c]

7 *Then King Ahasuerus said to Queen Esther and to Mordecai the Jew,*[a] *"Look, I have given Haman's property to Esther, and he has been hanged on the gallows because he*
lifted[b] *his hand against the Jews.* 8 *So now, you write concerning the Jews as you please*
in the king's name and seal it with the king's signet ring, for a decree written in the king's name and sealed[a] *with the king's signet ring cannot be revoked."*

SCENE 2. MORDECAI ISSUES THE COUNTERDECREE (8:9–17)
Time: 3/23, year 12

Episode 1. The counterdecree is written and promulgated (8:9–14)

9 *And so the royal scribes were summoned at that time, on the twenty-third day of the third*[a] *month, the month of Sivan.*[a] *And an edict was written,*[b] *exactly as*[c] *Mordecai directed, to*[d] *the Jews, and to the satraps, the governors, and the rulers of the provinces—the one hundred and twenty-seven provinces which stretched from India to Ethiopia*[e]*—to each province in its own script and to each people in their own language,*
and to the Jews in their script and in their language. 10 *It was written in the name of*
King Ahasuerus and sealed with his signet ring. And Mordecai sent dispatches by means of mounted[a] *couriers riding post-horses from the state service,*[b] *bred from the royal stud,*[b]
11 *to the effect that the king granted permission to the Jews in each and every city to assemble, to defend themselves,*[a] *to destroy, slay, and annihilate the forces*[b] *of any people or province attacking them,*[c] *women and children included, and to seize their goods as*
plunder, 12 *on one day, the thirteenth day of the twelfth month, the month of Adar, through-*
out all the provinces of King Ahasuerus. 13 *Also a copy of the edict was to be promulgated*
as law in every single province, being publicly displayed to all peoples,[a] *so that*[b] *the Jews*
might be ready[c] *for this day, to take vengeance on their enemies.* 14 *As the couriers went*
forth, mounted on post-horses from the state service[a] *and hastened and spurred by the king's command, the edict was issued in the Citadel of Susa.*

Episode 2. Mordecai leaves the king's presence with honor, and the Jews rejoice (8:15–17)

15 *Then Mordecai left the king's presence clad in a royal robe*[a] *of violet and white, wearing a large, gold turban and a purple cloak of fine linen. And the city of Susa rang*
with joyous cheers,[b] 16 *while for the Jews all was light, joy, gladness, and honor.* 17 *And in*
every single province and every single city which the king's command and edict reached, there was joy and gladness for the Jews, with feasting and celebration.[a] *And many of the peoples of the land professed to be Jews*[b] *because fear of the Jews had fallen upon them.*

Notes

1.a. Lit. "entered before the king." See *Comment.*

1.b. Lit. "made known what he was to her." See *Comment.* The readings of the LXX and Syr cited by *BHS* do not presuppose a different Heb. text. The LXX reading ἐνοικείωται, "he was related," merely explains the meaning of the Heb., while Syr *mnʾ hwʾ lh,* "what he was to her," involves a misreading of Heb. הוא, "he," as *hwʾ*, "was," instead of *hw*, "he" (Haupt, *AJSL* 24 [1907–8] 153–54).

2.a. The words "from his hand" found in a few MSS are most likely not original (contra Bardtke, 361) but were added in those texts under the influence of 3:10 (cf. *BHS* n.).

3.a. Lit. "the wickedness of Haman the Agagite and his scheme."
5.a. Lit. "in his eyes."
5.b. Lit. "the matter is right before the king." The idiom כשר לפני, "to be right, proper before," occurs in BH only here, while the verb כשר occurs elsewhere only in LBH (Eccles 10:10; 11:6). The comparable idiom in SBH is ישר בעיני, "to be right, correct in the eyes of." The lateness of the use of the idiom in Esther is indicated by the fact that כשר occurs elsewhere only in Sirach and MH; see Bergey, *JETS* 31 (1988) 165–66.
5.c. Lit. "let it be written."
5.d-d. Since the appositional phrase "son of Hammedatha, the Agagite" is lacking in the LXX, some would elide this whole phrase as a gloss (e.g., Haller, 130; Haupt, *AJSL* 24 [1907–8] 154; Ringgren, 397), but Haman's name must then be supplied since the sense of the following clause requires it (*BHS* n. 5c; cf. Bardtke, 363; Moore, 78). Such loosely attached appositional clauses are characteristic of the style of the book (Gerleman, 126 n. 5.b-b). Further, the proposal fails to catch the subtlety of Esther's language. By clearly dubbing the letters "Haman's scheme," she nicely avoids alluding to any personal responsibility on the part of the king, although the letters were sent out in his name and sealed with his signet ring (3:12; cf. Moore, 78).
5.e. A number of Heb. MSS and Syr read "all the Jews" (cf. *BHS* n.). Since the extent of the annihilation is indicated by the "all" of the next phrase, the reading of MT is to be preferred.
6.a. Though the sense of the expression is clear enough, the syntax of איככה אוכל וראיתי, lit. "how can I endure and I have seen," is not. It is variously explained in the grammars (see *GBH* § 177h; Brockelmann, *Syntax* § 143a). Gerleman (126 n. 6a), Haupt (*AJSL* 24 [1907–8] 154), and Paton (271) cite GKC § 112p. The reading of the LXX, σωθῆναι, "be delivered," for וְרָאִיתִי, "and I have seen," in the second occurrence of the clause in the verse (cf. *BHS* n.) can only be understood as a deliberate change by the Gr. translator.
6.b. Lit. "find." ימצא is masc, whereas its subject, רעה, is fem. As most scholars have noted, this is probably because the language here closely reflects that of Gen 44:34, where רע, the masc form of the noun, is used.
6.c. Lit. "kindred," i.e., all those related by blood.
7.a. Paton (270) considers the phrase "and to Mordecai the Jew" to be an interpolation because it is missing in LXX, OL, and Syr. However, all the verbs are pl, and the 2 m pl ind pron אתם, "you," is used at the beginning of v 8. Thus, the phrase clearly is original. Mordecai's presence is critical for what follows. Bardtke (367) argues that the introduction of Mordecai here, who has not been mentioned in vv 3–6, points to the beginning of a new scene, contending that several hours or even a day lay between Esther's petition and the king's reply. However, if there is no scenic break between v 2 and v 3 (for the argument for which, see *Form/Structure/Setting* below), then the narrator clearly intends to imply that Mordecai has been present throughout (cf. Moore, 79).
7.b. Lit. "sent."
8.a. There is no need to repoint this as a niphal ptcp (contra *BHS* n.). The inf abs can be used to continue a finite verb. See *Note* 2:13.e.
9.a. The LXX reads "the first month, the month of Nisan" (cf. *BHS* nn. a, b), undoubtedly a deliberate change; see the discussion in *Form/Structure/Setting*.
9.b. Lit. "it was written."
9.c. Lit. "according to all that . . ."
9.d. The emendation of אל to על and the omission of the waw on the following ואל with Syr (Haupt, *AJSL* 24 [1907–8] 155–56; Moore, 79–80; cf. *BHS* n. c) are to be rejected. These changes have been proposed on the grounds (cf. Moore, 80) that it is stated at the end of the verse that the edict was issued to the Jews as well as to the government officials and so to have the same information repeated here is superfluous. But this view quite misses the significance of the changes in and additions to the account of Mordecai's edict compared to that of Haman in 3:12–15; see *Form/Structure/Setting*. This also indicates how mistaken are those (e.g., BHK) who delete the final phrase.
9.e. Lit. "which were from India to Ethiopia, one hundred and twenty-seven provinces."
10.a. Lit. "couriers on horses."
10.b. The meanings of the Heb. terms here, אחשתרנים and רמכים, are uncertain; see *Comment*.
11.a. Lit. "to stand for their lives."
11.b. חיל, "(armed) force," is not to be deleted (*BHS* n.) as a gloss (contra Haupt, *AJSL* 24 [1907–8] 159).
11.c. הצרים is not to be emended to הצררים (Haller, 132; Haupt, *AJSL* 24 [1907–8] 159). הצרים is a qal ptcp < צור that can mean "fight, do battle with," as in Deut 2:9, 19 (cf. צור II, KB[3], 952).

13.a. On the syntax of this clause, see the *Comment* on 3:14.

13.b. The deletion of the waw on ולהיות (*BHS* n.) is unnecessary (contra Bardtke, 367; Gerleman, 126). Heb. frequently expresses clausal relationships paratactically.

13.c. Whether one reads the K עֲתוּדִים (qal pass ptcp on the Heb. pattern) or the Q עֲתִידִים (qal pass ptcp on the Aram. pattern), the meaning is not in doubt (see, e.g., KB[3], 854–55).

14.a. For this translation, see the *Comment* on the same phrases in v 10.

15.a. The word for robe, תכריך, occurs in BH only here. In SBH a wide variety of other terms are used for royal apparel. The lateness of the use of תכריך in Esther is indicated by the fact that it is found elsewhere only in MH (though not in a royal context); see Bergey, "Book of Esther," 139.

15.b. Lit. "shouted and rejoiced," a hendiadys.

17.a. Lit. "a good day."

17.b. The LXX and the OL clearly understood the word מתיהדים to mean full conversion, for they read "circumcised themselves and became Jews" (cf. *BHS* n.). See *Comment.*

Form/Structure/Setting

It is clear, in my opinion, that 8:1–17 comprises one act that divides unmistakably into two scenes, vv 1–8 and 9–17, on the basis of both content and form (contra Dommershausen, *Estherrolle,* 99–111; Bardtke, 361–77). As regards content, a new character is added to those of the previous acts, namely Mordecai (see the discussion below). Second, the unity of the two scenes is indicated by the cause-and-effect relationship between them. Thus, the first scene relates Esther's further appeal to the king on behalf of her people, which results in the king's permission to Esther and Mordecai to write whatever edict they please concerning the Jews, and the second describes the writing and promulgation of this decree. That the act divides into two scenes is indicated not only by this difference in content but also by the time statements with which each of the scenes begins: "on that day," v 1; "on the twenty-third day of the third month," v 9. For the question of the unity of venue and the difference in chronology between the two scenes, see the discussion below. As regards form, the mention of Mordecai provides a significant inclusio, binding the corpus into a unity. The statement that Mordecai was admitted into the king's presence (v 1b) in the short opening episode (vv 1–2) of the first scene (vv 1–8) is nicely balanced by the statement that he went forth from the king's presence (v 15a) in the short closing episode (vv 15–17) of the second scene (vv 9–17).

Each of the two scenes divides into two episodes as follows:

Scene 1. Esther and Mordecai acquire authority from the king to issue a counterdecree (vv 1–8)
- Episode 1. Mordecai is admitted into the king's presence (vv 1–2)
- Episode 2. The king grants Esther and Mordecai authority to issue a counterdecree (vv 3–8)

Scene 2. Mordecai issues the counterdecree (vv 9–17)
- Episode 1. The counterdecree is written and promulgated (vv 9–14)
- Episode 2. Mordecai leaves the king's presence with honor, and the Jews rejoice (vv 15–17)

There is considerable ambiguity, however, regarding two issues: (1) the point at which the previous act concludes and this new act begins and (2) whether these two scenes form a single act. The criteria are simply not as clear as they have been for previous acts.

(1) Regarding the point at which the act begins, clearly vv 1–8 divide into two sections: (a) vv 1–2, which relate the king's transference of Haman's property to Esther and his exaltation of Mordecai, and (b) vv 3–8, which describe Esther's new appeal to the king on behalf of her people, together with the king's grant of authority to her and Mordecai to promulgate a new decree. The narrator himself explicitly dates the events of the first section, vv 1–2, to the same day as those of the previous act ("on that day," v 1), so some have argued that they should be joined with that act as a conclusion. This has been argued on such grounds as: (a) these events are the immediate result of Haman's fall (Gerleman, 121), or (b) Mordecai's exaltation presents the consummation of the thwarting of Haman's attack upon him (Meinhold, 69; cf. also Ringgren, 397). The new act (or scene) then begins with 8:3. Bardtke (361–62), however, followed by Murphy (*Wisdom*, 166–67), sets the section off as a separate unit on the grounds that the events are only "reported," not presented as detailed dialogue. However, the very fact that it is given in the form of a brief report strongly argues that it is intended not as a separate entity but as a prelude and preparation for the events that are to follow, whose greater importance is indicated by their more detailed, dialogue form.

In my opinion the preponderance of the evidence is heavily in favor of joining 8:1–2 with 8:3–17, rather than joining them with the previous act or constituting them a separate unit (cf. also Clines, *Esther Scroll*, 98–99; Dorothy, "Books of Esther," 294–97). First, vv 1–2 introduce a character not present in the previous act, namely, Mordecai. He not only comes on the scene in a significant way with the statement that he "was admitted into the king's presence" (see *Comment*), but he is included in the king's response (v 7) to Esther's appeal (vv 3–6). Hence, he was present during that appeal (see *Note* 7.a.). Further, he is the major figure in the events that follow in vv 9–17. It is important to note that Mordecai has not been one of the major characters in any of the events of acts 4, 5, or 6 (5:1–7:10). He was not present at all in acts 4 and 6 (which relate Esther's entry into the king's presence and the accounts of the two banquets at which only she, the king, and Haman were present), and in act 5 he is entirely a secondary character, for he is the object of the discussion and the action, never the subject. The introduction of a character not present in the preceding acts argues strongly for a new act.

Second, the separation of 8:1–2 from the preceding act, 7:1–10, is strongly effected by the manner in which 7:1–10 is bound by form and content into a complete and cohesive whole (see *Form/Structure/Setting* thereto), indicated particularly by the strong closure of 7:10 (Fox, 89).

Third, the narrator has heretofore regularly indicated a new act or scene with a time designation or temporal clause (e.g., 1:10; 2:1; 3:1; 3:7, 12; 5:1, 9; 6:1; 7:1). Hence, the lack of a time designation at 8:3 and its presence in 8:1 strongly favor seeing vv 3–8 as a continuation of vv 1–2.

Fourth, Esther's appeal in v 3 clearly does not constitute a separate audience with the king (contra Paton, 269; see *Comment*), despite the king's extending to her the golden scepter. It is, rather, a continuation of her previous appeal, for the text says "Esther *spoke* again," not "Esther *came* again" (cf. Clines, *Esther Scroll*, 98; Moore, 77).

Finally, the conclusion that vv 1–8 are a single scene is not undercut by either questions of venue or chronology. Given that the nature of the events of vv 1–8 requires no special locale for their occurrence (such as the throne room; see below), the time designation "on that day" of v 1 naturally implies that they occurred in the same locale as the preceding events, namely, in the royal pavilion where Esther's banquet took place (see 7:7). It is certainly plausible that the events of both pericopes, vv 1–2 and 3–8, could have taken place there after Haman had been led away to execution. Bardtke's view (363) that the events of vv 3–6 took place elsewhere and some days later than those of vv 1–2 is based solely upon his judgment (the allusion to Isa 7:3–9, 10–17 proves nothing about Esther) that these verses begin a new scene. His argument that the locale is the throne room on the grounds that the king holds his scepter in his hand and stretches it out to Esther is belied by the fact that this procedure is not an act of clemency performed in the court ceremonial attendant upon an unbidden audience with the king (as Bardtke himself observes, 363; cf. 5:2) but a sign of favor in response to an act of supplication. Note that the narrator uses neither כרע nor השתחוה, the terms that normally express prostration, but the more general term נפל, "to fall" (cf. Clines, *Esther Scroll,* 98). As for the chronological question, it is not at all impossible that the events recorded in vv 1–8 could have taken place at the conclusion of the day that began in 6:1 with the king's insomnia. The events of the day would have been the following:

1. During the late night/early morning, the king asks Haman, who has arrived to request the king to hang Mordecai, what he should do for the man whom he desires to honor, since the king has just learned that Mordecai's report of the assassination attempt has gone without reward. Haman, thinking that the king is referring to him, describes what he should do for such a man. The king commands him to do such for Mordecai (6:1–10).
2. Later that morning Haman so honors Mordecai. Mordecai returns to the royal court. Haman goes home and complains to his wife and friends, and they proclaim that his doom is certain. Just then the king's servants arrive and bring Haman in haste to Esther's banquet (6:11–14).
3. In the early afternoon Esther's second banquet takes place, at the end of which, during the wine course, Haman's perfidy is discovered, and the king condemns him to execution (7:1–9).
4. That afternoon Haman is executed (7:10).
5. In the late afternoon/early evening the king gives to Esther the property of Haman. Esther informs the king of all that Mordecai is to her. Mordecai is admitted to the king's presence. The king gives him his signet ring, and Esther places him over Haman's property (8:1–2).
6. Later that evening Esther appeals again to the king on behalf of her people. Consequently, the king gives her and Mordecai permission to issue whatever edict they please concerning the Jews (8:3–8).

All of this could have taken place on one day since some events would doubtless have taken place at the same time. For instance, Mordecai's return to the royal court and Haman's return home would certainly have occurred simultaneously. Haman's execution and the complex of events in item 5 above involving the king, Esther, and Mordecai could well have taken place concurrently (cf. Fox, 96–97).

(2) Regarding whether these two scenes, vv 1–8 and 9–14, form a single act, it is not at all clear that they do. The greatest ambiguity in this regard relates to the chronology of the chapter, that is, the large gap that occurs between the time that Esther and Mordecai obtain the king's permission to issue their edict (v 8) and the date of the edict itself, the twenty-third day of the third month (8:9). This dating places the writing and promulgation of Mordecai's edict two months and ten days (or seventy days—perhaps symbolic; see below) later than the day (the thirteenth day of the first month) on which Haman issued his edict (3:12–15). This time period is far too long to be filled by the events related since the issuing of Haman's edict. The time that these events have consumed could not possibly have exceeded four days, or perhaps five depending upon whether an interval of a day might have elapsed between the issuance of Haman's edict in the Citadel of Susa (3:15) and the time by which "Mordecai learned of all that had been done" (4:1). Mordecai would have come into possession of a copy of the edict issued in Susa (4:8) almost immediately, but he also knows the exact amount of money Haman promised to pay into the royal treasury (4:7), and it might have taken him some time to learn these details from whatever were his sources within the inner circles of the court. It could hardly have taken more than a day for Esther to have learned of Mordecai's distress (4:4) and for the ensuing conversation between them to have taken place (4:5–16). Esther then appeared before the king (5:1) on the third day after her conversation with Mordecai, and the dramatic and climactic events that led to 8:1–8 transpired over just two days, as follows (for events of the second day, see above):

5:4 "Let the king and Haman come *today* to the banquet . . ."
5:8 ". . . let the king and Haman come to the banquet . . . *tomorrow* . . ."
5:9 "Haman left the banquet *that day* . . ."
5:12 ". . . and also *tomorrow* I have been summoned to come to her with the king."
6:1 "*That night* the king could not sleep . . ."
7:1 "Also on *the second day* the king said to Esther . . ."
8:1 "*That day* King Ahasuerus gave to Queen Esther . . ."

At the very most, then, from the issuance of Haman's decree to the events of 8:1–8 only four days (or perhaps five) can have elapsed. Nor does it help to begin a new act at 8:3, with a new venue and a later time (so, e.g., Bardtke; see the discussion above). Esther surely would not have delayed after the demise of Haman before appealing to the king for relief for her people from Haman's decree. In fact, it would have been to her advantage to strike while the iron was hot. Further, there might well have been a short period between the king's permission to Esther and Mordecai to write the decree (v 8) and Mordecai's writing of the decree itself (v 9). During this time, Mordecai presumably was determining that the best procedure was indeed to write a counterdecree. But this period could hardly have amounted to the lapse of time involved. Hence, we are faced with the incongruous fact that Esther and Mordecai received permission from the king to write a decree concerning the Jews on the seventeenth day of the first month (or at the most a day or so later) but did not issue the decree until the twenty-third day of the third month, a lapse of more than two months. (In this light there seems little doubt that the LXX reading of "the twenty-third of the first month, the month of Nisan" in 8:9 is a deliberate change.)

There does not seem to be any way from the distribution of the events themselves to account for this incongruous lapse of time (cf. also Fox, 97). Yet there are clear indications that the narrator (whose narrative skills have heretofore been amply demonstrated) intended the two scenes to be a unity. First, it is important to note that the narrator gives no absolute dates whatsoever for any of the events of his narrative between the date of Haman's decree (1/13, given in 3:12) and the date of Mordecai's decree (3/23, given in 8:9). Hence, it did not seem greatly to concern him exactly how much time has been consumed by the events that he has related. He apparently has made the general assumption that these events transpired in this interval of time. That this is the case is almost demanded by the fact that the narrator emphasizes the date by adding to it the phrase "at that time" (v 9). This naturally implies that the events he is about to relate are generally contemporaneous with those that immediately precede. Indeed, in this light it may well be that the narrator chose the date because of the symbolic value of the resulting seventy-day interval, even though he leaves it to his readers to make the calculation. He may well have subtly encouraged the calculation by the way in which he has emphasized the date. Perhaps indeed the date would have "struck a chord with every attentive post-exilic reader of the book: the seventy days are (are they not?) the seventy years of exile" (Clines, 316). In this view the seventy days of the interval would be not only a favorable symbol of "perfection and good" (Dommershausen, *Estherrolle,* 105) but also a signal that a reversal of the fate of the Jews was as certain as the return from the exile. However that may be, it nonetheless seems reasonably clear that the narrator, at least, assumed no significant time gap between the two scenes, thus constituting them a unity. On these grounds, then, I conclude that 8:1–17 constitutes a single act.

Finally, it is important to note that in the first episode of the second scene (vv 9–15) the narrator reports both Haman's edict itself and the specific circumstances of its writing and promulgation by using language virtually identical to that used in relating Haman's edict in 3:12–15. This can best be seen by a verse-by-verse comparison of the two accounts (the **changes** are marked in each account by bold type and the *pluses* in 8:9–16 by italicized type):

	3:12–15		8:9–16
12	And so the royal scribes were summoned on the **thirteenth day of the first month,**	9	And so the royal scribes were summoned *at that time* **on the twenty-third day of the third month,** *the month of Sivan.*
	and an edict was written, exactly as **Haman** directed,		And an edict was written, exactly as **Mordecai** directed,
	to the royal satraps, to the governors who are in charge of each province, and to the rulers of each people,		*to the Jews,* **and to the satraps, the governors, and the rulers of the provinces**—*the one hundred and twenty-seven provinces which stretched from India to Ethiopia*—
	to each province in its own script and to each people in their own language.		to each province in its own script and to each people in their own language, *and to the Jews in their script and in their language.*
	It was written in the name of King Ahasuerus and sealed with his signet ring.	10	It was written in the name of King Ahasuerus and sealed with his signet ring.

13	And dispatches were sent by means of **couriers** to all the provinces of the king,		And Mordecai sent dispatches by means of **mounted couriers riding post-horses from the state service, bred from the royal stud,**
	giving the order	11	to the effect that *the king granted permission to the Jews in each and every city to assemble, to defend themselves,*
	to destroy, slay, and annihilate		to destroy, slay, and annihilate
	all the Jews, young and old,		**the forces of any people or province attacking them,**
	women and children included,		women and children included,
			and to seize their goods as plunder,
	on one day, the thirteenth day of the twelfth month, the month of Adar,	12	on one day, the thirteenth day of the twelfth month, the month of Adar, *throughout all the provinces of King Ahasuerus.*
	and to seize their goods as plunder.		
14	Also a copy of the edict was to be promulgated as law in every single province, being publicly displayed to all peoples	13	Also a copy of the edict was to be promulgated as law in every single province, being publicly displayed to all peoples,
	so that **they** might be ready for this day.		so that **the Jews** might be ready for this day, *to take vengeance on their enemies.*
15	As the couriers went forth spurred by the king's command, the edict was issued in the Citadel of Susa.	14	As the couriers went forth, mounted on *post-horses from the state service and hastened and* spurred by the king's command, the edict was issued in the Citadel of Susa.
	Then **the king and Haman sat down to a banquet,** but the city of Susa **was confused and in tumult.**	15	Then **Mordecai left the king's presence** .... And the city of Susa rang with joyous cheers,
		16	*while for the Jews all was light, joy, gladness, and honor.*

Obviously, a number of the changes are simply required by the following facts: (1) the author of the decree is now Mordecai and not Haman, and (2) the recipients of the decree are now the Jews and not the generic "all peoples" to whom Haman's edict was addressed. Fox states that the reason that the wording of the decree and the details of its issuance match, almost exactly, those of the first decree is that it "becomes the means of neutralizing Haman's" decree (*Redaction,* 118). But surely Mordecai's decree and the circumstances of its issuance could have as effectively countered Haman's decree without the unmistakably conscious adoption of virtually identical language in both the decree itself and in relating the circumstances of its issuance. This conscious adoption of virtually identical language together with a number of significant changes and additions (beyond those necessitated by the changed decree) are significant (for which see *Explanation*).

Comment

1 נָתַן הַמֶּלֶךְ אֲחַשְׁוֵרוֹשׁ לְאֶסְתֵּר הַמַּלְכָּה אֶת־בֵּית הָמָן, "King Ahasuerus gave Queen Esther the property of Haman." As has often been noted, Herodotus (3.128–29) and Josephus (*Ant.* 11.17) report that in Achaemenid Persia the property of a traitor was confiscated by the state. The king presumably gives Haman's property to Esther because she was the one primarily wronged by his treachery. בית, lit. "house," is used here in the sense of all that one owned, real estate and moveable goods (as elsewhere, e.g., Gen 44:1; 1 Kgs 13:8), prompting the translation "property." It may have included Haman's family as well (Clines, 314), since בית, "house," is often used in that sense in the OT.

וּמָרְדֳּכַי בָּא לִפְנֵי הַמֶּלֶךְ, lit. "and Mordecai came into the king's presence." The expression doubtless means that Mordecai was admitted to the status of those who had access to the king (cf. "those who see the the king's face," 1:14) without being explicitly summoned, a status Haman apparently had (6:4).

מַה הוּא־לָהּ, lit. "what he was to her." It is best to keep the literal expression, for it is highly probable that it means more than simply the fact that Esther and Mordecai were related by blood (so Moore, 77). It doubtless implies in particular the quality of their relationship (note esp. 2:11, 20). The simple fact of blood relationship would more likely have been expressed by קרוב ל׳, "related to," or the like (cf. Ruth 2:20b, 2:1). It is really not at all extraordinary (so Paton, 267) that neither the king nor Haman heretofore knew of the relationship between Mordecai and Esther. The narrator has specifically stated that Esther did not make known her ethnic origins either in the harem itself (2:10) or in the court upon her accession to the queenship (2:20). Such a conspiracy of silence would doubtless also have included Esther's own personal attendants (cf. 4:5–16).

3 וַתּוֹסֶף אֶסְתֵּר וַתְּדַבֵּר לִפְנֵי הַמֶּלֶךְ, "And Esther spoke to the king again." The idiom, lit. "she added and she spoke," indicates the repetition of an action. It is clear that this is not a new audience with the king but a continuation of the one that began in the previous act and is continued in vv 1–2 (cf. esp. Clines, *Esther Scroll,* 98; Meinhold, 71; contra Bardtke, 363; Gerleman, 127). This is made clear by (1) the time reference "on that day" with which the events of vv 1–2 have been introduced, (2) the lack of any time reference in v 3, and (3) the specific language: "Esther *spoke* again to the king," not "Esther *entered* again to the king." Hence, Esther has not risked her life once more by coming into the king's presence unbidden (cf. Moore, 77, 82; Clines, 314; Fox, 91–92; contra Paton, 269). Here the king's action of extending to her the royal scepter in v 4 is not an act of clemency as it is in 5:2, but rather a sign of favor and encouragement (cf. Clines, 315; Moore, 78).

וַתִּפֹּל לִפְנֵי רַגְלָיו, "She fell down at his feet." This is not an act of obeisance, for which different verbs are used (כרע, השתחוה; cf. 3:2, 5), but of supplication (again indicating that this is not a new scene with a new audience with the king).

5 וְכָשֵׁר הַדָּבָר לִפְנֵי הַמֶּלֶךְ, lit. "(if) the matter is proper before the king." כשר occurs only in LBH. It is used outside Esther only in Ecclesiastes, where in the qal stem it means "to succeed" (11:6) and in the hiphil "to give success" (cf. also the related noun כִּשְׁרוֹן, "success, profit," Eccl 2:21; 4:4; 5:10). In post-biblical Hebrew, the verb means "to be fit, right, proper," so it seems possible in this context that the verb carries meanings in the range "to be agreeable, suitable; fitting, appropriate," or "proper, right" (hardly "to please," as *HALOT,* 503). Since Esther is about to propose the repeal of an edict issued in the king's name and sealed with his signet ring, which she must have known was improper and contrary to all established custom (cf. 1:19; 8:8), the context is highly in favor of the sense "proper, right."

וְטוֹבָה אֲנִי בְּעֵינָיו, lit. "(if) I am pleasing in his eyes." In context it is more likely that Esther uses טוב in the sense "pleasing in appearance, beautiful, lovely" (for the use of the word in this sense, see Exod 2:2; Judg 15:2) than in the sense "having approval" (so NRSV, NEB, REB). As Haupt (*AJSL* 24 [1907–8] 154; cf. Moore, 78) observes, the phrase is a "coquettish climax, equivalent to our *if you really care for me a little.*"

7 Most scholars have assumed that in the king's opening words he is expressing his goodwill or favorable disposition toward Esther and Mordecai by rehearsing what he has done for them (e.g., Gerleman, 128; Dommershausen, 102; Moore, 79). However, the use of the deictic or emphasizing particle הנה, "look!" with which he begins his reply here in v 7 and the use of highly emphatic independent pronoun ואתם, "and you," pleonastically added to the second person plural imperative verb "write" at the beginning of v 8, strongly suggest that the words are spoken in a sharp and exasperated tone of voice. He is saying, "Look! This is what I have done for you! Not only can you not expect me to do more, but I cannot do more" (v 8b). This understanding fits far better with the narrator's consistent characterization of the king as callously interested in little other than his own honor and power. It seems far more likely that he is no more concerned to be personally involved with the difficult task of saving this people from Haman's irrevocable decree than he was about their circumstances or identity when he gave Haman permission for the odious decree to be issued in the first place (see 3:10–11 and the *Explanation* thereto). He is simply telling Esther and Mordecai that he has done all he can do, the rest is up to them.

8 כִּי־כְתָב אֲשֶׁר־נִכְתָּב בְּשֵׁם־הַמֶּלֶךְ וְנַחְתּוֹם בְּטַבַּעַת הַמֶּלֶךְ אֵין לְהָשִׁיב, "for any decree written in the king's name and sealed with the king's signet ring cannot be revoked." Clines (*Esther Scroll,* 192 n. 6; cf. also 175 n. 6) wrestles with the question whether this clause gives the reason for the irreversibility of the previous decree issued by Haman or the new decree about to be issued by Mordecai. He concludes that it is quite possible that it refers to both. However, the response of the king is an exasperated concession in which he virtually washes his hands of the whole affair (see the entry above; Clines also so takes it), and his command to Esther and Mordecai is not specifically to write a counterdecree but to write whatever they please concerning the Jews. Hence, it seems far more probable that the king intends this clause to refer to the irrevocability of Haman's decree (so also Paton, 270–71; Bardtke, 367; Gerleman, 128). Moore's conclusion (77) that the clause could not have been spoken by the king but must be the "parenthetic aside" of the author or a glossator, since Esther would have known about the law's irrevocability, does not recognize that the king is not giving new information but denying the possibility of Esther's request that an order be given to revoke Haman's scheme (v 5).

10 רֹכְבֵי הָרֶכֶשׁ הָאֲחַשְׁתְּרָנִים בְּנֵי הָרַמָּכִים. Both here and in 1 Kgs 5:8, רכש (a collective) is a synonym for סוסים, "horses" (cf. also Mic 1:13). The word also occurs in Aramaic (see *DISO,* 1077; Driver, *Aramaic Documents,* 61; Naveh, "Aramaic Ostraca," 155) and Syriac, where it refers to some type of horse. Its exact nuance is, however, uncertain. Haupt (*AJSL* 24 [1907–8] 157) suggests "race-horses" or "swift dromedaries," while Bardtke (366) renders "post-horses" (cf. KB^3), both apparently simply from context. Recently, however, Klingbeil (*ZAW* 107 [1995] 301–3) has plausibly argued for the meaning "post-horses" on the grounds of the appearance of the term in the Aramaic ostraca from Arad (6:1; see Naveh, "Aramaic Ostraca," 155) dating to the Persian period. Since Arad seems to have functioned in this period as a border garrison and way station on the important trade and military route from Gaza to the interior (Naveh, "Aramaic Ostraca," 153, 176), Klingbeil (*ZAW* 107 [1995] 302) suggests that the use of the term at Arad, rather than the more common סוס, "horse," connotes a technical sense, "namely the team of horses used for the royal postal system." He then goes on to suggest that the use of such a technical term fits the context in Esther on the grounds that, since the whole series of obscure technical terms used here is missing in 3:13 (which describes the sending of Haman's decree), the author wished by their use here either to indicate that a different postal service is used by Mordecai or to stress that the speedy delivery of Mordecai's decree would decide the fate of the Jews. It seems most improbable that the Persian court had several types of postal services or, given that Mordecai's decree is promulgated on the twenty-third of the third month (v 9) and the proposed attack and defense is not to take place until the thirteenth of the twelfth month (v 12), that there is any need to stress the speed of its delivery. Nevertheless, it does seem appropriate that the author would reserve the technical terms for the famous and efficient Persian postal service for use here in order to stress the importance of the delivery of Mordecai's decree for the Jewish people (cf. Clines, *Esther Scroll,* 96). I have, then, with all due reserve, accepted the translation "post-horses" for רכש.

The meaning of the two terms in apposition to "riders of the post-horses" is also uncertain. Though syntactically they could be in apposition with either word of the construct phrase, they doubtless are modifying רכש, "post-horses," since רמכים seems clearly to be a term referring to animals (see below). אחשתרנים is generally seen as a loan word from Persian *ḫšaṣa,* "dominion, rule," plus the Persian adjectival suffix *ana.* Hence, it is most commonly taken to mean horses reserved for the imperial service and/or the personal use of the king (Haupt, *AJSL* 24 [1907–8] 157; Moore, 80; Paton, 273). I have therefore with all due reserve rendered רכבי הרכש האחשתרנים, "riding post-horses from the state service."

On the basis of cognate words in mishnaic Hebrew, late Aramaic, and Arabic, רמכים has been rendered "(swift) mare" (Bardtke, 366; Moore, 80; cf. KB³), yielding for בני הרמכים "offspring of the (swift) mares." Others, however, cite Syriac *ramkâ,* "herd," *rammâḵâ,* "herdsman" (Haupt, *AJSL* 24 [1907–8] 157–58), yielding "offspring of the (royal) herd [or 'stud']." In either case, the expression would mean animals specially bred for the royal service, and so I have tentatively taken it. Since Syriac *rammâḵâ* means "herdsman" and this noun pattern in Hebrew also signifies an occupation or profession (cf. *IBHS* § 5.4.a), it is highly probable that the word should be repointed הָרַמָּכִים (cf. Haupt, *AJSL* 24 [1907–8] 157). Gerleman's interesting proposal (129) to see in the term the Persian equivalent of the Greek term ἱππῶνες, "post-stations" (referring to the Persian practice of setting up resupply stations on the royal roads at intervals of a day's ride, described in a passage in Xenophon), yielding for בני הרמכים the translation "personnel of the post-stations," has in its favor only the fact that it fits the context; it is without lexical or textual support.

11 לְהַשְׁמִיד וְלַהֲרֹג וּלְאַבֵּד אֶת־כָּל־חֵיל עַם וּמְדִינָה הַצָּרִים אֹתָם טַף וְנָשִׁים וּשְׁלָלָם לָבוֹז, lit. "to destroy, slay, and annihilate all forces of people and province who attack them, children and women, and their plunder to seize." In the standard, almost universally accepted, interpretation of this clause, Mordecai's decree grants the Jews permission to destroy not only the national or provincial forces who would attack them but also their children and women. To avoid this ethical problem, Gordis (*JBL* 95 [1976] 49–53) reinterprets the text at two points (followed by Clines, *Esther Scroll*, 179 n. 3). (1) טף ונשים, "children and women," are the objects of the participle הצרים, "attacking," rather than the infinitives להשמיד ולהרג ולאבד, "to destroy, slay, and annihilate." (2) The following clause ושללם לבוז, "and their plunder to seize," is not to be understood as a second infinitival clause coordinate with the infinitives just mentioned, and hence part of the permission granted to the Jews, but as coordinate with the participle "attacking," so further describing the actions of the enemies of the Jews. Gordis then views these last five words of v 11, אתם טף ונשים ושללם לבוז, lit. "them, women and children, and their goods to plunder," as actually a citation of Haman's edict in 3:13. This reinterpretation yields the translation, "the king permitted the Jews . . . to destroy, kill, and wipe out every armed force of a people or a province attacking 'them, their children and their wives, with their goods as booty.'" Gordis seeks to justify this reinterpretation on the grounds that

> . . . an examination of the syntax and the linguistic usage of both passages (i.e., 3:13 and 8:11) indicates a radical difference between them. In 3:13, the clause *ʾet-kol-hayyehûdîm . . . ûšᵉlālām lābôz* ('all the Jews . . . and to plunder their goods') follows immediately after the verb *ûlᵉʾabbed* ('to destroy'), so that it is clear that the phrase is in the accusative and the object of the verbs. In 8:11, no less than seven words intervene between *ûlᵉabbēd* ('to destroy') and *ṭap wᵉnāšîm* ('children and women'). (*JBL* 95 [1976] 50, parentheses added)

However, the argument is "hardly relevant" (Fox, 284), for it obscures the full parallelism between the two passages:

3:13	*ûlᵉʾabbēd* to destroy	*ʾet-kol-hayyᵉhûdîm* all the Jews	*minnaʿar wᵉʿad-zāqēn* from young to old	*ṭap̄ wᵉnāšîm . . .* children & women . . .	*ûšᵉlālām lābôz* and to despoil them
8:11	*ûlᵉʾabbēd* to destroy	*ʾet-kol-ḥêl ʿam ûmᵉdînāh* all power of people and province	*haṣṣārîm ʾōtām* attacking them	*ṭap̄ wᵉnāšîm* children & women	*ûšᵉlālām lābôz* and to despoil them

The parallelism clearly reveals (Fox, 284) that the phrase *ṭap̄ wenašîm*, "children and women," is in apposition with the direct object phrase "all power of people and province" in 8:11, exactly as it is with the direct object phrase "all the Jews" in 3:13. Further, to understand the two nouns *ṭap̄ wenašîm*, "children and women," as further objects of the participle "attacking," they should not only carry the pronominal suffix "their," but the direct object marker *ʾe̱t* as well. Indeed, the very fact that they are indefinite coordinates them with the equally indefinite "all power of people and province," rather than the definite pronoun "them," which immediately precedes. Finally, as the parallelism also reveals, the final clause, being infinitival and not participial, must coordinate with "to destroy" and not with "attacking."

17 וְרַבִּים מֵעַמֵּי הָאָרֶץ מִתְיַהֲדִים, "and many of the peoples of the land professed to be Jews." It is striking that the narrator speaks of "peoples of the ארץ," "*land*," not "peoples of the מלכות," "*kingdom*," the word used everywhere else in Esther to refer to the kingdom or empire of Ahasuerus (cf. 1:14; 2:3; 3:6; 5:3, 6; 7:2). ארץ, "land," occurs elsewhere in Esther only in 10:1, where it is used in contrast to איי הים, "islands, coastlands," and doubtless means something like "mainland." The phrase "peoples of the land" occurs in the OT in texts from the post-exilic period (to be distinguished from the singular term "people of the land" in use in the pre-exilic period in a much different sense; cf. Healey, *ABD* 1:169). The designation ארץ, "land," means, of course, the land of Palestine, and the expression denotes the heterogeneous non-Jewish population that the exiles found occupying the land upon their return, a population that the post-exilic community viewed with disdain (cf. esp. Ezra 4:4; 6:21; 9:1, 2; 10:2; Neh 10:29–31 [Eng. 28–30]). Quite clearly the narrator uses a term for the non-Jewish elements of the Persian empire that was full of meaning for the post-exilic Palestinian Jewish community. Whether the term as used in the Jewish diaspora had the negative ring it has in the canonical texts of Ezra and Nehemiah is uncertain. It is certain, however, that it did not have the pejorative sense of "pagans, heathen" that it developed in later rabbinic usage.

The participle מִתְיַהֲדִים is a denominative verb from the noun יְהוּדִי, "Jew," built on the pattern of the hithpael stem. One of the frequent ranges of meaning expressed by this stem is the "estimative-declarative reflexive," i.e., "to esteem someone as in a state or to declare someone as existing in a state" (see *IBHS* § 26.2.f). Hence, the meaning here is "they esteemed themselves/declared themselves to be Jews." In context, does this mean "they pretended to be Jews" or "they (genuinely) adopted Jewish beliefs, customs, and practices"? There could have been no distinctive Jewish dress to adopt. If there had been such, Mordecai's fellow officials would have known that he was Jewish without his having to tell them (3:4; see Fox, *Redaction*, 112 n. 8). As Bardtke (376) notes, the members of each local Jewish community would have known exactly who its own members and genuine proselytes were, so a purely pro forma designation of oneself as a Jew could hardly have been successful, particularly when the Jews came to defending themselves from attack. Thus, in context, the word most probably must be taken to mean "they adopted Jewish beliefs, customs, and practices," i.e., they "joined the Jewish people" (Fox, *Redaction*, 112 n. 8). However, given that the motivation for such a change is that "the fear of the Jews had fallen upon them" (for the meaning of this clause see below), it may indeed have only been ostensibly genuine. Hence, it seems preferable to adopt an ambiguous translation such as "they professed themselves to be Jews" (so NJPS; cf. *IBHS* chap. 26, n. 26). Finally, it seems most probable (as Fox, 105, observes) that the change involved here was ethnic (becoming a Jew) more than religious (cleaving to God's law; cf. Neh 10:29).

כִּי־נָפַל פַּחַד־הַיְּהוּדִים עֲלֵיהֶם, "because fear of the Jews had fallen upon them." A number of scholars (e.g., Clines, 318–19; Dommershausen, *Estherrolle*, 110; Ringgren, 400) have argued that the fear involved here is religious awe, citing such OT passages as Josh 2:9; Exod 15:16; Ps 105:38. Clines states,

> It was a fear that had nothing to do with any perceived military prowess of the Jews, but rather with the sensitivity of these proselytes to the religious significance of the events that had befallen. The reversal of fortune of the Jewish people that had been achieved by a series of implausible coincidences (from the human point of view) infallibly dis-

> played where truth lay in matters of religion. . . . [I]t is solely the non-violent, political capability of the Jews and their God that provokes this rash of proselytism. . . . It is not indeed a fear precisely of the Jews, though the narrator is obliged to say that because he is avoiding specifically religious language, but of the God of the Jews . . . . (*Esther Scroll*, 40–41)

However, this view cannot be sustained on two grounds. First, it violates linguistic usage. The word פחד, "fear," in the OT does not refer only to the fear of God (Fox, 105; id., *Redaction*, 112; cf. Ps 64:2[Eng. 1]). Rather, as Williamson notes (*JTS* 37 [1986] 148), the idiom נפל פחד על, "fear fell upon," regularly refers to a fear of calamity that is generally of a military nature (cf. Exod 15:16; 1 Sam 11:7; Ps 105:38; Job 13:11). Second, it can only be made to fit the context with the greatest of difficulty. V 17 clearly refers to the Jews and the non-Jewish peoples spread throughout the empire in general, in contrast to both the Jewish and non-Jewish inhabitants of the capital city of Susa, which are referred to in vv 15–16. How then could the "peoples of the land," the non-Jewish ethnic groups spread throughout the huge Persian empire, be "sensitive to the religious significance of the events that have occurred"? How could they be presumed to have any knowledge of the "series of implausible coincidences" involved in the quite private series of events that have transpired in acts 4, 5, and 6 (5:1–7:10) involving Haman, Mordecai, Esther, and Ahasuerus? At most, they could have been aware of the public events that had transpired: (1) Haman's public honoring of Mordecai, (2) the hanging of Haman because he attempted to exterminate the Jews who were the people of Esther, the queen of Persia, (3) the elevation of Mordecai the Jew to Haman's position as the second in command to the king (cf. v 15), and (4) in particular, the contents of the public (cf. v 13) counterdecree, issued now under the authority of Mordecai the Jew, giving the Jews the right to defend themselves.

The narrator has also informed us (v 13) that, at the king's command, a copy of the decree was to be promulgated as law in each and every province and publicly displayed to all peoples, "so that the Jews might be ready for this day, to take vengeance on their enemies." Clearly, what the "peoples of the land" would have been aware of was the fact that it was not now Haman the Agagite and all those affiliated with him and his schemes who wielded power in the Persian empire but Mordecai the Jew and all those affiliated with him, the Jews. It is certainly the new-found "political capability" (Clines, see above) of the Jews that instigates the fear of them on the part of the non-Jewish peoples, but this can hardly have been considered "non-violent" when it sprang from their permission and ability to destroy any who dared attack them and to take vengeance on their enemies. The enemies of the Jews might have been aware of an unnamed power ranged on the side of the Jews (Fox, 105–6; id., *Redaction*, 112), but in the context it can hardly be some sense of the numinous that prompts the non-Jewish peoples to profess to be Jews, let alone a religious awe of the God of the Jews. It is surely, rather, the dread of the superior political and military power now wielded by Mordecai and the Jewish community that prompts their profession.

Explanation

It now must have been the evening of the long and emotionally charged day that began in 6:1 with the king's insomnia (see *Form/Structure/Setting*). During the course of this day, Esther's appeal to the king has succeeded in eliminating Haman, but that has removed from the scene only the source of the terrible edict that has decreed the annihilation of the Jews. The task, then, of saving the Jewish people, which Mordecai had laid upon Esther as the queen of Persia, has in a real sense only just begun. The threat to their very existence still lives on in the irrevocable edict that Haman had issued in the king's name and sealed with the king's signet ring (3:12–15).

SCENE 1. ESTHER AND MORDECAI ACQUIRE AUTHORITY TO ISSUE A COUNTERDECREE (8:1–8)

Episode 1. Mordecai is admitted into the king's presence (8:1–2). The process of dealing with Haman's edict begins when the king, surprisingly out of character, makes one of the very few decisions on his own volition in the whole story. He gives Haman's property to Esther. His action doubtless reflects the fact that it has been Esther's whole strategy thus far to have depicted herself as the one primarily wronged by Haman's treachery (cf. Fox, 89–90). Consequently, the king's anger had cooled as soon as the threat to his queen had been eliminated by Haman's execution (7:10). It was not the invidious plot against a whole people of his empire that had fueled his rage but the insult to his honor in the attack upon his queen. Little more can be expected from Ahasuerus. This is the situation that Esther must now modify by appealing again to the king, this time concerning the issue of relief from Haman's edict. It will be, however, a delicate matter indeed, for the king quite apparently has decided to leave that whole affair buried, undoubtedly because of his own complicity in it.

She begins by informing the king of all that Mordecai is to her (v 1b), which probably implies not just the fact of their blood relationship but the quality of that relationship (cf. 2:7, 10–11, 20) and of Mordecai's character (see *Comment*). As a result, Mordecai fully assumes Haman's position as the grand vizier. First, like Haman (6:4), he is admitted to the status of those who have access to the king without a specific summons (v 1b; see *Comment*). Then the king gives him his signet ring, which he had taken away from Haman (v 2a; cf. 3:10), thus transferring to him the power to act with the king's full authority that was previously Haman's (cf. 3:12c; 8:8). Finally, Esther appoints him to be the administrator of Haman's property (v 2b), thus giving him the resources appropriate to his new status. It is important to note that this is all effected by Esther. It is because she informs the king of all that Mordecai is to her that he is admitted into the royal presence and made vizier in Haman's place (he had already been rewarded for saving the king's life, 6:1–11). It is she who appoints him over Haman's estate. This, then, is all part of her preparations for dealing with Haman's edict, for Mordecai's position and power as vizier will play a critical role in nullifying that threat.

Episode 2. The king grants Esther and Mordecai authority to write an edict on behalf of the Jews (8:3–8). Having obtained for Mordecai the position of grand vizier, Esther wastes no time in confronting the matter of Haman's decree. It is important to seize the moment when all this is still fresh in the king's mind, so she once more importunes the king. This, as everyone knows (see 4:11), is always a dangerous game to play with an unstable and capricious monarch, but it is even more so now. She has already forced herself upon him by entering into his presence unsummoned and inviting him to a banquet, at which she did not present her request but instead invited him to a second banquet on the following day. There she precipitated a disturbing scene, unmasking his most favored courtier by exposing his plot that threatened her life. Further, in the specifics of this plot the king bore no small complicity. Hence, Esther must approach the whole matter of requesting relief from Haman's edict with great tact and subtlety. This she does.

Our narrator actually reports two separate appeals by Esther. In the first she turns on the charm, and in the second she employs skilled rhetoric (following Clines, *Esther Scroll,* 100–103). In relating her first appeal in v 3, the narrator describes the acts that accompany her words, thus portraying an emotional outburst: she collapses at the king's feet and bursts into tears. By reporting her words with indirect discourse, he skillfully implies that her outburst is so impassioned that only the gist of her meaning is clear. Yet even here her tact is evident. Not only does she dub the decree to annihilate her people "the wicked scheme of Haman the Agagite," but she modifies that phrase with the clause "which he plotted against the Jews," thereby virtually exonerating the king.

Then, after recounting the king's acceptance of her by extending to her the royal scepter, the narrator relates a second appeal, which he reports in *direct* discourse, in contrast to the previous one. In this appeal her perception of the great tact required is underlined by the skillful rhetoric she uses. The polite and deprecating conditional clauses with which she has previously introduced her requests to the king here reach their peak. In her invitation to the first banquet she had simply said, "If it please the king . . ." (5:4). In both the invitation to the second banquet and her request that her life and her people's be spared, she had added, "If I have found favor with the king" (5:8; 7:3). Now to these two she adroitly adds two others. The first of these, "If the matter is proper in the eyes of the king," recognizes how improper it is to request the rescinding of a decree authorized by the king. The second, with which she concludes, cleverly shifts the ground: "If I am pleasing in his eyes" (which is virtually equivalent to our "If the king really cares for me a little"; see *Comment*) alludes to the king's own obvious regard for her (cf. 2:17). From presenting polite conditions for requesting attention, she has unobtrusively shifted to giving reasons why her request should be heard. And this last, "though the least relevant (logically speaking) to her cause, is the reason which she may reasonably expect to linger most efficaciously in the king's mind" (Clines, *Esther Scroll,* 101).

With this skillful and subtle introduction, she turns to her request. She cannot avoid asking the king to revoke the dispatches that have gone out under his name and authority, but with utmost tact she once again carefully conceals his complicity. She first adds to the word "dispatches" an appositional phrase, "the scheme of Haman son of Hammedatha, the Agagite." Then she modifies that phrase with "which he wrote for the purpose of destroying the Jews who are in all the king's provinces." To this she adds, as a final reason for her request, "a little masterpiece of psychology and rhetoric" (Clines, *Esther Scroll,* 102). Her own life had been spared once already this day by a special appeal to the king, so she can hardly again make the threat to her life the basis of her appeal for her people. Further, she can scarcely appeal to the king's feelings for the Jewish people as a reason for her request (let alone to ethics, decency, or honor). The king has already demonstrated that he is largely unmoved by the invidious plot that threatens their existence. He *has* demonstrated, however, his solicitude for her, time and again. It is in this, therefore, that she grounds her appeal. She makes a tender plea to him to consider what terrible pain she, his queen, would feel to see the destruction of her people and all her relatives: "'how can I endure . . . how can I endure?' . . . She is her own trump card, and she plays it gallantly" (Clines, *Esther Scroll,* 102).

The great tact and care with which Esther has made her request were sorely needed, for the king's response to her appeal (vv 7–8) is sharp and exasperated (see *Comment*). Addressing both Esther and Mordecai, he reminds them of what he has already done for them. "Look," he says, "I have hanged Haman and given his property to Esther." In effect he is saying, "What more can I do?" He is trapped, he claims, "for a decree written in the king's name and sealed with the king's signet ring cannot be revoked" (v 8b), and Haman's decree met both these criteria (cf. 3:12). Hence, with the emphatic independent pronoun and the imperative verb, he once again (as he has done throughout the story) refuses to accept responsibility: "*You write,*" he says, "*you,* Esther and Mordecai, *write* whatever you please concerning the Jews" (v 8).

> Write what you like, says the king, as long as it doesn't overturn, revoke or contradict anything previously written. Write what you like to Jewish advantage, says the king, as long as you realize that Haman's decree still stands. Write what you like, says the king, it will bear my seal; but remember that so does every other official document, including Haman's letter. Write what you like, says the king, for I give up; the conundrum of how to revoke an irrevocable decree, as you, Esther have asked, is beyond me; but feel free to write what you like—if you can think of a way to reverse the irreversible. (Clines, *Esther Scroll,* 19)

SCENE 2. MORDECAI ISSUES THE COUNTERDECREE (8:9–17)

Episode 1. The counterdecree is written and promulgated (8:9–14). The conundrum is solved brilliantly by Mordecai. Some time later (for the significance and the difficulty of the chronology involved, see *Form/Structure/Setting*), the royal scribes are summoned, and Mordecai writes and promulgates a counterdecree that accords the Jews the right to defend themselves by annihilating any ethnic or political group who attacks them. In relating this, the narrator unmistakably presents Mordecai's edict as the complete reversal and annulment of Haman's edict.

First, this is skillfully effected in vv 9–10, 14 by relating the *circumstances* of the writing and promulgation of Mordecai's edict with the very language of the circumstances attendant upon the writing and promulgation of Haman's edict reported in 3:12–15. But, these verses are by no means a word-for-word copy of those of 3:12–15. On the contrary, they are modified in crucial respects so as to capture vividly the radically changed position of power and authority that Mordecai's edict has accorded the Jews throughout the empire of Ahasuerus (for a detailed comparison of the two passages, see *Form/Structure/Setting*). Thus, in v 9 the date of Mordecai's edict is emphasized by being proleptically introduced with the generic time indication "at that time," which probably alludes to the symbolic significance of the seventy-day period (see *Form/Structure/Setting*). Then, the three administrative entities in the Persian empire to whom the edict is addressed are modified by both changes in wording and three additions. The changes in wording are significant. The satraps are no longer dignified as "royal" (lit. "of the king"); nor are the governors identified as those "who are in charge of each province"; nor are the rulers modified by the genitive "of each people." Further, these three highest levels of administrative officialdom are no longer independently ranged alongside one another by each being separately governed by the preposition "to" and dignified by the appropriate administrative division or relationship. Rather, all three now become a single entity governed by the single preposition "to" and modified by the single genitive, "of the provinces." The significance of these changes is dramatically emphasized by the three additions. The first entity now addressed is the Jews. They are not only represented as on a par with satrap, governor, and ruler by being separately governed by the preposition "to" (cf. Bardtke, 369), but they also now stand first in the enumeration and thus rank before these three highest administrative officials. The same importance is stressed in the final clause dealing with the scripts and languages. Here the Jews are treated separately and so given equal status with "each province" and "each people." Finally, by adding to the genitive "of the provinces" the relative clause "which extend from India to Ethiopia, one hundred and twenty-seven provinces" (taken from 1:1), the narrator expresses just how widespread the Jewish diaspora is. Further changes and additions provide similar emphases. The "couriers" of Haman's edict (3:13) are now said to be riding mounts described with rare terms that probably stress both their swiftness and their royal source (v 10; see *Comment*). The vocabulary thus pictures both the speed and authority with which the edict in favor of the Jews is disseminated (cf. the similar force in the addition in 8:14 = 3:15a–b).

Second, the reversal of Haman's edict is effected by having Mordecai compose the edict (vv 11–13) using language virtually identical to that of Haman, except for two significant additions (and, of course, the necessary change in the object of the attack). The first addition states that "the king granted permission to the Jews in each and every city [cf. also the elaboration in v 12] to assemble and defend themselves" (v 11). Then, after the three infinitives from Haman's edict, "to destroy, slay, and annihilate," and the necessarily changed object of these actions, "the forces of any people or province," there follows the second addition, consisting of a restriction, "those attacking them." These changes accord the Jews no general right to attack whom they please but only the specific right to defend themselves by annihilating any ethnic or political group that attacks them. It is in this sense that the further addition allowing the Jews "to take vengeance on their enemies" in v 13 (= 3:14) must be understood.

All of this powerfully and expressively portrays the utter reversal of Haman's edict by skillfully capturing the radically changed position of power and authority that Mordecai's edict has accorded the Jews throughout the empire of Ahasuerus.

Episode 2. Mordecai leaves the king's presence in glory and honor, and the Jews rejoice (8:15–17). In the final episode of scene 2, the completeness of the reversal of the position and power of the Jews is further most effectively portrayed by the sharp contrast between the results of the two edicts. The picture of the king and Haman sitting down to a banquet to celebrate Haman's decree (3:15c), while Mordecai tears his clothes and goes forth into the city in sackcloth and ashes (4:1), has been replaced by the scene of Mordecai leaving the king's presence clothed in glory and honor (v 15a). The city of Susa in confusion and tumult (3:15d) has been replaced by the city of Susa ringing with joyous cheers (v 15b), while for the Jews of Susa all is light, joy, gladness, and honor (v 16). In the rest of the empire the "great mourning among the Jews, with fasting, weeping, and lamentation" (4:3a–b) has been transformed into "joy and gladness among the Jews, with feasting and celebration" (v 17a–b). Finally, the new status and position of the Jews is highlighted by the striking reversal of "*many* made their beds on sackcloth and ashes" (4:3c) to "*many* of the peoples of the land professed to be Jews because fear of the Jews had fallen upon them" (v 17c).

Clearly our story has reached its resolution. But that resolution is not yet complete. The crisis that set the story in motion was Haman's having written into immutable Persian law the edict that all the peoples of the empire were to be ready to annihilate all the Jews and to plunder their goods on one day, the thirteenth of the twelfth month, the month of Adar. Given the immutability of Persian law, it has not been possible simply to rescind Haman's edict. What Mordecai has been able to do is write and promulgate a counteredict that gives the Jews specific royal permission to defend themselves by destroying any and all who attack them. Hence, even though the Jews are now in the ascendancy with Esther as queen and Mordecai as grand vizier, the Jewish community is not yet safe, for Haman's edict still holds legal sway. It can in no way be taken for granted that, when 13 Adar comes, no one will rise against the Jews and seek to put the edict into effect. The crisis that set our story in motion still waits to be fully resolved, for 13 Adar still looms in the future as a day in which countervailing edicts and those that support them will yet face one another. Victory may seem secured, as the Jews' joy and celebrations affirm, but it is yet to be realized (cf. Fox, *Redaction,* 110–12).

Act 8
The Jews Are Victorious: They Put All Their Enemies to the Sword (9:1–5)

Bibliography

Anderson, B. W. "The Place of the Book of Esther in the Christian Bible." *JR* 30 (1950) 32–43. **Clines, D. J. A.** *The Esther Scroll: The Story of the Story.* JSOTSup 30. Sheffield: JSOT, 1984. **Dommershausen, W.** *Die Estherrolle.* Stuttgart: Katholisches Bibelwerk, 1968. **Dorothy, C. V.** "The Books of Esther: Structure, Genre, and Textual Integrity." Diss., Claremont, 1989. **Driver, S. R.** *Introduction to the Literature of the Old Testament.* Edinburgh: T. & T. Clark, 1913. **Fox, M.** *The Redaction of the Books of Esther: On Reading Composite Texts.* Atlanta: Scholars, 1991. **Huesman, J.** "Finite Uses of the Infinitive Absolute." *Bib* 37 (1956) 271–95. **Murphy, R. E.** *Wisdom Literature: Job, Proverbs, Ruth, Canticles, Ecclesiastes, and Esther.* FOTL 13. Grand Rapids, MI: Eerdmans, 1981. **Pfeiffer, R. H.** *Introduction to the Old Testament.* New York: Harper, 1948. **Williamson, H. G. M.** Review of *The Esther Scroll,* by D. J. A. Clines. *JTS* 37 (1986) 146–52.

Translation

[1]*The day arrived when the king's command and edict was to be carried out, the thirteenth day of the twelfth month, the month of Adar.*[a] *On this day, the day*[b] *in which the enemies of the Jews hoped to triumph over them, the very opposite occurred:*[c] *it was the Jews who triumphed over those who hated them.*[d] [2]*They assembled together in their cities in all the provinces of King Ahasuerus to attack*[a] *those who sought to do them harm, and no one could make a stand before them, for fear of them had overtaken everyone.*[b]
[3]*All the rulers of the provinces, the satraps, the governors, and the royal officials*[a] *were aiding the Jews out of fear of Mordecai,*[b] [4]*because he had come to occupy a position of great power*[a] *in the palace, while his fame was spreading through all the provinces. For the man Mordecai was growing more and more powerful.* [5]*So the Jews put all their enemies to the sword. They inflicted upon them slaughter and destruction,*[a] *and worked their will on*[b] *those who hated them.*

Notes

1.a. Lit. "in the twelfth month, the month of Adar, when the king's command and edict arrived to be carried out." By forefronting this temporal clause, the structure gives it prominence and hence emphasis. The translation attempts to do the same, consonant with good Eng. style.

1.b. Lit. "on the day in which." The repetition of ביום, "on the day," with which this second temporal clause begins, gives it emphasis, which the translation attempts to express.

1.c. Lit. "that was overturned"; see *Comment.*

1.d. For this force of the independent pron in apposition, see *GBH* § 146c.

2.a. Lit. "to send a hand upon."

2.b. Lit. "had fallen upon all the peoples."

3.a. Lit. "those who were carrying out the business of the king"; see *Comment.*

3.b. Lit. "because fear of Mordecai had fallen upon them."

4.a. Lit. "he was great."

5.a. The Heb. reads lit. "the Jews struck dead all their enemies with sword-blow, slaughter, and destruction."

5.b. Lit. "did according to their desire with."

Form/Structure/Setting

In my opinion, vv 1–5 of chap. 9 constitute a separate act in the development of the narrative, contrary to the almost universally held view that these verses should be included in a larger literary entity. In the division of the material most commonly encountered, 9:1–19 forms a pericope, often entitled "The Jews Are Victorious over Their Enemies" or the like (e.g., Dommershausen, 44; Gerleman, 130; Moore, 84; Dorothy, "Books of Esther," 297–303; cf. Clines, 320; Fox, 107). Others, on various grounds, separate 9:1–10 from 9:11–19 (so Bardtke, 377–89; Haller, 133–35; Murphy, *Wisdom,* 167–69; cf. Paton, 282–91, who divides the material into three pericopes, vv 1–10, 11–15, and 16–19). Dorothy ("Books of Esther," 299–300) separates vv 1–4, entitled "Stylized Battle Report, General," from vv 5–10, entitled "Battle Report, Specific." Not only does this miss the fact that vv 6–10 are clearly oriented to what follows since they are specifically concerned with what happened in Susa, but there is surely nothing "specific" about v 5!

Contrary to these views, there is a significant difference between vv 1–5 and what follows. The succeeding material unmistakably relates to the dénouement of the narrative, the establishment of the festival of Purim, and in particular to the explanation of why that festival is celebrated on two different days in two different parts of the Jewish diaspora, Susa and the provinces. But 9:1–5 does not really relate to this issue at all. Nothing here relates in any way either to the festival of Purim in general or to the question of the different days of its celebration. Contrast the way in which this latter issue comes to the fore immediately in v 6, the very first sentence of the next act, with its reference to the fighting in Susa alone, which leads directly to the king's question in vv 11–12 (see the discussion in the *Form/Structure/Setting* section thereto).

On the contrary, 9:1–5 relates the completion of the resolution of the crisis of the narrative, the threat to the existence of the Jewish people. By the end of chap. 8 the crisis has in essence been resolved, but how the confrontation between the two opposite and irreconcilable edicts will play itself out still waits to be told. So here, in summarizing, general statements, unencumbered by any detail whatsoever, the narrator relates the victory of the Jews, bringing closure to the resolution of the crisis that set the story in motion (see the discourse structure in the *Theme and Purpose* section of the *Introduction* to Esther). Only when this is complete will the narrator turn in the following act to the dénouement of his story, the establishment of the festival of Purim and its dates of celebration.

It has often been stated that the dénouement of the book, chaps. 9 and 10, is markedly inferior literarily to the rest of the book (see esp. Clines, *Esther Scroll,* 39–49; Fox, *Redaction,* 114–15; see the discussion in *Comment* below). This may be the case in 9:6–32 (see *Form/Structure/Setting* thereto), but it is hardly the case here. Though it is stated in the most general terms, the account of the Jewish victory is nevertheless skillfully crafted and carefully related to what has preceded, as the table reveals. Thus, the structure of the first verse, A, forefronts the temporal clauses, giving them primary focus (see *Comment*). The first temporal clause rings with significance, since it states in full detail (though in reverse order, with the month named first) the date that has already figured so prominently twice already, first in Haman's decree (3:13) and then most recently in Mordecai's opposing and irreconcilable edict (8:12; see esp. the table in the *Form/Structure/Setting* section of the previous act). In the same sentence the terseness and unusual syntax of the main clause (see *Comment*) emphasize this basic statement of Jewish victory. This general statement of the theme is followed by a nonsequential sentence (beginning with a perfect tense, not waw-consecutive imperfect; see *Comment*), B (v 2), which tells of Jewish actions and invincibility. This in turn is followed by a circumstantial, participial sentence, B´ (vv 3–4). This sentence gives two reasons for this state of affairs: (1) All the ruling authorities (including a significant addition to the threefold set of rulers who were addressed in the two opposing decrees; see *Comment* below) now aid the Jews (v 3), because (2) all these officials fear Mordecai, whose position of power and fame are then described (v 4). Finally, the pericope concludes with two sequential clauses (beginning with waw-consecutive imperfect; see *Comment*), A´ (v 5), which express in general terms the result of all this. This restatement of the theme provides an inclusio with the opening verse and hence closure for the act.

The Structure of 9:1–5

Verse	Style	Content	Relationship	
1	complex opening sentence with unusual structure and syntax	On 13 Adar, the day the king's edict arrived to be executed, the hope of the enemies of the Jews to triumph over them was overturned so that the Jews themselves triumphed over those who hated them.	theme sentence	A
2	nonsequential sentence that begins with perfect tense	The Jews assemble to attack those who seek to do them harm, and no one can make a stand before them, for fear of them has overtaken everyone.	further explanation of theme sentence, giving details of Jewish actions and invincibility	B
3–4	circumstantial, participial sentence	The ruling authorities are aiding the Jews out of fear of Mordecai, for his power and fame are growing greater.	the reason for this state of affairs	B´
5	sequential sentences that begin with waw-consecutive imperfects	The Jews strike all their enemies dead with sword, slaughter, and destruction and work their will on those who hate them.	the result of all this, the restatement of the theme sentence	A´

Comment

1–5 Clines (319–320; id., *Esther Scroll,* 39–49; followed by Dorothy, "Books of Esther," 221–38, 297–98, 386–90) argues that there are such logical narrative weaknesses and contradictions between the contents of 9:1–19 and the preceding eight chapters that this material must be a later edition to the book of Esther, which originally then ended at 8:17. Some of the differences that Clines alleges have merit, strongly suggesting that this material has a different literary prehistory than chaps. 1–8 (for a full discussion see *Unity and Redaction* in the *Introduction* to Esther). Nevertheless, at least four of the literary differences and contradictions between the two passages postulated by Clines are not valid (see Fox, *Redaction,* 110–13), and hence there is considerably more literary congruity between them than Clines perceives.

(1) Clines alleges that "the conceptual or documentary crisis (the conflict of the two decrees) of ch. 8 is not played out, but ignored in ch. 9" (*Esther Scroll,* 39). Rather, "the narrator of ch. 9 has presented a Jewish massacre of anti-Semites rather than Jewish self-defence against an imperially sponsored pogrom" (*Esther Scroll,* 40). It *is* true that the language of chap. 9 is different in some respects from that of chaps. 1–8. Haman's decree (3:12–14) authorized an officially sponsored attack. It was issued to the governing authorities ("to the royal satraps, to the governors . . . of each province, and to the rulers of each people," 3:12) ordering them "to destroy, slay, and annihilate all the Jews" (3:13). Mordecai's counteredict (8:11–12) permitted the Jews specifically to defend themselves (lit. "to stand for their lives") against "the (armed) forces of any people or province who attack them" (8:11). On the other hand, 9:1 speaks of both the enemies of the Jews and the Jews "getting the mastery [שלט] over" the other, and the elements opposing the Jews are referred to as "their enemies" (9:1b, 5a, 16c) and "those who hate them" (9:1d, 5b, 16d). The Jews do indeed adopt an offensive posture in chap. 9 rather than a purely defensive one. They "assembled together . . . to attack those who sought to do them harm" (9:2a), and it is the Jews who "put all their enemies to the sword, to slaughter, and to destruction" (9:5a). Nevertheless, in my opinion, Fox (*Redaction,* 110–11) is correct in arguing that Clines has badly overstated his case. The fighting in chap. 9 does presuppose both decrees.

First, the narrator of chap. 9 assumes that both Haman's and Mordecai's decrees exist and must be dealt with. The differences between the two chapters largely result from a change in emphasis. In chap. 9 only Mordecai's decree matters (Clines, 320), but this is not in open conflict with chap. 8. The dramatic portrayal in 8:15–17 of the joy of both the Jews and the general populace of the city of Susa (vv 15b–16), on the one hand, and the gladness, feasting, and celebration of the Jews in the rest of the kingdom (v 17a), on the other, are occasioned not only by the honor and power Mordecai now possesses (expressed in v 15a) but also, and principally, by his edict, which has just been described in such detail (vv 9–14). Further, the power of the Jews is now so great that fear of them prompts many people of the empire to "profess to be Jews" (v 17b). This surely demonstrates that it is equally the perspective of the author of chap. 8 that it is primarily Mordecai's decree that matters! As 9:3–4 reveals, this is clearly the understanding of the narrator in chap. 9.

Further, the fact that there is no imperially sponsored pogrom in chap. 9 is not in conflict with chap. 8 but is fully in keeping with the change created by Mordecai's counterdecree, a factor that the narrator of chap. 9 fully and adequately expresses. Mordecai's decree was issued to the same governing authorities as was Haman's (compare 3:12 with 8:9; see the table in the *Form/Structure/Setting* section of act 7), but it ordered them to permit the Jews not only to defend themselves but "to destroy, slay, and annihilate the forces of any people or province attacking them" (8:11). The Persian governing authorities were caught, then, between two contradictory orders. They could hardly carry out both, and that they chose to support the second decree is fully and adequately explained by the narrator of chap. 9: "All the rulers of the provinces, the satraps, the governors, and the royal officials were aiding the Jews out of fear of Mordecai, because he had come to occupy a position of great power in the palace" (9:3–4a). Indeed, the narrator here subtly emphasizes the support given to the Jews by adding to the list of Persian ruling authorities named in both decrees (3:12; 8:9) a most significant new category, the "royal officials" (lit. "those who perform the business of the king," for the significance of which see the *Comment* on 9:3).

Finally, Clines also alleges in this regard that chap. 8 permitted the Jews only a defensive posture ("to destroy . . . any armed force that might attack them," 8:11), but "In ch. 9 . . . there is no mention of any attack upon the Jews, but to the contrary it is the Jews who appear to take the initiative . . . . The narrator of ch. 9 has presented a Jewish massacre of anti-Semites rather than Jewish self-defence . . ." (*Esther Scroll,* 39–40). This again badly overstates the difference between the two passages. The narrator of chap. 8 also envisages a more active role for the Jews than a purely defensive one. He not only rewrites Haman's decree so as to grant the Jews permission to defend themselves by destroying those who attack them (8:11 vs. 3:13), but in the prescriptions that follow in each decree he makes a significant addition. Haman's command ordering that his edict be "publicly displayed to all peoples so that **they** might be ready for this day" (3:14) becomes Mordecai's command ordering that his edict be "publicly displayed to all peoples so that **the Jews** might be ready for this day *to take vengeance on their enemies*" (8:13). To blunt the force of this, Clines must deem it "superficial" and argue that its meaning is to be determined by "the precise wording of the imperial decree of v. 11" (*Esther Scroll,* 160), but this is to ignore the fact that this statement is also part of Mordecai's decree (see the table in the *Form/Structure/Setting* section of act 7). As Fox demonstrates (*Redaction,* 111), a careful reading of chap. 9 will reveal that it is not the Jews who instigate the fighting there. In v 2 the identification of those whom the Jews attack throughout the empire is significant. They are not described simply as "enemies" or "those who hate them" but as "those who sought to do them harm." Though this expression can elsewhere bear a meaning that is "solely volitional" (Clines, 321), it hardly seems likely that it has that sense in this context. On the contrary, "this 'seeking to harm' the Jews took the form of the licensed attack" (Fox, *Redaction,* 111). Likewise, the description in v 16 of the Jews "assembling together" (cf. also vv 2, 15) in order to "defend themselves" (lit. "make a stand for their lives") depicts "a body forming for defense, not a mob hunting down individuals it considers hostile" (Fox, *Redaction,* 111). This is not only fully in keeping with the intent of the decree in chap. 8 but uses the identical language (see 8:11). True, Jewish actions in 9:1–19 are not simply defensive but include significant offensive action (cf. v 5). In the nature of the case, this would have been necessary as part of an overall defensive strategy. In any case, their actions do not go beyond the "taking vengeance on their enemies" envisaged by the narrator in 8:11.

(2) Clines argues (*Esther Scroll,* 40–42) that the "fear of the Jews" in 9:2 is borrowed from 8:17, but to very different effect. In 8:17, the phrase refers to a "religious awe," whereas the narrator of chap. 9 misunderstands it to mean fear of the Jews' might and power (v 2a). However, as I have argued in the *Comment* to 8:17, the phrase there refers not to religious awe but to fear of the Jews' new position and power as a result of Mordecai's decree and his new stature in the court. Hence, as far as the meaning of this phrase is concerned, there is no conflict between the two chapters at all (cf. Fox, *Redaction,* 112).

(3) Clines contends (*Esther Scroll,* 42–46) that 9:1–5 contains a "set of references to the 'enemies' of the Jews and 'those who hated' them." But, ". . . in chs. 1–8 there are no *enemies* (in the plural!) of the Jews" (42). Rather, in chap. 8 "Haman is the only enemy the Jews have" (43). Again, in my opinion, Clines overstates his case. In chaps. 1–8 the enemy of the Jews par excellence is Haman, but the Jews have other enemies in these chapters. They but lurk in the background (Fox, *Redaction,* 113). Mordecai's command to Esther that she keep her ethnic identity a secret implies that some danger to her and to her people may be forthcoming if it becomes known that she is a Jew. Further, the fact that "a copy of the edict" giving the order to annihilate all the Jews "was to be promulgated as law in every single province, being publicly displayed to all peoples so that they might be ready for this day" (3:14), would have little meaning if there were not many enemies of the Jews among the peoples so commanded.

(4) For the "other minor conflicts of wording" that Clines finds between 9:1–5 and chap. 1–8 (*Esther Scroll,* 46–47), see the discussion in *Comment* below.

Hence, the confrontation related in chap. 9 between the enemies of the Jews, who act under the authority of Haman's edict, and the Jews themselves, who act under the authority of Mordecai's edict, is the natural and necessary continuation of the previous narrative (Fox, *Redaction,* 113). Indeed, does it seem at all probable "that a biblical story would stop short of an explicit resolution of the issue of Jewish survival?" (Williamson, *JTS* 37 [1986] 148). This victory of the Jews is precisely the "rounding off" of the narrative that Williamson (149) sensed was needed to bring completion to the story, for it is the logical conclusion of the resolution begun in chap. 8. True, at the end of that chapter the crisis has begun to be resolved and the tension consequently has abated, but the story is not complete.

1 The narrator begins in v 1 with a complex sentence that is remarkable for both its structure and its syntax. First, normal sentence order is significantly modified. The verse consists of a remarkably terse main clause, "that was overturned." This clause is prefaced by two long temporal clauses, (1) "in the twelfth month, the month of Adar, on the thirteenth day of it, when the command and edict of the king arrived to be carried out," and (2) "on the day when the enemies of the Jews hoped to triumph over them." These, in turn, are followed by a subordinate clause of result (or explanation), "so [or 'in'] that it was the Jews who triumphed over those who hated them." By beginning with the temporal clauses, both of which are fraught with significance from the previous events, the author throws them into relief, making them the focus of his sentence (for the significance of this, see *Form/Structure/Setting*). Second, the syntax of the main clause is highly unusual (see the next entry), thereby giving it emphasis also.

וְנַהֲפוֹךְ הוּא, lit. "that was overturned." This, in my opinion, is the main clause of the sentence. It consists of the infinitive absolute functioning in place of a finite verb. The infinitive absolute here is frequently understood to be subordinate to the preceding finite verb of the second temporal clause, שִׂבְּרוּ, "they hoped," and hence a second logical step in the temporal clause so begun (for which usage see *Note* 2:3.e.). The sense is then, "on the day when the enemies of the Jews hoped to triumph over them, but it was overturned, so that . . ." (so Huesman, *Bib* 37 [1956] 285; Fox, 107–8; cf. also RSV, NRSV). The syntax of this clause, however, is markedly different from that which occurs when the infinitive absolute is used to express temporal/logical sequence. Here an independent pronoun follows the infinitive absolute, forming its subject. This is a pattern, used most commonly with the first person pronoun, found also in Phoenician and in the Amarna Letters from Canaanite sites (see *IBHS* § 35.5.2.d n. 60). In this light, it seems far more probable that the clause is independent, not sequential. Hence, it forms the first main clause. By virtue of its unusual syntax, it is emphatic (cf. Bardtke, 380). A similar use of the idiom occurs in Eccles 4:2. That the clause then forms the summary and theme statement of the victory that follows (so JB, NAB, NASV, NJB, NIV; cf. Paton, 282) supports this interpretation. It seems hardly likely that "the victory of the Jews—in fact the entirety of the story"—would be "encapsulated in a clause embedded in a parenthesis" (Fox, 108).

2 נִקְהֲלוּ הַיְּהוּדִים בְּעָרֵיהֶם, lit. "the Jews assembled together in their cities." V 2 begins with a verb in the perfect tense. It does not then express temporal or logical sequence with what has preceded. Rather, as its content reveals, it gives further explanation, describing in general terms how the preceding theme sentence was effected (see *Form/Structure/Setting*). The expression "in their cities" does not necessarily imply that "the Jews dwell in particular cities" (Clines, *Esther Scroll,* 46) any more than the language of 8:11, which grants permission "to the Jews in each and every city to . . . defend themselves," implies that there are Jewish communities in every city. Both expressions must be understood to refer to those cities in which Jewish communities exist. In particular, then, there is no conflict in this instance between the wording of chap. 8 and that of chap. 9, as Clines alleges (*Esther Scroll,* 46).

וְאִישׁ לֹא־עָמַד לִפְנֵיהֶם, "no one could make a stand before them." Moore (86) interprets the idiom עמד לפני to mean "to be successful against," understanding the passage to mean that "no one could successfully sustain his attack against the Jews" (90), but the idiom clearly means "to resist, withstand," as its usage elsewhere attests (e.g., Judg 2:14; Dan 11:16; cf. also with the synonym בפני, "before," Josh 10:8; 21:44; 23:9; with התיצב, "to stand," Deut 11:25). In my opinion, Moore is right in understanding that this is in response to an attack upon the Jews, but that sense springs from the language of v 2a, which depicts the Jews "attacking those who sought to do them harm" (see the discussion in section [1] of the *Comment* on vv 1–5 above), not from the idiom here.

3 וְכָל־שָׂרֵי הַמְּדִינוֹת וְהָאֲחַשְׁדַּרְפְּנִים וְהַפַּחוֹת וְעֹשֵׂי הַמְּלָאכָה אֲשֶׁר לַמֶּלֶךְ מְנַשְּׂאִים אֶת־הַיְּהוּדִים, "and all the rulers of the provinces, the satraps, the governors, and the royal officials were aiding the Jews." The verse consists of waw + subject + participle and hence is highly circumstantial to the preceding sentence. Like v 2, then, it also is not temporally or logically sequential. The circumstance it relates gives the reason for the Jewish success and invincibility (see *Form/Structure/Setting*).

Here the list of Persian ruling authorities who are aiding the Jews is composed of the same three high officials of the empire who were ordered to implement the two opposing decrees (see 3:12; 8:9), but they are listed in a different order. Although there are slight variations in the way that these ruling authorities are designated in 3:12; 8:9 (see Clines, *Esther Scroll,* 46; and esp. the table in the *Form/Structure/Setting* section of the preceding act), they are listed in the correct order of descending rank, i.e., אחשדרפנים, "satraps," פחות, "governors," and שׂרים, "rulers" (i.e., ethnarchs or tribal chiefs; see Clines, *Esther Scroll,* 46, and *Comment* on 3:12). Here, however, the order is "the rulers, the satraps, and the governors." Clines argues that this difference is evidence of "another author who wrote more loosely of such matters" (*Esther Scroll,* 46). In my opinion, however, Bardtke's explanation (381) adequately accounts for the difference in order. In 3:12; 8:9 these ruling authorities are addressed as recipients of royal edicts and hence are named in order of rank. Here, however, they are regarded from the perspective of the Jews. Hence, the more local officials, the "ethnarchs" or "tribal chiefs," who would be far more effective in the matter of aiding the Jews than the governors or satraps, are lifted out of the order of rank and named first, leaving the order otherwise unchanged.

However one explains the change in order, the list nevertheless rings with significance from the previous narrative, since it is composed of the same ruling authorities as those ordered to implement the opposing edicts, who now aid the Jews. Moreover, it also contains a fourth category of officials, whose presence in the list is not inexplicable (contra Clines, *Esther Scroll,* 46) but significant. By including the "royal officials," lit. "those who carry out the king's business," the narrator subtly emphasizes the support given to the Jews. Even the lower functionaries, those who carry on the everyday work and activities of the royal court, now support the Jews. But, there is more; these are the very officials who deposited Haman's bribe in the royal treasury in 3:9 (Bardtke, 381; Dommershausen, *Estherrolle,* 113)!

4 כִּי־גָדוֹל מָרְדֳּכַי בְּבֵית הַמֶּלֶךְ, lit. "for Mordecai was great in the king's house." בית המלך, "the house of the king," has been used in the previous narrative to refer to the royal palace itself, as well as to various parts of it (see the discussion of the phrase in the *Comment* on its use in 5:1). Hence, it is most unlikely that it refers here to the entire capital city (contra Moore, 86). It most likely refers to the royal palace as the site of Mordecai's power and influence (cf. 8:1, 15).

5 וַיַּכּוּ הַיְּהוּדִים בְּכָל־אֹיְבֵיהֶם . . . וַיַּעֲשׂוּ בְשֹׂנְאֵיהֶם כִּרְצוֹנָם, lit. "the Jews struck all their enemies dead . . . and did as they pleased with those who hated them." For the first time in this pericope the sequence is now logical, for this is the force of the waw-consecutive + imperfect verbal forms with which each clause begins. The two clauses thus state the result of all that has been described, forming a conclusion to the whole (see *Form/Structure/Setting*).

Explanation

Having concluded the last act with Mordecai clad in splendor and glory, with the city of Susa ringing with joyous cheers, with the Jews engaged in feasting and celebration wherever Mordecai's edict reached, and with many peoples of the empire professing to be Jews, the narrator unmistakably presaged Jewish victory. So now, he wastes no words. In succinct and summary statement, hardly relieved by detail at all, he relates the result of the confrontation of Haman's and Mordecai's irreconcilable edicts.

He begins his report with a long, temporal clause, "in the twelfth month, the month of Adar, in the thirteenth day of it, when the king's command and edict arrived to be carried out." Thereby he highlights, on the one hand, the fateful date prescribed by each of the conflicting edicts. On the other hand, through its unnecessarily full and extended form, he keeps us for the briefest moment in suspense as to the outcome of the confrontation. But the suspense is no sooner created than it is relieved. Through a contrast highlighted by the unusual syntax of the main clause that forms its hinge (see *Comment*), he reports the utter reversal of the hope of the Jews' enemies to triumph over them (v 1). This statement is the clearest example in the book of the principle of "reversal" (or "peripety"), which the author has so effectively built into his story (see the role of God in the story in the *Theme and Purpose* section in the *Introduction* to Esther). In the sentences that follow, he describes in the most general of terms how this reversal was effected. Three elements enter into this dramatic success. First, the Jews go on the offensive. Assembling together in their localities, they attack all those who attempt to harm them (v 2a). Second, none could withstand their attack, for fear of them had overtaken all (v 2b). And third, all the Persian ruling authorities, not only those of high office charged with executing the conflicting decrees but even the lowly officials who carry on the everyday work and activities of the royal court, aid the Jewish offensive (v 3a), because they now fear the constantly increasing power and fame of Mordecai (vv 3b–4). Finally, the brief narrative comes full circle with a result clause expressing, again in general terms, the utter completeness of the Jewish success: "so the Jews put all their enemies to the sword . . . , and worked their will on those who hated them" (v 5). By relating the Jewish victory in such succinct statements and in such general terms, the narrator not only expresses its overwhelming nature and avoids going into the gory details, but he significantly subordinates this part of the resolution of the story to the previous detailed account in which Esther and Mordecai have obtained royal sanction for the Jewish defense. So, with the death and destruction of all their enemies, the terrible threat to the life of the whole Jewish community, which set our story in motion, has now been fully and completely resolved.

This victory of the Jews has frequently been interpreted in a very negative light. Paton interprets v 5 to mean that "all that were known to be hostile to the Jews were hunted out and killed" (283). Pfeiffer voices the opinion that the author contemplates "a massacre of defenseless Gentiles on a given day, within a great peaceful empire, with the connivance of the central government" (*Introduction,* 741; cf. also Driver, *Introduction,* 485–86). Anderson, for all his helpful analysis of the theological meaning of the book, yet can aver that the "Jews, in their actions, are not essentially different from the heathen. Mordecai and Esther merely put Haman's plan into reverse" (*JR* 30 [1950] 41). But this is a complete misreading of the actions of the Jewish forces in the narrative. The Jews' actions are strictly defensive. They do not instigate the fighting, for they attack "those who sought to do them harm" (v 5). They do take offensive action, but such action would have been necessary against an enemy acting upon a decree that licensed their complete extermination (see the discussion of Clines' views in the *Comment* on vv 1–5 above). As Fox demonstrates (220–26), their actions were necessary, defensive, and justified.

Indeed, if the purpose of our narrative had been simply to relate how the victory occurred, the story could well have ended here. But this is not its purpose (at least not in its present form, for which question see the *Introduction* to Esther). The narrator has a more important agenda, one that goes beyond this story of the resolution of the threat to the life of the Jewish community. This dramatic and overwhelming deliverance must be perpetually memorialized with an annual celebration. To this he now turns in the dénouement of his narrative.

Act 9
The Festival of Purim Is Instituted: Mordecai, Esther, and the Jewish Community Set Its Dates and Establish Its Character (9:6–32)

Bibliography

Barthélemy, D., et al. *Preliminary and Interim Report on the Hebrew Old Testament Text Project.* Vol. 2. New York: United Bible Societies, 1979. **Berg, S. B.** *The Book of Esther: Motifs, Themes and Structure.* SBLDS 44. Missoula, MT: Scholars, 1979. **Bergey, R. L.** "Post-exilic Hebrew Linguistic Developments in Esther." *JETS* 31 (1988) 161–68. **Brockington, L. H.** *The Hebrew Text of the Old Testament: The Readings Adopted by the Translators of the New English Bible.* Oxford: Oxford UP, 1973. **Childs, B.** *Introduction to the Old Testament as Scripture.* Philadelphia: Fortress, 1979. **Clines, D. J. A.** *The Esther Scroll: The Story of the Story.* JSOTSup 30. Sheffield: JSOT, 1984. **Dommershausen, W.** *Die Estherrolle.* Stuttgart: Katholisches Bibelwerk, 1968. **Driver, G. R.** "Abbreviations in the Massoretic Text." In *Textus: Annual of the Hebrew University Bible Project.* Jerusalem: Magnes, 1960. 1:112–31. ———. "Problems and Solutions." *VT* 4 (1954) 224–45. ———. "Problems in Judges Newly Discussed." ALUOS 4 (1962–63) 6–25. **Ehrlich, A.** *Randglossen zur hebräischen Bibel: Textkritisches, Sprachliches und Sachliches.* Vol. 7. 1914. Repr. Hildesheim: Georg Olms, 1968. **Fox, M.** *The Redaction of the Books of Esther.* Atlanta: Scholars, 1991. **Gordis, R.** *Megillat Esther.* New York: Ktav, 1974. ———. "Studies in the Esther Narrative." *JBL* 95 (1976) 43–58 (= Moore, *Studies,* 408–23). **Haupt, P.** "Critical Notes on Esther." *AJSL* 24 (1907–8) 97–186 (= Moore, *Studies,* 1–90). **Jones, B. W.** "Two Misconceptions about the Book of Esther." *CBQ* 39 (1977) 171–81. **Loewenstamm, S. E.** "Esther 9:29–32: The Genesis of a Late Addition." *HUCA* 42 (1971) 117–24 (= Moore, *Studies,* 227–34). **McKane, W.** "A Note on Esther IX and 1 Samuel XV." *JTS* 12 (1961) 260–61. **Murphy, R. E.** *Wisdom Literature: Job, Proverbs, Ruth, Canticles, Ecclesiastes, and Esther.* FOTL 13. Grand Rapids, MI: Eerdmans, 1981. **Niemann, H. M.** "Das Ende des Volkes der Perizziter." *ZAW* 105 (1993) 233–57. **Rudolph, W.** "Textkritisches zum Estherbuch." *VT* 4 (1954) 89–90. **Striedl, H.** "Untersuchungen zur Syntax und Stilistik des hebräischen Buches Esther." *ZAW* 14 (1937) 73–108.

Translation

SCENE 1. THE EVENTS THAT OCCASION THE CELEBRATION OF PURIM OVER TWO DAYS (9:6–19)
Time: 12/13 to 12/15, year 12

Episode 1. How the fighting in Susa took place on the thirteenth and on the fourteenth of Adar (9:6–15)

> [6]*Now in the Citadel of Susa itself the Jews slaughtered*[a] *five hundred men,* [7]*including*[a]
> *Parshandatha, Dalphon, Aspatha,* [8]*Poratha, Adalia, Aridatha,* [9]*Parmashta, Arisai,*
> *Aridai, and Vaizatha,* [10]*the ten sons of Haman son of Hammedatha, the enemy of the*
> *Jews. But they took*[a] *no plunder.* [11]*That very day the number of those killed in the Cita-*
> *del of Susa was reported to*[a] *the king.* [12]*So he said to Queen Esther, "In the Citadel of*
> *Susa alone the Jews have slaughtered*[a] *five hundred men and the ten sons of Haman.*

What, then, have they done in all the other provinces of the kingdom?[b] *So what more do you ask and what further do you request? Whatever it is, it shall be granted and it shall be done."*[c] 13 *Esther replied, "If it please the king, permit the Jews who are in Susa to do tomorrow what you have allowed them to do today,*[a] 14 *and let the bodies of Haman's ten sons be hanged*[a] *on the gallows." So the king commanded that this should be done, and an edict was issued in Susa. The bodies of Haman's ten sons were hanged,*[b] 15 *and the Jews who were in Susa assembled on the fourteenth day of the month of Adar also and killed three hundred men. But they took no*[a] *plunder.*

Episode 2. Why the Jews in Susa and the Jews elsewhere celebrate on two different days (9:16–19)

16 *The rest of the Jews throughout the king's provinces*[a] *had assembled together, defended themselves,*[b] *and gained relief*[c] *from their enemies. They slew seventy-five thousand men of those who hated them, but they took*[d] *no plunder.* 17 *This was on the thirteenth day of the month of Adar,*[a] *and on the fourteenth day of the month they had rested and made it a joyful day of feasting.*[b] 18 *But*[a] *the Jews in Susa had assembled together on the thirteenth and on the fourteenth day of the month, and had rested on the fifteenth and made it a joyful day of feasting.*[b] 19 *(Therefore,*[a] *the Jews who live outside the territory of Susa, those who live in places beyond its jurisdiction,*[b] *celebrate the fourteenth day of the month of Adar as a joyful holiday of feasting*[c] *and the sending of gifts of food to one another.)*

SCENE 2. MORDECAI, ESTHER, AND THE JEWISH COMMUNITY SET THE DATES OF PURIM AND COMMIT THEMSELVES TO ITS PERPETUAL CELEBRATION (9:20–32)

Episode 1. Mordecai writes to all the Jews to require them to celebrate annually the fourteenth or the fifteenth of Adar as days of joyful festivity (9:20–22)

20 *Then Mordecai wrote these things*[a] *down and sent letters to all the Jews who were in all the provinces of King Ahasuerus, both near and far,* 21 *to obligate them to celebrate annually the fourteenth and the fifteenth days of the month of Adar* 22 *in the same manner*[a] *as they did on the days*[b] *in which they gained relief from their enemies and the month which was transformed for them from sadness to joy and from mourning to a holiday.*[c] *That is, they were to make them*[d] *joyful days of feasting and of the sending of presents of food to one another and gifts to the poor.*

Episode 2. The Jews commit themselves, their descendants, and all who join them to the perpetual annual observance of the two-day festival of Purim (9:23–28)

23 *The Jews accepted*[a] [b]*what they had begun to do*[b] *and what Mordecai had written to them.* 24 *For Haman son of Hammedatha, the Agagite, the enemy of all the Jews, had plotted to destroy them and had cast* pur *(that is, the lot) in order to demolish them utterly.*[a] 25 *But when the matter*[a] *came before the king, he ordered in writing that*[b] *Haman's wicked plan which he had devised against the Jews should recoil on his own head, and that*[c] *he and his sons should be hanged upon the gallows.* 26 *(Therefore, these days are called Purim—from the word* pur.*)*

Therefore, because of all that was written in[a] *this letter, and what they had experienced in this regard,*[b] *and what had happened to them,* 27 *the Jews firmly obligated*[a] *themselves, their descendants, and all who would join them—never to be repealed*[b]*—to cel-*

ebrate these two days every year in the manner prescribed[c] *and on the days designated.*[d] [28]*These days are going to be celebrated as a memorial*[a] *throughout all generations and in every family, province, and city. The observance of these days of Purim shall never cease*[b] *among the Jews, and their commemoration shall not come to an end among their descendants.*

Episode 3. Esther writes to confirm the observance of Purim (9:29–32)

[29]*And Queen Esther, daughter of Abihail,*[a] *wrote a letter in which she used all her authority*[b] *to confirm this*[c] *letter about Purim.* [30]*So letters—expressing sentiments that were both kindly and authoritative*[a]*—were sent*[b] *to all the Jews in*[c] *the one hundred and twenty-seven provinces of*[d] *the empire of Ahasuerus* [31]*to confirm the observance of these days of Purim*[a] *on the days designated,*[b] *in the same manner that Mordecai the Jew*[c] *had obligated them, and in the same manner that they had obligated themselves and their descendants to the performance*[d] *of fasts and their accompanying laments.* [32]*So Esther's decree confirmed these regulations about Purim, and it was written down in the records.*[a]

Notes

6.a. Lit. "killed and destroyed." For the inf abs + waw, see *Note* 2:3.e.
7.a. Lit. "and."
10.a. Lit. "they did not stretch forth their hand to."
11.a. Lit. "came before."
12.a. Lit. "killed and destroyed." For the inf abs + waw, see *Note* 2:3.e.
12.b. Lit. "the rest of the king's provinces."
12.c. Lit. "What is your wish? It shall be granted. And what further is your request? It shall be done."
13.a. Lit. "according to this day's decree."
14.a. Since the ten sons of Haman have already been killed (v 6b), the idiom here means that their bodies were hung as a means of public humiliation.
14.b. Haller (134), following a few Heb. and LXX MSS and Syr, adds "on the gallows." Since the clause occurs at the end of the previous verse with this phrase, its presence here would be overloaded and unnecessary. The addition is undoubtedly prompted by its regular presence in the numerous other occurrences of the phrase (cf. *BHS* n.).
15.a. Lit. "they did not stretch forth their hand to."
16.a. Bardtke (386), appealing to 8:12, follows a number of Heb. MSS and Vg and reads "all the king's provinces" (cf. *BHS* n.). The appeal to 8:12, however, speaks not for the addition but against it. The phrase here is intended to provide a contrast with "the Jews who were in Susa" of v 15, and hence the addition is not only unnecessary but inappropriate, whereas the opposite is the case in 8:12. The Heb. MSS and Vg are undoubtedly influenced by the frequent occurrence of the full expression elsewhere in the book (1:16, 22; 2:3; 3:8, 13; 8:5, 12; 9:2, 20).
16.b. Lit. "made a stand for their lives." For the inf abs + waw, see *Note* 2:3.e.
16.c. There is no need to delete ונוח, "had rest" (Haupt, *AJSL* 24 [1907–8] 167; *BHS* n. c). Nor should the verb be emended to some form of נקם (Brockington, *Hebrew Text,* 101; cf. NEB; Paton, 291) or to ונחום, "avenged themselves" (cf. *BHS* n. c), as does Bardtke (386; following Rudolph, *VT* 4 [1954] 90); cf. also Driver (*VT* 4 [1954] 237), Clines (324), and Dommershausen (*Estherrolle,* 121). The verb presents the result of the Jews' assembling together and defending themselves, that is, the destruction of their enemies (cf. Barthélemy, *Preliminary and Interim Report,* 550). In that sense it is not in conflict with the statement that follows (contra Driver), which simply gives further detail. Nor does the use here of נוח מן, "to have rest from," conflict with the use of נוח, "to have rest," in vv 17, 18 (contra Fox, 285). For the inf abs + waw, see *Note* 2:3.e.
16.d. Lit. "they did not stretch forth their hand to."
17.a. The division of verses between v 16 and v 17 is problematical (the temporal clause logically belongs with the contents of v 16; cf. *BHS* n. d). The division probably indicates, however, that the Masoretes recognized that vv 16–17 are one complex sentence; see *Form/Structure/Setting.*

17.b. Lit. "a day of feasting and joy."

18.a. A few late Heb. MSS and Syr omit v 18 (cf. *BHS* n.) The verse, however, is essential to the sense of the pericope.

18.b. Lit. "a day of feasting and joy."

19.a. V 19 is clearly parenthetical but not, in my opinion, a gloss; see *Comment.*

19.b. For this translation of היהודים הפרזים and ערי הפרזות, see *Comment.*

19.c. Lit. "joy and feasting and a good day." "Joy and feasting" is a hendiadys: "joyful feasting."

20.a. The reading "*all* these things" with a few Heb. MSS and Vg (cf. *BHS* n.) is not original (contra Bardtke, 390–91; Haller, 134; Ringgren, 402). It is probably the sense that the phrase refers to more than just the events of 13 and 14 Adar that prompts the addition; see *Comment.*

22.a. The reading בימים of a few Heb. MSS, and apparently of the LXX and Vg (cf. *BHS* n.), cannot be original; see *Comment.*

22.b. Lit. "as the days . . ."; see *Comment.*

22.c. Lit. "a good day."

22.d. In the Heb. text, vv 20–22 form one long complex sentence, in which לעשות אותם, "to make them," resumes the idiom להיות עשים את יום, "to be making the (fourteenth and fifteenth) day," in v 21 (cf. *Comment*). Good Eng. style requires breaking the sentence into two.

23.a. The sg verb with pl subject, though rare, does occur (cf. GKC § 145o n. 1; Brockelmann, *Syntax* § 50a) and does not need to be emended (contra *BHS* n.; Haller, 134; Haupt, *AJSL* 24 [1907–8] 169; Moore, 92 n. c). The pl form found in many Heb. MSS and all the versions is undoubtedly *ad sensum.*

23.b-b. This clause is lacking in the LXX (*BHS* n.). Its originality, however, is demonstrated by its importance for the sense of the whole pericope (see *Comment*).

24.a. Lit. "to demolish and destroy them," a hendiadys. The root המם means not only "to throw into confusion, panic" but also "to demolish, crush, bring to ruin" (cf. Jer 51:34, where it is parallel with אכל, "to devour"). This must be its meaning here (contra NASV), as its parallelism with לאבד, "to destroy," reveals (cf. *TDOT* 3:421). It is probably chosen because *lĕhummām,* "to destroy them," creates a wordplay with Haman (Haupt, *AJSL* 24 [1907–8] 170; cf. Fox, 120).

25.a. Or "she" (i.e., Esther); see *Comment.*

25.b. The obj of אמר, "said, commanded," need not necessarily connote direct discourse. Indirect discourse may also be expressed asyndetically; see GKC § 120c.

25.c. The emendation of ותלו to the inf abs וְתָלוֹ (*BHS* n.) is unnecessary (contra Bardtke, 390; Gerleman, 137; Haller, 134). The waw-consec pf ותלו can equally well continue the impf ישוב.

26.a. Lit. "all the words of."

26.b. The idiom על ככה, lit. "concerning such," occurs in BH only here. SBH uses expressions such as ב-/ל-/על הדבר הזה, "about/concerning this matter." The lateness of the idiom in Esther is indicated by the fact that the expression occurs elsewhere only in a letter from Wadi Murabbaʿat dating to A.D. 132–35, while a very similar expression, ל + כך, occurs in MH (כך is the MH form of LBH ככה). See Bergey, *JETS* 31 (1988) 164–65.

27.a. Lit. "they made obligatory and accepted," a hendiadys. Following the pl verb קימו, one must read the Q (וקבלו), rather than the K (וקבל); cf. *BHS* n. a.

27.b. Lit. "and it will not pass away." The emendations suggested (cf. *BHS* n. c) are to be rejected; see *Comment.*

27.c. Lit. "according to their writing."

27.d. Lit. "according to their (appointed) times." The proposal to read בזמנם (*BHS* n.) on the basis of the Syr reading is to be rejected. The Syr is *ʾyk dktybyn bzbnhwn,* "according to the written stipulations [given?] at their [the two days?] time" (cf. Gerleman, 137), which not only makes difficult sense but also fits the context very poorly.

28.a. Lit. "these days are going to be remembered and celebrated," a hendiadys (cf. Ehrlich, *Randglossen,* 123). On this force of the ptcps, see *Comment.*

28.b. Lit. "these days of Purim shall not pass away."

29.a. Heb. adds "and Mordecai the Jew"; see *Additional Note on vv 29–32* below.

29.b. Lit. "wrote all authority," a difficult text (cf. *BHS* n.). For discussion, see *Comment.*

29.c. Heb. adds "second," which is lacking in the LXX and Syr (*BHS* n. b) and is most probably a later addition to the text. For discussion, see *Additional Note on vv 29–32* below.

30.a. The apposition comes at the end of the verse, which is acceptable syntax in Heb. but is hardly so in Eng. For the meaning, see *Comment.*

30.b. The Heb. reads וישלח, "and he sent," a most difficult form in the context (cf. *BHS* n. a). For discussion, see *Comment.*

30.c. Lit. "to."
30.d. In the Heb., "the empire of Ahasuerus" is in apposition to "the one hundred and twenty-seven provinces" (cf. *BHS* n. b).
31.a. Lit. "to confirm these days of Purim."
31.b. Lit. "at their appointed times."
31.c. Heb. adds "and Queen Esther," in my opinion a later addition to the text (cf. *BHS* n. b-b). For discussion, see *Additional Note on vv 29–32* below.
31.d. Lit. "matters/requirements."
32.a. Lit. "in the book/document."

Excursus: Additional Note on vv 29–32

There are three phrases that create such serious difficulties in making coherent sense of these verses that the vast majority of modern commentators consider them to be later additions to the text. Unfortunately, the ancient versions are of virtually no help whatsoever in deciding whether these phrases are part of the original Heb. text. Neither the A-text nor the LXX provides evidence upon which alternative Heb. readings may be posited; cf. Fox (286–87). The A-text lacks the whole pericope (for a translation of the ending of the A-text, see Clines, *Esther Scroll,* 245–47). The LXX lacks v 30 and presents an almost unintelligible text for the rest (for a literal translation of the LXX, see Fox, 286–87). The OL lacks vv 30–32, while Syr and Vg are highly literal renderings of the Heb. that present only one significant variant reading, for which see (1) below. For the character of the texts of both Syr and Vg, see Paton's comments, 16–18, 24–28.

Let us begin by noting that the pericope relates two facts that are important for correctly interpreting it and that are clear and create no problems. First, the letter that this passage states was sent to all the Jews in the empire (v 30) is a different letter from the one sent previously by Mordecai (v 20). Second, the purpose of this letter is "to confirm [לקים]" the celebration of Purim (lit. "these days of Purim at their appointed times"), v 31, a different purpose from that for which Mordecai's letter was sent. The purpose of Mordecai's letter was "to *require*" the Jews (קים עליהם, lit. "to make binding upon them"; see *Comment* on v 21) to celebrate Purim (vv 20–22). With these facts in mind, let us examine the difficulties of text and interpretation created by these phrases and the solutions that may be suggested to resolve them.

(1) The statement in v 29a that this new letter was written "to confirm this *second* letter about Purim" is highly problematic. Whether Esther alone is writing this new letter, or Esther and Mordecai together (see difficulty [3] below), it is clear that it is this new letter that is meant by the expression "this second letter," which is exactly the problem. It surely makes little sense to state that they are writing to confirm the letter that they are writing. Attempts to interpret the text as its stands are singularly unconvincing. Clines (*Esther Scroll,* 56) suggests that sense can be made of the text by ignoring the ʾatnah on תקף (under which word in the verse, then, would the ʾatnah be placed?). He then understands "this second letter" to be the object of the main verb ותכתב, "she wrote," rather than the inf לקים, "to confirm," yielding the translation "Esther wrote . . . this second letter about Purim to make its observance obligatory" (cf. also Gordis, *Megillat,* 61). (In actuality the translation should be "to *confirm* its observance," for לקים means "to confirm"; it is the idiom לקים על that means "to make obligatory"; see the discussion above.) But, even without the ʾatnah the only natural sense of the order of the words requires taking the phrase "this second Purim letter" as the object of the inf. For the sense suggested, this phrase would most naturally come *before* the inf. Further, whatever the position of the phrase, both meaning and syntax would require that the inf take at least a pron object, probably more, to express the sense "*its* (observance)." Equally problematic is the approach of Dommershausen (*Estherrolle,* 133–34), who takes the difficult expression

את־כל־תקף (for discussion of which, see *Comment* below) to be in constr with the inf לקים, yielding the translation "Esther wrote . . . this second Purim document with all the force of the obligation [*mit allem Nachdruck der Verpflichtung*]." However, the inf constr with the prep ל, "to/for," can hardly bear the gerundive sense. It is most naturally taken as a purpose/result clause subordinate to the main verb. Further, apart from this grammatical incongruity, what sense does it make to say that Esther wrote a second Purim letter "with all the force of the obligation (to observe Purim)" when the purpose of this letter was to confirm the obligation to observe Purim (v 31)?

Clearly it is the adj השנית, "second," that disturbs the meaning of the sentence, for without it "this letter about Purim" would naturally refer to the previous letter written by Mordecai. On this basis and on the basis that the position of השנית, "second," following הזאת, "this," is "peculiar," Rudolph proposes (*VT* 4 [1954] 90) that השנית be deleted as a corrupted dittogr of the first word of the following verse, וישלח. This explanation of the origin of the word is, in my opinion, most improbable (there is but one letter common to both words), but Rudolph's observation that the position of השנית, "second," is irregular is important. It indicates that, in addition to being problematic as far as sense is concerned, the word is problematic syntactically as well. For, when a noun is modified by an attributive and a demonstrative pron, the demonstrative pron almost invariably *follows* the attributive. This order can be observed dozens of times in the OT; Joüon (*GBH* § 143h) states that there is only one exception, Jer 13:10. Particularly pertinent in this regard is the order of the parallel expression לחדש השביעי הזה, "this seventh month," which occurs three times (Lev 23:27, 34; Num 29:7). Also, the Syr translation omits the word השנית, "second." Since the Syr of Esther is a highly literal translation of the Heb., this suggests that the word was missing in the Heb. text the translator used (Fox, 287). Finally, even though the LXX is a highly paraphrastic translation, particularly in this passage, it does not speak of a "second letter" (Fox, *Redaction,* 107; for a literal translation of the LXX, see Fox, 286–87).

Since, then, the word makes impossible sense in the context, is syntactically incorrect, and is absent in Syr and the LXX, it is highly plausible that it is not original but constitutes a later addition to the text. One must admit, however, that it is difficult to suggest a plausible reason for a later copyist to have added the word (cf. Fox, 125). One can only surmise that the word was added under the mistaken assumption that "this Purim letter" is the one that Mordecai and Esther are now writing. Or, perhaps, as Gerleman suggests (141), whoever added the word took "this Purim letter" to be the object of the verb "wrote" (understanding the sentence in the sense posited by Clines; see above) and added "the second" to make sure that this letter, said to have been written by Esther and Mordecai, was not confused with the previous letter written by Mordecai alone. Nevertheless, despite the difficulty of explaining how it arose, we shall delete the word as a gloss, a confusing later addition to the text.

(2) The second obvious difficulty in the pericope is that in v 31 both "Mordecai the Jew" and "Queen Esther" are said to have issued the first letter requiring the Jews to observe Purim. This is highly problematic, for it contradicts what has been stated earlier. According to the wording of vv 20–23, Mordecai alone sent out the letters establishing the festival. Hence, we have deleted the words "and Queen Esther" as a later addition to the text (along with most modern commentators, e.g., Bardtke, 399; Brockington, *Hebrew Text,* 101; Clines, *Esther Scroll,* 56; Gerleman, 141; Moore, 96; Paton, 301; cf. Fox, 123–25).

(3) The fact that in v 29 "Mordecai the Jew" joins Esther in writing this new letter seems problematic. First, it is apparently contradicted by v 32, which states that it was specifically the "command" (מאמר; cf. 1:15; 2:20) of *Esther* that confirmed the Purim regulations (cf. Fox, 124–25). Second, if Mordecai and Esther jointly are the authors of this new letter, then the 3 m sg form of the verb at the beginning of v 31 is syntactically incorrect. Though the verb preceding a compound subject is often sg (GKC § 146f), any following verb with

the same compound subject is necessarily pl (GKC § 146h). Hence, this syntactic incongruity strongly suggests that the previous compound subject is suspect. And to take the 3 m sg form of the verb to imply that Mordecai alone sent out the letters mentioned (NASV, NIV) is simply infelicitous after the immediately preceding compound subject. Further, it then makes the full reference to him in v 31 quite unnatural. One would surely expect the wording to be "as *he* had required of them" (cf. Bardtke, 398). Finally, it is evident that the major point of the pericope is that Esther now writes to use her royal authority for the purpose of "confirming" Mordecai's letter (v 31) calling for the observance of Purim. Hence, it certainly seems less than natural that Mordecai should participate in *her* confirmation of *his* appeal (cf. Clines, *Esther Scroll,* 56; Loewenstamm, *HUCA* 42 [1971] 227; Paton, 300). Note that some modern translations, apparently sensing the incongruity of the presence of Mordecai here, translate the waw-connective between the two names not as "and" but as "with" (NASV) or "along with" (NIV, NRSV, TEV). (Some of the difficulties alleged against the inclusion of Mordecai, however, are unconvincing. The agreement of the fem sg verb [ותכתב, "and she wrote"] with the fem 1st person noun ["Queen Esther"] of a fem sg + masc sg compound subject is perfectly acceptable BH [see Num 12:1; cf. GKC § 146g; contra Clines, *Esther Scroll,* 56; Paton, 302]. Also, that Mordecai is called "Mordecai the Jew" whereas Esther is called "Queen Esther" and is given her patronymic does not suggest that the reference to Mordecai is secondary [contra Clines, *Esther Scroll,* 56]. He is never identified in the book by any title expressing his position as the one who possesses the king's signet ring [cf. 8:2; such as the Persian equivalent of "Grand Vizier" or the like, nor was Haman before him]. The ethnicon is the only title he is given when not simply called Mordecai. Particularly pertinent is the fact that this is the way he is identified in the final encomium upon him in 10:2 [note also 8:7].)

Attempts to retain the name Mordecai and resolve the difficulty are most unpersuasive. Brockington's proposal (245; cf. id., *Hebrew Text,* 101; NEB, REB) to read "to Mordecai" instead of "and Mordecai," yielding the translation "Esther . . . gave full authority in writing to Mordecai . . . to confirm this second letter about Purim," makes most difficult sense in the context (cf. also Clines, *Esther Scroll,* 56), for, according to NEB's translation of vv 30–31, Mordecai writes not to "confirm this second letter about Purim" (whatever that means) but to require its observance. But why would Mordecai, who has already sent out a letter requiring the observance of Purim, need to send out a second letter requiring it, and why would he need Esther's authority to do so when no such authority was needed to send out the first letter? Haupt's proposal (*AJSL* 24 [1907–8] 172; followed in part by Haller, 136) to place "Mordecai the Jew" after את־כל־תקף, yielding the translation "Esther described all the power of Mordecai to enjoin this Purim message," makes even less sense. Vv 30–31 say nothing about any such message from Esther, even with Haupt's proposal to emend the first verb of v 30 to "she wrote" (see also the remarks of Clines, *Esther Scroll,* 183 n. 29). Finally, the words "and Mordecai the Jew" can hardly be intended to go with the preceding name, "Abihail," as a second patronymic (so NAB; cf. Berg, *Book of Esther,* 54 n. 48). Not only is such a double patronymic most improbable (she surely would have been known as the daughter of one or the other but not both), but the syntax would require the repetition of "daughter of" before the name "Mordecai."

Since, then, it is difficult to make coherent sense of the words "and Mordecai the Jew" here, and since they are problematic syntactically, we have deleted them as a later addition to the text (along with most modern commentators, e.g., Bardtke, 399, Clines, *Esther Scroll,* 56; Gerleman, 141; Moore, 95; Paton, 302; cf. Fox, 123–25). It seems quite plausible to surmise that someone sought to place the authority of both of these acknowledged leaders of the Jewish community behind both letters by adding the words "and Mordecai the Jew" to Esther's name in v 29 and the words "and Esther the queen" to Mordecai's name in v 31 (cf. Fox, 125).

Form/Structure/Setting

In my opinion, 9:6–32 forms a separate act from 9:1–5 (for the criteria, see *Form/Structure/Setting* to 9:1–5). One could question whether vv 6–10 belong with 9:1–5 as part of the account of the Jewish victory over their enemies, but a close look at these verses will demonstrate that they belong with what follows, not with what has preceded (contra Clines, 321–25; Dommershausen, *Estherrolle,* 114–17; Gerleman, 130–35; Moore, 84–91; Murphy, *Wisdom,* 167–68; Paton, 282–84). True, having just given us in 9:1–5 an account of the Jewish victory in only the most general terms, the narrator does now set forth some of the details of that victory by relating in vv 6–10 both the numbers slain in the Citadel of Susa and the death of the ten sons of Haman. His purpose, however, is not simply to fill in the details of the Jewish victory (contra Bardtke, 382; Dommershausen, *Estherrolle,* 115). Nor is he simply concerned to delineate its magnitude (although the statements of the numbers slain certainly make that clear). Rather, both content and form demonstrate that the passage is devoted specifically and exclusively to telling why the fighting in the city of Susa took place over two days, in contradistinction to what happened in the rest of the empire, and how this is related directly to the conflict in the dates of the celebration of Purim. Thus, as to content, the account of the number slain in the Citadel of Susa, vv 6–10, leads directly, v 11, to the king's recapitulation of that fact, v 12ab, and then to his offer to Esther to make a further request, v 12c. Esther's request for another day of fighting, vv 13–14a, leads directly to its implementation, v 14b, and to the account of the number slain in Susa the next day, v 15. All of this simply documents that two days of fighting took place in Susa. As to form, the emphatic forefronting of the locale of the events of vv 6–10 (see *Comment*) places the focus of the sentence there (and hence its purpose is not to describe the magnitude of the Jewish victory, for example, contra Fox, 110), in exactly the same way that the forefronting of the same locale does with the king's recapitulation of the same events in v 12. Likewise the emphatic forefronting of the temporal phrase "that day" in v 11 functions to contrast the events of the first day with the events that will transpire on the second as a result of Esther's request, to which this verse provides the lead in. Hence, vv 6–10 are inextricably linked with vv 11–15, and the main purpose of the whole is to explain how there came to be two days of fighting in Susa.

That the first episode concludes with v 15 is indicated not only by the tight coherence of the narrative content (see above) but also by the inclusio provided by the statement at the conclusion of the first sentence and the last that the Jews took no plunder.

The second episode comprises vv 16–19. This is indicated first by the change in venue, from Susa to the rest of the empire, and second by the change in time. The perfect verbs in vv 16, 18 and the series of sequential infinitives absolute that follow them constitute a "flashback" in time relative to the previous episode (hence their translation in the pluperfect in English), and the independence and coherence of the episode are effected by a striking congruity of form. Vv 16–18 comprise two closely related units, consisting of vv 16–17 on the one hand and v 18 on the other, tightly tied together by both content and structure (see table). Both units begin with the nonsequential inverted sentence order subject + perfect verb. The verbs in the opening clause of each unit are identical, נקהלו, "assembled," but the subjects

The Structure of vv 16–18

Unit 1

ושאר היהודים . . . נִקְהֲלוּ	the rest of the Jews . . . assembled
וְעָמֹד על נפשם	*and stood* . . . (inf abs)
וְנוֹחַ מאיביהם	*and had rest* . . . (inf abs)
וְהָרֹג בשׂנאיהם חמשׁה ושׁבעים אלף	*and slew* . . . (inf abs)
(ובבזה לא שׁלחו את־ידם)	(but on the booty . . .)
ביום שׁלושׁה עשׂר לחדשׁ אדר	[17] **on the 13th of Adar** (temp. ph.)
וְנוֹחַ	*and rested* (inf abs)
בארבעה עשׂר בו	**on the 14th of it** (temp. ph.)
וְעָשֹׂה אתו יום משׁתה ושׂמחה	*and made it* . . . (inf abs)

Unit 2

והיהודים אשׁר־בשׁושׁן נִקְהֲלוּ	[18] the Jews in Susa assembled
בשׁלשׁה עשׂר בו ובארבעה עשׂר בו	**on the 13th and 14th of it** (temp. ph.)
וְנוֹחַ	*and rested* (inf abs)
בחמשׁה עשׂר בו	**on the 15th of it** (temp. ph.)
וְעָשֹׂה אתו יום משׁתה ושׂמחה	*and made it* . . . (inf abs)

contrast "the rest of the Jews who are in the king's provinces" in the first unit, v 16, with "the Jews who are in Susa" in the second, v 18. In each unit the perfect verb is followed, in every case but one, by a series of short, summary clauses, each of which begins with the infinitive absolute (italicized in translation in the table) in place of the finite verbal form. The first unit, vv 16–17, consists of two statements that are semantically independent but bound together syntactically as a single compound sentence. This is accomplished first by the fact that all but one of the verbs following נקהלו, "assembled," consist of infinitives absolute, which must acquire their subject, tense/aspect, etc. from that verb. (The one exception, the clause about the booty, is negative and forefronts "on the booty," and so must use the finite verb.) Second, the two adverbial phrases of time ("on the fourteenth of Adar" and "on the fifteenth of it," in bold in translation in the diagram) form the hinge that binds the two statements together. They form a symmetrical arrangement that closes the first statement and opens the second, nicely flanking the main verbal idea, "rested," of the second statement. The second unit, v 18, though shorter, has exactly the same structure as the first. The opening clause (identical in structure to that of the first unit) forefronts the subject and hence contrasts the two groups, the Jews in the provinces and those in Susa. Then, after the appropriate adverbial phrases of time, follow two infinitive absolute clauses that are identical to the last two of the first unit, except for the appropriate change in the temporal phrase. The parallelism of the two units is also markedly effected by the fact that the main verbal idea of the second unit, "rested," identical to that of the first, is also symmetrically flanked by two temporal phrases. Finally, these two units, vv 16–17 and v 18, are closely bound together by the uniform way that the dates are stated throughout. After the first temporal phrase, v 17a, the month involved is not explicitly stated but is referred to by means of בו, "in it." This carefully balanced, tightly constructed structure reveals that the intent of vv 16–17 is not to give a report or account of the battles in the provinces (contra Dommershausen, *Estherrolle,* 121). The whole is directed narrowly and specifically to explaining why the celebration of the Jewish victory took place on two different days in these two different parts of the Jewish community.

The second episode is concluded by the etiological digression of v 19, which provides dramatic closure to the scene by contrasting the actions of the Jews who lived outside the jurisdiction of Susa with those of Susa, v 18, establishing the different dates of celebration of the festival, to which the entire previous narrative has been leading.

That 9:20–32 constitutes the second scene of the act is also unmistakably clear from both content and form. In content the narrative turns from the events that led to the celebration of the festival on two different days in the two different parts of the Jewish community to the events that led to the permanent institution of the festival as an annual celebration, namely, the letters sent out to the community by Mordecai, vv 20–22, and Esther, vv 29–32, and the communities' own actions and decisions, vv 23a, 26b–27. The boundaries of the scene are set by the inclusio provided by the initial statement, v 20, that Mordecai "wrote these things down" and sent out a letter requiring the observance of Purim and the closing statement that Esther's decree confirmed these regulations about Purim and "it was written down in the records," v 32.

The scene clearly divides into three episodes. The first, vv 20–22, relates the sending of Mordecai's letter, which delineates the dates and the character of the annual celebration of the festival of Purim. The second episode, vv 23–28, relates the acceptance of this appeal by the Jewish community, v 23, and the grounds for it, a brief retrospective of the facts that created the crisis and resolved it, vv 24–25. The episode concludes with a virtual peroration, a grand and emphatic recapitulation of the whole scene (see *Comment*), vv 26b–28. Episode 3, vv 29–32, concludes the scene by reporting that Esther (see *Comment*) also wrote a letter in which she used her authority as the queen to confirm the observance of Purim that Mordecai and the Jews themselves had already instituted.

Comment

6 וּבְשׁוּשַׁן הַבִּירָה הָרְגוּ הַיְּהוּדִים..., lit. "and in the Citadel of Susa the Jews killed . . ." The structure here forefronts the spatial clause, thus placing emphasis upon it (hence the translation "the Citadel of Susa *itself;* cf. Moore, 84 n. c, and the discussion of 9:1 above). The same structure occurs in the king's response to these facts in v 12 below (for the significance of this, see *Form/Structure/Setting*). Haupt (*AJSL* 24 [1907–8] 163) argues that הבירה, "the Citadel," is a later addition by a scribe who, ignorant of its meaning, wished to embellish the name, but the epithet is used coherently throughout the book (cf. esp. 3:15; 4:17). Further, the usage is consistent here. "The Citadel of Susa" is used by the narrator and the king in vv 6–12, and "Susa" by Esther and the narrator in vv 13–15 (contra Haupt). One would expect a later embellishing addition to be made randomly.

7–9 וְאֵת פַּרְשַׁנְדָּתָא... וְאֵת וַיְזָתָא, "and Parshandatha . . . and Vaizatha." Reasonable Persian/Elamite etymologies have been suggested for most of the names of the ten sons of Haman (see the bibliography given for the names of the king's personal attendants in the *Comment* on 1:10).

There is nothing in this succinct and spare narrative that demands the specific naming of each of Haman's ten sons. The point, then, must surely be to underline the terrible retribution that fell upon Haman in the obliteration of his whole house. In Hebrew MSS of Esther, the names of Haman's sons are written in one column on the righthand side of the page and the word ואת (*wĕʾet,* "and" + the sign of the definite direct object) in another column on the left side of the page (the names of the kings of Canaan are listed similarly in Josh 12:9–23; a modified form of this for both passages is followed in *BHS*). The reason for this is unknown (although later Jewish traditon has preserved a number of fanciful explanations, for which see Moore, 87; Bardtke, 383–84; cf. also Fox, 110 n. 60). With all due reserve, I suggest that the purpose of this arrangement is the same as that given above for naming all ten sons. By drawing sharp attention to the names, the arrangement simply further underlines the judgment meted out on Haman's house.

11 בַּיּוֹם הַהוּא בָּא מִסְפַּר הַהֲרוּגִים . . . לִפְנֵי הַמֶּלֶךְ, "that very day the number of those slain . . . entered before the king." Once again the adverbial clause is forefronted, thus laying stress on the time of the event (hence the translation "*very* day"). The emphatic position helps to make clear that all of this took place over just two days (see *Form/Structure/Setting*).

Gerleman's attempt (133) to overcome the infelicity of the expression "the number of those slain came before the king" by proposing that מספר means not "number" here but "report, account" (as in Judg 7:15) does not in the least commend itself. In this context, the expression "the report/account of the slain" is equally infelicitous, for the report clearly centers its attention on the numbers. Hence, one would expect "the report of the numbers slain came before the king" or the like (cf. Clines, *Esther Scroll,* 181 n. 28).

12 בְּשׁוּשַׁן הַבִּירָה הָרְגוּ הַיְּהוּדִים . . . בִּשְׁאָר מְדִינוֹת הַמֶּלֶךְ מֶה עָשׂוּ, "in the Citadel of Susa alone the Jews have killed . . . , in the rest of the king's provinces what have they done?" The king's statement forefronts both locales and hence not only contrasts but emphasizes them, revealing once again how centrally the content of this whole pericope is related to the issue of the fighting on the two days (see *Form/Structure/Setting*).

The exact force of the king's rhetorical question is difficult to determine from the context. Clearly the question implies that he knows about Mordecai's counteredict and that he does not doubt that it has been fully carried out (Bardtke, 386). The offer that immediately follows precludes the possibility that the question is said in consternation or anger (so *b. Meg.* 16b; cf. Paton, 286), and the narrator's negative characterization of the king throughout the story surely renders it most improbable that the author now puts into the king's mouth his own joy at the victory (Dommershausen, *Estherrolle,* 118; cf. also Clines, *Esther Scroll,* 181 n. 28). The whole tenor of the narrative renders utterly improbable Jones' interpretation that the narrator expected his readers to find the king's rejoicing in the slaughter humorous (*CBQ* 39 [1977] 180)! Clines interprets the king's reaction as astonishment, prompted by his calculation of the extent of the massacre when extrapolated over the whole empire (*Esther Scroll,* 47). However, the king's recapitulation of what has happened in Susa and his rhetorical question are obviously intended by the narrator as the grounds for his following invitation to Esther to make a further request. As Clines himself notes, a reaction of astonishment hardly provides the grounds for such a further request. (Even if one grants the correctness of Clines' conclusion that 9:1–19 must come from an author whose narrative skill is far inferior to that of the author of chaps. 1–8 [see *Comment* on 9:1–5], one must surely grant him the ability to write sentences that are logically coherent, at least until it is proven otherwise.) It is more plausible in my opinion that Fox (112) has correctly captured the tenor of the king's rhetorical question: "having willy-nilly taken sides, he has become a partisan of the Jews," and hence "admiration is the only possible tone here." Admiration at the Jewish slaughter is not out of character for the weak, pliable, and impulsive despot who could with indifference consign to oblivion a whole people of his empire without even inquiring as to their identity (see *Explanation* to 3:1–15).

וּמַה־שְּׁאֵלָתֵךְ וְיִנָּתֵן לָךְ וּמַה־בַּקָּשָׁתֵךְ עוֹד וְתֵעָשׂ, lit. "So what is your wish? It shall be granted you. And what further is your request? It shall be done." The king's offer is couched in exactly the same language as his previous offers to Esther, except that עוד, "more," replaces עד־חצי המלכות, "up to half the kingdom" (see 5:6; 7:2). Dommershausen suggests that the two questions "should be understood rhetorically, approximately in the sense 'Queen, what more do you ask?'" (*Estherrolle,* 118–19), but the actual sense of such a rhetorical question is "surely, Queen, you cannot ask for more!" This makes impossible sense, given the offer that follows. This offer, to be taken literally, is far more magnanimous than before. It gives Esther carte blanche. Clearly, since the narrative itself (v 11a) and the king's admiring recapitulation (v 12) both center on the issue of the number slain, he has in mind further slaughter.

13 יִנָּתֵן גַּם־מָחָר לַיְּהוּדִים אֲשֶׁר בְּשׁוּשָׁן לַעֲשׂוֹת כְּדָת הַיּוֹם, lit. "let the Jews be granted tomorrow also to do according to today's decree." Esther's request does not misunderstand the king's offer. She requests that the "Jews in Susa" may "do according to today's decree," that is, that they may both "defend themselves" (8:11) and "take vengeance on their enemies" (8:13), as they have already done (9:1–5). On the incongruency in the plot development of both the king's offer and Esther's response, and their significance, see *Form/Structure/Setting.*

16 וּבַבִּזָּה לֹא שָׁלְחוּ אֶת־יָדָם, "on the spoil they did not lay their hand." In portraying in this scene the circumstances by which the Jews engaged in two days of fighting in Susa but only one in the rest of the empire, the narrator has mentioned on three different occasions the number of Jewish enemies that have been slain: (1) in the Citadel of Susa on the first day of fighting, vv 6–10; (2) in Susa itself on 14 Adar, the second day of fighting, v 15; and (3) throughout the rest of the empire on 13 Adar, v 16. On each occasion he has then immediately stated that the Jews took no plunder (even though Mordecai's edict gave them express permission to do so). Obviously it was of great importance to him to stress this, but the reason for it is not at all clear. Commentators (e.g., Clines, 323; id., *Esther Scroll,* 200 n. 35; Moore, 87–88; Fox 115) have suggested that the narrator is contrasting the Jews' behavior here with that of their ancestors who, motivated by greed, took booty when they defeated Agag and the Amalekites in the time of Saul, the results of which were so disastrous (1 Sam 15), but the parallel is seriously flawed (contra Fox). The booty of the Amalekites was to have been taken but subjected to the ceremonious destruction of the "ban." Here the Jews lay no hand upon it at all. If the Jewish action here was intended to be "undoing their ancestors failure" (Fox, 115), one would surely expect a similar action (McKane,

JTS 12 [1961] 260–61). And if this is the explanation, it is strange that, when the narrator first mentions the failure to take booty in v 10, he does not call Haman the Agagite (so Clines, 323), as he does elsewhere (cf. 8:3 and his full identification in 3:10; 9:24). Since the statement about the booty is given each time that the narrator has stated the number of the slain (note that the statement is completely missing in vv 1–5), it seems highly probable that he wished to make it clear that the Jews' attacks were not motivated by greed and self-aggrandizement but solely by the need for self-preservation (see Moore, 87; Clines, 323; id., *Esther Scroll,* 160; other bibliography in McKane, *JTS* 12 [1961] 261).

19 הַיְּהוּדִים הַפְּרָוזִים הַיֹּשְׁבִים בְּעָרֵי הַפְּרָזוֹת, lit. "the *pĕrāzîm* Jews, those who live in *pĕrāzôt* cities." Given the reading פרזי in Deut 3:5; 1 Sam 6:18, the Q is undoubtedly the correct reading. In my opinion, the MH word פָּרוּז, "one living in an unwalled village," found only in Talmudic passages dealing with the halachic requirements for celebrating Purim (see Jastrow, *Dictionary,* 1218), does not help in determining the meaning here on the grounds that it is highly probable that that word is coined from the K reading in this passage. That the K form arises because the author deliberately altered the form of the word פְּרָזִים in order to create assonance with היהודים (Striedl, *ZAW* 14 [1937] 90–91; Bardtke, 386, 389) does not seem probable. The exact meanings of the terms היהודים הפרזים and ערי הפרזות remain uncertain. Driver's view (*VT* 4 [1954] 8–9) that the Q פְּרָזִי is a gentilic, meaning "persons living in isolated [i.e., 'unwalled'] villages," while ערי הפרזות means "isolated towns, i.e., open or unwalled market towns or hamlets dotted about the country" has been widely accepted (see KB^3, 909; *CHALOT,* 297). Recently, however, Niemann (*ZAW* 105 [1993] 233–43) has argued that the root פרז involves a semantic opposition between "here" and "there," or between "inside" and "outside." Hence, the term היהודים הפרזים, "the *pĕrāzîm* Jews," refers to the *Jews* "outside" the territory belonging to the jurisdiction of the capital city of Susa, while ערי הפרזות refers to the *cities* that lie outside this same jurisdiction. This interpretation of the meanings of the terms is much to be preferred, for it predicates the same contrast as that in vv 16–18, namely the contrast between שאר היהודים אשר במדינות המלך, "the rest of the Jews who are in the king's provinces" (v 16) and היהודים אשר בשושן, "the Jews who are in Susa" (v 18). It totally relieves the incongruity between the contrast in v 19 and that in vv 16–18, which the other interpretations entail. The contrast between "walled" and "unwalled" cities (e.g., Fox, 113; Moore, 85) sets up an opposition contrary to that of vv 16–18, since the Jews in the provinces (v 16) would undoubtedly have lived in both walled and unwalled cities (cf. Fox, 114). So does the contrast between "country-Jews" and "city-Jews" (Bardtke, 385, 389), since the Jews in the provinces would undoubtedly have lived in cities and in the "country," i.e., localities below the city level (cf. Niemann, *ZAW* 105 [1993] 242 n. 30). Even if v 19 was added by a later scribe, the statement would surely have been intended to make sense in the context. Given these facts, we have adopted the sense proposed by Niemann, since it alone fits the context. Finally, whichever of the suggested senses of the term is adopted, to modify the phrase "the *pĕrāzîm* Jews" by the participial clause "those who live in *pĕrāzôt* cities/places" is simply tautological and may well be a gloss (Paton, 292), probably to explain the K reading (Clines, *Esther Scroll,* 182 n. 12).

The verse is unmistakably parenthetical, since it strikingly shifts the focus of attention from the events of the past, the actions of the Jews of Susa and the Jews of the provinces, to the narrator's own day and time. Many commentators regard it as a gloss added by a later hand on the grounds that it (1) contradicts vv 21–22, which call for a universal two-day celebration, whereas this verse implies two separate days of celebration (see, e.g., Clines, 325; Moore, 89), and/or (2) does not follow naturally after v 18 since it breaks the continuity by reverting to the subject of the Jews of the provinces, which was discussed in v 16 (see, e.g., Moore, 89; Meinhold, 87). But this is by no means a necessary conclusion. In regard to (1), see the discussion in the *Comment* on v 21 below. In regard to (2), the verse simply is not as jarring in its context as it is claimed as soon as one realizes that it is to be understood as a parenthesis in which the narrator inserts information from his own day pertinent to the issue being addressed. Since v 19 is a parenthesis, v 20 continues the issue addressed in vv 16–18, namely, the celebration of the festival on two different days among the two different groups of Jews. Clines argues that if v 19 is understood to precede v 23 chronologically, there is then a contradiction between the two verses. For then "'what they (i.e., the Jews) had begun to do' would seem to refer to the continuing *commemoration* of the deliverance, on the *fourteenth*—which would be different from what 'Mordecai had written to them'" (*Esther Scroll,* 51), but this also does not necessarily follow. The statement in v 23 may very well refer to their ongoing celebrations in the sense that they now accept that this is not to be occasional and temporary but regular and permanent, which is what Mordecai's letter seeks to commit them to (cf. Fox, 118–19).

The LXX adds at the end of v 19 the statement "and those who dwell in the cities also celebrate the fifteenth of Adar with good cheer, sending portions to their neighbors." In my opinion, this addition cannot preserve an original reading (cf. Clines, *Esther Scroll,* 51; it is not even, as Paton, 291, designates it, "a happy conjectural emendation"). It totally misses the different days of celebration of the Jews in Susa and those in the provinces, which is established by vv 16–18 and is clearly understood by the explanation in the previous clause. By stating that "those who dwell in the cities *also* celebrate the fifteenth of Adar," the verse assumes a two-day celebration for these Jews. However, the correct statement would allude to a celebration for them only on the fifteenth, in keeping with the two days of fighting of the Jews in Susa on the thirteenth and fourteenth, followed by a day of rest on the fifteenth (v 18), in contrast to the custom of the Jews in the provinces (vv 16–17). It is highly probable, then, that it is a gloss from vv 21–22, these verses being understood by the LXX author to establish a two-day festival of Purim. (For additional evidence from LXX readings that the clause is secondary, see Clines, *Esther Scroll,* 51.) The "awkwardness" of v 19 in the MT created by its "concentration upon the Jews of the 'villages' and their custom without regard for Jews elsewhere" (Clines) is, in my opinion, adequately explained by the narrator's point of view being Susan, not only here (so Fox, 114) but throughout the previous narrative (cf. Bardtke, 389).

20 וַיִּכְתֹּב מָרְדֳּכַי אֶת־הַדְּבָרִים הָאֵלֶּה, "and Mordecai wrote these things down." This cannot mean that Mordecai was the author of the book of Esther (as medieval and other commentators assumed; cf. Clines, *Esther Scroll,* 177 n. 12; Bardtke, 391). Commentators differ over whether "these things" refers to what has preceded (and to how much of it) or to what follows. Dommershausen (*Estherrolle,* 123) and Paton (293) argue that the phrase refers specifically to the contents of Mordecai's letter, which they say appears in vv 21–22. These verses, however, set forth not the contents of Mordecai's letter but rather its purpose (Fox, 285). Dommershausen argues this case on the grounds that the demonstrative pronoun אלה, "these," usually refers to what follows, citing GKC § 136, but this is not borne out by the facts. To the contrary, הדברים האלה, "these things," occurs to the virtual exclusion of הדברים ההם/ההמה, "those things," and hence refers to either what has preceded or what follows (cf. GKC § 136b; BDB, 41). In my opinion, since Mordecai is writing to obligate the Jews to the annual celebration of the festival (v 21), his letter must have included at least a précis of the events that led to Haman's edict, for it would undoubtedly have been only the edict itself that most Jews, especially those outside Susa, would have been cognizant of. Such a précis occurs in vv 24–25, which may well be intended to reflect the gist of what Mordecai related since it is presented there as the reason the Jews accepted what Mordecai had written to them. In this light, then, it is most probable that the phrase refers not just to the recent Jewish victory in battle and the accompanying celebration (so Bardtke, 391; Gerleman, 138; Moore, 93) but at least to a summary account of what happened beginning with Haman's decree (cf. Fox, 117). Only such a story of threat, resolution, and salvation would be sufficient "to convince the people that the recent events justify a perpetual holiday" (Fox; cf. also Clines, *Esther Scroll,* 23). In the context, it can hardly mean that Mordecai had the narrative of the book of Esther recorded in the records of the Persian court (contra Clines, *Esther Scroll,* 23).

21 לְקַיֵּם עֲלֵיהֶם לִהְיוֹת עֹשִׂים, lit. "to impose upon them to be making." קַיֵּם, the piel infinitive construct < קום, is an LBH development (the SBH form is invariably the hiphil; see the discussion in LBH item [5] of *Date* in the *Introduction* to Ruth above). The verb is used seven times in scene 2 (vv 20–32) in two different idioms. In the first it occurs three times *without* the preposition על, "upon," and in each case the object is impersonal (v 29, "the letter about Purim"; v 31, "these days of Purim"; v 32, "these regulations about Purim"). In this usage the meaning is "to validate, confirm, effectuate." In the second idiom the verb occurs four times *with* the preposition על. In this usage there is a double object of the verbal action. The first object, governed by על, is personal ("them/themselves" [i.e., the Jews], vv 21, 27, 31; "their descendants," vv 27, 31; "all who joined them," v 27). The second object is the obligation enjoined ("to celebrate . . . ," vv 21, 27; "these days" [understood], v 31b; "the requirements of fasts . . . ," v 31c). The meaning, then, is "to make binding [על upon someone] something, to require [על of someone] something." In order to affirm that the meaning here is not "command, demand" (with which I agree), Fox (118) argues that the meaning throughout the passage is "to validate or confirm," appealing to its usage in Ruth 4:7; Ezek 13:6; Ps 119:106. However, each of these is an example of the first idiom. Rather, as Fox himself notes, the verb ". . . is used in Est 9:27 and 31 to report that the Jews made the Purim celebration binding upon themselves . . . ."

אֵת יוֹם אַרְבָּעָה עָשָׂר לְחֹדֶשׁ אֲדָר וְאֵת יוֹם־חֲמִשָּׁה עָשָׂר בּוֹ, "the fourteenth day of the month of Adar and the fifteenth day of it." Many commentators (e.g., Clines, 325; Moore, 89) interpret the language here to imply that Mordecai is calling for a two-day celebration applicable to all Jews everywhere, which contradicts vv 16–19 (see the discussion in *Comment* on v 19 above). But, even if this is Mordecai's intent, it is not necessarily in conflict with vv 16–19. Rather, one of the main purposes of Mordecai's letter may well be to adjudicate the differences in the dates of celebration by calling upon both groups to celebrate both days, since each day has been made legitimate by the experience of one of them. On the other hand, the language of vv 21–22 may also plausibly be taken to mean that there is to be one day of celebration each for the two groups, the Jews of Susa and the Jews of the provinces (so Fox, 114; Bardtke, 391–92). The distinction between two days of celebration has been clearly established by the two original days of celebration in the preceding narrative and does not need to be repeated here. It is simply taken for granted (Bardtke). In my opinion, this seems the more likely interpretation.

22 כַּיָּמִים אֲשֶׁר־נָחוּ בָהֶם הַיְּהוּדִים מֵאוֹיְבֵיהֶם, lit. "like the days on which the Jews had rest from their enemies." Most modern English translations of the passage translate the clause "*as* the days . . ." or equivalent (so NAB, NIV, NEB, REB, RSV, NRSV). As Clines points out (*Esther Scroll,* 201 n. 44), this is potentially misleading, for it can be taken to mean "*as being* the days . . ." This is not a possible rendering of the Hebrew, since כ, "like, as," cannot bear such a meaning (the so-called *kaph essentiae*). Rather, to celebrate these days "*like* the days on which they gained relief from their enemies" means to celebrate them by engaging in the same activities as they did on the original days of celebration (cf. Bardtke, 389, 392; Dommershausen, *Estherrolle,* 123). This is made clear by the epexegetical final clause, whose "to be making" resumes the clause in v 21 (see *Note* 22.d.), spelling out precisely what this means.

23 וְקִבֵּל הַיְּהוּדִים אֵת אֲשֶׁר־הֵחֵלּוּ לַעֲשׂוֹת, "the Jews accepted what they had begun to do." Given the object, "what they had begun to do," the verb קבל, lit. "to accept, receive," in this context must mean more than simply "to agree with, give assent to." It must mean "took upon themselves, adopted (as a custom)" (cf. esp. the remarks of Paton, 298). In the light of the preceding explanatory digression (v 19), the expression "what they had begun to do" refers not only to the original, spontaneous celebrations on the days following the fighting (vv 17–18) but also, and principally, to the differing regular practice that that etiology reveals has been going on since (cf. Clines, 326; Fox, 114).

24–25 These verses set forth a recapitulation of the narrative of chaps. 1–8 that differs significantly in details from the previous story, as summaries sometimes do (cf. Bardtke, 393; Clines, *Esther Scroll,* 54). In my opinion, one could well attribute the following to the imprecision of abridgment: (1) the statement that *pur,* "the lot," was cast to destroy the Jews, whereas it was actually cast to determine the day for the destruction (contra Clines, *Esther Scroll,* 53); (2) the statement that Haman's plot against the Jews comes back upon his own head, whereas in the story it was actually his plot against Mordecai (contra Clines, *Esther Scroll,* 53); (3) the compression of the hanging of Haman and of his sons into one event (Bardtke, 394; Clines, *Esther Scroll,* 53). Other differences, however, cannot be attributed simply to the demands of a summary presentation. On the grounds of these substantial differences, and on the grounds that the recapitulation at this point is superfluous, it has been argued that this material is a later addition to the book (see Paton, 58; Clines, *Esther Scroll,* 51–55).

Whatever one concludes in this regard, however, the material plays a significant and important role in the scene. Though it is not presented as a quotation from Mordecai's letter, it does give the substance of the retrospective that that letter contained, and it presents the reason (כִּי, "for") that the Jews took upon themselves "what Mordecai had written to them." This retrospective not only does *not* faithfully summarize the account that has already been told in chaps. 1–8; it differs from it deliberately. The reason for this has, in my opinion, been cogently argued by Fox (120; cf. also id., *Redaction,* 104). The situations of Mordecai, Esther, the Jews, and the king are now radically different from what they were in the original story. The Jews are no longer personae non gratae. The king's reason for executing Haman in 8:7 (quite different from what motivated him in 7:9) has revealed him as a protector of the Jews, and his recent question and offer to Esther in v 12 show him now to be their partisan (see the *Comment* above). Mordecai the Jew is now the grand vizier. Hence, Mordecai must now, as a skilled courtier and defender of the Jews, tell the story in such a way as to maintain the new status quo. Thus, it is only Haman who is given his full identity (unchanged but for the fact that he is now the enemy of *all* the Jews) and whose role remains the same as before (v 24a). In contrast, the role of each of the other protagonists of the story is significantly changed. In particular, Mordecai must portray the king in a far different role than he actually played in the story itself. Thus, he gives all the credit for foiling Haman's plot to the king, not to himself or to Esther. Both Esther's major role, and his own, are completely ignored (cf. Clines, *Esther Scroll,* 165). Second, he makes it appear that the moment Haman's plan came to the king's attention he gave orders for Haman's execution. The king, then, is made to appear as virtually the sole agent in the Jews' deliverance. Thus, Mordecai "flatters the king into adopting attitudes favorable to the Jews by speaking as if he already possessed them" (Fox, *Redaction,* 104). Third, and most important, with the little phrase "in writing" he subtly melds together his own decree to counter Haman's edict and the king's command to execute Haman (which, in point of fact, did ultimately happen because Haman's plan to annihilate the Jews "recoiled on his own head"). Hence, "the summary does not ignore the counter-decree but presents it as a direct expression of the king's anger at Haman" (Fox, *Redaction,* 104). Mordecai's retrospective, then, not only informs the Jews of the facts about the terrible crisis and its resolution, important to justify the call for a new holiday, but does so in such a way as to further enlist the king in the Jewish cause.

It is also important to note that the retrospective functions in another way in the passage. Since it provides the reason that the Jews accepted Mordecai's injunction to establish the festival ("what Mordecai had written to them," v 23), it is a further indication that the festival celebrates deliverance from terrible evil ("Haman's wicked plan"), not victory over enemies in battle and bloodshed (see the discussion of Purim in the *Theology* section of the *Introduction* to Esther).

25 וּבְבֹאָהּ לִפְנֵי הַמֶּלֶךְ, lit. "and when she/it came before the king." A number of the early versions (Syr, Tg, and Vg), modern commentators (e.g., Bardtke, 390; Ehrlich, *Randglossen,* 124; Haupt, *AJSL* 24 [1907–8] 170; Moore, 92), and translations (e.g., NAB, NRSV, RSV, TEV) take the third person feminine singular pronominal suffix on the infinitive construct to refer to Esther, since it was indeed her risky entry unbidden into the king's presence that led to Haman's undoing. But Esther has not been mentioned since episode 1 of the last scene (vv 12–13). Hence, it would surely require more than simply the feminine suffix to introduce her so suddenly into this scene. Rather, it would surely take a full reference to her (which therefore Ehrlich and Haupt posit must have been originally present in the text). Further, it is probably pertinent in this connection to note that the idiom here is the same one that occurs in 9:11 in reference to a report, בוא לפני, "to enter *before* the king," whereas when Esther is said to come to the king, the idiom is בוא אל, "to enter *to*" (4:8, 11, 16; so Dommershausen, *Estherrolle,* 126). Driver has postulated (followed by Bardtke and Moore) that the consonantal text ובבאה should be read וּבְב״א״ה, an abbreviation for וּבְבֹוא אֶסְתֵּר הַמַּלְכָּה, since the abbreviation "could be easily understood from the context" ("Abbreviations," 128). But, on the contrary, the context (see above) would have rendered it most difficult so to understand such an abbreviated reference. The LXX reads "when he came to the king," referring to Haman, the subject of the previous sentence (followed by JB, NJB), but this is doubtless an attempt to handle the problem, rather than evidence for a different Hebrew text. It is far preferable to understand the antecedent of the feminine suffix to be Haman's plot (Heb. מחשבת; see the following clause), which has just been mentioned (so also Clines, *Esther Scroll,* 53; Fox, 285). True, this interpretation means that the retrospective not only ignores Esther completely (as it does Mordecai) but makes it appear that the king learned somehow of the plot and acted immediately to reverse it. However, this can be accounted for as part of Mordecai's skillful transformation of the affair so as to present the king as the primary savior of the Jews (see the previous entry).

אָמַר עִם הַסֵּפֶר יָשׁוּב מַחֲשַׁבְתּוֹ הָרָעָה, lit. "he commanded with the writing/document that his evil device should recoil." The meaning of the expression עם הספר, lit. "with the writing/document," is wholly problematical. It is usually rendered "in writing" (e.g., NAB, NRSV, RSV) or the like, but such a meaning for עם is otherwise unattested. Haupt's view (*AJSL* 24 [1907–8] 170–71, followed by Gerleman, 139), that the phrase has the meaning "in spite of the letter," the "letter" referring to Haman's original decree ordering the extermination of the Jews (3:12), is fraught with problems. First, it is most difficult to ascribe to עם, "with," the adversative sense on the grounds of which the meaning "in spite of" is predicated (see Clines, *Esther Scroll,* 182 n. 14, who demonstrates that Neh 5:18 is no real parallel; cf. also BDB, 768). Second, the conciseness of the summary would render it most difficult to identify the "letter" as Haman's decree (Clines, 327–28). Also, the sense obtained is wholly problematical. Even if it were clear which "letter" was meant, it makes little sense to say that Haman's plot recoiled against him *in spite of* his letter ordering it (Fox, 285). In *HALOT* (840), the suggestion has been made (followed by Bardtke, 390, 394) that the phrase means "written simultaneously." However, aside from the difficulty of the expression ("together with" = "at the same time as"?), this likewise makes most difficult sense in the context. Apart from the fact that Haman was already long dead when Mordecai wrote his counterdecree (presumably "by letter" refers to Mordecai's decree), what point does such an inconsequential detail have in this briefest of summaries? Finally, Fox (285), following NJPV, renders the phrase "with the promulgation of this decree" and takes the words as part of Ahasuerus' words. However, this interpretation understands the preposition עם, "with," to have the sense "by means of," a meaning it bears nowhere else. For lack of anything better, we have adopted the traditional rendering, despite its weaknesses.

26 עַל־כֵּן קָרְאוּ לַיָּמִים הָאֵלֶּה פוּרִים עַל־שֵׁם הַפּוּר, "therefore, these days are called Purim—from the word *pur.*" Once again, as in v 19, the narrator inserts a digression. He leaves the context of his story and leaps to the setting of his own day to explain why these days of celebration are called Purim. (Hence, in the translation we have placed the clause in parentheses.) He obviously finds the reason in the retrospective drawn from Mordecai's letter (v 24), which mentioned that Haman "had cast *pur* (that is, the lot) in order utterly to demolish" the Jews (see 3:7). This is, however, a most tenuous explanation of the name. In his letter requiring the annual celebration, Mordecai does not require of his compatriots that it should be named after the foreign term *pur.* The narrator's etiological explanation, then, implies that the name was coined by the Jewish community independently of Mordecai's letter (vv 20–22) and the Jews' acceptance of it (vv 23, 26b–28). However, apart from the mentioning of Haman's casting of "*pur,* the lot" in Mordecai's brief retrospective (vv 24–25), the Jewish community at large would have known nothing whatever about either the event itself or the foreign term used. Hence, this really gives no explanation at all why the Jewish community would have named the festival after the foreign word for the lot that Haman cast in order to exterminate them (so Mordecai's retrospective, v 24b; in actuality, of course, the lot was cast *for* Haman to determine the propitious day for the extermination; see 3:7). If this is indeed the actual historical reason for the name, one can only suggest the rather weak explanation that the choice involves a kind of reverse psychology. The *pur* was to determine the day for the Jews' extermination, but it actually was a *pur* that produced the day of their vindication and victory. Further, the author himself clearly felt that the connection between what he has just related and the naming of the celebration Purim was not all that transparent. For he does not simply say "therefore these days are called Purim" but feels it necessary to make the connection explicit by including the clause of reason על שם הפור, "on account of the term *pur*" (Clines, *Esther Scroll,* 54). Finally, the etiology leaves totally unexplained why the name of the celebration is Purim, "lots," in the plural, when only one lot was cast. V 26a seems to suggest that the author understands that the term is plural because it is celebrated on "these (two) days," but that can hardly be the reason it is called "lots" (so Fox, 121). Clines (328; cf. id., *Esther Scroll,* 164) suggests that the narrator intends the plural name to signify the double lot or chance involved, one that determined disaster for the Jews and a second cast by God in the Jews' favor. However, there is not the slightest hint anywhere in the book of a second lot (Fox, 121), and there is not the slightest allusion in this portion of the narrative to divine providence. The victory of the Jews is not effected by any series of remarkable coincidences (such as those that so strikingly moved the narrative forward in the earlier story; see *Explanation* to 6:1–11), which could perhaps signal divine providence. On the contrary, the Jewish victory is a completely human achievement (cf. Gerleman, 131). It is effected by their own military offensive, by the fear of their prowess that has overtaken all their enemies, and by the aid afforded them by Persian officialdom at all levels (see 9:1–5 and *Explanation* thereto). Again, one might surmise that the Jewish community would have seen divine providence behind this effortless victory, but there is nothing in the narrative that hints in any way that this is intended by the narrator. Gerleman's convoluted attempt (25–28) to connect Purim, "lots," with *mānôt,* the "portions" (or gifts of food), exchanged in the celebration (vv 19, 22), by virtue of the fact that *gôrāl* may mean both "lot" and "that which is apportioned by lot," has been refuted by Clines (*Esther Scroll,* 201 n. 43). The plurality at least of the word may plausibly be explained by Clines' suggestion (*Esther Scroll,* 201 n. 43) that it results from assimilation of the name to the plurals by which most Jewish festivals were known, e.g., Weeks (*Šabûʿôṯ*), Booths (*Sukkôṯ*), Unleavened Bread/Passover (*maṣṣôt*), and Lights/Hanukkah (*ʾûrîm*).

עַל־כֵּן עַל־כָּל־דִּבְרֵי הָאִגֶּרֶת הַזֹּאת, lit. "therefore, because of all the statements of this letter." In my opinion, the introductory על־כן, "therefore," which grounds v 27 in what has preceded, is not at all as inappropriate in its context as Clines argues (*Esther Scroll,* 54–55). The statement to follow in v 27 is the grand conclusion that the narrator has been leading up to in all that he has related thus far in this whole act, and could have functioned well as a conclusion to the whole dénouement (cf. Loewenstamm, *HUCA* 42 [1971] 227). Hence, the "therefore" is intended to ground this conclusion in this account of the events that have led to the establishment of the festival. Indeed, in order to emphasize this very fact, the narrator, somewhat redundantly, but hence emphatically, restates these very grounds in the causal clause that follows. The contents of this causal clause are, in point of fact, an excellent summary of what has preceded. Thus, "all the statements of this letter" refers to vv 20–22, and "what they had experienced *in this regard* [i.e., 'in the foregoing'; see *IBHS* § 39.3.4.e, pp. 666–67] and what had happened to them" refers to the whole story of the crisis beginning with Haman's edict, which the narrator has just recapitulated in the retrospective drawn from Mordecai's letter, vv 24–25.

27 וְלֹא יַעֲבוֹר, lit. "and it will not pass away." It is entirely unnecessary to emend the singular יעבור to the plural יעברו (to give the sense "they [the Jews] will not transgress"; so Bardtke, 390; Moore, 93, 95; cf. Paton, 299). Nor should it be transposed to the end of the verse (to give the sense "they [the days] will not pass away"; so Haupt, *AJSL* 24 [1907–8] 172; cf. *BHS* n.). The subject of the singular verb is the obligation to celebrate Purim understood from the context and explicitly expressed in the clause that follows. The phrase is exactly the same as that used in 1:19. Hence, its purpose is to indicate that the obligation of Purim is as irrevocable as the laws of the Persians (cf. Dommershausen, *Estherrolle,* 127). The emendation quite misses the point.

28 וְהַיָּמִים הָאֵלֶּה נִזְכָּרִים וְנַעֲשִׂים, lit. "and these days are going to be remembered and celebrated." The syntactic structure of the previous sentence, "the Jews bound themselves . . . להיות עשים, to be celebrating," is not continued here, contra Paton (299). This clause breaks that pattern, since the subject "these days" is stated again. The significance of the participial predicate is, however, ambiguous. This construction usually expresses certainty, often with imminency, the sense expressed by the English "is going to" (see *IBHS* § 37.6.f). It could also be taken as a present tense, as does Fox (116; so also NJPV), but this seems less likely. A "continuous present tense" (so Fox, 132 n. 3) does not fit well with the following adverbial modifier בכל־דור ודור, "in every generation." (The perfect tense suggested by Berg, *Book of Esther,* 172–73, would require emendation of the text.) In my opinion, it is not, then, a continuation of the stipulations to which the Jews have bound themselves set forth in the previous verse, as it is almost universally rendered (e.g., Bardtke, 390; Moore, 93; Paton, 297; NASV, NEB, NIV, RSV). Rather, the narrator turns from relating what happened and prescribes for his readers the universal observance of Purim. This is indicated by his switch to the legal prohibitive (*IBHS* § 31.5.d; *GBH* § 113m), the negated imperfect, in the following two clauses.

29 וּמָרְדֳּכַי הַיְּהוּדִי, "and Mordecai the Jew." For defense of the view taken here that these words are a later addition to the text, see *Additional Note on vv 29–32* in the *Notes* to this act.

וַתִּכְתֹּב אֶסְתֵּר . . . אֶת־כָּל־תֹּקֶף, lit. "Queen Esther . . . wrote all power/authority," or perhaps "with all power/authority." The LBH word תקף occurs outside of this passage only in 10:2 and Dan 11:17, where it means "power, might" (cf. the verb תקף, "to overpower"). Hence, understanding the particle את to be the preposition "with," the phrase has been rendered adverbially, "with all force, emphatically" (e.g., Bardtke, 397; Paton, 300; Ringgren, 402) or, far more frequently, "with all/full authority" (e.g., NASV, NIV, NJB). However, it is the preposition ב, "in, by," that is used in the OT to express an adverbial sense of manner (cf. Haupt, *AJSL* 24 [1907–8] 76–77; Loewenstamm, *HUCA* 42 [1971] 228). The preposition את is never used in the OT in this way (the only use at all comparable is the expression of means in Judg 8:7; its use in Isa 30:8 is in no way comparable, contra Bardtke, 397). The particle, then, can only be the sign of the definite direct object, lit. "Queen Esther wrote all power/authority to confirm." The emendations suggested, to transpose "Mordecai the Jew" after תקף, yielding "Queen Esther . . . described all the power of Mordecai . . . (Haller, 136; Haupt, *AJSL* 24 [1907–8] 172), or to transpose תקף after לקים (cf. *BHS* n. a-a), have "no support in the versions" and are "strained and unconvincing" (Moore, 96). Loewenstamm, drawing upon an Akkadian analogy and on a reputed meaning in Nabatean, suggests the rendering "valid deed" for תקף, yielding the translation "Esther . . . and Mordecai . . . wrote the whole valid deed of this Purim epistle" (*HUCA* 42 [1971] 228–30). However, apart from the questionable validity of these parallels and the wholly problematic deletion of לקים (cf. Berg, *Book of Esther,* 54 n. 49), this simply makes no sense in the context. Much to be preferred is Fox's view (286), that תקף, "authority," is used figuratively here to mean "words of authority." The sentence, then, means "she wrote a letter in which she used all her authority (as queen) to confirm" Mordecai's letter enjoining the observance of Purim (cf. Gerleman, 141).

אֶת אִגֶּרֶת הַפּוּרִים הַזֹּאת הַשֵּׁנִית, "this letter about Purim, the second." For defense of the view taken here that the word השנית, "the second," is a later addition to the text, see *Additional Note on vv 29–32* in the *Notes* to this act.

30 וַיִּשְׁלַח, "and he sent." The pointing of this verb as third person masculine singular is difficult even with the compound subject in v 29 (see the discussion in section [3] of *Additional Note on vv 29–32* at the end of *Notes* above). If we delete "and Mordecai the Jew" from that verse (as seems required; see *Additional Note*), it is impossible. The difficulty can most simply be relieved, however, by repointing the verb as niphal third person masculine singular, which involves no change in the consonants (cf. Fox, 286). Noncoordination of number when the verb stands first is regular in BH in general (GKC § 145o) and in Esther in particular (e.g., 1:14; 2:21; 9:23a; so Fox). Once "and Mordecai the Jew" had been added to v 29, it would have been possible for the Masoretes to point the verb as qal (cf. Fox).

דִּבְרֵי שָׁלוֹם וֶאֱמֶת, lit. "words of peace and faithfulness." This phrase is in apposition to ספרים, "letters," though separated from it by the two intervening adverbial clauses. Such separation of an appositive from the noun it modifies does not violate Hebrew syntax; see esp. Fox (286; and the *Comment* on the phrase "the people of Mordecai" in 3:6). The precise sense of the apposition is, however, ambiguous.

Gordis (*JBL* 95 [1976] 57–58; so also Bardtke, 400) interprets it as the initial formula of greeting from the actual letter itself, of which only a summary is presented in v 31. However, the word אמת, "truth, faithfulness," is unattested as part of epistolary salutation formulae of the era (Clines, 330; Gerleman, 141), and Gordis does not make clear in any way what function a quote of the formula plays here. As Fox (286) notes, so understood, the phrase "hangs uselessly in the air." Nor is it clear how such an (abbreviated) quote would "evoke the effect of the actual letter" and so "enliven the whole portrayal" (Bardtke, 400). Since the phrase is in apposition to the word "letters," it intends to portray the character or quality of what Esther has written. And since Esther's letter intends to confirm the observance of Purim "as Mordecai had required of" the Jews, it is most reasonable to expect that it will not be out of character with that purpose. In this light, Gerleman's interpretation (141–42) is most persuasive. He argues that the word אמת is best rendered in this passage by "authority," since it designates that which gives to a person significance and validity, while שלום, used of "words" here, moves in the meaning range of "kindness, pleasantness," the sense it has when used in combination with verbs of speaking (e.g., Gen 37:4; Jer 9:7). The phrase then expresses that Esther's words were "kindly but authoritative."

31 וְאֶסְתֵּר הַמַּלְכָּה, "and Queen Esther." For defense of the view taken here that these words are a later addition to the text, see *Additional Note on vv 29–32* in the *Notes* to this act.

דִּבְרֵי הַצֹּמוֹת וְזַעֲקָתָם, lit. "matters of fasting and their laments." It has been alleged that the phrase is "syntactically awkward" (Clines, *Esther Scroll,* 57) or "lame" (Gerleman, 142) or "syntactically unrelated to the rest of the verse" (so Moore, 96), but this is hardly the case. The phrase is simply the direct object of the preceding verbal phrase, וכאשר קימו על־נפשם, "and as they had imposed upon themselves *matters* . . ." In the identical idiom in vv 21, 27, the direct object follows the prepositional phrase as here. It is not syntactically awkward or improper, but it is awkward in sense, for the phrase is unexpected to say the least. The parallelism strongly leads one to expect that this verbal phrase will have the same unexpressed object, "them" ("these days"), as the almost identical verbal phrase that precedes it. For this reason one is tempted to regard it as a later addition to the text (so Gerleman, 142; Moore, 96–97), but, since it is syntactically acceptable and does make tolerable sense, it seems inadvisable to delete it, even if it may have been added by a later hand. It is important to note that the text does not state that Esther is requiring the Jewish community to observe a fast as well as a festival (contra Bardtke, 401; Berg, *Book of Esther,* 37, 44; Paton, 301). Rather, the text states that Esther is *confirming* (לקים, not לקים על; see above) the observance of Purim *in the same manner as* (כאשר) Mordecai had required of them, that is, on the specified days and in the specified manner (vv 21–22, 27). Hence, the following phrase, "*and in the same manner as* they had imposed upon themselves . . . fasts and their accompanying laments" cannot be understood to be imposing a Purim fast. Esther is urging the Jewish community voluntarily to take upon themselves the Purim festival just as they have done with the fasts that they have imposed upon themselves on various occasions of national danger and disaster in the past, including the very recent occasions related in 4:3; 4:16 (see Loewenstamm, *HUCA* 42 [1971] 121–24; Clines, *Esther Scroll,* 167; and esp. the very helpful discussion of Fox, 125–27). In my opinion, the text does not imply that the Jewish community has already instituted a Purim fast (contra Clines, 330; id., *Esther Scroll*, 57; Haupt, *AJSL* 24 [1907–8] 174). The previous Purim obligation has said nothing whatsoever about a fast, but indeed just the opposite (v 22). And a Purim fast (on 13 Adar) is not attested in Jewish sources until the eighth century A.D. at the earliest (see Loewenstamm, *HUCA* 42 [1971] 123; Fox, 126 n. 74).

32 וּמַאֲמַר אֶסְתֵּר קִיַּם דִּבְרֵי הַפֻּרִים הָאֵלֶּה, "So Esther's decree confirmed these regulations about Purim." The LBH word מאמר is used elsewhere only in Esth 1:15; 2:20, where it means "command, order." If the MT text of vv 29–31 is maintained (i.e., including the three deletions discussed above), then this "command" of Esther must be distinguished from the "second" letter mentioned there (cf. Fox, 127). In that case the verse refers cryptically to some later command/edict of Esther that was preserved in written form, v 32b (probably in the daily court record; cf. 6:1). But this is made syntactically less probable by the fact that the text here does not use the waw-consecutive form of the verb, which would imply a subsequent event, but the subject + verb construction, which implies that this statement is coincident with the preceding (cf. Paton, 302). This speaks heavily in favor of the emended text. With that text, מאמר, "command," refers to the letter Esther has just issued confirming the observance of Purim, and the verse has the function of closing the episode with a summarizing statement.

Explanation

The previous act described the overwhelming Jewish victory over their enemies, which took place on 13 Adar. Though this victory has completed the resolution of the terrible threat to the life of the Jewish community created by Haman's edict, which crisis set our story in motion, it is not the conclusion to the final form of the book of Esther. In its present form, our story has not been told merely to relate how this resolution occurred (see *Unity and Redaction* in the *Introduction* to Esther). Nor, indeed, does it intend simply to relate how the festival of Purim emerged within the life of the Jewish community. It does do that, of course, but its primary purpose is a different one. The narrator now turns his attention to the institution of an annual celebration whose purpose is to memorialize the days of celebration and joy that occurred after the dramatic deliverance on 13 Adar (cf. the discussion of the genres established by the dénouement of the story in the *Genre* section of the *Introduction* to Esther). It intends to persuade the Jewish community that such a perpetual celebration is incumbent upon it. It is not narrational but legislative in purpose. At the time the narrator is writing, this festival has already begun to be celebrated by the Jewish community, as the etiological digressions in vv 19, 26a make clear. These etiologies transport the reader from the past time of the narrated events to the narrator's own present and ground an already extant celebratory practice (v 19) and name (v 26a) in the events of the story just related. Of similar import is v 23a, where the phrase "the Jews accepted what they had begun to do" refers not only to the original, spontaneous celebrations but also, and principally, to the (differing) regular celebrations that they have already adopted (v 19; see *Comment*). In this light, it is clear that the narrative is intended not simply to relate what happened but primarily to impose the festival upon the community. As I have understood v 28 (see *Comment*), it patently makes the case, for here the narrator ceases narrating past events and himself prescribes for his contemporaries what the community should do. The narrative indeed "... has shifted the focus of the story away from notions of victory ..., military prowess, and power ... to the hearers' present moment where the significance of the Esther story lies in the festal activities it has given birth to" (Clines, *Esther Scroll,* 161).

SCENE 1. THE EVENTS THAT OCCASION THE CELEBRATION OF PURIM OVER TWO DAYS (9:6–19)

Episode 1. How the fighting in Susa took place on the thirteenth and the fourteenth of Adar (9:6–15). The first scene, vv 6–19, is exclusively devoted to accounting for the two different dates on which different parts of the community celebrate the festival. The Jews who live outside of Susa celebrate it on 14 Adar (v 19), while the Jews of Susa celebrate it on 15 Adar (see *Comment* on v 18). That this is the purpose of this scene is indicated at every level of the narrative. Indeed, it is not only signaled by the content and form of the pericope (see *Form/Structure/Setting*) but also in a more subtle, and yet even more telling way, by its very narrative dynamics. Prior to this act the story has been told with great narrative skill, plot coherence, and sensitivity to characterization. Seldom, if ever, has the plot taken a sudden turn, or an event occurred, that has not been skillfully integrated into the narrative development. Nor have the characters acted in a manner that does not fit the way the narrator has previously characterized them. However, that is not the case here. Suddenly the narrative falls apart.

As numerous scholars have observed (e.g., Bardtke, 386–87; Clines, *Esther Scroll,* 47–49; Dommershausen, *Estherrolle,* 119–120; Fox, 112–13; id., *Redaction,* 115), Ahasuerus' offer in v 12c is anything but skillfully integrated into the plot development. Indeed, nothing in the preceding events has prepared us in the slightest way for the king's offer. His offer to fulfill Esther's request is worded almost identically to the three offers that he made to her previously (5:3; 5:6; 7:2), but on each of these occasions his offer was made because Esther had indicated by her actions and her words that she wished to make a request (in the first she entered his presence unbidden at the risk of her life, and in the next two she invited him to a banquet as the appropriate venue for her request). However, there is nothing whatsoever in the narrative here that would indicate to the king that Esther has a further request to make. Indeed, exactly the opposite is true. The overwhelming Jewish victory of the previous day has completely fulfilled the request she has already made (see 7:2). Why should the king suppose that she has any further request to make (Clines, *Esther Scroll,* 47)? Instead of being grounded in some indication that Esther has something further to ask, the king's offer is apparently grounded in his statement of the number of the slain in the Citadel of Susa and in his rhetorical question about how many must have been killed in the rest of the empire (v 12ab). Even if we grant that the tenor of these words is wonder and admiration at the extent of Jewish slaughter (see *Comment*), what possible grounds does this provide for him to conclude that Esther has a further request?

Second, the king's action here is strikingly out of character. In the previous narrative, Ahasuerus has been depicted as a weak and pliable despot who can make no decision on his own. He knew not what to do about Vashti without the advice of his wise men (1:13–22); his personal attendants must tell him how to find a new queen (2:1–4); he must turn to his grand vizier to find out how to reward the man who has saved his life (6:1–9; see esp. Clines, *Esther Scroll,* 47; Fox, 173–74). But now, without seeking any courtly advice, he acts decisively on his own in offering Esther carte blanche. On the basis of both plot development and characterization, the king's sudden offer is simply inexplicable.

Not only is the king's offer inexplicable but so also is the request that Esther then makes in response (vv 13–14a). It also is motivated by nothing in the preceding narrative. Haman's decree had limited any legally sanctioned attack on the Jewish community specifically to the one day, 13 Adar (see 3:13), and Mordecai's decree had likewise so limited the Jewish response (8:12). This day has come and gone, and the account of it has depicted an unmitigated Jewish victory. The Jews surely are now perfectly safe, since "they have put all their enemies to the sword" (9:5). Where, then, from the narrative's own point of view is there the need for a second day's fighting? True, one can logically surmise that there were still enemies of the Jews extant in Susa (Bardtke, 387; Moore, 91) or that the casualties have so far been in the Citadel as opposed to the city (Baldwin, 106), but any such surmises, and indeed the very need to make them, points up how incongruous the development is, for no surmise would be needed if there were the slightest hint in the preceding narrative that such enemies exist.

Finally, there is one further subtle incongruity in the narrative. Both the narrator's report of the fighting in vv 6–11 and the king's recapitulation of the same in v 12 speak only of events in the Citadel of Susa. But Esther's request in v 13 speaks rather of the city of Susa itself, as does both the account of the fulfillment of her request in vv 14–15 and the etiology explaining the two different dates of the celebration of Purim in vv 16–19. This sudden shift of locale also has no explanation from the plot development. Whether the incongruity is evidence for different authorship (so Clines, *Esther Scroll,* 181 n. 29) or not, the inexplicable shift of locale finds its only adequate explanation in the narrative (it can hardly be a scribal addition; see *Comment*) in the need for a second day's fighting in Susa in order to explain the geographical distinction between the dates of celebration of Purim by Jews of Susa and those elsewhere, v 19.

It is unmistakable, then, that the king's offer, Esther's request, and the sudden shift from the Citadel to the city of Susa are inexplicable on the grounds of the preceding narrative development. This does not mean, however, that they have no narrative purpose at all. On the contrary, as the next episode will reveal, their narrative purpose relates to what follows, rather than to what has preceded.

Episode 2. Why the Jews in Susa and the Jews elsewhere celebrate on two different days (9:16–19). With this episode, the purpose of the preceding account becomes immediately clear, for the narrator here contrasts the two days' fighting in Susa with what happened elsewhere. First he relates (v 16) the victory of the rest of the Jews throughout the empire of Ahasuerus (again in only the most general terms), sounding the same themes as before (giving the number slain and the fact that no plunder was taken). The purpose of this, however, is not simply to give an account of the fighting in the provinces. This is indicated even at the level of structure, for the description of the victory in v 16 is tightly bound together syntactically with v 17 as a single compound sentence, and both are closely correlated with v 18 (see *Form/Structure/Setting*). Its purpose is signaled primarily by content. The statements of v 18, tightly parallel with those of vv 16–17, provide a "flashback" to the actions of the Jews of Susa (related in episode 1), which is intended to contrast the actions of these two different parts of the Jewish community. The Jews in Susa had celebrated on 15 Adar, the Jews in the rest of the empire on 14 Adar. The narrator then immediately makes clear his purpose in drawing this contrast. With an explanatory digression, v 19, he transports us from the past time of his narrative to his own day to draw the conclusion to which his narrative has been leading. The contrast between the date of the day of rest and joyful feasting in Susa and that elsewhere explains why these events are now being celebrated (and presumably have been for some unspecified time) on two different days, on 14 Adar outside the jurisdiction of Susa and (by implication) on 15 Adar in Susa itself.

It is also important to note that the narrator has sounded a new theme in vv 16–18. Here for the first time he relates that the days of fighting were each followed by a day in which the Jews "had rest" and in which they made "a joyful day of feasting" (v 17). In his explanatory digression, v 19, he informs us that the Jews outside the jurisdiction of Susa (and by implication those in Susa) continued to celebrate these days of rest and joyful festivities "as a joyful holiday of feasting and the sending of gifts of food to one another." This theme will be resumed in the following scene and developed in an important way.

Finally, in this carefully integrated narrative and its concluding explanatory digression, the matter of adjudicating the different dates on which these two groups within the Jewish community will hold the festival commemorating the celebration clearly needs to be addressed. It is not surprising, then, that this is one issue that Mordecai will deal with in the message that he will send to all the Jews in the following scene.

SCENE 2. MORDECAI, ESTHER, AND THE JEWISH COMMUNITY SET THE DATES OF PURIM AND COMMIT THEMSELVES TO ITS PERPETUAL CELEBRATION (9:20–32)

In this, the second scene, the narrator turns to what constitutes his core concern in this act, the establishment of the festival of Purim. We already know from what he has told us in his explanatory digression in v 19 that the community has been continuing the spontaneous celebration that erupted on the days following the battles. He now proceeds to tell us how this has come about.

Episode 1. Mordecai writes to all the Jews to obligate them to celebrate annually the fourteenth and the fifteenth of Adar as days of joyful festivity (9:20–22). It is Mordecai first who, as the head of the community, writes to regularize the commemoration and make it permanent (vv 20–22). It is important to note that Mordecai does not write like a lawgiver from Sinai and simply "command" or "order" the community to observe the celebration annually (cf. Fox, 118). Rather, the narrator uses the LBH expression לקים על, "to require (something) of (someone), to obligate (someone) to (something)" (see *Comment*). That is, he is using moral suasion, appealing to their sense of what is fit, right, and proper. Second, Mordecai writes to set the dates of the festival. He obligates the Jews to celebrate it annually on "the fourteenth and on the fifteenth of the month of Adar" (v 21). Since the major point of the previous scene has been to account for the fact that the festival is being celebrated by different parts of the community on either of these two days, it seems highly probable that his purpose here is to adjudicate the dispute. He is either urging them all to celebrate both days, inasmuch as each day has been legitimately celebrated by a part of the community, or he is urging them to celebrate both days in the sense that each group celebrates the particular day appropriate to their location (see *Comment* on v 21). Third, Mordecai establishes the character of the festival. They are to celebrate these days "*like* the days in which they gained relief from their enemies and the month which was transformed for them from sadness to joy and from mourning to celebration." And to leave no doubt as to what this means, Mordecai concludes the sentence with a resumptive clause that spells it out, "to make them joyful days of feasting and of the sending of presents of food to one another and gifts to the poor" (see *Comment*). That is, these days are to be a commemoration of the days of rest and joyful feasting that followed the days of victory and slaughter (for the significance of this, see the *Theology* section in the *Introduction* to Esther).

Episode 2. The Jews commit themselves, their descendants, and all who join them to the perpetual annual observance of the festival of Purim (9:23–28). It is not only Mordecai's letter, however, that establishes the festival as a regular and permanent celebration. In episode 2 the narrator informs us that the Jewish community formally took the obligation upon itself as well (cf. Clines, *Esther Scroll,* 165–66). First we are told that the Jews "accepted what they had begun to do" (v 23a), which refers doubtless to both the original spontaneous celebrations (vv 17–18) and to the ongoing festal activities that these have given rise to (v 19; see *Comment*). However, he also alludes to the previous episode, affirming again that they accepted "what Mordecai had written to them" (v 23b). This is then followed by the retrospective from Mordecai's letter (vv 24–25; see *Comment*). Clearly, this indicates that Mordecai grounded the obligation to observe the festival primarily in the crisis and deliverance that they had experienced.

The narrator then emphatically affirms (v 27) that the Jews "*firmly* obligated themselves, their descendants, and all who would join them" to observe these two days "in the manner prescribed and on the days designated," referring to the character of the festival and the dates of its observance set forth in Mordecai's letter. This acquiescence is grounded not only in that letter (v 26b) but also in "what they had experienced in this regard and what had happened to them" (v 26cd), which doubtless refers to the whole story of the crisis that the narrator has just recapitulated in the retrospective drawn from Mordecai's letter (vv 24–25). That the community has committed itself to the regular and perpetual observance of the festival is made particularly clear in v 28, where the narrator stops telling what the Jewish community did. Suddenly, speaking directly to the community of his own day, to whom he has just related the firm commitment of those who have preceded them, he does not speak in the simple future but uses the language of obligation: These days "*are going to* be celebrated" throughout all generations and in every family, province, and city; their observance "*shall* never cease among the Jews"; their commemoration "*shall* not come to an end" among their descendants. The authority to establish this new festival lies not only in the leader of the community but also in the independent actions of the community, first in spontaneously beginning the celebration, and then in its decision to make that celebration permanent.

Finally, the narrator informs us in a second etiological digression (v 26a) that the name of the festival, Purim, derives from the word *pur,* the lot cast by Haman for their destruction mentioned in the preceding brief retrospective of the story (vv 24–25). Thus, the name of the festival is clearly connected with the story of dramatic deliverance from destruction (rather than with the account of military victory and the slaughter of their enemies; see the *Theology* section in the *Introduction* to Esther). But, it is also striking that the festival is not named Purim because Mordecai so designated it. Nor does the narrator relate that the Jewish community so named it when they took upon themselves its regular and perpetual celebration. Rather, the explanatory digression makes it clear that the name of the festival was already in existence in the narrator's own day, and presumably had been for some time, for he cites it as a known and accepted fact. Further, the narrator does not specifically state that the community so named the festival. He knows only its traditional etymology, for he cites it with the unspecified "they (named)," the third person masculine plural with unexpressed antecedent, the virtual equivalent of the passive in English. Hence, the exact origin of the name is buried in the traditions of the past.

Episode 3. Esther writes to confirm the observance of Purim (9:29–32). Finally, in the third episode the narrator relates that Esther also wrote to the Jewish community (not Esther and Mordecai; see *Comment*). She does not write, however, as Mordecai did, "to obligate" the community to the observance of the festival. Rather, she writes "to confirm" its observance (see *Comment*). Her function, then, is to corroborate what has already been done. She adds her authority as queen ("uses all her authority"; see *Comment* on v 29) to that of Mordecai and the Jewish community itself. It is also important to note, however, that her purpose is not only to confirm the dates of the festival ("at the appointed times," v 31a) and its character as a time of joyful feasting and the exchange of gifts ("in the same manner that Mordecai the Jew had obligated them," v 31b). In the present form of the text (see *Comment*), she is also said to confirm the observance of Purim "in the same manner" as the community "had obligated themselves and their descendants to the performance of fasts and their accompanying laments" (v 31c). The joy of the festival is not to obliterate the memory of the terrible danger that they had faced (see the *Theology* section in the *Introduction* to Esther).

So our story has reached its dénouement, a dénouement that is in many ways surprising, for it does not merely give the consequences of the crisis and its resolution for the protagonists of the story, but it also legislates a new and important cultic observance for Jews of the diaspora (for the significance of this, see the *Theology* section in the *Introduction* to Esther).

Act 10
Epilogue: An Encomium on Mordecai (10:1–3)

Bibliography

Clines, D. J. A. *The Esther Scroll: The Story of the Story.* JSOTSup 30. Sheffield: JSOT, 1984. **Daube, D.** "The Last Chapter of Esther." *JQR* 37 (1946–47) 139–47. **Driver, G. R.** "Problems and Solutions." *VT* 4 (1954) 224–45. **Ehrlich, A.** *Randglossen zur hebräischen Bibel: Textkritisches, Sprachliches und Sachliches.* Vol. 7. 1914. Repr. Hildesheim: Georg Olms, 1968. **Fox, M.** *The Redaction of the Books of Esther.* Atlanta: Scholars, 1991. **Haupt, P.** "Critical Notes on Esther." *AJSL* 24 (1907–8) 97–186 (= Moore, *Studies,* 1–90). **Humphreys, W. L.** "A Life-Style for Diaspora: A Study of the Tales of Esther and Daniel." *JBL* 92 (1973) 211–23. **Volkmann, H.** "Der Zweite nach dem König." *Philologus* 92 (1937) 285–316.

Translation

[1]*Then King Ahasuerus*[a] *imposed forced labor on the land and on the islands and coastlands of the sea.* [2]*And all the king's mighty accomplishments*[a] *and the full account of the high honor which he had conferred upon Mordecai,*[b] *are they not recorded in the Chronicles*[c] *of the Kings of Media and Persia?* [3]*For Mordecai the Jew was second in rank only to King Ahasuerus himself*[a] *and was pre-eminent among the Jews.*[b] *He was held in high esteem by all,*[c] *for he was constantly seeking the good of his people and promoting the welfare of*[d] *all their descendants.*

Notes

1.a. The K form of the name here, אחשרש, is closer to the original Persian, *Xšayāršān,* than the Q form, *ʾăḥašwērôš,* the form found elsewhere in the Heb. text (cf. Paton, 305). Nevertheless, this is undoubtedly a scribal *lapsus calami* rather than a different tradition of pronunciation.

2.a. Lit. "all the deeds of his power and his might."

2.b. Lit. "the account of the greatness of Mordecai (to) which the king had elevated him." Haupt's conjectural emendation (*AJSL* 24 [1907–8] 174; cf. BHS n. a-a) that this clause, minus the relative clause אשר גדלו המלך, "to which the king had elevated him," should be transposed to the beginning of the verse, so that the whole verse refers only to Mordecai, is to be rejected. It is without textual support (the LXX does not even mention Mordecai in the whole verse).

2.c. Lit. "the book/record of the events of the days."

3.a. Lit. "Second to King Ahasuerus," a formal Persian title; see *Comment.*

3.b. Lit. "great to the Jews," the exact nuance of which is not clear. Others render "held in respect among the Jews" (JB, NJB), "influential for the Jews" (Fox, 128), "influential among the Jews" (Moore, 98). The emendation to ביהודים (Haupt, *AJSL* 24 [1907–8] 174; followed by Bardtke, 401; Moore, 98; cf. *BHS* n.) is unnecessary.

3. c. Lit. "by the multitude of this brethren."

3. d. Lit. "speaking peace/well-being for."

Form/Structure/Setting

Content alone renders it unmistakable that these verses constitute a separate pericope from the preceding, for the subject is now an encomium for Mordecai, rather than the institution of the festival of Purim. In expressing his praise for Mordecai, the narrator draws on the conceptions and language of the traditions of his people in three striking instances: (1) in expressing the dramatic extent of the Persian empire, v 1; (2) in the rhetorical question expressing Mordecai's status, v 2; and (3) in the title "Second to the King," v 3 (for the parallels, see *Comment*).

Comment

1 וַיָּשֶׂם הַמֶּלֶךְ אֲחַשְׁרוֹשׁ מַס עַל־הָאָרֶץ וְאִיֵּי הַיָּם, lit. "then King Ahasuerus imposed forced labor [or 'tribute/tax'] upon the land and the islands-and-coastlands of the sea." Elsewhere in the OT the Hebrew word מס means "corvée, forced labor," always used collectively to refer to the persons so subjected. If it moves in that range of meaning here, it must bear the abstract sense "compulsory servitude." It is possible, however, considering the late date of Esther, that the word had already developed the related sense of "tribute, tax," which is its meaning in MH (cf. Ehrlich, *Randglossen,* 125). The Hebrew word אי means "island-and-coastland [cf. Isa 23:2] of the Mediterranean," which was for the Israelites the most distant part of the known world to the west (cf. Isa 24:15; 41:5). Here it is probably being used in the same sense to express the immense extent (cf. 1:1) of the empire of Ahasuerus (and his father Darius before him) in the west, i.e., in Ionia, western Turkey, and the islands of the Aegean. Herodotus' account of the tribute rendered to Darius (3.96) mentions "the islands and the inhabitants of Europe as far as Thessaly" as the farthest western reaches of the Persian empire (cf. Gerleman, 144). The unusual use of the word ארץ, "land," to refer to Ahasuerus' kingdom (the regular term in Esther has been the word מלכות, "kingdom" [1:14, 20; 2:3; 3:6, 8; 5:3, 6; 7:2; 9:30]) is doubtless required by the contrast with the "islands-and-coasts of the sea," since the use of מלכות here would be all-inclusive.

Whether מס is taken to mean "forced labor" or "tribute, tax," it is the relevance of this statement for the story that has troubled most commentators. Some of the explanations offered are simply not pertinent. Although they may be plausible reasons for the king to impose forced labor or a tax, they give no plausible reason for the narrator to include such a statement here (e.g., the views of Gunkel [see Fox, 129] or Rawlinson [see Paton, 303]). Daube (*JQR* 37 [1946–47] 140–46) suggests that the narrator presents the statement as Mordecai's alternative to the policy of the expropriation of the property of the Jews from which (in Daube's view) Haman's bribe of 10,000 talents (3:9) would have come. However, since it is not at all clear that Haman's bribe was to have come from the expropriation of Jewish property (see *Comment* on 3:9), the supposition is far too subtle to be at all convincing. Nothing in the text hints at any connection at all between this statement and either Haman's bribe (cf. Fox, 129; Clines, 332; id., *Esther Scroll,* 58) or some policy instituted by Mordecai. Fox (129) suggests that the narrator intends the statement to be taken as the opposite action to the "tax relief" the king granted in 2:18, implying that Jewish success benefits the king's subjects and is also "good for the royal coffers." Since 2:18 may not refer to a relief of taxes at all (see *Note* 2:18.b.), this suggestion also is far too subtle to be convincing. Nothing connects the two statements in any way (as Fox himself notes). In my opinion, the clue to the purpose of the statement is the unusual manner of referring to the Persian realm. A statement intended simply to record thc imposition of a corvée or a tax would surely have used the regular term for the empire, מלכות, "kingdom." The purpose, then, for using this unusual expression to describe the Persian empire, "the land and the islands-and-coastlands of the sea," must surely be to emphasize its vast expanse: it extends to the farthest western reaches of the known world. This serves to enhance the power and greatness of the king. In this light מס most likely means "forced labor" rather than "tribute, tax," for it would appear that the narrator is speaking hyperbolically in describing the power of the king to impress even the most distant parts of his empire into compulsory servitude (contra Fox, 129). Given the significance of this unusual way of designating the Persian empire, the statement is not as unintelligible and purposeless as is often alleged (e.g., Clines, *Esther Scroll,* 57–58). As the following statement reveals, the description of the king's power and greatness is intended to increase the stature of Mordecai, his Jewish prime minister (cf. Moore, 99).

2 וְכָל־מַעֲשֵׂה תָקְפּוֹ וּגְבוּרָתוֹ, lit. "and all the deeds of his power and his might." Since the subject of the previous sentence has been the king, the pronouns here can only refer to him, not to Mordecai (contra Ringgren, 403). In this context מעשׂה has the sense "deeds, accomplishments." It is not likely that the word means "story, affair," the sense that it developed in MH (contra Fox, 287), since in this verse the narrator patently draws upon the conceptions and even the language of the concluding formulas of the accounts of the kings of Judah and Israel in the books of Kings and Chronicles (see *Form/Structure/Setting*).

וּפָרָשַׁת גְּדֻלַּת מָרְדֳּכַי אֲשֶׁר גִּדְּלוֹ הַמֶּלֶךְ, lit. "and the account of the greatness of Mordecai (to) which the king had elevated him." Driver (*VT* 4 [1954] 237–38) avers that פרשׁה here (the same word used in 4:7 to express the "exact amount" of money Haman promised to pay for the extermination of the Jews) expresses the idea of a public record documenting his greatness, a "patent of nobility." In another context, the final clause could be understood to be modifying Mordecai, i.e., "Mordecai whom the king promoted" (so Moore, 98), but Mordecai surely needs no identification by this time in the story. Fox's view (287) that the relative clause is modifying פרשׁה, "details," yielding the translation, "the details . . . with respect to which the king promoted him," is not very convincing. The clause must modify "greatness" as a relative clause of degree.

הֲלוֹא־הֵם כְּתוּבִים עַל־סֵפֶר דִּבְרֵי הַיָּמִים לְמַלְכֵי מָדַי וּפָרָס, "are they not recorded in the Chronicles of the Kings of Media and Persia?" Here the narrator patterns his praise of Mordecai on the conceptions and language of the literary traditions of his people. The clause uses the identical form and language of the rhetorical question (which intends to make an emphatic statement) with which the editor(s) of the books of Kings and Chronicles concluded the accounts of the kings of Judah and Israel (e.g., "and the rest of the acts of Rehoboam and all that he accomplished, are they not recorded in the Chronicles of the Kings of Judah?" 1 Kgs 14:29; cf. also, e.g., 1 Kgs 15:23; 16:14; 2 Chron 25:26). In this way, Mordecai the Jew, the leader of the diaspora, acquires similar status to the leaders of the community of old.

3 כִּי מָרְדֳּכַי הַיְּהוּדִי מִשְׁנֶה לַמֶּלֶךְ אֲחַשְׁוֵרוֹשׁ, lit. "for Mordecai the Jew was second (in rank) to King Ahasuerus." By the title משׁנה למלך, "Second to the King," the narrator is describing Mordecai's position as second-in-command to the king by a term in actual use in the Achaemenid empire (see Volkmann, *Philologus* 92

[1937] 285–316). It is likely, however, that he also intends to extol Mordecai's status by drawing upon his readers' familiarity with a similar term in use in the biblical tradition. Thus, it would be reminiscent of Pharoah's mounting Joseph in his "chariot of the second (in command)" (Gen 41:43), and probably also of the reference to Jonathan as David's "second" (1 Sam 17:23). There were clearly priestly "seconds-in-command" (cf. 2 Kgs 25:18) and perhaps even a "Second to the King" (cf. Chron 28:7).

Explanation

Here, in a final epilogue, the narrator leaves the issue of the dates and character of the festival of Purim and picks up a theme from his previous narrative, the rise to power and the stature of Mordecai the Jew. In the previous narrative, the king had given to Mordecai his signet ring, which he had taken from Haman, apparently indicating that Mordecai had taken over the position of his enemy (8:2). This could doubtless, then, be taken to imply that Mordecai now occupied the position of grand vizier. However, Mordecai's role in these events had all been effected by Esther in her capacity as queen (8:1), and it was related almost in passing in connection with his issuance of the counteredict that annulled Haman's decree of extermination, the authority for which was specifically granted to him by the king (8:7–9). Indeed, nothing further has been said in this regard beyond the statements that, after the issuance of the counterdecree, he left the king's presence clad in royal attire (8:15a), and that, in connection with his role in the Jewish victory on 13 Adar, he was "great in the palace" and "was growing more and more powerful" (9:3–4). Furthermore, in order to magnify the role of the king in the retrospective of the events that led to the crisis (9:24–25), the joyful deliverance from which is celebrated by the festival of Purim, the narrator had totally ignored the part that Mordecai (and Esther) had played therein. Hence, in order to make clear that Mordecai indeed occupied the position of grand vizier successfully and permanently, he ties up the loose ends of his narrative with this encomium for him. Though it is not essential to his story, it is, nonetheless, a fitting conclusion (Fox, *Redaction,* 109).

The narrator begins with a statement that, at a subsidiary level at least, comes full circle as he alludes once more to both the extent of the Persian empire and the unrestricted power of Ahasuerus, its ruler (cf. 1:1–4 and *Explanation* thereto). But, the allusion here is not primarily for the purpose of extolling the might and the grandeur of the king. The highlighting of the greatness of Ahasuerus effectively serves, rather, to stress the importance and stature of Mordecai, his Jewish prime minister. This is made patently clear in v 2, where the narrator uses the identical form and language of the statements that conclude the accounts of the religious biographies of the kings of Judah and Israel (see *Comment*). By so doing, he implies that the stature of Mordecai as the head of the *Jewish* community (i.e., the diaspora; see *Theme and Purpose* in the *Introduction* to Esther) is commensurate with that of the royal rulers of Israel's distant past, the period of the monarchy. (That the parallel thus created could extend to character as well as stature [since the accounts of Israel's kings evaluate them so negatively] is rendered impossible by the grounds for Mordecai's repute that are delineated in the next verse.)

This high praise for Mordecai is grounded in two aspects of his role, service to the king and service to his people, the Jews (v 3). In regard to the former, he is the "Second" to the king, a rank that is at home in the Persian world and also reminiscent of both priestly and courtly rank in the world of Israel (see *Comment*). In regard to the latter, he is again identified as "Mordecai the Jew," emphasizing that the setting of this encomium is the world of the diaspora and that his preeminence among the Jews and the high esteem in which he is held by his compatriots does not result from his rank in the foreign court, as important as that is to the Jewish community. It is not even said to be the result of the role he has played in the deliverance from terrible evil that the story has related. It results rather from his continued actions in seeking the good of his people, the Jews of the diaspora, and promoting the welfare of all their descendants, as the present participles of the last two clauses stress.

Mordecai entered the story as a "Jew," a member of the diaspora who was a resident of the Citadel of Susa (2:5) and who served as a minor official in the Persian bureaucracy. At the end of the story he rules Persia as the grand vizier, second in power to the king alone, a power that he wields for the benefit of his people (Clines, 333). As such, Mordecai typifies for every diaspora community the possibility "of living a creative and rich life in the foreign environment, as part of the complex social, political, and economic dynamics of that world, and also of remaining a devoted and loyal member of his community of fellow Jews" (Humphreys, *JBL* 92 [1973] 216). Also, and far more significantly, he represents the need (and the hope) of the diaspora of having such a friend in high places whose dual loyalty may be the means of deliverance from the evil resident in that world.

Index of Authors Cited

Index of Principal Subjects

Index of Biblical and Other Ancient Sources

A. Old Testament

B. New Testament

C. Apocrypha

D. Old Testament Pseudepigrapha

E. Rabbinic Works

F. Dead Sea Scrolls

G. Classical and Hellenistic Works

H. Other Ancient Sources

Index of Key Hebrew Words